Foundations of Marketing
Fourth Edition

Foundations of Marketing
John Fahy and David Jobber

McGraw-Hill
Higher Education

London Boston Burr Ridge, IL Dubuque, IA Madison, WI New York San Francisco
St. Louis Bangkok Bogotá Caracas Kuala Lumpur Lisbon Madrid Mexico City Milan Montreal
New Delhi Santiago Seoul Singapore Sydney Taipei Toronto

Foundations of Marketing, Fourth Edition
John Fahy and David Jobber
ISBN-13 9780077137014
ISBN-10 0077137019

McGraw-Hill
Higher Education

Published by McGraw-Hill Education
Shoppenhangers Road
Maidenhead
Berkshire
SL6 2QL
Telephone: 44 (0) 1628 502 500
Fax: 44 (0) 1628 770 224
Website: www.mcgraw-hill.co.uk

British Library Cataloguing in Publication Data

A catalogue record for this book is available from the British Library

Library of Congress Cataloguing in Publication Data

The Library of Congress data for this book has been applied for from the Library of Congress

Executive Editor: Caroline Prodger
Commissioning Editor: Leiah Batchelor/Peter Hooper
Development Editor: Jennifer Yendell
Production Editor: James Bishop
Marketing Manager: Vanessa Boddington

Text Design by Hardlines
Cover design by Adam Renvoize
Printed and bound in Spain by Grafo Industrias Gráficas

Dedication

In memory of Prof. John A. Murray
a friend and mentor

John Fahy

About the Authors

John Fahy is Professor of Marketing at the University of Limerick in Ireland and Adjunct Professor of Marketing at the University of Adelaide, Australia. He has a distinguished track record of teaching and research in the fields of marketing and business strategy. In particular, he is known for his work in the area of marketing resources and capabilities and how these factors impact on organizational performance. He is a founder member of the MC21 group which has conducted research on marketing resources and performance across 15 countries. Other current research interests include evolutionary perspectives on marketing and strategic decision making. He is the author of 40 referred journal articles on marketing and strategy that have been published in leading titles, including *Journal of Marketing, Journal of International Business Studies, Journal of Business Research, Journal of Marketing Management, European Journal of Marketing, International Business Review* and *Sloan Management Review*. He is also the winner of several major international research awards such as the AMA Services Marketing Paper of the Year Award and the Chartered Institute of Marketing Best Paper Award at the Academy of Marketing Annual Conference. In addition, he serves on the Executive Committee of the European Academy of Marketing.

Professor Fahy is also a renowned teacher with a particular expertise in working with MBA and executive groups. His skills have been in demand around the world and he has worked with students in Australia, Japan, Hungary, Ireland, New Zealand, Singapore, the UK and the USA. The focus of his executive work is on bridging the gap between academic insight and the commercial realities facing organizations and he has been extensively involved in both open and in-company programmes in Ireland and the UK. As part of this activity he is the author of several award-winning business case studies and has also been involved in the development of new pedagogical materials such as a series of business videos where he interviews some leading marketing managers about recent strategic initiatives in their organizations. Further details can be found at www.johnfahy.net.

Professor Fahy currently holds the Chair in Marketing at the University of Limerick. Prior to this he worked at Trinity College, Dublin, and he holds a Master's degree from Texas A&M University and a Doctorate from Trinity College. Outside of work his passions include family, music, sport, food and travel.

David Jobber is an internationally recognized marketing academic. He is Professor of Marketing at the University of Bradford School of Management. He holds an Honours degree in Economics from the University of Manchester, a Master's degree from the University of Warwick and a Doctorate from the University of Bradford.

Before joining the faculty at the Bradford Management Centre, David worked for the TI Group in marketing and sales, and was Senior Lecturer in Marketing at the University of Huddersfield. He has wide experience of teaching core marketing courses at undergraduate, post-graduate and post-experience levels. His specialisms are industrial marketing, sales management and marketing research. He has a proven, ratings-based record of teaching achievements at all levels. His competence in teaching is reflected in visiting appointments at the universities of Aston, Lancaster, Loughborough and Warwick in the UK, and the University of Wellington, New Zealand. He has taught marketing to executives of such international companies as BP, Croda International, Allied Domecq, the BBC, Bass, Royal & Sun Alliance, Rolls-Royce and Rio Tinto.

Supporting his teaching is a record of achievement in academic research. David has over 150 publications in the marketing area in such journals as *International Journal of Research in Marketing, MIS Quarterly, Strategic Management Journal, Journal of International Business Studies, Journal of Management, Journal of Business Research, Journal of Product Innovation Management* and *Journal of Personal Selling and Sales Management*. David has served on the editorial boards of *International Journal of Research in Marketing, Journal of Personal Selling and Sales Management, European Journal of Marketing* and *Journal of Marketing Management*. David has acted as Special Adviser to the Research Assessment Exercise panel that rates research output from business and management schools throughout the UK. In 2008, he received the Academy of Marketing's Life Achievement award for distinguished and extraordinary services to marketing.

Brief Table of Contents

Detailed Table of Conten

Case list

www.mcgraw-hill.co.uk/textbooks/fahy

Vignette list

www.mcgraw-hill.co.uk/textbooks/fahy

Ethical Debate

www.mcgraw-hill.co.uk/textbooks/fahy

Social Media Marketing

www.mcgraw-hill.co.uk/textbooks/fahy

Preface to the Fourth Edition

In the three years since the last edition of this book, the world of business has undergone some radical transformations. In 2009, the global financial crisis (GFC) was just taking hold – few could have foreseen its dramatic consequences. The major economies of the USA, Britain and Western Europe have been struggling with the combined effects of recession, rising unemployment, spiralling sovereign and personal debt levels, and heightened consumer uncertainty. Businesses have been forced to deal with the most difficult economic environment since the Great Depression of the 1930s. In these circumstances, marketing capabilities have come under ever greater scrutiny. Businesses are competing more fiercely for reduced levels of consumer expenditure, so innovative products and services need to be developed, and delivered in ever more creative ways in a 'noisy' marketplace.

One of those interesting innovations to really take hold in the past three years has been social media. Facebook, which was founded in just 2004, has gone on to claim over 600 million members by 2011 making it one of the largest 'countries' in the world. Tweeting has become part of the general lexicon as more and more people use Twitter to find out about what is going on or to stay in touch. While some critics argue that social media may become a victim of its own hype, these large audiences provide interesting challenges and opportunities for organizations. Many are trying to develop a social media strategy or to figure out the role of social media in integrated marketing communications. Some have been successful in building their interactions with these communities; others much less so.

And in terms of how we think about marketing there have been some subtle changes also. While value has always been key to marketing, it is increasingly assuming centre stage. Many of the classic distinctions in marketing such as the marketing mix (4Ps) and products versus services have been losing some of their explanatory power. Instead value is the concept that captures the essence of modern marketing. In global, highly competitive and fast-moving markets, organizations of whatever type need to be clear about what value they are offering and communicate this value to their audiences. But the process is no longer one-way. In a networked world, value is often co-created between organizational partners and often jointly by organizations and consumers. This is the era of the consumer who can blog about their poor experiences with products, tweet their interesting ideas or upload videos of their innovations. A value-centred approach to marketing is more important than ever.

The fourth edition

Some of the exciting features of the fourth edition include the following.

A Focus on Value

Value is the central theme of this book. We examine its different forms and the core ways in which marketing contributes to the development and delivery of value.

Social Media Marketing

The nature of social media marketing is a core focus throughout the book. We examine the effective social media marketing and also include nine social media marketing vignettes. These contain insights on developing themes and effective practice and include questions for discussion and critical reflection.

Customer Behaviour and Market Research

The chapters on customer behaviour and market research have been extensively revised to incorporate new perspectives from the fields of consumer research and consumer psychology.

Services, Relationships and Experiences

The chapter on services marketing has been extensively revised to examine the creation of value through services, relationships and experiences which have become some of the central means through which organizations differentiate themselves in a competitive marketplace.

Digital Marketing

Theory and practice in the field of digital marketing continues to evolve at a rapid pace as it accounts for an ever greater percentage of marketing budgets. A completely revised and updated section on digital marketing in included is Chapter 10.

Ethical Debates

The book emphasizes a critical approach to both the theory and practice of marketing. For example, throughout the book, nine ethical debates are highlighted. These inserts provide conceptual arguments both for and against certain aspects of marketing with questions added to encourage critical reflection and debate.

Learning about Marketing

Marketing is an interesting and exciting subject that is at the core of our lives both as consumers and as employees or managers in organisations. Therefore the focus of this book has always been on blending conceptual insights with the contemporary world of marketing practice. As such it retains the popular features of previous editions and adds several new ones.

Insights from the world of practice feature in myriad ways. Each chapter begins with a marketing spotlight focusing on the marketing activities and challenges facing some well-known global enterprises that sets the scene for the content that follows. In addition to the social media marketing inserts discussed above, there are 37 marketing in action vignettes that focus on the activities of a variety of organizations, large and small, public and private. Roughly one-third of these organizations are based in the UK/Ireland, one-third in Western Europe and one-third are from around the world giving a wide geographic breadth. Each of these inserts contains discussion questions designed to improve critical thinking and learning. Eleven new and one updated end of chapter cases are included to provide more detailed problems for analysis and discussion.

Although the text is foundational, it also provides students with an introduction to many of the emerging themes in the marketing literature. Included, to name but a few, are consumer culture theory, semiotics, multi-sensory marketing, experiential marketing, search engine optimization, ambient marketing, value co-creation, marketing metrics, and so on. These concepts are presented in an accessible way to enable students to learn both the classic and contemporary elements of effective marketing.

Acknowledgements

Our thanks go to the following reviewers for their comments at various stages in the text's development:

Anne Marie Justinus Stærmose, Københavns Erhvervs Akademi
Andy Prothero, University College Dublin
Atanu Nath, University of Surrey
Birgit Wauters, Vrije Universiteit Brussels
Boris Maciejovsky, Imperial College London
Carsten Rennhak, EBS
Elisabeth Brüggen, Maastricht University
Glynn Atwall, ESC Rennes School of Business
Håkan Perzon, Luleå University of Technology
Jaya Sameera, University of East London
Jocelyn Hayes, University of York
John Nicholson, Hull University Business School

John Pallister, Cardiff University
Juliet Memery, University of Portsmouth
Kuldeep Banwait, University of Derby
Markus Wohlfeil, University College Cork
Mary Morgan, Cardiff University
Ming Lim, University of Leicester
Nadine Walter, TiasNimbus Business School
Nathalie Dens, Universiteit Antwerpen
Nik Yip, University of East Anglia
Patrik Gottfridsson, Karlstads Universitet
Rebecca Hughes, University of West England
Tony Willis, University of Surrey
Vicky Roberts, Staffordshire University

We would also like to thank the following contributors for the material which they have provided for this textbook and its accompanying online resources:

Brian Sealer, Loughborough University
David Cosgrave, University of Limerick
Deborah Sadd, Bournemouth University
Desmond Thwaites, Leeds University Business School
Glynn Atwall, ESC Rennes School of Business
Mark Durkin, Ulster University Business School
Marie O'Dwyer, Waterford Institute of Technology
Michael Gannon, Dublin University Business School
Yue Meng, Bournemouth University

Dan Germain, Innocent
Paulo Alves, BMW
Russell Jones, Diageo
Shane Lake, HungryHouse.co.uk

Authors' acknowledgements

We would like to thank colleagues, contributors and the reviewers who have offered advice and helped develop this text. We would also like to thank our editors Jennifer Yendell, Peter Hooper and Caroline Prodger for their invaluable support and assistance.

Every effort has been made to trace and acknowledge ownership of copyright and to clear permission for material reproduced in this book. The publishers will be pleased to make suitable arrangements to clear permission with any copyright holders whom it has not been possible to contact.

Picture acknowledgements

The authors and publishers would like to extend thanks to the following for the reproduction of company and advertising and/or logos:

Exhibits

1.1: Thanks to Alamy Stock Photography; 1.2: Thanks to Advertising Archives; 1.3: Thanks to The Hermès Group; 1.4: Thanks to PepsiCo; 1.5: Thanks to STA Travel; 1.6: Thanks to Oxfam; 2.1: Thanks to The Emirates Group; 2.2: Thanks to The Santander Group; 2.3: Thanks to Marks and Spencer plc; 2.4: Thanks to Statoil ASA; 2.5: Thanks to Advertising Archives; 2.6: Thanks to H&M; 2.7: Thanks to Mars; 2.8: Thanks to Fiji Water; 3.1: Thanks to Wm Morrison Supermarkets plc; 3.2: Thanks to Kohler Mira Ltd; 3.3: Thanks to Advertising Archives; 3.4: Thanks to comparethemarket.com; 3.5: Thanks to Volkswagen; 3.6: Thanks to Adidas; 3.7: Thanks to Greenpeace; 3.8: Thanks to Alamy Stock Photography; 3.9: Thanks to IKEA; 3.10: Thanks to Alamy Stock Photography; C3.1: Thanks to Tourism Queensland; 4.1: Thanks to Diageo; 4.2: Thanks to Alamy Stock Photography; 4.3: Thanks to Google; 4.4: Thanks to iStockphoto; 5.1: Thanks to Garmin Ltd; 5.2: 'Café' by Peter Lindbergh, Thanks to Leagas Delaney and Patek Philippe; 5.3: Thanks to Billabong Europe; 5.4: Thanks to The Gro Company; 5.5: Thanks to HSBC; 5.6: Thanks to Advertising Archives; 5.7: Thanks to The Coca-Cola Company; 5.8: Thanks to Panasonic; 6.1: Thanks to Nike; 6.2: Thanks to Tropicana; 6.3: Thanks to Ralph Lauren; 6.4: Thanks to Pernod-Ricard; 6.5: Thanks to NGN; 6.6: Thanks to Zara; 7.1: Thanks to nycvisit.com; 7.2: Thanks to IKEA; 7.3: Thanks to Vueling Airlines; 7.4: Thanks to B&Q; 7.5: Thanks to Xerox; 7.6: Thanks to Singapore Airlines; 7.7: Thanks to Guinness; 8.1: Thanks to MoneySupermarket.com; 8.2: Thanks to Apple Inc.; 8.3: Thanks to Advertising Archives; 8.4: Thanks to Rimmel/Cody Inc; 8.5: Thanks to Amazon; C8.1: Thanks to the Jelly Bean Factory; 9.1: Thanks to Apple Inc.; 9.2: Thanks to Nielsen Media Research UK; 9.3: Thanks to Diesel; 9.4: Thanks to Myriad PR/3M; 9.5: Thanks to Virgin Atlantic; 9.6: Thanks to Apple Inc; 9.7: Thanks to Belfast Zoo; 9.8: Thanks to Specsavers; 10.1: Thanks to John Harris; 10.2: Thanks to The Boots Company plc; 10.3: Thanks to Macmillan Cancer Support; 10.4: Thanks to Pantene Thailand; 10.5: Thanks to David Carroll; 10.6: Thanks to Blendtec; 11.1: Thanks to iStockphoto; 11.2: Thanks to Alamy Stock Photography; 11.3: Thanks to Toni and Guy; 11.4: Thanks to iStockphoto; 11.5: Thanks to Planet Beach; 11.6: Thanks to Calvin Klein, Cath Kidson, Dior, Disney, Helly Hansen, Hobbs, Hugo Boss, Nine West, Pandora and YSL; 11.7: Thanks to DHL; 12.1: Thanks to Philips and P&G; 12.2: Thanks to IBM; 12.3: Thanks to TAGHeuer; 12.4: Thanks to Kellogg's; 12.5: Thanks to Zappos; 12.6: Thanks to Neuroth; 12.7: Thanks to Toyota.

Figures

5.4: Thanks to Marriott International Inc.

Part opening images

Part 1: Thanks to innocent/The Coca-Cola Company; Part 2: Thanks to BMW; Part 3: Thanks to Diageo.

Chapter opening images

1: Thanks to Advertising Archives; 2: Thanks to innocent/The Coca-Cola Company; 3: Thanks to MoneySupermarket.com; 4: Thanks to Diageo; 5: Thanks to Billabong Europe; 6: Thanks to iStockphoto; 7: Thanks to Guinness; 8: Thanks to MoneySupermarket.com; 9: Thanks to Apple Inc; 10: Thanks to T-Mobile; 11: Thanks to DHL; 12: Thanks to TAGHeuer.

Marketing Spotlight images

1.1: Thanks to Alamy Stock Photography; 2.1: Thanks to Alamy Stock Photography; 3.1: Thanks to Sulake Corporation Oy. HABBO; 4.1: Thanks to iStockphoto; 5.1: Thanks to Blackberry; 6.1: Thanks to Nespresso; 7.1: Thanks to Build-A-Bear Workshop Inc.; 8.1: Thanks to Aldi; 9.1: Thanks to Barclays; 10.1: Thanks to T-Mobile; 11.1; Thanks to iStockphoto; 12.1: Thanks to Visa.

Case images

1: Thanks to Visit Britain; 2: Thanks to innocent/The Coca-Cola Company; 3: Thanks to Stefano Liboni; 4: Thanks to iStockphoto; 5: Thanks to iStockphoto; 6: Thanks to Carlsberg; 7: Thanks to ShredBank; 8: Thanks to iStockphoto; 9: Thanks to Getty Images; 10: Thanks to Diageo; 11: Thanks to Nielsen Media Research UK; 12: Thanks to iStockphoto.

Evert effort has been made to trace and acknowledge ownership of copyright and to clear permission for material reproduced in this book. The publishers will be pleased to make suitable arrangements to clear permission with any copyright holders whom it has not been possible to contact.

Guided Tour

Chapter Outline and Learning Outcomes

The topics covered and a set of outcomes are included at the start of each chapter, summarizing what to expect from each chapter.

MARKETING SPOTLIGHT

Nespresso

Traditionally, the coffee market comprised two broad segments, namely, the at-home market where consumption was largely pre-ground, instant coffee and contrasted with the on-trade segment in cafés and bars where, particularly in Europe, the coffee was ground from roasted beans generating the distinctive coffee aroma and full flavour. Some key trends have radically changed consumer behaviour in the at-home segment. First is the growth in entertaining at home rather than going out, which has driven the demand for everything from the recipes of celebrity chefs to changes in house design. Combined with a growing switch from tea to coffee, it meant that consumers became more discerning about the kind of coffee that they consumed at home, with an emerging preference towards more gourmet coffees. And, third, there is the trend towards individualization which is apparent in everything from telephones to beers to personal computers. This has given rise to a new business – portion coffees, in which Nespresso has been the undisputed market leader.

Marketing Spotlight

A lively vignette begins each chapter to introduce the main topic and show how marketing works in real life.

Marketing in Action 6.2   Gap's logo

Critical Thinking: Below is a review of the failed attemp discuss the extent to which a logo redesign was the correct tives should it have taken?

Before   After

1969 a
for me
right an
expans
increas
slide d
was to

Marketing in Action

In each chapter you'll find these fun, informative examples of marketing in action, which show how the issues covered in the chapter affect real life companies and products. Each Marketing in Action vignette has a Critical Thinking box to provoke discussion and encourage critical reflection on that topic.

Social Media Marketing

Critical Thinking: Below is a review of the succe of other brands that have tried to reposition. Cri

Old Spice is a brand of male grooming products and fragrances owned by the consumer goods group Procter & Gamble. Founded in the 1930s, the brand

Social Media Marketing

There are eight brand **new** social media marketing vignettes throughout the book. These contain insights on developing themes and effective practice and include questions for discussion and critical thinking.

Ethical Debate 11.1   Superma

Love them or hate them but you cannot ignore them. Superm gained enormous power over time. For example, the top four Asda and Morrisons – account for over 76 per cent of all gr large supermarkets and over 1,800 convenience stores, and it billion in 2011. It takes £1 of every £8 spent by consumers market concentration are even higher. For example in Australi control 70 per cent of the market and 23 cents in every dolla owned by either of these two companies.

Many critics contend that this level of power is unaccep them in a very difficult position because they are dependent o market demands lower supply prices, participation in special p

Ethical Debates

Ethical debate boxes are located throughout the book, designed to highlight ethical issues, provoke discussion and critical reflection.

Exhibit 2.1 This advert for Emirates Airlines reflects the economic growth of countries like China and the UAE

Advertisements, figures and tables

We've included a hand-selected array of contemporary advertisements and images to show marketing in action. Key concepts and models are illustrated using figures, tables and charts.

End of chapter case studies

Every chapter has its own case study, directly relating to the issues discussed and designed to bring the theories to life. See page xii for a full list of companies and issues covered. Questions are included for class work, assignments, revision and to promote critical reflection.

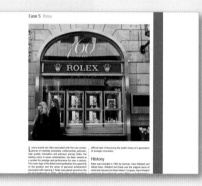

Summary

This chapter has examined the key activit
issues were addressed.

1. The process of market segmentatio
   them better by segmenting the ma
2. There are a variety of bases availa
   combination of bases is used to effe
   as benefits sought and purchase be
   are a key factor in segmenting orga

End of chapter material

The chapter Summary reinforces the main topics to make sure you have acquired a solid understanding. Study questions allow you to apply your understanding and think critically about the topics. Suggested reading and References direct you towards the best sources for further research.

Videos and Ad Insights

Look out for the Marketing Showcase and Ad Insight icons in the text to refer you to the digital support tools that accompany this book. Watch the videos and put your marketing skills into practice by answering the accompanying questions.

Tour our video and digital resources

In addition to the great study tools available for student and lecturers through **Connect** there are a host of support resources available to you via our website:

Online Learning Centre

Visit www.mcgraw-hill.co.uk/textbooks/fahy today

Resources for Students:
- Marketing weblinks
- Learning objectives
- Case study guidelines
- Glossary
- Ad Insight videos

Also available for lecturers:
- Case study teaching notes
- PowerPoint slides
- New case studies
- An image bank of artwork from the textbook
- Marketing Showcase videos

Ad Insight

On the student centre of the OLC you will find a wealth of TV advertising campaigns, many of which are linked to topics in the book. Look out for the Ad Insight icon in the text to refer you to watch the relevant clip and put your marketing skills into practice by answering the accompanying questions.

Marketing Showcase

We are excited to offer an exclusive set of new video cases to lecturers adopting this text. Each video illustrates a number of core marketing concepts linked to the book to help students to see how marketing works in the real world. This fantastic video resource will add real value to lectures, providing attention-grabbing content that helps students to make the connection between theory and practice.

What do the videos cover?

The videos offer students insights into how different organisations have successfully harnessed the elements of the marketing mix, including discussions about new product development, pricing, promotion, packaging, market research, relationship and digital marketing. The videos feature interviews with business leaders and marketing professionals, researched and conducted by Professor John Fahy to ensure seamless integration with the content of the new edition of this text.

How can I use them?

To ensure maximum flexibility for teaching purposes, the videos have been edited to focus on key topics so that short extracts can be easily integrated into a lecture presentation or be delivered in a tutorial setting to spark class discussion. To ensure painless preparation for teaching, each video is accompanied by teaching notes and discussion questions.

Some highlights of the video package include:

- **innocent's** Head of Creative responding to criticism of their pricing policy
- A first-hand account of how a young student entrepreneur set up the thriving **SuperJam** brand, taking his homemade preserves from the kitchen table to the supermarket
- How **Hungry House** took on the Dragon's Den and the take away market
- An interview with **BMW** reveals how they grow their market without damaging their reputation as a luxury brand

How do I get the videos?

The full suite of videos is available exclusively to lecturers adopting this textbook. For ultimate flexibility, they are available to lecturers:

- through **Connect**
- online at www.mcgraw-hill.co.uk/textbooks/fahy

If you are interested in this resource, please contact your McGraw-Hill representative or visit **www.mcgraw-hill.co.uk/textbooks/fahy** to request a demonstration.

Lecturer Test bank in EZ Test

A test bank of hundreds of questions is available to lecturers adopting this book for their module, either through Connect, or if preferred, direct through EZ Test online. A range of questions is provided for each chapter including multiple choice, true or false, and short answer or essay questions. The questions are identified by type, difficulty, and topic to help you to select questions that best suit your needs.

McGraw-Hill EZ Test Online is accessible to busy academics virtually anywhere. They also have access to hundreds of banks and thousands of questions created for other McGraw-Hill titles. Multiple versions of tests can be saved for delivery on paper or online through WebCT, Blackboard and other course management systems.

To register for this FREE resource, visit www.eztestonline.com or contact your McGraw-Hill representative.

 # STUDENTS...

Want to get **better grades**? *(Who doesn't?)*

Prefer to do your **homework online**? *(After all, you are online anyway...)*

Need **a better way** to **study** before the big test?

(A little peace of mind is a good thing...)

With **McGraw-Hill's** *Connect*™ *Plus Marketing,*

STUDENTS GET:

- **Easy online access** to homework, tests, and quizzes assigned by your instructor.

- **Immediate feedback** on how you're doing. (No more wishing you could call your instructor at 1 a.m.)

- **Quick access** to lectures, practice materials, eBook, and more. (All the material you need to be successful is right at your fingertips.)

- A Self-Quiz and Study tool that **assesses your knowledge** and **recommends** specific readings, supplemental study materials, and additional practice work.

- Access to the e-book of this text.

INSTRUCTORS...

Would you like your **students** to show up for class **more prepared**?
(Let's face it, class is much more fun if everyone is engaged and prepared...)

Want an **easy way to assign** homework online and track student **progress**?
(Less time grading means more time teaching...)

Want an **instant view** of student or class performance? *(No more wondering if students understand...)*

Need to **collect data and generate reports** required for administration or accreditation? *(Say goodbye to manually tracking student learning outcomes...)*

Want to **record and post your lectures** for students to view online?

With **McGraw-Hill's** *Connect*™ *Plus Marketing,*

INSTRUCTORS GET:

- Simple **assignment management**, allowing you to spend more time teaching.

- **Auto-graded** assignments, quizzes, and tests.

- **Detailed Visual Reporting** where student and section results can be viewed and analysed.

- Sophisticated **online testing** capability.

- A **filtering and reporting** function that allows you to easily assign and report on materials that are correlated to sections in the book and level of difficulty.

- An easy-to-use **lecture capture** tool.

- The option to **upload course documents** for student access.

Want an online, searchable version of your textbook?

Wish your textbook could be **available online** while you're doing your assignments?

Connect™ Plus Marketing eBook

If you choose to use *Connect™ Plus Marketing*, you have an affordable and searchable online version of your book integrated with your other online tools.

Connect™ Plus Marketing eBook offers a media-rich version of the book, including:

- Topic search
- Direct links from assignments
- Adjustable text size
- Jump to page number
- Print by section

Want to get more value from your textbook purchase?

Think learning marketing should be a bit more **interesting**?

Check out the STUDENT RESOURCES section under the *Connect™* Library tab.

Here you'll find a wealth of resources designed to help you achieve your goals in the course. Every student has different needs, so explore the STUDENT RESOURCES to find the materials best suited to you.

Part 1

A new Marketing Showcase video featuring an interview with innocent's Head of Creative is available to lecturers for presentation and discussion in class.

MARKETING
SHOWCASE

The Market-Led Organization

HERMÈS
PARIS
HERMÈS, LIFE AS A TALE

Chapter 1
The Nature of Marketing

Chapter outline

What is marketing?

The development of marketing

Marketing and business performance

The scope of marketing

Planning marketing activity

Learning outcomes

By the end of this chapter you will understand:

1. what marketing is
2. the nature of customer value
3. how marketing thought has developed over the years
4. the scope of marketing
5. the relationship between adopting a marketing philosophy and business performance
6. the role and importance of marketing planning.

Twitter

If there is one business that captures the essence of the current social media age, it is Twitter. Founded in 2006, the micro-blogging service has become a global phenomenon. Currently estimated to have 200 million users, Twitter is a service that allows members to post (or tweet!) short messages of no more than 140 characters. This critical difference from regular blogs has been one of the keys to its success. These short messages can be produced quickly and many are posted using mobile handsets which gives them a sense of immediacy. Tweets are then read by

'followers' and popular messages are 're-tweeted' by these followers in turn, to their readers. In any sphere, at any given time, whether it is business, politics, friends or celebrity one can quickly get a real-time sense of what is happening by following Twitter conversations and watching what is 'trending'.

Initially Twitter was very popular among technophiles and then quickly followed by celebrities. Those with the highest number of Twitter followers currently include Lady Gaga, Justin Beiber and Britney Spears. In 2011, controversial actor Charlie Sheen attained Guinness World Record status for gaining 1 million followers in just over 25 hours, demonstrating the powerful social potential of the medium. Along with social networks like Facebook and image and video sharing websites like Flickr and YouTube, Twitter exemplifies our current 'always on' society where people are spending a greater proportion of their time in front of a screen, connected to friends or work and providing real-time information.

So what are the implications of all of these developments for marketing? There are many. First, Twitter provides an illustration of the speed of change in marketplaces. The business is only five years old but it has dramatically altered how people receive information and has had a major impact on the operations of businesses like radio and newspapers. Second, marketers have been grappling with using Twitter as a marketing tool for updates about products, special offers, answering customer service queries and so on. The UK furniture firm, Habitat received negative coverage for using keywords relating to the Iranian elections in 2009 to drive traffic to its tweets. Third, organizations also need to be more careful than ever regarding issues such as the quality of service provided, socially responsible behaviour, etc. as criticisms and negative tweets will reach the public domain very quickly. Finally, one of the key attractions of marketing through Twitter is that followers have chosen to 'opt in' to receive messages, in contrast to traditional, interruptive forms of communication such as television advertising. Firms like the fruit drinks maker, innocent Ltd use Twitter to communicate its brand values through posting quirky messages on a variety of topics.

Although it hosts about 1 billion tweets per week and is estimated to be worth US$10 billion, Twitter's future remains uncertain. Despite its rapid growth and high usage levels, it has only begun to generate some income through both search and display advertising. Turning its popularity into cash will be one of its key challenges in the years ahead.[1]

The activities of companies both reflect and shape the world that we live in. For example, some have argued that the invention of the motor car has defined the way we live today because it allowed personal mobility on a scale that had never been seen before. It contributed to the growth of city suburbs, to increased recreation and to an upsurge in consumer credit. It gave us shopping malls, theme parks, motels, a fast-food industry and a generation of road movies. In a similar vein, many are now arguing that Facebook will have just as profound an impact on how we live, changing how we learn, how we interact with others and how companies do their marketing (see Exhibit 1.1).

Therefore, the world of business is an exciting one where there are new successes and failures every day. The newspaper industry was once all powerful and the main means by which consumers learned about what was happening in the world. It continued to thrive with the arrival of radio and television and complemented these media. But the Internet has changed the way that news is both captured and communicated with the result that many newspapers are either struggling or failing. Not too long ago, Sony dominated the gaming business with its PlayStation consoles and exciting range of games. While trying to strengthen the functionality of its PlayStation 3, it wasn't alive to the threat posed by the Nintendo Wii, whose ease of use, lower price points and broader appeal enabled it to capture a leading share in the market. And now both organizations must respond to an increasing customer preference for online play in virtual worlds.

At the heart of all of this change is marketing. Companies succeed and fail for many reasons but very often marketing is central to the outcome. The reason for this is that the focus of marketing is on customers and their changing needs. If you don't have customers, you don't have a business. Successful companies are those that succeed not only in getting customers but also in keeping them through being constantly aware of their changing needs. The goal of marketing is long-term customer satisfaction, not short-term deception or gimmicks. This theme is reinforced by the writings of top management consultant Peter Drucker, who stated:[2]

> *Because the purpose of business is to create and keep customers, it has only two central functions – marketing and innovation. The basic function of marketing is to attract and retain customers at a profit.*

What does this statement tell us? First, it places marketing in a central role for business success since it is concerned with the creation and retention of customers. The failure of many products, particularly those in sectors like information technology, is often attributed to a lack of attention to customer needs. A recent case in point was Google's Wave, which was one of the most technically sophisticated web applications ever built. The company had spent thousands of man-hours building the site but neither the company (nor the consumer) seemed to be sure what it was for and it was withdrawn in 2010 after only a few months in operation. Second, it is a reality of commercial life that it is much more expensive to attract new customers than to retain existing ones. Indeed, the costs of attracting new customers have been found to be up to six times higher than the costs of retaining existing ones.[3] Consequently, marketing-orientated companies recognize the importance of building relationships with customers by providing satisfaction and attracting new customers by creating added value. Grönroos stressed the importance of relationship building in his definition of marketing, in which he describes the objective of marketing as to establish, develop and commercialize long-term customer relationships so that the objectives of the

Exhibit 1.1 Facebook has quickly become a huge, global business

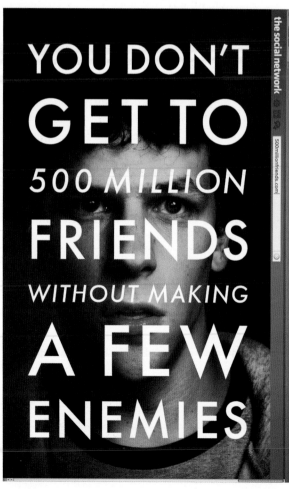

YOU DON'T GET TO 500 MILLION FRIENDS WITHOUT MAKING A FEW ENEMIES

the social network

500millionfriends.com

parties involved are met.[4] Third, since most markets are characterized by strong competition, the statement also suggests the need to monitor and understand competitors, since it is to rivals that customers will turn if their needs are not being met. The rest of this chapter will examine some of these ideas in more detail.

What is marketing?

The modern **marketing concept** can be expressed as 'the achievement of corporate goals through meeting and exceeding customer needs better than the competition'. For example, the mantra at Procter & Gamble, one of the world's leading consumer products companies, is that it must win at the first and second moments of truth – that is, in the shop where the consumer decides which brand to select and in the home when he/she uses it. Three conditions must be met before the marketing concept can be applied. First, company activities should be focused on providing **customer satisfaction** rather than, for example, simply producing products. This is not always as easy as it may first appear. Organizations almost by definition are inward looking with a focus on their people, their operations and their products. The customer may often appear to be at some remove from the organization and when their needs are changing rapidly, companies can lose touch with them. For example, until recently, Finland's Nokia was the world's dominant mobile-phone manufacturer by some distance. However, while it now still ships more phones than any of its competitors annually, it has fallen far behind Apple in terms of profitability and is not well positioned to exploit the shift in consumer tastes towards more technologically advanced smartphones.

Second, the achievement of customer satisfaction relies on integrated effort. The responsibility for the implementation of the concept lies not just within the marketing department but should run right through production, finance, research and development, engineering and other departments. The fact that marketing is the responsibility of everyone in the organization provides significant challenges for the management of companies. Finally, for integrated effort to come about, management must believe that corporate goals can be achieved through satisfied customers (see Figure 1.1). Some companies are quicker and better at recognizing the importance of the marketing concept than others. For example, Nike was a late entrant into the running shoe business dominated by brands such as Reebok and Puma, but it has established itself as the world's leading sportswear company, through the delivery of powerful brand values.

In summary, companies can be viewed as being either inward looking or outward looking. In the former, the focus is on making things or providing services but with significant attention being paid to the efficiency with which internal operations and processes are conducted. Companies that build strategy from the outside in start with the customer and work backwards from an understanding of what customers truly value. The difference in emphasis is subtle but very important. By maintaining an outside-in focus, companies can understand what customers value and how to consistently innovate new sources of value that keep bringing them back. Doing so efficiently, ensures that value is created and delivered at a profit to the company – the ultimate goal of marketing.

The nature of customer value

If delivering **customer value** is the key to building a successful business, how can a firm know if it is creating such value? This has proven to be a troublesome problem for many companies. For example, some firms add new features to products and hope that this will attract

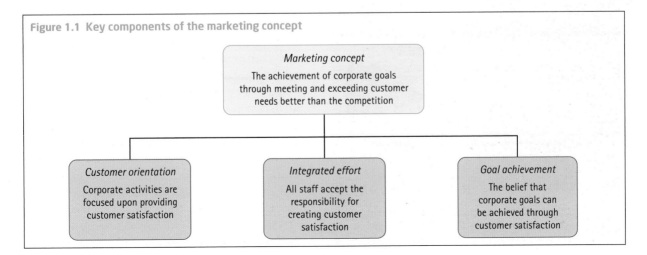

Figure 1.1 Key components of the marketing concept

customers. Others engage in new marketing activities such as advertising campaigns, Facebook competitions or the creation of retail experiences. And still others may seek to exploit consumer preferences for economy by offering products or services at lower prices. But the key is, do consumers see any of these changes as being beneficial to them and worth any of the costs that they may have to incur in order to obtain these benefits. Consequently, customer value is often expressed in terms of the definition below and it is important to note that it is customers and not organizations who define what represents value:

$$\text{customer value} = \text{perceived benefits} - \text{perceived sacrifice}$$

Perceived benefits can be derived from the product (for example, the hotel room and restaurant), the associated service (for example, how responsive the hotel is to the specific needs of customers) and the image of the company (for example, is the image of the company/product favourable?) (see Exhibit 1.2). Conveying benefits is a critical marketing task and is central to positioning and branding, as we shall see in Chapters 5 and 6.

Exhibit 1.2 L'Oréal Elvive advertisement

Go to the website to see how L'Oréal present the favourable benefits of using its Elvive shampoo.
www.mcgraw-hill.co.uk/textbooks/fahy

Perceived sacrifice is the total cost associated with buying the product. This consists not just of monetary costs, but also the time and energy involved in the purchase. For example, with hotels, good location can reduce the time and energy required to find a suitable place to stay. But marketers need to be aware of another critical sacrifice in some buying situations; this is the potential psychological cost of not making the right decision. Uncertainty means that people perceive risk when purchasing. Therefore, hotels like the Marriott or restaurants like McDonald's aim for consistency so that customers can be confident of what they will receive when they visit these service providers.

A further key to marketing success is to ensure that the value offered exceeds that of competitors. Consumers decide on purchases on the basis of judgements about the value offered by different suppliers. Once a product has been purchased, customer satisfaction depends on its perceived performance compared to the buyer's expectations and will be achieved if these expectations are met or exceeded. Expectations are formed through pre-buying experiences, discussions with other people and suppliers' marketing activities. Companies need to avoid the mistake of setting customer expectations too high through exaggerated promotional claims, since this can lead to dissatisfaction if performance falls short of expectations.

In the current competitive climate, it is usually not enough simply to match performance and expectations. Expectations need to be exceeded for commercial success so that customers are delighted with the outcome. In order to understand the concept of customer satisfaction, the Kano model (see Figure 1.2) helps to separate characteristics that cause dissatisfaction,

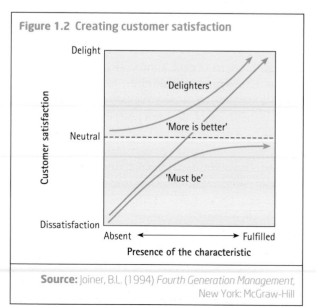

Figure 1.2 Creating customer satisfaction

Source: Joiner, B.L. (1994) *Fourth Generation Management*, New York: McGraw-Hill

satisfaction and delight. Three characteristics underlie the model: 'must be', 'more is better' and 'delighters'.

Those characteristics recognized as 'must bes' are expected and thus taken for granted. For example, commuters expect planes or trains to depart on time and for schedules to be maintained. Lack of these characteristics causes annoyance but their presence only brings dissatisfaction up to a neutral level. 'More is better' characteristics can take satisfaction past neutral and into the positive satisfaction range. For example, no response to a telephone call can cause dissatisfaction, but a fast response may cause positive satisfaction. The usability of search results is an example of 'more is better' and has become a key differentiating factor in the search engine industry, which has allowed Google to become the dominant player. 'Delighters' are the unexpected characteristics that surprise the customer. Their absence does not cause dissatisfaction, but their presence delights the customer. For example, tourists who have found that a holiday destination has exceeded their expectations through the quality of customer service that they have received will often be delighted and are likely to recommend the destination to friends and colleagues.

Over time, however, such 'delighters' become expected, which means that the bar is continually being raised. For example, some car manufacturers provided unexpected delighters such as CD players and delay mechanisms on interior lights so that there is time to find the ignition socket at night. These are standard on most cars now and have become 'must be' characteristics because customers have come to expect them. This means that marketers must constantly strive to find new ways of delighting; innovative thinking and listening to customers are key ingredients in this.

Four forms of customer value

Though modern organizations offer an innumerable variety of products and services, four core forms of customer value have been identified as follows:

Price value: one of the most powerful customer motivations to purchase is because a product is perceived as being cheaper than those offered by competitors. This has been exploited in many industries such as air travel (Ryanair), food retailing (Aldi), car rental (EasyCar), and so on. These types of organizations recognize that, in their markets, some consumers will forego extra product features in order to avail of low prices (see market segmentation in Chapter 5). They respond by providing basic products at low prices. For example, low fares airlines have stripped away many of the features that used to characterize air travel such as in-flight meals, airport check-ins and no baggage restrictions. Consumers who want these features are now charged extra for them and the profitability of low price companies is further enhanced by a high degree of attention that they pay to the efficiency of their operations. The food retailer Aldi has an estimated annual turnover of €40 billion and is one of Germany's most successful companies. Its business proposition is to offer customers a limited range of own-label products at permanently low prices in a no-frills environment.

Performance value: in the same way that some customers have a preference for low price, others are more concerned about product performance. What they are looking for is the latest features and they are attracted to products by their functionality and perceived quality levels. The priority for companies operating in this space is to be consistently innovative, exploiting changes and discontinuities in technology in order to deliver products with attractive features and functionality. For example, the UK electronic products manufacturer, Dyson has a team of 420 engineers and scientists working on product ideas and the firm has been responsible for innovations like the cyclonic vacuum cleaner, the Airblade electric hand dryer and the Contrarotator, which was the world's first washing machine with two counter-rotating drums for a better clean. Firms like Dyson aim to provide value to customers based on the functionality and performance features of their products and services.

Emotional value: one of the big challenges facing the modern firm is to find effective ways to differentiate products based on performance elements. If one looks at the car industry for example, the technical differences between cars in particular categories such as economy cars and family saloons are marginal. Most have very similar designs, functionality and features, and different manufacturers frequently share time on the same production lines. Similarly for a whole array of consumer products such as basic electrical appliances, the brands of competing firms are regularly manufactured by a small number of companies and technical differences between them are minimal. Consequently, the only real difference that exists between these brands is in the mind of the consumer and this is what is known as emotional value. Some consumers may prefer Volvo cars because they believe them to be safer than competing brands (technically this is not the case) and as a result remain loyal Volvo buyers. This kind of emotional value is created through marketing activity as we shall discuss throughout the book. It also helps to explain why some consumers will pay huge premiums for luxury brands (Chanel, Hermes) and why others will queue for hours to be the

Exhibit 1.3 Luxury brands like Hermès possess high levels of emotional value

first among their peers to own certain products (iPad, Kate Moss clothing) (see Exhibit 1.3).

Relational Value: Another important motive to purchase is the quality of service received by the customer. This presents a particular opportunity in the case of service businesses (see Chapter 7) such as a restaurant meal or business taxation services which are not easy to evaluate in advance of purchase. When the customer finds a good quality service provider, they may be willing to stay with this provider and as the relationship builds a high level of trust becomes established between the parties. Central to this is the notion of the **lifetime value of a customer** which is recognition by the company of the potential sales, profits and endorsements that come from a repeat customer who stays with the company for several years. But relational value is not restricted to just service businesses. All kinds of organizations are now becoming proficient users of **customer relationship management** (CRM) systems to get to know their customers better and to interact with them on a regular basis (see Chapter 7). Even fast-moving consumer goods brands such as innocent and Walkers have sought to build stronger relationships with core customers through running events that customers can enjoy (innocent village fetes, Walkers 'Do Us a Flavour') while in turn the company benefits from not only customer loyalty but also creation of new product ideas that come from the market place (see Exhibit 1.4). The role of social media in building relational value is explored in Social Media Marketing 1.1.

The challenge for organizations then is to try to become a value leader on one of these four dimensions. Those that do achieve these leadership positions such as Ryanair (price value leader in aviation) or Louis Vuitton (emotional value leader in luxury fashion goods) tend to be significantly more successful than their peers. This is because they have a clearly defined **customer value proposition** or unique selling point (USP) which is a reason why customers return to them again and again. It is not normally possible for companies to compete on more than one dimension as to do so would mean presenting a confusing message in the marketplace. However, the proposition may evolve over time. For example, innocent drinks initially captured a share of the market through the quality of their smoothies (performance value) but this was quickly supplanted by the personality of the brand – its humorous, quirky approach to business and its cause-related activity (emotional value). And as discussed above, some of its recent initiatives suggest a drive towards relational value.

Social Media Marketing 1.1 The return of Wispa

> **Critical Thinking:** Below is a review of the early success, failure and return to success of the Wispa brand. The product never changed but its sales levels changed dramatically. Critically evaluate why this was the case.

The Wispa chocolate brand made by Cadbury has had a chequered career. It was launched in 1984 and was so successful initially that the company's production system struggled to keep up with demand. Despite this early success, sales began to decline in the 1980s and several brand extensions such as Wispa Gold and Wispa Mint did little to alter this trend. In 2003, Cadbury made the decision to withdraw the brand and to place it within the Cadbury portfolio as Cadbury Dairy Milk Bubbly.

However, reflecting the level of customer attachment that had been created, consumers almost immediately began calling for the brand to be restored. This had happened in previous instances where confectionary brands had been withdrawn but what was different this time was that these disparate brand fans had a new forum – social networks, where they could voice their opinion. By 2007, over 10,000 fans had amassed on Facebook – then one of the largest Facebook groups – and they also took their campaign to the real world by storming the Iggy Pop stage during the Glastonbury festival with a 'Bring Back Wispa' banner. Cadbury decided to test if this demand would turn into real sales and brought back Wispa on a trial basis by producing 23 million bars. However, these sold out even before 50 per cent distribution could be reached and some purchasers even began trading them on eBay.

On the back of this success, Wispa was permanently relaunched in 2008. Building on its successful Facebook profile, the brand chose to put its fans at the heart of its communications strategy. It gave them a call to action by asking them what they would pledge as part of a 'For the Love of Wispa' campaign. 300 fans (from the over 2,000 pledges received) were selected to star in an advert celebrating the return of the brand. Involving fans in this way strengthened their relationship with the brand and also helped to grow Wispa's fan base. This was followed by the Wispa Gold Messages campaign where fans could broadcast messages to each other on Wispa-sponsored billboards. Using a social media focus, Wispa has reclaimed its position as the number one chocolate bar in the UK with sales of almost £60 million in 2010 and almost 1 million Facebook fans.

Based on: Farquhar, Barrie and Goodwin (2010);[5] Parry (2008)[6].

The key role of customer value enables us to offer the following definition of **marketing**:

Marketing is the delivery of value to customers at a profit.

Therefore we see that the two core elements of marketing are value and profit. Organizations must create and deliver some form of value for some customer group. But they also must be able to do this in a manner that enables them to generate a profit, otherwise their business will be unsustainable. Being consistently able to provide value and generate profit is a characteristic of the most successful companies such as Apple and Tesco.

The development of marketing

The origins of modern marketing can be traced to the Industrial Revolutions that took place in Britain around 1750 and in the USA and Germany around 1830.[7] Advances in production and distribution, and the migration of rural masses to urban areas, created the potential for large-scale markets. As business people sought to exploit these markets, the institutions of marketing such as advertising media and distribution channels began to grow and develop. Marketing as a field of study began in the early part of the twentieth century, growing out of courses that examined issues relating to distribution.[8] The focus of marketing courses

**Exhibit 1.4 The Walkers 'Do Us a Flavour campaign'
helped to build its relational value proposition**

Like the Walkers advert above, many of innocent
Ltd's marketing activities have been designed to build
its relational value.
www.mcgraw-hill.co.uk/textbooks/fahy

in the 1950s and 1960s was on 'how to do it', with an
emphasis on the techniques of marketing.[9] In more
recent times, attention has been paid to the philosophy
of marketing as a way of doing business, and to the
nature and impact of marketing on stakeholders and
society in general.

Despite this long tradition, there is no guarantee
that all companies will adopt a **marketing orientation**. Many firms today are characterized by an inward-
looking stance, where their focus is on existing products
or the internal operations of the company, that can be
traced all the way back to the emergence of mass production in the USA in the 1920s and 1930s. Figure 1.3a
illustrates **production orientation** in its crudest form.
The focus is on current production capabilities. The
purpose of the organization is to develop products or
services and it is the quality and innovativeness of these
offerings that are considered to be the key to success.
For example, a report on the funds management industry in the UK found that, in general, the sector was
characterized by a lack of customer focus and a lack
of effective market segmentation, with the result that
many products being offered were unsuitable and
potential sales were being lost.[10]

Many other organizations are characterized by
what can be described as an excessive sales focus.
They may possess good products and services but
believe that the focus of marketing should be on ensuring that customers buy these offerings (see Figure 1.3b).
This is an approach that is often traced back to the
post-Second World War period in the United States
when the engines of mass production generated a
surplus of products in the market and aggressive sales
efforts were required in order to persuade customers

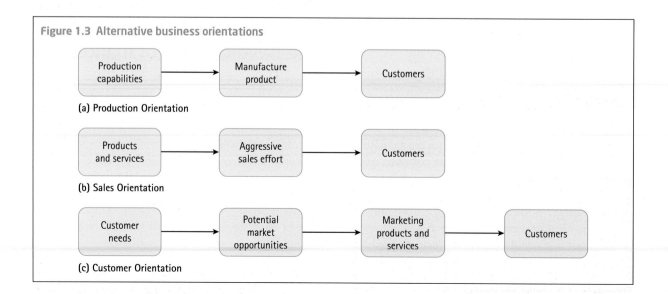

Figure 1.3 Alternative business orientations

(a) Production Orientation
Production capabilities → Manufacture product → Customers

(b) Sales Orientation
Products and services → Aggressive sales effort → Customers

(c) Customer Orientation
Customer needs → Potential market opportunities → Marketing products and services → Customers

to buy. Many industries such as pharmaceuticals rely heavily on sales forces to push products in the marketplace.

The failure of many businesses that were excessively product or sales focused then led to increasing attention to the needs of customers. This orientation is shown in Figure 1.3c. Because customer-orientated companies get close to their customers, they understand their needs and problems. When personal contact is insufficient or not feasible, formal marketing research is commissioned to enable the companies to understand customer motivations and behaviour. Part of the success of German machine tool manufacturers can be attributed to their willingness to develop new products with lead customers – those companies that, themselves, were innovative.[11] This contrasts sharply with the attitude of UK machine tool manufacturers, who saw marketing research only as a tactic to delay new product proposals and who feared that involving customers in new product design would have adverse effects on sales of their current products.

One of the great benefits of having satisfied customers is that they tell others of their experiences, further enhancing sales (see Exhibit 1.5). For example, recent research has shown that the experience of other customers with a product or service has a significant impact on purchase decisions in sectors like automobiles and financial services.[12] Online businesses are significant users of word-of-mouth marketing. For example, TripAdvisor is a website where satisfied and dissatisfied customers post their reviews of hotels and destinations that they have stayed at, and these kinds of reviews influence the purchase decision of other customers.

Sometimes these three orientations are presented as being chronological, with the production orientation

($c.$1930s), followed by the **sales orientation** ($c.$1950s) and then the customer orientation emerging in the 1960s and 1970s. But it is quite clear that in the world of practice all three orientations are still commonplace. Significant attention has also been paid to newer business orientations that have been emerging in recent years, particularly the **societal marketing concept**. One of the major concerns for both business and society is that the resources of the planet are finite and business activity places significant demands on these limited resources. The societal marketing concept holds that marketing strategy should deliver value to customers in a way that maintains or improves both the consumer's and society's well-being. This means that as well as meeting customer needs, businesses should also engage in activities such as reducing pollution as well as developing corporate social responsibility programmes. The societal marketing concept will be dealt with in greater detail in Chapter 2.

Finally, there is also an increasing recognition that a focus on customer needs does not always deliver the kinds of insights that businesses expect.[13] Consumers may not always be able to articulate their needs and wants and that it is also up to organizations to lead markets from time to time. These **market-driven or outside-in firms** seek to anticipate as well as identify consumer needs and build the resource profiles necessary to meet current and anticipated future demand. In the same vein, Vargo and Lusch have called for a move away from the economic model of marketing based on notions of manufactured goods and transactional exchanges to one that is based more clearly on relational exchanges between entities where value is co-created rather than determined by one entity and exchanged with another.[14] Recent developments such as the rapid growth of social media further illustrate the important role of the customer in co-creating value (see Social Media Marketing 1.1).

In short, the differences between market-orientated businesses and internally orientated businesses are summarized in Table 1.1. These can be considered to be two ends of a spectrum. Market-driven businesses display customer concern throughout the business; they understand the criteria customers use to choose between competing suppliers; they invest in market research, and track market changes; they regard marketing spend as an investment, and are fast and flexible in terms of their pursuit of new opportunities.

Efficiency versus effectiveness

We can gain another perspective on customer orientation if we understand the distinction between **efficiency**

Exhibit 1.5 **The STA Travel website enables students to blog about their travel experiences providing useful information for would-be travellers**

Table 1.1 Marketing-orientated businesses versus internally orientated businesses

Market-orientated businesses	Internally orientated businesses
Customer concern throughout business	Convenience comes first
Know customer choice criteria and match with marketing mix	Assume price and product performance key to most sales
Segment by customer differences	Segment by product
Invest in market research (MR) and track market changes	Rely on anecdotes and received wisdom
Welcome change	Cherish status quo
Try to understand competition	Ignore competition
Marketing spend regarded as an investment	Marketing spend regarded as a luxury
Innovation rewarded	Innovation punished
Search for latent markets	Stick with the same
Be fast	Why rush?
Strive for competitive advantage	Happy to be me-too

and **effectiveness**. *Efficiency* is concerned with inputs and outputs. An efficient firm produces goods economically – it does things right. The benefit is that cost per unit of output is low and, therefore, the potential for offering low prices to gain market share, or charging medium to high prices and achieving high profit margins, is present. However, to be successful, a company needs to be more than just efficient; it needs to be effective as well. *Effectiveness* means doing the right things. This implies operating in attractive markets and making products that consumers want to buy. Conversely, companies that operate in unattractive markets or are not producing what consumers want to buy will go out of business – the only question is one of timing. The link between performance and combinations of efficiency and effectiveness is illustrated in Figure 1.4.

A company that is both inefficient and ineffective will go out of business quickly because it is a high-cost producer of products that consumers do not want to buy. This was the case with many web-based businesses that were formed during the dotcom boom of the late 1990s. A company that is efficient and ineffective may last a little longer because its low cost base may generate more profits from the dwindling sales volume it is achieving. Firms that are effective but inefficient are

likely to survive because they are operating in attractive markets and are marketing products that people want to buy. The problem is that their inefficiency is preventing them from reaping the maximum profits from their endeavours. It is the combination of both efficiency and effectiveness that leads to optimum business success. Such firms do well and thrive because they are operating in attractive markets, are supplying products that consumers want to buy and are benefiting from a low cost base.

The global automotive industry is a classic study of the dynamics of efficiency and effectiveness. For many years now, the big three US auto manufacturers – Ford, General Motors and Chrysler – have been in trouble. In 2006, Ford and GM laid off some 55,000 workers between them in the USA, with Chrysler's German operations laying off a further 8,500. This was on top of previous rounds of heavy job losses in 1980, 1991 and 2001. Several rounds of efficiency drives had the effect only of lengthening the time period of the decline of these once leading firms. By January 2009, the US government provided almost $25 billion to GM and Chrysler to help keep them afloat and to allow them the financial breathing space to restructure their operations. In contrast, Toyota has risen to become the leading global car company through a combination of highly reliable, competitively priced vehicles (effectiveness) that are very efficiently produced using innovative and industry-leading production practices (efficiency). However, in 2009 and 2010, Toyota was forced to recall over 9 million vehicles worldwide due to problems with the acceleration system. This recall has damaged Toyota's reputation for effectiveness in the market and it demonstrates the dynamic nature of both efficiency and effectiveness (see Marketing in Action 1.1).

Figure 1.4 Efficiency and effectiveness

	Ineffective	Effective
Inefficient	Goes out of business quickly	Survives
Efficient	Dies slowly	Does well Thrives

Marketing in Action 1.1 Dell Inc.

Critical Thinking: Below is a review of the competitive challenges being faced by Dell Inc. Critically evaluate which has been more damaging for the company – the loss of its effectiveness lead or the loss of its efficiency lead?

The performance of Dell Inc. in the computer business is a classic illustration of the dynamics of efficiency and effectiveness. The company was famously founded by Michael Dell while he was still a student at the University of Texas in Austin and it was revolutionary in its approach to the personal computer business. At the time, other manufacturers produced computers that were sold through a specialist channel of value-added resellers (VARs), as it was felt that customers needed assistance in making their purchasing choices. However, as the technology changed quickly both manufacturers and VARs were often left holding unsold and outdated stock which was costly. Dell took a different approach. He pioneered a make-to-order model meaning that customers could have the latest technologies and a product that was designed to their specifications (effectiveness). This value was enhanced by the fact that Dell could deliver computers cheaply through the efficiencies in its production system. It adopted the same types of just-in-time production practices that were popular in the automotive business and its assembly line 'touches' or staff interventions were just 60 compared to an industry average of 130. The business thrived and its stock price rose by an amazing 29,600 per cent in the 1990s.

However, the past decade has been a significantly more demanding one for the company. Its efficiency lead is being challenged in many ways. Competitors have adopted similar production practices and some, like China's Lenovo, are based in lower cost regions. Consequently, Dell has ceased all of its production operations in the USA and Ireland and switched instead to manufacturing sites in Poland, Mexico, Malaysia and China. Its effectiveness lead has also been eroded in several ways. The make-to-order model is now the industry standard and all major manufacturers such as HP, Sony and Gateway offer similar features and benefits to Dell. Apple's success with portable devices like the iPod and the iPhone has revitalized interest in its computer brand – the iMac, and its attractive retail stores have become so important to its success that Dell has had to work with retailers for the first time. But perhaps the biggest threat of all comes once again from changes in technology and how consumers solve their computing needs. Tablet computers or simply tablets that combine computing, entertainment and news have become popular since 2010 with brands like Apple and Samsung assuming market leadership in this space. From a share price high of over US$50 in early 2000, Dell was trading at around $15 in 2011 and its profit margins had dropped to around 5 per cent.

Marketing and business performance

Does marketing work? Surprisingly this is a controversial question, with many people arguing that, yes, of course it does, while others are less sure. The difficulty surrounds both the definition and the intangibility of marketing. Many organizations think they are engaging in marketing but may simply be engaging in selling or promotion and, if these activities do not achieve their intended objectives, they may feel that their marketing efforts have been ineffective. But what we will learn throughout this book is that selling or promotion is only part of the marketing process. It can also be difficult to predict in advance whether a marketing or promotional campaign is going to work. Sometimes campaigns can be stunningly successful. For example, the celebrated Levi's 501 campaign from the 1980s, featuring Nick Kamen, had the effect of driving sales of Levi's 501s up by 800 per cent. Not only that but sales of all jeans (even those of competitors) went up. New campaigns can also drive the sales of stagnant brands as happened in the case of Magnum ice cream which had been suffering flat sales throughout Europe. Aimed at women and using a combination of television advertising, outdoor advertising and Internet advertising, the Magnum 7 Deadly Sins campaign lifted sales of the brand by 20 per cent in one year.[15]

In other companies, marketing is seen as the central engine of business growth (see Marketing in Action 1.2). For example, Nestlé is a huge global company with 8,000 products (a figure that grows to 20,000 when local variations are included) and an annual marketing budget of US$2.5 billion. These kinds of firms see marketing expenditure as an investment, not a cost, and continue to spend money on marketing even during recessions when sales and demand drops. A case in point in the Berocca vitamin tablet brand, owned by the German corporation, Bayer. It was launched on the Irish market in 2001 but thanks mainly to an investment level of 25 per cent of turnover on marketing, it has seen sales rise from an initial level of just €500,000 to over €4 million by 2010. This has given it a 40 per cent share of the Irish market, making it one of the best markets in the world for Berocca on a per capita basis.[16] But, for some, the issue is not whether marketing works but rather that it works too well. Marketing has been the subject of a great deal of criticism.[17] It has been equated with trickery and deception, and with persuading people (often those on low incomes) to buy products they do not really need. Some of the main controversies surrounding marketing are summarized in Ethical Debate 1.1.

In short, marketing works. Succeeding in making it work in any particular situation is the challenge. In this regard some issues relating to the nature and impact of marketing need to be borne in mind.

Marketing and performance

The adoption of the marketing concept will improve business performance – that is the basic premise. Marketing is not an abstract concept; its acid test is the effect that its use has on key corporate indices such as profitability and market share. In recent years, studies in both Europe and North America have sought to examine the relationship between marketing and performance. The results suggest that the relationship is positive.

Narver and Slater, for instance, looked closely at the relationship between business performance and

Marketing in Action 1.2 Tesco's drive for supremacy

Critical Thinking: Below is a review of the rise of Tesco over the past two decades. Read it and critically evaluate the role played by marketing in its success.

It is hard to believe that in the mid-1990s, Tesco was a struggling domestic grocery chain languishing in third place in the UK market behind Sainsbury's. By 2010, it was estimated that one in three British households were buying their weekly groceries there and 300,000 people were working for the company. It had become by far the market leader and had also expanded internationally to have operations in Europe, Asia and the USA.

The genesis of this remarkable turnaround came when Sir Terry Leahy was promoted to the board of the company in 1992 as Marketing Director (he subsequently became chief executive in 1997). His mantra for change was simple – know your customers and improve your stores. Tesco began moving from town centre locations to large suburban supermarkets carrying a wider product range than previously when they were known as a store that only appealed to customers looking for bargains. A loyalty card scheme – Clubcard – was introduced which enabled them to get to know their customer shopping habits better and to adjust their store ranges and special offers to these buying patterns. Each year, the company produced a customer research plan for all its markets which enabled it to innovate value for its customers quicker than its competitors, such as its Tesco Value and Tesco Finest ranges.

Over time, this enabled Tesco to appeal to all segments of the market while competitors like Asda or Waitrose were seen as targeting only specific segments. Its customer knowledge also enabled it to expand beyond food into non-food items and services including everything from household goods to car insurance. It was claimed that Tesco had become a giant by selling everything, to everyone, everywhere.

Based on: Rigby (2010)[18].

Ethical Debate 1.1 Marketing – good or evil?

It is possible to look at marketing from different standpoints. A positive view holds that marketing provides significant benefits to society. For example, the innovative efforts of companies provide us, as consumers, with a world of choice and diversity. A search on Google allows us to find information on anything that we want; with an Apple app on their iPhones, doctors no longer need a stethoscope to examine patients, and websites like Amazon and eBay allow us to shop from the comfort of our desks. The innovations of tomorrow will bring us new and appealing products, services and solutions. Second, as the practice of marketing improves, our particular needs are increasingly being met. If we eat only gluten-free products, love skydiving and have a passion for Japanese origami, there are organizations that will fulfil these needs. As firms collect more information about their customers, they will tailor solutions to meet specific user requirements. Finally, the competition between firms continually forces them to improve their services and products, and deliver extra value to customers. For example, low-fares airlines have revolutionized air travel and enabled people who traditionally flew infrequently to travel to new destinations much more often.

At the same time, marketing is also the subject of some trenchant criticism. For example, it is seen as not only fulfilling needs but creating unnecessary wants. Critics argue that companies use sophisticated marketing techniques to create aspirations and to get consumers to buy products that they don't really need, with the result that many consumers find themselves building up significant debts. Consumer credit levels are at an all-time high in many developed countries. Related to this is the rise of materialism in society. Proponents of this view suggest that the modern consumer has become obsessed with consumption, as illustrated, for example, by the growth in Sunday shopping. Psychologists argue that this rise in consumption has done little to make people feel happier and better about themselves. At the same time as materialism is rising, there are growing concerns that the world's resources are being rapidly depleted and that current levels of consumption are not sustainable into the future. Third, there are concerns with the way that marketers target vulnerable groups like children, where the skills of child psychologists are used to find more and novel ways to instil brand preferences in the very young. Finally, there are concerns with the ways that marketing activity appears to have invaded all aspects of society. Public leisure events such as sports, shows and concerts now usually have a corporate partner, with the result that events aimed at teenagers may be sponsored by an alcoholic drinks organization, for example. Pressures on the public funding of schools, hospitals, and so on also create opportunities for corporations to tie in with these entities, which is often ethically questionable.

Resolving such a debate is very difficult, but the core of the issue lies in the key components of the definition of marketing – namely, value and profit. When organizations provide genuine value to customers, marketing is doing what it should, and both firms and society benefit. When firms create an illusion of value or seek to exploit customers for profit, then consumers and society do not benefit. Like all professions, marketing has its unscrupulous practitioners and there will always be individuals and organizations who will seek to exploit vulnerable customers. But, in an information-rich world, such practitioners can and should be named and shamed.

Suggested reading: James (2007);[19] Klein (2000);[20] Linn (2004)[21].

Reflection: Critically evaluate the arguments above and develop your own opinion on whether marketing is good or evil.

---

marketing orientation.[22] They collected data from 113 strategic business units (SBUs) of a major US corporation. In the main, their study found that the relationship between market orientation and profitability was strongly linear, with the businesses displaying the highest level of market orientation achieving the highest levels of profitability, and those with the lowest scores on market orientation having the lowest profitability figures. As the authors state: 'The findings give marketing scholars and practitioners a basis beyond mere intuition for recommending the superiority of a market orientation.'

A study published in the UK by Hooley, Lynch and Shepherd[23] sought to develop a typology of approaches to marketing, and to relate those approaches to business performance. They identified four groups of companies, namely, 'marketing philosophers', 'sales supporters', 'departmental marketers' and 'unsures'. The marketing philosophers saw marketing as a function with prime responsibility for identifying and meeting customers' needs and as a guiding philosophy for the whole organization; they did not see marketing as confined to the marketing department, nor did they regard it merely as sales support. The sales supporters saw marketing's primary functions as being sales and promotion support. Marketing was confined to what the marketing department did, and had little to do with identifying and meeting customer needs. The departmental marketers not only shared the view of the marketing philosophers that marketing was about identifying and meeting customer needs, but also believed that marketing was restricted to what the marketing department did. The final group of companies – the unsures – tended to be indecisive regarding their marketing approach.

The attitudes, organization and practices of the four groups were compared, with the marketing philosophers exhibiting many distinct characteristics, as summarized below.

1 Marketing philosophers adopted a more proactive, aggressive approach towards the future.
2 They had a more proactive approach to new product development.
3 They placed a higher importance on marketing training.
4 They adopted longer time horizons for marketing planning.
5 Marketing had a higher status within the company.
6 Marketing had a higher chance of being represented at board level.
7 Marketing had more chance of working closely with other functional areas.
8 Marketing made a greater input into strategic plans.

Significantly, the marketing philosophers achieve a significantly higher return on investment (ROI) than the remainder of the sample. The departmental marketers performed at the sample average, while the unsures and sales supporters performed significantly worse. Hooley et al.'s conclusion was that marketing should be viewed not just as a departmental function but as a guiding philosophy for the whole organization.

It is surprising, then, that marketing has not had the influence in corporate boardrooms its importance would seem to justify. A study in the UK found that only 21 per cent of chief executive officers (CEOs) in the FTSE 100 had worked in marketing before going into general management, and only five of the FTSE 100 companies had dedicated marketing directors on their boards.[24] Research in the USA shows that the majority of chief executives in recent decades have had a finance background.[25] Doyle argues that the reason for marketing's relatively low status is that the links between marketing investments and the long-term profitability of the organization have not been made clear.[26] Too often, marketers justify their investments in terms of increasing customer awareness, sales volume or market share. Doyle proposes the concept of **value-based marketing**, where the objective of marketing is seen as contributing to the maximization of **shareholder value**, which has become the overarching goal of chief executives in more and more companies. This approach helps clarify the importance of investment in marketing assets such as brands and marketing knowledge, and helps to dissuade management from making arbitrary cuts in marketing expenditure, such as advertising, in times of economic difficulty.

To further explore the link between marketing activities and firm performance, Rust et al. have identified a **chain of marketing productivity** which demonstrates how marketing investments eventually are reflected in firm outcomes. The chain begins with a firm's strategy such as its product strategy or promotion strategy which is then translated into specific tactics such as an advertising campaign or a loyalty programme, for example. These campaigns have an impact on customers (attitudes or satisfaction) which in turn feed through to market impacts (e.g., market share) and financial impacts (e.g., profitability) and ultimately to the value of the firm. In other words, a variety of factors influenced by marketing activity such as marketing capabilities, marketing assets and marketing actions can impact upon firm value.[27,28] Further research has found that where this marketing activity is measured, significant performance benefits accrue.[29] As a result, the title Chief Marketing Officer (CMO) has emerged to reflect the importance of marketing to the overall performance of the organization. Chief Marketing Officers usually have a seat in the corporate boardroom.

The scope of marketing

Up to now our focus has been on the application of marketing in commercial contexts – that is, its use by companies with products or services to sell. But it is clear from simple observation that the marketing concept, and marketing tools and techniques, is in evidence in many other contexts too. For example, political parties are often criticized for their overuse of marketing. They are heavy users of marketing research to find out what the views of the voting public are; the candidates they put forward for election are often carefully selected and 'packaged' to appeal to voters. They are also extensive users of advertising and public relations to get their message across. This is because value exchange is a key element of marketing. Organizations create some form of value and exchange it for something that they need. In the case of politics it is the creation of policy platforms in exchange for votes in an election.

Evidence of the application of marketing can be found in many other contexts (see Social Media Marketing 1.2 and Exhibit 1.6). Educational institutions have become more market-led as demographic changes have given rise to greater competition for stu-

dents, whose choices are increasingly being influenced by the publication of performance-based league tables. Universities are responding by developing new logos and rebranding themselves, conducting promotional campaigns, and targeting new markets such as mature students and those from other countries around the world. They are also using the kinds of segmentation techniques employed by companies to identify potential 'customers', as well as customer service training to convert enquiries into 'sales'.[30] The use of marketing takes many forms in the arts and media. It has been argued that many media vehicles, such as newspapers and television channels, are being 'dumbed down' in order to appeal to certain market segments and to maximize revenues, in the same way many artistic organizations would be criticized for putting revenues ahead of quality and originality by producing art that appeals to a mass audience.

Social Media Marketing 1.2 Lady Gaga

Critical Thinking: Below is a review of the rise of Lady Gaga to the rank of the world's number one celebrity. Read it and critically evaluate her marketing approach to date.

The extent to which pop stars, television show presenters and sports stars use marketing to build their brands is clearly illustrated by Lady Gaga, the world's number one celebrity in 2010 as listed by Forbes. Nicknamed the 'Queen Monster', she may have grossed US$90 million from a 2010 world tour but her earnings were significantly enhanced by her mastery of social media. By 2011, she was able to boast over 38 million Facebook fans and her 10 million Twitter followers (little Monsters!) helped to move over 1 million digital downloads of her single 'Born This Way' in only five days.

Born Stefani Germanotta in New York, Lady Gaga came to public attention in 2008 with the success of her debut album *The Fame* which included the popular hit single 'Poker Face'. She followed this up with two more successful records, *The Fame Monster* (2009) and *Born This Way* (2011). Famous for her glamorous costumes and theatrical stage shows, by 2011 she had won a host of musical awards, was reputed to be the first artist to have achieved over 1 billion viral views on YouTube and was estimated to have sold 15 million albums and 51 million singles worldwide.

Marketing activity has been critical to her success. Her outrageous costumes, which have included, among others, a dress made from raw meat, have marked her out as being distinctive and worthy of attention. She has a string of product endorsements including Mac Cosmetics, Monster headphones and Android phones. She frequently partners with other leading brands to run social media competitions. For example, the build up to her *Born This Way* album launch featured a promotion with Starbucks, while another competition in conjunction with the UserFarm crowd-sourcing community in France invited entrants to create a video that represents the uniqueness of each human being. Perhaps the biggest challenge facing Lady Gaga is not a creative one but a brand management one. By attaching her brand to everything from scarves to swimwear to covers for mobile phones and laptops she runs the risk of extending it too far – a mistake that has been made many times in the past. And associations with the likes of Polaroid and Little Monster condoms may also turn out to have been unwise decisions.

Based on: Sauer (2010);[31] Shanyon (2011)[32]

arketing activity can be seen in many fields
for-profit, sport and music

The range of potential applications for marketing has given rise to much debate among marketing scholars regarding the scope of marketing.[33] In particular, the challenge has been to find a core concept that effectively integrates both business and non-business or social marketing. For example, initially the idea of a transaction was put forward, but not all marketing requires a transaction or sale. Kotler then put forward the notion of exchange, implying that any exchange between two parties can be considered marketing.[34] However, this is also clearly problematic as many exchanges, such as favours given by family members, are not marketing activities. For our purposes, the core of marketing is the notion of a customer and the importance of understanding and responding to the customer's needs.

Planning marketing activity

Finally, in many organizations, marketing can be a haphazard activity often done in response to particular opportunities or in times of difficulty or crisis. But attention to marketing must be consistent as markets change and nothing lasts forever. For example, even the book that you are reading is right at the centre of a rapidly

changing market environment. In 2010, the world's largest bookstore, Barnes and Noble, was put up for sale following the pattern of many other bookstores around the world that struggle to cope with the combined developments of Internet book selling, e-books and the recent emergence of e-book readers or e-readers such as Amazon's Kindle, the Apple iPad and the Sony e-reader.

For marketing efforts to be effective, it is essential that a planned approach is taken. Planning is about deciding where we want to go and how we are going to get there. The process of **marketing planning** involves analysing the environment and the organization's capabilities, and deciding on courses of action and ways to implement those decisions. Having a plan gives managers a focal point for decisions and actions. It also stimulates achievement by giving the organization clear targets to aim at, which can be helpful in generating change in an organization.

The marketing planning process is shown in Figure 1.5 and we will revisit the issue of marketing planning in more detail in Chapter 12. The planning process begins with an assessment of the situation that the organization currently finds itself in. This requires conducting both an external analysis of the industry and environment that it is operating in and an internal analysis or audit of its activities. When this information has been collected and considered, the organization can then begin to shape its strategy by considering which parts of the market to focus on and by deciding on the objectives that it seeks to achieve in the given planning period.

Once decisions have been made about where the organization wants to go, the next steps involve deciding on how to get there. This set of decisions has traditionally been described as the company's **marketing mix** which normally comprises the 4Ps of product, price, promotion and place. **Product** decisions refer to choices that are made regarding the products/services and benefits that are going to be offered to a particular customer group. **Price** refers to all the decisions that are made regarding the different price points used for products in the company's range as well as all those decisions regarding the raising or reducing of prices in response to competitor activity and consumer demand. The breadth of promotional activity that can be carried out by an organization is such that it has been labelled the promotions mix, a large and significant subset of the marketing mix. Decisions that are made regarding Facebook and Twitter campaigns, sponsorship, radio advertising and so on all constitute elements of a **promotional mix**. **Place** refers to distribution activity, that is, the processes by which products and services are

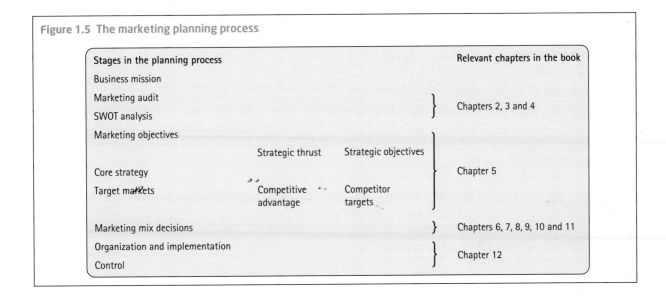

Figure 1.5 The marketing planning process

Stages in the planning process			Relevant chapters in the book
Business mission			
Marketing audit			} Chapters 2, 3 and 4
SWOT analysis			
Marketing objectives			
	Strategic thrust	Strategic objectives	
Core strategy			} Chapter 5
Target markets	Competitive advantage	Competitor targets	
Marketing mix decisions			} Chapters 6, 7, 8, 9, 10 and 11
Organization and implementation			} Chapter 12
Control			

delivered to customers. It entails decisions regarding which channels to use, for example selling online versus through retail stores, as well as the processes by which goods are physically moved from factories to shops. Finally, several other Ps have also been identified that can be considered as part of the marketing mix. These include people, process and physical evidence which are particularly relevant in the case of services industries (see Chapter 7). A total of 12 variables were initially identified by Borden which demonstrates the breadth of activities that need to be considered when putting marketing programmes into action.[35]

The final elements of the planning process involve organizing the people and structures to implement the chosen programme and carrying out all the necessary actions. Once the plan has been implemented all that remains is to assess whether it has been effective. One of the criticisms traditionally levelled at the marketing discipline was that it was weak on measurement and that it was not always possible to gauge whether marketing programmes had the desired effects. However, there is now a very wide suite of metrics available to the marketer and these are discussed in Chapter 12.

Summary

This chapter has introduced the concept of marketing and discussed how and why organizations become market-oriented. In particular, the following issues were addressed.

1. What is meant by the marketing concept? The key idea here is that it is a business philosophy that puts the customer at the centre of things. Implementing the marketing concept requires a focus on customer satisfaction, an integrated effort throughout the company and a belief that corporate goals can be achieved through customer satisfaction.

2. The idea of customer value, which is the difference between the perceived benefits from consuming a product or service and the perceived sacrifice involved in doing so. Customers are faced with a wide variety of choices in most instances, therefore companies need to clearly spell out what value they are offering and this forms their customer value proposition.

3. That marketing as both a field of study and a field of practice is constantly evolving. The way that we think about marketing has moved from an internal focus on production and sales towards a more outward-looking focus on customers and markets. These market-driven organizations are better placed to succeed in rapidly changing competitive environments.

4. That marketing works and there is a strong relationship between a marketing philosophy and business performance. Academic research in the field of market orientation and ample evidence from practice attest to the power of marketing in assisting organizations to achieve their goals.

5. That the scope of marketing is broad, involving non-business as well as business contexts. Political parties, educational institutions, sporting organizations, religious organizations and others are regular users of marketing.

6. That marketing is also controversial and that it has many negative connotations relating to the creation of unnecessary desires among consumers, that it exploits vulnerable groups and that it results in depletion of the world's resources. An informed perspective on both the merits and risks associated with marketing and commerce generally is important.

7. That marketing planning is an important activity to ensure marketing effectiveness. Organizations should avoid a haphazard approach to marketing and seek to conduct it in a carefully planned and structured manner.

Study questions

1. Discuss the development of marketing. What are the critical ways in which marketing has changed over the years?
2. Identify two examples of organizations that you consider provide customer value, and describe how they do it.
3. Marketing is sometimes considered to be an expensive luxury. Respond to this claim by demonstrating how a marketing orientation can have a positive impact on business performance.
4. Marketing is everywhere. Discuss.
5. Rather than assisting in the creation of value, marketing is responsible for many of society's ills. Discuss.
6. Visit www.marketingpower.com and www.cim.co.uk and discuss the different definitions of marketing presented by two of the world's leading marketing organizations.

Suggested reading

Comstock, B., **R. Gulati** and **S. Ligouri** (2010) Unleashing the Power of Marketing, *Harvard Business Review*, **88** (10), 90–8.

Court, D. (2007) The Evolving Role of the CMO, *McKinsey Quarterly*, **3**, 28–39.

Levitt, T. (1960) Marketing Myopia, *Harvard Business Review*, **38**, 45–56.

Rust, R., **C. Moorman** and **G. Bhalla** (2010) Rethinking Marketing, *Harvard Business Review*, **88** (1/2) January–February, 94–101.

Vargo, S. and **R. Lusch** (2004) Evolving to a New Dominant Logic for Marketing, *Journal of Marketing*, **86** (1), 1–17.

References

1. **Evans, M.** (2011) Twitter Users Publishes Fresh List of Super-Injunctions, *Telegraph.co.uk*, 30 May; **Mortimer, R.** (2009) How to be a Big Hitter when Using Twitter, *MarketingWeek.co.uk*, 5 November; **O'Reilly, L.** (2011) Twitter: A Five Year History in 140 Characters, *MarketingWeek.co.uk*, 21 March; **Walters, R.** (2009) Sweet to Tweet, *Financial Times*, 27 February, 10.

2. **Drucker, P.F.** (1999) *The Practice of Management*, London: Heinemann.

3. **Rosenberg, L.J.** and **J.A. Czepeil** (1983) A Marketing Approach to Customer Retention, *Journal of Consumer Marketing*, **2**, 45–51.

4. **Grönroos, C.** (1989) Defining Marketing: A Market-oriented Approach, *European Journal of Marketing*, **23** (1), 52–60.

5. **Farquhar, R., R. Barrie** and **T. Goodwin** (2010) For the Love of Wispa: A Social Media Driven Success Story, *Warc.com*.

6. **Parry, C.** (2008) Chocolate Bars Get Taste for Nostalgia, *MarketingWeek.co.uk*, 28 May.

7. **Fullerton, R.** (1988) How Modern is Modern Marketing? Marketing's Evolution and the Myth of the 'Production Era', *Journal of Marketing*, **52**, 108–25.

8. **Jones, D.** and **D. Monieson** (1990) Early Development of the Philosophy of Marketing Thought, *Journal of Marketing*, **54**, 102–13.

9. **Benton, R.** (1987) The Practical Domain of Marketing, *American Journal of Economics and Sociology*, **46** (4), 415–30.

10. **Davis, P.** (2005) Attack on 'Outdated' Marketing, *Financial Times*, Fund Management Supplement, 30 May, 1.

11. **Brown, R.J.** (1987) Marketing: A Function and a Philosophy, *Quarterly Review of Marketing*, **12** (3), 25–30.

12. **Satterthwaite, C.** (2004) Trust Me, and Martin and Sophie and the Boys, *Financial Times*, Creative Business, 16 November, 10.

13. **Graves, P.** (2010) *Consumer.ology: The Market Research Myth, the Truth about Consumers and the Psychology of Shopping*, London: Nicholas Brealey.

14. **Vargo, S.** and **R. Lusch** (2004) Evolving to a New Dominant Logic for Marketing, *Journal of Marketing*, **86** (1), 1–17.

15. **Coulter, D.** (2004) Magnum 7 Sins: Driving Women to Sin across Europe, *Warc.com*.

16. **O'Connell, S.** (2009) Vitamin Ad Provides Flat Market with Some Fizz, *Irish Times*, 15 October, 22.

17. **Klein, N.** (2000) *No Logo*, London: Flamingo Press.

18. **Rigby, E.** (2010) Fresh Horizons Uneasily Scanned, *Financial Times*, 20 September, 12.

19. **James, O.** (2007) *Affluenza*, London: Vermilion.

20. **Klein, N.** (2000) *No Logo*, London: Flamingo Press.

21. **Linn, S.** (2004) *Consuming Kids: The Hostile Takeover of Childhood*, New York: The New Press.

22. **Narver, J.C.** and **S.F. Slater** (1990) The Effect of a Market Orientation on Business Profitability, *Journal of Marketing*, **54** (October), 20–35.

23. **Hooley, G., J. Lynch** and **J. Shepherd** (1990) The Marketing Concept: Putting the Theory into Practice, *European Journal of Marketing*, **24** (9), 7–23.

24. **Terazono, E.** (2003) Always on the Outside Looking In, *Financial Times*, Creative Business, 5 August, 4–5.

25. **Fligstein, N.** (1987) Intraorganisational Power Struggles: The Rise of Finance Personnel to Top Leadership in Large Corporations, 1919–1979, *American Sociology Review*, **52**, 44–58.

26. **Doyle, P.** (2000) *Value-based Marketing*, Chichester: John Wiley & Sons.

27. **Rust, R., T. Ambler, G. Carpenter, V. Kumar** and **R. Srivastava** (2004) Measuring Marketing Productivity: Current Knowledge and Future Directions, *Journal of Marketing*, **68** (4), 76–89.

28. **Hanssens, D., R. Rust** and **R. Srivastava** (2009) Marketing Strategy and Wall Street: Nailing Down Marketing's Impact, *Journal of Marketing*, **73** (6), 115–18.

29. **O'Sullivan, D.** and **A. Abela** (2007) Marketing Performance Measurement Ability and Firm Performance, *Journal of Marketing*, **71** (2), 79–93.

30. **Boone, J.** (2007) Private School's Marketing Pays Off, *Financial Times*, 4 May, 3.

31. **Sauer, A.** (2010) Lady Gaga Pushes the Limits ..... of her Brand, *Brandchannel.com*, 23 February.

32. **Shanyon, S.** (2011) It's a Lady Gaga World (We Just Live in it), *Brandchannel.com*, 20 May.

33. See, for example, **Foxall, G.** (1984) Marketing's Domain, *European Journal of Marketing*, **18** (1), 25–40; **Kotler, P.** and **S. Levy** (1969) Broadening the Concept of Marketing, *Journal of Marketing*, **33**, 10–15.

34. **Kotler, P.** (1972) A Generic Concept of Marketing, *Journal of Marketing*, **36**, 46–54.

35. **Borden, N.** (1964) The Concept of the Marketing Mix, *Journal of Advertising Research*, June, 2–7.

When you have read this chapter

log on to the Online Learning Centre for *Foundations of Marketing* at **www.mcgraw-hill.co.uk/textbooks/fahy** where you'll find links and extra online study tools for marketing.

Appendix 1.1

Careers in marketing

Choosing a career in marketing can offer a wide range of opportunities. Table A1.1 outlines some of the potential positions available in marketing.

Table A1.1 Careers in marketing

Marketing positions	
Marketing executive/ co-ordinator	Management of all marketing-related activities for an organization.
Brand/product manager	A product manager is responsible for the management of a single product or a family of products. In this capacity, he or she may participate in product design and development according to the results of research into the evolving needs of their customer base. In addition, marketing managers develop business plans and marketing strategies for their product line, manage product distribution, disseminate information about the product, and co-ordinate customer service and sales.
Brand/ marketing assistant	At the entry level of brand assistant, responsibilities consist of market analysis, competitive tracking, sales and market share analysis, monitoring of promotion programmes, etc.
Marketing researcher/analyst	Market researchers collect and analyse information to assist in marketing, and determine whether a demand exists for a particular product or service. Some of the tasks involved include designing questionnaires, collecting all available and pertinent information, arranging and analysing collected information, presenting research results to clients, making recommendations.
Marketing communications manager	Manages the marketing communications activity of an organization manager such as advertising, public relations, sponsorships and direct marketing.
Customer service manager/executive	Manages the service delivery and any interactions a customer may have with an organization. Role can be quite varied, depending on industry.
Sales positions	
Sales executive/ business development	Aims to develop successful business relationships with existing and potential customers. Manages the company's sales prospects.
Sales manager	Plans and co-ordinates the activities of a sales team, controls product distribution, monitors budget achievement, trains and motivates personnel, prepares forecasts.
Key account executive	Manages the selling and marketing function to key customers (accounts). Conducts negotiations on products, quantities, prices, promotions, special offers etc. Networks with other key account personnel influential in the buying decision process. Liaises internally with all departments and colleagues in supplying and servicing the key account. Monitors performance of the key account.
Sales support manager	Provides sales support by fielding enquiries, taking orders and providing phone advice to customers. Also assists with exhibitions, prepares documentation for brochures and sales kits, and commissions market research suppliers for primary data.
Merchandiser	Aims to maximize the display of a company's point-of-sale displays, and ensures that they are stocked and maintained correctly.
Sales promotion executive	Aims to communicate product features and benefits directly to customers at customer locations through sampling, demonstrations and the management of any sales promotion activities.
Telesales representative	Takes in-bound or makes out-bound calls, which are sales related.
Advertising sales executive	Sells a media organization's airplay, television spot or space to companies for the purpose of advertising.
Retailing positions	
Retail management	Plans and co-ordinates the operations of retail outlets. Supervises the recruitment, training, conduct and work of staff. Maintains high levels of customer service. Manages stock levels.
Retail buyer	Purchases goods to be sold in retail stores. Manages and analyses stock levels. Obtains information about the range of products available. Manages vendor relations.

Table A1.1 *Continued*

Advertising positions	
Account executive	Helps devise and co-ordinate advertising campaigns. Liaises with clients, obtaining relevant information from them such as product and company details, budget and marketing goals, and marketing research information. Briefs other specialists in the agency (such as creative team, media planners and researchers) on client requirements, to develop the details of a campaign. May present draft campaign suggestions to clients along with a summary of the expenditure involved, and negotiate and arrange for modifications if required. May supervise and co-ordinate the work of the relevant production departments so that the campaign is developed as planned to meet deadlines and budget requirements.
Media planner/buyer	Organizes and purchases advertising space on television, radio, in magazines, newspapers or on outdoor advertising. Liaises between clients and sellers of advertising space to ensure that the advertising campaign reaches the target market.
Public relations positions	
Public relations executive	Helps to develop and maintain a hospitable, friendly public environment for the organization. This involves liaising with clients, co-ordination of special events, lobbying, crisis management, media relations, writing and editing of printed material.
Press relations/ corporate affairs	Develops and maintains a good working relationship with the media. Creates press releases or responds to media queries.

Jamie Oliver is a phenomenon in the world of food. He enjoyed huge success with his debut television series *The Naked Chef* in 1999. For over 10 years, he has graced television screens as a favourite celebrity chef, and has become a presence on the high street – both as the face of Sainsbury's, and by licensing the Jamie Oliver brand to numerous food and kitchenware producers. His commercial activities are anchored by his mission: to change the way people eat, both in the UK and, now, America. Jamie's CV is impressive, extending beyond books and television to include events, cooking schools, kitchen and lifestyle products, restaurants and wood-burning ovens.

Birth of *The Naked Chef*

Born on 27 May 1975, Jamie took an early interest in food, growing up in Essex, where his parents still run their own highly respected pub/restaurant. The extent of his brand is even more impressive, given Jamie's background which includes 'average' school grades, dyslexia and leaving school at 16 to complete his training at Westminster Catering College. After spending some time working in France, followed by a stint at Antonio Carluccio's Neal Street Restaurant, London, Jamie joined the acclaimed River Café where he worked for three and a half years alongside Rose Gray and Ruth Rogers. In 1997, he was featured in a television documentary about the River Café. Soon after the documentary was aired, Jamie was offered his own television show and *The Naked Chef* was born.

The Naked Chef first aired on the BBC in 1999. The concept behind *The Naked Chef* was to strip food down to its bare essentials. The show ran for six episodes as well as a Christmas special. The programme style was specifically designed to appeal to a young audience through Jamie Oliver's personal approach to developing a no-nonsense approach to food (see Figure C1.1 for Jamie's brand print). The show brought Jamie instant success, winning him a BAFTA Award for the best television series in the Features Category in 2000. The success from the television show also culminated in publishing opportunities. *The Naked Chef* book, published by Penguin Books, accompanied the first television series and it became an instant bestseller. A second and then a third television series were commissioned by the BBC, along with the second and third tie-in books: *The Return of the Naked Chef* and *Happy Days with the Naked Chef*, with the latter becoming the official Christmas No.1 in 2001 in the non-fiction chart. Jamie spent the autumn of 2001 conducting the Happy Days Tour which saw over 17,000 people packing theatres in the UK. Based on this success the tour moved to Australia and New Zealand, where he 'played' to sold out crowds in seven cities. Also in 2001, Jamie was cooking for the Italian Prime Minister at Tony Blair's invitation at Downing St and writing various columns in magazines including *GQ* and *The Times Magazine*, taking his brand to a greater audience.

Figure C1.1 Jamie's brand print

BRAND VISION
Get stuck in!

BRAND MISSION
Fresh ideas . . .
Better food . . .
Fantastic times . . .
Happy days . . . !

BRAND PERSONALITY
Accessible
Passionate
Inspiring
Eclectic
True Fun
Adventurous

BRAND BENEFITS
I feel guided, not instructed
I have the confidence to give it a bash
I love that feeling of accomplishment

BRAND PROMISE
To give people more than they expect

BRAND POSITION
Jamie Oliver takes the concept of cooking, food and fantastic times to a whole new level of accessibility.
By breathing passion and common sense into everything he touches, he inspires people, young and old, to keep things simple and Get Stuck In!

Source: Jamie Oliver Brand Consultancy

Jamie's programmes have now been broadcast in over 100 countries, including the USA, Australia, South Africa, Brazil, Japan and Iceland, and translated into over 30 languages. The accompanying cookbooks are bestsellers not only in the UK, but across the world (See Table C1.1 for a complete list of books and television shows). Autumn 2010

Table C1.1 List of Jamie Oliver's television shows and books

TV Show	Book
The Naked Chef	The Naked Chef
Return of The Naked Chef	Return of The Naked Chef
Happy Days with the Naked Chef	Happy Days with the Naked Chef
Jamie's Kitchen	Jamie's Kitchen
Oliver's Twist	Jamie's Dinners
Jamie's School Dinners	Jamie's Italy
Jamie's Great Italian Escape	Jamie's little book of big treats
Jamie's Return to School Dinners	Cook with Jamie
Jamie's Chef	Jamie at Home
Jamie at Home	Comic Relief 2009
Jamie at Home Christmas Special	Jamie's Ministry of Food
Jamie's Ministry of Food	Jamie's America
Jamie Cooks Christmas	Jamie Does . . .
Jamie's Fowl Dinners	30 Minute Meals
Jamie Saves our Bacon	Jamie's Great Britain
Jamie's American Roadtrip	
Jamie's Family Christmas	
Jamie's Food Revolution	
Jamie Does . . .	
30 Minute Meals	
Jamie's Dream School	
Jamie's Great Britain	

Source: Jamie Oliver Enterprises

▶ saw his first foray into UK 'daytime television' with the launch of *30 Minute Meals*, a daily television series at 5.30 p.m. in the UK, which aimed to show cooks of all levels how to cook a whole meal in half an hour. His 2010 book, *Jamie's 30 Minute Meals*, became his first million-selling book in the UK as well as being the fastest-selling non-fiction book since records began. Jamie Oliver has become only the second author to pass £100 million with book sales totalling £100.4 million to date. J.K. Rowling is the only other author to have passed the £100 million milestone.

Celebrity endorsement

In 2000, Jamie became the face of Sainsbury's in a deal worth approximately £2 million a year. Sainsbury's chain of supermarkets comprises 480 stores selling on average more than 56,000 different products in each store. This deal gave rise to the birth of one of the UK's longest-running celebrity endorsement campaigns. Oliver was selected for his passion and flair for food, which was seen as a key way of updating the retailer's historically reserved image, as Sainsbury's lost its long-held number-one place in the UK grocery retail market to Tesco in 1996. The relationship was highly productive, with Oliver not only fronting advertising, but also getting deeply involved in product development and colleague training and engagement. This endorsement also gave him access to Sainsbury's 14 million weekly shoppers. He fronted campaigns such as 'Try something new today' and 'Feed your family for a fiver'. The object of the 'Try' campaign was to get each consumer spending an extra £1.14 every time they shopped, in order to achieve Sainsbury's business goal of £2.5 billion additional sales over three years. By January 2008, the £2.5 billion goal had been achieved ahead of schedule. 'Feed your family for a fiver' created a range of 30 family meals with Sainsbury's products, all costing under £5, substantial enough for a hungry family of four. This campaign was estimated to have generated £1.12 billion of incremental revenue for the supermarket chain. However, Oliver has faced criticism during his relationship with Sainsbury's. In 2004, he appeared in a new Christmas advertisement, in which he visited a fish farm in Scotland. In the advertisement, he endorsed Sainsbury's sourcing of salmon from a Scottish loch, claiming the cold water made the fish healthy. Yet Oliver reportedly refused to serve any farmed fish in his restaurant, Fifteen, which prompted a backlash in the press. Similarly, after refusing a BBC demand that he drop his lucrative Sainsbury's contract, Oliver joined up with Channel Four to pursue his television shows. Oliver officially ended his relationship with Sainsbury's in July 2011.

Changing lives through food

Fifteen

In 2001, Oliver opened a training restaurant for young people who were not in full time education or employment. Followed by cameras that documented his every move, he spent the year setting up a training scheme, the restaurant and the charity into which all the profits would be channelled. The series, *Jamie's Kitchen*, broadcast by Channel 4 in the UK, became one of the biggest hit shows of the year. It has now been shown in over 40 countries and the book, also called *Jamie's Kitchen*, became a runaway success. The triumph of the restaurant was evident when it won Tatler Best Restaurant Award 2003 and the Academy Award of Excellence at the Tio Pepe Carlton London Restaurant Awards in the same year. Oliver was awarded an MBE in 2003 for his contribution to the hospitality industry. The Fifteen Foundation charity now owns Fifteen London and continues its work recruiting students for training in London. Fifteen has three restaurants worldwide – Amsterdam, Cornwall and London – all of which operate a pioneering Apprentice Programme for young people between the ages of 18 and 24. Again he has faced criticism from food critics claiming the food is overpriced and service levels are poor. Similarly, the apprentice programme has been criticized for having a low graduate rate. These claims have been strongly defended by Oliver who points out that the restaurant does not compromise on the quality of the ingredients along with setting a future benchmark of a 70 per cent graduate rate from the programme.

Feed Me Better

In 2004, motivated by the poor state of dinners in UK schools and their contribution to the childhood obesity rate of 25 per cent (the highest in Europe), Jamie embarked on one of his most ambitious ventures. He went back to school with the aim of educating and motivating the dinner ladies and kids to enjoy cooking and eating healthy, nutritious lunches rather than the processed foods that they were used to. He launched a national campaign called Feed Me Better (www.feedmebetter.com) and an online petition for better school meals. As a result of the 271,677 signatures on the petition, which he took to 10 Downing Street on 30 March 2005, the government pledged an extra £280 million; with £220 million to deliver a minimum ingredient spend of 50p per meal for primary schools and 60p for secondary schools, backed with minimum nutritional standards. This work culminated in the award-winning series *Jamie's School Dinners*, shown on Channel 4. The series prompted a public outcry for change to the school meals system. Between January and June 2005 there were a total of 1,016 articles with mentions of *Jamie's School Dinners*, including 21 key leader articles. Evaluation of print media coverage showed the public relations value was worth at least an additional £14.1 million.

The show was awarded Best Factual programme at the UK National TV Awards. Jamie also received a special award for his contribution to television at the National TV awards. A follow-up documentary, *Jamie's Return to School Dinners* aired on Channel 4 in September 2006 and, as a result of his new findings, the British government made further investment in school meals and food education for school children. The campaign revitalized Jamie Oliver's brand image, taking him from celebrity chef to a truly national hero and champion of change.

Ministry of Food

Jamie began 2008 fronting two major television programmes in the UK. *Eat To Save Your Life* used expert analysis as well as an autopsy by Dr Gunther von Hagens on a 25-stone man who literally 'ate himself to death', to try to change the dietary habits of a group of malnourished people. Meanwhile, *Jamie's Fowl Dinners* was an in-depth and challenging look at the British poultry industry with a message that unless British consumers were prepared to trade up to a higher welfare chicken and egg, the British poultry industry would suffer irreparably. Groups ranging from the RSPCA to farmers' organizations praised the programme and the immediate result was an increase in sales of free-range and organic chicken of up to 50 per cent. In 2008, he also appeared in *The Big Give*, the prime-time Oprah Winfrey-fronted hit show on ABC in the USA. His major project for 2008, however, was Jamie's *Ministry of Food*, a Channel 4 television series which showed how people could be inspired to cook with just a little encouragement and information. The series, filmed in Rotherham, explored how friends, family and work-mates could be inspired to pass on recipes to each other and cook using fresh ingredients. After the success of the Ministry of Food centre, Rotherham Council announced it would continue to fund the running of the centre and, by 2010, the Rotherham Ministry of Food centre was so successful that its classes were booked many weeks in advance with other centres opening across the UK.

Food Revolution

Jamie's Food Revolution combines the ambitions of both Jamie's Ministry of Food and Jamie's School Dinners and exists to tackle the obesity epidemic in America. The campaign seeks to educate people about food and cooking, address the quality of the food served in school lunch halls and inspire food retailers to provide good quality, fresh, local food to their customers. *Jamie Oliver's Food Revolution* premiered on ABC in America in March 2010, winning its slot each week with ratings peaking at 7.5 million. He appeared on Oprah to launch the campaign and also carried out high-profile interviews on *Letterman*, *Leno* and *Nightline* as well as press

interviews in *The New York Times* and *TIME* magazine. He became the recipient of the prestigious TED award for 2010 (previous winners have included Al Gore and Bono) at a ceremony in California. In August 2010, the *Food Revolution* series received an Emmy Award for Best Reality Series. One of the most impressive aspects of Jamie Oliver's Food Revolution is the grassroots support he has built for his cause. Over 709,493 Americans have signed up to support his Food Revolution with the campaign being funded solely by donations made from the US public. However, he has faced some criticism from the USA who view the Food Revolution as a cynical means of targeting the Jamie Oliver brand to American consumers rather than a campaign for social change.

Brand extensions – moving away from celebrity

Jamie has a wide range of food and kitchenware products. However, in 2009, Jamie Oliver Enterprises asked Pearlfisher to create an aspirational brand that communicates quality over celebrity to appeal to a more discerning consumer. Jme was launched online in March 2009, and via the Jamie at Home direct selling company. Jme is a diverse range of homeware and food products curated by Jamie Oliver and his buyers where products are chosen for beauty, efficacy and craft. The Jme stamp acts as a subtle endorsement, challenging the celebrity-led approach of so many lifestyle brands as his face or name does not appear anywhere on the brand. The Jme brand liberated him from his mainstream mass market audience and enabled him to appeal to a more discerning and aspirational consumer base. Sales to March 2011 are on track to reach an annual brand growth of 166 per cent. By 2012, target sales will have increased by 244 per cent. Achieving these targets will make Jamie at Home the largest Party Plan Direct Selling business in the UK. Jme has had a halo effect on the Jamie Oliver brand overall. His licensed goods have showed a 4 per cent increase in sales in the year since the launch of Jme, demonstrating that no cannibalization has occurred of other Jamie Oliver brands.

Conclusion

Jamie Oliver continues to effectively expand his brand using tactics such as reality television. The website jamieoliver.com has 1.5million unique users per month. Late in 2009, Oliver launched an iPhone app called 20 Minute Meals which quickly became a best-seller and a huge hit in the UK and overseas, as well as winning the much coveted Apple Design Award for applications. Similarly, Vodafone is to be the first operator to launch a made-for-mobile 3G television series. The series is being launched as a premium content download rather than a sponsored programme. In terms of social media Jamie Oliver has over 1,250,000 Twitter followers. The increasing popularity of the brand highlights the progression of Jamie Oliver using the traditional format of a cooking programme to the development of reality-based programmes.

▶| # Questions

1. What distinctive value proposition was initially offered by Jamie Oliver in his books and TV shows that explains his success?
2. Evaluate the techniques used to build his brand profile.
3. How has the Jamie Oliver brand proposition changed over time?
4. What are the risks faced by his brand at this time?

This case was prepared by David Cosgrave and Matthew Cannon, University of Limerick from published sources as a basis for class discussion rather than to illustrate either effective or ineffective management.

Chapter 2
The Global Marketing Environment

Chapter outline

The macroenvironment

Economic forces

Social forces

Political and legal forces

Physical forces

Technological forces

The microenvironment

Environmental scanning

Learning outcomes

By the end of this chapter you will understand:

1 what is meant by the term 'marketing environment'
2 the distinction between the microenvironment and the macroenvironment
3 the impact of economic, social, political and legal, physical and technological forces on marketing decisions
4 the importance of social responsibility and ethical marketing practices
5 how companies respond to environmental change.

Luxury brands in China

The shifting patterns in the consumption of luxury brands are a good indication of the directions in global commerce. Once upon a time, Europe was the home of luxury consumption, then the USA and now increasingly it would appear to be Asia and, in particular, China. A love for luxury brands has already become evident among Chinese consumers, including both those who are among the new wealthy in the country and those aspiring to be so. Global luxury sales are estimated to be worth US$168 billion in 2011 with China accounting for almost 20 per cent of this total.

Luxury goods purchases dropped dramatically in 2008 as a result of the global financial crisis (GFC). However, led by a quick recovery in Asia, its effects have not been long lasting. The world's biggest luxury good group, LMVH, saw its sales increase by almost 20 per cent in 2010 while Swatch, the Swiss watchmaker, and Richemont, the owner of Cartier, Montblanc and Hermes, saw their share prices rise by more than 50 per cent in the same year. Other brands like Gucci, Burberry and Prada all reported excellent results. The sales growth for luxury brands in China is estimated to be running above 30 per cent compared with global and European growth rates at just 5 per cent. This

is due to many factors ranging from the Chinese love of status to the rapid development of high-end shopping malls in a country experiencing significant economic growth. And when one considers that 71 million households in China are considered to be either wealthy or very wealthy (that is, with incomes of 300,000 renminbi or more), the size of the market is huge. Added to that, Chinese tourists account for a significant proportion of luxury spending around the world.

Not only do Asians love Western luxury brands, they also love the companies that make them. In 2000, the Hong Kong based S.C. Fang & Sons bought Pringle of Scotland. Li & Fung, also of Hong Kong, purchased Hardy Amies, the couturier to the British royal family, and other European luxury brands such as Escada from Germany are owned by Megha Mittal of India. As a further sign of a shift to the East, the stock market listing of the famous Italian brand Prada in 2011 took place not in Milan but in Hong Kong and was five times oversubscribed. Lower production costs in Asia mean that these investors believe that switching production from Europe will further increase the margins they can obtain from these famous labels.

These developments demonstrate the speed of global economic change. While former economic powers like the USA and Europe struggle with issues of debt and unemployment, new regions like Asia and Latin America are powering ahead and providing new opportunities. And in the same way that Japanese brands rose to dominate global markets in the 1980s, it may not be long before Chinese, Indian or Brazilian brands are doing the same.[1]

Figure 2.1 The marketing environment

A market-orientated firm needs to look outward to the environment in which it operates, adapting to take advantage of emerging opportunities and to minimize potential threats. In this chapter we will examine the **marketing environment** and how to monitor it. In particular, we will look at some of the major forces that impact upon organizations, such as economic, social, legal, physical and technological issues. Firms need to monitor the rapid changes taking place in these variables in order to exploit potential opportunities and to minimize potential threats.

The marketing environment is composed of the forces and actors that affect a company's ability to operate effectively in providing products and services to its customers. Distinctions have been drawn between the **microenvironment** and the **macroenvironment** (see Figure 2.1). The microenvironment consists of the actors in the firm's immediate environment or business system, that affect its capabilities to operate effectively in its chosen markets. The key actors are suppliers, distributors, customers and competitors. The macroenvironment consists of a number of broader forces that affect not only the company, but also the other actors in the microenvironment. These can be grouped into economic, social, political/legal, physical and technological forces. These shape the character of the opportunities and threats facing a company, and yet are largely uncontrollable.

The macroenvironment

This chapter will focus on the major macroenvironmental forces that affect marketing decisions. Four

forces – namely, economic, social, political/legal and technological – have been the focus of most attention, with the result that the acronyms PEST or STEP are often used to describe macroenvironmental analysis. The growing importance of the impact of marketing activity on the physical environment means that this issue, too, will be a focus of attention. Later in the chapter we will introduce the four dimensions of the microenvironment, which will then be dealt with in greater detail throughout the book. The changing nature of the supply chain and customer behaviour will be dealt with in detail in the next chapter. Distribution will be examined in Chapter 11 and competitive forces in Chapter 12.

Economic forces

Through its effect on supply and demand, the economic environment can have a crucial influence on the success of companies. It is important to identify those economic influences that are relevant and to monitor them. We shall now examine three major economic influences on the marketing environment of companies: economic growth and unemployment; interest rates and exchange rates; and taxation and inflation.

Economic growth and unemployment

The general state of both national and international economies can have a profound effect on an individual company's prosperity. Economies tend to fluctuate according to the 'business cycle'. Most of the world's economies went through a period of significant growth from the early to mid-2000s, driven mainly by rising demand in developing economies like China and the availability of cheap credit in the developed markets of the West. The fortunes of many sectors, such as retailing, services, consumer durables and commodities, closely mirror this economic pattern. For example, the rising demand for oil meant a rapid growth in wealth for oil-rich states like the United Arab Emirates (UAE) resulting in a retail, hotel and property boom in states such as Dubai (see Exhibit 2.1). The global financial crisis (GFC) of 2007 followed by a sudden scarcity of credit gave rise to significant financial losses for investors and much reduced consumer spending (see Marketing in Action 2.1). A major marketing problem is predicting the next boom or slump. Germany, which for years lagged average growth in Europe, has become the quickest country to recover from the GFC with many of its major firms reporting record profits. Investments made during periods of low growth can yield rich returns when economies recover.

Exhibit 2.1 This advert for Emirates Airlines reflects the economic growth of countries like China and the UAE

A place of priceless beauty.

The intricate pieces of fine china from the Ming Dynasty are prized for their rarity. Because Emirates flies to Beijing, Hong Kong, Shanghai and now Guangzhou, the hidden treasures of China need no longer be a mystery.

Emirates now flies to four destinations across China. Fly Emirates. Keep discovering.

BEIJING
SHANGHAI
GUANGZHOU
HONG KONG

emirates.com

Over 400 international awards and over 100 destinations worldwide. For more details contact your travel agent or visit emirates.com

Go to the website to see how this Emirates airlines advert conveys the global reach of the airline.
www.mcgraw-hill.co.uk/textbooks/fahy

Table 2.1 Growth rates and unemployment rates (percentage) in selected countries, 2011

Country	Growth Rate[1]	Unemployment Rate[2]
Canada	+2.6	7.8
United States	+3.3	8.9
Australia	+3.1	5.0
Japan	+1.7	4.6
Austria	+1.8	4.3
Belgium	+1.7	11.5
Czech Republic	+2.0	9.6
Denmark	+2.1	4.0
France	+1.7	9.6
Germany	+2.6	7.1
Greece	−4.0	14.8
Italy	+1.1	8.6
Netherlands	+1.8	5.1
Norway	+1.5	3.2
Poland	+4.2	13.2
Spain	+0.6	20.4
Sweden	+3.9	7.9
United Kingdom	+1.6	8.0
Euro Area	+1.6	9.9
China	+9.0	9.6
India	+9.0	10.8
Russia	+4.3	7.4
Brazil	+4.3	6.4

[1] Projected growth rate for 2011
[2] Unemployment rate, February 2011
Source: *The Economist.*

Low growth rates are reflected in high unemployment levels, which in turn affect consumer spending power. The variety of growth rates and unemployment levels throughout some of the world's major economies is illustrated in Table 2.1. In times of economic recession, consumers tend to postpone spending and/or become more cost conscious, shifting more of their spending to discount stores. This is also the time when companies tend to cut back on advertising budgets, which has particular implications for marketing. It was estimated that the advertising budget of the UK government was cut by 75 per cent in 2010.[2]

A key challenge for marketers will be to try to anticipate the implications of the changing patterns of global economic growth. While growth in the traditional powerhouses of the world economy such as Europe and the USA remains slow (see Table 2.1), other economies are racing ahead. China has grown so rapidly in the past decade that it is now the world's second largest economy. The remaining BRIC nations (Brazil, Russia and India, as well as China) are also growing strongly. As these countries build factories, roads and shopping centres, they need resources such as oil, copper, coal and so on, and the continent of Africa – traditionally the world's poorest region – is rich in these resources, with the result that huge levels of Chinese investment have poured into Africa. In specific industries, new opportunities are emerging all the time. For example, Nokia has been very successful in its efforts to gain a large share of the Indian market through its provision of low-cost telecommunications products. The publisher Condé Nast launched an Indian version of its *Traveller* magazine in 2010 to target the estimated 2 million people in India with a household income of greater than US$100,000.[3] These dramatic trends mean that European marketers need to be aware of the emerging opportunities and challenges.

Exhibit 2.2 **This advert by Europe's largest bank Santander demonstrates the nature of competition in retail financial services**

Be rewarded for switching your current account:

£100 for new customers

£200 for existing mortgage customers

£300 for existing mortgage customers with over £10,000 of savings with us

Visit your local branch
Call our UK call centres on 0800 80 80 80

Interest rates and exchange rates

One of the levers that the government uses to manage the economy is interest rates; the interest rate is the rate at which money is borrowed by businesses and individuals (see Exhibit 2.2). Throughout the world, interest rates are at historically low levels. One of the results of this has been a boom in consumer borrowing for capital investments such as housing. This has meant significant sales and profit rises for construction companies and global furniture retailers like IKEA. While taking on debt to buy homes and cars has traditionally been considered acceptable, what is worrying policy makers is the high levels of consumer debt arising particularly from the overuse of credit cards. Total household borrowing as a percentage of gross domestic product (GDP) has risen considerably over the past two decades, but the rate of growth has been variable. Debt levels are below 40 per cent of GDP in Italy but over 100 per cent in the UK, the Netherlands and Denmark. Overall, changes in interest rates are usually followed quickly by changes in consumer behaviour.

Exchange rates are the rates at which one currency buys another. With the formation of the European Union (EU), exchange rates between most European countries are now fixed. However, the rates at which major currencies like the US dollar, the euro, sterling and the yen are traded are still variable. These floating rates can have a significant impact on the profitability of a company's international operations. For example, the booming Australian economy and rising interest rates there in 2009 and 2010 have led to a significant strengthening of the Australian dollar against currencies like the euro and the US dollar. This in turn has meant that Australian goods became more expensive in Europe and the USA, creating challenges for Australian companies operating in these markets. However, the rising dollar also brings positive results, such as making the cost of travel abroad cheaper for Australian citizens.

Taxation and inflation

There are two types of taxes: direct and indirect. Direct taxes are taxes on income and wealth, such as income tax, capital gains tax, inheritance tax, and so on. Income tax is important for marketers because it determines the levels of disposable income that consumers have. When taxes fall, consumers keep a greater portion of their earnings and have more money to spend. It also increases the levels of discretionary income that they have – that is, the amount of money available after essentials, such as food and rent, have been paid for. At this point consumers move from needs to wants, and a great deal of marketing activity is aimed at trying to convince us where we should spend our discretionary income.

Indirect taxes include value added tax (VAT), excise duties and tariffs, and are taxes that are included in the prices of goods and services that we buy. They have major implications for marketing mix variables such as price. Changes in VAT rates need to be passed on to customers and this can cause problems for firms trying to compete on the basis of low price. Differences in indirect tax levels across national boundaries give rise to the problem of *parallel importing*, whereby goods are bought in a low-cost country for importation back into a high-cost country. This presents a challenge for distributors in the high-cost country, who are not permitted to get access to this source of supply. Variations in tax levels impact on consumer demand. For example, lower tax levels on wine have resulted in consumers switching from beer. As a result, some interesting disputes have arisen with regard to how products should be classified. For example, Marks & Spencer (M&S) had consistently argued that its teacakes should be classified as cakes (which carry a zero VAT rating) as opposed to chocolate biscuits, which carry a VAT rate of 20 per cent. The long-running legal battle between the company and the UK Treasury was finally ended in the European Court in 2008 when the court ruled in M&S's favour, resulting in a £3.5 million rebate to the company for VAT paid on the product.

Finally, inflation is a measure of the cost of living in an economy. The inflation rate is calculated by monitoring price changes on a basket of products such as rent/mortgage repayments, oil, clothing, food items and consumer durables. The rising price of commodities like oil and wheat feed through to consumers in the form of higher fuel bills and higher bread and pasta prices. Rapid rises in inflation also reduce the future value of savings, investments and pensions. Governments are acutely sensitive to inflation figures and increase interest rates to keep inflation under control.

Overall economic movements feed through to marketing in the form of influencing demand for products and services, and the level of profitability that accrues to the firm from the sales of goods. Economic movements can sometimes be sudden and severe in their level of impact, as shown in Marketing in Action 2.1.

Marketing in Action 2.1 The global financial crisis

Critical thinking: Below is a review of the recent global financial crisis. Read it and discuss what marketing approach firms should adopt during periods of economic recession.

The global financial crisis (GFC), which began with the collapse of the major US investment firm, Lehman Brothers in 2008, is a dramatic example of just how much economic events can affect consumers and businesses. Prior to the crisis, many major world economies were growing strongly. As a result, unemployment levels were low and consumer sentiment – in other words, their expectations about the future – was high. This in turn led them to spend their money in all sorts of ways. Typically during periods of growth and prosperity, demand for non-essential items such as multiple foreign holidays, spa treatments, restaurant meals, clothing and luxury goods increases. Consumers are also more likely to make investments in assets like shares, property and commodities, and when these rise strongly during periods of growth, they generate an additional wealth effect – consumers look at the value of their assets and consider themselves to be wealthier than they actually are. All of this demand is good for businesses who find that their sales and profits are growing. And because of this increased demand, they need to hire more staff or need to pay them more, which gives a further boost to consumer sentiment.

But just as this virtuous cycle can go upwards, it can quickly reverse. The GFC revealed that the growth in the early part of the last decade was not real but rather was fuelled by cheap credit and the lax lending policies of financial institutions around the world. Banks had lent money for consumers to invest or spend that in hindsight they were never going to be able to repay. They did this because new financial instruments enabled them to repackage these debts and sell them off to third parties who wanted to invest in growing economies. But once these loans began to fail, financial institutions everywhere began to panic, which was accelerated when major firms like Lehmans, AIG and Northern Rock went bankrupt. Suddenly credit became scarce or more expensive, so consumers struggled to pay back the debts on their loans. With more money going to support debt, there was less for day-to-day spending so demand for products and services started to drop. Now business sales begin to fall so they have to lay off employees which further depresses consumer sentiment leading them to consume less and save more given future uncertainty. Investors take their money out of property and shares causing the wealth effect to decrease and put it into commodities like oil, driving up oil prices and heaping further pressures on consumers. The GFC has been the worst economic event to hit the world since the Great Depression in the USA in the 1930s and several European countries such as Greece, Ireland and Portugal have had to receive major bailout loans from the International Monetary Fund in order to continue operating. It illustrates that major economic events have the power to not only impact consumers and businesses but even countries as well.

Social forces

There are four social forces, in particular, that have had implications for marketing. These are: changes in the demographic profile of the population; cultural differences within and between nations; **social responsibility** and marketing ethics; and the influence of the **consumer movement**. We will now examine each of these in turn.

Demographic forces

The term demographics refers to changes in population. The most significant factor from society's point of

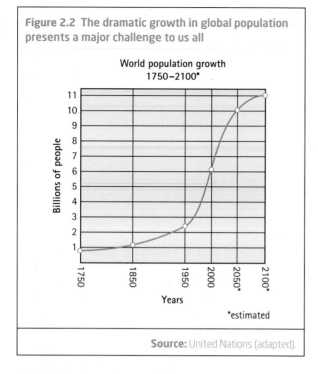

Figure 2.2 The dramatic growth in global population presents a major challenge to us all

Source: United Nations (adapted).

view is the dramatic growth in the world's population in the past 200 years (see Figure 2.2). On the one hand, this presents opportunities for marketers in the form of growing markets but on the other hand it raises questions about the sustainability of this global growth. The planet's resources are finite, meaning that pressure is increasing on the limited supplies of water, food and fuel. For example, the fishing industry supports 520 million people or 8 per cent of the global population but if current overfishing levels continue, commercial fishing will collapse before 2050. Innovative solutions to this challenge are likely to generate significant returns for organizations. Variations in population

growth are also important. China has a one-child policy, growth is slowing in the developed world and most increases are forecast in Africa, Asia and Latin America. In response, Unilever is trying to sell more soap in African countries, which improves hygiene and cuts down on diseases, while mobile phone companies like Vodafone in Africa and Digicell in the Caribbean have generated significant profits from providing telephony in these regions.

Globalization has given rise to two other interesting demographic effects, namely, population migration between countries and the rise of middle and wealthy classes in countries with a low average GDP per capita. The continued integration of Europe has resulted in significant movements of labour from the poorer areas of Central and Eastern Europe to the wealthier Western European countries. These patterns are being played out around the world, and the International Organization for Migration estimates that, in 2010, 214 million people settled outside the country in which they were born and that this number could reach 405 million by 2050. Changes in immigration controls such as the number of student visas issued impacts upon the level of demand for university places. Global economic prosperity has also given rise to significant segments of wealthy consumers in countries with low average wages, such as Russia and China (see Marketing Spotlight 2.1). For example, advertising expenditure in Nigeria has grown sixfold since 2000 as global companies seek to reach its growing middle class.[4]

A major demographic change that will continue to affect demand for products and services is the rising proportion of people over the age of 60 and the decline in the younger age group. Figure 2.3 shows projections for the growth of this segment up to 2050. The rise in

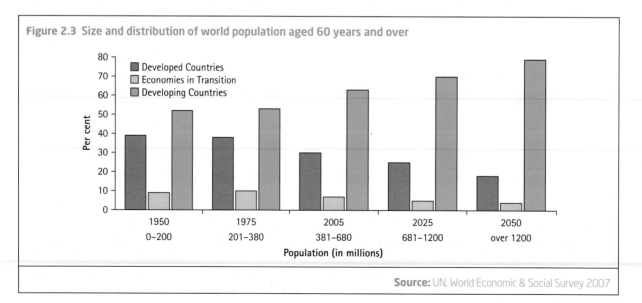

Figure 2.3 Size and distribution of world population aged 60 years and over

Source: UN, World Economic & Social Survey 2007

Exhibit 2.3 This advert from Marks & Spencer clearly targets a micro-household unit

the over-45-year-old group creates substantial marketing opportunities because of the high level of per capita income enjoyed by this group in developed countries. They have much lower commitments in terms of mortgage repayments than younger people, tend to benefit from inheritance wealth and are healthier than ever before. Pharmaceuticals, health and beauty, technology, travel, financial services, luxury cars, lavish food and entertainment are key growth sectors for this market segment. The overall implication of these trends is that many consumer companies may need to reposition their product and service offerings to take account of the rise in so-called 'grey' purchasing power.

Finally, one of the emerging demographic trends is the growth in the number of household units and falling household sizes. People are choosing to get married later or stay single, divorce rates are rising and family sizes are smaller than they traditionally have been. Combined with high incomes and busy lives, these trends have led to a boom in connoisseur convenience foods and convenience shopping. Companies like Northern Foods and Marks & Spencer, in particular, have catered for this market very successfully (see Exhibit 2.3). Demand for childcare and homecare facilities has also risen.

Cultural forces

Culture is the combination of values, beliefs and attitudes that is possessed by a national group or subgroup. Cultural differences have implications for the way in which business is conducted. For example, because of the growth of markets like China, India and Singapore, more and more westerners are doing business in these countries and are finding significant differences in the ways things are done. Westerners tend to view contracts as set in stone, while those from the East take a more flexible view. In the East, a penchant for harmony means that decision-making tends primarily to be a rubber-stamping of a consensus already hammered out by senior management. The Western obsession with using logic to unravel complex situations is likely to be viewed as naive by those in the East. These kinds of differences are deeply culturally bound in the complex social networks of the East versus the greater levels of independence experienced by those living in the West.[5]

International marketers need to pay particular attention to the possible impact of culture. For example, MTV – which was the traditional, all-American music channel – now has 141 channels broadcasting in 32 languages to 160 countries. While these could be viewed as vehicles for the export of American culture to new countries, the company is careful to reflect local cultures; for example, 45 per cent of what is shown on MTV Arabia in the Middle East is locally produced and the remainder is translated.[6]

Even within particular countries, however, it is important to bear in mind that many subcultures also exist. The rapid movement of global populations, described above, has meant that ethnically based subcultures have sprung up in most developed countries, creating potentially lucrative niche markets for products and services. For example, there is an estimated 3.5 million people of Turkish origin living in Germany, over 5.5 million Moroccans living in Spain, and over 800,000 people living in Italy are of Albanian origin. In addition, social trends and fashions give rise to their own particular subcultures, whose members dress and behave in certain ways.

Corporate social responsibility and marketing ethics

Companies have a responsibility to society that goes beyond their legal responsibilities, and they need to recognize this. Corporate social responsibility (CSR) refers to the ethical principle that a person or an organization should be accountable for how its actions might affect the physical environment and the general public. Concerns about the environment, business and public welfare are represented by pressure groups such as Greenpeace, Corporate Watch and Oxfam.

Marketing managers need to be aware that organizations are part of a larger society and are accountable to that society for their actions. Such concerns led Perrier to recall 160 million bottles of its mineral water in 120 countries after traces of a toxic chemical were found in 13 bottles. The recall cost the company a total of £50 million, even though there was no evidence that the level of the chemical found in the water was harmful to humans. Perrier acted because it believed the least doubt in the consumers' minds should be removed in order to maintain its brand's image of quality and purity. In contrast, Coca-Cola took a week to accept responsibility for a wave of sickness caused by the contamination of its products in Belgium, and

Exhibit 2.4 Oil companies such as Statoil have been very keen to stress their environmental credentials

Reliable energy production.
Powered by Norwegian gas.

Norwegian gas production from the Troll platform in the North Sea can supply millions of Europeans with power.
Due to its well-developed infrastructure and extremely high regularity, gas represents a safe and reliable source of
energy. Be enlightened at **goodideas**.statoil.com. There's never been a better time for good ideas.

Statoil

faces continued criticism over anti-union violence, worsening water shortages and childhood obesity. Companies are increasingly conscious of the need to communicate their socially responsible activities. The term 'Green marketing' is used to describe marketing efforts to produce, promote and reclaim environmentally sensitive products.[7]

The societal marketing concept is a label often used to describe how the activities of companies should not only consider the needs of customers but also society at large (see Exhibit 2.4). This notion has given rise to movements like the Fairtrade Foundation and also to the formation of companies like Edun, the Dublin-based fashion company. Founded by U2's Bono and his wife Ali Hewson, the company manufactures a line of organic cotton shirts, jeans and hemp blazers. Its fashion line is made from non-subsidized cotton sourced in Peru and manufactured in Africa, while its second brand, Edun Live, comprises mass-market clothes made from Tanzanian cotton and manufactured in Lesotho. The company's ethical goal is to support manufacturers in Africa and world farmers by championing organic, environmentally sustainable cotton products.[8]

Corporate social responsibility is no longer an optional extra but a key part of business strategy that comes under close scrutiny from pressure groups, private shareholders and institutional investors, some of whom manage ethical investment funds (see Marketing in Action 2.2). Businesses are increasingly expected to adapt to climate change, biodiversity, social equity and human rights in a world characterized by greater transparency and more explicit values.[9] Two outcomes of these developments have been the growth in social reporting and **cause-related marketing**.

A related issue is that of marketing ethics. **Ethics** are the moral principles and values that govern the actions and decisions of an individual or group.[10] They involve values about right and wrong conduct. There can be a distinction between the legality and ethicality of marketing decisions. Ethics concern personal moral principles and values, while laws reflect society's principles, and standards that are enforceable in the courts.

Not all unethical practices are illegal. For example, it is not illegal to include genetically modified (GM) ingredients in products sold in supermarkets; however, some organizations (such as Greenpeace) believe it is unethical to sell GM products when their effect on health has not been scientifically proven. Such concerns have led to supermarket chains, such as Iceland and Sainsbury's in the UK, removing GM foods from their own-label products. Similarly, mobile phone manufacturers are ensuring that handsets conform to

Marketing in Action 2.2   Allianz4Good

Critical thinking: Below is a brief overview of some of the corporate social responsibility activities conducted by Allianz. Read it, visit Allianz.com and critically evaluate the extent to which CSR is a core part of the organization's marketing strategy.

Allianz is one of the world's largest financial services companies and is headquartered in Germany. It operates in a range of businesses including general and life insurance for corporate and personal customers, banking, and investment and wealth management. It has more than 76 million customers in 70 countries and reported revenues of €106 billion and profits of €5 billion in 2010. One of its primary sponsorships is the Allianz Arena in Munich which is home to the city's two soccer teams, FC Bayern Munich and TSV 1860 Munich, and it is also a sponsor of Formula 1 motor racing and golf.

But Allianz also has a significant portfolio of CSR activities under the umbrella brand Allianz4Good. It has identified five core issues that are essential to both its success and that of its stakeholders which include access to finance, climate change, demographic change, digitalization and the stability of financial markets. These in turn convert into a variety of specific projects such as investments of €1.5 billion in wind power and photovoltaic projects (climate change), a target of 20 per cent CO_2 reduction by 2012 (climate change), My FinanceCoach where Allianz employees volunteer to provide financial literacy to schoolchildren (finance) and the Allianz Cultural Foundation which fosters mutual understanding by supporting artistic, cultural and educational projects. The company has also made donations to help relief efforts following on from natural disasters like the Indonesia earthquake, 2009 and the Pakistan floods, 2010 and is a major sponsor of the Paralympics for disabled athletes.

Because sustainable development is inherent to Allianz's business, the group has attempted to foster a culture of corporate responsibility in the organization through the Allianz Code of Conduct. As an insurer, all the initiatives that it takes to reduce insurance risks will ultimately benefit it in the long term. For example, it is estimated that 40 per cent of insurance claims arise from climate change. Its financial stability is also important in ensuring that it is there to meet the needs of its stakeholders.

Social reporting is where firms conduct independent audits of their social performance. These audits usually involve surveys of key stakeholders such as customers and employees. Social audits normally take the form of printed reports, but these are increasingly being replaced by the Internet as the main communication medium. The advantages of the Internet are that it is easy to update, the distribution of information is cost effective, it is searchable, can be produced swiftly and is environmentally friendly.

Cause-related marketing is a commercial activity by which businesses and charities or causes form a partnership with each other in order to market an image, product or service for mutual benefit. Cause-related marketing works well when the business and charity have a similar target audience. For example, American Express is a founding partner in Product Red, a corporate alliance that gives a share of profits from branded products to the Global Fund to fight AIDS, tuberculosis and malaria. One of the strongest commitments to cause-related marketing has been given by Canadian company MAC cosmetics, which is now part of the Estée Lauder group (see Exhibit 2.5). It gives away all of the sales revenues for its Viva Glam lipstick range to the MAC AIDS Fund, which in turn distributes it to HIV groups. To date, it has given away over US$100 million.[11]

international guidelines on the specific absorption rate of radiation emissions and the industry has contributed millions of dollars to research on the issue.[12]

Many ethical dilemmas derive from a conflict between profits and business actions. For example, by using child labour the cost of producing items is kept low and profit margins are raised. In 2006, secret footage aired on a news bulletin on the UK's Channel 4 showed clearly underage workers making Tesco own-label clothing in a factory in Bangladesh. Tesco, it emerged, was unaware that the factory produced clothes for it – it is a member of the Ethical Trading Initiative, which is a UK-based group that requires independent monitoring of the global supply chain. Because of the importance of marketing ethics, each of the chapters in this book includes a key ethical debate discussing the positions taken by supporters and critics of marketing on a variety of core themes. The debate on corporate social responsibility (CSR) is summarized in Ethical Debate 2.1.

Ethical Debate 2.1 CSR or PR?

For many years now, debate has raged regarding how socially responsible companies should be. Businesses do not operate in isolation, but are intrinsically linked to the economic, social, physical and political environments in which they operate. To many, their record in being sensitive to the needs of these environments is not one to be proud of. The abuse of human resources in the form of poorly paid workers, working in dangerous conditions and child labour has been highlighted. Environmental damage through pollution, deforestation and the illegal dumping of waste has rightly been criticized. There is also the exploitation of consumers through the maintenance of artificially high prices and the corruption of the political process throughout the world. The list goes on. Riots between protesters and police at major government and economic conferences highlight the extent of the divide between business and some sections of society.

As a result of societal pressure for change, corporate social responsibility (CSR) has become part of the language of the corporate boardroom. All major corporations have CSR initiatives and publicize these in their annual reports and on their websites. For example, in 1953, Shell Oil Company set up the Shell Oil Foundation, which, since its formation, has contributed in the region of US$500 million to the development of the communities where Shell employees live and work. Marks & Spencer has its 'Plan A', a list of 100 worthy targets over five years. These include helping 15,000 children in Uganda get a better education, saving 55,000 tonnes of CO_2, recycling 48 million clothes hangers, converting over 20 million garments to Fairtrade cotton, and so on. Triple bottom-line accounting has grown, whereby firms demonstrate not only their economic performance but also their social and environmental performances.

At the same time, however, there are commentators who trenchantly argue that these kinds of investments are completely wrong. This stance has been most famously taken by the US economist Milton Friedman. In his view, the mission of a business is to maximize the return to its owners and shareholders; he advocated that anything that detracts from that mission should be avoided, and that society's concerns are the responsibility of government. Similarly, Robert Reich, who served as US Labor Secretary under Bill Clinton, has argued that companies cannot be socially responsible and that activists are neglecting the important task of getting governments to solve problems. Added to this is the growing line of research which shows that CSR does not work – in other words, that CSR has a negative effect on corporate performance.

So it remains very much a matter of debate as to whether the current trend in CSR activity reflects a greater concern from businesses about their impact on the environment or whether this is simply a rather large public relations exercise. Many critics would suggest the latter as companies respond to increasing scrutiny from non-governmental organizations and the public at large. A CSR initiative may create a feel-good factor within a business and may satisfy commentators and shareholders, but the ultimate test is whether businesses will consistently put principle before profit. Ironically the two are not mutually exclusive as the experience of companies like the Body Shop, Ben & Jerry's, innocent Ltd and others has shown. Enlightened long-term self-interest would appear to be the best approach for corporations to take.

Suggested reading: Allen (2007);[13] Bakan (2004);[14] *The Economist* (2008);[15] James (2007)[16]

Reflection: Is it appropriate that business should put society's interests ahead of its own?

Exhibit 2.5 All revenue from MAC Cosmetics' Viva Glam range are donated to the MAC AIDS fund

Table 2.2 **Most ethically perceived brands in selected countries, 2008**

Ranking	UK	France	Germany
1	Co-op	Danone	Adidas
2	Body Shop	Adidas	Nike
3	Marks & Spencer	Nike	Puma
4	Green & Black's	Nestlé	BMW
5	Ecover	Renault	Demeter
6	Traidcraft	Peugeot	gepa
7	Cafédirect	Philips	Volkswagen
8	innocent	Carrefour	Sony
9	Divine	Coca-Cola	Trigema

Source: GfK NOP

The consumer movement

The 'consumer movement' is the name given to the set of individuals, groups and organizations whose aim is to safeguard consumer rights. For example, various Consumers' Associations in Europe campaign on behalf of consumers and provide information about products, often on a comparative basis, allowing consumers to make more informed choices between products and services.

As well as offering details of unbiased product testing and campaigning against unfair business practices, consumer movements have been active in areas such as product quality and safety, and information accuracy. Notable successes have been improvements in car safety, the stipulation that advertisements for credit facilities must display the true interest charges (annual percentage rates), and the inclusion of health warnings on cigarette packets and advertisements.

Such consumer organizations can have a significant influence on marketing practices. For example, the Belgian consumer group Test-Achats brought a case to the European Court of Justice on the equal treatment of males and females in the provision of goods and services. The court ruled in its favour meaning that insurance companies who have traditionally offered cheaper car insurance to female drivers will no longer

be able to do so from December 2012 with the result that the price of premiums for young female drivers is likely to rise.[17] In the UK, the Office of Fair Trading is seeking to enable consumers to more easily take legal action against companies that have harmed them through anti-competitive practices.

The consumer movement should not be considered a threat to business, but marketers should view its concerns as offering an opportunity to create new products and services to satisfy the needs of these emerging market segments. For example, growing concern over rising obesity levels in the developed world has led McDonald's to make significant changes to its menu items and marketing approach. It introduced a number of healthy options to its menus, including salads and fruit bags, which helped the company to return to profitability after some years of poor performance. Some of the leading ethical brands in Europe are listed in Table 2.2.

Political and legal forces

Marketing decisions can also be influenced by political and legal forces, which determine the rules by which business is conducted. Political forces describe the close connections that politicians and senior business people often have. These relationships are often cultivated by organizations, both to monitor the political mood and also to influence it. Companies sometimes make sizeable contributions to the funds of political parties in an attempt to maintain favourable relationships. The importance of political connections has been demonstrated by a study which showed that 'politically connected firms' are three times more likely to be bailed out during a financial crisis than those that are not.[18] During the global financial crisis, Lehman Brothers was allowed to fail but Goldman Sachs was rescued, leading it to earn the nickname – 'Government Sachs'. The extent to which businesses try to influence the political process is illustrated by the level of lobbying that takes place. It is estimated that there are 15,000 lobbyists in Brussels trying to influence EU policy-making by its 732 Members of the European Parliament (MEPs).[19] Some of the proposals that businesses have lobbied against include restrictions on online and mobile phone advertising to reduce spam, tougher packaging rules to reduce waste, and stricter testing and labelling for chemicals.

Political decisions can have major consequences for businesses. This is sharply illustrated by the US decision to invade Iraq, which resulted in some leading American companies becoming the targets for attack and some American products being boycotted. Usually, political forces have a more gradual and subtle effect, as illustrated by European politicians' pursuit of a common European union.

The European Union

In the past, the basic economic unit has been the country, which was largely autonomous with regard to the decisions it made about its economy and levels of supply and demand. But for the past three decades, all this has been changing rapidly, driven mainly by the globalization of business. The world's largest companies, like Microsoft, General Electric, Wal-Mart and others, are now larger than most countries in economic terms. At the same time, countries have been merging together into economic areas to more effectively manage their affairs. Most European countries are now part of the European Union (EU), the North American countries have grouped together into an economic area known as NAFTA (North American Free Trade Agreement), and the Pacific Rim countries are part of a group known as the ASEAN (Association of South East Asian Nations).

The advent in 1986 of the Single European Act was the launch pad for an internal market in the EU. The intention was to create a massive deregulated market of 320 million consumers by abolishing barriers to the free flow of products, services, capital and people among the then 12 member states. The current EU members are Austria, Belgium, the Czech Republic, Cyprus, Denmark, Estonia, Finland, France, Germany, Greece, Hungary, Ireland, Italy, Latvia, Lithuania, Luxembourg, Malta, the Netherlands, Poland, Portugal, Slovakia, Slovenia, Spain, Sweden and the UK. The common currency, the euro, is in use in 17 countries, making travel, price comparisons and cross-border trade easier.

One of the main outcomes of economic union is that the prospects for adopting what is known as a pan-European or standardized strategy across Europe are improved. Standardization appears to depend on product type. In the case of many industrial goods, consumer durables (such as cameras, toasters, watches, radios) and clothing (Gucci shoes, Benetton sweaters, Levi's jeans) standardization is well advanced (see Exhibit 2.6). However, for many fast-moving consumer goods (fmcg), standardization of products is more difficult to achieve because of differences in local tastes. Nevertheless, it is an approach that is being increasingly adopted by companies. For example, Lastminute.com, which is aiming to position itself as a leisure, entertainment and travel retailer, has created a European-wide promotional campaign based on the idea of customers telling unforgettable stories under the tagline 'Stories start here'. Similarly, Mars employed the television personality, Mr T in their advertising as the centrepiece of efforts to develop a more coordinated campaign for the Snickers brand throughout Europe (see Exhibit 2.7).

Pro-competitive legislation

Political action may also translate directly into legislation and less formal directives, which can have a profound influence on business conduct. One of the key areas in

Exhibit 2.6 The Swedish brand H&M favours the use of pan-European advertising through simply designed posters that work well in different markets

Exhibit 2.7 Mars used the television personality, Mr T to front its Euro-wide promotion of the Snickers brand

which regulators act is ensuring that competition is fair and legal and operates in a way so that consumers and society benefit. Formerly, the control of monopolies in Europe was enacted via Article 86 of the Treaty of Rome, which aimed to prevent the 'abuse' of a dominant market position. However, control was increased in 1990 when the EU introduced its first direct mechanism for dealing with mergers and takeovers: the Merger Regulation. This gave the Competition Directorate of the European Commission jurisdiction over 'concentrations with a European dimension'. Over the years, the Commission has challenged the activities of major global companies, most notably Microsoft. After a legal battle lasting nine years, Microsoft finally admitted defeat in 2007 after the European Commission charged that it had abused its dominance in the software market. It had to pay fines totalling €777 million and was forced to provide information to other companies in order that their software would 'interoperate' with Microsoft's software. In 2011, the Commission ordered an investigation into Google after three online companies alleged that its search functions were penalizing their businesses.[20] Competition bodies also operate at a national level, such as the Office of Fair Trading in the UK and the Competition Authority in Ireland, where they monitor local-level competition issues.

Consumer legislation

Regulators also enact legislation designed to protect consumers. Many countries throughout Europe have some form of Consumer Protection Act that regulates how businesses interact with consumers and how they advertise their products. These acts typically outlaw practices that are deemed to be unfair, misleading or aggressive. For example, promotions and product information must be clear and claims – such as that a product is friendly to the environment – must be backed up with evidence. This legislation is then enforced through a body such as the National Consumer Agency in Ireland. For example, because of a global obesity epidemic, restaurants around the world are being required to state the number of calories in everything on their menus. The need for this kind of consumer protection is illustrated by the marketing of products like breakfast cereals and soft drinks, as shown in Marketing in Action 2.3.

In short, political and legal decisions can change the rules of the business game very quickly. For example, in 2006, the mayor of San Paulo in Brazil introduced the Clean City Law requiring that all of the city's extensive outdoor advertising be removed, with the result that Brazilian advertisers quickly adapted to using social media to reach their customers.[21] Similarly, the European Court's ruling in 2007 that the Baileys Minis series could remain on sale represented an important victory for Diageo, which had invested heavily in the development of the brand extension. In many instances, firms and industries create voluntary codes of practice in order to stave off possible political and legal action.

Codes of practice

On top of the various laws that are in place, certain industries have drawn up codes of practice – sometimes as a result of political pressure – to protect consumer interests. The UK advertising industry, for example, has drawn up a self-regulatory Code of Advertising Standards and Practice designed to keep advertising 'legal, decent, honest and truthful' and in 2010 this code was extended to cover Facebook pages, Twitter feeds and online banner advertising. Similarly, the marketing research industry has drawn up a code of practice to protect people from unethical activities such as using marketing research as a pretext for selling. However, many commentators are critical of the potential effectiveness of voluntary codes of conduct in industries like oil exploration and clothing manufacture.[22] Firms like Coca-Cola and PepsiCo in the USA have begun to restrict sales of soft drinks in schools, in an effort to appease critics and stave off regulation such as that imposed in France, which banned school-based vending machines.

Marketing management must be aware of the constraints on its activities brought about by the political and legal environment. It must assess the extent to which there is a need to influence political decisions that may affect operations, and the degree to which

Marketing in Action 2.3 What is a healthy breakfast?

Critical Thinking: Below is a review of some research that is critical of marketing to children. Read it and critically evaluate how consumers, regulators and companies should respond to the issues raised.

The breakfast cereal market is a huge one, estimated to be worth £1.23 billion in the UK, and is critical for companies like Kellogg's. The major target for most breakfast cereal marketing is children, and cartoon characters such as Shrek, Tony the Tiger and the Simpsons regularly appear in advertising and on packaging. But what is in breakfast cereals and are they as healthy as they often claim to be? A study by the Consumers' Association of Ireland found that none of the 36 children's cereals that it studied scored a healthy rating, meaning that it was high in fibre and low in sugar, salt and saturated fat. Two-thirds of the cereals contained at least 30 per cent sugar, with some own-label brands reaching 38 per cent sugar content. Kellogg's rejected the findings of the study, claiming that it did not take account of the vitamins and minerals included in its products.

Controversies like these are important because of the growing problem of obesity in society and particularly among children. For example, obesity levels in UK children aged 2–15 are estimated to have risen from around 11 per cent in 1995 to almost 16 per cent in 2008. As a result there are increasing calls for a ban on the advertising of certain kinds of foods to children. Ofcom, the UK communications regulator, proposed a series of restrictions, including no advertising or sponsorship by food and drinks firms in programmes aimed at pre-school children, that celebrities and licensed characters not be used in food and drink adverts, and that promotional offers not be targeted at children aged under 10. These types of promotional offer have a powerful effect on children and research has even found that obese children double their intake of food after watching food advertisements on television.

Based on: Cullen (2007);[23] NHS (2010);[24] Terazono (2006);[25] Wiggins (2007)[26].

industry practice needs to be self-regulated in order to maintain high standards of customer satisfaction and service.

Physical forces

As we have seen, the consumer movement aims to protect the rights of consumers; environmentalists, in turn, aim to protect the physical environment from the costs associated with producing and marketing products and services. They are concerned with the *social* costs of consumption, not just the *personal* costs to the consumer. Six environmental issues are of particular concern. These are climate change, pollution, scarce resource conservation, recycling and non-wasteful packaging, environmentally friendly ingredients, and animal testing. Marketers need to be aware of the threats and opportunities associated with each of these issues.

Climate change

Climate change has been one of the most hotly debated topics in recent years. Most commentators argue that human activity is hastening the depletion of the ozone layer, resulting in a gradual rise in world temperatures, which is melting the polar ice caps and causing more unpredictable weather extremes like droughts and hurricanes. Movies like Al Gore's *An Inconvenient Truth* have helped to bring the debate into the mainstream. Contrarian views suggest that global warming is largely the result of a natural cycle. To date, the Kyoto Protocol, a global agreement on climate change, has been signed and ratified by 191 countries and seeks agreed reductions in greenhouse gas emissions from all parties signed up to the agreement. In effect, for businesses, this means seeking ways to reduce CO_2 emissions and a ban on the use of chlorofluorocarbons (CFCs). For example, Land Rover, whose sports utility vehicles (SUVs) are a prime target for green-minded law-makers, aims to cut its fleet's average carbon dioxide emissions by 20 per cent before 2012. Such initiatives will be necessary as higher taxes on SUVs have caused their sales levels in Western Europe to fall quickly. Opportunities are also being created by the use of route-planning software for transport companies to reduce emissions, and Internet matching systems to fill empty vehicles.

Climate change has the potential to have a major impact on business and society. For example, air travel is very much taken for granted and has boomed in recent years due to economic prosperity and the marketing activities of low-cost airlines. But aeroplanes are significant users of limited fossil fuels like oil, and CO_2 emissions from international aviation have doubled since 1990. Ultimately, this may mean consumers choosing to fly less or even being encouraged to fly less, which will have significant implications for the aviation industry. These kinds of changes have already happened in the business of patio heaters, which grew in popularity due to smoking bans and a preference by consumers for eating and drinking outdoors. But the gas-powered heaters can emit as much CO_2 per year as one and half cars, and companies like B&Q have decided to stop selling them.

Pollution

The quality of the physical environment can be harmed by the manufacture, use and disposal of products. The production of chemicals that pollute the atmosphere, the use of nitrates in fertilizer that pollutes rivers, and the disposal of by-products into the sea have caused considerable public concern. Rapidly growing economies like China and India have particular problems in this regard, with China having overtaken the USA as the world's biggest emitter of CO_2. Coal provides 80 per cent of China's energy and it is anticipated that it will continue to do so for the next half-century. Factory and car emissions have meant that air pollution has become a major problem in Beijing. Water pollution has also reached serious levels, with an estimated 90 per cent of the water running through cities being polluted.[27]

Pressure from regulators and consumer groups helps to reduce pollution. Denmark has introduced a series of anti-pollution measures including a charge on pesticides and a CFC tax. In the Netherlands, higher taxes on pesticides, fertilizers and carbon monoxide emissions are proposed. Not all of the activity is simply cost raising, however. In Germany, one of the marketing benefits of its involvement in green technology has been a thriving export business in pollution-control equipment.

Conservation of scarce resources

Recognition of the finite nature of the world's resources has stimulated a drive towards conservation. This is reflected in the demand for energy-efficient housing and fuel-efficient motor cars, for example. In Europe, Sweden has taken the lead in developing an energy policy based on domestic and renewable resources. The tax system penalizes the use of polluting energy sources like coal and oil, while less polluting and domestic sources such as peat and woodchip receive favourable tax treatment. The UK is experiencing a boom in the installation of solar panels in response to the creation of incentives for households that generate surplus electricity which is exported back into the grid.[28] Companies manufacturing solar panels and related products stand to benefit from this trend. Toyota's development of its Prius model – a hybrid petrol-electric car – has been an unprecedented success; so much so, that the company has struggled to meet demand for it.

There is increasing recognition that water may become the next scarce resource that needs to be conserved as it is estimated that only 1 per cent of the world's water is fit for human consumption. This has major implications for the lucrative global bottled water industry. A US study has found that global consumption of bottled water had grown by over 57 per cent in the five-year period to 2006 and the amount being spent on it was seven times the sum invested in providing safe drinking water in developing countries.[29] The lifestyle brand, Fiji water is sourced in Fiji but travels 10,000 miles to Europe and beyond while one in three Fijians do not have access to safe drinking water (see Exhibit 2.8). Furthermore, millions of barrels of crude oil are used in the making of 300 billion plastic bottles per year, 90 per cent of which are disposed of after one use and take 1000 years to biodegrade. Water scarcity also has implications for soft drinks manufacturers like PepsiCo and Coca-Cola, which are accused of causing water shortages near production plants in developing countries.

Organizational responses to the issue of scarce resources can have interesting effects. For example, because of the finite supply of fossil fuels like oil, there has been a significant growth in bio-fuels, which are manufactured from grain. This has resulted in less grain available to make products like bread, which has driven up food prices around the world.

Recyclable and non-wasteful packaging

The past 20 years or so have seen significant growth in recycling throughout Europe. Cutting out waste in packaging is not only environmentally friendly but also makes commercial sense. Thus companies have introduced concentrated detergents and refill packs, and removed the cardboard packaging around some brands of toothpaste, for example. The savings can be

Exhibit 2.8 The 'lifestyle' brand Fiji Water is a particular favourite with celebrities

substantial: in Germany, Lever GmbH saved 30 per cent by introducing concentrated detergents, 20 per cent by using lightweight plastic bottles, and the introduction of refills for concentrated liquids reduced the weight of packaging materials by a half. Many governments have introduced bans on the ubiquitous plastic bags available at supermarkets and convenience stores as they give rise to pollution and are slow to bio-degrade, which has major implications for packaging manufacturers.

The growth in the use of the personal computer has raised major recycling issues as PCs contain many harmful substances and pollutants. EU legislation is forcing manufacturers to face up to the issue of how these products are recycled, with some of the costs being absorbed by the companies and the rest by the consumer. Hewlett Packard has set up a team to re-examine how PCs are made and to design them with their disposal in mind. The team has conducted projects such as using corn starch instead of plastic in its printers, redesigning packaging and cutting down on emissions from factories.[30] The Waste Electrical and Electronic Equipment (WEEE) Directive became

European law in 2003 and imposed the responsibility for the disposal of electrical products on manufacturers. Consumers are entitled to return old electrical goods to sellers, which are charged with recycling them, though the cost of this activity has largely been passed on to consumers through an additional recycling levy. One of the consequences of the Directive has been an increased focus by manufacturers on the ease of recycling of their products.

Use of environmentally friendly ingredients

The use of biodegradable and natural ingredients when practicable is favoured by environmentalists. The toy industry is one that has come in for criticism for its extensive use of plastics and other environmentally unfriendly products. Consequently, startup companies like Green Toys and Anamalz have used a different approach. The former makes toys from recycled plastic milk containers, which are sold in recycled cardboard, while Anamalz uses wood instead of plastic. The humble light bulb is a classic example of a product made from environmentally unfriendly ingredients. It wastes huge amounts of electricity, radiating 95 per cent of the energy it consumes as heat rather than light, and its life span is relatively short. This is because existing light bulbs use electrodes to connect with the power supply and also include dangerous materials like mercury. Researchers at a company called Ceravision in the UK have developed an alternative that does not require electrodes or mercury, uses very little energy and should never need changing. These types of innovations illustrate the business opportunities that are created through the monitoring of the marketing environment.

Animal testing of new products

To reduce the risk of them being harmful to humans, potential new products such as shampoos and cosmetics are tested on animals before launch. This has aroused much opposition. One of the major concepts underlining the initial success of UK retailer the Body Shop was that its products were not subject to animal testing. This is an example of the Body Shop's ethical approach to business, which also extends to its suppliers. Other larger stores, responding to Body Shop's success, have introduced their own range of animal-friendly products.

In summary, while care for the physical environment represents a major challenge for commercial enterprises, it also represents a huge opportunity. New products or solutions that are environmentally friendly are likely to be received positively in the marketplace.

Technological forces

People's lives and companies' fortunes can both be affected significantly by technology. Technological advances have given us body scanners, robotics, camcorders, computers and many other products that have contributed to our quality of life. Many technological breakthroughs have changed the rules of the competitive game. For example, the launch of the computer has decimated the market for typewriters and has made calculators virtually obsolete. Companies, like Skype, that have pioneered telephone calls over the Internet threaten to revolutionize the telecoms business and reduce revenues for international calling to virtually zero. Mobile phone services are being used by pharmaceutical companies to tackle the damaging trade in counterfeit drugs in developing countries like Ghana and Nigeria. Consumers in these countries that buy medicines scratch off a panel on the packaging that reveals a code. They text this code to a computer system that comes back with a message that the drug is genuine and safe.[31] Monitoring the technological environment may result in the spotting of opportunities and major investments in new technological areas. For example, parallel parking of a car is something that many people find difficult with the result that many car brands now come with a facility made by the French company Park4U, which requires the driver to control only the accelerator and brake while the car's park assist system does the rest.

New potential applications for technology are emerging all the time. For example, money – which has been the foundation for the market economy for generations – is becoming increasingly redundant. For example, in Japan there has been a huge growth in the use of e-cash facilities where consumers buy smart cards which are topped up on a monthly basis and can be used for everything from transport systems to shops and cafés. Other consumers pay using their mobile phones with the result that leading firms like 7 Eleven and McDonald's have installed e-money readers.[32]

The speed with which technology can become part of our lives is illustrated by the rapid penetration of application software or apps. An app is a computer program that allows a user to perform a single or several related tasks. When the last edition of this book was being written applications for devices such as smartphones were only in the process of being developed. Now they are ubiquitous – over 10 billion have been downloaded from the Apple App Store alone as of 2011, and they assist with a wide range of activities as illustrated in Table 2.3. The impact of society's love affair with technology is reviewed in Social Media Marketing 2.1. The key to successful technological investment is, however, market potential, not technological sophistication for its own sake. The classic example of a high-technology initiative driven by technologists rather than pulled by the market is Concorde. Although technologically sophisticated, management knew before its launch that it never had any chance of being commercially viable. Large numbers of Internet businesses have failed for the same reason.

Nikon's 'I Am Nikon' campaign illustrates how consumers embrace technology in their lives.
www.mcgraw-hill.co.uk/textbooks/fahy

Table 2.3 Ten most popular free and paid iPhone applications

Free Apps		Paid Apps	
Application	**Explanation**	**Application**	**Explanation**
Facebook	Social networking	Doodle Jump	Simplistic platformer
Pandora Radio	Internet radio	Tap Tap Revenge 3	Rhythm game
Google Mobile	Web search	Pocket God	God game
Shazam	Music discovery	Angry Birds	Catapulting game
Flixter	DVD rental	Tap Tap Revenge 2.6	Rhythm game
The Weather Channel	Weather forecasts	Bejewled 2 + Blitz	Gemstone puzzles
Google Earth	Mapping services	Traffic Rush	Traffic jam puzzles
Bump	Data sharing between two iphones	Tap Tap Revenge Classic	Rhythm game
Skype	VoIP calling	App Box Pro Alarm Clock	Utilities suite
Paper Toss	Video game	Flight Control	Air traffic control simulator

Source: *Telegraph,* April 2011.

Social Media Marketing 2.1 Always on technology

Critical Thinking: Below is a review of the increasing pervasiveness of technology in people's lives. Read it and critically reflect on its marketing implications.

For every age group either at home, school or work, technology has become a major part of our lives. For example, a report in the Korean Herald claimed that 52 per cent of Korean infants aged 3–5 regularly use the Internet, spending an average of four hours per week online. It is estimated that British school children aged 10–11 spend 900 hours per year at school, 1,300 hours with their family but at least 2,000 hours in front of a screen – whether it is a computer, phone or television. According to a 2009 study in the USA, an average of 2,272 text messages per month are sent and received via a teenager's mobile phone. In the UK, those aged 15–24 spend 6.5 hours per day on media and communication and 29 per cent of the time they are multitasking. Overall, it is estimated the average person's intake of information increased by 300 per cent between 1960 and 2008. Inevitably the impact of all this exposure to technology is going to impact on how young people, in particular, think and behave. According to Watson (2010), some key ways in which screenagers are likely to behave differently include the following:

- Screenagers prefer multitasking, parallel processing and personalized experiences, read text in a non-linear fashion and prefer images over words.
- Memory is something that is found on a hard drive. If they need information, they Google it.
- The screenage brain is hyperalert to multiple streams of information, although attention and understanding can be shallow.
- The digital generation demands sensory-laden environments, instant response, and frequent praise and reward.
- Visualisation is removing the need for direct human contact.

Based on: Watson (2010)[33].

The microenvironment

In addition to the broad macroeconomic forces discussed above, a number of microeconomic variables also impact on the opportunities and threats facing the organization. We shall introduce each of these in turn, and deal with them in greater detail throughout the book.

Customers

As we saw in Chapter 1, customers are at the centre of the marketing effort and we shall examine customer behaviour in great detail in the next chapter. Ultimately customers determine the success or failure of the business. The challenge for the company is to identify unserved market needs and to get and retain a customer base. This requires sensitivity to changing needs in the marketplace and also having the adaptability to take advantage of the opportunities that present themselves.

Distributors

Some companies, such as mail-order houses, online music companies and service providers, distribute directly to their customers. Most others use the services of independent wholesalers and retailers. As we shall see in Chapter 11, these middlemen provide many valuable services, such as making products available to customers where and when they want them, breaking bulk and providing specialist services such as merchandising and installation. Developments in distribution can have a significant impact on the performance of manufacturers. For example, the growing power of grocery retailers such as Wal-Mart and Tesco has affected the profitability of consumer foods manufacturers.

Suppliers

Not only are the fortunes of companies influenced by their distributors, they can also be influenced by their suppliers. Supply chains can be very simple or very complex. For example, the average car contains about 15,000 components. As a result the car industry is served by three tiers of suppliers. Tier-one companies make complete systems such as electrical systems or braking systems. They are served by tier-two suppliers, who might produce cables, for example, and are in turn supplied by tier-three suppliers who produce basic commodities such as plastic shields or metals. Just like distributors, powerful suppliers can extract profitability from an industry by restricting the supply of essential components and forcing the price up (see Chapter 12).

Competitors

Levels of competition vary from industry to industry. In some instances, there may be just one or two major players as is often the case in formerly state-run industries like energy or telecommunications. In others, where entry is easy or high profit potential exists, competition can be intense. For example, when Perrier launched its mineral water in response to a growing concern with healthy living, it spawned a rash of competitors in a rapidly growing industry. To be successful in the marketplace, companies must not only be able to meet customer needs but must also be able to gain a differential advantage over competitors. We will examine the issue of competition in greater detail in Chapter 12.

Environmental scanning

The practice of monitoring and analysing a company's marketing environment is known as **environmental scanning**. Two key decisions that management need to make are what to scan and how to organize the activity. Clearly, in theory, every event in the world has the potential to affect a company's operations, but a scanning system that could cover every conceivable force would be unmanageable. The first task, then, is to define a feasible range of forces that require monitoring. These are the 'potentially relevant environmental forces' that have the most likelihood of affecting future business prospects – such as, for example, changes in the value of the yen for companies doing business in Japan. The second prerequisite for an effective scanning system is to design a system that provides a fast response to events that are only partially predictable, emerge as surprises and grow very rapidly. This has become essential due to the increasing turbulence of the marketing environment.

In general, environmental scanning is conducted by members of the senior management team, though some large corporations will have a separate unit dedicated to the task. The most appropriate organizational arrangement for scanning will depend on the unique circumstances facing a firm. A judgement needs to be made regarding the costs and benefits of each alternative. The size and profitability of the company and the perceived degree of environmental turbulence will be factors that impinge on this decision. Environmental scanning provides the essential informational input to create strategic fit between strategy, organization and the environment (see Figure 2.4). Marketing strategy should reflect the environment even if this requires a fundamental reorganization of operations.

Companies respond in various ways to environmental change (see Figure 2.5).

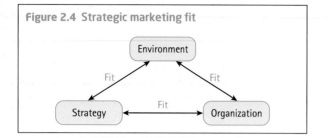

Figure 2.4 Strategic marketing fit

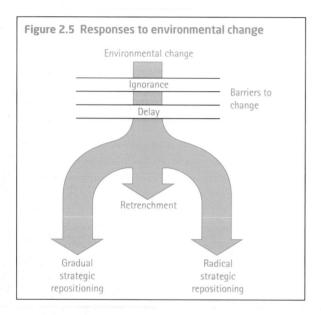

Figure 2.5 Responses to environmental change

Delay

The next response, once the force is understood, is to delay action. This can be the result of bureaucratic decision processes that stifle swift action. The slow response by Swiss watch manufacturers to the introduction of digital watches, for example, was thought, in part, to be caused by the bureaucratic nature of their decision making. 'Marketing myopia' can slow response through management being product focused rather than customer focused. A third source of delay is 'technological myopia'; this occurs where a company fails to respond to technological change. The fourth reason for delay is 'psychological recoil' by managers who see change as a threat and thus defend the status quo. These are four powerful contributors to inertia.

Retrenchment

This sort of response deals with efficiency problems but disregards effectiveness issues. As sales and profits decline, the management cuts costs; this leads to a period of higher profits but does nothing to stem declining sales. Costs (and capacity) are reduced once more, but the fundamental strategic problems remain. Retrenchment policies only delay the inevitable.

Gradual strategic repositioning

This approach involves a gradual, planned and continuous adaptation to the changing marketing environment.

Radical strategic repositioning

If its procrastination results in a crisis, a company could have to consider a radical shift in its strategic positioning – the direction of the entire business is fundamentally changed. For example, the UK clothing retailer Hepworths was radically repositioned as Next, a more upmarket outlet for women's wear targeted at 25–35-year-old working women. Radical strategic repositioning is much riskier than gradual repositioning because, if unsuccessful, the company is likely to fold.

Ignorance

If environmental scanning is poor, companies may not realize that salient forces are affecting their future prospects. They therefore continue as normal, ignorant of the environmental issues that are threatening their existence, or the opportunities that could be seized. No change is made.

Summary

This chapter has introduced the concept of the marketing environment. In particular, the following issues were addressed.

1. That the marketing environment comprises a microenvironment and a macroenvironment. What happens in these environments is largely uncontrollable by firms but can have a significant impact on organizational performance.

2. There are five key components of the macroenvironment: economic forces, social forces, legal/political forces, technological forces and physical forces. Changes on each of these dimensions can present either opportunities or threats to the firm.

3. Economic forces comprise economic growth and unemployment, interest rates and exchange rates, as well as taxation and inflation. They largely impact upon how well-off consumers feel, and their resulting propensity to buy goods and services.

4. Social forces comprise demographic forces, cultural forces, corporate social responsibility and marketing ethics, as well as the consumer movement. The latter two forces have become particularly important as the impact of business on society receives greater attention.

5. 'Political and legal forces' describes the regulatory environment in which organizations operate. Regulation may be enacted at a national or European level, and is mainly designed to protect the interests of consumers and to ensure a fair competitive playing field for organizations.

6. Changes in the physical environment have been the focus of a great deal of attention in recent years. This encompasses concerns regarding climate change, pollution, scarce resource conservation, recycling and non-wasteful packaging, environmentally friendly ingredients and animal testing.

7. The term technology is used widely to describe information technology but also developments in nanotechnology, automation and so on. Technology is the engine as well as one of the outputs of modern business and needs to be carefully monitored as changes in this area can make businesses obsolete very quickly.

8. There are four key components of the microenvironment: suppliers, distributors, customers and competitors. These will be discussed in detail throughout the book.

9. That environmental scanning is the process of examining the company's marketing environment. Firms exhibit a number of different responses to environmental change, including no change through ignorance, delay and retrenchment, through to gradual or radical repositioning.

Study questions

1. Visit www.trendwatching.com. Select five key trends that you feel marketers need to monitor closely and discuss their likely impact on marketing activity.

2. Corporate social responsibility (CSR) activities are largely an exercise in public relations by major corporations. Discuss.

3. Discuss the alternative ways in which companies might respond to changes in the macroenvironment.

4. Discuss five business opportunities arising from the growth in concern for the physical environment.

5. Visit http://business-ethics.com/. Select any two of its 'popular stories' and discuss their implications for both business and society.

When you have read this chapter

log on to the Online Learning Centre for
Foundations of Marketing at
www.mcgraw-hill.co.uk/textbooks/fahy
where you'll find links and extra online study tools for marketing.

Suggested reading

Bakan, J. (2004) *The Corporation*, London: Constable & Robinson.

Brownlie, D. (1999) Environmental Analysis, in M.J. Baker (ed.) *The Marketing Book*, Oxford: Butterworth-Heinemann.

The Economist (2008) Just Good Business: A Special Report on Corporate Social Responsibility, 19 January, 1–22.

Enkvist, P., T. Naucler and **J. Oppenheim** (2008) Business Strategies for Climate Change, *McKinsey Quarterly*, **2**, 24–33.

James, O. (2007) *Affluenza*, London: Vermilion.

Royte, E. (2008) *Bottlemania: How Water Went on Sale and Why We Buy It*, London: Bloomsbury Publishing Inc.

Sekerta, L. and **D. Stimel** (2011) How Durable is Sustainable Enterprise? Ecological sustainability meets the reality of tough economic times, *Business Horizons*, **54**, 115–24.

References

1. **Jack, A.** (2007) Bitter Pills: The Fast-Growing, Deadly Industry in Fake Drugs, *Financial Times*, 14 May, 13; **Lambkin, M.** and **Y. Tyndall** (2007) Stealing Beauty, *Marketing Age*, Summer, 71–5; **Rigby, E.** (2005) Fashionistas May Soon Find Being up to Date Too Costly, *Financial Times*, 18 August, 22. **Atsmon, Y., V. Dixit** and **C. Wu** (2011) *McKinsey Quarterly.com*, April; **Daneshkhu, S.** (2010) Boom in Luxury Goods to Cool Off, *Financial Times*, 18 October, 25; **Ritson, M.** (2011) World Domination is in the Hands of China, *MarketingWeek.co.uk*, 2 February; **Sender, H.** and **V. Friedman** (2010) Relocated Labels, *Financial Times*, 1 September, 9.

2. **Bradshaw, T.** (2010) Government Advertising Cuts Concern Agencies, *Financial Times*, 18 October, 5.

3. **Leahy, J.** (2010) Condé Nast in Push to Court India's Affluent, *Financial Times*, 24 August, 19.

4. **Green, M.** (2008) Nigerians Heed the Call of Marketing, *Financial Times*, 8 April, 10.

5. **Matthews, R.** (2005) US Grapples with 'Language of Love', *Financial Times*, 13 January, 9.

6. **Edgecliffe-Johnson, A.** (2007) MTV Tunes into a Local Audience, *Financial Times*, 16 October, 16.

7. For a discussion of some green marketing issues, see **Pujari, D.** and **G. Wright** (1999) Integrating Environmental Issues into Product Development: Understanding the Dimensions of Perceived Driving Forces and Stakeholders, *Journal of Euromarketing*, **7** (4), 43–63; **Peattie, K.** and **A. Ringter** (1994) Management and the Environment in the UK and Germany: A Comparison, *European Management Journal*, **12** (2), 216–25.

8. **Carter, M.** (2005) Ethical Business Practices Come into Fashion, *Financial Times*, 19 April, 14.

9. **Elkington, J.** (2001) *The Chrysalis Economy*, Capstone.

10. **Berkowitz, E.N., R.A. Kerin, S.W. Hartley** and **W. Rudelius** (2000) *Marketing*, Boston, MA: McGraw-Hill.

11. **Hunt, B.** (2005) Companies with Their Reputations on the Line, *Financial Times*, 24 January, 10.

12. **Jack, A.** (2008) An Unusual Model for Good Causes, *Financial Times*, 5 June, 16.

13. **Allen, K.** (2007) *The Corporate Takeover of Ireland*, Dublin: Irish Academic Press.

14. **Bakan, J.** (2004) *The Corporation*, London: Constable.

15. **Anonymous** (2008) Just Good Business: A Special Report on Corporate Social Responsibility, *The Economist*, 19 January.

16. **James, O.** (2007) *Affluenza*, London: Vermilion.

17. **Anonymous** (2011) A Boy-Racer's Dream, *The Economist*, 5 March, 74.

18. **Faccio, M., R. Masulis** and **J. McConnell** (2006) Political Connections and Corporate Bailouts, *Journal of Finance*, **61** (6),

19. **Minder, R.** (2006) The Lobbyists Have Taken Brussels By Storm, *Financial Times*, 19 January, 11.

20. **Ahmed, K.** (2011) Google under Investigation for Alleged Breach of EU Competition Rules, *Telegraph.co.uk*, 11 June.

21. **Bevins, V.** (2010) Advertising Goes Underground, *Financial Times*, 7 September, 14.

22. **Klein, N.** (2000) *No Logo*, London: HarperCollins.

23. **Cullen, P.** (2007) Survey Finds 36 Children's Cereals Cannot Be Rated Healthy, *Irish Times*, 4 June, 3.

24. **NHS** (2010) *Statistics on Obesity, Physical Activity and Diet: England, 2010*, February, ic.nhs.uk.

25. **Terazono, E.** (2006) Ban on Junk Food Adverts 'Should be Bolder', *Financial Times*, 29 March, 5.

26. **Wiggins, J.** (2007) Fat Children Double Eating After Adverts, *Financial Times*, 25 April, 5.

27. **Coonan, C.** (2008) Great Pall of China, *Innovation*, January, 36–7.

28. **Harvey, F.** and **L. Simpson** (2010) Outlook Sunny for Solar Panels as Homeowners Go Green, *Financial Times*, 25 August, 8.

29. **Ward, A.** (2006) Global Thirst for Bottled Water Attacked, *Financial Times*, 13 February, 9.

30. **Harvey, F.** (2004) PC Makers Set to Face Costs of Recycling, *Financial Times*, 4 February, 13.

31. **Anonymous** (2011) Not Just Talk, *The Economist*, 29 January, 61–2.

32. **Birchall, J.** (2005) US Supermarket Encourages Shoppers to Keep in Touch, *Financial Times*, 13 July, 22.

33. **Watson, R.** (2010) *Future Minds: How the Digital Change is Changing Our Minds, Why this Matters and What We Can Do About it*, London: Nicholas Brealey & Co.

In a world of big commercial brands that promise to make you feel younger, look better or live longer, occasionally there are those that come along that try to be more grounded, more real and more authentic. innocent Ltd is one of those companies. It has built a very successful business in the smoothie market by offering quality, fresh products and by behaving in an openly ethical manner. But a distribution agreement with McDonald's and a takeover by Coca-Cola has threatened to take the gloss off its ethical image.

Company background

innocent was founded in 1998 by three college friends – Richard Reed, Adam Balon and Jon Wright. In the summer of that year, the trio set up a stall at a small music festival in London. They started with £500 of fresh fruit and set up two bins, one with a 'yes' sign and the other with a 'no' sign. They also had another sign that asked customers 'Should we give up our jobs to make these drinks?' By the end of the festival, the 'yes' bin was overflowing and innocent Ltd was born. The vision of its founders, in the words of Richard Reed, was to be 'Europe's favourite little juice company', and innocent set about making products that contained 100 per cent pure, fresh ingredients with no additives. The unconventional approach that has characterized its development was illustrated through the use of both a lower-case 'i' rather than a capital letter 'I' in its name and its claim on its packaging that its smoothies contained no preservatives, no concentrates, no sweeteners, no additives and no funny business. Based on its initial success, its vision was subsequently broadened to be the Earth's favourite little food company by 2030.

Capitalizing on the growing trend towards healthy eating and living, innocent quickly became a marketing phenomenon. Its products were ideal for cash-rich, time-poor, health-conscious consumers, who do not eat enough fruit or have the time to prepare healthy meals. It achieved year-on-year sales growth levels of 100 per cent and reached an annual turnover in excess of £100 million in 2007. Its primary markets were the UK and Ireland, where estimates put its market share at 64 per cent, but the product was also sold in a variety of other countries throughout Europe, including the Netherlands, France, Germany and Scandinavia.

Company values and branding

The company's core values were to be responsible, entrepreneurial, generous, commercial and natural. The choice of the innocent name, which was a very unusual name for a brand of soft drinks, deliberately reflects this ethos. It represents the naturalness of the products and also that the company wants to do the right things in its key business decisions. These values were also reflected in how the company communicated with its customers, which was in a very relaxed and non-corporate style. Product packaging was bright and colourful and contained text that was designed to bring a smile to your face. It included statements like 'shake before opening, not after' and invited customers to 'enjoy by' rather than 'use by'. Another label read 'Thou shall not commit adultery . . . that's one guideline we follow religiously; our smoothies are 100 per cent pure fruit. We call them innocent because we refuse to adulterate them in any way.' This kind of statement effectively got the message across that the product was made from real fruit, but it did so in a humorous, non-preachy, non-corporate way.

Dan Germain, Head of Creative at innocent, has been quoted as saying 'lots of businesses spend a lot of money on creating an image and then telling people about it. What we do is tell people about our reality. Being innocent informs everything we are trying to do . . . paper from sustainable resources, a fresh tone on our labels, vans painted like cows, staff games in the park, going into the country to help pick elderberries for our juice. If we call the company innocent, we have a responsibility to be innocent.' He highlighted that innocent's major focus was on getting its products right and when that occurred it made branding easier.

Marketing activities

innocent's main business was smoothies. Having started off with three recipes, it has come up with almost 30 others over the years. Some of its most popular varieties have included strawberry and banana, mango and passion fruit, and pineapple, banana and coconut. It also introduced a range of kids' smoothies, which came in kid-friendly flavours complete with straws, and thickies, which were made with yoghurt and were thicker than regular smoothies. These products came in three different-sized packages, including 250 ml bottles, which were suitable for individuals who may want to consume the product while on the move, small cartons for its kids' range and large cartons for family consumption.

Because the product was a 100 per cent pure fruit smoothie, innocent was able to command a premium price for its range in the marketplace. List prices ranged from 99p for small bottles to £3.49 for its large cartons, prices that were generally higher than those of competitors such as own-label brands offered by supermarkets like Tesco. It cleverly deflected potential criticism of its prices by saying things like 'we would make them cheaper but they wouldn't be as tasty or as healthy because we'd have to use concentrates and other nasty stuff'. It was also innovative in how it has used sales promotions to encourage consumers to buy its product. An example of this is its 'Buy-one-get-one-tree' promotion, where a tree was planted by the company for every carton of smoothie purchased during the promotional period. Over 165,000 trees were planted in Africa and India.

Brightly coloured packaging and company vehicles are a key part of how the brand has built its presence in the marketplace. In terms of promotion, it initially held a music festival called 'Fruitstock', which had the dual objective of thanking customers for their support as well as creating awareness of the brand. This was replaced by the 'innocent village fete', which has also been highly effective in enabling the company to reach its primary target markets. In 2007, a village fete was held in Regent's Park, London, and attracted over 60,000 people as well as raising over £150,000 for three chosen charities: the Samaritans, Friends of the Earth and Well Child.

Consumers were invited to contact the company on the 'banana' phone number, which was a hotline that anyone at head office would answer, or to visit the company any time at its headquarters in London – Fruit Towers. They were encouraged to submit smoothie recipes as well as content and slogans for product packaging and advertising, and any 'sorry smoothie' stories, if they'd had a bad innocent experience. Its website, innocentdrinks.co.uk, provided entertainment through images and videos from various village fetes, and it also had pages on YouTube and Facebook.

Sustainability

In keeping with its core values, innocent aimed to be an ethical company that 'wanted to leave things a little better than we find them'. Each year, it gave 10 per cent of its profits to charity, most of which goes to the innocent Foundation set up in 2004, with the aim of building sustainable futures for the world's poorest people. The foundation has worked with 18 partner organizations around the world such as Womankind Worldwide and the Microloan Foundation. Its partnership with Womankind supported Irula tribal women living in the Nadu coastal region of India, which was devastated by the 2004 tsunami and subsequent flooding. It helped to support over 430 families in setting up a brick production unit, which provided the income and bricks needed to rebuild homes. The Microloan Foundation provided small loans, basic business training and continuing guidance to vulnerable groups of women in sub-Saharan Africa.

Ethical behaviour has also permeated the company's key strategic decisions. All its bananas are bought from plantations that have been accredited by the Rainforest Alliance, an independent ethical auditing body that looked at farm workers' rights and well-being, as well as protecting ecosystems on the farms and encouraging biodiversity. One hundred per cent recycled materials are used in packaging and labelling. Bottles are made from recycled plastic, while bottle caps are made from polyethylene, which is completely recyclable. Labels are made from 25 per cent recycled paper and 75 per cent paper from forests that have been certified by the Forest Stewardship Council. In 2007, innocent started measuring its carbon footprint from farm to fridge to recycling bin and, by the end of the year, had reduced it by 15 per cent. It has also encouraged its suppliers to go green and in the space of eight months, one of its carton co-packers had reduced its footprint by 60 per cent.

New challenges

In a short space of time, innocent Ltd has had a remarkable rise to fame. But having built a reputation as an ethical and 'innocent' company, it has faced many challenges in sustaining that reputation. For example, in May 2007, it was accused by one of its customers of having sold its soul to Satan when it announced its decision to trial its kids' smoothies in McDonald's. It has also been in trouble with the Advertising Standards Authority (ASA) for its campaigns for the 'Superfoods smoothie', where it claimed that the product was a 'natural detox'. It said the drink contained even more antioxidants than the average five a day, referring to the government's recommendation to eat at least five portions of fruit and vegetables per day. The ASA criticized the advertisement, claiming that 'neutralizing' free radicals did not amount to removing toxins and that innocent could not provide scientific evidence to support its detox claim.

But perhaps most controversial has been its take-over by the Coca-Cola corporation. innocent initially sold a minority stake to the global drinks giant in 2009 for £30 million which it justified on the basis that it would get its products to more people in more places by financing its expansion into Italy and Spain. Coke captured a majority shareholding in the company in 2010. Predictably many of its customers were outraged and these moves received a very negative response on social media sites like Twitter and Facebook and on the company's own blog. Accused of a sell-out, Richard Reed and his co-directors responded that they would personally answer all comments, that they were still in full operational control of the company and that they would continue donating 10 per cent of their profits to charity. The investment, they said, would assist them in their goal of bringing healthy drinks to the rest of the world.

Questions

1. What environmental trends created the opportunity for innocent to build its dominant position in the smoothie market?
2. Evaluate innocent's marketing mix. What are its strengths and weaknesses?
3. Analyse innocent's relationships with its customers. How have these relationships assisted with the development of the brand?
4. Should the company have sold a majority shareholding to Coca-Cola?

This case was prepared by Professor John Fahy, University of Limerick, from various published sources as a basis for class discussion rather than to illustrate either effective or ineffective management.

A new Marketing Showcase video featuring an interview with innocent's Head of Creative is available to lecturers for presentation and discussion in class. In the video, innocent's Head of Creative talks to Professor John Fahy about the innocent brand, its meaning and resonance with customers, and innocent's marketing communications strategies. Go to **www.mcgraw-hill.co.uk/textbooks/fahy**

Chapter 3
Understanding Customer Behaviour

Chapter outline

The dimensions of customer behaviour

Who buys?

How they buy

What are the choice criteria?

Influences on consumer behaviour

Influences on organizational buying behaviour

Learning outcomes

By the end of this chapter you will understand:

1 the dimensions of customer behaviour, who buys, how they buy and the choice criteria used

2 the role of rational versus emotional criteria in purchase decisions

3 the differences between consumer and organizational buyer behaviour

4 the main influences on consumer behaviour – personal and social influences

5 the main influences on organizational buying behaviour – the buy class, product type and purchase importance

6 the marketing implications of the various dimensions of consumer behaviour.

MARKETING SPOTLIGHT

Habbo

One of the most fascinating dimensions of the rise of the Internet has been the growth in popularity of virtual worlds which are essentially interactive, usually three-dimensional (3D) environments where users create objects, communicate with each other and play games. At their simplest, virtual worlds take the form of chat rooms or forums where interactions between visitors are simply text based, but with improved functionality many now allow users to represent themselves graphically using 3D multisensory avatars visible to others. As

such, these virtual worlds can depict a real world with all of its rules, actions and communications or fantasy worlds limited only by the imagination. *Second Life*, founded in 1999, was one of the earliest entrants into this space and other leaders include *World of Warcraft* – the multiplayer online game developed by Blizzard Inc, Sony's *PlayStation Home* and *The Sims 3* which is currently available to play on smartphones. The attraction of a virtual world is that it is a social community of like-minded people offering users the opportunity to share passions and experiences and to meet new people.

Habbo, originally known as Habbo Hotel, is owned by the Finnish company, Sulake Corporation. It originally started out in 1999 as a chat room called Mobile Discos for a Finnish band before emerging as a virtual hotel called Finnish Hotelli Kultakala in 2000 which was renamed Habbo Hotel in early 2001. Users can decorate their 'hotel rooms', hang out in public spaces, participate in virtual events and trade in virtual gifts. Its growth has been phenomenal and it is the largest virtual community for teenagers (over 90 per cent of its users are aged between 13 and 18) with over 170 million users spread across 31 countries. Some of its other metrics include 3 million new characters created each month, 120 million user-created rooms and an average user session of 42 minutes.

Unlike World of Warcraft whose users are primarily male, Habbo is more popular with teenage girls. Not surprisingly, the size and nature of its audience is of interest to marketers. In 2006, Habbo signed a deal with RealNetworks which gave users a bespoke radio station where they could vote for their favourite bands. Using branded goods to decorate rooms and trading in branded gifts are two other ways in which 'real' brands reach this 'virtual' audience. For example, *Seventeen* magazine promoted its content by sponsoring a free virtual beauty salon while a partnership with *American Idol* allowed sponsors the opportunity to sign on for event signage and virtual goods in the Habbo universe. Aside from attracting sponsorship, Habbo generates revenues through the sale of credits to users which can be used to buy furniture (or furni!) to decorate rooms or trade with others as well as through the sale of premium services such as Habbo Club and VIP. Its focus on revenue generation is reflected in the fact that it provides users with 150 payment channels in the 31 countries within which it operates. Sulake reported first quarter sales of US$20 million in 2010 generating a profit of US$3 million.

The speed with which users are keen to create virtual worlds to sit alongside the real world that we live in raises all sorts of interesting questions about consumer behaviour which is the focus of this chapter.[1]

Our lives are full of choices. We choose which universities we would like to attend, what courses we would like to study, what careers we would like to pursue. On a daily basis we make choices about the food we eat, the clothes we buy, the music we listen to, and so on. The processes by which we make all these choices and how they are influenced are of great interest to marketers as well as to consumer researchers. Companies with products or services to sell want to know us, what we like and dislike, and how we go about making these consumption decisions.

As we saw in Chapter 1, this kind of in-depth knowledge of customers is a prerequisite of successful marketing; indeed, understanding customers is the cornerstone upon which the marketing concept is built. How customers behave can never be taken for granted and new trends emerge all the time, such as the current popularity of social networking. There are a variety of influences on the purchasing habits of customers and our understanding of these influences is constantly improving. Successful marketing requires a great sensitivity to these subtle drivers of behaviour and an ability to anticipate how they influence demand. In this chapter we will explore the nature of customer behaviour; we will examine the frameworks and concepts used to understand customers; and we will review the dimensions we need to consider in order to grasp the nuances of customer behaviour and the influences upon it.

The dimensions of customer behaviour

At the outset, a distinction needs to be drawn between the purchases of private consumers and those of organizations. Most consumer purchasing is individual, such as the decision to purchase a chocolate bar on seeing an array of confectionery at a newsagent's counter, though it may also be by a group such as a household. In contrast, in organizational or business-to-business (B2B) purchasing there are three major types of buyer. First, the industrial market concerns those companies that buy products and services to help them produce other goods and services such as the purchase of memory chips for mobile telephones. These industrial goods can range from raw materials to components to capital goods such as machinery. Second, the reseller market comprises organizations that buy products and services to resell. Online retailers and supermarkets are examples of resellers and we will look at these in some detail in Chapter 11. Third, the government market consists of government agencies that buy products and services to help them carry out their activities. Purchases for local authorities and defence are examples of this.

Understanding the behaviour of this array of customers requires answers to the following core questions (see Figure 3.1).

- *Who* is important in the buying decision?
- *How* do they buy?
- *What* are their choice criteria?
- *Where* do they buy?
- *When* do they buy?

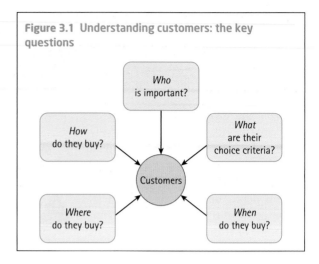

Figure 3.1 Understanding customers: the key questions

The answers to these questions can be derived from personal contact with customers and, increasingly, by employing marketing research, which we will examine in Chapter 4. In this chapter we examine consumer and organizational buyer behaviour. The structure of this analysis will be based on the first three questions: who, how and what. These are often the most intractable aspects of customer behaviour; it is usually much more straightforward to answer the last two questions, about where and when customers buy.

Who buys?

Blackwell, Miniard and Engel[2] describe five roles in the buying decision-making process.

1 *Initiator:* the person who begins the process of considering a purchase. Information may be gathered by this person to help the decision.
2 *Influencer:* the person who attempts to persuade others in the group concerning the outcome of the decision. Influencers typically gather information and attempt to impose their choice criteria on the decision.
3 *Decider:* the individual with the power and/or financial authority to make the ultimate choice regarding which product to buy.
4 *Buyer:* the person who conducts the transaction. The buyer calls the supplier, visits the store, makes the payment and effects delivery.
5 *User:* the actual consumer/user of the product.

Multiple roles in the buying group may, however, be assumed by one person. In a toy purchase, for example, a girl may be the initiator and attempt to influence her parents, who are the deciders. The girl may be influenced by her sister to buy a different brand. The buyer may

Exhibit 3.1 The Morrisons' 'Disney Magical Moments' TV campaign was banned for targeting children

Exhibit 3.1 The Morrisons' 'Disney Magical Moments' TV campaign was banned for targeting children

be one of the parents, who visits the store to purchase the toy and brings it back to the home. Finally, both children may be users of the toy. Although the purchase was for one person, in this example marketers have four opportunities – two children and two parents – to affect the outcome of the purchase decision. For example, Samsung has sponsored the European Computer Gaming Championships in a bid to build its brand image among young people, who are known to have a significant influence on the purchasing behaviour of adults when it comes to buying technology. While it does not have a very favourable image among over-40s, the company's research has found that positive attitudes towards the Samsung brand have increased by 25 per cent in the 18–29 age group since it changed its marketing focus.[3]

The role of children in influencing household purchasing is very significant. The expression 'pester power' is often used by advertisers to describe the process by which children subtly influence or more overtly nag their parents into buying a product (see Exhibit 3.1). Young children are very brand aware. Studies show that over 80 per cent of children aged between 3 and 6 recognize the Coca-Cola logo.[4] The charity Childwise estimated that children in the UK spend £4.2 billion annually, demonstrating the size of the potential market.[5] It is also estimated that over two-thirds of households buying a new car are influenced in the decision by their children. Therefore Toyota in Australia has very successfully included chickens, puppies and kittens in its advertising.[6] Overt efforts by firms to target children in their marketing continues to be a significant source of controversy as shown in Ethical Debate 3.1.

The roles played by the different household members vary with the type of product under consideration and the stage of the buying process. For example, men now do a very significant portion of household grocery shopping, while women are increasing visitors to DIY and hardware shops. Other interesting differences have also been observed. Women, who tend to take their time and browse in a retail environment, are more time conscious and goal directed online, while males tend to surf and browse many websites when shopping on the Internet. Also, the respective roles may change as the purchasing process progresses. In general, one or other partner will tend to dominate the early stages, then joint decision-making tends to occur as the process moves towards final purchase. Joint decision-making is more common when the household consists of two income-earners.

Most organizational buying tends to involve more than one individual and is often in the hands of a decision-making unit (DMU), or **buying centre**, as it is sometimes called. This is not necessarily a fixed entity and may change as the **decision-making process** continues. Thus a managing director may be involved in the decision that new equipment should be purchased, but not in the decision as to which manufacturer to buy it from. The marketing task is to identify and reach the key members in order to convince them of the product's worth. But this is a difficult task as the size of the decision-making groups in organizations is on the increase. It can also be difficult as the 'gatekeeper' is an additional role in organizational buying. Gatekeepers are people like secretaries who may allow or prevent access to a key DMU member. The salesperson's task is to identify a person from within the decision-making unit who is a positive advocate and champion of the supplier's product. This person (or 'coach') should be given all the information needed to win the arguments that may take place within the decision-making unit.

The marketing implications of understanding who buys lie within the areas of marketing communications and segmentation. An identification of the roles played within the buying centre is a prerequisite for targeting persuasive communications. As we saw earlier, the person who actually uses or consumes the product may not be the most influential member of the buying centre, nor the decision-maker. Even when they do play the predominant role, communication to other members of the buying centre can make sense when their knowledge and opinions act as persuasive forces during the decision-making process. For example, recommendations from plumbers influence the majority of shower purchase decisions by consumers planning to install or replace shower units in their homes. Therefore, brands like Mira have sought to build awareness in the consumer market to reduce the influence of these 'deciders' in the purchasing decision (see Exhibit 3.2).

Ethical Debate 3.1 Marketing to children

Few issues in marketing generate as much heated debate and discussion as the question of marketing to children. To many it represents the ugly and sinister face of capitalism. They see companies as deliberately targeting children in their advertising and communications to encourage them to pester their parents to buy products and services that in many instances they may not be able to afford. In contrast, those in favour argue that children should be exposed to marketing communications as part of their education because we live in a consumer society and children need to understand marketing.

The opponents of marketing to children have highlighted the systematic ways in which firms target younger and younger consumers. Children are carefully researched and firms employ the skills of child psychologists to devise ways to reach inside developing minds and 'implant' brand preferences through sponsorship, advertising and product placement. Many of the products that children are encouraged to pester their parents for have negative consequences as illustrated by the dramatic growth in childhood obesity in some countries. To some commentators, the obesity problem and the fact that a firm like McDonald's is the largest owner and operator of children's playgrounds in the world is not a coincidence. Other negative consequences identified include the perpetuation of stereotypes (dolls for girls, war games for boys, etc.), the rise of materialism, the economic hardship placed on families during key gift-giving times and the sexualization of young girls (such as when Tesco offered pole dancing kits aimed at young girls on its website).

Consequently, many countries have placed restrictions on advertising to children, most notably Germany, France and the Scandinavian countries who have placed limits on both the type and amount of advertising that is allowed. However, these measures have also come in for criticism. Because of the proliferation of ways in which marketers can reach children such as through programme and video-game sponsorship, marketing in schools and using cross-national television channels, marketing to children is very hard to police fairly. Others have pointed to the fact that some countries have suffered a reduction in the quality of children's programming when they have banned advertising. And anyway these critics argue that kids need to be exposed to marketing so that they can understand it and make informed decisions.

While it will continue to generate fierce debate, one thing seems certain and it is that firms under more and more competitive pressures will continue to experiment with all sorts of ways of reaching and influencing the next generation of consumers.

Suggested reading: Barber (2007)[7].

Reflection: In your view, what kinds of restrictions (if any) should be placed on advertising to children?

How they buy

Attempting to understand how consumers buy and what influences their buying decisions have been the core questions examined in the field of consumer behaviour. It is a rich arena of study drawing on perspectives from disciplines as wide ranging as economics, psychology, sociology, cultural anthropology and others. The dominant paradigm in consumer behaviour is known as the **information processing approach** and has its roots in cognitive psychology. It sees consumption as largely a rational process – the outcome of a consumer recognizing a need and then engaging in a series of activities to attempt to fulfil that need. But an alternative paradigm, known as **consumer culture theory (CCT)** (Arnould and Thompson 2005),[8] has

emerged in recent years which views consumption as a much less rational or conscious activity. In it, consumption is seen as a more sociocultural or experiential activity that is laden with emotion and helps to explain, for example, why consumers derive pleasure from shopping or search for certain meanings in the brands that they choose.

Both traditions enrich our understanding of why consumers behave as they do and we also need to take account of the different kinds of decisions that consumers engage in (see Figure 3.2). *Extended problem solving* occurs when consumers are highly involved in a purchase, perceive significant differences between brands and there is an adequate time available for deliberation.[9] It involves a high degree of information search, as well as close examination of the alternative solutions using

Exhibit 3.2 Advertising by the shower manufacturer Mira has enabled it to build a high level of consumer recognition

wakes up while I'm still snoozing.

Figure 3.2 Types of consumer decisions

Extended problem solving	Habitual problem solving
Limited problem solving	Variety seeking behaviour

many choice criteria.[10] It is commonly seen in the purchase of cars, audio equipment, houses and expensive clothing, where it is important to make the right choice. Information search and evaluation may focus not only on which brand/model to buy, but also on where to make the purchase. The potential for post-purchase dissatisfaction or **cognitive dissonance** is greatest in this buying situation.

A great deal of consumer purchases come under the mantle of *limited problem solving*. The consumer has some experience with the product in question so that information search may be mainly internal through memory. However, a certain amount of external search and evaluation may take place (e.g. checking prices) before the purchase is made. This situation provides marketers with some opportunity to affect the purchase by stimulating the need to conduct a search (e.g. advertising) and reducing the risk of brand switching (e.g. warranties).

Habitual problem solving occurs in situations of low consumer involvement and a perception of limited dif-

ferences between brands. It will take place, for example, when a consumer repeat buys a product while carrying out little or no evaluation of the alternatives, such as groceries purchased on a weekly shopping trip. He or she may recall the satisfaction gained by purchasing a brand, and automatically buy it again. Advertising may be effective in keeping the brand name in the consumer's mind and reinforcing already favourable attitudes towards it.

Finally, consumers also engage in *variety seeking behaviour* in situations characterized by low product involvement but where there are significant perceived differences between brands. For example, consumers may switch from one brand of biscuit to another, simply to try something new. The use of sales promotions by firms such as extra free products and product sampling are designed to encourage variety seeking behaviour.

The typical decision-making process for consumers and organizations is shown in Figure 3.3. This diagram shows that buyers typically move through a series of stages, from recognition that a problem exists to an examination of potential alternatives to a purchase and the subsequent evaluation of the purchase. Organizational buying is typically more complex and may involve more stages. However, as we saw above, the exact nature of the process will depend on the type of decision being made. In certain situations some stages will be omitted; for example, in a routine re-buy situation such as reordering photocopying paper, the purchasing officer is unlikely to pass through the third, fourth and fifth stages of organizational decision making (search for suppliers and analysis, and evaluation of their proposals). These stages will be bypassed as the buyer, recognizing a need, routinely reorders from an existing supplier. In general, the more complex the decision and the more expensive the item, the more likely it is that each stage will be passed through and that the process will take more time.

Need recognition/problem awareness

Need recognition may be functional and occur as a result of routine depletion (e.g. petrol, food) or unpredictably (e.g. the breakdown of a car or washing machine). In other situations, consumer purchasing may be initiated by more emotional needs or by simply imagining or day-dreaming about what an experience may be like. For example, the purchase of Chanel perfume is likely to be motivated by status or experiential needs rather than by any marginal functional superiority over other perfumes (see Exhibit 3.3).

The need recognition stage has a number of implications for marketing. First, marketing managers must be aware of the needs of consumers and the problems

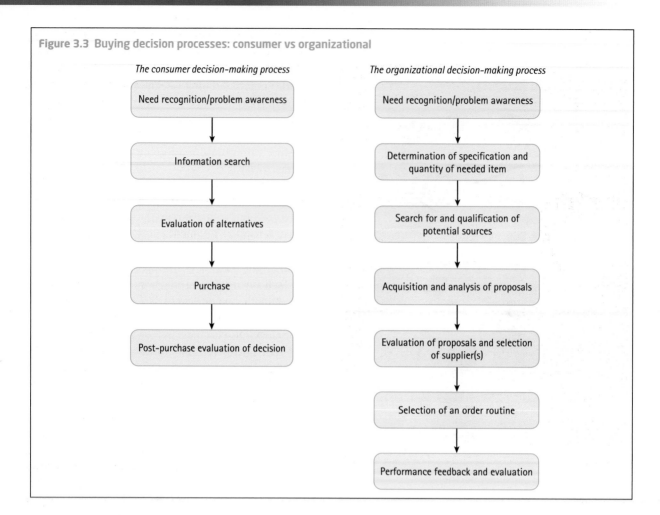

Figure 3.3 Buying decision processes: consumer vs organizational

they face. Sometimes this awareness may be due to the intuition of the marketer who, for example, spots a new trend (such as the early marketing pioneers who spotted the trend towards fast food, which has underpinned the global success of companies like McDonald's and KFC). Alternatively, marketing research could be used to assess customer problems or needs (see Chapter 4). Second, marketers should be aware of need inhibitors, that is, those factors that prevent consumers from moving from need recognition to the next stage of the buying decision process. For example, eBay has recognized that overcoming the need inhibitor – lack of trust in being sent the product – is important. To overcome this inhibitor, it introduced its PayPal system, which acts as financial insurance against non-receipt of goods and has developed a feedback system that allows buyers to post information on their transactions and their experiences with particular buyers. Third, marketing managers should be aware that needs may arise because of stimulation. Their activities, such as developing advertising campaigns and training salespeople to sell product benefits, may act as cues to need arousal.

Information search

The second stage in the buyer decision-making process will begin when problem recognition is sufficiently strong. In the case of an organizational buying decision, the decision-making unit (DMU) will draw up a description of what is required and then begin a search for potential alternatives. When marketers can influence the specification that is drawn up, it may give their company an advantage at later stages in the buying process.

In a consumer situation, the search may be internal or external. Internal search involves a review of relevant information from memory. This review would include potential solutions, methods of comparing solutions, reference to personal experiences and marketing communications. If a satisfactory solution is not found then an external search begins. This involves personal sources such as friends, family, work colleagues and neighbours, and commercial sources such as advertisements and salespeople. Third-party reports, such as *Which?* reports and product testing reports in print and online media, may provide unbiased information, and

Exhibit 3.3 **The latest Chanel No 5 campaign features the well-known French actress Audrey Tautou**

Go to the website to watch the Chanel Coco Mademoiselle advert.
www.mcgraw-hill.co.uk/textbooks/fahy

personal experiences may be sought such as asking for demonstrations, and viewing, touching or tasting the product. A great deal of information searching now takes place on the Internet and one of the significant growth businesses has been intelligent agents – that is, websites such as buy.com and mysimon.com, which allow buyers to find out information about a wide range of products and compare online vendors. Many of these sites also provide product reviews and price comparisons free of charge (see Marketing in Action 3.1). In addition, sites like Amazon.com provide ongoing product and service recommendations for their customers. The objective of **information search** is to build up the **awareness set** – that is, the array of brands that may provide a solution to the problem.

Evaluation of alternatives and the purchase

Reducing the awareness set to a smaller group of options for serious consideration is the first step in evaluation. The awareness set passes through a screen-ing filter to produce an **evoked set**: those products or services that the buyer seriously considers before making a purchase. In a sense, the evoked set is a shortlist of options for careful evaluation. The screening process may use different choice criteria from those used when making the final choice, and the number of choice criteria used is often fewer.[11] In an organizational buying situation, each DMU member may use different choice criteria. One choice criterion used for screening may be price. For example, transportation companies whose services are below a certain price level may form the evoked set. Final choice may then depend on criteria such as reliability, reputation and flexibility. The range of choice criteria used by customers will be examined in more detail later in this chapter.

Consumers' level of involvement is a key determinant of the extent to which they evaluate a brand. Involvement is the degree of perceived relevance and personal importance accompanying the brand choice.[12] When engaging in extended problem solving, the consumer is more likely to carry out extensive evaluation. High-involvement purchases are likely to include those incurring high expenditure or personal risk, such as car or home buying. In contrast, low-involvement situations are characterized by simple evaluations about purchases. Consumers use simple choice tactics to reduce time and effort rather than maximize the consequences of the purchase.[13] For example, when purchasing baked beans or breakfast cereals, consumers are likely to make quick choices rather than agonize over the decision. Research by Laurent and Kapferer has identified four factors that affect involvement.[14]

1 *Self-image*: involvement is likely to be high when the decision potentially affects one's self-image. Thus purchase of jewellery, clothing and cosmetic surgery invokes more involvement than choosing a brand of soap or margarine.

2 *Perceived risk*: involvement is likely to be high when the perceived risk of making a mistake is high. The risk of buying the wrong house is much higher than that of buying the wrong chewing gum, because the potential negative consequences of the wrong decision are higher. Risk usually increases with the price of the purchase.

3 *Social factors*: when social acceptance is dependent upon making a correct choice, involvement is likely to be high. Executives may be concerned about how their choice of car affects their standing among their peers in the same way that peer pressure is a significant influence on the clothing and music tastes of teenagers.

Marketing in Action 3.1 Online information search

Critical Thinking: Below is a review of the ways in which the Internet assists with the information search phase of the buying decision process. Read it and critically evaluate the extent to which consumer behaviour is rational (information processing approach) or emotional (CCT approach).

The Internet is an information medium and, from its inception, has promised to revolutionize consumer buying behaviour. Its impact on the information search stage of the buying process can be seen at three levels, namely, host websites, comparison websites and peer websites.

Host websites are those of product vendors. Most buying decisions are preceded by a visit to a company website to examine the product and read detailed information about it. For service companies, this can be an important way of bringing the experience to life for customers. For example, many hotels now offer web-surfers an opportunity to take a video tour of their facilities so that prospective customers can have an idea of what to expect before booking.

Comparison websites are those that use intelligent agents to speedily search online stores and aggregate results in a form of one-stop shopping. Searches generate product and price information as well as reviews of products and online stores. Some of the global leaders include yahoo.com, kelkoo.co.uk and shopping.com, but there are many others. Specialist comparison websites have also been developed, such as those for the financial services industry (e.g. moneysupermarket.com, comparethemarket.com and confused.com). These sites compare the cost of loans, mortgages, insurance and the like, and facilitate online purchasing (see Exhibit 3.4).

Finally, peer-to-peer websites play an important role in the information search phase. For example, a site like TripAdvisor.com has had a significant impact on the travel industry. It contains reviews of destinations, airlines, hotels and restaurants written by other consumers, which can be checked in advance of a travel decision. Sites like Ratemyprofessors.com are becoming popular with university students for obvious reasons. For some popular products like the Harry Potter book series, thousands of reviews have been submitted to Amazon.com. Despite the fact that potential purchasers are unlikely to read all these reviews, the mere volume of reviews has been seen to have a positive effect on sales. However, like the reviews that are posted on sites like Amazon and elsewhere, it is important to remember that such sites are open to manipulation, such as consumers being paid to write favourable reviews. Social networks like Facebook and MySpace can also be a source of information on consumption decisions. In short, the biggest challenge facing the modern shopper is sifting through all the product information that is available in advance.

Based on: The Economist (2009);[15] Fenton (2008)[16].

4 *Hedonistic influences*: when the purchase is capable of providing a high degree of pleasure, involvement is usually high. The choice of restaurant when on holiday can be highly involving since the difference between making the right or wrong choice can severely affect the amount of pleasure associated with the experience.

The distinction between high-involvement and low-involvement situations is important because the variations in how consumers evaluate products and brands lead to contrasting marketing implications. The complex evaluation in the high-involvement situation suggests that marketing managers need to provide a good deal of information to assist the purchase decision such as through employing a well-trained, well-informed sales force. In low involvement situations, providing positive reinforcement through advertising as well as seeking to gain trial (e.g. through sales promotion) is more important than providing detailed information.

Post-purchase evaluation of the decision

The creation of customer satisfaction is the real art of effective marketing. Marketing managers want to create positive experiences from the purchase of their products or services. Nevertheless, it is common for customers to experience some post-purchase concerns; this is known as cognitive dissonance. Such concerns arise because of an uncertainty surrounding the making

Exhibit 3.4 The comparethemarket.com meerkat advertising campaign has been very effective in building the comparison website's brand profile

of the right decision. This is because the choice of one product often means the rejection of the attractive features of the alternatives.

There are four ways in which dissonance is likely to be increased: owing to the expense of the purchase; when the decision is difficult (e.g. there are many alternatives, many choice criteria, and each alternative offers benefits not available with the others); when the decision is irrevocable; and when the purchaser is inclined to experience anxiety.[17] Thus it is often associated with high-involvement purchases. Shortly after purchase, car buyers may attempt to reduce dissonance by looking at advertisements and brochures for their model, and seeking reassurance from owners of the same model. Some car dealers, such as Toyota, seek to reduce this 'buyer remorse' by contacting recent purchasers by letter to reinforce the wisdom of their decision and to confirm the quality of their after-sales service.

Many leading US retailers are aiming to reduce dissonance by posting customer reviews of products and services online. Companies like Target, Home Depot and Macy's have all launched online product reviews. The risks of a negative review are outweighed by the value of obtaining customer feedback and also by providing future customers with a better idea of what to expect (see also Marketing in Action 3.1).[18] Managing expectations is a key part of reducing dissonance.

What are the choice criteria?

The various attributes (and benefits) a customer uses when evaluating products and services are known as **choice criteria**. They provide the grounds for deciding to purchase one brand or another. Different members of the buying centre may use different choice criteria. For example, purchasing managers who are judged by the extent to which they reduce purchase expenditure are likely to be more cost conscious than production engineers who are evaluated in terms of the technical efficiency of the production process they design. Four types of choice criteria are listed in Table 3.1, which also gives examples of each.

Technical criteria are related to the performance of the product or service, and include reliability, durability, comfort and convenience. Many consumers justify purchase decisions in rational technical terms but as we shall see, the true motives for purchasing are often much more emotional. Some technical criteria such as reliability are particularly important in industrial purchasing. Many buying organizations are unwilling to trade quality for price. For example, Qantas Airlines had significant problems with the Rolls-Royce engines in its Airbus A380 planes in 2010 resulting in the grounding of flights while inspections were carried out. Rolls-Royce's quick and effective diagnosis of the problem not only limited any potential damage but also

Table 3.1 Choice criteria used when evaluating alternatives

Type of criteria	Examples
Technical	Reliability Durability Performance Style/looks Comfort Delivery Convenience Taste
Economic	Price Value for money Running costs Residual value Life cycle costs
Social	Status Social belonging Convention Fashion
Personal	Self-image Risk reduction Morals Emotions

resulted in the company winning further orders from British Airways and Air China.

Economic criteria concern the cost aspects of purchase and include price, running costs and residual values (e.g. the trade-in value of a car). However, it should not be forgotten that price is only one component of cost for many buying organizations. Increasingly, buyers take into account life-cycle costs – which may include productivity savings, maintenance costs and residual values as well as initial purchase price – when evaluating products. Marketers can use life-cycle cost analysis to break into an account. By calculating life cycle costs with a buyer, new perceptions of value may be achieved.

Social and personal criteria are particularly influential in consumer purchasing decisions. Social criteria concern the impact that the purchase makes on the person's perceived relationships with other people, and the influence of social norms on the person. For example, in the early days the manufacturers of personal computers and mobile phones, such as Apple, IBM and Motorola, sought to sell them on the basis of their technical and economic criteria. But as the technology underpinning these products becomes similar for all vendors, new forms of differentiation, such as colour, shape, materials and appearance all become important. Recent research has demonstrated the powerful social effects of consumption. Simply wearing clothes sporting well-known labels such as Lacoste and Tommy Hilfiger has been shown to generate perceptions of higher status, increase participation in shopping mall surveys and improve the wearer's job prospects and the wearer's ability to solicit funds for a charity.[19]

Personal criteria concern how the product or service relates to the individual psychologically. Emotions are an important element of customer decision-making (see Exhibit 3.5).

Personal criteria are also important in organizational purchasing. Risk reduction can affect choice decisions since some people are risk averse and prefer to choose 'safe' brands. The IBM advertising campaign that used the slogan 'No one ever got fired for buying IBM' reflected its importance. Suppliers may be favoured on the basis that certain sales people are liked or disliked, or due to office politics where certain factions within the company favour one supplier over another.

Marketing managers need to understand the choice criteria being used by customers to evaluate their products and services. Such knowledge has implications for priorities in product design, and the appeals to use in advertising and personal selling.

Influences on consumer behaviour

The main influences on consumer behaviour are summarized in Figure 3.4. Personal influences describe

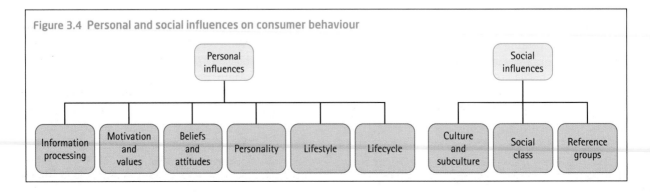

Figure 3.4 Personal and social influences on consumer behaviour

Exhibit 3.5 This humourous Volkswagen Passat commercial has been hugely popular, with almost 50 million YouTube views

those drivers that relate to the individual while social influences takes account of the drivers that arise from the contexts in which we live.

Personal influences

The six personal influences on consumer behaviour are: information processing, motivation, **beliefs** and **attitudes**, personality, lifestyle and life cycle.

Information processing

The term **information processing** refers to the process by which a stimulus is received, interpreted, stored in memory and later retrieved.[20] It is therefore the link between external influences including marketing activities and the consumer's decision-making process. Two key aspects of information processing are perception and learning.

Perception is the complicated means by which we select, organize and interpret sensory stimulation into a meaningful picture of the world.[21] We receive these external stimuli through our different senses such as hearing a familiar jingle, seeing a YouTube video or encountering the familiar smell of a favourite coffee shop. The sensation of touch has been important in the success of Apple's products. Companies now place a significant emphasis on trying to present a multi-sensory experience for their customers as a way

of attracting our attention (often sub-consciously) and of differentiating their offerings from competitors (see Marketing in Action 3.2).

Three processes may be used to sort, into a manageable amount, the masses of stimuli that could be perceived. These are **selective attention**, **selective distortion** and **selective retention**. Selective attention is the process by which we screen out those stimuli that are neither meaningful to us nor consistent with our experiences and beliefs. In our information-rich world, selective attention represents a major challenge for marketers. Various studies have shown that consumers are exposed to a huge volume of marketing messages but attend to a very small percentage of them. For example, one study has found that consumers could recall only an average of 2.21 advertisements that they had ever seen.[22] Creative approaches such as humour, shock, sex and mystery are used by advertisers to try to capture consumer attention. Position is also critical; objects placed near the centre of the visual range are more likely to be noticed than those on the periphery. This is why there is intense competition to obtain eye-level positions on supermarket shelves. We are also more likely to notice those messages that relate to our needs (benefits sought)[23] and those that provide surprises (for example, substantial price reductions).

When consumers distort the information they receive according to their existing beliefs and attitudes

Marketing in Action 3.2 Wrigley 5 gum

Critical Thinking: The launch of Wrigley 5 gum is reviewed below. Read it and evaluate the techniques used by Wrigley to create a high level of consumer attachment to a product category that would be generally seen as being low-involvement. Also look at 5 gum advertising on YouTube and visit 5gum.com.

Teenagers and young adults in the 12–24 age group are the life blood of the gum category and this group alone accounts for 32 per cent of sales. However, gum consumption among this age group was falling and of more concern for marketers was that teenagers did not express a high affinity for gum brands – certainly nothing close to the passion with which they talked about their iPods, Wiis, clothes or shoes. This presented a challenge for the leading gum manufacturer Wrigley who launched a new brand 5 which set out to challenge the conventions of this low involvement category.

As Wrigley set about developing 5, one of the critical consumer insights was that teenagers are always on the quest for new experiences and that they like telling peers about these experiences as a way of gaining social capital. Wrigley decided to create a gum brand that would be experienced rather than just chewed. Three flavours were launched – Rain, Cobalt and Flare – in sleek black packaging that was viewed as modern, innovative and mysterious. The television advertising to support the launch featured an explorer who guided the viewer through a sensory experiment to the tagline – Stimulate Your Senses. The brand was also integrated into Guitar Hero 3 and at 5gum.com a multiplayer, rock, paper, scissors online game was created. Through this approach, consumers not only get to smell and taste the gum but also to see, hear and feel it!

The approach was highly successful. 5 reached a 45 per cent level of awareness within nine months of its launch in summer 2007 and was rated by 42 per cent of survey respondents as a cool brand to be seen with compared with an average of 22 per cent for the gum category. It has since become the number three gum brand behind Orbit, the market leader which is also made by Wrigley.

Based on: Advertising Research Foundation (2010);[24] Silverstein (2010)[25].

this is known as selective distortion. We may distort information that is not in accord with our existing views. Methods of doing this include thinking that we misheard the message, and discounting the message source. Consequently it is very important to present messages clearly without the possibility of ambiguity and to use a highly credible source. **Information framing** or priming can affect interpretation. 'Framing' refers to ways in which information is presented to people. Levin and Gaeth[26] asked people to taste minced beef after telling half the sample that it was 70 per cent lean and the other half that it was 30 per cent fat. Despite the fact that the two statements are equivalent, the sample that had the information framed positively (70 per cent lean) recorded higher levels of taste satisfaction. Priming involves using stimuli to encourage people to behave in certain ways. For example, when consumers arrive at a supermarket it takes a while for the mind to get into shopping mode. Therefore retailers term the area just inside the entrance as the decompression zone – where people

are encouraged to slow down and look at special offers which is then followed by the chill zone containing books, magazines and DVDs.[27] Colour is another important influence on interpretation. Blue and green are viewed as cool, and evoke feelings of security. Red and yellow are regarded as warm and cheerful but have also been found to have an aphrodisiac effect on men without an awareness on their part that this is so.[28] By using the appropriate colour in pack design it is possible to affect the consumer's feelings about a product. However, it is important to remember that colour is also subject to different interpretations across different cultures.

Selective retention refers to the fact that only a selection of messages may be retained in memory. We tend to remember messages that are in line with existing beliefs and attitudes. Marketers are also interested in how we make sense of marketing stimuli such as the processes by which a leading sportsperson can cause us to select particular brands.

Learning takes place in a number of different ways. These include conditioning and cognitive learning.

Classical conditioning is the process of using an established relationship between a stimulus and a response to cause the learning. Thus, advertising of soft drinks will typically show groups of people having fun and when this type of advertising is constantly repeated a certain level of conditioning takes place creating an association between drinks consumption and happiness. This helps to explain why big, well-known brands repeatedly advertise. For example, the energy drink Red Bull repeatedly uses quirky, humorous advertising to appeal to its target market of young adults.

Operant conditioning differs from classical conditioning in terms of the role and timing of the reinforcement. In this case, reinforcement results from rewards: the more rewarding the response, the stronger the likelihood of the purchase being repeated. Operant conditioning occurs as a result of product trial. The use of free samples is based on the principles of operant conditioning. For example, free samples of a new shampoo are distributed to a large number of households. Because the use of the shampoo is costless it is used (desired response), and because it has desirable properties it is liked (reinforcement) and the likelihood of its being bought is increased. Thus the sequence of events is different for classical and operant conditioning. In the former, by association, liking precedes trial; in the latter, trial precedes liking. A series of rewards (reinforcements) may be used over time to encourage the repeat buying of the product.

The learning of knowledge, and the development of beliefs and attitudes without direct reinforcement is referred to as **cognitive learning** which stresses the importance of internal mental processes. The learning of two or more concepts without conditioning is known as **rote learning**. Having seen the headline 'Lemsip is for flu attacks', the consumer may remember that Lemsip is a remedy for flu attacks without the kinds of conditioning and reinforcement previously discussed. **Vicarious learning** involves learning from others without direct experience or reward. It is the promise of the reward that motivates. Thus we may learn the type of clothes that attract potential admirers by observing other people. In advertising, the 'admiring glance' can be used to signal approval of the type of clothing being worn or the alcoholic beverage being consumed. We imagine that the same may happen to us if we dress in a similar manner or drink a similar drink (see Exhibit 3.6). **Reasoning** is a more complex form of cognitive learning and is usually associated with high-involvement situations. For example, a detailed online product review or a sales presentation enables the consumer to draw their own conclusions through reasoning, having been presented with some facts or

Exhibit 3.6 The Adidas 'originals' campaign leverages vicarious learning

assertions. Whatever form of learning is used, marketers are particularly interested in both the recognition and recall of messages as we shall see in Chapter 9.

Our understanding of how people perceive stimuli and learn is improving all the time. **Semiotics** is the study of the correspondence between signs and symbols and their roles in how we assign meanings. Symbols in logo design and advertising are given meanings by the consumers that interpret them as such. For example, the striding man on a bottle of Johnnie Walker whisky symbolizes the journey we take through life and this journey is the centrepiece of the Johnnie Walker 'Keep Walking' campaign. In psychology and brain research, significant attention is being devoted to trying to understand the subconscious as it would appear that much of our decision-making is done there without us realizing it. For example, it has been argued that we often make snap judgements that are superior to those that we think a great deal about.[29]

Motivation

Given the endless array of choices that are available to us, what are the motives that cause us to select one experience over another or choose to spend our time or money in certain ways? A key part of this issue (and of the debates about marketing generally) is the distinction between needs and wants. Critics of marketing argue that it creates excessive wants and desires among consumers leading to all types of maladaptive behaviours such as addictive consumption, compulsive shopping disorder (CSD), consumer debt and the waste of the planet's scarce resources (see Exhibit 3.7).

Exhibit 3.7 This Greenpeace advert shows us the dark side of consumption

One of the best known theories of motivation is Maslow's Hierarchy of Needs. The psychologist Abraham Maslow sought to explain how people grow and develop and proposed that we move through a hierarchy of motives. First we must satisfy our basic *physiological needs* for food, clothing and shelter, then we move to *safety needs* such as protection from danger and accidents, then to the need for *belongingness* such as love and family relationships, then to the needs for *esteem and status* and then to the final highest level of need, namely, *self-actualization* which is essentially our understanding of whatever the meaning of life is for us. From a marketing point of view, different products can be seen as fulfilling different needs such as security systems for safety, club memberships for status and travel and education for self-actualization. However, consumers do not progress rigidly up the hierarchy but may place emphasis on different levels and different times and the same product may satisfy different needs for different people.

Consequently, new explanations of fundamental human needs are becoming more popular. For example, evolutionary psychologists argue that we have four basic human needs that have derived from our

evolution as a species and can be observed in different cultures during different time periods. These are the need to survive, to reproduce, to select kin and to reciprocate. These fundamental motives can be observed in the consumption of everything from cookery books (survival) to cosmetic surgery (reproduction) to Christmas gift giving (reciprocation).[30]

Beliefs and attitudes

A thought that a person holds about something is known as a 'belief'. Beliefs about oneself, which is known as the **self-concept**, are very important because this drives a signification element of consumption. For example, the viral video from Dove called *Evolution*, which was part of the Real Beauty campaign, has been a significant hit because it shows how perceptions of beauty are distorted in the media (see Exhibit 3.8).

Consumers increasingly use brands to convey their identity by wearing branded clothes or even having brands tattooed on their bodies (see Exhibit 3.9). Marketing people are also very interested in consumer beliefs because these are related to attitudes. In particular,

Exhibit 3.8 Dove's 'Real Beauty' campaign challenges society's concept of beauty

Go to the website to watch an advert from the 'Real Beauty' campaign.
www.mcgraw-hill.co.uk/textbooks/fahy

misconceptions about products can be harmful to brand sales. Duracell batteries were believed by consumers to last three times as long as Ever Ready batteries, but in continuous use they lasted over six times as long. This prompted Duracell to launch an advertising campaign to correct this misconception.

An 'attitude' is an overall favourable or unfavourable evaluation of a product or service. The consequence of a set of beliefs may be a positive or negative attitude towards the product or service. Changing attitudes is an important step in convincing consumers to try a brand. For example, the marketers of Skoda cars first had to overcome significantly negative attitudes towards the brand before they succeeded in growing its sales levels in the UK market.

Understanding beliefs and attitudes is an important task for marketers. For example, the attitudes of the 'grey market', those over the age of 50 years, are not well understood. Some companies, such as Gap, have explicitly targeted this segment, but Gap was forced to close its Forth & Towne outlets after heavy losses. Brands like Amazon's Kindle and Apple's iPhone and iPad have proved to be particularly popular with the grey market because they are larger than other portable devices and are very easy to use. This large and relatively well-off group is likely to be the subject of significant marketing effort in the years to come.

Personality

Just from our everyday dealings with people we can tell that they differ enormously in their personalities. **Personality** is the sum of the inner psychological characteristics of individuals, which lead to consistent responses to their environment.[31] There are several theories of personality but the most accepted today is the Big Five, and the extent to which one varies on these dimensions ranges from high to low.[32] The big

five are openness to new experience, novelty seeking etc.; conscientiousness, which is self-control, reliability etc.; agreeableness, which is warmth, friendliness etc.; stability such as emotional stability, and extraversion, that is, the extent to which people are outgoing and talkative or not. The extent to which we possess each of these traits will be reflected in our behaviour and in our consumption choices. For example, conscientiousness is generally low in juveniles and it increases with age. The consumption of high-maintenance products, pets, personal grooming and home fitness equipment are all indicators of high conscientiousness.

This concept – personality – is also relevant to brands (see Marketing in Action 3.3). 'Brand personality' is the characterization of brands as perceived by consumers. Brands may be characterized as 'for young people' (Tommy Hilfiger), 'for winners' (Nike), or 'self-important' (L'Oréal). This is a dimension over and above the physical (e.g. colour) or functional (e.g. taste) attributes of a brand. By creating a brand personality a marketer may generate appeal to people who value that characterization. For example, one of the longest-running fictional brands is James Bond; a variety of car makers and technology companies have attempted to bring his cool, suave and sexy personality into their brands by placing them in Bond movies.

Lifestyle

Lifestyle patterns have been the subject of much interest as far as marketing research practitioners are concerned. The term 'lifestyle' refers to the pattern of living as expressed in a person's activities, interests and opinions (the AIO dimensions). Lifestyle analysis (psychographics) groups consumers according to their beliefs, activities, values and demographic characteristics (such as education and income). For example, the

Exhibit 3.9 The role of brands in identity formation

Marketing in Action 3.3 The rise, fall and rise again of Tayto

Critical Thinking: The successful revival of the Tayto brand on the Irish market is reviewed below. Read it and critically evaluate the role of brand personalities in building brand loyalty in consumer markets.

Tayto is an iconic Irish brand of potato crisps which was founded in 1954 and became so successful and dominant in the market that it became a generic name for crisps in Ireland. As with many crisps brands, it originally appeared as a salted potato flavour but it was the creation of a cheese and onion variant that catapulted the brand to success. However, the arrival of the leading UK brand, Walkers, using the same marketing approach featuring the famous English soccer star and television personality, Gary Lineker, that had proved so successful in its home country, soon changed all that. Tayto's share of market declined rapidly and the brand was sold by its owner C&C to Largo Foods in 2006 for €62.3 million.

Largo quickly set about trying to re-establish Tayto to its pre-eminent position in Ireland. The centrepiece of the campaign was to focus on Mr Tayto – the brand's core personality. The perfect opportunity arose in 2007 – a year when there was a general election in Ireland. Mr Tayto ran as a fake election candidate. It provided light relief from the serious business of election campaigning and enabled Mr Tayto to have a public visibility as he canvassed for votes. It also reminded consumers who may have forgotten the brand that Tayto was still there. This was followed in 2008 with a digital campaign, where Mr Tayto began looking for a suitable Mrs Tayto which was a huge publicity success as he was frequently pictured in the media with leading models and celebrities. In 2009, his fictional autobiography – *The Man Inside the Jacket* was published and became an unprecedented success. It sold 60,000 copies and was the number one bestseller for six weeks as well as going on to become the third highest recalled campaign of 2009. This sequence of campaigns focusing on the Tayto personality helped to re-establish the Irish consumers' love of Tayto and also restored it to its position of being the dominant brand in the Irish market.

advertising agency Young & Rubicam identified seven major lifestyle groups that can be found throughout Europe and the USA.

1   *The mainstreamers*: the largest group. Attitudes include conventional, trusting, cautious and family centred. Leisure activities include spectator sports and gardening; purchase behaviour is habitual, brand loyal and in approved stores.
2   *The aspirers*: members of this group are unhappy, suspicious and ambitious. Leisure activities include trendy sports and fashion magazines; they buy fads, are impulse shoppers and engage in conspicuous consumption.
3   *The succeeders*: those that belong to this group are happy, confident, industrious and leaders. Leisure activities include travel, sports, sailing and dining out. Purchase decisions are based on criteria like quality, status and luxury.
4   *The transitionals*: members of this group are liberal, rebellious, self-expressive and intuitive. They have unconventional tastes in music, travel and movies;

and enjoy cooking and arts and crafts. Shopping behaviour tends to be impulsive and to involve unique products.
5   *The reformers*: those that belong to this group are self-confident and involved, have broad interests and are issues orientated. They like reading, cultural events, intelligent games and educational television. They have eclectic tastes, enjoy natural foods, and are concerned about authenticity and ecology.
6   *The struggling poor*: members of this group are unhappy, suspicious and feel left out. Their interests are in sports, music and television; their purchase behaviour tends to be price based, but they are also looking for instant gratification.
7   *The resigned poor*: those in this group are unhappy, isolated and insecure. Television is their main leisure activity and shopping behaviour is price based, although they also look for the reassurance of branded goods.

Lifestyle analysis has implications for marketing since lifestyles have been found to correlate with purchasing

Exhibit 3.10 The IKEA 'Kitchen Party' campaign reflects a young, modern, urban lifestyle

behaviour.[33] A company may choose to target a particular lifestyle group (e.g. the mainstreamers) with a product offering, and use advertising that is in line with the values and beliefs of this group (see Exhibit 3.10). For example, Benecol's range of cholesterol-lowering foods are marketed at consumers who seek to have a healthy lifestyle. As information on the readership/viewership habits of lifestyle groups becomes more widely known so media selection may be influenced by lifestyle research.

A typical example of a niche lifestyle that has grown significantly in recent years is surfing. Originating in the south Pacific, surfing was formerly popular in just some select areas such as Hawaii, California and Australia. In the past decade, its popularity has soared and participation rates around the world have grown dramatically. It is characterized by its own surf culture such as dressing in boardshorts or driving 'woodies', that is, station wagons used to carry boards. Many brands have capitalized on this opportunity, most notably the Australian clothing brand Billabong, and marketers aiming to target surfers can do so through particular magazines, events, television programmes and social networks.

Life cycle

In addition to the factors we have already examined, consumer behaviour may depend on the 'life stage'

people have reached. A person's life-cycle stage is of particular relevance since disposable income and purchase requirements may vary according to life-cycle stage. For example, young couples with no children may have high disposable income if both work, and may be heavy purchasers of home furnishings and appliances since they may be setting up home. When they have children, their disposable income may fall, particularly if they become a single-income family and the purchase of baby and child-related products increases. At the empty-nester stage, disposable income may rise due to the absence of dependent children, low mortgage repayments and high personal income. Research has shown that when children leave a home, a mother is likely to change 80 per cent of the branded goods she buys regularly and that they are more likely than any other group to decide which brands they want to buy once in a store than beforehand.[34] Both these issues have important marketing implications.

Social influences

The three social influences on consumer behaviour are: culture, social class and reference groups.

Culture

As we noted in Chapter 2, **culture** refers to the traditions, taboos, values and basic attitudes of the whole society within which an individual lives. It provides the framework within which individuals and their lifestyles develop, and consequently affects consumption. For example, in Japan it is generally women that control the family finances and make all the major household spending decisions. As a result, many financial services firms are developing investment products targeted specifically at Japanese women. Within cultures there are also a variety of sub-cultures that influence consumer behaviour and marketing as we saw in Chapter 2.

The most notable trend in the past three decades has been the increased internationalization of cultures. Products and services that, previously, may only have been available in certain countries are now commonplace. For example, speciality cuisines like Japanese sushi, Korean barbeque and Cajun food can now be found in major cities throughout the world. Allied to this, though, is the growing domination of some cultures. For example, the successes of American fast-food chains and movie production companies represent a major challenge to smaller, local enterprises in many parts of the world.

Social class

Long regarded as an important determinant of consumer behaviour, the idea of social class is based largely on occupation (often that of the chief income earner). This is one way in which respondents in marketing research surveys are categorized, and it is usual for advertising media (e.g. newspapers) to give readership figures broken down by social class groupings. Some countries are significantly more class conscious than others such as the UK and India and movement between

Exhibit 3.11 Demand growth for luxury brands has been increasing in many Asian markets

the classes is difficult. In others, such as Brazil and China rising incomes are creating large new middle- and upper-class segments which is significantly driving demand for international and luxury brands respectively (see Exhibit 3.11). For example, such is the demand for golf courses in China that many are being built without planning permission and others are not being called golf courses to get around planning legislation.

However, the use of traditional social class frameworks to explain differences in consumer behaviour has been criticized because certain social class categories may not relate to differences in disposable income (for example, many self-employed manual workers can have very high incomes). The National Statistics Socio-economic Classification system (NSSEC) in the UK aims to take account of this situation by identifying eight categories of occupation, as shown in Table 3.2.

Table 3.2 Social class categories

Analytic class	Operational categories	Occupations
1	Higher managerial and professional occupations	Employers in large organizations; higher managerial and professional
2	Lower managerial and professional occupations	Lower managerial occupations; higher technical and supervisory occupations
3	Intermediate occupations	Intermediate clerical/administrative, sales/service, technical/auxiliary and engineering occupations
4	Small employers and own-account workers	Employers in small, non-professional and agricultural organizations, and own-account workers
5	Lower supervisory and technical occupations	Lower supervisory and lower technical craft and process operative occupations
6	Semi-routine occupations	Semi-routine sales, service, technical, operative, agricultural, clerical and childcare occupations
7	Routine occupations	Routine sales/service, production, technical, operative and agricultural occupations
8	Never worked and long-term unemployed	Never worked, long-term unemployed and students

Consumption patterns are likely to vary significantly across these categories. For example, research on the social class of British grocery shoppers has found that the highest proportion of AB (managerial/professional) shoppers frequent Sainsbury's; Asda attracts a significantly higher share of people in lower supervisory and technical occupations; while Tesco's profile mirrors that of society in general.[35] An interesting trend in the growing middle-class segment is that consumers are becoming more cost-conscious but are also willing to splash out on luxury items. Brands that have targeted the middle market such as Maxwell House coffee owned by Kraft will be challenged by this development.[36]

Reference groups

A group of people that influences an individual's attitude or behaviour is called a **reference group**. Where a product is conspicuous (for example, clothing or cars) the brand or model chosen may have been strongly influenced by what buyers perceive as acceptable to their reference group; this may consist of the family, a group of friends or work colleagues. Some reference groups may be formal (e.g. members of a club or society), while others may be informal (friends with similar interests). Reference groups influence their members in a number of ways such as providing peers with information about products, by influencing peers to buy products and by individual members choosing certain products because they feel that this will enhance their image within the group. The role of reference groups is now more important than ever given that certain groups choose to live a very 'public' life through social networks. Different types of reference groups exist. *Membership*

groups are those to which a person already belongs and can be with friends, club members or class mates. An interesting marketing development has been the growth of brand communities which are social relationships based around interest in a product (see Chapter 6). *Aspirational* groups are those which a person would like to belong, for example, people often aspire to the lifestyle of sports stars or celebrities. Finally, *avoidance* groups are those that people choose to distance themselves from because they do not share the values of such a group.

A key role in all reference groups is played by the opinion leader. Opinion leaders are typically socially active and highly interconnected within their groups. They also have access to product information and influence the behaviour and purchase choices of group members. Given advances in social networking technology, their influence can be highly significant. Therefore, they are the focus of attention from marketers who aim to identify them and to encourage them to influence their peers through buzz marketing techniques (see Chapter 10). They are also critical to the adoption of new products as demonstrated in Figure 3.5.

A related issue is the 'herd mentality' of consumption behaviour. People are social animals and tend to follow the crowd, therefore companies are looking at ways of exploiting this to increase sales. For example, researchers in the USA created an artificial music market in which people downloaded previously unknown songs. What they found was that when consumers could see how many times the tracks had been downloaded, they tended to select the most popular tracks. As a result, many websites now include features like 'other customers have bought' tabs. Similarly, 'smart cart' technology is being pioneered in supermarkets to

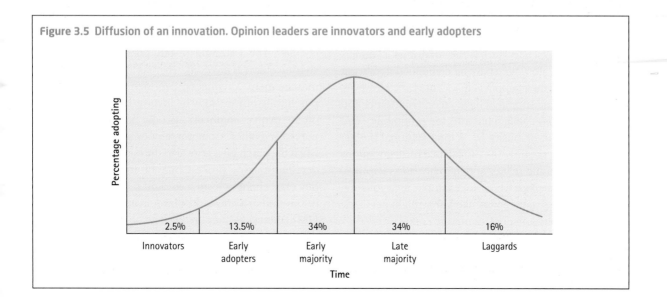

Figure 3.5 Diffusion of an innovation. Opinion leaders are innovators and early adopters

Percentage adopting

| 2.5% | 13.5% | 34% | 34% | 16% |

| Innovators | Early adopters | Early majority | Late majority | Laggards |

Time

exploit this herd instinct. Each cart has a scanner that reads products that have been chosen and relays it to a central computer. When a shopper walks past a shelf of goods, a screen on the shelf can tell her/him how many people in the shop have already selected that particular product. Studies have shown that if the number is high, he or she is more likely to choose it, so this method can be used to increase sales without offering discounts, for example.

In summary, the behaviour of consumers is affected by a variety of factors. There is a range of personal influences and some social influences that all combine to make up the nature of the relationships that individuals have with products and services. We will now turn to the factors that influence the buying behaviour of organizations.

Influences on organizational buying behaviour

Organizational buying is characterized by a number of unique features. Typically, the number of customers is small and order sizes large. For example, in Australia just two companies, Coles and Woolworths account for over 70 per cent of all products sold in supermarkets, so getting or losing an account with these resellers can be crucial. Organizational purchases are often complex and risky, with several parties having input into the purchasing decision as would be the case with a major information technology (IT) investment. The demand for many organizational goods is derived from the demand for consumer goods, which means that small changes in consumer demand can have an important impact on the demand for industrial goods. For example, the decline in the sale of VCRs has had a knock-on effect on the demand for VCR component parts. When large organizational customers struggle, this impacts on their suppliers. Most major car manufacturers such as Ford, General Motors, Daimler-Chrysler and Volkswagen have all demanded significant price cuts from their suppliers in recent years. However, at the same time suppliers have faced rising steel and raw material costs, which has affected profitability and forced some out of business.[37] Organizational buying is also characterized by the prevalence of negotiations between buyers and sellers; and in some cases reciprocal buying may take place where, for example, in negotiating to buy computers a company like Volvo might persuade a supplier to buy a fleet of company cars.

Figure 3.6 shows the three factors that influence organizational buying behaviour and the choice criteria that are used: the buy class, the product type and the importance of purchase.[38]

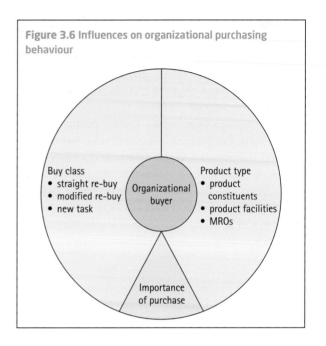

Figure 3.6 Influences on organizational purchasing behaviour

The buy class

Organizational purchases may be distinguished as either a **new task**, a **straight re-buy** or a **modified re-buy**.[39] A new task occurs when the need for the product has not arisen previously so that there is little or no relevant experience in the company, and a great deal of information is required. A straight re-buy occurs where an organization buys previously purchased items from suppliers already judged acceptable. Routine purchasing procedures are set up to facilitate straight re-buys. The modified re-buy lies between the two extremes. A regular requirement for the type of product exists, and the buying alternatives are known, but sufficient change (e.g. a delivery problem) has occurred to require some alteration to the normal supply procedure.

The buy classes affect organizational buying in the following ways. First, the membership of the DMU changes. For a straight re-buy possibly only the purchasing officer is involved, whereas for a new buy senior management, engineers, production managers and purchasing officers may be involved. Modified re-buys often involve engineers, production managers and purchasing officers, but not senior management, except when the purchase is critical to the company. Second, the decision-making process may be much longer as the buy class changes from a straight re-buy to a modified re-buy and to a new task. Third, in terms of influencing DMU members, they are likely to be much more receptive to new task and modified re-buy situations than straight re-buys. In the latter case, the purchasing manager has already solved the purchasing problem and has other problems to deal with.

The first implication of this buy class analysis is that there are big gains to be made if a company can enter the new task at the start of the decision-making process. By providing information and helping with any technical problems that can arise, the company may be able to create goodwill and 'creeping commitment', which secures the order when the final decision is made. The second implication is that since the decision process is likely to be long, and many people are involved in the new task, supplier companies need to invest heavily in sales personnel for a considerable period of time. Some firms employ 'missionary' sales teams, comprising their best salespeople, to help secure big new task orders.

The product type

Products can be classified according to four types: materials, components, plant and equipment, and maintenance, repair and operation (MRO):

1 materials – to be used in the production process, e.g. aluminium
2 components – to be incorporated in the finished product, e.g. headlights
3 plant and equipment – for example, bulldozers
4 products and services for MRO – for example, spanners, welding equipment and lubricants.

This classification is based on a customer perspective – how the product is used – and may be employed to identify differences in organizational buyer behaviour. First, the people who take part in the decision-making process tend to change according to product type. For example, senior management tend to get involved in the purchase of plant and equipment or, occasionally, when new materials are purchased if the change is of fundamental importance to company operations, e.g. if a move from aluminium to plastic is being considered. Rarely do they involve themselves in component or MRO supply. Similarly, design engineers tend to be involved in buying components and materials, but not normally MRO and plant equipment. Second, the decision-making process tends to be slower and more complex as product type moves along the following continuum:

> MRO → components → materials
> → plant and equipment

The importance of purchase

A purchase is likely to be perceived as being important to the buying organization when it involves large sums of money, when the cost of making the wrong decision, e.g. in terms of production downtime, is high and when there is considerable uncertainty about the outcome of alternative offerings. In such situations, many people at different organizational levels are likely to be involved in the decision and the process will be long, with extensive search for and analysis of information. Thus extensive marketing effort is likely to be required, but great opportunities present themselves to sales teams who work with buying organizations to convince them that their offering has the best pay-off; this may involve acceptance trials (e.g. private diesel manufacturers supply railway companies with prototypes for testing), engineering support and testimonials from other users. Additionally, guarantees of delivery dates and after-sales service may be necessary when buyer uncertainty regarding these factors is pronounced.

Features of organizational purchasing practice

Within the purchasing function, a number of trends have occurred that have marketing implications for supplier firms. The relentless drive for efficiency by businesses has been one of the key factors behind the growth of just-in-time purchasing, online purchasing and centralized purchasing. At the same time, these developments have often strengthened relationships between buyers and their suppliers, and we have seen a significant growth in relationship marketing and reverse marketing.

The **just-in-time (JIT)** concept aims to minimize stocks by organizing a supply system that provides materials and components as they are required. The total effects of JIT can be enormous. Purchasing inventory and inspection costs can be reduced, product design can be improved, delivery streamlined, production downtime reduced and the quality of the finished item enhanced. Very close co-operation is required between a manufacturer and its suppliers. An example of a company that employs a JIT system is the Nissan car assembly plant in Sunderland in the UK. Nissan adopts what it terms 'synchronous supply': parts are delivered only minutes before they are needed. For example, carpets are delivered by Sommer Allibert, a French supplier, from its facility close to the Nissan assembly line in sequence for fitting to the correct model. Only 42 minutes elapse between the carpet being ordered and its being fitted to the car. This system also carries risks, however. For example, the 2011 earthquake in Japan caused delays to the introduction of two new Toyota Prius models and impacted on production in other global companies such as Caterpillar and General Motors.

Social Media Marketing 3.1   LinkedIn

Critical Thinking: Below is a review of the rapid growth of the business network, LinkedIn. Read it and consider how business social networking can impact on your own career.

LinkedIn is a business-related social networking website that was launched in 2003 and is mainly used for professional networking. It has grown rapidly and currently claims over 100 million registered users in 200 countries. Members create an online profile which is essentially a brief career résumé and then form connections with people whom they know or have worked with in the past. These lists of connections are then used in a wide variety of ways. For example, employers can list jobs and search for potential candidates. Many LinkedIn users will carry recommendations from former contacts on their profiles to increase their attractiveness to employers or potential business partners and customers. Job seekers can review the profile of hiring managers and discover which of their existing contacts can introduce them. Users can join any of LinkedIn's 500,000 groups to find people who share similar interests and can also research companies to find out information like the ratio of male/female staff, the location of the company and its offices and lists of present and former staff.

LinkedIn is a highly successful company and when it went public in 2011, its shares tripled with hours of flotation. It generates revenue in a number of different ways including LinkedIn Jobs – a recruiting and hiring service, text and display advertising sales and also subscription services such as Business, Business Plus and Pro accounts that provide extra features including lists of who has searched you or your company. This approach of collecting money from both individuals and companies enabled it to report revenues of US$243 million and profits of US$15 million in 2010.

Based on: Kim (2011);[40] Wall (2011)[41]

The growth in the use of the Internet has given rise to the development of online purchasing. Two main categories of marketplaces, or exchanges, have been created: **vertical electronic marketplaces** are industry specific, such as sites for the paper industry (e.g. www.paperexchange.com) or the automotive and healthcare industries (e.g. www.covisint.com); **horizontal electronic marketplaces** cross industry boundaries and cater for supplies such as MROs (e.g.www.dgmarket.com) and services (www.elance.com). Companies seeking supplies post their offers on these websites. Potential vendors then bid for the contracts electronically. Some companies report significant improvements in efficiency from managing their purchasing this way, through reducing the amount of procurement staff involved in processing orders and increasing the potential global spread of vendors. This heightened competition presents challenges for suppliers. Social media platforms such as Facebook and LinkedIn have become a popular mechanism for firms to source employees and suppliers (see Social Media Marketing 3.1).

Where several operating units within a company have common requirements and where there is an opportunity to strengthen a negotiating position by bulk buying, centralized purchasing is an attractive option. Centralization encourages purchasing specialists to concentrate their energies on a small group of products, thus enabling them to develop an extensive knowledge of cost factors and the operation of suppliers.[42] For example, increasing concerns over the costs of healthcare has meant that many hospitals have centralized purchasing in procurement departments rather than devolving the activity to doctors and nurses as had been the case in the past. As a result, many contracts are put out to tender, often on a pan-European basis, with vendors selected on the basis of quality, cost and ability to deliver over a number of years. The net effect of this is that orders are much more difficult to secure but, once secured, are likely to be more long lasting. At the same time, organizational buying has become increasingly characterized by very close relationships between buyers and sellers. **Relationship marketing** is the process of creating, developing and enhancing relationships with customers and other stakeholders. For example, Marks & Spencer has trading relationships with suppliers that stretch back almost a century. Such long-term relationships can have significant advantages for both buyer and seller. Risk is reduced for buyers as they get to know people in the supplier organization and know who to contact when problems arise. Communication is thus improved, and joint problem solving and design management can take place with suppliers becoming, in effect, strategic partners. Sellers gain through closer knowledge of buyer requirements, and many companies have reorganized their sales forces to reflect the importance of managing customer relationships effectively – a process known as key account management. New product development can benefit from such close relationships. The development of machine-washable lamb wool fabrics and easy-to-iron cotton shirts came about because of Marks & Spencer's close relationship with UK manufacturers.[43] The issue of relationship marketing will be dealt with in more detail in Chapter 7.

The traditional view of marketing is that supplier firms will actively seek out the requirements of customers and attempt to meet those needs better than the competition. However, purchasing is now taking on a more proactive, aggressive stance in acquiring the products and services needed to compete. This process, whereby the buyer attempts to persuade the supplier to provide exactly what the organization wants, is called **reverse marketing**.[44] Syngenta, an international supplier of chemicals, uses reverse marketing very effectively to target suppliers with a customized list of requirements concerning delivery times, delivery success rates and how often sales visits should occur. The growth of reverse marketing presents two key benefits to suppliers who are willing to listen to the buyer's proposition and carefully consider its merits: first, it provides the opportunity to develop a stronger and longer-lasting relationship with the customer; second, it could be a source of new product opportunities that may be developed to a broader customer base later on.

Finally in B2B contexts, a firm may not actually make a purchase but rather it simply leases a product. A lease is a contract by which the owner of an asset (e.g. a car) grants the right to use the asset for a period of time to another party in exchange for the payment of rent.[45] The benefits to the customer are that a leasing arrangement avoids the need to pay the cash purchase price of the product or service, is a hedge against fast product obsolescence, may have tax advantages, avoids the problem of equipment disposal and, with certain types of leasing contract, avoids some maintenance costs. These benefits need to be weighed against the costs of leasing, which may be higher than outright buying.

When you have read this chapter
log on to the Online Learning Centre for *Foundations of Marketing* at **www.mcgraw-hill.co.uk/textbooks/fahy** where you'll find links and extra online study tools for marketing.

Summary

This chapter has examined the nature of customer behaviour and the key influences on customer behaviour. The following key issues were addressed.

1. The differences between consumer and organizational buying behaviour. In the latter, the buying decision process involves more stages, the input of more parties and greater levels of negotiation. Technical and economic choice criteria tend to play a greater role in organizational buying.

2. Who buys – the five roles in the buying decision-making process: initiator, influencer, decider, buyer and user. Different people may play different roles, particularly in a family purchase and, for marketers, identifying the decider is critical.

3. The buying decision process, involving the stages of need recognition, search for alternatives, evaluation of alternatives, purchase and post-purchase evaluation. In the case of high-involvement purchases, consumers will typically go through all these stages, whereas in a low-involvement situation, they may move directly from need recognition to purchase.

4. The main choice criteria used in making purchase decisions – namely, technical, economic, social and personal criteria. In consumer buyer behaviour, social and personal criteria are very important as consumers build their identities through product and service selection.

5. The main influences on consumer buying behaviour: personal influences and social influences. At any given time, there are myriad factors that may influence a consumer's purchase decision. Deeply embedded emotional elements such as conditioning, learning, attitudes and personality are key drivers of consumption decisions.

6. The main influences on organizational buying behaviour: the buy class, the product type and the importance of purchase. For example, a major investment in plant and equipment that is critical to the organization and is a new task purchase will necessitate the involvement of many parties in the organization and will take time before a decision is made.

7. The key features of organizational purchasing practice: just-in-time purchasing, online purchasing, centralized purchasing, relationship marketing, reverse marketing and leasing. Organizational purchasing at one level presents opportunities for reverse marketing and relationship building with suppliers, but at a different level is driven by efficiency concerns that are managed through centralized and online purchasing.

Study questions

1. What are the differences between organizational buying behaviour and consumer buying behaviour?

2. Choose a recent purchase that included not only yourself but also other people in making the decision. What role(s) did you play in the buying centre? What roles did these other people play and how did they influence your choice?

3. Review your decision to choose the educational establishment you are attending in terms of need recognition, information search, evaluation of alternatives and post-selection evaluation.

4. Review the choice criteria influencing some recent purchases such as a hairstyle, a meal, etc.

5. Describe the recent trends in just-in-time purchasing, online purchasing and centralized purchasing. Discuss the implications of these trends for marketers in vendor firms.

Suggested reading

Anderson, J.C., J.A. Narus and **W. van Rossum** (2006) Customer Value Propositions in Business Markets, *Harvard Business Review*, **84** (3), 90–9.

Arnould, E. and **C. Thompson** (2005) Consumer Culture Theory (CCT): Twenty Years of Research, *Journal of Consumer Research*, **31** (4), 868–82.

Gladwell, M. (2005) *Blink: The Power of Thinking Without Thinking*, London: Allen Lane.

Miller, G. (2009) *Spent: Sex, Evolution and the Secrets of Consumerism*, London: William Heinemann.

Mollen, A. and **H. Wilson** (2010) Engagement, Telepresence and Interactivity in Online Consumer Experience: Reconciling Scholastic and Managerial Perspectives, *Journal of Business Research*, **63** (9/10), 919–25.

Underhill, P. (2000) *Why We Buy: The Science of Shopping*, London: Texere.

References

1. **Anonymous** (2006) Habbo Hotel Signs RealNetworks Radio Deal, *MarketingWeek.co.uk.*, 14 December; **Brady, S.** (2010) Habbo, *Brandchannel.com*, 7 May; **Kiss, J** (2010) Ten Years of Virtual Worlds: Habbo Hits a Decade, *Guardian.co.uk*, 5 July.
2. **Blackwell, R.D., P.W. Miniard** and **J.F. Engel** (2000) *Consumer Behavior*, Orlando, FL: Dryden, 174.
3. **Pesola, M.** (2005) Samsung Plays to the Young Generation, *Financial Times*, 29 March, 11.
4. **Jones, H.** (2002) What Are They Playing At? *Financial Times*, Creative Business, 17 December, 6.
5. **Pidd, H.** (2007) We Are Coming for your Children, *Guardian. co.uk*, 31 July.
6. **Lindstrom, M.** (2003) The Real Decision Makers, *Brandchannel. com*, 11 August.
7. **Barber, B.** (2007) *Consumed: How Markets Corrupt Children, Infantilize Adults and Swallow Citizens Whole*, London: W. H. Norton & Co.
8. **Arnould, E.** and **C. Thompson** (2005) Consumer Culture Theory (CCT): Twenty Years of Research, *Journal of Consumer Research*, **31** (4), 868–82.
9. **Engel, J.F., R.D. Blackwell** and **P.W. Miniard** (1990) *Consumer Behavior*, Orlando, FL: Dryden, 29.
10. **Hawkins, D.I., R.J. Best** and **K.A. Coney** (1989) *Consumer Behavior: Implications for Marketing Strategy*, Boston, MA: Irwin, 30.
11. **Kuusela, H., M.T. Spence** and **A.J. Kanto** (1998) Expertise Effects on Prechoice Decision Processes and Final Outcomes: A Protocol Analysis, *European Journal of Marketing*, **32** (5/6), 559–76.
12. **Blackwell, R.D., P.W. Miniard** and **J.F. Engel** (2000) *Consumer Behavior*, Orlando, FL: Dryden, 34.
13. **Elliott, R.** and **E. Hamilton** (1991) Consumer Choice Tactics and Leisure Activities, *International Journal of Advertising*, **10**, 325–32.
14. **Laurent, G.** and **J.N. Kapferer** (1985) Measuring Consumer Involvement Profiles, *Journal of Marketing Research*, **12** (February), 41–53.
15. **The Economist** (2009), Fair Comment, *Technology Quarterly*, March 7, 11.
16. **Fenton, B.** (2008) Counting the Cost of the Online Land Grab, *Financial Times*, 19 February, 21.
17. **Hawkins, D.I., R.J. Best** and **K.A. Coney** (1989) *Consumer Behavior: Implications for Marketing Strategy*, Boston, MA: Irwin.
18. **Birchall, J.** (2006) Retailers Give Customers the Final Word, *Financial Times*, 6 October, 13.
19. **Anonymous** (2011) I've Got You Labelled, *The Economist*, 2 April, 74.
20. **Engel, J.F., R.D. Blackwell** and **P.W. Miniard** (1990) *Consumer Behavior*, Orlando, FL: Dryden, 363
21. **Williams, K.C.** (1981) *Behavioural Aspects of Marketing*, London: Heinemann.
22. **Lindstrom, M.** (2009) *Buyology: How Everything We Believe About Why We Buy is Wrong,* London: Random House Books, 38.
23. **Ratneshwar, S., L. Warlop, D.G. Mick** and **G. Seegar** (1997) Benefit Salience and Consumers' Selective Attention to Product Features, *International Journal of Research in Marketing*, **14**, 245–9.
24. **Advertising Research Foundation** (2010) Wrigley's 5 Gum, Warc.com.
25. **Silverstein, B.** (2010) A Gum that Willy Wonka Would Love, Brandchannel.com, 11 May.
26. **Levin, L.P.** and **G.J. Gaeth** (1988) Framing of Attribute Information Before and After Consuming the Product, *Journal of Consumer Research*, **15** (December), 374–8.
27. **Anonymous** (2008) The Way the Brain Buys, *The Economist*, December 20, 99–101.
28. **O'Morain, P.** (2008) The Fascinating Facts About Ladies in Red, *Irish Times HealthPlus*, November 11, 14.
29. **Gladwell, M.** (2005) *Blink: The Power of Thinking Without Thinking*, London: Allen Lane.
30. **Saad, G.** (2007) *The Evolutionary Bases of Consumption*, Hillsdale, NJ: Lawrence Erlbaum.
31. **Kassarjian, H.H.** (1971) Personality and Consumer Behavior: A Review, *Journal of Marketing Research*, November, 409–18.
32. **Miller, G.** (2009) *Spent: Sex, Evolution and the Secrets of Consumerism*, London: William Heinemann.
33. **O'Brien, S.** and **R. Ford** (1988) Can We At Last Say Goodbye to Social Class?, *Journal of the Market Research Society*, **30** (3), 289–332.
34. **Carter, M.** (2005) A Brand New Opportunity in the Empty Nest, *Financial Times*, 5 December, 14.
35. **Anonymous** (2005) This Sceptred Aisle, *The Economist*, 6 August, 29.
36. **Anonymous** (2006) The Disappearing Mid-Market, *The Economist*, 20 May, 70–2.
37. **Simon, B.** (2005) Car Parts Groups Face a Depressed Future, *Financial Times*, 18 May, 31.
38. **Cardozo, R.N.** (1980) Situational Segmentation of Industrial Markets, *European Journal of Marketing*, **14** (5/6), 264–76.
39. **Robinson, P.J., C.W. Faris** and **Y. Wind** (1967) *Industrial Buying and Creative Marketing*, Boston, MA: Allyn & Bacon.
40. **Kim, R.** (2011) LinkedIn Preps a Bigger IPO, but it's no Facebook, Businessweek.com, 9 May.
41. **Wall, E.** (2011) LinkedIn IPO: Is this a Tech Bubble? Telegraph. co.uk, 13 June.
42. **Briefly, E.G., R.W. Eccles** and **R.R. Reeder** (1998) *Business Marketing*, Englewood Cliffs, NJ: Prentice-Hall, 105.
43. **Thornhill, J.** and **A. Rawsthorn** (1992) Why Sparks Are Flying, *Financial Times*, 8 January, 12.
44. **Blenkhorn, D.L.** and **P.M. Banting** (1991) How Reverse Marketing Changes Buyer–Seller Roles, *Industrial Marketing Management*, **20**, 185–91.
45. **Anderson, F.** and **W. Lazer** (1978) Industrial Lease Marketing, *Journal of Marketing*, **42** (January), 71–9.

Case 3 Tourism Queensland: 'The Best Job in the World'

On 1 July 2009, Ben Southall from the UK took up his position in what was described as 'The Best Job in the World'. Ben was named Caretaker of the Islands of the Great Barrier Reef. He was paid a generous salary of AU$150,000 for 6 months' work, with luxury accommodation on Hamilton Island included during his post. 'The Best Job in the World' campaign, launched on 11 January 2009, was created for Tourism Queensland, a government industry body designed to promote Queensland as a tourist destination throughout the world and specifically through this campaign, to raise international awareness of the Islands of the Great Barrier Reef.

Background to the campaign

Despite the fact that the Great Barrier Reef is a world-heritage listed Natural Wonder of the World, the islands of the region are relatively unknown. In fact, approximately two million tourists visit the reef each year, but most are on day trips rather than long-stay holidays. In the years prior to the campaign, international visits to Australia had stagnated (less than 1 per cent growth in 2006). Even with Tourism Australia's much talked about 'Where the bloody hell are you' campaign in 2007, figures only grew by 2 per cent. Queensland's international visitor arrivals were declining (−1 per cent in 2007) mostly due to fewer tourist visits from key international markets (see Table C3.1). Significantly, tourism was directly responsible for 122,000 jobs and indirectly responsible for an additional 100,000 jobs, or 10.3 per cent of Queensland's workforce. The Queensland tourism industry faced a number of difficult challenges. There was a pending State election, and as Tourism Queensland is a government linked agency, this created some uncertainty as to timing and government responses to funding. The global financial crisis was in full swing and taking its toll on tourism, airlines and travel companies around the world. Consumer spending in most markets was reducing and unemployment rising, creating a mood of uncertainty. Therefore, Tourism Queensland turned to agency CumminsNitro to deliver a compelling central idea that would resonate with people across the world, across varying cultures and backgrounds, with a nominal AU$1.2 million budget (including all production and media).

Table C3.1 Country of origin of Great Barrier Reef visitors

Market	UK	Europe	USA	Japan	Germany	Other*
%	29	23	12	11	9	16

*Other includes New Zealand, New Caledonia, Ireland and the Nordic regions, Singapore, Malaysia, India, China, Taiwan and Korea.

Exhibit C3.1 The Tourism Queensland Marketing Communications mix

The campaign itself

The campaign 'The Best Job in the World' launched in January 2009. The campaign created a reason for people all over the world to engage with the Australian destination and aspire to experience it. The Best Job campaign utilized a very simple communications strategy. Classified ads, job listings and small banner advertisements were strategically placed in target markets directing people to a central URL: islandreefjob.com. The purpose of the campaign was to drive traffic to this website to stimulate mass social media and mainstream media coverage. The website aimed to capture consumer interest on two levels: (1) the primary motivation, job application or interest of applicants; (2) engaging and aspirational content about the Islands of the Great Barrier Reef. The website was supported by a presence on Myspace, Facebook, YouTube and Twitter. The campaign launch was targeted to coincide with the northern hemisphere's winter ensuring that the campaign would have heightened appeal in the primary markets. A comprehensive PR strategy fed the world's media a rare 'good news' story in a time of rising unemployment, raising awareness and directing traffic online to apply. Candidates were asked to submit a one minute video application demonstrating their knowledge of the region, generating content for the website.

The competition itself allowed Tourism Queensland the opportunity to develop more publicity at a number of stages. The potential candidates for the position were narrowed down to 150. From this, a shortlist of 50 applicants from 22 countries were narrowed down to a final 16, 15 of whom were chosen by Tourism Queensland, and a sixteenth 'wild card' applicant chosen by popular vote. This maintained huge interest in the campaign over a sustained period before the winner was announced on 6 May 2009 (see Exhibit C3.1).

The target audience for the campaign was defined as 'Global Experience Seekers': self-challengers, youthful travellers with high education, with access to new technology, and with a preference for holiday immersion beyond major cities. This segment was primarily targeted across key markets that have a higher propensity to travel to Australia. The Best Job campaign set a number of objectives. Firstly it was hoped that mainstream media coverage would exceed overall investment in the campaign. The campaign also targeted news coverage in key population markets and to gain travel industry recognition (by wholesalers, travel agents, airlines and local tourism operators). Specifically for the campaign activity the target response objectives were: to receive 14,000 job applications, for specific content of the Islands to become viral, as well as extensive social media use of campaign content and consumer-generated content over and above the applicant videos through blogs, social network sites and in other Web 2.0 portals.

Campaign results

The campaign results far exceeded any expectations. In total, Tourism Queensland received 34,684 video job applications from 201 countries. Therefore, at least one person from every country in the world applied for the position. Tourism Queensland also received over 20,000 emails. The organization had initially prepared three or four people to watch 4,000 videos but due to the huge response they needed 35–40 people to vet the final 9,000 videos over the last weekend. Total visitors to The Best Job in the World website exceeded 8.7 million with 53,889,455 page views and 8.25 minutes average time spent. News updates from the site were subscribed to by 154,437 individuals. There were also over 475,000 votes for Wild Card applicants. A Google search for 'best job in the world island' returned around 52,500,000 listings and 43,603 news story listings. In terms of social media, Facebook referred 371,126 visits, the highest referrer after Yahoo and Google. The showcase video for the Islands of the Great Barrier Reef was viewed on YouTube almost 300,000 times. In terms of consumer generated content, there were over 578 hours of content on YouTube from the video applications alone. These videos and Ben's videos showing what it was like to work as the Island Caretaker have been viewed almost 400,000 times. A 'best job in the world' search on FLIKR showed over 3,500 pictures. A Google Blog search for 'best job in the world' generated 231,355 blogs.

Ben has been very successful in his role as Island Caretaker promoting Queensland. He has approximately 4,000 followers on Twitter and 1,300 people 'like' Ben on Facebook. He has also gained significant media attention including a guest appearance on The Oprah Winfrey Show, viewed by approximately 9.7 million in the USA alone and broadcast internationally to an additional 145 counties worldwide. The estimated publicity value for the interview was US$440,952 in America alone. The Best Job campaign received huge exposure in the UK where BBC1 ran an hour-long documentary screened during prime-time, attracting 5.7 million viewers. The estimated publicity value for the first screening of this documentary was more than £9 million. This documentary also featured on all Air New Zealand and Cathay Pacific's in-flight programmes. Ben made regular appearances on domestic television including several guest appearances presenting the weather on Channel 7's Sunrise and hosting a Getaway crew on Hamilton Island. The estimated publicity value for these segments was $570,000 and $970,000 respectively. Sixty media from around the globe attended the job announcement on Hamilton Island attracting coverage from BBC, CNN, *Good Morning America*, Canada TV, Sky News, *The Times* and the *Shanghai Morning Post*. Tourism Queensland generated further media exposure through the National Geographic Channel's International 'Best Job in the World' six-part documentary series following Ben's exploits during his tenure as Island Caretaker.

To date, the campaign has generated $430 million in publicity. This figure represents approximately $94 million in domestic media coverage in Australia and $326 million in international media coverage (and excludes the value of social media coverage and consumer content). The Best Job campaign also received a number of awards, most notably stealing the show at the world's most prestigious advertising awards, the Cannes Lions International Advertising Festival, by winning more of the ultimate Grand Prix awards than any other campaign in the Festival's 55-year history. The key for Tourism Queensland now was turning the success of the campaign into bookings.

Tourism

The campaign was launched at the height of the global financial crisis, which saw a massive decline in travel globally. This coupled with the effects of swine flu and a strong Australian dollar, all contributed to a decline in overall visitors to Australia. The campaign has significantly impacted tourism figures in Queensland. Despite overall numbers for Australian tourism decreasing, Queensland tourism increased 20 per cent since the campaign launch with 50 per cent of all Australia trips now including a Queensland component. The stability in international visits that Australia experienced in 2009 represented a comparatively strong performance compared with a number of other regions around the world, with the United Nations World Tourism Organization (UNWTO) estimating that international tourist arrivals declined worldwide by 4 per cent in 2009. Owing to the social networking nature of the Best Job in the World campaign, the youth market (under 30 years old) has been particularly important for Queensland. Youth visitors from continental Europe increased 6 per cent over the year ended December 2009. Similarly, Tourism Research Australia's International Visitor Survey for the year ended June 2010 revealed growth in the number of UK (8 per cent) and continental European (10 per cent) visitors aged under 30 years who visited the Whitsundays on holidays. Queensland now has the second largest share of the international youth market in Australia with 42 per cent.

Several operators reported significant referrals from the campaign website in the first few weeks, with the Mantra Group receiving more than 1400 enquiries in a single day after the campaign launched. In Germany, wholesaler FTI's booking numbers to Queensland increased steadily, up 8.7 per cent year ending December 2009, while Wholesaler Dertour announced that while numbers for Australia were declining, numbers to Queensland were increasing steadily with more bookings than the other states. Boomerang Reisen recorded a 7 per cent increase in visitors to Queensland throughout 2009 stating that they use the Best Job in the World campaign in almost every second customer pitch. Media exposure generated as a result of the Best Job in the World also resulted in a decision by Amway Australia to hold its 500 delegate conference on Hamilton Island in November 2010 which helped to generate approximately $580,000 in expenditure for Queensland. In May 2010, two major US travel companies, online booking agent Orbitz and luxury travel wholesaler Signature, became the first US travel sellers to promote the Islands of the Great Barrier Reef as a stand-alone destination. This decision was due to the profile gained by the Islands through the Best Job in the World campaign. Throughout their campaign Orbitz. com and their other international websites generated 6,524 room nights of Queensland accommodation sales in May and June. This figure equates to year-on-year growth of 170 per cent for Queensland room nights booked through Orbitz during the two-month period.

Tourism Queensland's 14 international offices have also achieved success from a series of spin-off campaigns from the Best Job in the World, such as the Great Barrier Reef sale which ran shortly after the campaign launched in the Nordic region, generating just under 5000 passengers to Queensland. In early 2009, Tourism Queensland's UK office created six 'Best' theme packages. For example, The Best Holiday in the World run in partnership with Ethiad and Austravel, generated 1,584 passengers for Queensland from the UK. The Best Adventure in the World, run in partnership with Backpacking Queensland and Kilroy Travels in the Nordic region, reported their results for Queensland were up 58 per cent on the same time the previous year. The Best Experience in the World viral campaign in the UK which began in September 2009, reached more than 250,000 trade and end consumers and resulted in a combined click through rate of 24.29 per cent. In August 2009, Tourism Queensland launched the Best Holiday in the World domestic marketing campaign which featured four of the Best Job in the World candidates set to the theme song of The Monkees. The 10-month television, print, radio and online campaign drove visitors to look at more than 552,000 Best Holiday campaign pages during the campaign period August 2009–June 2010. Throughout October–December 2009, Tourism Queensland Europe coordinated a digital campaign themed The Best Holiday in the World, which resulted in more than 75,000 page views with more than 32,000 participating in the game. Tourism Queensland's Europe office also ran an activity with one of the Queensland tourism ambassadors in Europe themed Best Holiday in the World. This activity reached more than 64,000 consumers and potential visitors to Queensland.

Hamilton Island, the base of the Best Job in the World Island Caretaker Ben Southall, enjoyed impressive international visitor numbers in 2009. Room night sales were up 21 per cent in November 2009 compared with the same month in 2008. The European market also performed well with room night sales 29 per cent stronger year on year. Hamilton Island also reported in December 2009 that Japanese arrivals for the year were up 59 per cent, while the national average was down 24 per cent. Korean, Indian and Chinese arrivals were also up, 84 per cent, 41 per cent and 34 per cent respectively.

Conclusion

Ben finished his contract as Island Caretaker on 31 December 2009. Owing to the success of the campaign and high publicity value generated, he continued as a Queensland Tourism Ambassador. In this role he continues to work closely with Tourism Queensland's international offices and continues to appear at a range of high-profile media and trade events in the USA, Canada, Japan, New Zealand, the UK, China, Hong Kong, Taiwan and the Middle East. In May 2011, Ben embarked on 'The Best Expedition in the World' exploring the Great Barrier Reef by kayaking and sailing over 1600 km. As his journey progresses, he will again report by blogging and photographing through his website www.bestexpeditionintheworld.com. Tourism Queensland plans to continue to capitalize on the opportunities this global attention has presented.

Questions

1. Based on your understanding of who is important in the buying decision process, evaluate the potential roles in the decision to apply to the Best Job advertisement. How are these roles significant in terms of generating greater awareness for Queensland?
2. How would you characterize the level of involvement in the decision to apply for the 'Best Job in the World'?
3. The target audience for this campaign were defined as 'Global Experience Seekers'. Discuss the influences on consumer behaviour in applying for the Best Job in the World with reference to the target market.
4. Discuss the growth in importance of social media as a tool in the consumer decision-making process.

This case was prepared by Deborah Sadd, Bournemouth University and David Cosgrave, University of Limerick from published sources as a basis for class discussion rather than to illustrate either effective or ineffective management.

Chapter 4

Marketing Research and Customer Insights

<table>
<tr><td>

Chapter outline

The role of customer insights

Types of marketing information

Internal market information

Market intelligence

Approaches to conducting
marketing research

Stages in the marketing
research process

Marketing information systems

The use of marketing information
systems and marketing research

</td><td>

Learning outcomes

By the end of this chapter you will understand:

1. the importance of marketing information and customer insights
2. the different types of marketing information available
3. the main types of internal market information
4. what is meant by market intelligence
5. the main approaches to conducting marketing research
6. the main stages in the marketing research process
7. the differences between qualitative and quantitative research
8. the nature and purpose of marketing information systems.

</td></tr>
</table>

MARKETING SPOTLIGHT

IKEA

The privately owned, Swedish company IKEA is the world's largest home furnishings brand, operating over 300 stores in Europe, Asia, North America and Australia. It employs 127,000 people in 41 countries and reported a profit of €2.5 billion in 2010 on the back of sales of €23.1 billion. It has been claimed that one in every three Europeans is now conceived in an IKEA bed!

IKEA is renowned for its competitively priced, Scandinavian-designed, self-assembly furniture. Its huge stores, often up to 50,000 square metres in size, are stocked with all household requirements ranging from kitchens right down to small items like candlesticks. To achieve global consistency, the company standardizes its operations and procedures such as the management of its supply chain and the familiar look of its blue and yellow stores as much as possible. However, this presents a challenge as it moves to new markets because the brand risks being seen as cold and global and not connected to the needs of local customers. This is a particular issue in the furniture business because household designs, climatic conditions and living patterns vary enormously around the world. So in Australia, IKEA conducted an ethnographic study of 80 homes to observe and talk to people about how they live – getting into details such as where they sit to watch the television, where they really eat their dinner and where they leave their keys, handbags or wallets when they come home. This type of study enabled the researchers to uncover just how passionately people felt about their homes.

Go to the website to see the IKEA 'Kitchen Party' campaign.
www.mcgraw-hill.co.uk/textbooks/fahy

During the analysis of the findings, a critical insight emerged which was that the right furniture can facilitate a better home life such as allowing families to watch television together or have dinner together. Because of the flexible, modern design of its home furnishings, IKEA felt it was perfectly positioned to capitalize on this opportunity. So it created an advertising campaign called 'This is Home', which aimed to demonstrate how furniture can change one's life. A further six households were selected in key segments such as families with school-age kids, young couples living on their own, etc. Cameras were placed in kitchens, living rooms and bedrooms and people were filmed for several weeks during which the rooms were made over with IKEA furniture. The cameras recorded the new behaviours and emotions that this change created. This 'reality'-style advertising worked and 50 per cent of people who saw the campaign said they would consider visiting an IKEA store. The ethnographic methodology used to research the market had become the core of the brand's promotional campaign.[1]

The role of customer insights

Would the likes of New Coke, WAP technology or the Millennium Dome not have been such disastrous failures had more or better consumer research been conducted in advance? We will never know but what is certain is that truly market-led companies recognize that they need to always be in touch with what is happening in the marketplace. Customer needs are continually changing, often in ways that are very subtle. To innovate new forms of value for customers, accurate and timely customer insights are very important. These insights can inform everything from product innovation, product design and features, advertising campaign themes and so on. For example, the famous Johnnie Walker 'Keep Walking' campaign was created after research insights which showed that modern men (their key target market) increasingly saw life as one long journey. The successful television and viral advertisement featuring the Scottish actor Robert Carlyle, is over five minutes long, serving to illustrate this journey (see Exhibit 4.1).

For some companies, no major strategic decisions are made without first researching the market. But this activity goes far beyond commercial organizations. For example, political parties and record companies are heavy users of marketing research and often stand accused of overdependence on it to shape everything from manifestos to new albums. Therefore organizations have a huge appetite for information to help them make the correct decisions. This information can play a key role in a whole variety of decisions including whether there is a market for a new product, what our current customers think of our service levels, how our brands are performing in the market, how effective our latest promotional campaign has been and so on. This chapter will examine the types of information that are available and how they can be used to assist better decision making. Given the information age that we live in, this is a crucial activity, as organizations frequently suffer more from a surplus rather than a deficit of information. Being able to intelligently sort through all the information that is potentially available and convert it into usable customer insights is an important marketing task.

Exhibit 4.1 Johnnie Walker's 'Walk with Giants' campaign is a series of inspiring personal stories

Table 4.1 Global marketing research expenditure 2009 (selected countries)

Country	Turnover in US$ million	Spend per capita in US$
UK	2332	52.55
France	1930	42.94
Sweden	261	39.38
Germany	2080	35.32
Norway	102	29.22
Denmark	112	28.29
USA	6144	27.84
Switzerland	146	27.56
Australia	414	26.33
Finland	94	24.33
Netherlands	262	22.15
Ireland	68	21.32
Belgium	148	19.05
Canada	453	18.72
New Zealand	53	17.18
Japan	1270	13.87
Italy	543	12.66
Singapore	42	12.20
China	659	0.69

Source: Esomar Global Market Research, 2010.

As a result, the marketing research industry is a huge one, estimated to be worth over US$28.95 billion globally in 2009 and US$13.30 million in Europe, or just under half the total global spend.[2] Table 4.1 provides details of levels of marketing research expenditure throughout the world. Market research also tends to follow market development. For example, some of the highest growth rates for market research have been in countries and regions like Indonesia and East Africa, whose growing economies have attracted the interest of marketers.[3] The highest expenditure per capita is to be found in Europe (see Table 4.1). Defining the boundaries of marketing research is not easy. Casual discussions with customers at exhibitions or through sales calls can provide valuable informal information about their requirements, competitor activities and future happenings in the industry. More formal approaches include the conduct of marketing research studies or the development of marketing information systems. This chapter focuses on these formal methods of information provision.

Types of marketing information

Given the wide variety of information sources that an organization can potentially access, decisions about which types of information to gather are crucial. In the main, these are driven by what questions need to be answered. For example, if a company wants to examine whether there have been any changes in attitudes towards its brand following on from recent marketing activities, it may informally monitor conversations that are happening in various websites or more formally carry out periodic market research using customer panels that track changes in how the brand is perceived. For every research question, there is always a menu of answers. A preliminary analysis of a foreign market can be done relatively cheaply using secondary data available online and reports held in libraries, or more expensively using a research firm in the target country to conduct a detailed study. The major types of marketing information available are outlined below.

Internal market information

A very good place for an organization to begin answering a research problem is by looking at what information it currently already has available to it. This can take many forms. For example, personnel working in the organization such as salespeople or customer service people may have useful information regarding what is happening in the market. Studies conducted in one part of the organization may help to answer questions elsewhere. Advances in information technology mean that the retention of this type of information has improved dramatically. Internal market information is particularly useful when companies want to get to know their current customers better. To do this the following techniques are used.

Marketing databases

Companies collect data on customers on an ongoing basis. The data are stored on marketing databases, containing each customer's name, address, telephone number, past transactions and, sometimes, demographic and lifestyle data. Information on the types of purchase, frequency of purchase, purchase value and responsiveness to promotional offers may be held (see Chapter 10). For example, retailers collect these data through loyalty card schemes, which are popular with supermarkets, department stores and so on (see Exhibit 4.2). Customers collect points that can be redeemed for cash or gifts while at the same time the retailer collects valuable information about the customer each time the card is used.

Exhibit 4.2 Loyalty card schemes are used extensively by organizations to build up databases of customers

Banks have become heavy users of this type of information as they seek to manage more carefully consumers that have taken on debts such as mortgages and credit cards. Banks get information from a number of sources, including their own records, their links to other payment organizations, such as Visa and MasterCard, and specialist credit-checking agencies. Through the examination of this information, they can develop relatively accurate predictions of which customers are likely to default on a loan, or they can intervene earlier before debts become significant. For example, if consumers have switched more of their regular shopping, such as groceries, from cash to credit cards, this may indicate a cash shortage and the increased risk of a missed payment on a loan.

Customer relationship management (CRM) systems

A potential problem with the growth of marketing databases is that separate ones often exist in different departments in an organization. For example, the sales department may have an account management database containing information on customers, while call-centre staff may use a different database created at a different time also containing information on customers. This fragmented approach can lead to problems, when, for example, a customer transaction is recorded on one but not the other database. Issues like this have led to the development of **customer relationship management (CRM)** systems where a single database is created from customer information to inform all staff who deal with customers. CRM is a term for the methodologies, technologies and e-commerce capabilities used by companies to manage customer relationships[4] (see Chapter 10). Good CRM systems throw up all sorts of unusual patterns in consumer behaviour, such as when Tesco

found that one segment of its customers were buying beer and nappies during the same shopping trip and it was then able to target more carefully these young fathers (see Marketing in Action 4.1).

The effective use of CRM allows organizations to conduct a rigorous analysis of their customers. Businesses frequently find that they are subject to the Pareto Principle or 80/20 rule, that is, that 80 per cent of their profits may come from 20 per cent of their customers. At a very simple level what this means is that some customers may be more important than others and that from a marketing point of view perhaps the company should invest more in those valuable customers. Other researchers have recommended classifying customers on the basis of their value to the organization using labels such as platinum, gold, silver and lead.[5] Silver and gold customers need to be moved up the scale while lead customers are gradually 'fired'. Customer relationship management allows firms to measure the following:

1 *Customer retention*: What proportion of customers is staying with the firm and are these the customers that it wants to retain?
2 *Customer defection*: What proportion of customers is leaving the firm? Are these the customers that firm would want to 'fire' or the ones that it would rather retain?
3 *Customer acquisition*: What proportion of new customers is arriving onto the firm's books as a result of its marketing activities?

Website analysis

Customer information can also be provided by analysing website behaviour. Measurements of the areas of the site most frequently visited, which products are purchased and the payment method used can be made. Indeed, one of the challenges of website analysis is coping with the vast volumes of data that can be produced. Whatever the challenges of measuring the size of the audience from an advertising point of view, there are several aspects of how consumers behave while visiting a website that owners should record and monitor. First, where did they come from – for example, did they come via a search engine or from a link on another site? Second, where do they go once they are on the site? What options are selected, what visuals are viewed, and so on. How long did they spend on the website and what proportion of visitors 'bounced' away from the site within a few seconds? Did they respond to particular offers, promotions or site design changes? Most websites use Google Analytics to monitor these patterns and results are available on a daily or weekly basis (see Exhibit 4.3). And, if the company is an online retailer,

Marketing in Action 4.1 Boots Advantage card

Critical Thinking: Below is a review of a Christmas promotion conducted by Boots using its Advantage card information. Read it and critically evaluate why the promotion was so successful and the ways in which firms can use existing customer information better.

Boots is the leading pharmacy chain in the UK as well as having operations in Ireland, Norway and Sweden. It launched its Advantage card loyalty scheme in 2001. Customers sign up for the card and collect points for each purchase that they make at Boots which can then be redeemed against future purchases. Each £1 purchase generates four points for the customer but all sorts of additional activities such as special promotions and in-store events garner additional 'bonus' points – an approach which subtly creates a focus on points collection and consequently more purchases. It has extended its scheme to allow customers to collect points at other retailers, such as Thomas Cook, Toys 'R' Us and Asos.com, which can be redeemed at Boots. Most retailers operate similar schemes but the key to successful loyalty programmes rests on the company's ability to use the information it is collecting on its customers and their buying habits to target them more effectively.

For example, Boots ran a special Christmas promotion in 2009 with the aim of showing customers that they could get gifts for everyone under one roof and at the same time collect bonus points for themselves. It sent a direct mail package to 6 million of its customers to drive them to special in-store events and this effort was complemented by press and television promotions. But its customer knowledge meant that it was able to send out 400,000 different versions of the mailing tailored to a customer's previous purchasing patterns. This deep customer knowledge enabled the promotion to be highly successful at a time of year when all retailers are marketing very aggressively. Coupon redemption rates, which are generally very low, rose by 25 per cent because customers were receiving more relevant offers. Incremental sales from the in-store events rose by 90 per cent year on year and incremental profits rose by 60 per cent.

Based on: Baker (2010);[6] Direct Marketing Association (2010)[7].

Exhibit 4.3 Consumer behaviour on websites can be analysed using Google Analytics

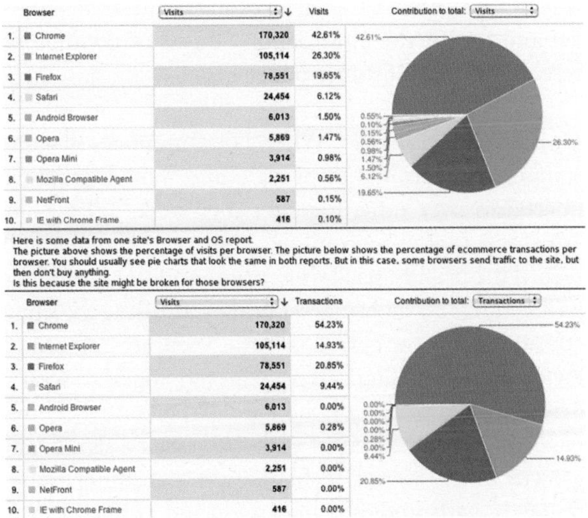

	Browser	Visits	Visits	Contribution to total: Visits
1.	Chrome	170,320	42.61%	
2.	Internet Explorer	105,114	26.30%	
3.	Firefox	78,551	19.65%	
4.	Safari	24,454	6.12%	
5.	Android Browser	6,013	1.50%	
6.	Opera	5,869	1.47%	
7.	Opera Mini	3,914	0.98%	
8.	Mozilla Compatible Agent	2,251	0.56%	
9.	NetFront	587	0.15%	
10.	IE with Chrome Frame	416	0.10%	

Here is some data from one site's Browser and OS report.
The picture above shows the percentage of visits per browser. The picture below shows the percentage of ecommerce transactions per browser. You should usually see pie charts that look the same in both reports. But in this case, some browsers send traffic to the site, but then don't buy anything.
Is this because the site might be broken for those browsers?

	Browser	Visits	Transactions	Contribution to total: Transactions
1.	Chrome	170,320	54.23%	
2.	Internet Explorer	105,114	14.93%	
3.	Firefox	78,551	20.85%	
4.	Safari	24,454	9.44%	
5.	Android Browser	6,013	0.00%	
6.	Opera	5,869	0.28%	
7.	Opera Mini	3,914	0.00%	
8.	Mozilla Compatible Agent	2,251	0.00%	
9.	NetFront	587	0.00%	
10.	IE with Chrome Frame	416	0.00%	

what percentage of consumers proceeded to the checkout and, for those that didn't, at what stage in the buying process did they drop out?

Some of the key metrics for website analysis include the number of unique visitors, information on these visitors and their levels of engagement with the site. Measurement of these variables is improving all the time, although some are still open to manipulation. *Unique users* (when a person visits a website) is a popular metric for measuring the number of visitors to a site. But it is problematic because 2 million unique users could mean anything from 2 million people visiting the site once, to one person visiting it 2 million times. It is impossible to know for sure. Information about website visitors is best captured by having them register to use the site where they provide details of who they are and what they are interested in. *Page views* has been a popular way of measuring website engagement but many modern websites use a technology that allows pages to update parts of themselves, such as a share-price ticker, without having to reload and redraw the rest of the page. Therefore a user spending the entire day on Yahoo! Finance, for example, counts as only one page view. Therefore, more emphasis is now being put on website *interactivity*. 'Duration' and 'time spent' suggest how long one or more people are interacting with a page, which in turn gives an indication of how 'engaged' they are as does counting the number and types of comments left by visitors.

Market intelligence

Internal market information is very useful for developing deep insights about current customers but is less useful for learning about potential new customers and competitor activity. For answers to these questions, the organization needs to begin looking outward to what is happening in the marketplace. **Market intelligence** is something of a catch-all term to describe the systematic collection of publicly available data on what is happening in a market including gathering information on customers, competitors and market developments. It can take many forms. Information on both current and potential customers can be found by monitoring Internet conversations in blogs and chat rooms. Potential market trends can be considered by participating in future trends discussion groups or reading publicly available books and reports. And information on competitors can be collected by visiting competitor stands at trade shows or in extreme cases going through the rubbish bins of rivals. The most important component of market intelligence is secondary data and as this is publicly available and relatively cheap, it is often the first source to which organizations will go when attempting to answer a research problem.

Secondary research

Because the data come to the researcher 'second-hand' (i.e. other people have compiled it), it is known as **secondary research**. (When the researcher actively collects new data – for example, by interviewing respondents – this is called primary research.) Secondary research should be carried out before primary research. Without the former, an expensive primary research survey might be commissioned to provide information that is already available from secondary sources. Increasingly a significant amount of market information is available for purchase through companies like Mintel, Euromonitor and others.

There is a very wide variety of secondary sources of data available. These include government and European Commission statistics, publishers of reports and directories on markets, countries and industries, trade associations, banks, newspapers, magazines and journals. Given the amount of potential sources of

information that are available globally, for many the first port of call is an Internet search engine. The search engine business has grown dramatically in recent years and has led to expressions such as 'to google', after the popular search engine Google, entering the general lexicon. The range of sources of information available to researchers in the European Union is included in Appendix 4.1 (at the end of this chapter), which lists some of the major sources classified by research question.

Marketing research

If organizations cannot find the answers they are looking for through either existing internal information or market intelligence, then there is always the option of a marketing research study. **Marketing research** is defined as the systematic design, collection, analysis and reporting of data relevant to a specific marketing situation. Marketing research describes a broad range of potential activities many of which are quite different from each other and therefore it can be classified in a number of different ways. For example, distinctions are drawn between ad hoc and continuous research, custom and syndicated research and also between exploratory, descriptive and casual research.

Ad hoc and continuous research

Ad hoc research focuses on a specific marketing problem and involves the collection of data at one point in time from one sample of respondents such as a customer satisfaction study or an attitude survey. **Continuous research** involves conducting the same research on the same sample repeatedly to monitor the changes that are taking place over time. This form of research plays a key role in assessing trends in the market and one of the most popular forms of continuous research is the consumer panel.

Consumer panels When large numbers of consumers are recruited to provide information on their purchases over time, together they make up a **consumer panel**. For example, a grocery panel would record the brands, pack sizes, prices and stores used for a wide range of supermarket brands. By using the same consumers over a period of time, measures of brand loyalty and switching can be achieved, together with a demographic profile of the type of person who buys particular brands. Recent years have seen a significant growth in the use of technology in consumer panel research, with studies being conducted online or over the telephone as well as face to face. Once participants are familiar with the researchers and have indicated a willingness to participate, then these more remote research approaches can work very effectively. For example, Metro Ireland, which markets a free newspaper to Dublin commuters, set up an online panel of 2,000 18- to 44-year-old urban dwellers to which it sent six waves of questions and a series of mini-polls over 18 months. The insights derived from the panel informed Metro's decisions regarding everything from its editorial content to its marketing strategies to attract advertising.

The rapid growth of online blogs and discussion forums has given rise to a variant on the traditional customer panel. These types of discussion boards are everywhere on the Internet, discussing anything from the fat content of potato crisps to the merits of new electronic gadgets. In most instances, they have not been formally created by corporations but the frank nature of the debate that often takes place on them makes them appealing to managers (see Social Media Marketing 4.1). Some companies track these discussion groups to see what is being said about their brands and what trends are emerging. It is also a very cost-effective form of research as much of the monitoring can be

Social Media Marketing 4.1 Social media and market research

Critical Thinking: Below is a review of some of the recent developments in social media research. Begin a social media conversation on a brand or topic of your choice and then monitor this conversation for a period of time. Assess what you have learned.

The rise of social media has begun to drastically change the market research landscape. Hundreds of millions of personal pages, feeds, status updates, tweets, profiles and blogs have been created and the numbers are growing all the time. To date, this potential source of market information is largely untapped but is likely to become increasingly important in the years ahead.

For example, Facebook has been described as a 'confessional' society where people are *marketing* themselves by acting out their desirable personalities. So researchers need to examine the motives behind decisions to join Facebook groups such as brand fan pages, for example. Does everyone become a Starbuck's fan for the same reason or are there different motives at play? What do the comments that they post about a brand say about it and its future prospects? Similarly, brand owners can monitor and analyse conversations on blogs or micro-blogs like Twitter. Are they broadly positive or negative? One of the most famous brand blogs became known as Dell Hell, when blogger Jeff Jarvis began writing negatively about the company and its products. What kinds of problems if any are being encountered with organizations? These types of conversations could be the genesis of anything from a new product idea to a new service solution

to an advertising campaign idea. Social media sites like LinkedIn and ChubbyBrain can be used to research competitors while Google Trends and Trendpedia enable important trends to be tracked.

Conducting marketing research through social media raises many interesting possibilities. As consumers tire of being constantly surveyed and asked for their opinions, social media creates the opportunity for people to be participants in a dialogue rather than 'respondents'. Consumers are now willing to record and share information in ways never seen before, so user-generated content may be both more insightful and accurate. Comments may be more natural and spontaneous and more emotionally rich. Research techniques like netnography (online ethnography) are being developed to monitor online conversations, and social communities are being created to get a better understanding of consumer needs. For example, Mercedes Benz USA set up GenBenz, an online community to help it understand Generation Y who will be the Mercedes purchasers of the future. But as with offline research, issues of sampling, data collection and data analysis remain crucially important to ensure that erroneous conclusions are not drawn.

Based on: Beer (2008);[8] Cooke (2008);[9] Precourt (2010)[10].

done electronically. However, because this monitoring is generally covert, it may be disturbing for participants to learn that what they have to say is being studied by companies.

Custom and syndicated research

Custom research is research that is conducted for a single organization to provide specific answers to the questions that it has. But because companies have such an appetite for market information, an industry has grown up in the provision of **syndicated or omnibus research**. This is research that is collected by firms on a regular basis and then sold to other firms. Among the most popular types of syndicated research are retail audits and television viewership panels.

Retail audits   Major research firms like the Nielsen Company conduct **retail audits**. By gaining the co-operation of retail outlets (e.g. supermarkets), sales of brands can be measured by means of laser scans of barcodes on packaging, which are read at the checkout. Although brand loyalty and switching cannot be measured, retail audits can provide an accurate assessment of sales achieved by store. For example, Nielsen's BookScan service provides weekly sales data on over 300,000 titles collected from point-of-sale information from a variety of retailers.

Television viewership panels   A television viewership panel measures audience size on a minute-by-minute basis. Commercial breaks can be allocated ratings points (the proportion of the target audience watching) – the currency by which television advertising is bought and judged. In the UK, the system is controlled by the Broadcasters' Audience Research Board (BARB) and run by AGB and RSMB. AGB handles the measurement process and uses 'people meters' to record whether a set is on/off, which channel is being watched and, by means of a hand console, who is watching. Because of concerns about the extent to which viewers actually watch advertising, audience measurement companies are now providing measures of the viewership of advertising breaks as well as programmes. Technological developments continue to revolutionize television audience measurement. Personal video recorders (PVRs), build up a profile of viewers' likes and dislikes, and record their favourite programmes automatically, but the box also relays every button press on its remote control back to the manufacturer, providing exact details of what programmes people watch on what channels.

Exploratory, descriptive and causal research

Finally, distinctions can also be drawn between exploratory, descriptive and causal research. **Exploratory research** is employed to carry out a preliminary exploration of a research area to gain some initial insights or to form some research hypotheses. It can be conducted in a variety of ways such as examining secondary data that is available, conducting a focus group interview with some key customers or depth interviews with industry experts. To develop stronger conclusions about a research problem, **descriptive research** needs to be conducted. This may involve a survey of a large sample of customers that is representative of a population as a whole and allows the researchers to be confident that their views accurately represent those of the market. Finally, **causal research** seeks to establish cause-and-effect relationships. The most popular form of causal research is experimentation where different variables are manipulated such as a packaging design or advertising theme and the effects of these changes on consumers are monitored. The processes through which these different forms of research are conducted are examined next.

Approaches to conducting marketing research

There are two main ways for a company to carry out marketing research, depending on the situation facing it. It might either carry out the work itself or employ the services of a market research agency. Where the study is small in scale, such as gathering information from libraries or interviewing a select number of industrial customers, companies may choose to conduct the work themselves. This is particularly feasible if a company has a marketing department and/or a marketing research executive on its staff. Other companies prefer to design the research themselves and then employ the services of a fieldwork agency to collect the data. Alternatively, where resources permit and the scale of the study is larger, companies may employ the services of a market research agency to conduct the research. The company will brief the agency about its market research requirements and the agency will do the rest. The typical stages involved in completing a market research study are described next; full-service agencies generally conduct all the activities described below.

The leading marketing research firms in the world are shown in Table 4.2.

Table 4.2 World's leading marketing research firms, 2009

Name	Country	Employees	Turnover (US$ million unless stated)
The Nielsen Company	USA	40,000	4,808
IMS Health, Inc.	USA	7,250	2,190
The Kantar Group	UK	N/A	2,927 (£)
GfK AG	Germany	10,058	1,165 (€)
Ipsos Group SA	France	8,761	944 (€)
Symphony/IRI	USA	3,600	706
Synovate	UK	N/A	521 (£)
Westat, Inc.	USA	N/A	502
Arbitron, Inc.	USA	971	385
Intage Inc.	Japan	1,966	34,526 (Yen)

Source: Esomar, Global Market Research, 2010.

Stages in the marketing research process

Figure 4.1 provides a description of a typical marketing research process. Each of the stages illustrated will now be discussed.

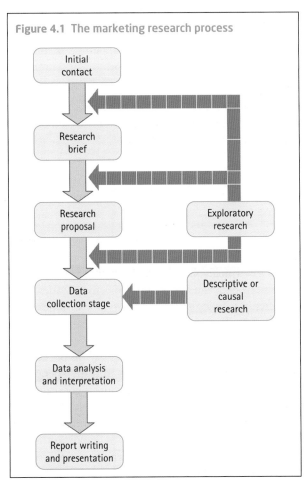

Figure 4.1 The marketing research process

Initial contact

The process usually starts with the realization that a marketing problem requires information to aid its solution. Marketing management may contact internal marketing research staff or an outside agency. Where an outside agency is being used a meeting will be arranged to discuss the nature of the problem and the client's research needs. If the client and its markets are new to the agency, some exploratory research (e.g. a quick online search for information about the client and its markets) may be conducted prior to the meeting.

Research brief

At a meeting to decide what form the research will need to take, the client explains the marketing problem and outlines the company's research objectives. The information that should be provided for the research agency includes the following.[11]

1 *Background information*: the product's history and the competitive situation.
2 *Sources of information*: the client may have a list of industries that might be potential users of the product. This helps the researchers to define the scope of the research.
3 *The scale of the project*: is the client looking for a 'cheap and cheerful' job or a major study? This has implications for the research design and survey costs.
4 *The timetable*: when is the information required?

The client should produce a specific written **research brief**. This may be given to the research

Table 4.3 Market research expenditure by type (%*), 2009

Method	France	Germany	Holland	Ireland	Norway	Sweden	UK
Focus groups	7	2	0	16	4	6	N/a
Depth interview	3	3	0	4	1	3	N/a
Online qualitative	4	2	0	0	0	0	N/a
Other qualitative	0	0	9	0	4	0	N/a
Total qualitative	**14**	**7**	**9**	**20**	**9**	**9**	**10**
Telephone survey	12	39	20	23	31	32	17
Postal survey	2	6	5	0	14	15	9
Face-to-face	14	18	11	40	7	5	24
Online survey	13	29	30	12	18	27	26
Other quantitative	10	0	10	0	13	8	2
Total quantitative	**51**	**92**	**76**	**75**	**83**	**87**	**78**

Source: Esomar, Global Market Research, 2010.
* Figures may not add up to 100 due to rounding.

agency prior to the meeting and perhaps modified as a result of it but, without fail, should be in the hands of the agency before it produces its **research proposal**. The research brief should state the client's requirements and should be in written form so that misunderstandings are minimized.

Research proposal

A research proposal lays out what a marketing research agency promises to do for its client, and how much this will cost. Like the research brief, the proposal should be written in a way that avoids misunderstandings. A client should expect the following to be included.

1 *A statement of objectives*: to demonstrate an understanding of the client's marketing and research problems.
2 *What will be done*: an unambiguous description of the research design – including the research method, the type of sample, the sample size (if applicable) and how the fieldwork will be controlled.
3 *Timetable*: if and when a report will be produced.
4 *Costs*: how much the research will cost and what, specifically, is/is not included in those costs.

Data collection

During the main data collection phase of the study, a variety of techniques can be employed to deal with the questions under consideration. Researchers usually draw a distinction between qualitative and quantitative research. **Qualitative research** involves a semi-structured, in-depth study of small samples in order to

gain deep customer insights. Some of the key qualitative techniques include focus-group interviews, depth interviews, observation studies and ethnographic research. **Quantitative research** is a structured study of small or large samples using a pre-determined list of questions or criteria and the statistical analysis of findings. Typical quantitative techniques include surveys and experiments. Traditionally, qualitative research was seen as being useful during exploratory research but then needed to be supplemented by quantitative research if a descriptive study was necessary. However, this is no longer the case. The findings of many quantitative studies have proven to be erroneous while improvements in qualitative research techniques mean that they may yield more useful insights (see Table 4.3 for a breakdown of research expenditure patterns). We will now examine some of the major data collection techniques in more detail.

Focus group discussions

Focus groups involve unstructured or semi-structured discussions between a moderator or group leader, who is often a psychologist, and a group of consumers (see Exhibit 4.4). The moderator has a list of areas to cover within the topic, but allows the group considerable freedom to discuss the issues that are important to them. By arranging groups of six to twelve people to discuss their attitudes and behaviour, a good deal of knowledge may be gained about the consumer. This can be helpful when constructing questionnaires, which can be designed to focus on what is important to the respondent (as opposed to the researcher) and worded in language the respondent uses and understands.

Exhibit 4.4 Focus group interviews such as this one are a very popular form of market research

Sometimes focus groups are used to try to generate new product ideas, through the careful selection of participants who have a flair for innovation or a liking for all things new.

Focus groups takes place face to face, but the rise of the Internet has led to the creation of online focus groups. The Internet offers 'communities of interests', which can take the form of chat rooms or websites dedicated to specific interests or issues (see Social Media Marketing 4.1). These are useful forums for conducting focus groups or at least for identifying suitable participants. Questions can be posed to participants who are not under time pressure to respond. This can lead to richer insights since respondents can think deeply about the questions put to them online. Another advantage is that they can comprise people located all over the world at minimal cost. Furthermore, technological developments mean it is possible for clients to communicate secretly online with the moderator while the focus group is in session. The client can ask the moderator certain questions as a result of hearing earlier responses. Clearly, a disadvantage of online focus groups compared with the traditional form is that the body language and interaction between focus group members is missing.[12]

Depth interviews

Depth interviews involve the interviewing of individual consumers about a single topic for perhaps one or two hours. The aims are broadly similar to those of the group discussion, but depth interviews are used when the presence of other people could inhibit the expression of honest answers and viewpoints, when the topic requires individual treatment (as when discussing an individual's decision-making process) and where the individual is an expert on a particular topic. For example, depth interviews have been used to conduct research

on wealthy Americans to try to understand their attitudes and opinions on money and how they spend it. This was deemed to be a method that was superior to focus groups or surveys, where it was felt that respondents would be reluctant to talk about these issues. A technique called 'snowballing' was also used, where interviewees would recommend others that they thought would be willing to participate in the research.[13]

Care has to be taken when interpreting the results of these kinds of qualitative research because the findings are usually based on small sample sizes, and the more interesting or surprising viewpoints may be disproportionately reported.

Observation

Observation research involves gathering primary data by observing people and their actions. These types of studies can be conducted in real situations such as traffic counts on public streets or in contrived situations such as hall tests where research subjects are presented with a mock shopping aisle and their behaviour is monitored. Observation studies can have a number of advantages. First, they do not rely on the respondent's willingness to provide information; second, the potential for the interviewer to bias the study is reduced; and, third, some types of information can be collected only by observation (for example, a traffic count). Observation studies are particularly popular in the retail trade where a great deal can be learned by simply watching the behaviour of shoppers in a supermarket or clothing shop. Many retail innovations including store layout and the positioning of products have arisen as a result of observation studies of consumer behaviour.

Observation studies can be conducted by either human or increasingly mechanical means, such as video recording, and may be conducted with or without the customer's knowledge. Camera phones are the latest technology to be used for observation studies, with problems arising when they are used covertly. Samsung, the world's leading manufacturer of camera phones, has even banned their use in its factories, fearing industrial espionage.[14] Some technologies allow researchers to bypass what consumers say and observe instead what they do. For example, by using eye tracking technology researchers observe which parts of an advertisement are viewed first by a subject and the design of print advertisements is greatly influenced by this kind of research. **Neuro-marketing** research, which involves observing brain responses to marketing stimuli, promises to provide an even deeper understanding of why consumers behave in the ways that they do (see Marketing in Action 4.2).

Marketing in Action 4.2 The growth of neuro-marketing

Critical Thinking: Read the review of recent developments in neuro-marketing described below and consider whether you think this type of research is ethical or not.

Neuro-marketing is the application of the techniques of neuroscience to the field of marketing. Neuroscience is the study of the brain and the nervous system and it also draws on perspectives from fields as diverse as genetics and evolutionary biology. Marketers hope that increased understanding of brain functioning and patterns will also assist them in gaining deeper insights in the minds of consumers in ways that have not traditionally been possible, using techniques such as surveys and focus group interviews.

A typical neuro-marketing study is an experiment that was carried out on the impact of Pepsi and Coke advertising on preferences for these brands. Subjects were asked to take sips of Pepsi and Coke from unmarked cups and were also shown visual images of the brands. The respondents expressed a significant preference for Coke but it was clear from the brain scans that this was due to the advertising imagery rather than the taste. Neuro-imaging studies frequently reveal preferences that contradict what consumers report in conventional research. For example, a study during the Super Bowl in the USA found that viewers reported that a Bud Light advert was their favourite while brain research suggested a preference for a Disney World commercial.

In short, brain research can reveal the emotions that consumers may be unwilling or unable to articulate. A neuro-imaging study using the famous Dove Evolution viral advert revealed the emotional patterns followed by viewers as they watched the ad and helped to explain why it was so successful. At the point where it becomes clear that the film is about the creation of a billboard, a peak in emotion and cognition is reached followed by more negative emotions as the implications sink in. Another interesting brain study at Stanford University in the USA, found that student preferences for certain wines increased when they were told that these wines were more expensive. Is it possible that neuro-marketing can unlock all the deep emotions and biases inside consumer minds?

Based on: Page (2010)[15].

Ethnographic research

One of the criticisms of research techniques like focus-group interviews is that they are somewhat contrived. Groups of people, who may or may not know each other, are brought together in boardroom-type settings and expected to provide insights into their thoughts, feelings and opinions. In such settings consumers may find it difficult or be unwilling to fully engage. As a result, many research companies are borrowing from the kinds of techniques that are employed by anthropologists and biologists, which place an emphasis on the observation of species in their natural settings. This type of research is known as **ethnographic research** and it may involve a combination of both observation and in-depth or focus-group interviewing.

In ethnographic studies, researchers decide what human behaviours they want to observe. They then go out into the field and record what consumers do, how they live their lives, how they shop, and so on. One of the key advantages of the ethnographic approach is that researchers often find things they didn't even realize they should have been looking for (see Marketing in Action 4.3). Having recorded these activities, consumers are interviewed to try to gain insights into the motivations and attitudes that underpin their actions. When all these data have been collected, they are analysed using qualitative software packages that search for common patterns of behaviour and generate clusters of consumers. Ethnographic findings are often reported using visual as well as written means. This provides a mechanism for senior executives to get close to consumer groups they may never come into contact with in their own daily lives because of physical distance and/or social class disparities.

Waitrose's 2011 TV campaign featuring chef Heston Blumenthal reflects changing consumer attitudes towards home cooking and entertaining.
www.mcgraw-hill.co.uk/textbooks/fahy

Marketing in Action 4.3 L'Oréal

Critical Thinking: Below is a brief discussion of the types of observation and ethnographic research conducted by the French cosmetics brand, L'Oréal. Think of a research problem and devise an ethnographic research study to tackle it.

Fast-moving consumer goods companies typically spend 2–3 per cent of sales on the research and development of new products and many are spreading their wings geographically and digging ever deeper into consumers' lives in order to try to develop offerings that will succeed in the market. For example, L'Oréal has experimented with bathroom photography to understand how consumers in different markets use beauty products. This research has revealed that Korean women apply more potions and cosmetics to their faces than anyone else – a total of more than 25 creams and cosmetics at any one time which is more than double the amount used by European women. Japanese women may apply 50 coatings of mascara at one time compared with five to 10 for Europeans.

L'Oréal's research takes place both in 'labs' decked out as bathrooms as well as through cameras in people's homes. The latter, more ethnographic approach has been found to be more effective as mistakes are sometimes made in lab settings. For example, when reviewing the in-home footage, L'Oréal found that many Japanese women used a tiny razor as part of their routine. It was slid around the nose, below the eyebrows and on the nape of the neck to remove any hairs and get a better effect when powder was applied. These razors had not even been made available in the lab setting. All this research provides information on both what consumers are doing and what they are trying to achieve. This is then taken to the product development departments where new products are created or existing ones modified. For example, L'Oréal's lipstick gloss is lighter in Japan to allow for the constant reapplication beloved of Japanese women.

Based on: Lucas (2010)[15].

Surveys

Surveys remain the major market research technique (see Table 4.3) and typically involve the following key decisions.

- Who and how many people to interview: the sampling process.
- How to interview them: the survey method.
- What questions to ask: questionnaire design.

The sampling process   Figure 4.2 offers an outline of the **sampling process**. This starts with the definition of the population – that is, the group that forms the subject of study in a particular survey. The survey objective will be to provide results that are representative of this group. Sampling planners, for example, must ask questions like 'Do we interview purchasing managers in all software development firms or only those that employ more than 50 people?'

Once the population has been defined, the next step is to search for a sampling frame – that is, a list or other record of the chosen population from which a

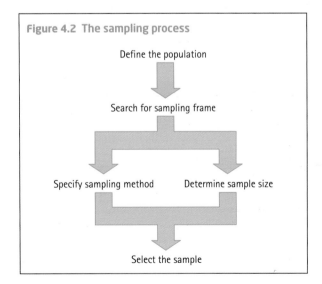

Figure 4.2 The sampling process

Define the population

Search for sampling frame

Specify sampling method   Determine sample size

Select the sample

sample can be selected. Examples include the electoral register and the *Kompass* directory of companies. Researchers then choose between three major sampling methods: simple random sampling (where the sample is drawn at random and each individual has a known and equal chance of being selected); stratified random sampling (where the population is broken into groups and a random sample is drawn from each group); and quota sampling (where interviewers are instructed to ensure that the sample comprises a required number of individuals meeting pre-set conditions, such as a set percentage of small, medium-sized and large companies).

Finally, the researcher must select an appropriate sample size. The larger the sample size the more likely it is that the sample will represent the population. Statistical theory allows the calculation of sampling error (i.e. the error caused by not interviewing everyone in the population) for various sample sizes. In practice, the number of people interviewed is based on a balance between sampling error and cost considerations. Fortunately, sample sizes of around 1000 (or fewer) can provide measurements that have tolerable error levels when representing populations counted in their millions.

The survey method Four options are available to those choosing a survey method: face-to-face interviews, telephone interviews, mail surveys or online surveys. Each method has its own strengths and limitations. Table 4.4 gives an overview of these.

A major advantage of face-to-face interviews is that response rates are generally higher than for telephone interviews or mail surveys.[17] It seems that the personal element in the contact makes refusal less likely. Face-to-face interviews are more versatile than telephone and mail surveys. The use of many open-ended questions on a mail survey would lower response rates[18]

and time restrictions for telephone interviews would limit their use. Probing for more detail is easier with face-to-face interviews. A certain degree of probing can be achieved with a telephone interview, but time pressure and the less personalized situation will inevitably limit its use.

Face-to-face interviews do, however, have their drawbacks. They are more expensive than telephone, mail and Internet surveys. The presence of an interviewer can cause bias (e.g. socially desirable answers) and lead to the misreporting of sensitive information. For example, O'Dell[19] found that only 17 per cent of respondents admitted borrowing money from a bank in a face-to-face interview compared with 42 per cent in a comparable mail survey.

In some ways, telephone interviews are a halfway house between face-to-face and mail surveys. They generally have a higher response rate than mail questionnaires but a lower rate than face-to-face interviews; their cost is usually three-quarters of that for face-to-face but higher than for mail surveys; and they allow a degree of flexibility when interviewing. However, the use of visual aids is not possible and there are limits to the number of questions that can be asked before respondents either terminate the interview or give quick (invalid) answers in order to speed up the process. The use of computer-aided telephone interviewing (CATI) is growing. Centrally located interviewers read questions from a computer monitor and input answers via the keyboard. Routing through the questionnaire is computer-controlled, thus assisting the process of interviewing.

Table 4.4 A comparison of survey methods

	Face to face	Telephone	Mail	Online
Questionnaire				
Use of open-ended questions	High	Medium	Low	Low
Ability to probe	High	Medium	Low	Low
Use of visual aids	High	Poor	High	High
Sensitive questions	Medium	Low	High	Low
Resources				
Cost	High	Medium	Low	Low
Sampling				
Widely dispersed populations	Low	Medium	High	High
Response rates	High	Medium	Low	Low
Experimental control	High	Medium	Low	Low
Interviewing				
Control of who completes questionnaire	High	High	Low	Low/high
Interviewer bias	Possible	Possible	Low	Low

Given a reasonable response rate, mail survey research is normally a very economical method of conducting research. However, the major problem is the potential for low response rates and the accompanying danger of an unrepresentative sample. Nevertheless, using a systematic approach to the design of a mail survey, such as the total design method (TDM),[20] has been found to have a very positive effect on response rates. The TDM recommends, as ways of improving response rates, both the careful design of questionnaires to make them easy to complete, as well as accompanying them with a personalized covering letter emphasizing the importance of the research. Studies using the TDM on commercial populations have generated high response rates.[21]

The Internet has become a very popular medium for conducting survey research. Online research is now the most popular form, accounting for 23 per cent of all research expenditure globally. The countries with the highest spend on online research as a percentage of total spend include Bulgaria (43 per cent), Canada (39 per cent) and Japan and New Zealand (36 per cent each).[22] The Internet questionnaire is usually administered by email or signals its presence on a website by registering key words or using banner advertising on search engines to drive people to the questionnaire. The major advantage of the Internet as a marketing research vehicle is its low cost, since printing and postal costs are eliminated, making it even cheaper than mail surveys. In other ways, its characteristics are similar to mail surveys: the use of open-ended questions is limited; control over who completes the questionnaire is low; interviewer bias is low; and response rates are likely to be lower than for face-to-face and telephone interviews.

When response is by email, the identity of the respondent will automatically be sent to the survey company. This lack of anonymity may restrict the respondent's willingness to answer sensitive questions honestly. A strength of the Internet survey is its ability to cover global populations at low cost, although sampling problems can arise because of the skewed nature of Internet users. These tend to be from the younger and more affluent groups in society. For surveys requiring a cross-sectional sample this can be severely restricting.

Questionnaire design To obtain a true response to a question, three conditions are necessary. First, respondents must understand the question; second, they must be able to provide the information; and, third, they must be willing to provide it. Figure 4.3 shows the three stages in the development of the questionnaire: planning, design and pilot.

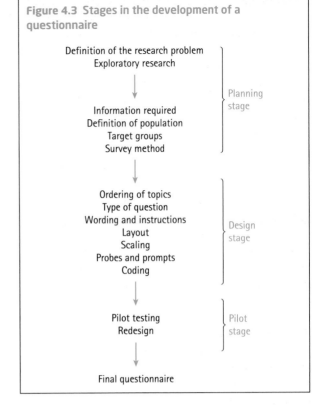

Figure 4.3 Stages in the development of a questionnaire

The planning stage involves the types of decision discussed so far in this chapter. It provides a firm foundation for designing a questionnaire, which provides relevant information for the marketing problem that is being addressed.

The design stage deals with the actual construction of the survey instrument and involves a number of important decisions. The first relates to the ordering of topics. It is sensible to start with easy-to-answer questions, in order to relax the respondent, and leave sensitive questions until last. Effective questionnaires are well structured and have a logical flow. Second, the type of question needs to be decided. Generally, three types are used: dichotomous questions (allow two possible answers, such as 'Yes'/'No'), multiple-choice questions, which allow more than two answers, and open questions, where the respondents answer by expressing their opinions.

Great care needs to be taken with both the wording and instructions used in the questionnaire and its layout. Questionnaire designers need to guard against asking ambiguous or leading questions, and using unfamiliar words (see Table 4.5). In terms of layout, the questionnaire should not appear cluttered and, where possible, answers and codes should each form a column so that they are easy to identify.

The use of 'scales' is very common in questionnaire design. For example, respondents are given lists of

Table 4.5 Poorly worded questions

Question	Problem and solution
What type of wine do you prefer?	'Type' is ambiguous: respondents could say 'French', 'red' or 'claret', say, depending on their interpretation. Showing the respondent a list and asking 'from this list . . .' would avoid the problem
Do you think that prices are cheaper at Asda than at Aldi?	Leading question favouring Asda; a better question would be 'Do you think that prices at Asda are higher, lower or about the same as at Aldi?' Names should be reversed for half the sample
Which is more powerful and kind to your hands: Ariel or Bold?	Two questions in one: Ariel may be more powerful but Bold may be kinder to the hands. Ask the two questions separately
Do you find it paradoxical that X lasts longer and yet is cheaper than Y?	Unfamiliar word: a study has shown that less than a quarter of the population understand such words as paradoxical, chronological or facility. Test understanding before use

statements (e.g. 'My company's marketing information system allows me to make better decisions') followed by a choice of five positions on a scale ranging from 'strongly agree' to 'strongly disagree'. 'Probes' are used to explore or clarify what a respondent has said. Following a question about awareness of brand names, the exploratory probe 'Any others?' would seek to identify further names. Sometimes respondents use vague words or phrases like 'I like going on holiday because it is nice'. A clarifying probe such as, 'In what way is it nice?' would seek a more meaningful response. 'Prompts', on the other hand, aid responses to a question. For example, in an aided recall question, a list of brand names would be provided for the respondent. Coding involves the assignment of numbers to specific responses in order to facilitate analysis of the questionnaire later on.

Once the preliminary questionnaire has been designed it should be piloted with a representative sub-sample, to test for faults. Piloting tests the questionnaire design and helps to estimate costs. Face-to-face piloting, where respondents are asked to answer questions and comment on any problems concerning a questionnaire read out by an interviewer, is preferable to impersonal piloting where the questionnaire is given to respondents for self-completion and they are asked to write down any problems found.[23] Once the pilot work proves satisfactory, the final questionnaire can be administered to the chosen sample.

Data analysis and interpretation   Basic analysis of questionnaire data may be at the descriptive level (e.g. means, frequency tables and standard deviations) or on a comparative basis (e.g. t-tests and cross-tabulations). More sophisticated analysis may search for relationships (e.g. regression analysis), group respondents (e.g. cluster

analysis), or establish cause and effect (e.g. analysis of variance techniques used on experimental data).

When interpreting marketing research results, great care must be taken. One common failing is to infer cause and effect when only association has been established. For example, establishing a relationship that sales rise when advertising levels increase does not necessarily mean that raising advertising expenditure will lead to an increase in sales. Other marketing variables (e.g. sales force effect) may have increased at the same time as the increase in advertising. A second cautionary note concerns the interpretation of means and percentages. Given that a sample has been taken, any mean or percentage is an estimate subject to 'sampling error' – that is, an error in an estimate due to taking a sample rather than interviewing the entire population. A market research survey which estimates that 50 per cent of males but only 45 per cent of females smoke, does not necessarily suggest that smoking is more prevalent among males. Given the sampling error associated with each estimate, the true conclusion might be that there is no difference between males and females.

Report writing and presentation   Crouch suggests that the key elements in a research report are as follows:[24]

1   title page
2   list of contents
3   preface – outline of agreed brief, statement of objectives, scope and methods of research
4   summary of conclusions and recommendations
5   previous related research – how previous research has had a bearing on this research
6   research method

7 research findings

8 conclusions

9 appendices.

Sections 1–4 provide a concise description of the nature and outcomes of the research for busy managers. Sections 5–9 provide the level of detail necessary if any particular issue (e.g. the basis of a finding, or the analytical technique used) needs checking. The report should be written in language the reader will understand; jargon should be avoided.

Marketing information systems

By carefully following each of the stages described above, researchers can improve the quality of the market information and customer insights that they collect. However, the variety of information that is currently available to companies means that it is sensible to set up a **marketing information system**. A marketing information system is defined as:

> a system in which marketing information is formally gathered, stored, analysed and distributed to managers in accord with their informational needs on a regular planned basis.[25]

The system is built on an understanding of the information needs of marketing management, and supplies that information when, where and in the form that the manager requires it. Marketing information system (MkIS) design is important since the quality of a marketing information system has been shown to influence the effectiveness of decision-making.[26] The MkIS comprises four elements: internal market information, market intelligence, marketing research and environmental scanning (see Figure 4.4). The first three elements of the system have been discussed in this chapter while environmental scanning was discussed in Chapter 2. The volume of market information and insight that is to be managed clearly shows how important it is to effectively design and use a MkIS system.

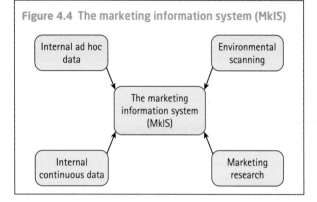

Figure 4.4 The marketing information system (MkIS)

- Internal ad hoc data
- Environmental scanning
- The marketing information system (MkIS)
- Internal continuous data
- Marketing research

The use of marketing information systems and marketing research

Marketing information systems should be designed to provide information and insights on a selective basis where it is useful in assisting decisions. Senior management should conspicuously support use of the system.[27] These recommendations are in line with Ackoff's view[28] that a prime task of an information system is to eliminate irrelevant information by tailoring what is provided to the individual manager's needs. It is also consistent with Kohli and Jaworski's view that a market orientation is essentially the organization-wide generation and dissemination of, and responsiveness to, market intelligence.[29]

Marketing research is more likely to be used if researchers appreciate not only the technical aspects of research, but also the need for clarity in report presentation and the political dimension of information provision. It is unlikely that marketing research reports will be used in decision-making if the results threaten the status quo or are likely to have adverse political repercussions (see Ethical Debate 4.1). Therefore, perfectly valid and useful information may sometimes be ignored in decision-making for reasons other than difficulties with the way the research was conducted. However, accurate and timely customer insights are crucial to an organization becoming a truly market-led enterprise.

Ethical Debate 4.1 Market research – fact or fiction?

Market research is one of the most visible faces of marketing. At some stage or other, nearly everyone participates in a survey, whether it is in a retail environment, a university or at home via telephone, post or, increasingly, by pressing the red button on their television remote controls. Consumers are also invited to participate in focus groups, depth interviews and ethnographic research. While all this research provides answers, it also seems to be raising some very fundamental questions.

The first concerns the widespread usage to which research is being put. It is virtually impossible now to pick up a newspaper or watch the television without seeing the results of some survey or other being presented. It may be about the most mundane of matters, such as how much time is spent cleaning the kitchen floor or who people think is the most eligible film star. The more outrageous the survey or its findings, the more likely it is to be picked up by news bulletins or discussed on radio talk shows. In other words, surveys have become the news and for 24-hour news channels they represent a relatively cheap and useful time filler. For example, many people missed the irony of Sky News charging viewers to vote by text on whether they thought they were paying too much for their mobile phone bills.

The sheer prevalence of surveys and their findings raises two other fundamental questions: who sponsored the study and how was it conducted? The former is crucial because it demonstrates that many of the surveys in the media are, in truth, public relations pieces being put out by particular companies or brands. For example, our floor cleaning survey is likely to have originated from a cleaning products company; that the majority of workers favour emailing colleagues over face-to-face meetings is likely to come from a business communications company, and so on. Sometimes, this can be relatively harmless fun but in other instances it can be very serious if the subject matter relates to food, family health and the like. The surfeit of visual, audio and print media means that there is always an outlet for these kinds of PR exercises. The consumer should take care to know who sponsored any study that receives media coverage.

After reading this chapter, you should also be critical of how studies are being conducted. What were the sampling frame and the sample size? Are the findings valid (the research measured what it intended to measure), reliable (similar findings would be found if the study was repeated) and representative (the study accurately represents the larger population)? For all the survey findings that are presented regularly, this type of detail rarely is. In its absence, it is impossible to conclude that the research was conducted scientifically. Unfortunately, time-pressed consumers rarely seek out this information and tend to take survey results at face value.

Market research suffers from other problems, too. In some instances it is used to gather competitor intelligence. Questionable practices include using student projects to gather information without the student revealing the identity of the sponsor of the research, pretending to be a potential supplier who is conducting a telephone survey to understand the market, posing as a potential customer at an exhibition, bribing a competitor's employee to pass on proprietary information, and covert surveillance such as through the use of hidden cameras. The practice of selling in the guise of marketing research, commonly known as 'sugging', also occurs from time to time. Despite the fact that it is not usually practised by bona fide marketing research agencies but, rather, unscrupulous selling companies who use marketing research as a means of gaining compliance to their requests, it is the marketing research industry that suffers from its aftermath.

Market research is an important vehicle by which organizations can learn more about their customers, and develop products and services that meet their needs. Properly conducted, it can yield invaluable insights, and can be the difference between success and failure in business. But its reputation is being sullied by the prevalence of 'bogus' surveys and other questionable practices. This raises the issue of whether research deals with the facts or is an exercise in fiction.

Reflection: Select any three studies that you have heard or seen being publicized in the media. Investigate them and evaluate the quality of the research that has been undertaken using the criteria discussed above.

Summary

This chapter has examined the nature and role of marketing information and customer insights. The following key issues were addressed.

1. The importance of marketing research and customer insights: customer insights are key if an organization is to be truly market-led. They can provide answers to all sorts of marketing questions that the organization may face.

2. The three main types of market information: internal market information involves the collection and examination of data available internally to the organization; market intelligence involves the gathering of information on what is happening in the marketplace generally; while marketing research is conducted to examine specific research questions that the firm has.

3. The approaches to conducting research: marketing research can be conducted either by the organization itself or by employing the services of a professional marketing research firm. Large-scale, complex research work is best conducted by a professional firm.

4. The stages in the market research process: these include initial contact, the research brief, the research proposal, exploratory research, the main data collection phase, data analysis and report writing/presentation.

5. Qualitative research techniques: a range of semi-structured research techniques including focus groups, depth interviews, observation studies, ethnographic research and so on.

6. The four main survey methods, namely face-to-face, telephone, mail and Internet: each has its unique advantages and disadvantages, and the decision as to which to use should be guided by the nature of the study, the respondents and the cost.

7. The nature of marketing information systems: these are systems in which marketing information is formally gathered, stored and distributed on a regular, planned basis.

Study questions

1. What are the differences between qualitative and quantitative research? Explain the roles played by each.
2. Outline the main stages in the marketing research process, identifying particularly the kinds of difficulties that might be faced at each stage.
3. Market research is being trivialized by the number of surveys that are being reported in the media. Discuss
4. Many firms are now investing heavily in analyzing their own customers through CRM and website analysis. What are the advantages and disadvantages of this trend for both firms and consumers?
5. Discuss the recent mechanical methods such as neuro-marketing that are being used to study consumer behaviour. What are the ethical implications of these approaches?
6. Visit www.surveymonkey.com and learn about how to create and administer a survey.

Suggested reading

Carson, D., A. Gilmore and **K. Gronhaug** (2001) *Qualitative Marketing Research*, London: Sage Publications.

Davenport, T. (2006) Competing on Analytics, *Harvard Business Review*, **84** (1), 98–107.

Graves, P. (2010) *Consumerology*, London: Nicholas Brealey.

Poynter, R. (2010) *The Handbook of Online and Social Media Research: Tools and Techniques for Market Researchers*, London: John Wiley & Sons.

Mueller, S., L. Lockshin and **J. Louviere** (2010) What You See May Not Be What You Get: Asking Consumers What Matters May Not Reflect What They Choose, *Marketing Letters*, **21**, 335–50.

Ulwick, A. and **L. Bettencourt** (2008) Giving Customers a Fair Hearing, *Sloan Management Review*, **49** (3), 62–8.

References

1. **Aitken, L.** (2010) IKEA – An Improbable Tale: How a Research Methodology Became a Big Creative Idea, *Warc.com*; **Armitstead, L.** (2010) IKEA Reveals Profit for the First Time to Dispel 'Secretive' Image, *Telegraph.co.uk*, 1 October.

2. **Esomar** (2010) *Global Market Research*.

3. **Esomar** (2010) *Global Market Research*.

4. **Foss, B.** and **M. Stone** (2001) *Successful Customer Relationship Marketing*, London: Kogan Page.

5. **Zeithaml, V., R. Rust** and **K. Lemon** (2001) The Customer Pyramid: Creating and Serving Profitable Customers, *California Management Review*, **43** (4), 118–42.

6. **Baker, R.** (2010) Boots Advantage Card Signs up Third Parties, *MarketingWeek.co.uk*, 5 October.

7. **Direct Marketing Association** (2010) Boots: Christmas, *Warc.com*.

8. **Beer, D.** (2008) Researching a Confessional Society, *International Journal of Market Research*, **50** (5), 619–29.

9. **Cooke, M.** (2008) The New World of Web 2.0 Research, *International Journal of Market Research*, **50** (5), 569–72.

10. **Precourt, G.** (2010) Mercedes Benz USA: The Move from Traditional Research to Consumer Communities, *Warc.com*.

11. **Crouch, S.** and **M. Housden** (1999) *Marketing Research for Managers*, Oxford: Butterworth Heinemann, 253.

12. **Gray, R.** (1999) Tracking the Online Audience, *Marketing*, 18 February, 41–3.

13. **Birchall, J.** (2005) Rich, But Not Fortune's Fools, *Financial Times*, 13 December, 13.

14. **Harper, J.** (2003) Camera Phones Cross Moral, Legal Lines, *Washington Times*, Business, 15 July, 6.

15. **Page, G.** (2010) Neuroscience: A New Perspective, *Warc.com*.

16. **Lucas, L.** (2010) Up Close and Personal Brands, *Financial Times*, 14 October, 15.

17. **Yu, J.** and **H. Cooper** (1983) A Quantitative Review of Research Design Effects on Response Rates to Questionnaires, *Journal of Marketing Research*, 20 February, 156–64.

18. **Falthzik, A.** and **S. Carroll** (1971) Rate of Return for Close v Open-ended Questions in a Mail Survey of Industrial Organisations, *Psychological Reports*, **29**, 1121–2.

19. **O'Dell, W.F.** (1962) Personal Interviews or Mail Panels?, *Journal of Marketing*, **26**, 34–9.

20. **Dillman, D.** (1978) *Mail and Telephone Surveys: The Total Design Method*, New York: John Wiley & Sons.

21. See **Fahy, J.** (1998) Improving Response Rates in Cross-cultural Mail Surveys, *Industrial Marketing Management*, **27** (November), 459–67; **Walker, B., W. Kirchmann** and **J. Conant** (1987) A Method to Improve Response Rates in Industrial Mail Surveys, *Industrial Marketing Management*, **16** (November), 305–14.

22. **Esomar** (2010) *Global Market Research*.

23. **Reynolds, N.** and **A. Diamantopoulos** (1998) The Effect of Pretest Method on Error Detection Rates: Experimental Evidence, *European Journal of Marketing*, **32** (5/6), 480–98.

24. **Crouch, S.** (1992) *Marketing Research for Managers*, Oxford: Butterworth Heinemann, 253.

25. **Jobber, D.** and **C. Rainbow** (1977) A Study of the Development and Implementation of Marketing Information Systems in British Industry, *Journal of the Marketing Research Society*, **19** (3), 104–11.

26. **Van Bruggen, A., A. Smidts** and **B. Wierenga** (1996) The Impact of the Quality of a Marketing Decision Support System: An Experimental Study, *International Journal of Research in Marketing*, **13**, 331–43.

27. **Piercy, N.** and **M. Evans** (1983) *Managing Marketing Information*, Beckenham: Croom Helm.

28. **Ackoff, R.L.** (1967) Management Misinformation Systems, *Management Science*, **14** (4), 147–56.

29. **Kohli, A.** and **B. Jaworski** (1990) Market Orientation: The Construct, Research Propositions and Marketing Implications, *Journal of Marketing*, **54**, 1–18.

When you have read this chapter

log on to the Online Learning Centre for
Foundations of Marketing at
www.mcgraw-hill.co.uk/textbooks/fahy
where you'll find links and extra online study tools for marketing.

Appendix 4.1: Sources of European marketing information

Is there a survey of the industry?

Euromonitor GMID Database has in-depth analysis and current market information in the key areas of country data, consumer lifestyles, market sizes, forecasts, brand and country information, business information sources and marketing profiles.

Reuters Business Insight Reports are full-text reports available online in the sectors of healthcare, financial services, consumer goods, energy, e-commerce and technology.

Key Note Reports cover size of market, economic trends, prospects and company performance.

Mintel Premier Reports cover market trends, prospects and company performance.

Snapshots on CD-Rom The 'Snapshots' CD series is a complete library of market research reports, providing coverage of consumer, business-to-business and industrial markets. Containing 2000 market research reports, this series provides incisive data and analysis on over 8000 market segments for the UK, Europe and the USA.

British Library Market Research is a guide to British Library Holdings. It lists titles of reports arranged by industry. Some items are available on inter-library loan; others may be seen at the British Library in London.

International Directory of Published Market Research, published by Marketsearch.

How large is the market?

European Marketing Data and Statistics Now available on the Euromonitor GMID database.

International Marketing Data and Statistics Now available on the Euromonitor GMID database.

CEO Bulletin

A–Z of UK Marketing Data

European Marketing Pocket Book

The Asia Pacific Marketing Pocket Book

The Americas Marketing Pocket Book

Where is the market?

Regional Marketing Pocket Book

Regional Trends gives the main economic and social statistics for UK regions.

Geodemographic Pocket Book

Who are the competitors?

British companies can be identified using any of the following.

> *Kompass* (most European countries have their own edition)
>
> *Key British Enterprises*
>
> *Quarterly Review – KPMG*
>
> *Sell's Products and Services Directory* (Gen Ref E 380.02542 SEL)

For more detailed company information consult the following.

> *Companies Annual Report Collection Carol:* Company Annual Reports online at www.carol.co.uk
>
> *Fame DVD* (CD-Rom service)
>
> *Business Ratio Reports*
>
> *Retail Rankings*

Overseas companies sources include:

> *Asia's 7,500 Largest Companies*
>
> *D&B Europa*
>
> *Dun's Asia Pacific Key Business Enterprises*
>
> *Europe's 15,000 Largest Companies*
>
> *Major Companies of the Arab World*
>
> *Million Dollar Directory (US)*
>
> *Principal International Businesses*

What are the trends?

Possible sources to consider include the following.

> *The Book of European Forecasts* Now available on the Euromonitor GMID database.
>
> *Marketing in Europe*
>
> *European Trends*
>
> *Consumer Europe* Now available on the Euromonitor GMID database.
>
> *Consumer Goods Europe*
>
> *Family Expenditure Survey*
>
> *Social Trends*
>
> *Lifestyle Pocket Book*
>
> *Drink Trends*
>
> *Media Pocket Book*
>
> *Retail Business*

Mintel Market Intelligence

OECD (Organisation for Economic Co-operation and Development)

EU statistical and information sources

'Eurostat' is a series of publications that provide a detailed picture of the EU; they can be obtained by visiting European Documentation Centres (often in university libraries) in all EU countries; themes include general statistics, economy and finance, and population/ social conditions.

Eurostat Yearbook

European Access is a bulletin on issues, policies, activities and events concerning EU member states.

Marketing and Research Today is a journal that examines social, political, economic and business issues relating to Western, Central and Eastern Europe.

European Report is a twice-weekly news publication from Brussels on industrial, economic and political issues.

Abstracts and indexes

Business Periodicals Index

ANBAR Marketing and Distribution Abstracts

ABI Inform

Research Index

Times Index

Elsevier Science Direct

Emerald

Wiley Interscience and Boldideas

Guides to sources

A great variety of published information sources exists; the following source guides may help you in your search.

Marketing Information

Guide to European Marketing Information

Compendium of Marketing Information Sources

Croner's A–Z of Business Information Sources

McCarthy Cards: a card service on which are reproduced extracts from the press covering companies and industries; it also produces a useful guide to its sources: *UK and Europe Market Information: Basic Sources*

Statistics

Guide to Official Statistics

Sources of the Unofficial UK Statistics

Sources: the authors thank the University of Bradford School of Management Library for help in compiling this list.

Retail Eyes UK is a subsidiary of an American company founded in 1995. Located in Milton Keynes (UK), Retail Eyes is the UK's leading research agency providing customized solutions to its clients that focus on mystery shopping, retail audits and online customer surveys. The company offers customer experience improvement programmes across a variety of sectors by combining innovative approaches and new technologies. Its international scale and experience enables it to benefit from the most updated technologies and research expertise in the market. The latter are sources of differentiation in an industry populated by several competitors all stating that they offer 'the best service' to their clients.

Marketers are increasingly using innovative ways to better understand and to reach customers more effectively. To enhance their understanding of customers' needs and effectively design marketing strategies, marketers need to deeply analyse the elements influencing customers' buying experiences. In fact, the quality of customer experience in a retailer's shop is one of the most cost-effective methods of differentiating competing retailers. Moreover, customers generally do not complain when they receive a poor service; they simply go to shop elsewhere. Therefore, it is fundamental to monitor the quality of customer service in order to make an early identification of any strengths or weaknesses. As a result, mystery shopping has become popular among marketers since it is a powerful technique to evaluate the company's customer service (i.e. staff attitude and appearance, product knowledge). Mystery shoppers are defined as 'individuals trained to experience and measure any customer service process, by acting as potential customers and in some way reporting back on their experience in a detailed and objective way'.[1] Mystery shoppers are normal people who play the role of real customers getting a monetary reward in exchange for auditing retailers. In doing this, they must not reveal their identity. They buy products, ask questions, identify problems and finally they write reports helping companies to identify training needs or to evaluate training programmes, but also to boost staff morale through incentives.

Retail Eyes commenced business in the UK in 2003 and it has grown rapidly since, at a time when competing research companies nationwide are struggling to maintain revenues. In 2010, the company saw an increased turnover of 31 per cent making it one of the largest customer experience agencies in the UK. The company has worked for several major retailers and service providers in various sectors throughout the UK, undertaking over 200,000 mystery visits per year. Clients include Subway, HMV, O2, William Hill, BAA, Intercontinental Hotels Group, JD Sports Fashion, Pret a Manger, Lloyds Pharmacy, Thomas Cook, and JD Wetherspoon. In 2009, the company was ranked 27th according to *Marketing*'s market research league table and 57th in the *Sunday Times* Tech Track 100 fastest-growing technology companies.

The company's key promise is to open the eyes of retailers in order that they understand who their real customers are. Mystery shopping programmes are used to identify the key touch-points in the customers' journey that may lead to sales' improvement, customer advocacy and higher profits. This type of research can provide both customer and competitor intelligence. Mystery shoppers often follow a prescribed evaluation form in order to anonymously assess a specific business against specific criteria. Further, the evaluation may take into consideration various aspects of the retailer's business (or of a product) comprising the simple factual observation of points of sale or services, focusing especially on courtesy and preparation of the sales force, cleanliness, waiting time, response time, commercial signage, the state of the equipment in use, adherence to the company's standards and so on. The evaluation might go further to making a purchase or enquiry as an actual or potential customer. Moreover, from the report, the company will know if their training is working, or if their staff need different or additional training.

Today, the traditional customer research methodologies (i.e. surveys) used by retailers and other operators are considered primitive as they often provide unreliable and generic results and customer knowledge that is deemed to be outdated. On the contrary, mystery shopping is a market research technique providing accurate findings in the short term. Retail Eyes' mystery shoppers provide real-time, consistent and updated knowledge on a specific retailer. This is fundamental in an economy in which customers' tastes, preferences and needs can change quickly. Accordingly, Retail Eyes recommends its mystery shoppers to return their reports as soon as possible after completing each assignment (normally the same day or the day after at the latest). Increasingly, the company uses software (re:view™) enabling clients to access all results in genuine real-time, 24 hours per day, seven days a week so they can monitor and analyse the latest results as they occur.

Another problem with traditional surveys was that the results are often biased according to the availability and willingness of a certain population. Retail Eyes has tried to overcome this problem by enlarging the number of mystery shoppers available for each assignment. The company may choose among more than 250,000 'real' mystery shoppers, whose ages range from 16 to 96 years old, with several interests and hobbies and who represent potential customers to its clients. The quantity and heterogeneity of this sample differentiates Retail Eyes from other research agencies that often employ a small team of professional shoppers to conduct an evaluation of prescripted situations where they would not otherwise be. According to Simon Boydell, Marketing Manager for Retail Eyes: 'It is great to see an increased interest into the world of mystery shopping – consumers are becoming aware that not only can they get paid to go shopping, eat out at a restaurant or stay the night in a hotel, but they will be providing valuable feedback to assist retailers in providing a more enjoyable shopping experience for everyone.'[2]

In addition, it is not difficult to become a mystery shopper. Mystery shoppers are generally asked to fill in a form in which they are asked about their socio-demographic data. They may be asked to audit a retailer in different ways, either personally at the business establishment through observation or visits, or impersonally through other media such as Internet, mail/fax or telephone. The completion of the final report requires good observational skills, reliability, accuracy, objectivity, honesty and professionalism. Also, it is normal practice for any organization using mystery shoppers to advise their staff that they will be used periodically to check their service delivery performance.

There are a number of usual stages involved in conducting a piece of mystery shopping research. The first step consists of identifying the client's target market and qualifying the company's database of mystery customers. Then, suitable candidates are selected from a vast community of shoppers in order to assess the business in a natural setting. Matching the right mystery shopper to the right situation is critical to providing accurate feedback. According to Tim Ogle, founder and marketing director of Retail Eyes, 'There is nothing more valuable than understanding how real customers perceive a business.'[3]

Retail Eyes aims to differentiate itself from its competitors by ensuring that its mystery shoppers do not have to simply tick the box of simple questions like: did employees wear a name badge? Did they smile when they took your money? Did they say would you like anything else like that? Rather they are more focused in getting the whole picture by collecting additional qualitative data. In doing so, it aims to provide clients with more detailed feedback.

The company's business activities are based on an online reporting system enabling mystery shoppers registered with the company to easily select tasks and to provide feedback on their mystery shopping experience. Another innovation in the service offered by Retail Eyes comes from the use of a tablet PC instead of paper and pencil to complete compliance-led audits. The introduction of this innovation has helped the company to speed up and secure the audit process; increasingly, mystery shoppers can also integrate digital photography and video as part of the audit process. Videos are useful to reinforce the message and to show more clearly some of the aspects of the service. Thanks to its leading-edge technology, Retail Eyes then provides its clients with fast and easy access to information in virtually any format.

The emergence of online reviews

Retail Eyes and other market research companies offering mystery shopping programmes have currently to face the emergence of customers' reviews on the Internet. Online reviews are any positive or negative statement made by potential, actual or former customers about a product or company that is made available via the Internet. They may represent a substitute to mystery shopping reports; therefore they constitute a real threat to the business. The use of online reviews is constantly growing among customers; for example, Tripadvisor.com enables customers to publish reviews on travel products and services. In January 2005, this website hosted 1 million reviews and opinions; today it hosts over 20 million monthly visitors, 15 million registered members and over 30 million reviews and opinions. The growth of this and other websites such as Epinions.com and booking.com suggests that those reviews are widely used and the sources are perceived as reliable and credible among both customers and companies. This has enticed marketers to encourage consumers to post product reviews on retailers' websites. Therefore, retailers can start to analyze the comments and reviews available before conducting a mystery shopping audit or they can encourage customers to directly publish reviews on the company's website or send them by email.

References

1. **Market Research Society** (2003) MRS Code and Guidelines on Mystery Customer. mrs.org.uk (accessed 4 August 2011).
2. **RetailEyes** (2011) Retail Eyes Signs Up Record Number of Mystery Shoppers, retaileyes.co.uk/latest_news/item/162/start//num// (accessed 6 August 2011).
3. **Mystery Shopper Special Report** (2007) Open Up Your Retail Eyes, *Frontier Magazine*, frontiermagazine.co.uk/article/Open-up-your-retail-eyes-71.html (accessed 6 August 2011).

Questions

1. Analyse under which conditions a retailer may decide to use a mystery shopping research technique.
2. Identify a set of typical research questions which should be answered by a mystery shopper.
3. Discuss the advantages and disadvantages of the mystery shopping technique compared to other market research methods.
4. Discuss the innovations introduced by Retail Eyes in its mystery shopping programmes.

This case was prepared by Dr Raffaele Filieri, Lecturer in Marketing, Newcastle Business School, Northumbria University from published sources as a basis for class discussion rather than to illustrate either effective or ineffective management.

Chapter 5

Market Segmentation, Targeting and Positioning

Chapter outline

Segmenting consumer markets

Consumer segmentation criteria

Segmenting organizational markets

Criteria for successful segmentation

Target marketing

Positioning

Repositioning

Learning outcomes

By the end of this chapter you will understand:

1 the process of market segmentation and why it is important

2 the methods used to segment both consumer and organizational markets

3 the criteria for effective segmentation

4 the process of market targeting and the four target market strategies – undifferentiated, differentiated, focused and customized marketing

5 the concept of positioning and the keys to successful positioning

6 the concept of repositioning and the repositioning options available to the firm.

MARKETING SPOTLIGHT

BlackBerry

The power of some innovations to impact upon work, culture and society is illustrated by BlackBerry, one of the early brands of smartphone. Manufactured by the Canadian firm, Research in Motion (RIM), the BlackBerry was first launched in 1999. Containing a full QWERTY keyboard combined with a 'push' email software facility which meant that email was delivered instantaneously, it became the essential business tool. So revolutionary was the ability to check emails on the move that the BlackBerry was nicknamed the 'Crackberry' – a reference to the addictiveness of crack cocaine, because of the extent to which it was used by its owners. It helped to change the nature of work, with company representatives able to send and receive emails 24/7 and even led to a Canadian minister imposing a BlackBerry 'blackout' after office hours in order that his staff could maintain a work–life balance.

Despite taking the name of a fruit, the BlackBerry quickly became the dominant smartphone brand. It was initially targeted at the business market and hundreds of devices were given to senior business people, journalists and politi-

"This is one change I won't make!"

Some habits are hard to break, which is why President-Elect Barack Obama, against the wishes of attorneys and his own secret service, just can't give up the ease, convenience and reliability of his BlackBerry.

≡≡ BlackBerry.

cians to encourage them to adopt the product and influence their peers. Some major events had the effect of further cementing its reputation. For example, during the 2001 attacks on the Twin Towers in New York, the only people able to get messages out were those using their BlackBerrys as the network remained functional. And many major political figures, most famously Barak Obama and Nicolas Sarkozy, attested to the value of the product in enabling them to keep in touch with their staff and supporters. Obama's endorsement alone was estimated to have been worth US$50 million to the company. The brand was supported by a major global campaign 'Love What You Do (and Do What You Love)', using the famous Beatles song 'All You Need Is Love', and more recent social media efforts have asked users to visit the BlackBerry.com website and share their 'why I love my BlackBerry' stories.

But having dominated the business segment of the market, BlackBerry faces some serious challenges. The biggest threat is coming from brands like the Apple iPhone and Samsung Galaxy, which having been initially popular in consumer markets are rapidly making inroads into the business segment as they offer not only email and web-browsing functions but also access to software applications (apps) and podcast libraries. BlackBerry has responded with the Torch series which provides access to BlackBerry's App World and is designed to appeal to consumer as well as business markets, through offering music, video, access to social networks and tools for controlling their personal video recorders (PVRs). But given that its major competitors have a significant technology, not to mention branding, lead in the consumer market, it is uncertain how well it is going to fare. And as they make inroads into the business market, BlackBerry's legendary addictiveness will be tested to the full. Although RIM has sold 40 million BlackBerrys to date and there are 16 million active BlackBerry subscriptions, it has fallen to fifth place with a 15 per cent share of the smartphone market behind Nokia, Samsung, LG and Apple.[1]

our review of customer behaviour in Chapter 3, we saw that there are a variety of influences on the purchase decisions of customers. Their needs and wants vary and no matter how good a company's product or service is, not all customers will want it or will be willing to pay the same price for it. For example, some consumers may feel that saving their money in order to be able to travel to New Zealand to do a bungee jump is a good idea, while others might rather spend their money now on the latest fashions in order to look good. While both these groups of consumers may have some similarities in their preferences, they also have some key differences. Therefore, to implement the marketing concept and satisfy customer needs successfully, different product and service offerings must be made to the diverse customer groups that typically comprise a market.

The technique used by marketers to get to grips with the diverse nature of markets is called **market segmentation**. Market segmentation is defined as 'the identification of individuals or organizations with similar characteristics that have significant implications for the determination of marketing strategy'.

Thus, market segmentation involves the division of a diverse market into a number of smaller submarkets that have common features. The objective is to identify groups of customers with similar requirements so that they can be served effectively, while being of a sufficient size for the product or service to be supplied efficiently (see Exhibit 5.1). Usually, it is not possible to create a marketing mix that satisfies every individual's particular requirements exactly. Market segmentation, by grouping together customers with similar needs, provides a commercially viable method of serving these customers. It is therefore at the heart of strategic marketing, since it forms the basis by which marketers understand their markets and develop strategies for serving their chosen customers better than the competition.

There are a number of reasons why it is sensible for companies to segment their markets (see Figure 5.1). Most notably, it allows companies the opportunity to enhance their profits. Many customers are willing to pay a premium for products or services that match their needs. For example, first-class air travellers regularly pay thousands of pounds for long-haul flights, though the additional costs of catering for these customers is only marginally higher than that of catering for economy-class customers. In emerging product categories like 'All-In-One' PCs, where all the key internal computer parts such as processors and graphic cards are encased with the monitor, consumers have the option of paying over €1,200 for a top of the range Apple iMac or approximately half that amount for models on offer from companies like Samsung and Hewlett Packard.

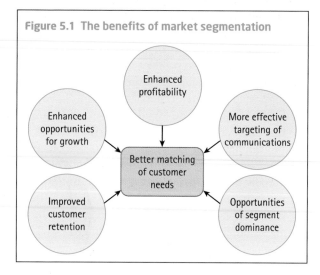

Figure 5.1 The benefits of market segmentation

Both of these price points and product offerings will appeal to different segments of the market.

Second, through segmenting markets, companies can examine growth opportunities and expand their product lines. For example, in marketing its over-the-counter cough medicines, the Pfizer corporation offers different products for different types of cough under the Benylin brand. In its children's medicines range, it offers separate products for chesty coughs, dry coughs and night coughs, while there are five different cough brands in its adult range. Finally, in many competitive markets, companies are not able to compete across all segments effectively; by segmenting markets, companies can identify which segments they might most effectively compete in and develop strategies suited for that segment. For example, in the audio equipment business, one of the leading brands is Bose, which has built a global reputation as a manufacturer of high-quality sound systems that are only available through select stores and at premium prices. By pursuing this strategy, Bose has successfully differentiated itself from competitors like Sony, Samsung and Pioneer and, despite its premium prices, still has sales revenues of over US$2 billion per annum.

Segmenting consumer markets

Consumer segmentation criteria may be divided into three main groups: behavioural, psychographic and profile variables. Since the purpose of segmentation is to identify differences in behaviour that have implications for marketing decisions, behavioural variables, such as benefits sought from the product and buying patterns, may be considered the ultimate basis for segmentation. **Psychographic segmentation** is used when researchers believe that purchasing behaviour is correlated with the personality or lifestyle of consumers. Having found these differences, the marketer needs to describe the people who exhibit them and this is where **profile segmentation** such as socio-economic group or geographic location is valuable.[2] For example, a marketer may see whether there are groups of people who value low calories in soft drinks and then attempt to profile them in terms of their age, socio-economic groupings, etc. Figure 5.2 shows the major segmenta-

Table 5.1 Consumer segmentation methods

Variable	Examples
Behavioural	
Benefits sought	Convenience, status, performance
Purchase occasion	Self-buy, gift, special occasions
Purchase behaviour	Brand loyal, brand switching, innovators
Usage	Heavy, light
Media behaviour	Primarily online, primarily offline
Psychographic	
Lifestyle	Trendsetters, conservatives, sophisticates
Personality	Conscientious, agreeable, extrovert
Profile	
Age	Under 12, 12–18, 19–25, 26–35, 36–49, 50–64, 65 and over
Gender	Female, male
Life cycle	Young single, young couples, young parents, middle-aged empty-nesters, retired
Social class	Upper middle, middle, skilled working
Terminal education age	16, 18, 21 years
Income	Income breakdown according to study objectives and income levels per country
Geographic	North vs south, urban vs rural, country
Geodemographic	Upwardly mobile young families living in larger owner-occupied houses, older people living in small houses, European regions based on language, income, age profile and location

tion variables used in consumer markets and Table 5.1 describes each of these variables in greater detail.

Consumer segmentation criteria

Table 5.1 shows the variety of criteria that might be considered when segmenting a consumer market. In

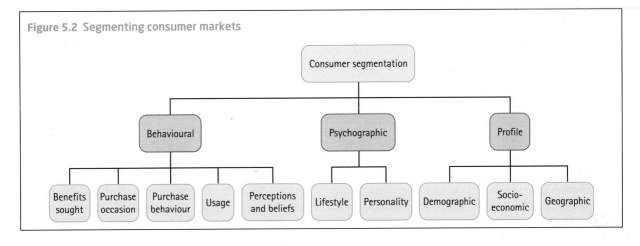

Figure 5.2 Segmenting consumer markets

practice there is no prescribed way of segmenting a market, and different criteria and combinations of criteria may be used. In the following paragraphs we will examine some of the more popular bases for segmentation. It is also critical for marketers to remember that consumer psychographics and behaviour patterns change over time, so that consumers do not necessarily remain in the same segments but may move between them. It is important therefore that segmentation analyses are done with the most up-to-date information.

Benefits sought

Benefit segmentation provides an understanding of why people buy in a market, and can aid the identification of opportunities. It is a fundamental method of segmentation because the objective of marketing is to provide customers with benefits that they value. For example, a basic product like toothpaste can confer a variety of benefits, ranging from decay prevention to fresh breath, and great taste to white teeth. Colgate has developed sub-brands that provide each of these benefits, such as Colgate Cavity Protection (decay prevention), Colgate Max Fresh (fresh breath), Colgate Kids (taste), Colgate Sparkling White and Ultrabrite Advanced Whitening (white teeth), and Colgate Sensitive (sensitive teeth). Luxury watch brands like Omega, Hermes and Patek Philippe convey the benefits of status and prestige to their owners as well as being considered to be a good long-term investment (see Exhibit 5.2). Focusing on benefits helps companies to spot business development opportunities.

Purchase behaviour

The degree of brand loyalty in a market is a useful basis for segmenting customers. Some buyers are totally brand loyal, buying only one brand in the product group. For example, a person might invariably buy Ariel Automatic washing powder. Most customers, however, practise brand-switching behaviour. Some may have a tendency to buy Ariel Automatic but also buy two or three other brands; others might show no loyalty to any individual brand but switch brands on the basis of special offers (e.g. money-off promotions) or because they are variety seekers who look to buy a different brand each time. A recent trend in retailing is 'biographics'. This is the linking of actual purchase behaviour to individuals. The growth in loyalty schemes in supermarkets, such as the Tesco Clubcard scheme, has provided the mechanism for gathering this information (see Marketing in Action 4.1). Such biographic data can be used to segment and target customers very precisely. For example, it would be easy to identify a

Exhibit 5.2 This advertisement for Patek Philippe uses powerful emotional appeal to convey the benefits of ownership

group of customers who were ground coffee purchasers and target them through special offers. Analysis of the data allows the supermarkets to stock products in each of their stores that are more relevant to their customers' age, lifestyle and expenditure.

Usage

Another way of segmenting customers is on the basis of whether they are heavy users, light users or non-users of a selected product category. The profiling of heavy users allows this group to receive the most marketing attention (particularly promotion efforts) on the assumption that creating brand loyalty among these people will pay great dividends. Sometimes the 80:20 rule applies, where about 80 per cent of a product's sales come from 20 per cent of its customers. Skype is an example of a telecommunications company that has focused very effectively on the opportunities created by the growing need for telephone contact among people living in different parts of the world. By offering free calls over the Internet, Skype quickly built a customer base of over 600 million registered user accounts worldwide, resulting in a 13 per cent market share of international calls in just seven years.[3] However, attacking the heavy-user segment can have drawbacks if all of the competition are also following this strategy. Analysing the light and non-user categories may provide insights that permit the development of appeals that are not being mimicked by the competition. The identity of heavy, light and non-user categories, and their accompanying profiles for many consumer goods, can be accomplished by using survey information such as that provided by the Target Group Index (TGI). This is a large-scale annual survey of buying and media habits and is available in over 60 countries around the world.

Lifestyle

Lifestyle segmentation aims to categorize people in terms of their way of life, as reflected in their activities, interests and opinions (see Exhibit 3.3). As we saw in Chapter 3, lifestyle is an important personal factor driving consumer behaviour, and advertisers have identified several different lifestyle groupings. Lifestyle is also a powerful method of segmentation as particular lifestyle groups have fairly predictable media habits (see Marketing in Action 5.1). For example, people who enjoy outdoor activities such as hiking and water sports will be likely to read magazines, watch television programmes, visit websites and join social networks dealing with these topics. Marketers can then use these media to reach their chosen segments (see Exhibit 5.3).

An interesting example of the successful use of **lifestyle segmentation** is provided by a small US frozen foods firm, the SeaPak Shrimp Company. Although operating in a low-involvement product category that is often dominated by retailer own-brands, it identified two core but completely different lifestyle groups, namely, those that 'live-to-cook' and those that 'cook-to-live' and set about creating separate brands for each segment. The live-to-cook lifestyle has a passion for cooking, for discovering new recipes and for preparing unique meals. SeaPak surrounded these shoppers with content that enabled their passion such as access to famous chefs through online events, original seafood recipes and monthly emails. Other elements of the brand offering included higher-end unbreaded seafood products, upscale packaging and placement near the fresh seafood counter in supermarkets where these types of customers shop. For the cook-to-live group, the emphasis was on product quality and ease of preparation, with quick-bake breaded items in the frozen food section of shops. This two-segment approach yielded the firm a 15 per cent sales increase in a declining category.[4]

Exhibit 5.3 The Billabong brand is closely associated with active, outdoor lifestyles epitomized by images such as this

Marketing in Action 5.1   The Porsche lifestyle

Critical Thinking: Below is a review of some recent product and branding decisions made by Porsche. Read it and critically evaluate how the market segments for Porsche are changing and the advantages and disadvantages of these developments.

The Porsche 911 is seen by many as the embodiment of the good life. Images of the venerable two-seater cruising along cliff-top roads on a sunny day have marked out the kind of lifestyles enjoyed by some and aspired to by many. Consequently, Porsche has built up a staunchly loyal following since the 911 brand was launched in 1964 after some motor racing success with the Porsche 550 Spyder. It is seen as a brand that provides legacy, performance and pricing. There are faster cars available for less money, but not ones that perform as well on the road. And there are many supercar brands such as Maserati and Lamborghini, but these are far less affordable than the German brand.

However, in recent years Porsche has aimed to broaden the appeal and the range of its vehicles. In 2004, it launched a high-performance, sports utility vehicle (SUV), the Cayenne. This sub-brand was initially not welcomed by Porsche loyalists. Its size, weight and lack of any racing circuit sanctioning was criticized but, nevertheless, the Cayenne has gone on to be very successful and outsells the 911 in the US market. But it was the launch of the Panamera brand in 2009 that really convinced some Porsche fans that the marque was changing for the worse. It is a four-seater luxury car designed to compete in the space occupied by global leaders such as the Mercedes S Class, the Audi 8, the BMW 7 Series and the Lexus 460. This is a very different market segment, where customers are looking for size, power, a beautiful cabin with state-of-the-art technology and a car that both announces their arrival and allows them to carry their friends around in style. It is also a market segment where Porsche is not in the consumer's evoked set because it is seen as a sports car rather than a luxury car. Yet, again, the Panamera has also been a success, with over 43,000 units sold since it was launched.

And what of the 911? Well, it would appear that Porsche wants to broaden its appeal too. Owing to falling sales in the USA, it has decided to reposition the brand as an 'everyday' vehicle. In a campaign where the car is labelled as a 'snowmobile', 'pet-carrier' and 'school bus', its television advertisements show Porsche owners collecting kids from school and taking a big dog for a fun drive – somewhat more mundane events than the aspirational lifestyle of old. On PorscheEveryday.com, visitors are invited to share their everyday stories of 911 practicality.

Based on: Buss (2011);[5] Ross (2010)[6].

Age

Age is a factor that has been used in the segmentation of a host of consumer markets.[7] As we saw in Chapter 3, children have become a very important market believed to be worth about $1 trillion per year and now have their own television programmes, cereals, computer games and confectionery. The Gro Company's Gro Clock is an example of a successful product launch in the children's market. This market has traditionally been dominated by simple mechanical devices using static illustrations such as cartoon characters like Thomas the Tank Engine. The Gro Clock contains animated imagery of the sun and the stars to communicate wake up times for very young children (see Exhibit 5.4). The product launch exceeded sales forecasts by over 300 per cent and it has quickly become a market leader in its category. Similarly, a KPMG study found that only one-fifth of fund management firms were targeting 'Generation Y' customers – that is, those born in the 1980s – even though this group will have to be more financially adept than their parents owing to changes in pension regimes.[8]

As we saw in Chapter 2, age distribution changes within the European Union are having a profound effect on the attractiveness of various age segments to marketers, with people over 50 years of age likely to become increasingly important in the future. Labelled the 'grey market', people are now living longer, with life expectancies rising into the eighties in developed

Exhibit 5.4 The Gro Clock - a successful product launch in the children's market segment

countries around the world. Many 'grey consumers' are healthy, active, well educated, financially independent and have a lot of leisure time, making them a very attractive market. For example, in the music business, record companies have been struggling with the fact that its core market (young people) are buying less music, preferring to download it, often for free, from file-sharing websites. Therefore, Universal Music Group brought out a CD of songs for people who grew up in the 1950s named 'Dreamboats and Petticoats'. It was so successful, it was followed by a West End musical and three other albums that have sold over 2.3 million copies.[9] Other media companies such as television stations, radio stations and newspapers are increasingly realizing that the best potential for their offerings may lie with the grey market.

Social class

Social class is another important segmentation variable. As we saw in Chapter 3, social class groupings are based primarily on occupation. However, people who hold similar occupations may have very dissimilar lifestyles, values and purchasing patterns. Nevertheless, research has found that social class has proved to be useful in discriminating between owning a dishwasher, having central heating and privatization share ownership, for example, and therefore should not be discounted as a segmentation variable.[10] In addition,

social classes tend to vary in their media consumption, meaning that these groups can be targeted effectively by advertisers. For example, tabloid newspapers tend to target working-class people, whereas traditional broadsheets see the middle and upper classes as their primary audience.

Geography

At a very basic level, markets can be segmented on the basis of country or regions within a country or on the basis of city size. More popular in recent years has been the combination of geographic and demographic variables into what are called **geodemographics**. In countries that produce population census data, the potential exists for classifying consumers on the combined basis of location and certain demographic (and socio-economic) information. Households are classified into groups according to a wide range of factors, depending on what is asked on census returns. In the UK, variables such as household size, online behaviour, occupation, family size and ethnic background are used to group small geographic areas (known as enumeration districts) into segments that share similar characteristics. Two of the best known geo-demographic systems are ACORN (from its full title – A Classification Of Residential Neighbourhoods) produced by CACI Market Analysis and MOSAIC produced by Experian. The main ACORN groupings and their characteristics are shown in Table 5.2. CACI uses 125 demographic statistics and 287 lifestyle variables to produce a detailed consumer picture of the UK; all 1.9 million postcodes are classified in this way, enabling some very precise targeting of the market.

Using a similar classification system, MOSAIC Global is available in 24 countries, including most in Western Europe. Based on the assumption that the world's cities share common patterns of residential segregation, it uses 10 distinct types of residential neighbourhood, each with a characteristic set of values, motivations and consumer preferences, to generate consumer classifications ranging from 'Comfortable Retirement' to 'Metropolitan Strugglers'. Geodemographic information has been used to select recipients of direct mail campaigns, to identify the best locations for stores and to find the best poster sites. This is possible because consumers in each group can be identified by means of their postcodes. Another area where census data are employed is in buying advertising spots on television. Agencies depend on information from viewership panels, which record their viewing habits so that advertisers can get an insight into who watches what. This means that advertisers who wish to reach a

Table 5.2 The ACORN targeting classification

Categories	% in UK population	Groups	% in UK population
A: Wealthy Achievers	25.4	1 Wealthy Executives	8.6
		2 Affluent Greys	7.9
		3 Flourishing Families	9.0
B: Urban Prosperity	11.5	4 Prosperous Professionals	2.1
		5 Educated Urbanites	5.5
		6 Aspiring Singles	3.8
C: Comfortably Off	27.4	7 Starting Out	3.1
		8 Secure Families	15.5
		9 Settled Suburbia	6.1
		10 Prudent Pensioners	2.7
D: Moderate Means	13.8	11 Asian Communities	1.5
		12 Post-Industrial Families	4.7
		13 Blue Collar Roots	7.5
E: Hard Pressed	21.2	14 Struggling Families	13.3
		15 Burdened Singles	4.2
		16 High Rise Hardship	1.6
		17 Inner City Adversity	2.1

Source: © CACI Limited (data source BMRB and OPCS/GRO(S)); © Crown Copyright; all rights reserved; ACORN is a registered trademark of CACI Limited; reproduced with permission.

Note: Due to rounding, the percentages total 99.2.

particular geodemographic group can discover the type of programme they prefer to watch and buy television spots accordingly. Advertising on social media sites like Facebook can also be targeted very specifically at customer groups based on the profile information submitted by members when they create their accounts.

A major strength of geodemographics is that it can link buyer behaviour to customer groups. Buying habits can be determined by means of large-scale syndicated surveys – for example, the TGI and MORI Financial Services – or from panel data (for example, the grocery and toiletries markets are covered by AGB's Superpanel). By 'geocoding' respondents, those ACORN groups most likely to purchase a product or brand can be determined. This can be useful for branch location since many service providers use a country-wide branch network and need to match the market segments to which they most appeal to the type of customer in their catchment area. The merchandise mix decisions of retailers can also be affected by customer profile data. Media selections can be made more precise by linking buying habits to geodemographic data.[11]

In short, a wide range of variables can be used to segment consumer markets. Flexibility and creativity are the hallmarks of effective segmentation analysis.

Often, a combination of variables will be used to identify groups of consumers that respond in the same way to marketing mix strategies.

Segmenting organizational markets

As we noted in Chapter 3, organizational markets, in contrast to consumer markets, tend to be characterized by relatively small numbers of buyers. Nevertheless, there are also many cases where it will be appropriate to segment organizational markets.

Organizational segmentation criteria

Some of the most useful bases for segmenting organizational markets are described below.

Organizational size

Market segmentation in this case may be by size of buying organization. Large organizations differ from medium-sized and small organizations in having greater order potential, more formalized buying and management processes, increased specialization of function, and special needs (e.g. quantity discounts). The result is that they may form important target market segments and require tailored marketing mix strategies. For example, the sales force may need to be organized on a key account basis where a dedicated sales team is used to service important industrial accounts. List pricing of products and services may need to take into account the inevitable demand for volume discounts from large purchasers, and the sales force will need to be well versed in the art of negotiation.

Industry

Industry sector – sometimes identified by the Standard Industrial Classification (SIC) codes – is another common segmentation variable. Different industries may have unique requirements from products. For example, software applications suppliers like Oracle and SAP can market their products to various sectors, such as banking, manufacturing, healthcare and education, each of which has unique needs in terms of software programs, servicing, price and purchasing practice. By understanding each industry's needs in depth, a more effective marketing mix can be designed. In some instances, further segmentation may be required. For example, the education sector may be further divided into primary, secondary and further education, as the product and service requirements of these sub-sectors may differ.

Geographic location

The use of geographic location as a basis for differentiating marketing strategies may be suggested by regional variations in purchasing practice and needs. The purchasing practices and expectations of companies in Central and Eastern Europe are likely to differ markedly from those in Western Europe. Their more bureaucratic structures may imply a fundamentally different approach to doing business that needs to be recognized by companies attempting to enter these emerging industrial markets. These differences, in effect, suggest the need for regional segments since marketing needs to reflect these variations.

Choice criteria

The factor of choice criteria segments the organizational market on the basis of the key criteria used by buyers when they are evaluating supplier offerings (see Exhibit 5.5). One group of customers may rate price as the key choice criterion, another segment may favour productivity, while a third may be service orientated. These varying preferences mean that marketing and sales strategies need to be adapted to cater for each segment's needs. Three different marketing mixes

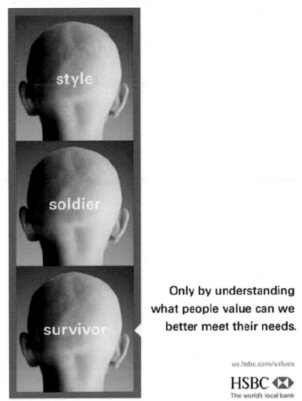

Exhibit 5.5 This advertisement from HSBC bank reflects the importance of understanding choice criteria in business-to-business marketing

Only by understanding what people value can we better meet their needs.

us.hsbc.com/values

HSBC
The world's local bank

would be needed to cover the three segments, and salespeople would have to emphasize different benefits when talking to customers in each segment. Variations in key choice criteria can be powerful predictors of buyer behaviour.

Purchasing organization

Another segmentation variable is that of decentralized versus centralized purchasing, because of its influence on the purchase decision.[12] Centralized purchasing is associated with purchasing specialists who become experts in buying a range of products and are particularly popular in sectors like grocery retailing. Specialization means that they become more familiar with cost factors, and the strengths and weaknesses of suppliers than do decentralized generalists. Furthermore, the opportunity for volume buying means that their power to demand price concessions from suppliers is enhanced. They have also been found to have greater power within the decision-making unit (DMU – see Chapter 3) than decentralized buyers who often lack the specialist's expertise and status to counter the view of technical members like designers and engineers. For these reasons, purchasing organization provides a good base for distinguishing between buyer behaviour, and can have implications for marketing activities. For example, the centralized purchasing segment could be served by a national account sales force, whereas the decentralized purchasing segment might be covered by territory representatives.

Interesting opportunities often appear at the intersection of consumer and industrial markets. For example, a small German technology company called Wagner has become the biggest supplier of spray guns for painting in the USA, with an 85 per cent market share. It used its expertise, built up through working with professional painters, to make products that also appeal to DIY painters. Its vast range of 3,000 products enables it to span both consumer and industrial markets, with prices ranging from US$50 up to US$2 million for large industrial systems. Though most manufacturers concentrate on industrial segments, two-thirds of Wagner's sales in the USA now come from consumer spray guns.

Criteria for successful segmentation

To determine whether a company has properly segmented its market, five criteria are usually considered.

1 *Effective*: the segments identified should consist of customers whose needs are relatively homogeneous within a segment, but significantly different from those in other segments. If buyer needs in different segments are similar, then the segmentation strategy should be revised.
2 *Measurable*: it must be possible to identify customers in the proposed segment, and to understand their characteristics and behaviour patterns. For example, some personality traits, like 'extrovert' or 'conscientious', might be difficult to pin down, whereas variables like age or occupation would be more clear-cut.
3 *Accessible*: the company must be able to formulate effective marketing programmes for the segments that it identifies. In other words, it must be clear what kinds of promotional campaign might work best for the segment, how the products might best be distributed to reach the segment, and so on.
4 *Actionable*: the company must have the resources to exploit the opportunities identified through the segmentation scheme. Certain segments – for example, in international markets – might be identified as being very attractive but the company may not have the resources or knowledge necessary to serve them.

5 *Profitable*: most importantly, segments must be large enough to be profitable to serve. This is what is meant by the clichéd expression 'Is there a market in the gap?' Very small segments may be unprofitable to serve, though advances in production and distribution technologies mean that, increasingly, micro-segments can be profitable (see the section on customized marketing, below).

Target marketing

Once the market segments have been identified, the next important activity is the selection of target markets. **Target marketing** refers to the choice of specific segments to serve, and is a key element in marketing strategy. An organization needs to evaluate the segments and to decide which ones to serve using the five criteria outlined above. For example, CNN targets its news programmes to what are known as 'influentials'. This is why, globally, CNN has focused so much of its distribution effort into gaining access to hotel rooms. Business people know that, wherever they are in the world, they can see international news on CNN in their hotel. Its sports programming is also targeted, with plenty of coverage of upmarket sports such as golf and tennis.

The aim of evaluating market segments is for a company to arrive at a choice of one or more segments to concentrate on. Target market selection is the choice of what and how many market segments in which to compete. There are four generic target marketing strategies from which to choose: undifferentiated marketing, differentiated marketing, focused marketing and customized marketing (see Figure 5.3). Each option will now be examined.

Figure 5.3 Target marketing strategies

Undifferentiated marketing

Marketing mix → Whole market

Differentiated marketing   Focused marketing

Marketing mix 1 → Segment 1
Marketing mix 2 → Segment 2 ← Marketing mix
Marketing mix 3 → Segment 3

Customized marketing

Marketing mix 1 → Customer 1
Marketing mix 2 → Customer 2
Marketing mix 3 → Customer 3

Undifferentiated marketing

Market analysis will occasionally reveal no pronounced differences in customer characteristics that have implications for a marketing strategy. Alternatively, the cost of developing a separate marketing mix for different segments may outweigh the potential gains of meeting customer needs more exactly. Under these circumstances a company may decide to develop a single marketing mix for the whole market. This absence of segmentation is called **undifferentiated marketing**. Unfortunately this strategy can occur by default. For example, companies that lack a marketing orientation may practise undifferentiated marketing through lack of customer knowledge. Furthermore, undifferentiated marketing is more convenient for managers since they have to develop only a single product/marketing strategy. Finding out that customers have diverse needs, which can be met only by products with different characteristics, means that managers have to go to the trouble and expense of developing new products, designing new promotional campaigns, training the sales force to sell the new products, and developing new distribution channels. Moving into new segments also means that salespeople have to start prospecting for new customers. This is not such a pleasant activity as calling on existing customers who are well known and liked.

Differentiated marketing

Specific marketing mixes can be developed to appeal to all or some of the segments when market segmentation reveals several potential targets. This is called **differen-**

tiated marketing; it is a very popular market targeting strategy that can be found in sectors as diverse as cars, hotels and fashion retailing (see Figure 5.4). For example, Arcadia's segmentation of the fashion market revealed distinct customer groups for which specific marketing mixes could be employed. In response the group has a portfolio of shops that are distinctive in terms of shop name, style of clothing, décor and ambience. In all, the company has seven separate brands including, for example, Miss Selfridge (aimed at the 18–24 age group), Dorothy Perkins (aimed at women in their twenties and thirties) and Evans (which stocks women's clothes that are size 16+). Similarly, as part of its turnaround strategy, Marks & Spencer sought to move away from one brand (St Michael) with wide market appeal to a range of sub-brands such as Autograph (an upmarket brand) and Per Una, which is aimed at fashion-conscious women up to the age of 35. A differentiated target marketing strategy exploits the differences between marketing segments by designing a specific marketing mix for each segment. One potential disadvantage of a differentiated compared to an undifferentiated marketing strategy is the loss of cost economies. However, the use of flexible manufacturing systems can minimize such problems. The challenges of pursuing a differentiated marketing strategy are outlined in Marketing in Action 5.2.

Focused marketing

Just because a company has identified several segments in a market does not mean that it should serve them all. Some may be unattractive or out of step with its

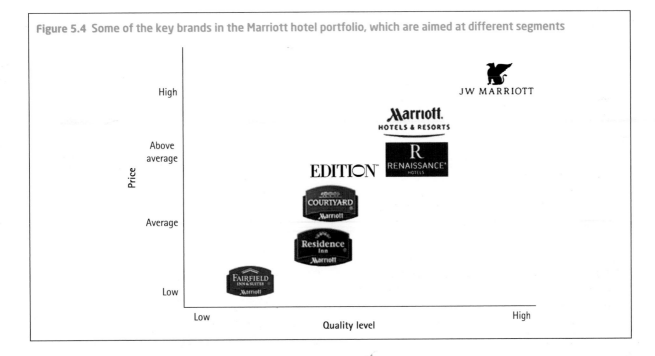

Figure 5.4 Some of the key brands in the Marriott hotel portfolio, which are aimed at different segments

Marketing in Action 5.2 The perils of differentiated marketing

> **Critical Thinking:** Below is a review of some of the risks associated with differentiated marketing strategies. Read and critically evaluate both the advantages and disadvantages of this approach.

Two of the risks associated with using a differentiated marketing strategy are creating confusion in the marketplace and spreading the organization's resources too thinly. The casual clothing retailer Gap Inc. is a classic case of the former. There are different segments of the market for casual clothes ranging from those who want to shop in discount outlets to those looking for smart casual garments for work or social events. To meet the needs of these different segments, Gap Inc. acquired both the Old Navy (discount fashions) and Banana Republic chains (smart casual). But a lack of sufficient differentiation between the three brands led to cannibalization of each other's sales, with first Old Navy taking sales from Gap and then Gap taking sales from Banana Republic as it tried to position itself away from the discount retailer.

Confusion and reputational damage can also be caused by how a brand owner chooses to differentiate. From example, the leading wine brand Wolf Blass chooses to identify most of its range by the colour of the label with variants like Yellow Label and Red Label sold in supermarkets while its more exclusive wines like Gold, Grey and Platinum Label are only available in specialist wine shops. However, because all of these brands share the Wolf Blass name, some consumers may associate the brand only with the low price (and moderate quality) wines that they see in supermarkets and not select it when choosing to buy an expensive wine.

A differentiated approach also puts great pressure on a management team to ensure that they understand and respond to the needs of different segments. Therefore when Alan Mulally took over the leadership of the Ford Motor Company he set about selling off a variety of prestigious brands that it had acquired, such as Land Rover, Jaguar, Aston Martin and Volvo, despite the fact that many of these were selling profitably. Instead, the plan was to put all the company's resources into the Ford brand under the umbrella of the OneFord strategy. For example, although the 2011 Fiesta was produced in five plants and sold in five continents, the car itself was the same. Focusing the company's energies in this way meant that Ford could generate above average profitability for its products. So while some of its peers like GM and Chrysler relied on government bailouts to stay afloat, Ford's more focused approach allowed it to survive more comfortably.

Based on: Gayatri and Madhav (2004);[13] Ritson (2010)[14].

business strengths. Perhaps the most sensible route would be to serve just one of the market segments. When a company develops a single marketing mix aimed at one target (niche) market it is practising **focused marketing**. This strategy is particularly appropriate for companies with limited resources. Small companies may stretch their resources too far by competing in more than one segment. Focused marketing allows research and development expenditure to be concentrated on meeting the needs of one set of customers, and managerial activities can thus be devoted to understanding and catering for those needs. Large organizations may not be interested in serving the needs of this one segment, or their energies may be so dissipated across the whole market that they pay insufficient attention to their requirements.

An example of a firm pursuing a focused marketing approach is Bang & Olufsen (B&O), the Danish audio electronics firm; it targets its stylish music systems at up-market consumers who value self-development, pleasure and open-mindedness. Anders Kwitsen, the company's chief executive, describes its positioning as 'high quality, but we are not Rolls-Royce – more BMW'. Focused targeting and cost control mean that B&O defies the conventional wisdom that a small manufacturer could not make a profit by marketing consumer electronics in Denmark.[15] One of the challenges for focused marketers is effectively evolving their targeting strategy as the market grows. For example, the sports nutrition supplements company Maximuscle traditionally focused on the narrow niche of bodybuilders but has evolved the brand through its marketing

Exhibit 5.6 Maximuscle aimed to overcome consumer resistance to using sports food supplements by including both images of leading athletes and product information in their advertising

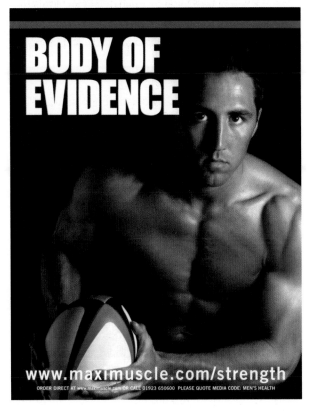

communications to target a broader base of lifestyle gym-goers and those active in sports (see Exhibit 5.6). To do this, it was necessary to overcome consumer resistance to sports supplements which has connotations of steroids and other banned substances. Similarly low-cost airlines that have traditionally focused on budget travellers have begun to expand their appeal to budget-conscious business travellers by offering some flights to primary airports like London's Gatwick and Paris Charles De Gaulle as well as offering priority boarding and access to frequent flyer, loyalty schemes.[16]

Customized marketing

The requirements of individual customers in some markets are unique, and their purchasing power sufficient to make viable the design of a discrete marketing mix for each customer. Segmentation at this disaggregated level leads to the use of **customized marketing**. Many service providers, such as advertising and marketing research agencies, architects and solicitors, vary their offerings on a customer-by-customer basis. They will discuss face to face with each customer their requirements, and tailor their services accordingly. Customized marketing is also found within organizational markets because of the high value of orders and the special needs of customers. Locomotive manufacturers will design and build products according to specifications given to them by individual rail transport providers. Similarly, in the machine tools industry, the German company Emag is a global leader in making 'multitasking' machines that cut metals used in industries like aerospace and vehicles. It practises customized marketing by manufacturing basic products at a cost-effective production site in eastern Germany but then finishing off or customizing these products in factories around the world that are located close to the customer.[17] Customized marketing is often associated with close relationships between suppliers and customers in these circumstances because the value of the order justifies a large marketing and sales effort being focused on each buyer.

One of the most fascinating developments in marketing in recent years has been the introduction of **mass customization** in consumer markets. This practice was initially pioneered by Japanese companies, who exploited their strengths in production systems and logistics to deliver customized products such as men's suits, bicycles and golf clubs to private consumers.[18] More and more products are now being customized to the needs of particular individuals. For example, at the Mercedes Sindelfingen plant near Stuttgart, every model passing through the plant has a pre-assigned customer, many of whom configure their cars via the Internet. Furthermore, many customers take delivery of their cars at the plant rather than from a dealer as has traditionally been the case. Online firms like Google allow customers to create a personalized iGoogle page that contains all key information sources, favourite websites and 'gmail' messages. But, increasingly, this is happening not just with technology companies but all leading brands. For example, NikeiD enables customers to design their own personal versions of Nike shoes and apparel. Initially only available online, Nike has followed up the success of this service by opening NikeiD studios in Nike Town stores around the world. Consumers create designs in the studio which can then be delivered either via the Nike Town stores or direct to their homes (see Exhibit 5.7).

Future technological developments are likely to significantly increase the prospects for true mass customization. For example, 3D printing is already enabling the production of individually customized items that are as cheap to make as production runs in the thousands thus eliminating the role of economies of scale.[19] Using a process known as additive manufacturing,

Exhibit 5.7 Diet Coke and Coke Zero: virtually identical drinks that are positioned very differently

Go to the website to see the best bits of Coca-Cola's advertising from the past 125 years.
www.mcgraw-hill.co.uk/textbooks/fahy

objects are created first from blueprints that can be adjusted and customized on a computer screen, and are then 'printed' out one layer at a time until the new product is built up. Because this kind of production does not need to happen in a factory, high levels of customization and niche production will be feasible.

Positioning

So far, we have examined two key aspects of the marketing management process, namely, market segmentation (where we look at the different needs and preferences that may exist in a market) and market targeting (where we decide which segment or segments of the market we are going to serve). We now arrive at one of the most important and challenging aspects of marketing: **positioning**. Positioning can be defined as:

the act of designing the company's offering so that it occupies a meaningful and distinct position in the target customer's mind.

This is the challenge that faces all organizations. All firms make products or provide services but, as we saw in Chapter 1, consumers buy benefits. Positioning is essentially that act of linking your product or service to the solutions that consumers seek and ensuring that, when they think about those needs, your brand is one of the first that comes to mind. For example, there is a segment of the car-buying market that values safety as one of its key purchasing criteria. Over the years, Swedish

car manufacturer Volvo successfully positioned itself as one of the safest cars in the market through a combination of its design and its advertising messages. When asked which car they thought was the safest, Volvo was consistently mentioned by customers though technical tests showed that it was not significantly safer than other brands in the market. This is the power of effective positioning: ensuring that your brand occupies a meaningful and distinct place in the target customer's mind. Volvo typically sells over 200,000 units globally and has been consistently profitable in recent years. The clarity of Volvo's positioning contrasts markedly with that of Saab, another Swedish car brand whose image declined so badly that it had to be rescued from bankruptcy by the Dutch car firm Spyker in 2010.

Effective positioning created an interesting problem for Coca-Cola (see Exhibit 5.6). Though not exclusively marketed towards females, 80 per cent of Diet Coke sales are to women. Research by the company showed that men were also interested in a low-calorie drink but were reluctant to drink Diet Coke. So Coca-Cola Zero, which has been dubbed 'bloke Coke', was targeted at the male market using very male-orientated advertising. Though its ingredients are virtually indistinguishable from those of Diet Coke, its market appeal is very different.[20]

Positioning is both important and difficult. It is important because today we live in an over-communicated society.[21] Consumers are constantly exposed to thousands of marketing messages per day and as we saw in Chapter 3, as few as 5 per cent of these messages may gain the attention of the target audience. To cut through this clutter, a company needs messages that are simple, direct and that resonate with the customer's needs. Failure to gain a position in the customer's mind significantly increases the likelihood of failure in the marketplace.

Developing a positioning strategy

Deciding what position to try to occupy in the market requires consideration of three variables, namely, the customers, the competitors and the company itself. In terms of customers we must examine what attributes matter to them – there is little point in seeking a position that is unimportant from the customer's point of view. In many markets, competitors are already well entrenched, so the next challenge is to find some differential advantage that ideally cannot easily be matched. Third, as implied by the resource-based view of the firm, the company should look at building a position based on its unique attributes as this increases the likelihood that advantage can be sustained.[22]

Once the overall positioning strategy is agreed, the next step is to develop a positioning statement. A positioning statement is a memorable, image-enhancing, written summation of the product's desired stature. The statement can be evaluated using the criteria shown in Figure 5.5. Coca-Cola has become one of the world's most valuable brands through its effective exploitation of catchy positioning slogans like 'Things go better with Coke' in the 1960s and 'It's the real thing' in its 1970s advertising.

1 *Clarity*: the idea must be perfectly clear, both in terms of target market and differential advantage. Complicated positioning statements are unlikely to be remembered. Simple messages such as 'BMW – The Ultimate Driving Machine', 'Carlsberg – Probably the Best Lager in the World' and 'L'Oréal – Because I'm Worth it' are clear and memorable (see Figure 5.6 and Exhibit 5.8).

2 *Consistency*: because people are bombarded with messages daily, a consistent message is required to break through this noise. Confusion will arise if, this year, we position on 'quality of service' and next year change this to 'superior product performance'. Some companies, like BMW, have used the same positioning – in BMW's case, 'The Ultimate Driving Machine' – for decades.

3 *Credibility*: the selected differential advantage must be credible in the minds of target customers. An attempt to position roll-your-own cigarette tobacco as an upmarket exclusive product failed due to lack of credibility. Similarly, Toyota's lack of credibility as an upmarket brand caused it to use 'Lexus' as the brand name for its top of the range cars.

4 *Competitiveness*: the chosen differential advantage must possess a competitive edge. It should offer something of value to the customer that the com-

Figure 5.6 Some classic advertising slogans

'We try harder.'	Avis
'Go to work on an egg.'	Egg Marketing Board
'Guinness is good for you.'	Guinness
'Don't be vague. Ask for Haig.'	Haig Scotch Whisky
'Happiness is a cigar called Hamlet.'	Hamlet
'Heineken refreshes the parts other beers cannot reach.'	Heineken
'Beanz Meanz Heinz.'	Heinz
'It is. Are you?'	The Independent
'Just do it.'	Nike
'Think small.'	Volkswagen

Source: www.adslogans.co.uk

petition is failing to supply. For example, the success of the iPod was based on the differential advantage of seamless downloading of music from iTunes, Apple's dedicated music store, to a mobile player producing high quality sound.

The perceptual map is a useful tool for determining the position of a brand in the marketplace. It is a visual representation of consumer perceptions of a brand and its competitors, using attributes (dimensions) that are important to consumers. The key steps in producing a perceptual map are as follows.

1 Identify a set of competing brands.

2 Identify – using qualitative research (e.g. group discussions) – the important attributes consumers use when choosing between brands.

3 Conduct quantitative marketing research where consumers score each brand on all key attributes.

4 Plot brands on a two-dimensional map (or maps).

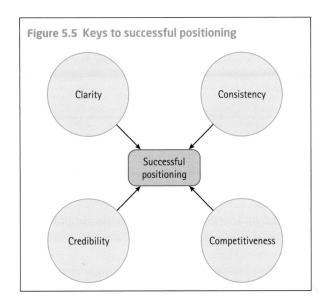

Figure 5.5 Keys to successful positioning

Exhibit 5.8 This advertisement for Lumix digital cameras powerfully illustrates its core value proposition

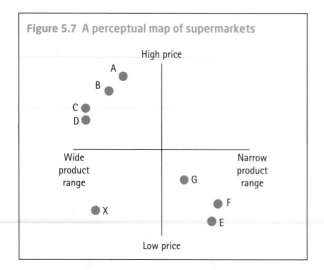

SUBMERGEABLE UP TO 10 METERS

LUMIX | Panasonic

Go to the website to see Lumix's advert for the T23 and how Panasonic highlight the camera's key features.
www.mcgraw-hill.co.uk/textbooks/fahy

Figure 5.7 shows a perceptual map for seven supermarket chains. The results show that the supermarkets are grouped into two clusters: the high-price, wide product range group; and the low-price, narrow product range group. These are indicative of two market segments and show that supermarkets C and D are close rivals, as measured by consumers' perceptions, and have very distinct perceptual positions in the marketplace compared with E, F and G. Perceptual maps are a visually appealing way of presenting a diverse market. They are also useful in considering strategic moves. For example, an opportunity may exist to create a differential advantage based on a combination of wide product range and low prices (as shown by the theoretical position at X).

Figure 5.7 A perceptual map of supermarkets

High price

- A
- B
- C
- D

Wide product range

Narrow product range

- G
- X
- F
- E

Low price

Repositioning

Frequently, perhaps because of changing customer tastes or poor sales performance, a product or service will need to be repositioned. **Repositioning** involves changing the target markets, the differential advantage, or both (see Figure 5.8). The first option is to keep product and target market the same but to change the image of the product. For example, many companies

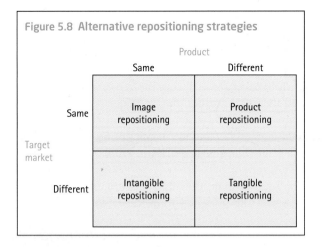

Figure 5.8 Alternative repositioning strategies

marketing products to older customers are realizing that they need to be very careful in not portraying this group as kindly, slightly doddery souls when many remain reasonably healthy and active into old age. Therefore, the Complan brand of powdered energy drinks has changed its image from one of a caring, sickbed 'meal replacement' drink to a proactive brand with a sense of humour, by using tongue-in-cheek cartoon characters on its packaging and in its advertising, engaged in lively activities like skateboarding and crowd surfing.[23] An alternative approach is to keep the same target market but to modify the product. For example, in the intensely competitive mass car market, Ford brands like the Mondeo have had a reputation for being dull, so Ford is investing heavily in trying to make its car designs more appealing to the consumer. A new design team was assembled and at the 2005 Frankfurt Motor Show, the new Ford Iosis was unveiled with a radical new design featuring doors that opened upwards, a sharply sloping windscreen and large wheels.

Some repositioning strategies involve retaining the product but changing the market segment it is aimed at. Lucozade, a carbonated drink, is a famous example of this kind of so-called 'intangible repositioning'.

Manufactured by Beecham's Foods, it was initially targeted at sick children. Marketing research found that mothers were drinking it as a midday pick-me-up and the brand was consequently repositioned to aim at this new segment. Subsequently the energy-giving attributes of Lucozade have been used to appeal to a wider target market – young adults – by means of advertisements featuring leading athletes and soccer players. The history of Lucozade shows how a combination of repositioning strategies over time has been necessary for successful brand building. Several other brands have sought to repeat what Lucozade has done. For example, Rubex, the vitamin C drink, has transformed its positioning from a cold and flu drink to one that assists young people in overcoming the effects of a hard night's clubbing, while Red Bull has moved from a drink associated with clubbing to a more mainstream energy drink. Cadbury's has sought to reposition Roses and Flake into the rapidly growing premium chocolate segment, while Jose Cuervo spent US$65 million on a promotional campaign entitled 'Vive Cuervo' (Live Cuervo) to broaden the appeal of tequila, which has traditionally been associated with student parties.[24]

When both product and target market are changed, a company is said to be practising 'tangible repositioning' (see Social Media Marketing 5.1). For example, a company may decide to move up- or down-market by introducing a new range of products to meet the needs of its new target customers. British Midland found it necessary to use both target and product repositioning in the face of growing competition in the airline business. The company was worried about its local British image and set about transforming itself into a global airline. It joined the Star Alliance led by Lufthansa and United Airlines, and commenced a long-haul service to the USA. It also spent £15 million on a corporate rebranding initiative to change its name from British Midland to bmi to create a more international appeal.

Social Media Marketing 5.1 Repositioning Old Spice

Critical Thinking: Below is a review of the successful repositioning of Old Spice. Read it and think of other brands that have tried to reposition. Critically assess the reasons for success or failure.

Old Spice is a brand of male grooming products and fragrances owned by the consumer goods group Procter & Gamble. Founded in the 1930s, the brand came to dominate the shaving foam and aftershave market and was promoted using a nautical theme with the ocean frequently appearing in its advertising and sailing ships on its packaging. By the time P&G took over the brand in 1990, it had become somewhat stale and old-fashioned.

But in the past decade, the brand's image has been revitalized through a combination of product development and effective social media marketing, most notably the viral marketing campaign featuring Isaiah Mustafa. In 2003, Old Spice introduced a body wash for men and even though the category was growing by almost 10 per cent per year, it faced stiff competition from rival brands like Lynx and Dove for Men. Unlike some of the new entrants into this space, Old Spice had a high level of masculine credibility – its most famous slogan being 'Old Spice – The Mark of a Man'. However research also showed that 60 per cent of body wash products were purchased by women. Therefore Old Spice needed a creative campaign that would appeal to and impact on both men and women in what is a low-involvement category.

This resulted in 'The Man Your Man Could Smell Like' campaign. It featured Mustafa – a US actor and former NFL footballer – and contained lines like 'Look at your man, now back at me' which clearly targeted women but was equally appealing to men. A key element of the campaign was to create a buzz about the advert and a conversation between men and women. The advert ran first on YouTube and Facebook, to coincide with a major push by rival Dove during the 2010 Super Bowl, and then on television during major shows where couples would be watching together such as *Lost* and *American Idol* and in cinema during Valentine's weekend. The advert quickly got millions of views and dozens of parodies.

To continue the conversation, Old Spice recorded 186 responses from Mustafa to fans who had commented on Facebook, Twitter and YouTube which generated further huge amounts of buzz. For example, in one video he proposes to a woman on behalf on one of his Twitter followers (she said yes, apparently!). In three days, the response campaign had generated 20 million views, Facebook fans increased by 60 per cent to 800,000 and Twitter followers increased by 2,700 per cent. Both the initial advert and the response campaigns were multiple award winners and helped to both humanize and modernize the brand. At the height of the campaign in June 2010, sales of Old Spice products rocketed by over 100 per cent.

Based on: Effie Worldwide (2011);[25] Sauer (2010)[26]

Summary

This chapter has examined the key activities of market segmentation, market targeting and positioning. The following issues were addressed.

1. The process of market segmentation: not all consumers in the market have the same needs and we can serve them better by segmenting the market into groups with homogeneous needs.

2. There are a variety of bases available for segmenting both consumer and industrial markets, and often a combination of bases is used to effectively segment markets. In consumer markets, behavioural variables such as benefits sought and purchase behaviour are particularly powerful bases for segmentation. Choice criteria are a key factor in segmenting organizational markets.

3. The five criteria for successful segmentation: effective, measurable, accessible, actionable and profitable.

4. The four generic target marketing strategies: undifferentiated marketing, differentiated marketing, focused marketing and customized marketing. Differentiated and focused marketing have their unique strengths and weaknesses, while customized marketing continues to grow in popularity.

5. What is meant by the concept of positioning, why it is important, and the need for clarity, consistency, credibility and competitiveness in a positioning statement. Consumers buy benefits, not products or services, and positioning is the key to conveying these benefits.

6. The concept of repositioning and the four repositioning strategies: image repositioning, product repositioning, intangible repositioning and tangible repositioning. Repositioning is challenging and should be undertaken with great care.

Study questions

1. Discuss the advantages of market segmentation.
2. You have been asked by a client company to segment the ice cream market. Use at least three different bases for segmentation and describe the segments that emerge.
3. Many consumer goods companies have recently been experimenting with the possibilities of a customized target marketing strategy. What are the advantages and limitations of such a strategy?
4. A friend of yours wants to launch a new breakfast cereal on the market but is unsure how to position the product. Develop a perceptual map of the breakfast cereal market identifying brands that compete in the same space and also if there are gaps where there are currently no major brands.
5. What is the difference between positioning and repositioning? Choose a brand that has been repositioned in the marketplace and describe both its old positioning and its new positioning. Is its repositioning strategy best described as image, product, intangible or tangible repositioning?
6. Visit Experian.co.uk and review the Mosaic Global geodemographic system. Select any one Mosaic group (e.g. Sophisticated Singles) and identify some products that could be targeted at this group and what kind of marketing strategy would be most appropriate for reaching the group.

Suggested reading

Agarwal, J., N. Malhorta and **R. Bolton** (2010) A Cross-National and Cross-Cultural Approach to Global Market Segmentation: An Application Using Consumers' Perceived Service Quality, *Journal of International Marketing*, **18** (3), 18–40.

Court, D. and **L. Narashiman** (2010) Capturing the World's Emerging Middle Class, *The McKinsey Quarterly*, **3,** 12–17.

Dibb, S. and **L. Simkin** (2009) Implementation Rules to Bridge the Theory/Practice Divide in Market Segmentation, *Journal of Marketing Management*, **25** (3/4), 375–96.

Pine, J.B. and **J.H. Gilmore** (2000) *Markets of One – Creating Customer-unique Value through Mass Customization*, Boston, MA: Harvard Business School Press.

Ries, A. and **J. Trout** (2001) *Positioning: The Battle for Your Mind*, New York: Warner.

Yankelovich, D. and **D. Meer** (2006) Rediscovering Market Segmentation, *Harvard Business Review*, **84** (2), 122–31.

References

1. **Hesseldal, A.** (2008) BlackBerry vs iPhone: RIM Takes It Up a Notch, *Businessweek.com*, 11 September; **Silverstein, B.** (2010) BlackBerry Lights Torch as Android Advances, *Brandchannel.com*, 4 August.
2. **Van Raaij, W.F.** and **T.M.M. Verhallen** (1994) Domain-specific Market Segmentation, *European Journal of Marketing*, **28** (10), 49–66.
3. **Hodson, S.** (2010) Skype Commands 13 Percent of International Calls, *The Inquisitor*, 3 May.
4. **Heile, C.** (2009) Brands: Taking a Narrow View, *Brandchannel.com*, 5 January.
5. **Buss, D.** (2011) Porsche 911 Makes U-Turn as Everyday Vehicle, *Brandchannel.com*, 28 March.
6. **Ross, M.** (2010) Porsche Passion, *Warc.com*.
7. **Tynan, A.C.** and **J. Drayton** (1987) Market Segmentation, *Journal of Marketing Management*, **2** (3), 301–35.
8. **Anonymous** (2007) The Boomers' Babies, *The Economist*, 11 August, 60.
9. **Anonymous** (2011) Peggy Sue Got Old, *The Economist*, 9 April, 67–8.
10. **O'Brien, S.** and **R. Ford** (1988) Can We at Last Say Goodbye to Social Class? *Journal of the Market Research Society*, **30** (3), 289–332.
11. **Mitchell, V.W.** and **P.J. McGoldrick** (1994) The Role of Geodemographics in Segmenting and Targeting Consumer Markets: A Delphi Study, *European Journal of Marketing*, **28** (5), 54–72.
12. **Corey, R.** (1978) *The Organisational Context of Industrial Buying Behavior*, Cambridge, MA: Marketing Science Institute, 6–12.
13. **Gayatri, D.** and **T. Phani Madhav** (2004) Gap and Banana Republic: Changing Brand Strategies with Fashion, Case 504-087-1, *European Case Clearing House*.
14. **Ritson, M.** (2010) Why Ford's Focus is the Best in the Business, *MarketingWeek.co.uk*, 4 August.
15. **Richards, H.** (1996) Discord Amid the High Notes, *The European*, 16–22 May, 23.
16. **Anonymous** (2011) In the Cheap Seats, *The Economist*, 29 January, 56.
17. **Marsh, P.** (2004) Mass-Produced for Individual Tastes, *Financial Times*, 22 April, 12.

18. **Westbrook R.** and **P. Williamson** (1993) Mass Customisation: Japan's New Frontier, *European Management Journal*, **11** (1), 38–45.

19. **Anonymous** (2011) The Printed World, *The Economist*, 12 February, 69–71.

20. **Madden, C.** (2007) Coca-Cola Zero: The Real Thing or the Same Thing? *Irish Times*, 16 March, 12.

21. **Ries, A.** and **J. Trout** (2001) *Positioning: The Battle For Your Mind*, New York: Warner.

22. **Fahy, J.** (2001) *The Role of Resources in Global Competition*, London: Routledge.

23. **Dowdy, C.** (2005) Advertisers Smoke Out Images of Pipes and Slippers, *Financial Times*, 7 November, 30.

24. **Silver, S.** (2003) Tequila Tries to Get Out of the Slammer, *Financial Times*, 22 May, 15.

25. **Effie Worldwide** (2011) Old Spice: The Man Your Man Could Smell Like, *Warc.com*.

26. **Sauer, A.** (2010) Media Too Quick to Label Old Spice Man a Failure, *Brandchannel.com*, 23 July.

Luxury brands are often associated with the core competences of creativity, exclusivity, craftsmanship, precision, high quality, innovation and premium pricing. Rolex, the leading name in luxury wristwatches, has been viewed as a symbol for prestige and performance for over a century. The crown logo of the Rolex brand symbolizes the superiority of the product and the sense of personal achievement associated with wearing it. Rolex was placed second on the list of Superbrands in 2010, which rates leading products based on reputation, quality, reliability and distinction of offerings, based on the emotional and functional benefits they provide when compared with competitors. Rolex has maintained its position as a market leader in the luxury watch market by engaging in a successful segmentation, target marketing and positioning strategy. However, this strategy presents a new challenge to Rolex, as it faces the difficult task of becoming the watch choice of a generation of younger consumers.

History

Rolex was founded in 1905 by German, Hans Wilsdorf and Alfred Davis. Wilsdorf and Davis was the original name of what later became the Rolex Watch Company. Hans Wilsdorf registered the trademark name 'Rolex' in Switzerland in 1908. It was selected as it was easy to pronounce in every language and short enough to figure on the dial of the watch. At that time, Swiss workshops produced mostly pocket watches as it was still difficult to manufacture small enough movements that could be used in a wristwatch. In 1910, a Rolex watch was the first wristwatch in the world to receive the Swiss Certificate of Precision, granted by the Official Watch Rating Centre in Bienne. In 1914, Kew Observatory in Great Britain awarded a Rolex wristwatch a class 'A' precision certificate which until that point had been reserved exclusively for marine chronometers. This led to Rolex watches becoming synonymous with precision. Wilsdorf later relocated Rolex to Geneva in 1919. In 1926, the company took a major step towards developing the world's first waterproof wristwatch named the Oyster. The Oyster watch featured a sealed case providing optimal protection. The following year the Oyster was worn by Mercedes Gleitze, a young English swimmer who swam the English Channel. The watch remained in perfect working order after the 10-hour swim. This gave rise to the use of testimonials by Rolex to convey the superiority of the brand.

In 1931, Rolex invented the world's first winding mechanism with a perpetual rotor. This system remains at the origin of every modern automatic watch. In the early 1950s, Rolex developed professional watches whose function went beyond that of simply telling time. The Submariner, launched in 1953, was the first watch guaranteed waterproof to a depth of 100 metres. In the same year, the expedition led by Sir Edmund Hillary, equipped with the Oyster Perpetual, became the first to reach the summit of Mount Everest.

Before his death in 1960, Hans Wilsdorf created a private trust run by a board of directors to ensure the company could never be sold. Today, Rolex is the largest single luxury watch brand, with estimated revenues of around US$3 billion and annual production of between 650,000 and 800,000 watches. Rolex has remained independent even as many major competitors have sought the shelter of conglomerates. It currently has 28 affiliates worldwide and maintains a network of 4,000 watchmakers in over 100 countries.

Watch industry

The world of luxury is not just exclusive, it is highly secretive too. Several of the large luxury brands are privately held, like Rolex, and therefore are not required to report annual or quarterly results. Many publicly listed companies, e.g. Louis Vuitton and Gucci, are part of much bigger companies which makes assessing the individual performance of these brands difficult to do with any accuracy. Many brands have responded to competition by merging into conglomerates. LVMH Louis Vuitton Moët Hennessy, the world's largest luxury goods company, with annual sales of more than US$15 billion, includes watch brands such as Tag Heuer, Zenith and Dior Watches. Compagnie Financière Richemont, the world's third largest luxury goods maker, owns watch brands such as Cartier, Baume and Mercier, Piaget, Jaeger-LeCoultre and Officine Panerai. Well-known brands Movado, Patek Philippe and Breitling remain essentially independent. In terms of watches, Switzerland possesses close to 100 per cent of the luxury market value which represents 48 per cent of the watch market value (see Table C5.1).

Recent trends in the luxury market

Exports of Swiss watches dropped 22 per cent in 2009 which represented the biggest drop since the Great Depression. The USA had the biggest decline of any importing country. Rolex depends on the USA for one-third of its sales, so it was particularly affected. Competitors such as Omega are less dependent on the US market for sales (only about 10 per cent).

Table C5.1 World's top luxury brands

Top luxury brands			
	Brand value $m	Brand contribution	Brand momentum
Louis Vuitton	19781	5	8
Hermès	8457	5	7
Gucci	7588	5	4
Chanel	5547	4	4
Hennessy	5368	5	9
Rolex	4742	2	6
Moët & Chandon	4279	5	9
Cartier	3964	3	2
Fendi	3199	2	5
Tiffany & Co	2383	1	6

Source: Millward Brown Optimer
Brand contribution is the proportion of financial value driven purely by brand equity.
Brand momentum is an indicator of short-term growth.

This fact, combined with the widely held perception of younger consumers that Omega is trendier, helped Swatch Group AG's Omega gain market share from Rolex. One reason may be that Omega was associated with more recent James Bond movies (worn by Pierce Brosnan in 1995 and Daniel Craig in 2006). Rolex, on the other hand, was favoured in earlier Bond movies starring Sean Connery. Rolex still maintained estimated sales three times the size of Omega's. Luxury watchmakers cut production in 2009 to adjust to lower demand from consumers owing to the economic conditions. Although most luxury watchmakers did not reduce prices, some had to adjust to currency fluctuations in specific markets. The strength of the Swiss franc, which gained 19 per cent against the euro, had an impact on profitability. This will continue to intensify the pressure to use Asian components in watches because Swiss-made parts are becoming more expensive.

In 2010, watch exports reached a value of 16.2 billion Swiss francs. This represents growth of 22.1 per cent compared with 2009, with the record levels of 2008 expected in the first half of 2011. Swiss watch manufacturers exported 26.1 million finished watches in 2010, an increase of 20.4 per cent, the highest since 2002. Asia was responsible for more than 50 per cent of the value of these exports, i.e. 8.5 billion Swiss francs. It also registered the highest growth, with an increase of 34.6 per cent compared with 2009. In terms of the number of watches, the proportion falls to 38.6 per cent, meaning that on average Asian customers purchased more expensive timepieces, with an average export price of nearly 800 francs. Europe accounted for slightly less than a third of Swiss watch exports (31.1 per cent) by value and registered growth of 10.4 per cent. Despite a lower share than Asia in value terms, Europe imported a larger volume of watches: 11.2 million timepieces compared to 10.1 million for Asia, with an average price of 415 Swiss francs. The USA recorded a higher increase than Europe, but from a lower base.

Growth of emerging markets

Despite signs of recovery in markets of Western countries, emerging markets such as China offer the brightest prospect for luxury goods in the near future. China has become the world's second largest consumer of luxury goods, surpassing the USA in 2008, with an annual growth in demand of 20 per cent. Today, China has an estimated 18,000 billionaires, 440,000 multi-millionaires, and a fast rising middle class of around 250 million who have high purchasing power, spending US$8 billion on luxury goods in 2007. Luxury Swiss watches have become the latest must-have accessory for newly affluent Chinese consumers, who invariably shop by brand rather than model. The most aspirational brand is Rolex,

cited by 31 per cent of Chinese consumers living in households with a monthly income in excess of US$1,300 (€883). According to *Time* (2007), 22 per cent of affluent consumers in China own a Rolex. Hong Kong is the world's biggest buyer of premium watches, but it has been estimated that 30 per cent of these are purchased by mainland Chinese consumers keen to avoid the 20 per cent luxury tax imposed on brands priced above US$1,200.

Challenges for Rolex

Rolex faces a number of significant challenges in the luxury market, which are outlined below.

Over-dependence on current target market – this represents a key challenge. Rolex is faced with building relevance among a younger audience. A new generation of affluent consumers is needed to generate a vital source of business in both established and emerging markets. Unfortunately, many younger consumers see Rolex as an older status symbol and not a contemporary icon of achievement. A large majority view Rolex as the watch choice of their predecessors and parents. The average Rolex customer is 45 or older and the brand now needs to build interest, relevance and aspiration among consumers in their thirties and younger, in order to drive long-term growth. It is in danger of being seen as an older symbol of personal wealth, instead of a crowning symbol of timeless human achievement. Similarly, the brand has been characterized as having a more 'male' identity. The opportunity of increasing its presence in the female segment has been identified as an area for development, but the company still appears to have difficulty in attracting new female customers. The positioning strategy that has been so successful for Rolex is in danger of isolating a new generation of consumers.

Counterfeit – like many high-priced, brand-name accessories, Rolex watches are among the most counterfeited brands of watches, illegally sold on the street and on the Internet. According to the FH, the association of the Swiss watch industry, counterfeiting causes damage of 800 billion Swiss francs to Swiss watchmakers. These fake watches are mainly produced in China owing to the ease of copying the general design (EU figures show that 54 per cent of fakes seized in 2004 originated in China) and retail anywhere from US$5 upwards to US$1000 for high-end replicas fabricated in gold. It is estimated that over 75 per cent of all replica watches produced annually are copies of Rolex Oyster Perpetual designs. It is widely accepted that the number of counterfeits on the market is larger than the number of original pieces. This figure serves as proof of the brand's aspirational quality.

Distribution – Rolex maintains its positioning strategy by limiting production, even as demand increases. For luxury goods, scarcity in the marketplace can influence value, spur demand and contribute to long-term appreciation. Rolex also ensures that its watches are sold only in designated stores. The crystal prism that indicates a store is an 'Official Rolex

Table C5.2 Price segmentation in the watch market

Price segmentation in the watch market (factory-gate)			
Price category	**Definition**	**Technology***	**Brand examples**
Over CHF3,000 (over EUR2,000) Between CHF500 and CHF3,000	'Exclusive luxury' segment	M	*Patek Philippe, Breguet*
(between EUR350 and EUR2000) Between CHF200 and CHF 500	'Accessible luxury' segment	M/Q	*Rado, Zenith, IWC*
(between EUR150 and EUR350) Below CHF200 (below EUR150)	Mid-priced segment Low-priced segment	Q/M Q	*Tissot, Maurice Lacroix Swatch, Coach*

Sources: Pictet, FH.

*Q = Quartz movement; M = Mechanical movement; Bold typeface indicates dominant technology.

Dealer' is highly prized. Rolex seeks dealers with high-end images, relatively large stores and attractive locations that can provide outstanding service. Maintaining this standard is not always easy. The company previously had a dispute with Tiffany because the retailer was imprinting its name on the Rolex watches it sold. When Tiffany refused to stop, Rolex dropped Tiffany as an official retailer. Similarly, in the 1990s, as part of an effort to control sales of their goods in the grey market, Rolex cancelled agreements with 100 dealers. More recently it fought a lengthy court battle with online retailer eBay seeking an injunction to prevent the sale of Rolex-branded watches by the online auctioneer. The Supreme Court stated in its decision that eBay must take preventative measures to ensure that no counterfeit goods are sold under the pretence of being authentic Rolex watches.

Branding – Rolex has also focused on maintaining the purity of its brand image. Many luxury-goods makers have used their original product as a springboard for brand extensions, e.g. Cartier and Mont Blanc, while others have licensed their brand to other manufacturers. Rolex has, so far, not diversified into the production of parallel products. However, it did launch the Tudor brand, aimed at competing with Tag Heuer and other competitors within the accessible luxury market. For example, the price tag on a typical Rolex started at US$2,000 and could go as high as US$180,000 whereas a Tudor watch ranges from US$850 to US$4,000. (see Table C5.2 for price segmentation). There is no direct reference to the Tudor brand on the official Rolex website and as it is owned by Rolex, no financial information is made available to the public. In an effort to reposition the Tudor line as a more youthful and accessible brand, Tudor previously endorsed Tiger Woods. The clear distinction between both brands has prevented any dilution of the value of the Rolex brand in the luxury market. However, the launch of Tudor in this market segment may have contributed to Rolex being ineffective at reaching a younger market.

Communications – Rolex uses a number of marketing communication tools to effectively convey its posi-
tioning strategy. Print advertising in upmarket publications such as the *Financial Times* and *Vogue* remain popular. Sponsorship and testimonials remain central to its marketing communications. Rolex aims to select people who have achieved something so that it can reinforce the similar values of the brand. Rolex has links to the arts (Michael Bublé), motor sports (Jackie Stewart), equestrian, exploration, skiing and yachting. It has had a long association with golf since 1967, when Arnold Palmer endorsed the brand. Today it sponsors major events such as the Open, the Augusta Masters and the Ryder Cup and in a bid to attract younger consumers, Rolex has sponsored current players such as Ricky Fowler, Adam Scott and Martin Kaymer. Finally, the brand remains a partner of the Wimbledon tennis tournament since 1978, with the Rolex clock synonymous with the scoreboard on Centre Court. Similarly, Rolex is robustly involved in philanthropy. It is the initiator of a mentoring programme, the Rolex Mentor and Protégé Arts Initiative, launched in 2002 as well as the Rolex Awards for Enterprise launched in 1978. These carefully selected methods of communication all reinforce its positioning.

Conclusion

In the future, Rolex will face greater competition, particularly in Asia, as competitors search for new ways to gain market share. The large luxury goods conglomerates enjoy certain advantages over independent firms. Many have restructured operations to take advantage of size and significantly reduce costs, enjoying synergies in advertising and marketing. The conglomerates may also be more willing to source from Asia, where labour costs are considerably lower than Switzerland. These conglomerates also have successful brands targeted at a younger market. With an ageing target market and difficulty in attracting a younger consumer base Rolex could become a prisoner of its own strategy. The strategy has been so well defined that it would be difficult for the company to change radically or become more innovative. It might be difficult to communicate any new strategy to customers without confusing them, leaving some market opportunities unattainable in the future.

▶ # Questions

1. Evaluate the alternative bases that Rolex might use to segment its market. Which base would you recommend and why?
2. Evaluate the current market targeting strategy being used by Rolex. Is it appropriate?
3. Discuss the key factors contributing to the success of Rolex's positioning strategy.
4. 'Rolex could become a prisoner of its own strategy.' Critically evaluate the advantages and disadvantages of implementing a repositioning strategy for Rolex.

This case was prepared by David Cosgrave, University of Limerick from published sources as a basis for class discussion rather than to illustrate either effective or ineffective management.

Part 2

**MARKETING
SHOWCASE**

A new Marketing Showcase video featuring an exclusive interview with BMW's General Manager for Marketing Communications (UK) is available to lecturers for presentation and discussion in class.

Creating Customer Value

Chapter 6
Value through Products and Brands

Chapter outline

What is a product?

Product differentiation

Branding

Building brands

Managing brands

Managing product and brand portfolios

Managing brands and product lines over time: the product life cycle

New product development

Learning outcomes

By the end of this chapter you will understand:

1 what is meant by a product in marketing terms
2 the differences between products and brands
3 the alternative ways of differentiating products
4 the key aspects of building and managing a successful brand
5 how to manage a diverse product or brand portfolio
6 how product performance evolves over time
7 the importance of innovation and the new product development process.

Nespresso

Traditionally, the coffee market comprised two broad segments, namely, the at-home market where consumption was largely pre-ground, instant coffee and contrasted with the on-trade segment in cafés and bars where, particularly in Europe, the coffee was ground from roasted beans generating the distinctive coffee aroma and full flavour. Some key trends have radically changed consumer behaviour in the at-home segment. First is the growth in entertaining at home rather than going out, which has driven the demand for

everything from the recipes of celebrity chefs to changes in house design. Combined with a growing switch from tea to coffee, it meant that consumers became more discerning about the kind of coffee that they consumed at home, with an emerging preference towards more gourmet coffees. And, third, there is the trend towards individualization which is apparent in everything from telephones to beers to personal computers. This has given rise to a new business – portion coffees, in which Nespresso has been the undisputed market leader.

The Nespresso system consists of individually portioned aluminium capsules of five grams of roast and ground coffee made for exclusive use in specially designed coffee machines. The capsules are sealed to preserve the freshness for six months after production and the Nespresso system has the advantage of being clean and easy to use compared with traditional, hand-measured espresso coffee. Each capsule corresponds to a single cup of coffee and consumers can choose from eight coffee varieties. The brand's owner Nestlé does not make any money from the sale of the machines – it is the capsules, with a profit margin of up to 50 per cent, that drive the profitability of the business.

Nespresso was initially targeted at the office market, but sales in this segment were disappointing. It was then that Nestlé decided to target high-income households who were more likely to be discerning coffee drinkers. Distribution through supermarkets was rejected in favour of department stores and other premium retail outlets. The company also developed the *Nespresso Club*, which offered customers around-the-clock order-taking, prompt delivery and personalized advice. It now has 7 million members worldwide. Using a CRM system heavy users were tracked and if orders were not received by anticipated dates, these users could be contacted to ensure that their machines were working properly, etc. The brand's positioning has been unashamedly upmarket. Its slogan is simply 'What else?' and the popular US actor, George Clooney, has been the face of the brand since 2007. He is renowned for his suave, sophisticated yet personable style which is seen as perfect for an up-market brand that Nestlé now wants to have broader appeal.

Nestlé's product innovation and brand building efforts have revolutionized home coffee consumption. The Nespresso brand has achieved an annual sales growth of over 30 per cent since 2000 and it has been enhanced by the opening of over 200 Nespresso boutiques (retail outlets) in leading cities around the world. While many coffee shops struggle due to the recession, in-home coffee consumption has risen by 17 per cent, much of this growth due to consumers trading up to the more expensive portion coffee options.[1]

As we saw in Chapter 1, the essence of marketing is the delivery of value to some customer group. Products and brands are often the embodiment of that value proposition. For example, Kodak may well manufacture film but it understands that its business is allowing its customers to collect and retain memories. That is just as well because film technology is rapidly being replaced by digital technology and by consumers collecting and sharing memories via mobile phones and online. Old 'technologies' like 35 mm film and paper printing are quickly becoming outdated, with up to 30 per cent of digital camera owners never printing their pictures. Kodak has been attempting to respond to these changes by focusing on digital photography but the pace of change in its sector has been so quick that, once one of the world's leading brands, it had fallen out of the Interbrand Top 100 global brands by 2008. In the same way, the printed book that you are now reading may become an outdated technology. In 2010, Amazon reported that e-books were outselling printed versions for the first time. The benefit which you are seeking, namely, learning about marketing can be satisfied in different ways and it is the job of the marketer to anticipate these types of changes and develop the appropriate solutions that customers are looking for.

This chapter will deal with all these issues. First, we will begin by examining what we mean by the term 'product' and then explaining the difference between a product and a brand, which is one of the most important distinctions that students of marketing must grasp. Then we will take a comprehensive look at the different aspects of managing modern brands. Many firms, such as global corporations like Diageo or Colgate, can have an extensive range of brands, so we will also examine how to manage these portfolios of brands or products. As the Kodak example shows, the demand for products can change very rapidly, so we will look, too, at how to manage products and brands effectively over time. An important element of this is innovation and ensuring a steady supply of new products, which is also discussed.

What is a product?

Conventionally, when thinking about products, people tend to think of tangible items such as a mobile phone, a plasma screen television or a kettle and so on. These are all products but in marketing terms, the definition of what comprises a product is much broader. A visit to a theme park like Legoland is a product, so is a sports star like Usain Bolt, so is the running of the bulls in Pamplona, the fund-raising efforts of the International Red Cross and the political activities of the Liberal Democratic party (see Exhibit 6.1). In marketing terms, any form of value that is offered in exchange for money, votes or time is a product. In recent years, we have seen an increase in the marketing of ideas. For example, **social marketing** has emerged as a field of study due to the increase in marketing efforts behind socially beneficial causes such as the reduction in obesity, alcoholism and the promotion of wilderness protection, human rights and so on.

One of the most effective ways to think about products is in terms of their mix of tangible and intangible components (see Figure 6.1). Some products are high on tangible components and the company's marketing of these products places a great deal of emphasis on these tangible elements. Those at the intangible end of the spectrum are usually referred to as services and in Chapter 7 we will focus more specifically on the types of marketing efforts that are employed when creating value through service, experiences and relationships. But it is important to remember that almost all value offerings combine elements of both tangible and intangible components. Apple markets innovative handheld items like smartphones and tablets but the experience of the Apple store is an important part of its offering. A consultation with a psychotherapist is largely an intangible, mental activity but it will take place in a physical setting such as a consultation room (that probably contains a couch!).

The next important distinction that needs to be made is between products and brands. As we saw above a product can be anything that has the capacity to satisfy customer needs by providing some form of benefit or value. **Brands**, on the other hand, fulfil the very important function of distinguishing the offering of one company from those of others in a competitive environment. The word 'brand' is derived from the old Norse word 'brandr', which means 'to burn' as brands were and still are the means by which livestock owners mark their animals to identify ownership.[2] As we shall see below, branding has become an ever more important aspect of marketing. This is due to the fact that the technical differences between products are becoming fewer and fewer. For example, the competing brands of many basic consumer electronics like DVD players may all be made in the same factory on the same production line. The technical features of the product are mainly the same – the only element that differs is the name. In these situations, value is derived less from the actual product and more from the brand associations. The power of brands to affect perceptions is particularly noticeable in blind product testing, where customers often fail to distinguish between competing

Exhibit 6.1 Top US basketball player LeBron James has astutely managed his personal brand to win multiple endorsement contracts with leading firms like Nike, McDonald's and State Farm

Figure 6.1 The physical goods-service continuum

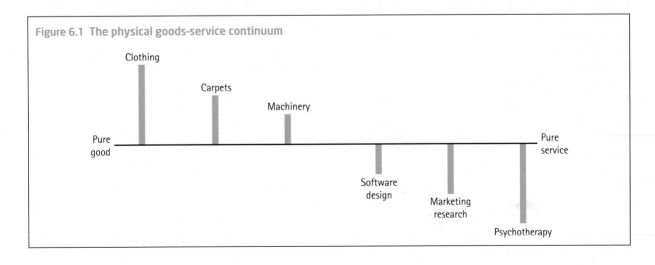

offerings even though they may have a high level of loyalty to one brand. The power of brands over products can also be seen in the way that some products are more commonly known by the brand name than by the product name.

Product differentiation

To understand fully both the nature of the product offering and how it can be best distinguished from those of competitors, it has been customary to think in terms

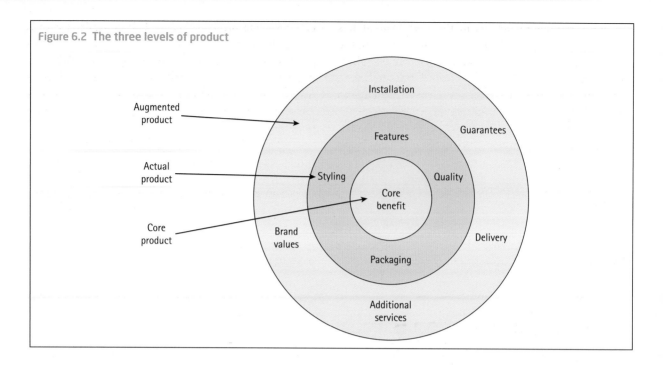

Figure 6.2 **The three levels of product**

of the different levels of product (see Figure 6.2). At the most basic level, there is the core benefit provided by the product, such as cars that provide transportation or telephones that provide a means of communication. Products will quickly decline if the core benefit can be met most effectively in another way as we saw in the case of Kodak above. Around the basic benefit is the 'actual product' the consumer purchases, which comprises certain features, styling, and so on. For example, a Neff electric oven is an actual product, which is a blend of design, style, features and packaging assembled to meet the needs of the market. There is also a third level of product, namely the 'augmented product'. This is the additional bundle of benefits that are added to a product, and typically include elements like guarantees, additional services and additional **brand values**. For example, the Lexus GS includes extras like a keyless entry system, air-conditioned front seats, Bluetooth connectivity for mobile phones, parking-assist sensors and a rear electric sunshade. Product differentiation can take place at any of these three levels.

Core differentiation

The most radical product differentiation takes place at the core level and usually arises when there are significant technological breakthroughs. Therefore, the core benefit of keeping track of our appointments has moved from paper diaries to electronic ones stored on PCs or mobile phones with significant implications for paper diary manufacturers like Filofax. Similarly, the music industry

has been transformed many times as technological changes enabled consumers to switch first from albums to CDs and then from CDs to digital downloading. The first change meant a significant rise in profits for music companies, the second, a significant fall. Core differentiation also occurs due to shifts in strategic thinking. For example, for years, airlines have been trying to outdo each other by competing on actual differentiation such as expanding menu items on flights. Low-cost carriers have made huge inroads in the business by simply focusing again on the core benefit, namely, moving people from one location to another and by removing – or charging customers for – any extras.

Actual differentiation

Actual differentiation occurs when organizations aim to compete on the basis of elements of the product such as its quality, its design, its features or its packaging. Quality is a key aspect of the product and has long been positively associated with corporate performance. It refers to both the fact that a product is free from defects and that it meets the needs of customers. Around the world, most companies look to the uniform standards of the International Organization for Standardization (ISO) for quality guidelines through its various certifications such as ISO 9001. Operational systems such as total quality management (TQM) are employed to emphasize the relentless pursuit of quality. Problems with quality regularly undermine the marketing efforts of companies. For example, Toyota is one of the most renowned brands in the world but it has suffered significant quality problems involving both the acceleration and braking of some of its car brands in 2009 and 2010. In all, a total of over 9 million Toyota vehicles have had to be recalled resulting in damage to the brand as well as potentially expensive legal judgments against it. Product safety is particularly crucial in industries such as food, transport and medicines. How firms deal with these problems is also very important.

Tropicana aims to differentiate itself through the quality of its products.
www.mcgraw-hill.co.uk/textbooks/fahy

With the increased difficulty of differentiating products based on their features many companies turn to elements like product design. For example, Evian is one of Europe's leading bottled water brands, but its position was being eroded by a range of local competitors in different countries. Water bottles had traditionally been designed to meet the needs of retailers allowing for easy storage on shelves, but Evian's research had indicated that consumers wanted a bottle that fitted with their lifestyles. It released a new looped bottle cap and demand in France tripled in the year of the bottle's launch[3]. Other leading firms like Dyson, Apple and Sony are renowned for their design capability. Key to effective design is a deep understanding of customer lifestyles and preferences as illustrated by the example of Danish firm, Biomega bikes (see Marketing in Action 6.1).

Marketing in Action 6.1 Biomega

Critical Thinking: Below is a review of the innovative bicycle designs made by Biomega. Read it and, using Figure 6.2, evaluate how Biomega is differentiating its products from its competitors'.

Bicycle theft is one of the biggest challenges facing urban bike owners and many people attempt to solve it by investing heavily in expensive locking devices or choosing to ride around on very old, cheap bikes. The Danish firm, Biomega, has come up with a revolutionary bike design that integrates the lock within the structure of the frame. If a would-be thief tries to cut the wire, the bike becomes unrideable, but repairable and there is no need for the customers to carry an extra lock. Named the Boston and made in collaboration with the lifestyle brand, Puma, the bike was launched in 2009. It has a stylish design and is also foldable, allowing for easy transportation.

In 2010, Biomega launched a further five designs with Puma that each combine chosen aspects of BMXs, cruisers, folding bikes and fixed-wheel designs. They were again designed for urban use enabling riders to switch between fixed and single gears and were targeted at both men and women. They offer more than 120 varieties of optional extras and colour choices which gives customers the option of individualizing their own bicycle. Each bike is supplied with a sticker book of bike names allowing customers to choose one or create one of their own. They are sold both online and through dedicated bike retailers. Biomega focuses solely on urban bike design and development and its vision is to change the way society imagines urban transportation. It claims to be the first bicycle manufacturer to see the bike as a lush piece of 'furniture for locomotion' and it considers cars to be its primary competitor.

Packaging involves all those decisions on the kind of container or wrapper used for the product. In the past, the primary purpose of packaging was simply to protect the product but in modern marketing it has a much more significant role in terms of attracting attention, carrying information about 'the product and conveying elements of the product's positioning. For example, the packaging of Apple products is highly distinctive with a focus on style and minimalism. Organizations frequently change their product packaging as part of their marketing strategy but this is a difficult and risky thing to do (see Exhibit 6.2). For example, the fair trade tea and coffee company Cafédirect, changed its packaging in 2009 to draw a clearer link between its products and the actual farmers who grow them to reflect the product's authenticity. A major packaging change may mean that some existing customers no longer recognize or can find the product.

There are several important ethical dimensions to packaging as well. Slack packaging describes the

Exhibit 6.2 The change to the packaging of Tropicana orange juice from the old on the left to the new on the right was controversial. What are your thoughts on the packaging?

Old   New

situation where products are packaged in oversized containers giving the impression that they contain more than they actually do. Accurate labelling is also a significant issue, particularly in the case of food products. For example, in the UK, the 'country of origin' is only the last country where the product was 'significantly changed'. So oil pressed from Greek olives in France can be labelled 'French' and foreign imports that are packed in the UK can be labelled 'produce of the UK'. Consumers should be wary of loose terminology. For example, Bachelors Sugar Free Baked Beans actually contain 1.7 g of sugar per 100 g, Kerry LowLow Spread, which is marketed as low in fat, contains 38 g of fat per 100 g and Walkers Lite crisps are a hefty 22 per cent fat. Attempts by consumer groups to have labelling systems that highlight this information have been resisted by leading manufacturers and retailers, who favour a system whereby levels of sugar, fats and salt are given as a percentage of an adult's 'guideline daily amount'.[4] Similarly EU legislation aims to outlaw vague claims such as 'vitalize your body and mind' (Red Bull) or 'cleanse and refresh your body and soul' (Kombucha).[5]

Augmented differentiation

Finally, organizations may choose to differentiate their offerings on the augmented dimensions. Most differenti-

ation efforts take place at this level. Firms are constantly looking for new features that they can add which will give them an advantage in the marketplace. For example, mobile phone manufacturers are constantly trying to improve dimensions like screen size and resolution, weight and portability, navigation features and reliability. However, these types of advantages are often short-lived, being quickly imitated by competitors or becoming standard parts of the offering of all major rivals. As a result, firms are putting greater efforts into intangible changes which cannot be so easily imitated. These intangible elements are captured in the brand and it is to this key decision that we now turn.

Branding

Developing a brand is difficult, expensive and takes time. We have seen that brands enable companies to differentiate their products from competitive offerings, but we must look at the benefits of brands for both organizations and consumers in more detail.

The benefits of brands to organizations

Strong brands deliver the following benefits to organizations.

Company value

The financial value of companies can be greatly enhanced by the possession of strong brands. The concept of **brand equity** is used to measure the strength of the brand in the marketplace and high brand equity generates tangible value for the firm in terms of increased sales and profits. For example, Nestlé paid £2.5 billion (€3.6 billion) for Rowntree, a UK confectionery manufacturer – a sum six times its balance sheet value. However, the acquisition gave Nestlé access to Rowntree's stable of brands, including KitKat, Quality Street, After Eight and Polo.

Consumer preference and loyalty

Strong brand names can have positive effects on consumer perceptions and preferences. This in turn leads to brand loyalty where satisfied customers continue to purchase a favoured brand. Over time some brands, such as Apple, Harley-Davidson and Virgin, become cult brands: consumers become passionate about the brand and levels of loyalty go beyond reason[6] (see Social Media Marketing 6.1). The strength of brand loyalty can be seen when companies try to change brands, such as Coca-Cola's proposed introduction of New Coke, or when the brand is threatened with extinction such as Bewley's Cafés in Dublin.[7]

Social Media Marketing 6.1 Facebook fans and brand communities

> **Critical Thinking:** Below is a review on the growth of Facebook fan pages. Read it and evaluate the pages where you are currently a fan. Why have these pages appealed to you? Reflect on your level of attachment to the brand or organization.

Brand communities have been formally defined as a 'specialized, non-geographically bound community based on a structured set of relationships among admirers of a brand'. Some have emerged organically and in other instances leading brands have attempted to create communities of followers. Among the most famous have been cult brands like Harley-Davidson

The Harley Owners Group – initially set up to counter the damage to the company's image caused by an association with Hell's Angels – consists of 866,000 members who organize bike rides, training courses, social events and charity fund-raisers. They pore over motorcycle magazines and wear Harley-branded gear to feel like rugged individualists. Over 250,000 attended the brand's centenary, held in Milwaukee in 2003.

Facebook has become the new vehicle through which brands can communicate with their communities of fans. The largest Facebook brand fan communities in 2011 were:

1 YouTube – 39.9 million fans
2 Coca-Cola – 31.1 million
3 Disney – 26.2 million
4 Starbucks – 23.2 million
5 Oreo – 21.5 million

Facebook pages can be used for brand communications, running competitions, handling complaints, new announcements and so on. The creation of original, entertaining and shareable content such as videos and applications is critical to the popularity of a fan page. Pages also provide a forum for fans to share stories about the brand, to show how it is a part of their lives and to connect with like-minded devotees.

Several different metrics can be used to assess the overall effectiveness of a Facebook page. Total fan numbers are important but so also are the trends in these numbers. Many pages are growing in popularity while others are falling quickly. This is influenced by levels of page engagement which can also be measured in a variety of ways including number of posts, number of comments, participation in competitions, and so on. Some leading brands, nervous about possible negative commentary, do not allow fans to post comments on their official pages. These companies see their page more as a channel of communication to customers rather than a forum that is created by both the brand owners and its community of users. As such, Facebook pages may lure brand owners into thinking that they have a brand community when in reality they do not. True brand communities have a much higher level of connection and engagement with their favoured brands.

Based on: Balwani (2009),[8] Shayon (2011)[9].

Barrier to competition

The impact of the strong, positive perceptions held by consumers about top brands means it is difficult for new brands to compete. Even if the new brand performs well on blind taste tests, this may be insufficient to knock the market leader off the top spot. This may be one of the reasons that Virgin Coke failed to dent Coca-Cola's domination of the cola market.

High profits

Strong, market-leading brands are rarely the cheapest. Brands such as Kellogg's, Coca-Cola, Mercedes, Apple and Intel are all associated with premium prices. This is because their superior brand equity means that consumers receive added value over their less powerful rivals. Strong brands also achieve distribution more readily and are in a better position to resist retailer demands for price discounts. Research into return on investment for US food brands supports the view that strong brands are more profitable. The number one brand's average return was 18 per cent, number two achieved 6 per cent, number three returned 1 per cent, while the number four position was associated with a minus 6 per cent average return on investment.[10]

Base for brand extensions

A strong brand provides a foundation for leveraging positive perceptions and goodwill from the core brand to brand extensions. Examples include Pepsi Max, Lucozade Sport, Smirnoff Ice and Google Scholar. The new brand benefits from the added value that the brand equity of the core brand bestows on the extension.

The benefits of brands to consumers

Brands also provide consumers with a variety of benefits as follows.

Communicates features and benefits

In the first instance, brands are a source of information about a product. Through their associated marketing communications, they communicate information about a product and its benefits which assist consumers in making a buying decision. The associated brand elements also make it easier for consumers to identify products.

Reduces the risk in purchasing

As we saw in Chapter 3, consumers experience a range of potential risks when they are making a purchase including functional risks (that the product does not perform to expectations), financial risk (that is not worth the price that is paid) as well as social risk (that the product produces social embarrassment). Brands reduce these risks because consumers can trust the brands they choose based on past experiences.

Simplifies the purchase decision

As we have seen already, we live in an over-communicated society where consumers are faced with a proliferation of product choices. To rationally evaluate all these options is impossible, so brands make consumers' lives easier by providing shortcuts for product choices. Trusted and preferred brands are purchased again and again giving rise to the notion of brand loyalty.

Symbolic value

Most importantly of all, brands provide consumers with the opportunity for self-expression. Brands of clothing, music, cars, perfume and so on are powerful indicators of the consumer's personality-type (see Exhibit 6.3). For example, recent research has demonstrated the role of brands in signalling one's desirability to potential mates.[11]

Brands are not just a consumer phenomenon. They are also increasingly important in the worlds of industrial and technology marketing. For example, although many people would not recognize a microprocessor, the chances are that they have heard of Intel, one of the world's leading technology firms who have invested heavily in branding. But it is not something that is simple, as Microsoft found in its forays into brand building. An advertising campaign featuring its founder Bill Gates and comedian Jerry Seinfeld confused many consumers.[12] The widespread development of brands in politics, popular culture and elsewhere means that the ethical dimensions of branding have taken on even greater importance (see Ethical Debate 6.1).

Exhibit 6.3 Brands like Ralph Lauren's Polo use celebrities such as professional polo player Ignacio Figueras in its advertising to convey symbolic value

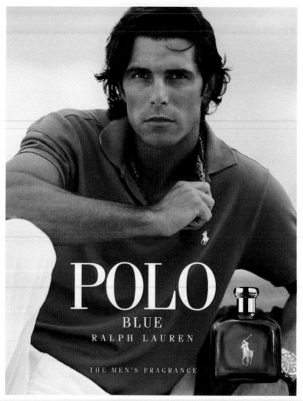

Ethical Debate 6.1 Brand values and the value of a brand

Inherent in the notion of a brand is the concept of value. When a consumer chooses a certain brand, they are doing so on the basis that a given brand delivers a certain level of value. But how accurate is this perception? For example, when a consumer buys a leading brand of running shoe, is she buying a higher level of value than if she bought a lesser-known brand or a cheaper running shoe? Consumers who are brand loyal would typically argue that a leading brand equates with better quality, but the research evidence does not always support this position. For example, a study published in the *British Journal of Sports Medicine* in 2007 showed that low- to medium-cost running shoes in each of three brands provided the same (if not better) cushioning of in-shoe pressure than high-cost running shoes.[13] A high-price brand, in this case, does not equate to greater levels of value as measured by product quality.

Critics of branding argue that brands do not provide value but rather an illusion of value. Vast sums are spent creating brands that are essentially not really all that different. Consumers pay more for leading brands in the belief that these are superior to other brands in terms of quality and specifications, when often this is not the case. A way out of this dilemma is to fully understand what we mean by consumer value. As shown in Chapter 3, consumers choose products for rational as well as emotional reasons. Brands are selected not only for their technical attributes but also for personal and social reasons. Should a consumer not have the option to select a brand if that brand, for example, makes them feel good about themselves or gives them the feeling that they are impressing their peers? Consumer societies are about choice and, increasingly, consumers have the information that they need to make informed choices. But, despite this, the debate concerning the real value of brands is likely to continue to rage into the future.

Suggested reading: Adamson (2006);[14] Klein (2000)[15].

Reflection: Critics of marketing contend that brand creation is unnecessary. Consider the points above and decide how you would respond.

Building brands

Building brands involves making decisions about the brand name and how the brand is developed and positioned in the marketplace.

Naming brands

Three brand name strategies can be identified: family, individual and combination.

A **family brand name** is used for all products – for example, Philips, Heinz and Google. The goodwill attached to the family brand name benefits all brands, and the use of the name in advertising helps the promotion of all of the brands carrying the family name. The risk is that if one of the brands receives unfavourable publicity or is unsuccessful, the reputation of the whole range of brands can be tarnished. This is also known as 'umbrella branding'. Some companies create umbrella brands for part of their brand portfolios to give coherence to their range of products. For example, Sony has created PlayStation for its range of video game consoles.

The **individual brand name** does not identify a brand with a particular company – for example, Procter & Gamble does not use its company name on its brands Duracell, Head & Shoulders, Pampers, Pringles, and so on (see Table 6.4). This may be necessary when it is believed that each brand requires a separate, unrelated identity. In some instances, the use of a family brand name when moving into a new market segment may harm the image of the new product line. One famous example is the decision to use the Levi's family brand name on a new product line – Levi's Tailored Classics – despite marketing research information which showed that target customers associated the name Levi's with casual clothes, thus making it incompatible with the smart suits the company was launching. This mistake was not repeated by Toyota, which abandoned its family brand name when it launched its up-market executive car, the Lexus.

In the case of combination brand names, family and individual brand names are combined. This capitalizes on the reputation of the company while allowing the individual brands to be distinguished and identified (e.g. Kellogg's All Bran, Nokia N Series, Microsoft Windows XP).

Much careful thought should be given to the choice of brand name since names convey images. For example, Renault chose the brand name Safrane for one of its executive saloons because research showed that this brand name conveyed an image of luxury, exotica, high technology and style. The brand name Pepsi Max was chosen for the diet cola from Pepsi targeted at men as it conveyed a masculine image in a product category that was associated with women. So, one criterion for deciding on a good brand name is that it evokes positive associations.

Another important criterion is that the brand name should be memorable and easy to pronounce. Short names such as Esso, Shell, Daz, Ariel, Novon and Mini fall into this category. Interesting examples of name shortening are taking place online. Facebook has used the domain name for Montenegro – .me – for fb.me. There are exceptions to this general rule, as in the case of Häagen-Dazs, which was designed to sound European in the USA where it was first launched. A brand name may suggest product benefits – as in the case of Right Guard (deodorant), Alpine Glade (air and fabric freshener) and Head & Shoulders (anti-dandruff shampoo) – or express what the brand is offering in a distinctive way, such as Toys 'R' Us. Technological products may benefit from numerical brand naming (e.g. Audi A4, Airbus A380, Yamaha YZF R125). This also overcomes the need to change brand names when marketing in different countries.

Some specialist companies have been established to act as brand-name consultants. Market research is used to test associations, memorability, pronunciation and preferences. The value of a good brand name can be seen in the prices paid for some of the top domain names in the world, such as diamond.com (US$7.5 million), vodka.com (US$3 million) and cameras.com (US$1.5 million).[16] It is important to seek legal advice to ensure that a brand name does not infringe an existing brand name. Interesting controversies can arise relating to brand names and trademarks such as Victoria Beckham's efforts to stop Peterborough United Football Club trademarking their decades-old nickname 'Posh'. More controversially, some companies are also trying to obtain the legal rights to slogans – such as Nestlé for the KitKat slogan 'Have a Break'.

Legal protection for a brand name, brand mark or trade character is provided through the registration of **trademarks**. As brands assume greater importance so too does their legal protection. The Nike swoosh, the Starbuck's mermaid and the Apple icon are all highly valuable to their owners and these registered trademarks can be legally protected from copying by rivals. For example, Apple Computers won a recent court case against Apple Corporation – the owners of the Beatles Music company who had sued against its use of the apple logo. Trademarks also need to be protected online. Search advertising regulations allow firms to use trademarks as keywords and in display ads, increasing the costs of trademark protection for brand owners.[17]

Table 6.1 summarizes those issues that are important when choosing a brand name, while Table 6.2 shows how brand names can be categorized.

Table 6.1 Brand name considerations

A good brand name should:	
1	evoke positive associations
2	be easy to pronounce and remember
3	suggest product benefits
4	be distinctive
5	use numerals when emphasizing technology
6	not infringe an existing registered brand name

Table 6.2 Brand name categories

People:	Cadbury, Mars, Heinz
Places:	Singapore Airlines, Deutsche Bank
Descriptive:	I Can't Believe it's Not Butter, the Body Shop, T-mobile
Abstract:	KitKat, Kodak, Prozac
Evocative:	Egg, Orange
Brand extensions:	Dove Deodorant, Virgin Direct, Playtex Affinity
Foreign meanings:	LEGO (from 'play well' in Danish), Thermos (meaning 'heat' in Greek)

Source: adapted from Miller, R. (1999) Science Joins Art in Brand Naming, *Marketing*, 27 May, 31–2.

Developing brands

Building successful brands is an extremely challenging marketing task. In fact, of Britain's top 50 brands, only 18 per cent have been developed since 1975.[18] This also implies that when a brand becomes established, it tends to endure for a very long time. Table 6.3 lists the world's leading brands, some of which are over 100 years old, so we can see that brand building is a long-term activity. There are many demands on people's attention; generating awareness, communicating brand values and building customer loyalty usually takes many years, which is why the rapid rise to prominence of brands like Amazon and Google is so admirable. Similarly, the Korean company, Samsung has moved from being seen as a company that produced cheap televisions and microwave ovens to a leading global premium brand in sectors like mobile phones, memory chips and flat panels. This was achieved through doubling its marketing spend to US$3 billion, advertising that showed the company's prowess in technology, product placement in futuristic films like *Matrix Reloaded* and sponsorship of the Athens Olympics, which increased general awareness of the brand.[19] The value of the Samsung brand is now greater than that of the once dominant Sony. League tables like those presented in Table 6.3

Table 6.3 The top 20 most valuable brands worldwide

Company	2010 brand value (US$ billions)	Country of origin	% change from 2009
Google	114.26	USA	14
IBM	88.38	USA	30
Apple	83.15	USA	32
Microsoft	76.34	USA	0
Coca-Cola	67.98	USA	1
McDonald's	66.00	USA	−1
Marlboro	57.05	USA	15
China Mobile	52.62	China	−14
General Electric	45.06	USA	−25
Vodafone	44.04	UK	−17
ICBC	43.93	China	15
Hewlett-Packard	39.72	USA	48
Wal-Mart	39.42	USA	−4
BlackBerry	30.71	Canada	12
Amazon	29.46	USA	29
UPS	26.49	USA	−5
Tesco	25.74	UK	12
Visa	24.88	USA	52
Oracle	24.82	USA	16
Verizon	24.66	USA	39

Source: Brandz Top 100.

are also illustrative in charting both the demise of venerable brands like Toyota, Gap, Nokia, Dell and Motorola, and the rise of powerful new brands like Visa, BlackBerry and Allianz. Management must be prepared to provide a consistently high level of brand investment to establish and maintain the position of a brand in the marketplace. Unfortunately, it can be tempting to cut back on expenditure in the short term, particularly when there is a downturn in the economy. Such cutbacks need to be resisted in order for the brand to be supported, as it is one of the key drivers of shareholder value.[20]

Figure 6.3 is an analytical framework that can be used to dissect the current position of a brand in the marketplace, and to form the basis of a new brand positioning strategy. The strength of a brand's position in the marketplace is built on six elements: brand domain, brand heritage, brand values, brand assets, brand personality and brand reflection. The first of these, brand domain, corresponds to the choice of target market (where the brand competes); the other five elements provide avenues for creating a clear differential advantage with these target consumers. These elements are expanded on briefly below.

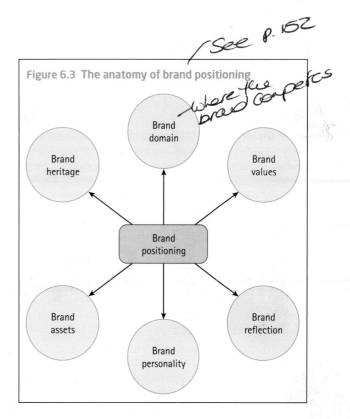

See p. 152

Figure 6.3 The anatomy of brand positioning

where the brand competes

1 *Brand domain*: the brand's target market, i.e. where it competes in the marketplace.
2 *Brand heritage*: the background to the brand and its culture. How it has achieved success (and failure) over its life. For example, English wines like Chapel Down have been successful despite the country's lack of a wine heritage.
3 *Brand value*: the core values and characteristics of the brand.
4 *Brand assets*: what makes the brand distinctive from other competing brands (symbols, features, images and relationships, etc.).
5 *Brand personality*: the character of the brand described in terms of other entities, such as people, animals or objects. Celebrity endorsement of brands gives them personality. Sales of Kia Kaha, a small New Zealand-based company, were significantly boosted when Michael Campbell won the US Open golf tournament wearing its clothing.[21]
6 *Brand reflection*: how the brand relates to self-identity; how the customer perceives him/herself as a result of buying/using the brand (see Exhibit 6.4).

Brand managers can form an accurate portrait of how brands are positioned in the marketplace by analysing each of the elements listed above. Brand building is expensive and great care needs to be taken with brand investment decisions. A classic case in point has been the decision by Gap to change its logo (see Marketing in Action 6.2).

Exhibit 6.4 The Chivas whisky brand's campaign 'Live with Chivalry' implies that the Chivas man is a good guy who gives something back.

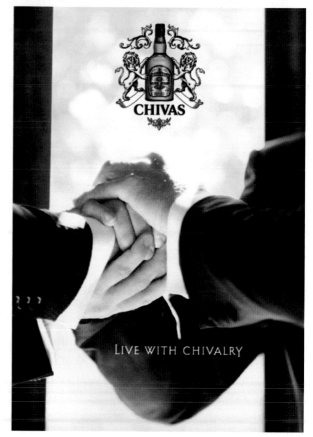

LIVE WITH CHIVALRY

Marketing in Action 6.2 Gap's logo disaster

Critical Thinking: Below is a review of the failed attempt to redesign the Gap logo. Read it and discuss the extent to which a logo redesign was the correct response to Gap's problems. What initiatives should it have taken?

Before   After

Gap is a leading US casual clothing brand. Its parent company, Gap Inc. was founded in San Francisco in

1969 and its range of casual clothes and accessories for men, women and children has become popular right around the world. However, due to its rapid global expansion, problems in brand management and increased competition, its sales and profits began to slide during the 2000s. One of its strategic responses was to unveil a new logo for the brand in 2010. Out went its iconic blue box logo to be replaced by the word Gap with a blue box located behind the p.

In doing so, Gap adopted an interesting approach. It quietly unveiled the new logo on its website without any fanfare and waited to see what kind of response came from customers and brand fans. Almost immediately, it was apparent that the new logo was not going to be well received and was criticized for being bland, uninspiring and more reminiscent of a technology company than a fashion retailer. Some of the most trenchant criticism argued that it fitted Gap perfectly – a brand that had lost its way and lacked vision and creativity! Also devastating were two Twitter accounts @OldGapLogo and @Gap Logo that began a satirical dialogue with each other including tweets from @OldGapLogo that said 'Help I've Been Taken Hostage!' Within three days, Gap had reverted to its original logo on its website claiming that it was listening and responding to the views of its fans. It then commenced a crowd-sourcing project – inviting its Facebook and Twitter fans to suggest new ideas for its logo. But in another twist and all within just seven days, it announced that it was withdrawing its crowd-sourcing project as well.

The manner in which the new Gap logo was introduced and then scrapped, led many to claim that this was a deliberate and clever ploy on the part of the company to engineer publicity about the brand in the news and on social media. However, with hindsight it is clear that it was a major logo redesign disaster. Marka Hansen, president of Gap North America who oversaw the project, resigned in February 2011.

Based on: Anonymous (2010);[22] Ritson (2010);[23] Sauer (2010)[24].

Managing brands

Once brands have been established, several important management decisions need to be made. The first of these is whether or not to extend or stretch the brand. A **brand extension** is the use of an established brand name on a new brand within the same broad market. For example, the Anadin brand name has been extended to related brands: Anadin Extra, Ultra, Soluble, Paracetamol and Ibuprofen. Unilever has successfully expanded its Dove soap brand into deodorants, shower gel, liquid soap and bodywash.[25] **Brand stretching** is when an established brand name is used for brands in unrelated markets. Among the most famous examples of brand stretching is the Virgin brand which began life as Virgin Music (music publishing) and Megastores (music retailing) but grew to encompass over 200 businesses in everything from financial services, to modelling to rail travel.

The question of whether or not, the same brand can be marketed in the same way across geographic boundaries is an important decision facing brand managers when an organization internationalizes. The expansion of economic unions and the growing globalization of business are forces that seem to favour the use of standardized or **global branding** strategies, which help to reduce campaign costs and generate global uniformity for brands. Major multinational corporations adopt different approaches to the global/local choice. Unilever has cut its brand portfolio from over 1600 down to just 400 big brands that are marketed across international boundaries. Similarly, the luxury goods group, LVMH, cut its range from 73 in 2000 to 58 in 2006. Other companies have spent heavily on renaming local brands such as Mars' decision to rename Marathon as Snickers, and P&G's decision to rename its popular Fairy laundry detergent as Dawn, with the aim of giving these brands global consistency.

In contrast, the German consumer group Henkel is going in the opposite direction. Like Unilever, Henkel has grown through the acquisition of local companies, but rather than focusing on global leaders it maintains a portfolio of national and international brands. Persil, its premium brand in the laundry detergent business, is not suitable for the USA market where washing machines on average use more water at lower temperatures than Europe, so for this reason it paid US$2.9 billion for the Dial group in 2003 to acquire the US washing powder, Purex. After the failure of Fa, its range of personal care products, in the USA, it acquired the deodorants Right Guard, Soft & Dri and Dry Idea from P&G for US$275 million. In the company's view, Americans tend to prefer to suppress sweating, while continental Europeans want to conceal any odour without blocking perspiration, illustrating the kinds of differences that can exist between markets.

Finally, a popular strategy for some companies today is co-branding where two brands are combined. This may take the form of **product-based co-branding** or **communications-based co-branding**. Product-based co-branding involves the linking of two or more existing brands from different companies to form a product in which both brand names are visible to the consumer. There are two variants of this approach.

Parallel co-branding occurs when two independent brands join forces to form a combined brand such as HP and Apple iPod to form the HP iPod. **Ingredient co-branding** is where one supplier explicitly chooses to position its brand as an ingredient of a product, such as when U2 launched the album *How to Dismantle an Atomic Bomb* pre-installed on an Apple iPod. Intel is one of the best-known ingredient brands through its popular slogan 'Intel inside', seen on PCs worldwide.

There are a number of advantages to product-based co-branding. First, the co-branding alliance can capture multiple sources of brand equity and therefore add value and provide a point of differentiation. Combining Häagen-Dazs ice cream and Bailey's liqueur creates a brand that adds value through distinctive flavouring that is different from competitive offerings. Second, a co-brand can position a product for a particular target market. For example, Volkswagen teamed up with Trek mountain bikes to develop the Jetta Trek, a special edition of the Volkswagen Jetta. The car was equipped with a bike rack and a Trek mounted on top, and appealed to some 15 million mountain bikers. Finally, co-branding can reduce the cost of product introduction since two well-known brands are combined, accelerating awareness, acceptance and adoption.[26]

Communications-based co-branding involves the linking of two or more existing brands from different companies or business units for the purpose of joint communications. For example, one brand can recommend another, such as Whirlpool's endorsement of Ariel washing powder.[27] Also the alliance can be used to stimulate interest or provide promotional opportunities, such as the deal between McDonald's and Disney, which gives the former exclusive global rights to display and promote material relating to new Disney movies in its outlets. Communications alliances are very popular in sponsorship deals, such as Shell's brand name appearing on Ferrari cars.

Whatever basis is used to differentiate products in a market, three important product management issues remain, namely, managing large portfolios of products and brands, managing products over time and developing new products. We now turn to each of these questions.

Managing product and brand portfolios

Some companies have a large portfolio of products or brands (see Table 6.4). They can be described in terms

Table 6.4 Sample brand portfolios of leading companies

Johnson & Johnson	Procter & Gamble	Nestlé	Unilever	L'Oréal	Diageo
Band-Aid	Always	Nescafé	Omo	Vichy	Guinness
Neutrogena	Bounce	Perrier	Surf	Garnier	Baileys
RoC	Duracell	Vittel	Comfort	La Roche-Posay	Smirnoff
Johnson's	Pantene	KitKat	Domestos	Maybelline	J&B
bebe	Pampers	Quality Street	Cif	Lancôme	Bundaberg
Clean & Clear	Tampax	Purina	Dove	Ralph Lauren perfumes	Captain Morgan
Aveeno	Crest	Rolo	Timotei	Helena Rubinstein	Moët & Chandon
Acuvue	Vicks	Nespresso	Organics	Giorgio Armani perfumes	Jose Cuervo
Pepcid	Head & Shoulders	Carnation	Knorr	Cacherel	Tanqueray
Tylenol	Gillette Fusion	Lean Cuisine	Ben & Jerry's	Biotherm	Malibu
Imodium	Camay	Buitoni	Lipton	Body Shop	Archers
Stayfree	Hugo	Nesquik	Ragu	Diesel	Bells
Piz Buin	Cover Girl	Libby's	Pot Noodle	Redken	Piat d'Or
Benecol	Old Spice	Chef	Hellmann's		Bertrams VO
Reach toothbrushes	Pringles	Purina	SlimFast		Hennessey
	Oral B	Friskies	Lux		
	Naomi Campbell	Dreyer's	Impulse		
	Lacoste	Poland Spring	Bertolli		

Figure 6.4 The Boston Consulting Group growth-share matrix

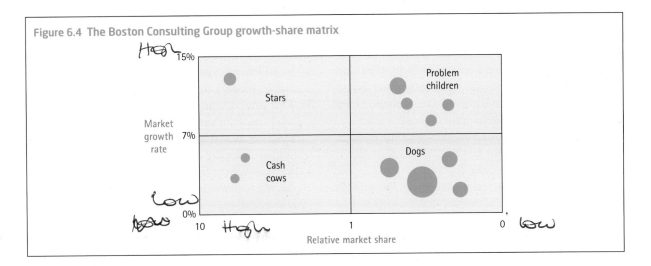

of a company's product line and mix. A **product line** is a group of products that are closely related in terms of their functions and the benefits they provide (e.g. Dell's range of personal computers or Samsung's line of television sets). The *depth* of the product line refers to the number of variants offered within the product line. A 'product mix' is the total set of brands or products marketed in a company. It is the sum of the product lines offered. Thus, the *width* of the product mix can be gauged by the number of product lines an organization offers. Philips, for example, offers a wide product mix comprising the brands found within its product lines of television, audio equipment, DVDs, camcorders, and so on. Coca-Cola, for example, is deemed to be more vulnerable to market trends than its rival Pepsi because of its greater dependence on sales of sugary drinks, whereas Pepsi has a broader portfolio of drinks and food.

The process of managing groups of brands and product lines is called **portfolio planning**. This can be a very complex and important task. Some product lines will be strong, others weak. Some will require investment to finance their growth, others will generate more cash than they need. Somehow companies must decide how to distribute their limited resources among the competing needs of products so as to achieve the best performance for the company as a whole. Specifically, management needs to decide which products to invest in, hold or withdraw support from.

The Boston Consulting Group's (BCG's) growth-share matrix is a technique borrowed from strategic management that has proved useful in helping companies to make product mix and/or product line decisions (see Figure 6.4). The matrix allows portfolios of products to be depicted in a 2 × 2 box, the axes of which are based on market growth rate and relative market share. The size of the circles reflects the proportion of revenue generated by each product line. Market growth rate forms the vertical axis and indicates the annual growth rate of the market in which each product line operates; in Figure 6.4 this is shown as 0–15 per cent although a different range could be used depending on economic conditions. Market growth rate is used as a proxy for market attractiveness.

Relative market share refers to the market share of each product relative to its largest competitor, and is shown on the horizontal axis. This acts as a proxy for competitive strength. The division between high and low market share is 1. Above this figure a product line has a market share greater than its main competitor. For example, if our product had a market share of 40 per cent and our main competitor's share was 30 per cent this would be indicated as 1.33 on the horizontal axis. Having plotted the position of each product on the matrix, a company can begin to think about setting the appropriate strategic objective for each line.

The market leaders in high-growth markets are known as *stars*. They are already successful and the prospects for further growth are good. Resources should be invested to maintain/increase the leadership position. Competitive challenges should be repelled. These are the cash cows of the future (see below) and need to be protected.

Problem children (also known as *question marks*) are cash drains because they have low profitability and require investment to enable them to keep up with market growth. They are so called because management has to consider whether it is sensible to continue the required investment. The company faces a fundamental choice: to increase investment (build) to attempt to turn the problem child into a star, or to withdraw support, either by harvesting (raising the price while lowering marketing expenditure) or divesting (dropping or selling it). In a few cases a third option may be viable: to find a small market segment (niche) where dominance can be achieved.

The high profitability and low investment associated with high market share in low-growth markets mean that *cash cows* should be defended. Consequently, the appropriate strategic objective is to hold sales and market share. The excess cash that is generated should be used to fund stars, problem children that are being built, and research and development for new products. For example, the C&C group sold its soft drinks business (a cash cow) to Britvic for €249 million, a deal aimed to fund its star division: cider.[28]

Dogs are weak products that compete in low-growth markets. They are the also-rans that have failed to achieve market dominance during the growth phase and are floundering in maturity. For those products that achieve second or third position in the marketplace (*cash dogs*) a small positive cash flow may result and, for a few others, it may be possible to reposition the product into a defendable niche. For the bulk of dogs, however, the appropriate strategic objective is to *harvest* – that is, to generate a positive cash flow for a time – or to *divest*, which allows resources and managerial time to be focused elsewhere.

The strength of BCG's growth-share matrix is its simplicity. Once all of the company's products have been plotted it is easy to see how many stars, problem children, cash cows and dogs there are in the portfolio. Cash can be allocated as necessary to the different product lines to ensure that a balanced portfolio is maintained. For example, the world's biggest maker of alcoholic drinks, Diageo, sold off its food businesses such as Burger King in order to focus on its global brands in whiskey, vodka and stout. However, the tool has also attracted a litany of criticism.[29] Some of the key problems with using the technique are as follows.

1   The matrix was based on cash flow but perhaps profitability (e.g. return on investment) is a better criterion for allocating resources.

2   Since the position of a product on the matrix depends on market share, this can lead to an unhealthy preoccupation with market share gain. In addition, market definition (which determines market share) can be very difficult.

3   The matrix ignores interdependences between products. For example, a dog may need to be marketed because it complements a star or a cash cow (it may be a spare part or an accessory, for example). Alternatively, customers and distributors may value dealing with a company that supplies a full product line. For these reasons dropping products because they fall into a particular box may be naive.

4   Treating market growth rate as a proxy for market attractiveness, and market share as an indicator of competitive strength is to oversimplify matters.

There are many other factors that have to be taken into account when measuring market attractiveness (e.g. market size, the strengths and weaknesses of competitors) and competitive strengths (e.g. exploitable marketing assets, potential cost advantages) besides market growth rates and market share. This led to the introduction of more complex portfolio matrices such as the McKinsey/GE market attractiveness–competitive position matrix, which used a variety of measures of market attractiveness and competitive strength.

The main contribution of the portfolio matrices generally has been to demonstrate that *different products should have different roles* in the product portfolio. For example, to ask for a 20 per cent return on investment (ROI) for a star may result in underinvestment in an attempt to meet the profit requirement. On the other hand, 20 per cent ROI for a cash cow or a harvested product may be too low. However, the models should be used only as an aid to managerial judgement, and other factors that are not adequately covered by the models should be considered when making product mix decisions (see Marketing in Action 6.3).

Marketing in Action 6.3: Sony's portfolio decisions

Critical Thinking: Below is a review of some of the leading product lines in Sony's portfolio. Read it, plot along the lines mentioned on a BCG matrix and advise Sony on what it should do.

Sony is one of Japan's most famous companies; its unique ability to produce top-quality miniature consumer electronics gave the world products like the Walkman personal stereo and the camcorder.

However, for the past few years the company has been struggling to maintain its once dominant position. The reason for this is that too many of Sony's products are in unprofitable and declining businesses – in other words, it has too many 'dogs' in its portfolio.

For example, Sony is one of the top manufacturers of cathode-ray televisions. It sold over 7 million of these sets in 2005 and this product range was one of its biggest cash generators. But this business has collapsed in the developed world in recent years as consumers have switched to flat-panel televisions, and Sony has ceded market leadership to brands like Samsung and Panasonic. It has now entered the rapidly growing home theatre system and flat-screen television business, but does not have market leadership in this sector (a problem child division). It also has a presence in the personal computer (PC) business, through its Vaio brand, but here again it is faced with some tough choices. PCs are an intensely price-competitive, low-margin and low-growth business, where Sony faces entrenched competitors like Dell, HP and Lenovo. Given its inability to differentiate the Vaio from the other brands in the marketplace it is questionable whether Sony should persist in this business. Other 'dog' businesses in which it is operating include its compact disc and minidisc product ranges, its car audio equipment and Sony Chemical – all low-growth or declining sectors.

The company has other divisions in its portfolio that appear to offer greater prospects. For example, its main 'cash cow' business is its camcorders. Although the business is no longer rapidly growing, Sony is the unquestioned market leader, and because it makes most of the product's components in-house, camcorders still deliver double-digit margins. Its 'star' division in recent years has been its video games business. The PlayStation brand is one of the best known in the industry and contributed two-thirds of Sony's operating profit in 2005. As this business matures, Sony needs to maintain a dominant position against rivals like the Xbox and Nintendo Wii, which it is trying to do with its PlayStation 3, in order to make this division a future cash cow. Sony has plenty of 'problem children' too, like its Walkman MP3 range, which trails well behind the dominant Apple iPod, though this is a growing business. But it is its investment in the Blu-ray disc, the next generation of DVD technology, that is likely to be its new 'star'. Having succeeded in convincing most of the big Hollywood studios to adopt its technology instead of the HD-DVD technology being promoted by Toshiba and Microsoft, Sony has won an intensely fought format war, which should drive sales of its high-definition DVD players and discs into the future.

Sony demonstrates the dynamic nature of company portfolios. Brands and divisions that were the stars or cash cows of the past may need to be divested in order to concentrate resources on delivering new stars for the future as consumer tastes and technologies change rapidly.

Based on: Anonymous (2008);[30] Gapper (2006);[31] Nakamoto (2005)[32].

Managing brands and product lines over time: the product life cycle

Both individual brands and product lines need to be managed over time. A useful tool for conceptualizing the changes that may take place during the time that a product is on the market is called the **product life cycle**. The classic product life cycle (PLC) has four stages (see Figure 6.5): introduction, growth, maturity and decline.

The PLC emphasizes the fact that nothing lasts forever. For example, the drop in demand for elaborate tea services has seen dramatic declines at the makers of porcelain and fine bone china products, like Royal Worcester and Royal Doulton. There is a danger that management may fall in love with certain products, as in the case of a company that was founded on the success of a particular product. The PLC underlines the fact that companies have to accept that products need to be terminated and new products developed to replace them. Without this sequence, a company may find itself with a group of products all in the decline stage of their PLC. A nicely balanced product array would see the company marketing some products in the mature stage of the PLC, a number at the growth stage and the prospect of new product introductions in the near future.

The PLC emphasizes the need to review marketing objectives and strategies as products pass through the various stages. Changes in market and competitive conditions between the PLC stages suggest that marketing strategies should be adapted to meet them. Table 6.5 shows a set of stylized marketing responses to each stage. Note that these are broad generalizations rather

The product life cycle

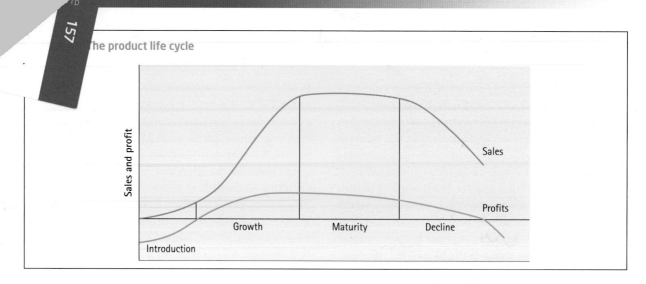

Table 6.5 Marketing objectives and strategies over the product life cycle

	Introduction	Growth	Maturity	Decline
Strategic marketing objective	Build	Build	Hold	Harvest/manage for cash
Strategic focus	Expand market	Penetration	Protect share	Productivity
Brand objective	Product awareness/trial	Brand preference	Brand loyalty	Brand exploitation
Products	Basic	Differentiated	Differentiated	Rationalized
Promotion	Creating awareness/trial	Creating awareness/ trial repeat purchase	Maintaining awareness/ repeat purchase	Cut/eliminated
Price	High	Lower	Lowest	Rising
Distribution	Patchy	Wider	Intensive	Selective

than exact prescriptions, but they do serve to emphasize the need to review marketing objectives and strategies in the light of environmental change.

Introduction

When a product is first introduced on to the market its sales growth is typically low and losses are incurred as a result of heavy development and initial promotional costs. Companies will be monitoring the speed of product adoption and, if it is disappointing, may terminate the product at this stage.

The strategic marketing objective is to build sales by expanding the market for the product. The brand objective will be to create awareness so that customers will become familiar with generic product benefits. The product is likely to be fairly basic, with an emphasis on reliability and functionality rather than special features to appeal to different customer groups. Promotion will support the brand objectives by gaining awareness for the brand and product type, and stimulating trial. Advertising has been found to be more effective at the

start of the life of a product than in later stages[33] (see Exhibit 6.5). Typically, price will be high because of the heavy development costs and the low level of competition. Distribution will be patchy as some dealers will be wary of stocking the new product until it has proved successful in the marketplace.

Growth

This second stage is marked by a period of faster sales and profit growth. Sales growth is fuelled by rapid market acceptance and, for many products, repeat purchasing. Profits may begin to decline towards the latter stages of growth as new rivals enter the market attracted by the twin magnets of fast sales growth and high profit potential. For example, the Internet search engine business has been growing rapidly and delivering very high profits for some incumbent firms like Google. But the profitability of this sector has attracted a range of new entrants, such as Jeteye.com, Blinkx.com and Icerocket.com, all of which are providing new and innovative search solutions. Similarly,

Exhibit 6.5 This advert for NGN targets innovators and early adopters in movie downloads

in developed countries, the growth in pet ownership has given rise to a rapidly growing pet products and pet services sector (see Marketing in Action 6.4). The end of the growth period is often associated with 'competitive shake-out', whereby weaker suppliers cease production.

The strategic marketing objective during the growth phase is to build sales and market share. The strategic focus will be to penetrate the market by building brand preference. To accomplish this task the product will be redesigned to create differentiation, and promotion will stress the functional and/or psychological benefits that accrue from the differentiation. Awareness and trial are still important, but promotion will begin to focus on repeat purchasers. As development costs are defrayed and competition increases, prices will fall. Rising consumer demand and increased sales-force effort will widen distribution.

Maturity

Sales will eventually peak and stabilize as saturation occurs, hastening competitive shake-out. Mobile phone adoption rates, for example, have surpassed 100 per cent

in some Western European countries. The survivors now battle for market share by introducing product improvements, using advertising and sales promotional offers, dealer discounting and price cutting; the result is strain on profit margins, particularly for follower brands. The need for effective brand building is felt most acutely during maturity and brand leaders are in the strongest position to resist pressure on profit margins.[34] Careful strategic decisions are very important in mature markets. For example, the falling profitability of Starbucks in 2007 was attributed to decisions that sought to grow the business too rapidly (it has now over 17,000 outlets worldwide) in a mature market, which has led to market saturation and poor control over cafés.[35]

Decline

During the decline stages – when new technology or changes in consumer tastes work to reduce demand for the product – sales and profits fall. Suppliers may decide to cease production completely or reduce product depth. Promotional and product development budgets may be slashed, and marginal distributors dropped as suppliers seek to maintain (or increase) profit margins. Products like cathode ray tube (CRT) televisions have fallen out of favour as consumers have switched to flat-panel screens. For example, Dixons dropped the price of a CRT television from £1300 in 2004 to £300 in 2005, and the range still failed to sell.[36] The increase in consumers making their travel arrangements online has led to a significant fall in the number of travel agents operating in the UK. In 2000, there were 1820 registered members of the Association of British Travel Agents (ABTA) but by 2005 this had fallen to 1397.[37]

A key ethical consideration is the speed with which many products move through the product life cycle. For example, mobile phone models and computer software become quickly outdated. Fast fashion retailers like Zara aim to change the range of clothing in their retail outlets every two weeks. This 'planned obsolescence' is a significant boom for organizations as consumers need to repurchase updates or new models and discard old ones. Critics argue that this kind of consumption is not only expensive from the consumer's point of view but significantly wasteful from society's viewpoint. Clothes or computers that are perfectly 'fit for purpose' are being discarded simply because newer models are available.

Like BCG's growth-share matrix, the PLC theory has been the subject of a significant amount of criticism. First, not all products follow the classic S-shaped curve. The sales of some products 'rise like a rocket then fall like a stone'. This is normal for fad products such

Marketing in Action 6.4: Pedigree dog food

Critical Thinking: Below is a review of the marketing of Pedigree dog food. Read it and using Table 6.5 as a guide, decide which stage of the life cycle the Pedigree brand is in and make appropriate marketing strategy recommendations.

Pedigree dog food is part of the Mars group portfolio of pet care products which also includes Kitekat, Wiskas and Sheba. Together these brands account for almost 50 per cent of turnover at Mars, a group that is better known for its sales of confectionary products. Pedigree is the number one dog food brand in the world and has been expanding into emerging markets like Brazil, China and Russia where the growth of the middle class has fuelled the demand for pet products. Even throughout Europe, dog food is a market that is growing at a rate of approximately 10 per cent per year with some sub-segments of the market such as dog treats and snacks growing much faster.

To capitalize on these growing markets, Pedigree has focused on increasing the depth of its product line. Brand extensions such as Pedigree Dentastix helps clean the dog's teeth and reduce plaque while Pedigree Joint Care is a beef-flavoured product containing omega 3, glucosamine and other ingredients commonly found in products aimed at alleviating joint stiffness in humans. Packaging changes have taken place as well with single-use pouch packages becoming popular as consumers seek greater convenience.

Pedigree has traditionally held the quality positioning in dog food which was achieved through a focus on the quality and nutritional value of its products, the use of slogans like 'what champions are made of' as well as the brand's name. More recently, the brand has shifted to a global positioning approach encapsulated in the slogan 'we're the dogs' which aims to make an emotional connection with the owner rather than talk about the product itself. This has been important given the rise in the number of own-label dog food brands sold by large supermarkets such as Tesco and Aldi. It has also been supported by CSR initiatives that raise money for dog shelters and societies for the prevention of cruelty to animals. Labelled the Pedigree Adoption Drive and launched in the USA in 2006, the campaign began telling some of the unique stories of a few of the millions of dogs left in shelters around the world, further strengthening the emotional connection between the brand and dog lovers.

Based on: Effie Worldwide (2010),[38] Skelly (2008)[39].

---

as Rubik's cubes, which in the 1980s saw phenomenal sales growth followed by a rapid sales collapse as the youth market moved on to another craze. Blockbuster movies have a similarly short life cycle. For example, *X-Men, The Last Stand* grossed US$123 million in its first four days in cinemas, which was more than it earned for the remaining four months of its run.[40] Second, the duration of the PLC stages is unpredictable. The PLC outlines the four stages a product passes through without defining their duration. For example, e-books have languished in the introduction stage of the product life cycle for longer than anticipated before finally taking off. Clearly this limits its use as a forecasting tool since it is not possible to predict when maturity or decline will begin. Finally, and perhaps most worryingly, it has been argued that the PLC is the *result* of marketing

activities, not the cause. Clearly, sales of a product may flatten out or fall simply because it has not received enough marketing attention, or because there has been insufficient product redesign or promotional support. Using the PLC, argue its critics, may lead to inappropriate action (e.g. harvesting or dropping the product) when the correct response should be increased marketing support (e.g. product replacement, positioning reinforcement or repositioning). Like many marketing tools, the PLC should not be viewed as a panacea to marketing thinking and decision-making, but as an aid to managerial judgement.

Nevertheless, the dynamic nature of brands and product lines focuses attention on the key marketing challenge of developing new products and services. It is to this issue that we turn next.

New product development

The introduction of new products to the marketplace is the lifeblood of corporate success. Changing customer tastes, technological advances and competitive pressures mean that companies cannot afford to rely on past product successes. Instead they have to work on new product development programmes and nurture an innovative climate in order to lay the foundations for new product success. But new product development is inherently risky. Pharmaceutical companies research hundreds of molecular groups before coming up with a marketable drug and less than 2 per cent of films account for 80 per cent of box office returns.[41] However, failure has to be tolerated; it is endemic in the whole process of developing new products. One of the outcomes of the innovative process is the large number of interesting product ideas that emerge that never go on to be commercially successful and join lists such as the top 20 most useless gadgets (see Table 6.6).

Some new products reshape markets and competition by virtue of the fact that they are so fundamentally different from products that already exist. However, a shampoo that is different from existing products only by means of its brand name, fragrance, packaging and colour is also a new product. In fact four broad categories of new product exist.[42]

1 *Product replacements*: these account for about 45 per cent of all new product launches, and include revisions and improvements to existing products (e.g. the Ford Focus replacing the Fiesta), repositioning (existing products such as Lucozade being targeted at new market segments) and cost reductions (existing products being reformulated or redesigned so that they cost less to produce).

2 *Additions to existing lines*: these account for about 25 per cent of new product launches and take the form of new products that add to a company's existing product lines. This produces greater product depth. An example is the launch by Weetabix of a brand extension, Oatabix, to compete with other oat-based cereals.

3 *New product lines*: these total around 20 per cent of new product launches and represent a move into a new market. For example, in Europe, Mars has launched a number of ice cream brands, which made up a new product line for this company. This strategy widens a company's product mix.

4 *New-to-the-world products*: these total around 10 per cent of new product launches, and create entirely new markets. For example, the video games console, the MP3 player and the camcorder have created new markets because of the highly valued customer benefits they provide.

Of course, the degree of risk and reward involved will vary according to the new product category. New-to-the-world products normally carry the highest risk since it is often difficult to predict consumer reaction. Often, market research will be unreliable in predicting demand as people do not really understand the full benefits of the product until it is on the market and they get the chance to experience them. For example, initial market testing yielded very negative results for products like Red Bull and Nespresso coffee machines which went on to become global leaders. At the other extreme, adding a brand variation to an existing product line lacks significant risk but is also unlikely to proffer significant returns (see Table 6.7 for a list of the world's most innovative companies).

Table 6.6 Top 10 most useless gadgets

1. Electric nail files
2. Laser guided scissors
3. Electric candles
4. Soda stream
5. Foot spas
6. Fondue sets
7. Hair crimpers
8. Egg boiler
9. Electric fluff remover
10. Electric carving knife

Source: Irish Times

Table 6.7 The world's most innovative companies

Company	Business
1. Apple	Consumer electronics
2. Google	Information technology
3. Toyota	Automotive
4. General Electric	Industrial
5. Microsoft	Information technology
6. Tata Group	Industrial
7. Nintendo	Gaming
8. Procter & Gamble	Consumer products
9. Sony	Consumer electronics
10. Nokia	Telecommunications

Source: Business Week

Managing the new product development process

New product development is expensive, risky and time consuming – these are three inescapable facts. Gillette, for example, spent in excess of £100 million over more than 10 years developing its Sensor razor brand. The new product concept was to develop a non-disposable shaver that would use new technology to produce a razor that would follow the contours of a man's face, giving an excellent shave (due to two spring-mounted platinum-hardened chromium blades) with fewer cuts. This made commercial sense given that shaving systems are more profitable than disposable razors and allow more opportunity for creating a differential advantage. Had the brand failed, Gillette's position in the shaving market could have been irreparably damaged.

A seven-step new product development process is shown in Figure 6.6; this consists of idea generation, screening, concept testing, business analysis, product development, market testing and commercialization. Although the reality of new product development may resemble organizational chaos, the discipline imposed by the activities carried out at each stage leads to a greater likelihood of developing a product that not only works, but also confers customer benefits. We should note, however, that new products pass through each stage at

varying speeds: some may dwell at a stage for a long period while others may pass through very quickly.[43]

Idea generation

The sources of new product ideas can be internal to the company: scientists, engineers, marketers, salespeople and designers, for example. Some companies use the **brainstorming** technique to stimulate the creation of ideas, and use financial incentives to persuade people to put forward ideas they have had. 3M's Post-it adhesive-backed notepaper was a successful product that was thought of by an employee who initially saw the product as a means of preventing paper falling from his hymn book as he marked the hymns that were being sung. Because of the innovative culture within 3M, he bothered to think of commercial applications and acted as a product champion within the company to see the project through to commercialization and global success.

Sources of new product ideas can also be external to the company and the turnaround at P&G was largely attributable to its chief executive officer (CEO) AG Lafley setting a goal that 50 per cent of innovation in the company should come from external sources.[44] Examining competitors' products may provide clues to product improvements. Distributors can also be a source of new product ideas directly, since they deal with customers and have an interest in selling improved products. A major source of good ideas is the customers themselves. Their needs may not be satisfied with existing products and they may be genuinely interested in providing ideas that lead to product improvement. For example, the Dutch electronics group Philips employs anthropologists and cognitive psychologists to gather insights into the desires and needs of people around the world to enable it to compete more effectively with Asian rivals such as Sony who are more renowned for their design capabilities.[45] Internet-based social communities are a powerful source of innovation, with like-minded individuals willing to share ideas and innovations for the common good. Companies like Lego and Walkers have worked with consumers to generate new products and the open source software movement is one of the most powerful examples of consumer-led innovation.

In organizational markets, keeping in close contact with customers who are innovators and market leaders in their own marketplaces is likely to be a fruitful source of new product ideas.[46] These 'lead customers' are likely to recognize required improvements ahead of other customers as they have advanced needs and are likely to face problems before other product users.

Figure 6.6 The seven-stage new product development process

- Idea generation
- Screening
- Concept testing
- Business analysis
- Product development
- Market testing
- Commercialization

New products

Some recent innovations such as GE's Light Speed VCT, which provides a three-dimensional image of a beating heart, and Staples' Wordlock, a padlock that uses words instead of numbers, have been developed in co-operation with lead customers.

A 2006 study by IBM of global chief executives found that, overall, employees were the most significant source of innovative ideas, followed by business partners, customers and consultants – in that order.[47]

Screening

Once new product ideas have been developed they need to be screened in order to evaluate their commercial value. Some companies use formal checklists to help them judge whether the product idea should be rejected or accepted for further evaluation. This ensures that no important criterion is overlooked. Criteria may be used that measure the attractiveness of the market for the proposed product, the fit between the product and company objectives, and the capability of the company to produce and market the product. Other companies may use a less systematic approach, preferring more flexible open discussion among members of the new product development committee to gauge likely success.

Concept testing

Once a product idea has been deemed worthy of further investigation, it can be framed into a specific concept for testing with potential customers. The concept may be described verbally or pictorially so that the major features are understood. In many instances the basic product idea will be expanded into several product concepts, each of which can be compared by testing with target customers. **Concept testing** thus allows the views of customers to enter the new product development process at an early stage. The buying intentions of potential customers are a key factor in judging whether any of the concepts are worth pursuing further.

Business analysis

Estimates of sales, costs and profits will be made, based on the results of the concept test, as well as on considerable managerial judgement. This is known as the **business analysis** stage. In order to produce sensible figures a marketing analysis will need to be undertaken. This will identify the target market, its size and projected product acceptance over a number of years. Consideration will be given to various prices and the implications for sales revenue (and profits) discussed. By setting a tentative price this analysis will provide

sales revenue estimates. Costs will also need to be estimated. If the new product is similar to existing products (e.g. a brand extension) it should be fairly easy to produce accurate cost estimates. For radical product concepts, costings may be nothing more than informal guesstimates.

When the quantity needed to be sold to cover costs is calculated, *break-even analysis* may be used to establish whether the project is financially feasible. *Sensitivity analysis*, in which variations from given assumptions about price, cost and customer acceptance, for example, are checked to see how they impact on sales revenue and profits, can also prove useful at this stage. 'Optimistic', 'most likely' and 'pessimistic' scenarios can be drawn up to estimate the degree of risk attached to a project. If the product concept appears commercially feasible, this process will result in marketing and product development budgets being established based on what appears to be necessary to gain customer awareness and trial, and the work required to turn the concept into a marketable product.

Product development

This stage involves the development of the actual product. It is usually necessary to integrate the skills of designers, engineers, production, finance and marketing specialists so that product development is quicker, less costly and results in a high-quality product that delights customers. For example, marketing plays a key role in Hewlett Packard's Innovation Program Office where all products are designed with a specific 'persona' in mind, that is a target user who is given a name, lifestyle and personality which ensures that a product design is kept relevant to a potential user.[48] Costs are controlled by a method called target costing. Target costs are worked out on the basis of target prices in the marketplace, and given as engineering/design and production targets.

A key marketing factor in many industries is the ability to cut time to market by reducing the length of the product development stage. There are two reasons why product development is being accelerated. First, markets such as those for personal computers, consumer electronics and cars change so fast that to be slow means running the risk of being out of date before the product is launched. Second, cutting time to market can lead to competitive advantage. This may be short-lived but is still valuable while it lasts. For example, Zara's ability to reduce time to market for new styles gave it a competitive advantage in the fashion industry (see Exhibit 6.6). Marketing has an important role to play in the product development stage. R&D and engineering may focus on the functional aspects of the

product, whereas seemingly trivial factors may have an important bearing on customer choice.

Product testing concentrates on the functional aspects of a product, as well as on consumer acceptance. Functional tests are carried out in the laboratory and in the field to check such aspects as safety, performance and shelf-life. Products also need to be tested with consumers to check their acceptability in use. Care at this stage can avoid expensive product recalls as we saw earlier in the case of Toyota. For consumer goods this often takes the form of in-house product placement. 'Paired companion tests' are used when the new product is used alongside a rival so that respondents have a benchmark against which to judge the new offerings. Alternatively, two (or more) new product variants may be tested alongside one another. A questionnaire is administered at the end of the test, which gathers overall preference information as well as comparisons on specific attributes. For example, two soups might be compared on taste, colour, smell and richness.

Market testing

Up to this point in the development process, although potential customers have been asked if they intend to buy the product, they have not been placed in the position of having to pay for it. **Market testing** takes measurement of customer acceptance one crucial step further than product testing, by forcing consumers to put their money where their mouth is, so to speak. The basic idea is to launch the new product in a limited way so that consumer response in the marketplace can be assessed. There are two major methods: the simulated market test and **test marketing**.

Simulated market tests take a number of forms, but the main idea behind them is to set up a realistic market situation in which a sample of consumers choose to buy goods from a range provided by the organizing company (usually a market research organization). For example, a sample of consumers may be recruited to buy their groceries from a mobile supermarket that visits them once a week. They are provided with a magazine in which advertisements and sales promotions for the new product can appear. This method allows the measurement of key success indicators such as penetration (the proportion of consumers who buy the new product at least once) and repeat purchase (the rate at which purchasers buy again) to be made. If penetration is high but repeat purchase low, buyers can be asked why they rejected the product after trial. Simulated market tests are therefore useful as a preliminary to test marketing by spotting problems, such as in packaging and product formulation, that can be rectified before test market launch. They can also be useful in eliminating new products that perform so badly compared with the competition in the marketplace that test marketing is not justified.

When the new product is launched in one, or a few, geographical areas chosen to be representative of its intended market, this is known as test marketing. Towns or television areas are chosen in which the new product is sold into distribution outlets so that performance can be gauged face to face with rival products. Test marketing is the acid test of new product development since the product is being promoted as it would be in a national launch, and consumers are being asked to choose it against competitor products as they would if the new product went national. It is a more realistic test than the simulated market test and therefore gives more accurate sales penetration and repeat purchasing estimates. By projecting test marketing results to the full market an assessment of the new product's likely success can be gauged. However, test marketing does have a number of potential problems. Test towns and areas may not be representative of the national market, and thus sales projections may be inaccurate. For this reason, when Guinness was test-marketing its brand extension Guinness Mid-Strength, a low-alcohol version of Guinness, it chose Limerick as the most nationally representative location in the Irish market. Competitors may invalidate the test market by giving distributors incentives to stock their product, thereby denying the new product shelf space. Also, test markets need to run for long enough to enable the measurement of repeat purchase rates for a product since this is a crucial indicator of success. One of the main advantages of test marketing is that the information it provides facilitates the 'go/no go' national launch decision.

Commercialization

The final stage of this rigorous process is the launch of the product in the marketplace. As an indication of the scale of the process, Hewlett Packard generates 1,800 raw ideas per year with the goal of examining 200 in detail and then commercializing two.[49] An effective commercialization strategy relies on marketing management making clear choices regarding the target market (*where* it wishes to compete), and the development of a marketing strategy that provides a differential advantage (*how* it wishes to compete). These two factors define the new product positioning strategy, as discussed in Chapter 5.

An understanding of the **diffusion of innovation** process is a useful starting point for choosing a target market.[50] This explains how a new product spreads throughout a market over time. Particularly important is the notion that not all people or organizations who comprise a market will be in the same state of readiness to buy a new product when it is launched. In other words, different actors in the market will have varying degrees of 'innovativeness' – that is, their willingness to try something new. For example, some consumers will be much quicker to adopt a new technology like a smartphone than others. Firms launching new products initially aim to target innovators and early adopters. For example, innovators are often adventurous and like to be different; they are willing to take a chance with an untried product.[51] In consumer markets they tend to be younger, better educated, more confident and more financially affluent, and consequently can afford to take a chance on buying something new. In organizational markets, they tend to be larger and more profitable companies if the innovation is costly, and have more progressive, better-educated management. They may themselves have a good track record in bringing out new products, and may have been the first to adopt innovations in the past. As such they may be easy to identify.

In summary, bringing out new products and services is the key to long-term corporate success. It is a risky activity, but a systematic approach is likely to improve the chances of success.

Summary

In this chapter we have explored a number of issues involved in the marketing of products and brands. The following key issues were addressed.

1. In marketing terms, products are anything that delivers benefits and value to a consumer and all products contain some tangible and some intangible elements.

2. The important distinction between products and brands. A product is anything that is capable of satisfying customer needs. Brands are the means by which companies differentiate their offerings from those of their competitors.

3. The three different levels of product, namely, the core, the actual and the augmented product and how differentiation can take place at any of these levels.

4. The key aspects involved in building brands, including decisions regarding the brand name, and developing and positioning brands. Firms can choose from family, individual and combination brand names, and developing the brand requires key decisions regarding its customer value proposition.

5. The challenge of managing a diverse group of products and brands, and the role of portfolio planning in assisting with this process. Many firms own significant portfolios of products and ongoing decisions need to be made regarding which ones should be invested in and which should be wound down.

6. The challenge of managing products and brands over time and the role of the product life cycle concept in assisting with this process. Products at different stages of growth require different marketing strategies and, despite its weaknesses, the product life cycle offers a helpful way of thinking about these decisions.

7. The importance of new product development and the process by which products are taken from the idea stage through to commercialization. Careful management is required during all the main stages, including idea generation, screening, concept testing, business analysis, product development, market testing and commercialization.

Study questions

1. Explain the difference between a product and a brand.

2. Think of five brand names. To what extent do they meet the criteria of good brand naming as laid out in Table 6.1? Do any of the names legitimately break these guidelines?

3. Examine a product like bottled water through the lens of the core, actual and augmented product. What types of differentiation strategies are being used by brands in this sector? Can you suggest any new sources of differentiation?

4. The product life cycle is more likely to mislead marketing management than provide useful insights. Discuss.

5. Many companies comprise a complex group of business units, which in turn often have wide product lines. Discuss the techniques available to the marketer for managing this complexity.

6. Outline the main stages in the new product development process, identifying the potential sources of failure at each stage.

7. Visit www.rdtrustedbrands.com. Review the most trusted brands in different categories in your area. How do these brands go about building this trust?

Suggested reading

Gerzema, J. and **E. Lebar** (2008) *The Brand Bubble: The Looming Crisis in Brand Value and How to Avoid it*, London: Jossey-Bass.

Gladwell, M. (2000) *The Tipping Point: How Little Things Can Make a Big Difference*, London: Abacus.

Hill, S., R. Ettenson and **D. Tyson** (2005) Achieving the Ideal Brand Portfolio, *Sloan Management Review*, **46** (2), 85–91.

Holman, R., H. Kaas and **D. Keeling** (2003) The Future of Product Development, *McKinsey Quarterly*, **3**, 28–40.

Kumar, N. and **J.B. Steenkamp** (2007) *Private Label Strategy: How to Meet the Store Brand Challenge*, Harvard Business School Press.

Moon, Y. (2005) Break Free From the Product Life Cycle, *Harvard Business Review*, **83** (5), 86–95.

References

1. **Millar, J.** and **K. Kashani** (2000) Innovation and Renovation: The Nespresso Story, *International Institute for Management Development*, IMD-5-0543; **Teather, D.** (2010) Clooney's Nespresso Steams Ahead With 35.5% Sales Growth in UK, *Guardian.co.uk*, 9 April.

2. **Keller, K.** (2003) *Strategic Brand Management*, Upper Saddle River, NJ: Pearson.

3. **O'Shaughnessy, H.** (2007) Getting a Good Look, *Innovation*, June, 26–30.

4. **Pope, C.** (2007) New Labels Hit a Red Light, *Irish Times*, 15 January, 13.

5. **Hegarty, S.** (2003) You Are What You Think You Eat, *Irish Times*, Weekend Review, 19 July, 1.

6. **Roberts, K.** (2004) *The Future Beyond Brands: Lovemarks*, New York: Powerhouse Books.

7. **Healy, A.** (2004) Campaigners Appeal for Cafes to be Rescued, *Irish Times*, 25 November, 6.

8. **Balwani, S.** (2009) 5 Elements of a Successful Facebook Fan Page, *Mashable.com*, 30 March.

9. **Shayon, S.** (2011) BMW, Clinique and Audi Top Facebook Luxury Brands Ranking, *Brandchannel.com*, 6 June.

10. **Reyner, M.** (1996) Is Advertising the Answer? *Admap*, September, 23–6.

11. **Anonymous** (2011) I've Got You Labelled, *The Economist*, 2 April, 74.

12. **Waters, R.** (2008) Microsoft Says 'We're human too', *Financial Times*, 9 September, 16; **Anonymous** (2008) Postmodern Wriggle, *The Economist*, 13 September, 72.

13. **Clingham, R., G.P. Arnold, T.S. Drew, L.A. Cochrane** and **R.J. Abboud** (2007) Do You Get Value for Money When You Buy an Expensive Pair of Running Shoes? *British Journal of Sports Medicine*, October, 1–5.

14. **Adamson, A.** (2006) *Brand Simple: How the Best Brands Keep it Simple and Succeed*, New York: Palgrave Macmillan.

15. **Klein, N.** (2000) *No Logo*, London: HarperCollins.

16. **Palmer, M.** (2007) What's in a Name? A Lot if it's Your Domain, *Financial Times*, 14 March, 24.

17. **O'Connor, R.** (2010) Question Marks over Trademarks, *Marketing Age*, **4** (1), 49–51.

18. **Brady, J.** and **I. Davis** (1993) Marketing's Mid-life Crisis, *McKinsey Quarterly*, **2**, 17–28.

19. **Anonymous** (2005) As Good As It Gets, *The Economist*, 15 January, 60–2.

20. **Doyle, P.** (2000) *Value-based Marketing*, Chichester: John Wiley & Sons.

21. **Richards, H.** (2005) A Clothing Hit – On the Back of a Golfing Hero, *Financial Times*, 13 July, 16.

22. **Anonymous** (2010) Is This Clever Crowdsourcing or a Genuine Brand Gaff? *MarketingWeek.co.uk*, 21 October.

23. **Ritson, M.** (2010) Is this Gap's Idea of 360 Degree Branding? *MarketingWeek.co.uk*, 13 October.

24. **Sauer, A.** (2010) Gap Rebrands Itself into Oblivion, *Brandchannel.com*, 6 October.

25. **Pandya, N.** (1999) Soft Selling Soap Brings Hard Profit, *Guardian.co.uk*, 2 October, 28.

26. **Brech, P.** (2002) Ford Focus Targets Women with *Elle* Tie, *Marketing*, 8 August, 7.

27. **Keller, K.** (2003) *Strategic Brand Management*, Upper Saddle River, NJ: Pearson.

28. **Brown, J.M.** (2007) Soft Drinks Sale to Britvic Enables C&C to Concentrate on High Margin Alcohol, *Financial Times*, 15 May, 22.

29. See, e.g., **Day, G.S.** and **R. Wensley** (1983) Marketing Theory with a Strategic Orientation, *Journal of Marketing*, Fall, 79–89; **Haspslagh, P.** (1982) Portfolio Planning: Uses and Limits, *Harvard Business Review*, January/February, 58–73; **Wensley, R.** (1981) Strategic Marketing: Betas, Boxes and Basics, *Journal of Marketing*, Summer, 173–83.

30. **Anonymous** (2008) Everything's Gone Blu, *The Economist*, 12 January, 53.

31. **Gapper, J.** (2006) Sony is Scoring Low at its Own Game, *Financial Times*, 6 November, 17.

32. **Nakamoto, M.** (2005) Screen Test: Stringer's Strategy Will Signal to What Extent Sony Can Stay in the Game, *Financial Times*, 21 September, 17.

33. **Vakratsas, D.** and **T. Ambler** (1999) How Advertising Works: What Do We Really Know? *Journal of Marketing*, **63**, January, 26–43.

34. **Doyle, P.** (1989) Building Successful Brands: The Strategic Options, *Journal of Marketing Management*, **5** (1), 77–95.

35. **Anonymous** (2008) Starbucks v McDonald's: Coffee Wars, *The Economist*, 12 January, 54–5.

36. **Rigby, E.** and **A. Edgecliffe-Johnson** (2006) Dixons to Pull the Plug on Old Fashioned TV Sets, *Financial Times*, 19 January, 4.

37. **Garrahan, M.** (2005) Is this Journey's End for the Travel Agent? *Financial Times: Global Traveller*, 14 November, 2.

38. **Effie Worldwide** (2010) Pedigree Adoption Drive, *Warc.com*

39. **Skelly, B.** (2008) Man About a Dog, *Marketing Age*, May–June, 34–8.

40. **Anonymous** (2007) Endless Summer, *The Economist*, 28 April, 69–70.

41. **Anonymous** (2011) Fail Often, Fail Well, *The Economist*, 16 April, 66.

42. **Booz, Allen** and **Hamilton** (1982) *New Product Management for the 1980s*, New York: Booz, Allen & Hamilton.

43. **Cooper, R.G.** and **E.J. Kleinschmidt** (1986) An Investigation into the New Product Process: Steps, Deficiencies and Impact, *Journal of Product Innovation Management*, June, 71–85.

44. **O'Dea, A.** (2008) Open for Innovation, *Marketing Age*, September/October, 22–6.

45. **Tomkins, R.** (2005) Products That Aim Straight For Your Heart, *Financial Times*, 29 April, 13.

46. **Parkinson, S.T.** (1982) The Role of the User in Successful New Product Development, *R&D Management*, **12**, 123–31.

47. **Anonymous** (2007) The Love-In, *The Economist, Special Report on Innovation*, 13 October, 18.

48. **Lillington, K.** (2008) Taking Invention Out of the Lab, *Innovation*, May, 32–4.

49. **Lillington, K.** (2008) Taking Invention Out of the Lab, *Innovation*, May, 32–4.

50. **Rogers, E.M.** (1983) *Diffusion of Innovations*, New York: Free Press.

51. **Rogers, E.M.** (1983) *Diffusion of Innovations*, New York: Free Press.

When you have read this chapter

log on to the Online Learning Centre for *Foundations of Marketing* at **www.mcgraw-hill.co.uk/textbooks/fahy** where you'll find links and extra online study tools for marketing.

connect

Go to the website to watch Carlsberg's 'Spaceman' campaign.
www.mcgraw-hill.co.uk/textbooks/fahy

Carlsberg, one of the world's premium beer brands, is getting its most significant makeover since the beer's origination in 1847. The company has decided to call time on the 'probably the best lager in the world' tagline. Carlsberg Group's new brand proposition for its flagship Carlsberg brand is supported by a range of marketing initiatives and innovations being rolled out simultaneously across over 140 markets and will be visible from packaging through to point-of-sale and other marketing communications. The global campaign will centre on the tagline 'That calls for a Carlsberg'. This rebranding comes as part of a global over-haul of the lager aimed at boosting the drink's appeal to younger drinkers in current and emerging markets.

History of Carlsberg

In 1835, following the death of his father, J.C. Jacobsen, aged 24, took over full responsibility for his father's brewery. In 1847, to cope with the increasing demand for his beer, J.C. Jacobsen established Carlsberg. The first brew was carried out on 10 November 1847 and sold under the name Carlsberg Lager Beer. The lager beer was an undisputed success, and from the first test brews until 1861, production increased from 300 barrels to more than 20,000 barrels. Carlsberg first began exporting in 1868, when a single test sample was sent to a grocer in Edinburgh, Scotland. Jacobsen became internationally recognized as a brewing pioneer by introducing science into brewing. In 1873, Jacobsen was awarded a prestigious progress medal for brewing. He repeated this success at the 1878 World Trade Exhibition in Paris, where he took the Grand Prix. In 1875, J.C. Jacobsen established the Carlsberg Laboratory to study the malting, brewing and fermenting processes, and one year later the Carlsberg Foundation which remains central to the group's organizational structure. Today the foundation serves as an important part of Carlsberg's governance structure. The foundation must hold at least 51 per cent of the votes and more than 25 per cent of the share capital.

The Carlsberg Laboratory has been at the forefront of breakthroughs in brewing. In 1883, the species of yeast used to make lager (Saccharomyces carlsbergensis) was discovered at the Carlsberg laboratory. This achievement revolutionized brewing. Jacobsen offered samples of the new pure yeast to breweries all over the world rather than main-taining the discovery as a source of competitive advantage. This point has been illustrated in some of Carlsberg's most recent advertising campaigns. Other notable achievements from the laboratory included the discovery of a method to analyse nitrogen and protein in food and feedstuff, the establishment of the concept of pH and research into the dynamic nature of proteins. One of the laboratory's most recent achievements is the development of a new type of barley. The new Null-LOX barley is being tipped as a source of competitive advantage for Carlsberg, since it will be able to keep beer fresh for a longer time while also providing better foam for the beer. As part of the global relaunch of the Carlsberg brand, Null-LOX will be used first in the Group's Carlsberg brand beers and is currently being rolled out across its markets.

Currently, the Carlsberg Group is one of the leading brewery groups in the world employing more than 43,000 people, with a large portfolio that includes more than 500 brands. These brands vary significantly in volume, price, target audience and geographic penetration. The portfolio includes the well-known international premium brands Carlsberg, Tuborg, Baltika and Kronenbourg 1664, and strong local beers such as Ringnes (Norway), Feldschlösschen (Switzerland), Lav (Serbia) and Wusu (Western China). The strength of the group's portfolio is highlighted by the fact that Baltika, Carlsberg and Tuborg are among the six biggest brands in Europe, with Baltika ranked as number one. Kronenbourg also features within the top 10. The Carlsberg Group's brands are sold in more than 150 markets. In 2010, the Carlsberg Group sold more than 135 million hectolitres of beer (about 40 billion bottles of beer) and competes in three regions: Northern and Western Europe, Eastern Europe and Asia (see Table C6.1). In Northern and Western Europe, the Carlsberg Group is the second largest brewer with market leader positions in a large number of countries and significant positions in others. It holds the number one position in Eastern Europe and states its ambition is to be the fastest growing global beer company.

Current global beer market

The current situation in the global beer market reflects the global economic crisis. Global beer market growth slowed from an average of 4.5 per cent growth in the period 2005–08 to just 0.8 per cent in 2009. Global per capita consumption remains low at just 28.7 litres compared with an average per capita consumption of 66 litres in West Europe and 75 litres in North America. However, most Asian markets saw very little disruption to their impressive growth patterns. For example, the Chinese beer market grew by 7.1 per cent in 2009 and is now almost twice the size of the US beer market.

Brewers

The global beer industry has consolidated dramatically over the past 10 years. In 2000, the top 10 brewing companies accounted for 37 per cent of the global market. By 2010 this had risen to 63 per cent. Acquisitions within the industry have given rise to the emergence of four global brewing giants: Anheuser-Busch InBev, SABMiller, Heineken and Carlsberg in order of sales. In 2010, these four companies accounted for an estimated 48 per cent of all beer consumed worldwide.

Table C6.1 Carlsberg Group financial information

DKK million	2006	2007	2008	2009	2010
Sales volumes, gross (million hl)					
Beer	100.7	115.2	126.8	137.0	136.5
Other beverages	20.2	20.8	22.3	22.2	22.5
Sales volumes, pro rata (million hl)					
Beer	72.6	82.0	109.3	116.0	114.2
Other beverages	17.5	17.8	19.8	19.8	19.3
Income statement					
Net revenue	41,083	44,750	59,944	59,382	60,054
Operating profit before special items	4,046	5,262	7,978	9,390	10,249
Special items, net	−160	−427	−1,641	−695	−249
Financial items, net	−857	−1,201	−3,456	−2,990	−2,155
Profit before tax	3,029	3,634	2,881	5,705	7,845
Corporation tax	−858	−1,038	312	−1,538	−1,885
Consolidated profit	2,171	2,596	3,193	4,167	5,960
Attributable to:					
Non-controlling interests	287	299	572	565	609
Shareholders in Carlsberg A/S	1,884	2,297	2,621	3,602	5,351

Brands and segmentation

In almost all markets, premium beer brands are outperforming mainstream brands, even in the face of the economic downturn. In part, this is due to consumers seeking better value. A parallel development has been the growth of strong beers (above 5.6 per cent abv). Many of these brands are moving away from their downmarket image towards a more upscale speciality positioning.

One of the paradoxes of the consolidation of the global beer industry has been the proliferation of brands and brand extensions, and the fact that there are still no real global beer brands. The growth of emerging markets often driven by local brands has limited the development of truly international brands.

Distribution

The biggest consequence of the economic downturn has been the acceleration of the decline in on-premise consumption in favour of off-premise. In West Europe, the decline in on-premise consumption was 6 per cent in 2009. Generally, on-premise consumption in the southern European markets and in the UK accounts for half or more of total beer consumption, whereas in the northern and eastern European countries off-premise consumption is much more prevalent, accounting for approximately 80 per cent or more of total beer consumption. In Asia, the consumption patterns are more fragmented.

Outlook

Global beer markets showed early signs of recovery in 2010, though not to the pre-2008 level. Carlsberg are forecasting global average growth of 2.8 per cent for the period 2011–15. This is in line with worldwide beer consumption, which is expected to grow by 2–3 per cent annually. Global consumption is forecast to reach 2 billion hectolitres by 2013. However, underlying growth forecasts for the different regions vary substantially. Asia will continue to grow faster than the rest of the world markets and is expected to account for nearly 40 per cent of all global beer consumption by 2015, which is more than Europe and North America combined. Despite this growth, global per capita consumption is not expected to reach more than 30 litres per capita by 2015–16, suggesting that there is considerable potential for further growth in the longer term. Carlsberg outlined its mid-term operating margin targets of 15–17 per cent in Northern and Western Europe, 26–29 per cent in Eastern Europe and 15–20 per cent in Asia in its annual report. The greatest strategic risks identified by Carlsberg are excise duties, legal restrictions, price increases and volatility in commodity prices.

Reasons for change

So why has Carlsberg launched this new campaign? Carlsberg's famous tagline, 'Probably the best beer in the world' was created in 1973 by Saatchi and Saatchi with the voiceover for the original by Orson Welles. This tagline remains popular and easily recognizable to consumers. However, while global brand recognition is high, sales of Carlsberg are worrying. *The Wall Street Journal* reports that the Carlsberg brand represents only 10 per cent of the company's total revenues, with the majority of revenue coming from the sales of local brews in individual markets. Carlsberg has made no secret of its desire to establish the brand as a global icon, with unity of image and marketing message seen as key to achieving this much sought-after status. There is also the possibility of significant cost savings in a 'glocal' approach.

Another valid reason for the new slogan is that the phrase 'probably the best lager in the world' does not translate well. The playful humour associated with the tagline is lost on consumers with the 'probably' message becoming a source of confusion in relation to the quality of the beer in some markets. Given that Carlsberg seeks fresh growth in Eastern Europe and Asia, a new unified tagline seems appropriate. However, this new campaign represents a significant risk for the company considering that the UK market currently delivers 40 per cent of the Carlsberg brand's profits. In order to prevent a negative reaction Carlsberg have said that the phrase will continue to appear on the UK packaging. However, the 'If Carlsberg did' aspect of the campaign which portrays idealized versions of everyday life will be cancelled.

The new campaign

The global relaunch of the Carlsberg brand was announced on 5 April 2011, after a two-year process. It bids to add a greater sense of essence to the brand to appeal to a new generation of drinkers. The new positioning of the brand celebrates Carlsberg's heritage and values, while connecting with today's active, adventurous generation of beer drinkers. The proposition encourages consumers 'to step up and do the right thing', rewarding themselves with a Carlsberg for their deeds, and carries the tagline 'That calls for a Carlsberg'.

New innovations

Carlsberg is keen to emphasize its rich heritage in scientific discovery. As part of the new campaign, the Null-LOX barley has been developed and is being rolled out across its markets.

New modernized identity

Carlsberg brand's visual identity has been modernized to aim to increase its appeal to today's young adult consumers. The visual identity has been developed around four design principles: bold, authentic, modern and approachable. The Danish royal crown has been made more simple and distinctive and allows Carlsberg to continue to tell the story of its authenticity and premium quality. The dominant green used since 1904 has been made more vibrant, while the antique gold has been replaced by a more sophisticated alloy of gold and silver. In addition, the brand's logo now carries three elements together for the first time: the brewer's star, the hop leaf and the inclusion of 'Copenhagen 1847,' the city where and date when Carlsberg was first brewed. Carlsberg believes the inclusion of all three elements reiterates the brand's quality, natural and authentic credentials.

New packaging

The new packaging, carrying the modernized visual identity, is now being rolled out across over 140 markets. Carlsberg is now establishing an embossed bottle with a new neck-shape label as the key bottle design across all bottle sizes. The majority of beer bottles are characterized by the brand name printed across the face of an elliptical or rectangular paper label. The brand has opted to replace the conventional paper label with glass embossing of the brand name on the bottle itself. This feature aims to differentiate the brand from other beers both on the shelf and in the hand of consumers. Carlsberg has also introduced a simpler and more distinctive version of the crown icon. Overall, the new bottle is meant to appear more modern and refined to appeal to a younger target market. However, competitor brands such as Heineken also feature the trademark green colour so Carlsberg cannot depend on visual identity alone to stand out.

New marketing communications

A total of 350 different creative materials, including 90-second cinema spots and point of sale panels, will be utilized by Carlsberg marketers worldwide. The introduction of updated pack graphics and an embossed bottle has led to 55 production lines across the globe being specially adapted. The brewer has also created its own soundtrack that will be used in different styles and tempos across all media channels. Brands can pay upwards of £250,000 to use single songs in just one market, so the initiative will deliver significant cost savings. The new campaign coincides with the announcement of Carlsberg Group's international design competition to transform the New Carlsberg Brewhouse into a Brand and Experience Centre hoping to attract 500,000 visitors each year. Carlsberg Group has also announced the sponsorship of UEFA European Soccer Championships in 2012. It has also launched its first global digital initiative which features content for YouTube and Facebook all reinforcing the new tagline. The new strategy was devised by creative agency Fold7. Jorgen Bulh Rassmussen, CEO, said the brewer aimed to double the profits of the Carlsberg brand by 2015 at the minimum.

Conclusion

Some critics have already labelled this decision by Carlsberg as 'probably not the best rebranding in the world'. The new campaign represents an idea that consumers can connect to on a personal level. The new slogan aims to create a new voice that resonates with a younger market who like to dream big and reward themselves. In its step towards new brand positioning, Carlsberg will have to be wary of alienating brand loyalists in its northern European stronghold and ensure that the idea behind the new campaign meets with the brand's core identity. In attempting to appeal to all its consumers globally with a single positioning, it may risk connecting with none. This major investment in a global branding strategy demonstrates Carlsberg's ambition to achieve iconic status for its flagship brand. Will this rebranding be successful in terms of reaching its target of doubling profits by 2015?

Questions

1. Identify Carlsberg's current stage in terms of its product life cycle.
2. Carlsberg Group has a portfolio of over 500 brands varying significantly in volume, price, target audience and geographic penetration. Outline the benefits of using the Boston Consulting Group growth-share matrix to manage this portfolio to the Carlsberg Group. In what quadrant of the matrix would you place the Carlsberg brand?
3. Discuss using Figure 6.3 (the anatomy of brand positioning) the effect of Carlsberg's new tagline on the positioning of the Carlsberg brand.
4. Critically evaluate the advantages and risks associated with utilising a single global branding strategy for Carlsberg. Explain what is meant by a 'glocal' approach.

This case was prepared by David Cosgrave, University of Limerick, from various published sources as a basis for class discussion rather than to illustrate either effective or ineffective management.

Chapter 7
Value through Services, Relationships and Experiences

Chapter outline

The unique characteristics of services

Managing services enterprises

Relationship marketing

Experiential marketing

Marketing in non-profit organizations

Learning outcomes

By the end of this chapter you will understand:

1   the nature and special characteristics of services
2   the key issues in managing services enterprises
3   the nature of service quality
4   the nature of relationship marketing
5   the management of customer relationships
6   the management of customer experiences
7   the nature and characteristics of not-for-profit marketing.

Build-a-Bear

The first Build-a-Bear store was founded in St Louis, USA, in 1997 and today there are over 400 located right around the world. The concept is a relatively simple one – instead of buying a pre-made teddy bear, children get the option of creating a teddy that is customized to their particular preferences. The company's founder Maxine Clark explains its approach using the example of McDonald's. Its founder, Ray Croc, did not invent the hamburger but, rather, a better way to sell it. In the same way, Build-a-Bear transforms the humble teddy bear from a product to a service business with an emphasis on the customer experience.

On entering a Build-a-Bear store, the process begins at the 'Choose Me' station, where customers select an unstuffed animal such as an Endless Hugs teddy or Sparkly snow leopard from a bin. At the 'Hear Me' station customers can choose from a range of pre-recorded sounds or record their own message which gives their new bear a voice. They then move to the 'Stuff Me' station where, with the assistance of a Build-a-Bear 'associate', the child operates a foot pedal that blows in the desired amount of filling for 'ideal huggability'. Plastic hearts that beat when you squeeze the creature can also be included. From there, customers move through the remaining five stations, including 'Stitch Me' where a barcode is included in case the bear is ever lost; 'Fluff Me' where children can comb their new cuddly friend's hair; 'Dress Me' where a wide range of clothes and accessories are available, and finally the 'Name Me' and 'Take Me Home' stations where the teddy receives a name and birth certificate complete with eye colour and weight.

Adopting this self-service model brings many benefits to the company. Teddy bears do not need to be manufactured in advance or held in stock which reduces the risk of product obsolescence as children's preferences may change quickly. Each additional item included in a custom-built bear increases its final price with the result that toys are often sold at a premium. And the experiential and entertainment elements of the Build-a-Bear store means that it has become popular for family days out, children's parties and even among adults buying toys for each other. The company reported profits of US$162 million on sales of US$400 million in 2010.

Build-a-Bear is expanding rapidly around the world with a mix of over 400 wholly owned and franchised outlets throughout Europe, North America, South East Asia and Australia. In 2007, the company launched buildabearville.com where children can play games with their new furry friends and earn Bear Bills which can be used to purchase clothes and other items or to trade with other guests which continues the link with Build-a-Bear long after they have left the store.[1]

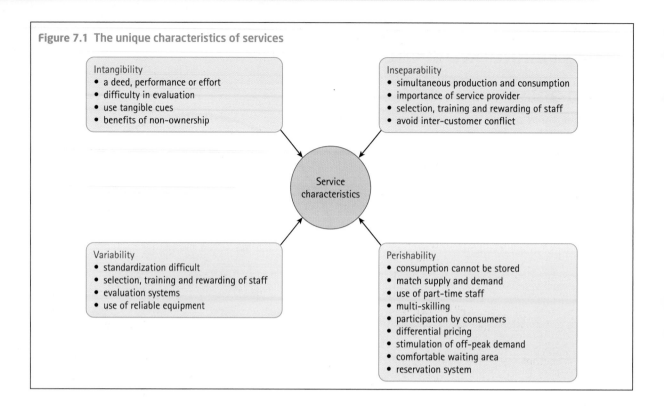

Figure 7.1 The unique characteristics of services

In the previous chapter, we saw that almost all goods that are offered in a marketplace contain elements that are both tangible and intangible (see Figure 6.1). Those that are high on tangible elements, we tend to think of as products and those that are high on intangible elements, we think of as services. A wide variety of activities such as going on holidays, visiting the dentist, receiving an education and getting legal advice are all generally thought of as service activities because of their high levels of intangibility. Throughout much of the developed world, services activity is reckoned to account for up to 60 to 70 per cent of the gross national product of some countries, thus far outweighing that of manufacturing and agriculture. This level of importance, along with some unique characteristics means that services is an important area of study.

The unique characteristics of services

There are four key distinguishing characteristics of **services**, namely, intangibility, inseparability, variability and perishability (see Figure 7.1).

Intangibility

Services can be thought of as a deed, performance or effort, not an object, device or thing, and are therefore intangible.[2] This **intangibility** may mean that a cus-

tomer may find difficulty in evaluating a service before purchase. For example, it is virtually impossible to judge how enjoyable a holiday will be before taking it because the holiday cannot be shown to a customer before consumption. The contrasts with physical products where, at a minimum, the customer has an opportunity to pick up a new product like a smartphone and examine how it looks and feels. Therefore products are characterized by *search* properties (they can be examined in advance) while services exhibit *experience* properties (they can be assessed only after they have been experienced) with a result that service choices are often riskier. Some services such as a medical operation or a car service possess *credence* properties, that is, it is not possible to evaluate them even after they have been consumed which means that these types of choices are particularly difficult for consumers.[3]

The challenge for the service provider is to use tangible cues to service quality. For example, a holiday firm may show pictures of the holiday destination, display testimonials from satisfied holidaymakers and provide details in a brochure of the kind of entertainment available (see Exhibit 7.1). The staff of US-based computer services company the Geek Squad are clearly distinguishable through their short-sleeved white shirts, black ties and badges, and their colourful 'Geek Mobiles' in which they drive to house calls.[4] Service companies, like hotels, invest heavily in tangibles such as the decor of rooms and staff uniforms (see Marketing in Action 7.1).

Marketing in Action 7.1 Rebranding Holiday Inn

Critical Thinking: Below is a review of the rebranding of the Holiday Inn hotel chain, with a focus on the changes being made to hotel tangibles. Read it and think of an example of another service business. Identify the tangibles in this business and how they might be updated.

Holiday Inn is part of the Intercontinental Hotels Group (IHG), which is one of the world's largest hotel groups, with almost 4000 outlets in over 100 countries. The original Holiday Inn chain was founded in the USA in 1952 and quickly grew its reputation as a middle-market family hotel. As well as continuing to serve this segment, it also targets business travellers and competes in a crowded sector against a variety of other well-known brands, such as Ramada Inn, Best Western and Quality Inn. Its sister brand, Holiday Inn Express, targets more budget-conscious travellers.

In 2007, IHG decided to rebrand Holiday Inn to take advantage of what it determined to be a gap in the market between it and more upmarket brands such as Marriott and Hilton. The overall cost of the initiative was estimated to be US$1 billion, with a minimum investment of US$200,000 from each hotel owner. The rebranding was expected to move at a rate of 150 hotels per month and finish by 2010.

A particular focus of the effort was on tangibles such as the hotel signage and upgrading of lobbies, which influence the important first impressions that customers get. For example, the group spent two years developing perfumes and a music list to complement its image. Holiday Inns will smell of fresh odours such as lemongrass, paired with the music of bands like U2, while the Express chain will have a musky, woody scent and be complemented by the soft pop sounds of Jack Johnson and John Mayer.

The decision to rebrand Holiday Inn was taken after research on 18,000 customers, which took two years and cost £20 million. The overall level of investment in the tangible aspects of the hotel experience demonstrates how important they are perceived to be when delivering services. Holiday Inn expects that the investment will deliver a memorable customer experience as well as increased room revenue.

Based on: Blitz (2007);[5] Ranson (2007);[6] Sibun (2007)[7].

The task is to provide an indication of likely service quality. McDonald's does this by controlling the physical settings of its restaurants and by using the golden arches as a branding cue. By having a consistent offering, the company has effectively dealt with the difficulties that consumers have in evaluating the quality of a service. Standard menus and ordering procedures have also ensured uniform and easy access for customers, while allowing quality control.[8]

Intangibility also means that the customer cannot own a service. Payment is for use or performance. For example, a car may be hired or a medical operation performed. Service organizations sometimes stress the benefits of non-ownership such as lower capital costs and the spreading of payment charges.

Inseparability

Unlike physical goods, services have **inseparability** – that is, they have simultaneous production and consumption. For example, a haircut, a medical operation, psychoanalysis, a holiday and a pop concert are produced and consumed at the same time. This contrasts with a physical good that is produced, stored and distributed through intermediaries before being bought and consumed. It also highlights the importance of the service provider, who is an integral part of the satisfaction gained by the consumer. How service providers conduct themselves may have a crucial bearing on repeat business over and above the technical efficiency of the service task. For example, how courteous and friendly the service provider is may play a large part in the customer's perception of the service experience. The service must be provided not only at the right time and in the right place but also in the right way.[9]

Often, in the customer's eyes, the photocopier service engineer or the insurance representative *is* the company. Consequently, the selection, training and rewarding of staff who are the front-line service people is of fundamental importance in the achievement of high standards of service quality. This notion of the inseparability of production and consumption means that both internal marketing and relationship marketing

their decision making. A study into service interactions in IKEA stores found that almost all customer–employee exchanges related to customer concerns about 'place' (e.g. 'Can you direct me to the pick-up point?') and 'function' (e.g. 'How does this chair work?'). However, interactions between customers took the form of opinions on the quality of materials used in products, advice on bed sizes and how to move around the in-store restaurant. Many customers appeared to display a degree of product knowledge or expertise bordering on that of contact personnel.[11]

Variability

Service quality may be subject to considerable **variability**, which makes standardization difficult (see Exhibit 7.2). Two restaurants within the same chain may have variable service owing to the capabilities of their respective managers and staff. Two marketing courses at the same university may vary considerably in terms of quality, depending on the lecturer. Quality variations among physical products may be subject to tighter controls through centralized production, automation and quality checking before dispatch. Services, however, are often conducted at multiple locations, by people who may vary in their attitudes

Exhibit 7.2 The Kitchen Squad campaign saw IKEA transform kitchens and offer tips on design and planning to help customers create a kitchen that suits their lifestyle

are important in services, as we shall see later. In such circumstances, managing buyer–seller interaction is central to effective marketing and can be fulfilled only in a relationship with the customer.[10]

Furthermore, the consumption of the service may take place in the presence of other consumers. This is apparent with restaurant meals, air, rail or coach travel, and many forms of entertainment, for example. Consequently, enjoyment of the service is dependent not only on the service provided, but also on other consumers. Therefore service providers need to identify possible sources of nuisance (e.g. noise, smoke, queue jumping) and make adequate provision to avoid inter-customer conflict. For example, a restaurant layout should provide reasonable space between tables and non-smoking areas so that the potential for conflict is minimized.

Marketing managers should not underestimate the role played by customers in aiding other customers in

(and tiredness), and are subject to simultaneous production and consumption. The last characteristic means that a service fault (e.g. rudeness) cannot be quality checked and corrected between production and consumption, unlike a physical product such as misaligned car windscreen wipers.

The potential for variability in service quality emphasizes the need for rigorous selection, training and rewarding of staff in service organizations. Training should emphasize the standards expected of personnel when dealing with customers. *Evaluation systems* should be developed that allow customers to report on their experiences with staff; for example, many service organizations invite feedback from customers through comment cards or online surveys. Some service organizations, notably the British Airports Authority, tie reward systems to customer satisfaction surveys, which are based, in part, on the service quality provided by their staff.

Service standardization is a related method of tackling the variability problem. For example, a university department could agree to use the same software platform when developing course delivery. The use of reliable equipment rather than people can also help in standardization – for instance, the supply of drinks via vending machines or cash through bank machines. However, great care needs to be taken regarding equipment reliability and efficiency. For example, the perceived security of Internet banking facilities impacts upon consumers' willingness to use this medium for financial transactions.

Perishability

The fourth characteristic of services is their **perishability** in the sense that consumption cannot be stored for the future. A hotel room or an airline seat that is not occupied today represents lost income that cannot be gained tomorrow. If a physical good is not sold, it can be stored for sale later. Therefore it is important to match supply and demand for services. For example, if a hotel has high weekday occupancy but is virtually empty at weekends, a key marketing task is to provide incentives for weekend use. This might involve offering weekend discounts, or linking hotel use with leisure activities such as golf, fishing or hiking (see Exhibit 7.3).

Service providers also have the problem of catering for peak demand when supply may be insufficient. A physical goods provider may build up inventory in slack periods for sale during peak demand. Service providers do not have this option. Consequently, alternative methods need to be considered. For example, supply flexibility can be varied through the use of part-time staff doing peak periods. Multi-skilling means that

Exhibit 7.3 Adverts like this from Spain's Vueling Airlines reflect the perishability of services

employees may be trained in many tasks. Supermarket staff can be trained to fill shelves, and work at the checkout at peak periods. Participation by consumers may be encouraged in production (e.g. self-service breakfasts in hotels). Demand may be smoothed through differential pricing to encourage customers to visit during off-peak periods (for example, lower-priced cinema and theatre seats for afternoon performances). If delay is unavoidable then another option is to make it more acceptable, for example, by providing effective queuing systems or a comfortable waiting area with seating and free refreshments. Finally, a reservation system as commonly used in restaurants, hair salons, and theatres can be used to control peak demand and assist time substitution.

In summary, intangibility, inseparability, variability and perishability combine to distinguish services from products. As we noted at the outset, products and services are not completely distinct and in most instances it is a matter of degree. For example, a marketing research study would provide a report (physical good) that represents the outcome of a number of service activities (discussions with client, designing the research strategy, interviewing respondents and analysing the results). As many firms are finding it increasingly difficult to differentiate themselves on the basis of the products, opportunities for adding value are provided by the service components. For example, staff at a Niketown store may do much more than just assist customers with finding a running shoe that fits correctly. These stores also provide additional services such as gait analysis and advice on training and running techniques – as well as selling Nike products of course!

Managing services enterprises

Because of the unique characteristics described above, managing services enterprises involves some special challenges. Four key issues are physical evidence, people, process and branding and we shall now examine each of these in detail.

Physical evidence

As we saw above, customers look for clues to the likely quality of a service by inspecting the tangible evidence or the **servicescape**. For example, prospective customers may look through a restaurant window to check the appearance of the waiters, the decor and furnishings. The ambience of a retail store is highly dependent on decor, and colour can play an important role in establishing mood because colour has meaning. For example, the reception area of the Petshotel chain in the USA is typically furnished with floral soft furnishings, armchairs, a wide-screen television and stainless steel bowls filled with doggie biscuits. This and its slogan,

Exhibit 7.4 Advertising from service businesses like this one from B&Q regularly feature company employees. This type of advertising is aimed at both employees (to motivate them to deliver the service promise) and customers (to reassure them that company employees are there to serve them)

'All the comforts of home', is designed to put pet owners at ease that their dogs will be well looked after while they are away.[12]

The layout of a service operation can be a compromise between the operation's need for efficiency and marketing's desire for effectively serving the customer. For example, the temptation to squeeze in an extra table in a restaurant or seating in an aircraft may be at the expense of customer comfort. Changes in the physical evidence are often part of a marketer's effort to reposition a brand. For example, the desire by McDonald's to improve the image of its brand has seen it invest in lime-green 'egg' chairs in many of its European restaurants, as well as putting in iPods so that customers can sit and listen to music. This moves the brand much closer to a company like Starbucks rather than its traditional competitors such as Burger King.

People

Because of the simultaneity of production and consumption in services, the firm's personnel occupy a key position in influencing customer perceptions of product quality.[13] The term **service encounter** is used to describe an interaction between a service provider and a customer. These encounters may be short and quick such as when a customer picks up a newspaper at a newsstand or long and protracted involving multiple encounters such as receiving a university education. Jan Carlzon, head of the airline SAS, called these interactions 'moments of truth'. He explained that SAS faced 65,000 moments of truth per day (that is the number of interactions between company personnel and people outside the company) and that the outcome of these interactions determined the success of the company. Research on customer loyalty in service industries has shown that only 14 per cent of customers who stopped patronizing service businesses did so because they were dissatisfied with the quality of what they had bought. More than two-thirds stopped buying because they found service staff indifferent or unhelpful.[14]

In order for service employees to be in the frame of mind to treat customers well, they need to feel that their company is treating them well. This has given rise to the idea of the *service profit chain* whereby having a happy work force leads to having happy customers and ultimately superior profitability – a maxim that has been adopted by many leading companies such as the Virgin Group. The evidence to support the existence of a service profit chain is mixed, with some findings showing a correlation between happy staff and happy customers while others have found that having a happy work force is more important than having happy customers in terms of profitability.[15] An important marketing task, then, is **internal marketing**, that is, selecting, training and motivating staff members to provide customer satisfaction. Without this type of support, employees tend to be variable in their performance, leading to variable service quality (see Exhibit 7.4).

The selection of suitable people is the starting point of the process as the nature of the job requires appropriate personality characteristics. Once selected, training is required to familiarize recruits to the job requirements and the culture of the organization. Socialization then allows recruits to experience the culture and tasks of the organization. Service quality may also be affected by the degree to which staff are empowered or given the authority to satisfy customers and deal with their problems. For example, each member of staff of Marriott Hotels is allowed to spend up to £1000 on their own initiative to solve customer problems.[16] Maintaining a motivated work force in the face of irate customers, faulty support systems and the boredom that accompanies some service jobs is a demanding task. Some service companies give employee-of-the-month awards in recognition of outstanding service. Reward and remuneration is also important. For example, the US retailer Costco competes against Wal-Mart in the discount warehouse sector. But its pay and conditions are far superior to its main rival and it has a staff turnover rate of 17 per cent annually compared with 70 per cent for the sector.[17]

Process

The service process refers to the procedures, mechanisms and flow of activities by which a service is acquired. The service process usually contains two elements, namely, that which is visible to the customer and where the service encounter takes place and that which is invisible to the customer but is still critical to service delivery. For example, waiting staff in a restaurant are a key part of the service encounter and they need to be well selected and well trained. How they treat customers is a key element of the service experience. But what happens in the kitchen, even though it is invisible to the customer is also critical to the service experience. Both parts of the service process need to be carefully managed.

Service process decisions usually involve some trade-off between levels of service quality (effectiveness) and service productivity (efficiency). Productivity is a measure of the relationship between an input and an output. For instance, if more people can be served (output) using the same number of staff (input), productivity per employee has risen. For example, a doctor who reduces consultation time per patient, or a university that increases tutorial group size, raises productivity at the risk of lowering service quality. Clearly, a balance

must be struck between productivity and service quality. There are ways of improving productivity without compromising quality. As we saw earlier, customers can be involved in the service delivery process, such as in self-service restaurants and petrol stations, and supply and demand for services can be balanced through either capacity expansion or demand management techniques.

The service process will also be significantly influenced by the service provider's attitude towards investments in technology (see Exhibit 7.5). Owing to some of the challenges involved in delivering services through people that we discussed above, firms have begun to look at technological solutions. For example, banks have been using automatic cash dispensers, telephone banking and Internet banking to improve the number of transactions per period (productivity) while reducing waiting times and increasing the availability of banking facilities (service quality). For many customers this means that the service encounter is no longer with a banking representative but rather a piece of technology. This may be advantageous in terms of service consistency but it also removes the opportunity to build a personal relationship with the customer, as we shall see later. The potential offered by technology has caused some service providers to focus more on

Exhibit 7.5 This advert by Xerox shows the role its technology plays in automating the invoice processes of the Marriott hotel chain

productivity rather than on service quality. Significant investments have been made in outsourcing customer service to call centres from which levels of service quality is often variable leading to customer frustration and dissatisfaction.

Service branding

Because of the intangible nature of services, branding is of crucial importance. As we saw earlier in the chapter, service decisions are difficult to make because services may be high on experience and credence properties. The reputation of the service provider becomes ever more important as a result and trust is an important factor in the customer buying decision. One way for service providers to differentiate themselves is through the strength of their brand equity. The brand name of a service influences the perception of that service. Research on service organizations has identified four characteristics of successful brand names, as follows.[18]

Premier Inn's 'Big Time' campaign featuring Lenny Henry conveys its brand proposition.
www.mcgraw-hill.co.uk/textbooks/fahy

1 *Distinctiveness*: it immediately identifies the service provider and differentiates it from the competition.
2 *Relevance*: it communicates the nature of the service and the service benefit.
3 *Memorability*: it is easily understood and remembered.
4 *Flexibility*: it not only expresses the service organization's current business but also is broad enough to cover foreseeable new ventures.

Wagamama, the successful Japanese noodle chain, literally translates as 'wilful naughty child', but the distinctiveness of its name and service has proven to be attractive in foreign markets. Credit cards provide examples of effective brand names: Visa suggests internationality and MasterCard emphasizes top quality. Obviously the success of the brand name is heavily dependent on the service organization's ability to deliver on the promise it implies. Sometimes service brand names are changed, such as the decision by Aviva, the UK's biggest insurer group, to drop its Norwich Union brand, which had existed for over 200 years, and by Eagle Star to change its name to that of its parent, Zurich (see Marketing in Action 7.2).

Marketing in Action 7.2 AXA: changing the brand proposition

Critical Thinking: Below is a review of a repositioning exercise conducted by the financial services group, AXA. Read it and critically evaluate the role of the brand in the service enterprise.

AXA is a French global insurance group headquartered in Paris. It provides life, health and other forms of insurance as well as investment management and operates throughout Western Europe, North America and Asia. Originally founded in the nineteenth century, the company grew through the acquisition of new businesses and in 1982 selected the name AXA because it was easy to pronounce and remember and could be used throughout its growing global markets.

In 2005, it set about attempting to become the first-choice provider, whether for customers, commercial partners or employees. Its key task was to differentiate itself from its rivals who all offer similar products and services and it was also concerned that its slogan, 'be life confident', was no longer appropriate. It conducted a detailed analysis of executives, employees and customers and developed a new slogan 'redefining/standards' which would underpin its efforts to win the trust of customers through being

'available', 'attentive' and 'reliable'. Another appeal of the new slogan was its flexibility – it could be adjusted to read 'redefining/car insurance', 'redefining/pensions' etc.

However, AXA quickly found that repositioning involved a lot more than simply changing the slogan. What being available, attentive and reliable meant to employees, in practical terms, needed to be spelled out. Similarly employee expectations regarding how management treated them also changed. Therefore, the repositioning exercise involved not only marketing but also human resources and communications executives. Early evidence would suggest that AXA's efforts to become first-choice provider are being successful with its rise to the number one position in the *Interbrand* rankings for insurance firms in both 2009 and 2010.

Based on: Michel (2011)[19].

Dimensions of the service brand may also be difficult to communicate. For example, it may be difficult to represent courtesy, hard work and customer care in an advertisement. Once again the answer is to use tangible cues that will help customers understand and judge the service. A hotel, for example, can show the buildings, swimming pool, friendly staff and happy customers; an investment company can provide tangible evidence of past performance; testimonials from satisfied customers can also be used to communicate services benefits. Netto, the Danish-based supermarket chain, used testimonials from six customers in its UK advertising to explain the advantages of shopping there. External communications that depict service quality can also influence internal staff if they include employees and show how they take exceptional care of their customers.

Word of mouth is critical to success for services because of their experiential nature. For example, talking to people who have visited a resort or hotel is more convincing than reading holiday brochures. Promotion, therefore, must acknowledge the dominant role of personal influence in the choice process and stimulate word-of-mouth communication. Cowell suggests four approaches:[20]

1 persuading satisfied customers to inform others of their satisfaction (e.g. American Express rewards customers who introduce others to its service)
2 developing materials that customers can pass on to others
3 targeting opinion leaders in advertising campaigns
4 encouraging potential customers to talk to current customers (e.g. open days at universities).

Managing service quality

One of the core means of providing value to customers is to focus on the issue of service quality and how it can be improved. All kinds of organizations are making increasing use of customer satisfaction research to guide their marketing activity. This type of research may range from customer comment cards, to mystery shoppers to online customer satisfaction studies. In a world of Internet communications and social networking, those organizations with a reputation for poor service or for not handling customer complaints effectively will be quickly named and shamed with a result that their performance often suffers. Conversely, research has shown that companies that are rated higher on service quality perform better in terms of market share growth and profitability.[21] Yet for many companies high standards of service quality remain elusive. There are four causes of poor perceived quality (see Figure 7.2). These

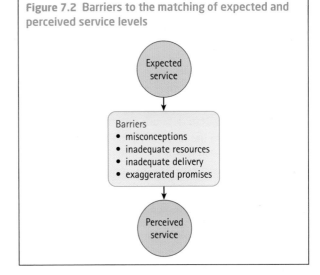

Figure 7.2 Barriers to the matching of expected and perceived service levels

are the barriers that separate the perception of service quality from what customers expect.[22]

Barriers to the matching of expected and perceived service levels

1 **Misconceptions barrier**. This arises from management's misunderstanding of what the customer expects. Lack of marketing research may lead managers to misconceive the important service attributes that customers use when evaluating a service, and the way in which customers use attributes in evaluation.

2 **Inadequate resources barrier**. Managers may understand customer expectations but be unwilling to provide the resources necessary to meet them. This may arise because of a cost reduction or productivity focus, or simply because of the inconvenience it may cause.

3 **Inadequate delivery barrier**. Managers may understand customer expectations and supply adequate resources but fail to select, train and reward staff adequately, resulting in poor or inconsistent service. This may manifest itself in poor communication skills, inappropriate dress and unwillingness to solve customer problems.

4 **Exaggerated promises barrier**. Even when customer understanding, resources and staff management are in place, a gap between customer expectations and perceptions can still arise through exaggerated promises. Advertising and selling messages that build expectations to a pitch that cannot be fulfilled may leave customers disappointed even when receiving a good service. Therefore, it is important not to over-promise in marketing communications.

Meeting customer expectations

A key to providing service quality is the understanding and meeting of customer expectations. To do so requires a clear picture of the criteria used to form these expectations, recognizing that consumers of services value not only the outcome of the service encounter but also the experience of taking part in it. For example, an evaluation of a haircut depends not only on the quality of the cut but also the experience of having a haircut. Clearly, a hairdresser needs not only technical skills but also the ability to communicate in an interesting and polite manner. Consequently, five core dimensions of service quality have been identified.[23]

1 *Reliability*: is the service consistent and dependable?
2 *Assurance*: that customers can trust the service company and its staff.
3 *Responsiveness*: how quickly do service staff respond to customer problems, requests and questions?
4 *Empathy*: that service staff act in a friendly and polite manner and care for their customers.
5 *Tangibles*: how well managed is the tangible evidence of the service (e.g. staff appearance, decor, layout)?

Improving service quality delivery requires an understanding of both customer expectations and the barriers that cause a difference between expected and perceived service levels. One approach has emphasized the closing of four gaps which are the main cause of service quality problems.[24]

Gap 1

This is the gap between what customers expect from a service provider and what the senior management team in the service organization thinks that customers expect. The gap is caused by senior managers being too far removed from customers – a problem that arises particularly in large organizations. Effective research of customers' expectations can be used to close this gap.

Gap 2

This is the gap between senior management perceptions and the service level criteria that they set for the organization. All organizations have some service level criteria such as the speed with which phones should be answered or the number of breakdowns that should be fixed within a day and so on. This gap can be closed by ensuring that customer service goals are an important part of the organization's targets for the planning period.

Gap 3

This is the gap between the service level targets set by the organization and the actual level of service that is delivered by front-line staff. This gap can arise due to there being inadequate resources committed to service delivery or poor selection, training and motivation of staff. Good internal marketing practices can assist in closing this gap.

Gap 4

Finally, this is the gap between what firms tell their customers to expect in their external communications and what they actually deliver. Therefore, service promises need to be managed very carefully. Overpromising causes customer expectations to rise and failure to deliver on these promises leads to dissatisfaction.

In summary, delivering service quality requires constant attention to the four potential gaps in the service delivery system. This is why consistently high levels of service are so difficult and why only very few firms, such as service leaders like Singapore Airlines and Marriott Hotels, manage to achieve them (see Exhibit 7.6).

Service recovery

Because services involve people, mistakes will inevitably occur even in the best managed service systems. Service recovery strategies should be designed to solve the problem and restore the customer's trust in the firm, as well as improve the service system so that the problem does not recur in the future.[25] They are crucial because an inability to recover service failures and mistakes loses customers directly as well as through their tendency to tell other actual and potential customers about their negative experiences. This is particularly the case where consumers have paid a great deal for a service, such as first-class airline passengers.

The first ingredient in a service recovery strategy is to set up a tracking system to identify system failures. Customers should be encouraged to report service problems since it is those customers that do not complain that are least likely to purchase again. Second, staff should be trained and empowered to respond to service complaints. This is important because research has shown that the successful resolution of a complaint can cause customers to feel more positive about the firm than before the service failure. For example, when P&O had to cancel a round-the-world cruise because of problems with its ship, the *Aurora*, it reportedly offered passengers their money back plus a discount on their next booking. Many passengers said they planned to travel on a P&O cruise in the future.[26]

Exhibit 7.6 The iconic Singapore girl is used in Singapore Airlines' advertising to illustrate the company's passion for service quality

THE SINGAPORE AIRLINES
BUSINESS CLASS
MOST SPACIOUS THE WORLD HAS EVER SEEN

Singapore Airlines Business Class – the widest in its class – invites you to be reacquainted with the joys of relaxing on your favourite sofa. The premium seat unfolds to reveal the largest ever full-flat bed in Business Class; offering you plenty of room to stretch out and enjoy a rejuvenating night's rest. Unrivalled space and direct access to the aisle are signatures of our innovative seat. With these unique features, and the inflight service even other airlines talk about, the Singapore Airlines Business Class brings you travel in a new light. Available onboard the A340-500, A380 and 777-300ER aircraft. Visit **singaporeair.com** for more information.

SINGAPORE AIRLINES
A great way to fly

The Singapore Airlines' 'Across the World' campaign illustrates the company's reputation for outstanding service quality. **www.mcgraw-hill.co.uk/textbooks/fahy**

Finally, a service recovery strategy should encourage learning so that service recovery problems are identified and corrected. Service staff should be motivated to report problems and solutions so that recurrent failures are identified and fixed. In this way, an effective service recovery system can lead to improved customer service, satisfaction and higher customer retention levels.

Relationship marketing

The intangible nature of services means that customers may also value having a close relationship with a service provider. For example, if a customer finds an organization that she can trust, she may want to go back to this provider again and again as this saves her having to conduct a new information search each time a purchase is made. The relationship may also benefit the service provider as it is generally believed that it is cheaper for the organization to retain its existing customers than it is to gain new ones. These elements have underpinned the rise of **relationship marketing** which has grown in popularity in recent times.

The idea of relationship marketing can be applied to many industries. It is particularly important in services since there is often direct contact between service provider and consumer – for example, doctor and patient, hotel staff and guests. The quality of the relationship that develops will often determine its length. Not all service encounters have the potential for a long-term relationship, however. For example, a passenger at an international airport who needs road transportation will probably never meet the taxi driver again, and the choice of taxi supplier will be dependent on the passenger's position in the queue rather than free choice. In this case the exchange – cash for journey – is a pure transaction: the driver knows that it is unlikely that there will ever be a repeat purchase.[27] Organizations therefore need to decide when the practice of relationship marketing is most applicable. The following conditions suggest the use of relationship marketing activities.[28]

■ There is an ongoing or periodic desire for the service by the customer, e.g. insurance or theatre service versus funeral service.

- The customer controls the selection of a service provider, e.g. selecting a hotel versus entering the first taxi in an airport waiting line.
- The customer has alternatives from which to choose, e.g. selecting a restaurant versus buying water from the only utility company service in a community.

The existence of strong customer relationships brings benefits both for organizations and customers. There are six benefits to service organizations in developing and maintaining strong customer relationships.[29] The first is *increased purchases*. Customers tend to spend more because, as the relationship develops, trust grows between the partners. Second is *lower costs*. The start-up costs associated with attracting new customers are likely to be far higher than the cost of retaining existing customers. Third, loyal customers generate a significant *lifetime value*. If a customer spends €80 in a supermarket per week, resulting in €8 profit, and uses the supermarket 45 times a year over 30 years, the lifetime value of that customer is almost €11,000. Fourth, the intangible aspects of a relationship are not easily copied by the competition, generating a *sustainable competitive advantage*. Fifth, satisfied customers generate additional business due to the importance of *word-of-mouth* promotion in services industries. Finally, satisfied, loyal customers raise *employees' job satisfaction* and decrease staff turnover.

The net result of these six benefits of developing customer relationships is high profits. A study has shown across a variety of service industries that profits climb steeply when a firm lowers its customer defection rate.[30] Firms can improve profits from 25 to 85 per cent (depending on industry) by reducing customer defections by just 5 per cent. The reasons are that loyal customers generate more revenue for more years and the costs of maintaining existing customers are lower than the costs of acquiring new ones.

Entering into a long-term relationship can also reap benefits for the customer. First, since the intangible nature of services makes them difficult to evaluate beforehand, purchase relationships can help to reduce the risk and stress involved in making choices. Second, strong relationships allow the service provider to deliver a higher-quality service, which can be customized to particular needs. Maintaining a relationship reduces the customer's switching costs and, finally, customers can reap social and status benefits from the relationship, such as when restaurant managers get to know them personally.

Relationship marketing strategies vary in the degree to which they bond the parties together. One framework that illustrates this idea distinguishes between three levels of retention strategy based on the types of bond used to cement the relationship.[31]

1   *Level 1*: at this level the bond is primarily through financial incentives – for example, higher discounts on prices for larger-volume purchases, or frequent flyer or loyalty points resulting in lower future prices. The problem is that the potential for a sustainable competitive advantage is low because price incentives are easy for competitors to copy even if they take the guise of frequent flyer or loyalty points.
2   *Level 2*: this higher level of bonding relies on more than just price incentives and consequently raises the potential for a sustainable competitive advantage. Level 2 retention strategies build long-term relationships through social as well as financial bonds, capitalizing on the fact that many service encounters are also social encounters. Customers become clients, the relationship becomes personalized and the service customized. Characteristics of this type of relationship include frequent communication with customers, providing personal treatment like sending cards, and enhancing the core service with educational or entertainment activities such as seminars or visits to sporting events. Some hotels keep records of their guests' personal preferences such as their favourite newspaper and alcoholic drink.
3   *Level 3*: this top level of bonding is formed by financial, social and structural bonds. Structural bonds tie service providers to their customers through providing solutions to customers' problems that are designed into the service delivery system. For example, logistics companies often supply their clients with equipment that ties them into their systems.

Customer loyalty and retention

Relationship marketing strategies focus attention on the important issue of customer loyalty. At the most basic level, it has been suggested that a potential ladder of loyalty exists and that customers progress up or down this ladder (see Figure 7.3). Basically, the firm's marketing activity may revolve around trying to move customers up this ladder until they become advocates or partners of the organization. Advocates are an important group because they not only purchase an organization's products but they actively recommend it to their friends and colleagues. At the top of the ladder are partners who trust and support the organization and actively work with it.

The ladder of loyalty also helps organizations to reflect on the different types of loyalty that may exist.

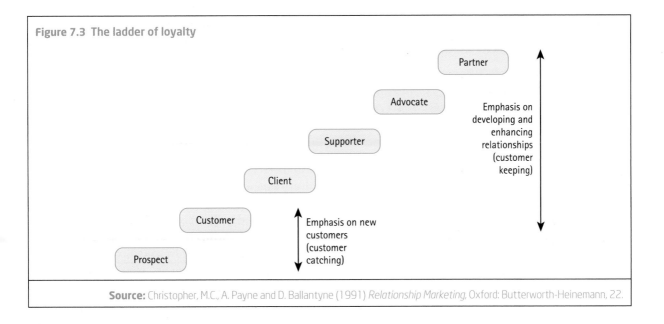

Figure 7.3 The ladder of loyalty

Emphasis on developing and enhancing relationships (customer keeping)

Emphasis on new customers (customer catching)

Source: Christopher, M.C., A. Payne and D. Ballantyne (1991) *Relationship Marketing*, Oxford: Butterworth-Heinemann, 22.

For example, some customers may continue to engage in high levels of repeat business with an organization but this may happen for reasons of inertia rather than true loyalty. This has occurred in sectors like retail banking where consumers have demonstrated a reluctance to switch. Similarly, many of the loyalty schemes run by organizations aim to attract and retain customers on a purely financial basis. Again, this is not true loyalty with customers tending to engage in repeat business only for as long as the financial incentives remain. A much greater understanding of customers' needs and a willingness to meet those needs on an ongoing basis is required for true loyalty to occur.

Finally, the link between customer loyalty and profitability is a very important one in marketing. Associations between a small increase in customer retention and a large increase in profitability have been identified.[32] This has been explained by the propensity of loyal customers to spend more with the organization and the decreased cost of serving such customers. However, other research has highlighted that this relationship may be more complex. For example, in some instances it has been found that long-standing customers are only marginally profitable while some short-term customers have been highly profitable.[33] This reaffirms that it is the nature of loyalty rather than the length of time customers have been with a firm that is most important.

Experiential marketing

Allied to the provision of service quality and relationships, the creation of customer experiences is another avenue for organizations to deliver value for customers, as we saw in the marketing spotlight at the beginning of the chapter. It aims to capitalize on consumer trends in the Western world, where experiences are perceived by many as being more important than the ownership of goods. Through **experiential marketing**, organizations either partner with existing events or create entirely new ones.

For example, one of the most popular forms of experiential marketing has been the increased association of brands with events like rock concerts and music festivals. This allows marketers to use relevant ways of communicating with audiences for such events, such as through online media and buzz marketing. The Guinness brand has been associated with the Witness music festival in Ireland, where even the altered spelling of the word 'witness' highlighted the Guinness association. Pre-publicity for the event also featured a play on the idea of a witness. Consumers and the media joined in a search for clues and were invited to participate in the discovery of Witness. This generated huge publicity about the event and the various acts that would be performing there. Because the target audience was considered to be marketing literate and cynical with regard to corporate marketing efforts, this approach was more subtle and gave consumers a feeling of ownership and involvement with the event. In a similar fashion, the Guinness brand has been behind the creation of the hugely successful Arthur's Day (see Marketing in Action 7.3 and Exhibit 7.7).

Experiential marketing has also become very popular within the retail trade as stores and locations seek to find new ways of appealing to potential

Marketing in Action 7.3 Arthur's Day

Critical Thinking: Below is a review of the hugely successful Arthur's Day celebrations run by the Guinness brand. Read it and critically assess the key ingredients of successful experiential marketing campaigns.

The iconic drinks brand Guinness, which is sold in over 150 countries around the world, faced an interesting challenge as it considered how best to celebrate its 250th birthday in 2009. How could it stay true to its long history but at the same time say happy birthday in a way that resonated with its current generation of customers? The answer was Arthur's Day – a planned mass celebration of the brand.

There were three main elements to the original Arthur's Day idea, namely, recognize the iconic status of the brand, make a positive statement of intent about it and engage both existing and new drinkers with the brand. In the lead-up to the big day, classic print and television advertisements were shown again highlighting the brand's long legacy. The statement of intent involved the launch of the Arthur Guinness Fund to deliver philanthropy to good causes. With every signature up to one million, Guinness pledged to donate €2.50 generating a fund of €2.5million, a move which engaged its

customers with the brand. The first ever global advertisement for the brand was aired in summer 2009 showing people around the world toasting to Arthur's birthday. Then on Thursday 9 September 2009 at 17.59 Arthur's birthday was 'officially' celebrated in bars all over Ireland. Sixty music acts, including many surprise guests, played. The attendant media coverage for the event which aired right around the world was worth millions and some 16,000 fans signed a petition on Facebook to make Arthur's Day a national holiday.

One measure of its success was that over 800 bands applied for a chance to play in Arthur's Day 2010, which too turned out to be a huge success selling over 18,000 tickets for events on Ticketmaster and the number of Facebook fans rising to 170,000. By building an international event that takes place in pubs and clubs, the Guinness brand is not only providing an experience for its customers but also assisting its channel partners to achieve their business goals through increased revenues.

Exhibit 7.7 Guinness' Arthur's Day, which celebrates the founding of the company, has been a huge global success for the brand

customers. The focus has moved from being a venue where products are sold to one where consumers can have a shopping experience or where they can shop as part of other activities. Many major shopping malls now have cinemas attached, others have leisure facilities such as gymnasiums and swimming pools, and some have theatres and galleries. Luxury store Prada, New York, has a cultural performance space, Louis Vuitton's Paris flagship store has an art gallery and a bookstore, while Gucci's Ginza store in Tokyo also has an art gallery as well as an event space. Nespresso has opened a number of Nespresso Boutiques to create the 'ultimate coffee experience'.

The ideal experiential marketing effort is an ownable, sensory brand experience that makes customers feel like the product or service is theirs. These motivated customers then become product advocates, who influence family, friends and co-workers to try the product. For example, Delta Airlines has developed its SKY360 lounge in New York to create a customer experience. Visitors to the lounge are met by actual flight attendants and ticket agents. They sample food items available on Delta and are asked to try new entertainment systems that are built into the backs of seats. The lounge has WiFi connections and computer terminals for anyone who wants to book a flight with Delta.[34]

Marketing in non-profit organizations

Non-profit organizations attempt to achieve some other objective than profit. This does not mean that they are uninterested in income as they have to generate cash to survive. However, their primary goal is non-economic – for example, to provide cultural enrichment (an orchestra), to protect birds and animals (Royal Society for the Protection of Birds, Royal Society for the Prevention of Cruelty to Animals), to alleviate hunger (Oxfam), to provide education (schools and universities), to foster community activities (community associations), and to supply healthcare (hospitals) and public services (local authorities) (see Exhibit 7.8). Their worth and standing is not dependent on the profits they generate. They are discussed in this chapter as most non-profit organizations operate in the services sector. Indeed, non-profit organizations account for over half of all service provision in most European countries.

Marketing is of growing importance to many non-profit organizations because they need to generate funds in an increasingly competitive arena. Even organizations that rely on government-sponsored grants need to show how their work is of benefit to society; they must meet the needs of their customers. Many

Exhibit 7.8 A clever print advertising visual used to create awareness of a French Film Festival

non-profit organizations rely on membership fees and donations, which means that communication to individuals and organizations is required, and they must be persuaded to join or make a donation. This requires marketing skills, which are increasingly being applied. As we saw in Chapter 1, political parties, universities, hospitals and aid agencies are now frequent users of marketing.

Characteristics of non-profit marketing

There are a number of characteristics of non-profit marketing that distinguish it from that conducted in profit-orientated organizations.[35]

Education vs meeting current needs

Some non-profit organizations see their role not only as meeting the current needs of their customers but also educating them in terms of new ideas and issues, cultural developments and social awareness. **Social marketing** is the term that is used to describe efforts, mainly by public sector organizations, to encourage positive social change such as healthy eating, reduced cigarette and alcohol consumption, safe sex, safe driving, human rights and racial equality. Commercial marketing techniques such as consumer research, segmentation and marketing mix development are frequently used to achieve these types of goals.

Multiple publics

Most non-profit organizations serve several groups, or publics. The two broad groups are *donors*, who may be individuals, trusts, companies or government bodies, and *clients*, who include audiences, patients and beneficiaries.[36] The need to satisfy both donors and clients is a complicated marketing task. For example, a community association may be partly funded by the local authority and partly by the users (clients) of the association's buildings and facilities. To succeed, both groups have to be satisfied. The BBC has to satisfy not only its viewers and listeners, but also the government, which decides the size of the licence fee that funds its activities. Non-profit organizations need to adopt marketing as a coherent philosophy for managing multiple public relationships.[37]

Measurement of success and conflicting objectives

For profit-orientated organizations success is ultimately measured in terms of profitability. For non-profit organizations, measuring success is not so easy. In universities, for example, is success measured in terms of research output, number of students taught, the range of qualifications or the quality of teaching? The answer is that it is a combination of these factors, which can lead to conflict – more students and a larger range of courses may reduce the time available for research. Decision making is therefore complex in non-profit-orientated organizations.

Public scrutiny

While all organizations are subject to public scrutiny, public-sector non-profit organizations are never far from the public's attention. The reason is that they are publicly funded from taxes. This gives them extra newsworthiness and they have to be particularly careful not to become involved in controversy.

Marketing procedures for non-profit organizations

Despite these differences, the marketing procedures relevant to profit-orientated organizations can also be applied to non-profit organizations. Target marketing, differentiation and tactical marketing decisions need to be made. We will now discuss these issues with reference to the special characteristics of non-profit organizations.

Target marketing and differentiation

As we have already discussed, non-profit organizations can usefully segment their target publics into donors and clients (customers). Within each group, sub-segments of individuals and organizations need to be identified. These will be the targets for persuasive communications and the development of services. The needs of each group must be understood. For example, donors may judge which charity to give to on the basis of awareness and reputation, the confidence that funds will not be wasted on excessive administration, and the perceived worthiness of the cause. The charity needs, therefore, not only to promote itself but also to gain publicity for its cause (see Marketing in Action 7.4). Its level of donor funding will depend upon both these factors. The brand name of the charity is also important. 'Oxfam' suggests the type of work the organization is mainly concerned with – relief of famine – and so is instantly recognizable. 'Action in Distress' is also suggestive of its type of work.

Market segmentation and targeting are key ingredients in the marketing of political parties. Potential voters are segmented according to their propensity to vote (obtainable from electoral registers) and their likelihood of voting for a particular party (obtainable from door-to-door canvassing returns). Resources can then be channelled to the segments most likely to switch votes in the forthcoming election, via direct mail and doorstep visits. Focus groups provide a feedback mechanism for testing the attractiveness of alternative policy options and gauging voters' opinions on key policy areas such as health, education and taxation. By keeping in touch with public opinion, political parties have the information to differentiate themselves from their competitors on issues that are important to voters. While such marketing research is unlikely to affect the underlying beliefs and principles upon which a political party is based, it is a necessary basis for the policy adaptations required to keep in touch with a changing electorate.[38]

Developing a marketing mix

Many non-profit organizations are skilled at *event marketing*. Events are organized to raise funds, and include dinners, dances, coffee mornings, book sales, sponsored walks and theatrical shows. Not all events are designed to raise funds for the sponsoring organization. For example, the BBC has organized the Comic Relief and Children in Need telethons to raise money for worthy causes.

Marketing in Action 7.4   Remember a Charity (in your will)

Critical Thinking: Below is a review of a promotional campaign run by the Remember a Charity organization. Review it and evaluate the reasons for its success.

Remember a Charity is a UK not-for-profit organization that was established in 1999 to encourage those making their wills to consider including a charity as one of the beneficiaries. It is a challenging remit as it is estimated that only 8 per cent of people leave a legacy to charity in any given year, though this accounts for over one-third of the income generated by charities. It is also a unique business in that the effectiveness (or otherwise) of its current marketing efforts may not be seen for years or even decades.

Legacy values are very closely tied to economic performance so since the global financial crisis of 2008, forecast income for charities from legacy donors has fallen sharply. Added to that was the fact that in the main, people generally left their estates to their children so it was important that any marketing efforts would not be seen as attempting to put charity ahead of family. As a result the message became – 'In your will, take care of your loved ones first, and then consider a little for charity'. And finally, legacies were something that were usually not talked about so Remember a Charity decided to bring the issue out in the open with a series of daytime television and radio advertising. It also took the decision to use humour in the creative execution – a difficult decision when dealing with such sensitive topics as death and legacies.

The promotional approach was highly successful. Within one month of the campaign, the number of people reporting that they had seen legacy advertising doubled. The risky use of humour also proved to be a success with over half of those interviewed reporting that they enjoyed the adverts. Attendant press coverage and the publicity surrounding the launch of a Legacy Awareness Week in 2009 were estimated to have reached 20 million UK consumers. Post-campaign research also showed that people had more positive attitudes to legacies and that more consumers intended to leave some of their legacy to charity.

Based on: Hill, Ringshall and Vass (2010)[39].

The pricing of services provided by non-profit organizations may not follow the guidelines applicable to profit-orientated pricing. For example, the price of a nursery school place organized by a community association may be held low to encourage poor families to take advantage of the opportunity. Some non-profit organizations exist to provide free access to services – for example, the National Health Service in the UK. In other situations, the price of a service provided by a non-profit organization may come from a membership or licence fee. For example, the Royal Society for the Protection of Birds (RSPB) charges an annual membership fee; in return members receive a quarterly magazine and free entry to RSPB bird watching sites. The BBC receives income from a licence fee, which all television owners have to pay. The level of this fee is set by government, making relations with political figures an important marketing consideration.

Like most services, distribution systems for many non-profit organizations are short, with production and consumption simultaneous. This is the case for hospital operations, consultations with medical practitioners, education, nursery provision, cultural entertainment and many more services provided by non-profit organizations. Such organizations have to think carefully about how to deliver their services with the convenience that customers require. For example, Oxfam has 750 shops around the UK that sell second-hand clothing, books, music and household items that have been donated to it. It has also formed alliances with online retailers such as abebooks.co.uk to list and sell second-hand books, from which Oxfam receives a commission.

Many non-profit organizations are adept at using promotion to further their needs. The print media are popular with organizations seeking donations for worthy causes such as famine in Africa. Direct mail is also used to raise funds. Mailing lists of past donors are useful here, and some organizations use lifestyle geodemographic analyses to identify the type of person who is more likely to respond to a direct mailing. Non-profit organizations also need to be aware of publicity opportunities that may arise because of their activities.

Many editors are sympathetic to such publicity attempts because of their general interest to the public. Sponsorship is also a vital income source for many non-profit organizations.

Public relations have an important role to play in generating positive word-of-mouth communications and establishing the identity of the non-profit organization (e.g. a charity). Attractive fundraising settings (e.g. sponsored lunches) can be organized to ensure that the exchange proves to be satisfactory to donors. A key objective of communications efforts should be to produce a positive assessment of the fundraising transaction and to reduce the perceived risk of the donation so that donors develop trust and confidence in the organization and become committed to the cause.[40]

Summary

In this chapter, we examined the particular issues that arise when marketing services businesses. The following key issues were addressed.

1. There are four unique characteristics of services, namely intangibility, inseparability, variability and perishability. As a result marketers must find ways to 'tangibilize' services, must pay attention to service quality, must find ways to ensure service consistency, and must find ways to balance supply and demand for services.
2. The four key elements of managing services enterprises, namely, physical evidence, people, process and service branding.
3. Internal marketing to frontline employees is critical to the success of a service organization and great attention needs to be paid to their selection, training and motivation. Employee empowerment is a key element of service quality and service recovery.
4. Service quality is an important source of value creation. Essentially, it involves measuring how service perceptions match up against the expectations that customers have of the service provider and taking the types of remedial action necessary to close any service delivery gaps.
5. Relationship marketing is another important source of value creation. Organizations can engage in marketing activities that raise levels of attitudinal loyalty.
6. Value can also be created through the provision of customer experiences which can be used to improve the consumer's relationship with the organization.
7. Non-profit organizations attempt to achieve some objectives other than profit. Their two key publics are donors and clients; the needs of these two groups often conflict. In managing this complexity, non-profit organizations use conventional services marketing techniques.

Study questions

1. Discuss the implications of the unique characteristics of services for the marketing activities of services enterprises.
2. What are the barriers that can separate expected from perceived service? What must service providers do to eliminate these barriers?
3. Discuss the role of service staff in the creation of a quality service. Can you give examples from your own experiences of good and bad service encounters?
4. Discuss the benefits to organizations and customers of developing and maintaining strong customer relationships.
5. Select any three music, sport or cultural events that you have attended in the past year. What industry partners were involved in the events and what role did they play in each one?
6. How does marketing in non-profit organizations differ from that in profit-orientated companies? Choose a non-profit organization and discuss the extent to which marketing principles can be applied.
7. Visit www.epinions.com and www.tripadvisor.com. Discuss the impact of the existence of these websites on organizations that provide good and poor levels of service.

Suggested reading

Ahmed, P.K. and **R. Mohammed** (2003) Internal Marketing: Issues and Challenges, *European Journal of Marketing*, **37** (9), 1177–87.

Berry, L.L., V. Shankar, J. Turner Parish, S. Cadwallader and **T. Dotzel** (2006) Creating New Markets Through Service Innovation, *Sloan Management Review*, **47** (2), 56–63.

Dixon, M., K. Freeman and **N. Toman** (2010) Stop Trying to Delight Your Customers, *Harvard Business Review*, **88** (7/8), 116–22.

Kumar, V., J.A. Petersen and **R.P. Leone** (2007) How Valuable is Word of Mouth? *Harvard Business Review*, **85** (10), 139–56.

McDermott, L., M. Steed and **G. Hastings** (2005) What is and What is Not Social Marketing: The Challenge of Reviewing the Evidence, *Journal of Marketing Management*, **21** (5/6), 545–53.

Moeller, S. (2010) Characteristics of Services – A New Approach Uncovers Their Value, *Journal of Services Marketing*, **24** (5), 359–68.

References

1. **DeMesa, A.** (2005) Marketing and Tweens, *Brandchannel.com*, 10 October; **Woods, J.** (2009) Build-a-Bear: The Last Resort for the Middle Class, *Telegraph.co.uk*, 18 August.
2. **Berry, L.L.** (1980) Services Marketing is Different, *Business Horizons*, May–June, 24–9.
3. **Zeithaml, V.** (1984) How Consumer Evaluation Processes Differ Between Goods and Services, in C.H. Lovelock (ed.) *Services Marketing*, Engelwoods Cliffs, NJ., Prentice-Hall, 191–9.
4. **Foster, L.** (2004) The March of the Geek Squad, *Financial Times*, 24 November, 13.
5. **Blitz, R.** (2007) Holiday Inn in $1bn Makeover, *Financial Times*, 25 October, 21.
6. **Ranson, K.** (2007) Holiday Inn Gets a $1bn Rebrand, *Travelweekly.co.uk*, 24 October.
7. **Sibun, J.** (2007) £1bn Rebrand for Holiday Inn Chain, *Telegraph.co.uk*, 25 October.
8. **Edgett, S.** and **S. Parkinson** (1993) Marketing for Services Industries: A Review, *Service Industries Journal*, **13** (3), 19–39.
9. **Berry, L.L.** (1980) Services Marketing is Different, *Business Horizons*, May–June, 24–9.
10. **Aijo, T.S.** (1996) The Theoretical and Philosophical Underpinnings of Relationship Marketing, *European Journal of Marketing*, **30** (2), 8–18; **Grönoos, C.** (1990) *Services Management and Marketing: Managing the Moments of Truth in Service Competition*, Lexington, MA: Lexington Books.
11. **Baron, S., K. Harris** and **B.J. Davies** (1996) Oral Participation in Retail Service Delivery: A Comparison of the Roles of Contact Personnel and Customers, *European Journal of Marketing*, **30** (9), 75–90.
12. **Birchall, J.** (2005) Top Dogs Lead the Way as Pet Market Grooms and Booms, *Financial Times*, 3 August, 28.
13. **Rafiq, M.** and **P.K. Ahmed** (1992) The Marketing Mix Reconsidered, *Proceedings of the Annual Conference of the Marketing Education Group*, Salford, 439–51.
14. **Schlesinger, L.A.** and **J.L. Heskett** (1991) The Service-driven Service Company, *Harvard Business Review*, September–October, 71–81.
15. **Anonymous** (2007) Doing Well By Being Rather Nice, *The Economist*, 1 December, 74; **Mitchell, A.** (2007) In the Pursuit of Happiness, *Financial Times*, 14 June, 14.
16. **Bowen, D.E.** and **L.L. Lawler** (1992) Empowerment: Why, What, How and When, *Sloan Management Review*, Spring, 31–9.
17. **Birchall, J.** (2005) Pile High, Sell Cheap and Pay Well, *Financial Times*, 11 July, 12.
18. **Berry, L.L., E.E. Lefkowith** and **T. Clark** (1980) In Services: What's in a Name? *Harvard Business Review*, September–October, 28–30.
19. **Michel, S.** (2011) Axa's Rebranding, *Ft.com*, 9 March.
20. **Cowell, D.** (1995) *The Marketing of Services*, London: Heinemann, 35.
21. **Buzzell, R.D.** and **B.T. Gale** (1987) *The PIMS Principles: Linking Strategy to Performance*, New York: Free Press, 103–34.
22. **Parasuraman, A., V.A. Zeithaml** and **L.L. Berry** (1985) A Conceptual Model of Service Quality and its Implications for Future Research, *Journal of Marketing*, Fall, 41–50.
23. **Parasuraman, A., V.A. Zeithaml** and **L.L. Berry** (1985) A Conceptual Model of Service Quality and its Implications for Future Research, *Journal of Marketing*, Fall, 41–50.
24. **Berry, L.L., A. Parsuraman** and **V.A. Zeithaml** (1988) The Service-Quality Puzzle, *Business Horizons*, **31** (5), 35–44.
25. **Reichheld, F.F.** and **W.E. Sasser Jr** (1990) Zero Defections: Quality Comes To Services, *Harvard Business Review*, September–October, 105–11.
26. **Reinartz, W.J.** and **V. Kumar** (2002) The Mismanagement of Customer Loyalty, *Harvard Business Review*, **80** (7), 86–94.
27. **Egan, C.** (1997) Relationship Management, in Jobber, D. (ed.) *The CIM Handbook of Selling and Sales Strategy*, Oxford: Butterworth-Heinemann, 55–88.
28. **Berry, L.L.** (1995) Relationship Marketing, in Payne, A., M. Christopher, M. Clark and H. Peck (eds) *Relationship Marketing for Competitive Advantage*, Oxford: Butterworth-Heinemann, 65–74.
29. **Zeithaml, V.A.** and **M.J. Bitner** (2002) *Services Marketing*, New York: McGraw-Hill, 174–8.
30. **Reichheld, F.F.** and **W.E. Sasser Jr** (1990) Zero Defections: Quality Comes To Services, *Harvard Business Review*, Sept–Oct, 105–11.
31. **Berry, L.L.** and **A. Parasuraman** (1991) *Managing Services*, New York: Free Press, 136–42.
32. **Kasper, H., P. van Helsdingen** and **W. de Vries Jr** (1999) *Services Marketing Management*, Chichester: Wiley, 528.
33. **Witzel, M.** (2005) Keep your Relationship with Clients Afloat, *Financial Times*, 31 January, 13.

34. **Borden, J.** (2008) Experiential Marketing Takes the Industry by Storm in 2008, *Marketing Week*, 15 January, 23–6.

35. **Bennett, P.D.** (1988) *Marketing*, New York: McGraw-Hill, 690–2.

36. **Shapiro, B.** (1992) Marketing for Non-Profit Organisations, *Harvard Business Review*, September–October, 123–32.

37. **Balabanis, G., R.E. Stables** and **H.C. Philips** (1997) Market Orientation in the Top 200 British Charity Organisations and its Impact on their Performance, *European Journal of Marketing*, **31** (8), 583–603.

38. **Butler, P.** and **N. Collins** (1994) Political Marketing: Structure and Process, *European Journal of Marketing*, **28** (1), 19–34.

39. **Hill, R., S. Ringshall** and **A. Vass** (2010) Remember a Charity – Pennies from Heaven, *Warc.com*.

40. **Hibbert, S.** (1995) The Market Positioning of British Medical Charities, *European Journal of Marketing*, **29** (10), 6–26.

When you have read this chapter

log on to the Online Learning Centre for
Foundations of Marketing at
www.mcgraw-hill.co.uk/textbooks/fahy
where you'll find links and extra online study tools for marketing.

Case 7 ShredBank: differentiating document destruction services

ShredBank is a mobile document shredding business based in Belfast, Northern Ireland (NI). The company was set up in 2007 by local business man James Carson and business graduate and entrepreneur, Philip Bain. Bain focused on business development within the company while Carson managed logistics and operations. According to Carson, 'the company aspires to be the leading on-site document destruction company in Ireland through technological innovation, creative marketing and superior customer service'.

ShredBank secured ISO 9001:2008 within six months of trading and was also awarded the shredding standard Code of Practice BS EN 15713:2009. Two years from inception, and during the beginnings of the global recession, ShredBank grew to employ 10 staff. The company secured Investors in People in April 2010 and has won numerous business awards including the Northern Ireland Chamber of Commerce 'Most Promising New Business of 2009', while Bain himself has been named Northern Ireland's Entrepreneur of the Year in 2010 and Young Business Person of the Year in 2011. The business has grown on average by 30 per cent per annum since start-up and, as of year-end 2010, it had secured some 30 per cent of the Northern Ireland mobile shredding market.

The document disposal market

Internationally the market for confidential document disposal services is growing – in the USA alone the market was worth $3 billion in 2005 and has been growing at 10 per cent per annum. The US market is highly fragmented with over 90 per cent of players in the shredding business sector turning over less than $1.5 million. Although specific market information relating to the size of the on-site shredding market in the UK and Ireland is limited, the growth trend is in line with that of the international market.

In parallel with these global growth trends, in 2006–07 there was an explosion in local media stories which 'named and shamed' organizations that had lost documents that contained confidential information. Often this information related to personal details of members of the general public (e.g. perhaps in relation to medical or financial detail).

In late 2007, James Carson and Philip Bain sensed a shift in mood around this issue of confidential document destruction, both among their own business contact networks and more generally at a societal level. At a business level, this change was characterized by a move away from a sense of relative indifference regarding how documents were disposed of to an approach increasingly characterized by firms putting policies in place to ensure the safe disposal of documents. Indeed, at a company level, a catalyst for this change of attitude was the fact that companies now had to comply with the UK's Data Protection Act (1998) and a failure to comply meant up to £500,000 in fines could be imposed by the Information Commissioner's Office.

Exhibit C7.1 ShredBank Paper Bank

Therefore, if a company were now to be found negligent in how it disposed of confidential documents there were real financial risks. In a more personal sense, there was also a general recognition of the need for more environmentally friendly waste management activities to be embraced – a movement encouraged by government in terms of positively influencing recycling behaviours amongst consumers and householders.

ShredBank's business

ShredBank was set up in 2007 to exploit this perceived market opportunity and sought to provide a highly secure and customer-focused solution to the growing challenge of secure document disposal. It was established to create a customer-oriented offering which was differentiated through convenience, reassurance and friendly service. Bain says, 'We had a desire to create and develop an organization that had meaning and that could make a difference to those who worked for us and for our customers who would use our service. In some way, through the supply of what has been seen as a largely functional service, we have to capture the aspect of "being likeable and memorable" through our branding.'

The ShredBank solution was designed to ensure that business customers were offered complete peace of mind regarding the disposal of their company's confidential waste as well as a guarantee that the process was legally and environmentally compliant. For the client the process works by company staff members depositing their confidential paper waste documents into storage units provided to them. These lockable 'Paper Banks' (see Exhibit C7.1) are branded 'ShredBank' and are usually located throughout the client staff offices. Once full the Paper Banks are then collected by ShredBank staff, sealed and the contents shredded on-site using mobile shredding trucks.

ShredBank seeks to eliminate the risk of documents being lost in transit or viewed by third parties by providing ▶

the shredding service on-site. Documents are therefore shredded at the client's premises using mobile shredding trucks with the drivers providing a certificate of destruction immediately to the customer on completion of the job. All driving staff are uniformed security guards and wear ShredBank identity badges. Clients are issued with an Annual Environmental Certificate which indicates how many trees were saved by recycling their shredded material. The company ensures that all shredded material is recycled into tissue products, such as kitchen towels.

The ShredBank brand

At inception, ShredBank's key competitors were major multinational companies that were well established and respected in the Northern Ireland marketplace. When it commenced trading in October 2007, it was an unknown brand in a relatively small and niche market. The global economic recession had begun to impact on the NI economy with business confidence beginning to deteriorate as the international financial crisis unfolded. Many local businesses were reducing costs and there was a reluctance to engage with new services or new suppliers. This relatively hostile environment meant that trading conditions for the young company were initially very difficult. In that context, the key strategic aim for ShredBank's branding strategy was deemed to be:

- to create and develop a high quality brand to an international standard that would differentiate the company on convenience, reassurance and friendly service.

This was to be achieved through meeting the following objectives:

- to continuously work with the media and to position co-owner Bain as an industry expert and authority figure
- to build a high level of brand visibility relative to competitors
- to create positive brand associations through CSR activities
- to always provide superior and friendly customer service
- to be consistently excellent in operational activity.

ShredBank engaged a leading design house to develop the brand identity and logo. The aim of the design was to create an impression that it was '*big, international, large-scale*' so that the fledgling small company may be seen as operating on a more level playing field with its global competitors. Over 10 per cent of initial start-up costs were invested in brand design and registering the name (and logo) both nationally and internationally. The brand logo was used in all literature including brochures, mail-shots, letter heads, business cards, promotional items, the paper banks and on the mobile shredding trucks themselves.

In order for the company to create brand awareness in the marketplace it positioned itself with the local media as subject matter expert in areas relating to the document shredding industry such as data protection legislation, environmental responsibility and identity fraud. There were already a series of stories in the media relating to public sector bodies and private companies losing important data relating to the public and ShredBank was able to comment on these stories, contribute to the debate and provide solutions to the problem of sensitive data constantly ending up in the public domain. Within three weeks of trading, ShredBank were in the media and have appeared there on average twice per month over a three-year period. It achieved this by being proactive in approaching the media with relevant stories, developing good relationships and by being highly responsive to journalists and editors when they needed information or to comment on a particular story. On one occasion, after a phone call with a local journalist, the company got a full page article about their business in the newspaper at no cost.

Given the fact that few people knew about ShredBank, it had two fundamental challenges: (1) to be more visible than the competition and (2) to achieve that visibility on a marketing budget that was a fraction of its competitors' budgets. Therefore, the strategy was to set an affordable budget and focus that budget on only the key media that businesses would use to find a shredding provider. Therefore, it focused on having a strong Internet presence, high impact mail-shots using 'branded stress trucks' and proactive telesales directed towards the target businesses. ShredBank began by targeting organizations that generated significant volumes of confidential information (at least 300 kg per annum) and which required regular disposal for this confidential information. The sectors it initially targeted included finance, accounting and legal companies.

Creating positive associations through CSR activity

ShredBank wanted to engender a positive image of the brand in society more generally, not just at the level of the end-customer. Bain believed that it was necessary to engage in high-profile CSR activities. These CSR activities can be subdivided into essentially two activities:

1 *Shredathon®* In 2009, it launched a new service into the Northern Ireland market-place called 'Shredathon®'. Shredathon® is a unique creation in Northern Ireland that allows the general public to bring confidential

documents that they may wish to dispose of and to have them destroyed in one of the company's shredding trucks without charge. This free service is provided across Northern Ireland in the car-parks of large supermarkets. This facility highlights the importance of securely disposing of personal confidential information in a secure as well as environmentally friendly way.

2 *Schools recycling competitions* ShredBank runs annual schools recycling competitions. Three competitions have taken place to date which have received thousands of entries and some 36 prizes have been awarded – including three iMac computers to three schools and three iPod Nanos to winning pupils. The winning schools also are hosts to ShredBank's Shredathon® so children can see the importance of recycling.

These events and subsequent media exposure significantly enhanced its corporate image in the market place as a company that had a strong commitment to the local community and the environment.

Friendly customer service

ShredBank believed that the core to customer service excellence was delivering a standardized, consistent and efficient service. To underpin this approach, it developed a range of robust standard operating procedures that were implemented throughout the organization through continuous training. The company received its ISO 9001:2008 accreditation within six months of trading and this is sustained through ongoing internal audits and external auditing.

The commitment of the owners to differentiating ShredBank on convenience, reassurance and a customer service ethos dominated the emerging business approach. Through staff training programmes they ensured that customer service was given top priority and that all staff, from the person answering the telephone to the truck drivers themselves, had a commitment to, and were competent in, the provision of an excellent and friendly service.

Relationship marketing is a key pillar of its business approach, with a customer relationship management system heavily used. The system has details of all their customers' unique requirements and the company monitors customer shredding trends and service requirements on an ongoing basis. Many of the clients who receive 'large shreds' (as the bigger customers are known) receive branded ShredBank cupcakes in order to reinforce the brand after purchase and to create a 'buzz' about the firm in the customer's office environment.

This service innovation is highly personal and has proved very popular with client staff. The initiative serves to ensure that the ShredBank name is kept to the fore in the minds of the client's staff and creates the friendly and approachable image it is striving for. This initial impression is then maintained and built upon through ongoing direct mail contact, courtesy calls and social media activity. The information provided through these channels is mainly of an educational nature relating to document disposal trends, legislation and processes and is designed to add value to the relationship. This approach allows the communication to be seen as informed, timely and relevant rather than potentially intrusive, thereby reinforcing the image of the company as being customer oriented, expert and reliable.

While this investment in relationship management and service is deemed critical it has also been important for the company to invest in the technology that actually delivers the core benefit to the customer – the mobile shredding trucks themselves. ShredBank has invested significantly in purchasing and maintaining mobile shredding trucks that are of the highest quality in the industry. Even the presentation of the trucks is of a particular pride to the company – they are regularly washed and cleaned. Such attention to the appearance of the trucks is unusual in the sector but is a key distinguishing factor for this company.

Questions

1. In what way has ShredBank sought to differentiate its brand from the established competitors?
2. Discuss how ShredBank makes use of tangibles in its marketing activity. Why is this important?
3. Examine ShredBank's customer service initiatives. Comment on their strengths and weaknesses.

This case was prepared by Professor Mark Durkin, University of Ulster and Philip Bain, Shredbank. Copyright © Mark Durkin and Philip Bain (2012). The material in the case has been drawn from a variety of published sources, interviews, archival records and research reports.

Chapter 8
Value through Pricing

Chapter outline

Basic methods of setting prices

Key factors influencing price-setting decisions

Managing price changes

Customer value through pricing

Learning outcomes

By the end of this chapter you will understand:

1 the three basic approaches to setting prices
2 the importance of adopting an integrated approach to price setting
3 the key factors that influence price-setting decisions
4 the major issues involved in managing pricing decisions over time
5 delivering value through price.

Aldi

One of the most enduring value propositions that an organization can offer is a competitive price for its products and services and the strength of this proposition becomes particularly evident during times of economic recession. Foremost among a number of discount grocery retailers is Europe is the German group, Aldi. The company name, which is short for *Al*brecht *Di*scount, was the brainchild of two of Germany's most famous businessmen, Karl and Theo Albrecht. Its two main subsidiaries, Aldi Nord and Aldi Sud (reputedly

In taste tests 173 liked Birds Eye, 89% of them also liked Aldi.

formed after a disagreement between the brothers over whether cigarettes should be sold at the checkout or not) operate over 4,000 stores between them in Germany, and a further 4,000 outlets throughout Europe, Australia and North America making Aldi the world's largest discount retailer.

Simplicity is a key element of the Aldi marketing strategy. Stores typically carry just 1,000 items compared with over 20,000 items for many of their competitors. So if for example, only one brand of toothpaste is carried then there is little need for gigabytes of stock control data or endless alterations to orders and store displays. All of the trappings of high-end grocery stores such as background music, product tastings and extravagant product displays are eschewed in favour of simple product presentation. The company's promotional activities are equally limited. It does not have a slogan and spends just 0.3 per cent of its turnover on advertising – a simple newsletter of weekly specials. This relentless drive for efficiencies combined with careful management of a small number of suppliers adds up to a very simple proposition – good quality at a consistently low price. Although the company remains privately held and is highly secretive, its global sales were estimated to be worth €45 billion in 2008.

However, competition in the discount grocery sector means that Aldi does not have the playing field to itself. Its main rival is another German firm Schwartz which operates the Kaufland and Lidl brands, while the growth of the Edeka-owned Netto chain has given rise to a strong third player. Schwartz in particular has been more aggressive in expanding into Eastern Europe and has developed a stronger presence than Aldi in this growing region. Price wars between the major rivals are commonplace with discounts and special offers rapidly matched by rivals. Added to this are the efforts by mainstream retailers such as Carrefour and Tesco to present themselves as also offering discount ranges to customers. This demonstrates one of the weaknesses of a low-price marketing strategy. The basis upon which a company differentiates itself is relatively easy to understand and if it can be successfully matched by rivals, its leadership can be eroded.[1]

Setting prices and managing prices over time is another set of important decisions that must be made by the organization. Several factors are likely to have an influence in these decisions. If input costs such as the price of energy in the form of electricity or oil are rising, then these input costs may need to be passed on to the customer in terms of increased prices. But if customers are struggling because of an economic downturn, they may be unwilling to accept these increased prices and therefore decide to consume less, thereby reducing organizational sales. And then there is also the role played by competitors. Pricing decisions need to take account of the prices being offered by competitors for alternative products or potential substitutes. Some of these firms may also be seeking to differentiate themselves based on the prices that they charge and will therefore tend to defend their price positions very aggressively.

All these dimensions need to be considered in terms of the principal relationship between price and the ultimate goal of the business, which is profit. This was starkly illustrated by the example of the Harry Potter series of books which have been the best-selling books of all time. But such was the demand for the books that each of the different sales channels such as major chains like Tesco and KwikSave, online retailers like Amazon and specialist book stores like Waterstones competed aggressively to get as big a share of the market as possible. The major competitive tool used was special price reductions on the books, with the result that some retailers made very little overall profit on the sales of this successful series. The importance of the price–profit relationship is also illustrated by the launch of the Mercedes A Class model in Germany. Initially, the company had chosen a price tag of DM29,500, based on the belief that the DM30,000 mark was psychologically important. However, after further market research that examined the value offered to customers in comparison with competitor brands such as the BMW 3 series and the VW Golf, the price was set at DM31,000. Mercedes still hit its sales target of 200,000, but the higher price increased its income by DM300 million per year.[2]

Exhibit 8.1 Price comparison websites like moneysupermarket.com enable consumers to compare the prices of different vendors in a variety of product and service categories

In many businesses, greater price competition is becoming a fact of life, with the use of technology helping to drive down costs, greater levels of globalization and retail competition helping to depress price levels, and developments like the Internet and the introduction of the euro giving rise to greater levels of price transparency (see Exhibit 8.1). Economic downturns focus further attention on price levels and increase demands for greater price transparency so that consumers can understand the true cost of goods such as personal loans or telephone services. As a result, firms must think carefully when setting prices initially and when adjusting them to changing circumstances.

Basic methods of setting prices

Shapiro and Jackson[3] identified three methods used by managers to set prices (see Figure 8.1). The first of these – cost-based pricing – reflects a strong internal orientation and, as its name suggests, is based on costs (see Marketing in Action 8.1). The second is competitor-orientated pricing, where the major emphasis is on the

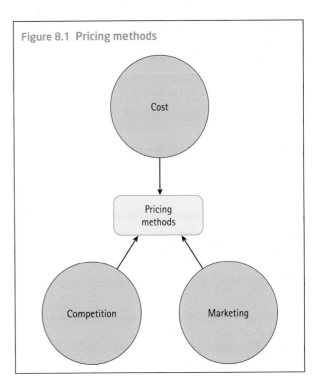

Figure 8.1 Pricing methods

Marketing in Action 8.1 The success of Renault's Logan

Critical Thinking: Below is review of the pricing strategy used for the launch of the Renault Logan. Read it and consider the advantages and disadvantages of cost-based pricing.

To take advantage of the growing prosperity of Central and Eastern Europe, the French motor company Renault bought the ageing Romanian manufacturer Dacia in 1999. Its strategy was to produce a car that was modern, reliable and affordable for sale in developing markets in Europe, Asia and Latin America. Driving efficiencies were a key part of this strategy and every effort was made to keep costs to a minimum. Expensive curves and creases in the car design were eliminated, and components from other vehicles were even reused. The result was a cheap-looking saloon car. The model was priced inexpensively and was only expected to cover its investment costs and make a modest contribution to profits.

But the car has turned out to be a runaway success. Priced at €7,500 in France, it sold 9,000 units in three months after going on sale there in June 2005, despite receiving no advertising support. Global sales in 2005 were expected to hit 160,000

units, well ahead of the planned level of 100,000 units. By the end of 2006, over 450,000 vehicles had been sold, which was substantially ahead of targeted sales levels. The brand has also been a hit in Romania, to such an extent that the company has raised its prices there and did not even bother to launch the planned cheapest version at €5,000. Profits were far ahead of expectations and the success of the car has left its Romanian factory struggling to keep up with demand. In 2006, an estate version of the car was launched, in 2007 the Logan van was launched and a pick-up version was planned for 2008.

This example illustrates the risks of cost-based pricing. Fortunately for the company, sales exceeded expectations but the opportunity to reap larger profits had been missed. It demonstrates the need to understand the potential level of value that consumers can attribute to a new innovation.

Based on: English (2004);[4] Mackintosh (2005)[5].

price levels set by competitors and how our prices compare with those. The final approach is market-led pricing, so called because it focuses on the value that customers place on a product in the marketplace and the nature of the marketing strategy used to support the product. In this section we will examine each of these approaches, and draw out their strengths and limitations.

Cost-based pricing

Cost-based pricing is a useful approach to price setting in that it can give an indication of the minimum price that needs to be charged in order to break even. Cost-based pricing can best be explained by using a simple example (see Table 8.1). Imagine that you are given the task of pricing a new product and the cost figures given in Table 8.1 apply. Direct costs such as labour and materials work out at €2 per unit. As output increases, more people and materials will be needed and so total costs increase. Fixed costs (or overheads) per year are calculated at €200,000. These costs (such as office and manufacturing facilities) do not change as output increases. They have to be paid whether 1 or 200,000 units are produced.

Once we have calculated the relevant costs, it is necessary to estimate how many units we are likely to sell. We believe that we produce a good-quality product and therefore sales should be 100,000 in the first year. Therefore total (full) cost per unit is €4 and using the

Table 8.1 Cost-based pricing

Year 1	
Direct costs (per unit)	= €2
Fixed costs	= €200,000
Expected sales	= 100,000
Cost per unit	
Direct costs	= €2
Fixed costs (200,000 ÷ 100,000)	= €2
Full costs	= €4
Mark-up (10 per cent)	= €0.40
Price (cost plus mark-up)	= €4.40
Year 2	
Expected sales	= 50,000
Cost per unit	
Direct costs	= €2
Fixed costs (200,000 ÷ 50,000)	= €4
Full costs	= €6
Mark-up (10 per cent)	= €0.60
Price (cost plus mark-up)	= €6.60

company's traditional 10 per cent mark-up a price of €4.40 is set.

So that we may understand the problems associated with using **full cost pricing**, we should assume that the sales estimate of 100,000 is not reached by the end of the year. Because of poor economic conditions or as a result of setting the price too high, only 50,000 units are sold. The company believes that this level of sales is likely to be achieved next year. What happens to price? Table 8.1 gives the answer: it is raised because cost per unit goes up. This is because fixed costs (€200,000) are divided by a smaller expected sales volume (50,000). The result is a price rise in response to poor sales figures. This is clearly nonsense and yet can happen if full cost pricing is followed blindly. A major UK engineering company priced one of its main product lines in this way and suffered a downward spiral of sales as prices were raised each year, with disastrous consequences.

So, the first problem with cost-based pricing is that it leads to an increase in the price as sales fall. Second, the procedure is illogical because a sales estimate is made *before* the price is set. Third, it focuses on internal costs rather than the customer's willingness to pay. And, finally, there may be a technical problem in allocating overheads in multi-product firms. Nevertheless the cost-based approach is popular in practice. For example, Apple aims to cover costs plus receive a 40 per cent margin on all its new product launches.

The real value of this approach is that it gives an indication of the minimum price necessary to make a profit. Once direct and fixed costs have been measured, 'break-even analysis' can be used to estimate the sales volume needed to balance revenue and costs at different price levels. Therefore, the procedure of calculating full costs is useful when other pricing methods are used since full costs may act as a constraint. If they cannot be covered then it may not be worthwhile launching the product. In practice, some companies will set prices below full costs (known as direct cost pricing or **marginal cost pricing**). As we saw in the previous chapter this is a popular strategy for services companies. For example, where seats on an aircraft or rooms in hotels are unused at any time, that revenue is lost. In such situations, pricing to cover direct costs plus a contribution to overheads is sensible to reduce the impact of excess capacity, although this approach is not sustainable in the long term.

Competitor-orientated pricing

Competitor-orientated pricing may take any one of three forms:

Exhibit 8.2 Advertising for the iPad 2 which was launched in 2011 has focused heavily on its low price level relative to competing tablets

The iPad 2011 official advert illustrates its wide range of applications in a typically minimalist Apple style.
www.mcgraw-hill.co.uk/textbooks/fahy

1 where firms follow the prices charged by leading competitors
2 where producers take the going-rate price
3 where contracts are awarded through a **competitive bidding** process.

Some firms are happy simply to benchmark themselves against their major competitors, setting their prices at levels either above, the same as or below them (see Exhibit 8.2). This is very popular in the financial services area where, for example, the price of a loan (that is, the interest rate) is often very similar across a wide range of competitors. It can be a risky approach to take, particularly if the firm's cost position is not as good as that of its competitors (see 'Cost-based pricing' above).

In other circumstances, all competitors receive the same price because it is the going rate for the product. **Going-rate prices** are most typically found in the case of undifferentiated commodities such as coffee beans or cattle meat. The challenge for the marketer in this situation is to find some creative ways of differentiating the product in order to charge a different price.

In addition, many contracts are won or lost on the basis of competitive bidding. The most usual process is the drawing up of detailed specifications for a product and putting the contract out to tender. Potential suppliers quote a price, which is known only to themselves and the buyer (known as a 'sealed bid'), or the bidding may take place in a public auction where all competitors see what prices are being bid. All other things being equal, the buyer will select the supplier that quotes the lowest price. A major focus for suppliers, therefore, is the likely bid price of competitors. Increasing price pressures, European competition legislation and the growing use of technology has resulted in more and more supply contracts being subject to competitive

bidding. For example, traditionally, many hospital supply companies sold directly to doctors and nurses in hospitals, which meant that suppliers invested in developing selling skills and building relationships with these customers. Now, the norm is that supply contracts are put out to tender, with the winning bidder often securing the contract for a period of three to five years. Thus supply firms have had to develop skills in different areas such as tender preparation and pricing. Online auctions present suppliers with a whole new set of demands (see Chapter 3).

The main advantage of the competitor-orientated pricing approach is that it is simple and easy to use, except in the case of competitive bidding, where it may be difficult to guess what prices competitive bids will come in at. Increased price transparency in Europe, brought about by the introduction of the euro and the growing use of the Internet as a tool for comparing prices, will perhaps increase the level of attention being given to competitor-orientated pricing. It also suffers, however, from two significant flaws. First, it does not take account of any differential advantages the firm may have, which may justify its charging a higher price than the competition. As we have seen, the creation of a differential advantage is a fundamental marketing activity, and firms should seek to reap the rewards of this investment. Second, as noted above, competitor-orientated pricing is risky where a firm's cost position is weaker than that of its competitors.

Market-led pricing

A key marketing consideration when setting prices is estimating a product's value to the customer. In brief, the more value a product gives compared to the competition, the higher the price that can be charged (see Exhibit 8.3). Simply because one product costs less

Exhibit 8.3 **Products like those from luxury brand company Louis Vuitton command premium prices due to their association with high value**

Sold exclusively in Louis Vuitton stores. Tel: 020 7399 4050 www.louisvuitton.com

LOUIS VUITTON

to make than another does not imply that its price should be less. The logic of this position is borne out by Glaxo's approach when it launched Zantac, an ulcer treatment drug. It set the price for the drug at 50 per cent more than that of SmithKline Beecham's Tagamet, which was then the world's best-selling drug. Thanks to its fewer side effects, Zantac overtook Tagamet and the resulting superior revenues transformed Glaxo from a mid-sized UK company to a global powerhouse.[6]

In this section we shall explore a number of ways of estimating value to the customer. Marketers have at their disposal three useful techniques for uncovering customers' value perceptions: **trade-off analysis**, experimentation and **economic value to the customer (EVC)** analysis.

Trade-off analysis

Measurement of the trade-off between price and other product features – known as trade-off analysis or conjoint analysis – enables their effects on product preference to be established.[7] Respondents are not asked direct questions about price but instead product profiles consisting of product features and price are described, and respondents are asked to name their preferred profile. From their answers the effect of price

and other product features can be measured using a computer model. For example, respondents are shown different combinations of features such as speed, petrol consumption, brand and price in the case of a car and asked which combinations they prefer. This exercise enables one to measure the impact on preferences of increasing or reducing the price. Companies like 3M, who are renowned for their product innovation, use trade-off analysis at the test marketing stage for new products. Different combinations of variables such as the brand, packaging, product features and price are tested to establish the price level customers are prepared to pay.[8]

Experimentation

A limitation of trade-off analysis is that respondents are not asked to back up their preferences with cash expenditure. Consequently, there can be some doubt whether what they say they prefer would be reflected in an actual purchase when they are asked to part with money. 'Experimental pricing research' attempts to overcome this drawback by placing a product on sale at different locations with varying prices. Test marketing (see Chapter 6) is often used to compare the effectiveness of varying prices. For example, the same product could be sold in two areas using an identical promotional campaign, but with different prices between areas. The areas would need to be matched (or differences allowed for) in terms of target customer profile so that the result would be comparable. The test needs to be long enough so that trial and repeat purchase at each price can be measured. This is likely to be between 6 and 12 months for products whose purchase cycle lasts more than a few weeks.

EVC analysis

Experimentation is more usual when pricing consumer products. However, industrial markets have a powerful tool at their disposal when setting the price of their products: economic value to the customer (EVC) analysis. Many organizational purchases are motivated by economic value considerations since reducing costs and increasing revenue are prime objectives for many companies. If a company can produce an offering that has a high EVC, it can set a high price and yet still offer superior value compared to the competition. A high EVC may be because the product generates more revenue for the buyer than competition or because its operating costs (such as maintenance, operation or start-up costs) are lower over its lifetime. EVC analysis is usually particularly revealing when applied to products whose purchase price represents a small proportion of the lifetime costs to the customer.[9]

For example, assume a manufacturer is buying a robot to use on its production line-cycle costs. An additional €50,000 is required for start-up costs such as installation and operator training, while a further €150,000 needs to be budgeted for in post-purchase costs such as maintenance, power, etc. Assume also that a new product comes on the market that due to technological advances reduces start-up costs by €20,000 and post-purchase costs by €50,000. Total costs then have been reduced by €70,000 and the EVC that the new product offers is €170,000 (€300,000 − €130,000). Thus the EVC figure is the total amount that the customer would have to pay to make the total life-cycle costs of the new and existing robot the same. If the new robot was priced at €170,000 this would be the case – any price below that level would create an economic incentive for the buyer to purchase the new robot.

The main advantage of market-led pricing is that it keeps customer perceptions and needs at the forefront of the pricing decision. However, in practice it is sensible for a company to adopt an integrated approach to pricing, paying attention not only to customer needs but also to cost levels (cost-based pricing) and competitor prices (competitor-orientated pricing).

Key factors influencing price-setting decisions

Aside from the basic dimensions of cost, competitive prices and customer value, various aspects of the firm's marketing strategy will also affect price-setting decisions. In particular, marketing decisions such as positioning strategies, new product launch strategies, product-line strategies, competitive marketing strategies, distribution channel strategies and international marketing strategies will have an impact on price levels.

Positioning strategy

As we saw in Chapter 5, a key decision that marketing managers face is positioning strategy, which involves the choice of target market and the creation of a differential advantage. Each of these factors can have an enormous impact on price. Price can be used to convey a differential advantage and to appeal to a certain market segment (see Exhibit 8.4). Leading European retail chains such as Aldi and Lidl target cost-conscious grocery shoppers through a policy of lowest prices on a range of frequently purchased household goods. At the other end of the spectrum, many firms will charge very high prices in order to appeal to individuals with a high net worth. Products such as yachts, luxury cars, golf club memberships, luxury holidays, and so on, are sold in this way. Price is a powerful positioning tool because, for many people, it is an indicator of quality. This is particularly the case for products where objective measurement of quality is not possible, such as

Exhibit 8.4 Rimmel cosmetics was traditionally positioned as 'beauty on a budget' but moved to a more up-market 'beauty made in London' positioning which involved raising prices by almost 30 per cent in two years

Rimmel's London Glam eyes campaign reflects its new positioning.
www.mcgraw-hill.co.uk/textbooks/fahy

drinks and perfume, and for services where quality cannot be assessed before consumption.

Because price perceptions are so important to customers, many companies engage in what is called **psychological pricing** – that is, the careful manipulation of the reference prices that consumers carry in their heads. Consequently, the price of most grocery products ends in '.99' because the psychological difference between €2.99 and €3.00 is much greater than the actual difference.

New product launch strategy

When launching new products, price should be carefully aligned with promotional strategy. Figure 8.2 shows four marketing strategies based on combinations of price and promotion. Similar matrices could also be developed for product and distribution, but for illustrative purposes promotion will be used here. A combination of high price and high promotion expenditure is called a 'rapid skimming strategy'. The high price provides high-margin returns on investment and the heavy promotion creates high levels of product awareness and knowledge. The launches of Microsoft's Xbox and Apple's iPod and iPhone are examples of a rapid skimming strategy (see Marketing in Action 8.2). A 'slow skimming strategy' combines high price with low levels of promotional expenditure. High prices mean big profit margins, but high levels of promotion are believed to be unnecessary, perhaps because word of mouth is more important and the product is already well known (e.g. Rolls-Royce) or because heavy promotion is thought to be incompatible with product image, as with cult products. One company that uses a skimming pricing policy effectively is German car components supplier Bosch. It has applied an extremely profitable skimming strategy, supported by patents, to its launch of fuel injection and anti-lock brake systems.[10] Companies that combine low prices with heavy promotional expenditure are practising a 'rapid penetration strategy'. In a break with its traditional policy of rapid skimming, Apple changed to a rapid penetration

strategy with its launch of the iPad due to intense competition with rival tablets makers (see Exhibit 8.2). Finally, a 'slow penetration strategy' combines low price with low promotional expenditure. Own-label brands use this strategy: promotion is not necessary to gain distribution and low promotional expenditure helps to maintain high profit margins for these brands. This price/promotion framework is useful when thinking about marketing strategies at launch.

The importance of picking the right strategy is illustrated by the failure of TiVo in the UK. TiVo makes personal video recorders (PVRs), which are high-technology recorders capable of storing up to 40 hours of television and with features such as the facility to rewind live television programmes and memorize selections so that favourite programmes are automatically recorded. But the product has failed to take off and TiVo has withdrawn from the UK market. Part of the reason for the failure is that consumers did not seem to fully understand what PVRs can do and therefore could not justify spending in the region of £300 plus a monthly subscription fee for a recorder. Some analysts estimate that the product should be priced in the region of £100 for it to take off, suggesting that a penetration rather than a skimming strategy would have been more appropriate.[11]

High price (skimming) strategies and low price (penetration) strategies may be appropriate in different situations. A skimming strategy is most suitable in situations where customers are less price sensitive, such as where the product provides high value, where customers have a high ability to pay and where they are under high pressure to buy. However, setting the price too high can lead to problems generating sales. For example, when Nissan launched its 350Z sports car, it was priced at levels similar to top sports cars like the Porsche Boxster and BMW Z4. However, poor sales levels forced it to cut its retail price by €10,000, a move that brought it closer to the next level of sports cars like the Mazda RX-8. Penetration pricing strategies are more likely to be driven by company circumstances where the company is seeking to dominate the market, where it is comfortable to establish a position in the market initially and make money later, and/or where it seeks to create a barrier to entry for competitors.

Product-line strategy

Marketing-orientated companies also need to take account of where the price of a new product fits into its existing product line. Where multiple segments appear attractive, modified versions of the product should be designed, and priced differently, not according to differences in costs, but in line with the respective values that each target market places on a

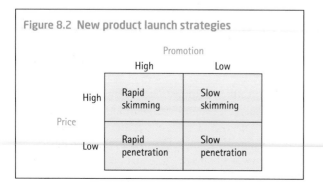

Figure 8.2 New product launch strategies

		Promotion	
		High	Low
Price	High	Rapid skimming	Slow skimming
	Low	Rapid penetration	Slow penetration

Marketing in Action 8.2 Skimming the market

Critical Thinking: Below is a review of price skimming strategies in some popular product categories. Read it and critically evaluate the pros and cons of price skimming from both the firm's and the customer's points of view.

In a number of product markets, like phones, MP3 players and games consoles, rapid skimming strategies are becoming ever more prevalent. A particular case in point is the Apple iPhone. An 8-gigabyte version of the phone was launched in July 2007 with a price tag of US$599. But, by just September of that year, its price had fallen by US$200 and a new 16-gigabyte model was launched on the market at a price of US$499. Innovators and early adopters who had purchased the phone at the full initial price were outraged and were ultimately offered a US$100 gift voucher by Apple.

The iPhone is an example of a classic rapid skimming strategy. Buzz marketing was used intensively to generate demand for the product, with a promise that it would do for mobile phones what the iPod had done for MP3 players. Its ease of use, combined with its functionality and its Apple 'cool', were extolled in blogs, reviews and commentaries. This low-cost form of promotion, combined with a high initial price, meant high profits for Apple. By 2011, Apple still only commanded a mere 4 per cent of the global mobile phones market in terms of sales but took in over 50 per cent of all profits in the industry.

There are several explanations for the rise in the use of rapid skimming strategies. The first is the cost of production. Products like the iPhone represent the convergence of several technologies, such as music players, computers and telecommunications. Packing all this functionality into one product is expensive. Second is the speed of imitation by competitors. Innovative new designs are now very quickly reverse-engineered and replicated, with new low-cost versions quickly reaching the shop floor. A rapid skimming strategy is the best way to recoup the high costs of research and development before competitors erode margins. Finally, consumer behaviour also plays an important role. The desire to be the first person with a new product is a strong feature of today's consumers, as demonstrated by the queues that frequently form for new telephones, games consoles and fashion items. Price does not seem to be a major factor for these early adopters, and technology companies are exploiting this.

However, managing a skimming strategy is easier said than done. Drop the price too quickly and you risk the wrath of customers, as Apple has done. Drop the price too slowly, as Sony did with its PlayStation 3, and you risk losing out on sales and market penetration. On the back of the global success of its PlayStation 2, Sony launched the PlayStation 3 at a price of US$600 in 2006, compared with US$399 for the Microsoft Xbox and US$249 for the Nintendo Wii. By the time the PlayStation 3 brand was eventually retailing at US$399 one year later, Sony had seen its dominant position in the global games console market eroded and it had fallen to number three behind Microsoft and Nintendo. The timing of pricing decisions is critical for the success of new products.

Based on: Anonymous (2011);[12] Sanchanta (2007);[13] Stern (2008)[14].

product. All the major car manufacturing companies have products priced at levels that are attractive to different market segments, namely, economy cars, family saloons, executive cars, and so on. In 2009, iTunes abandoned its long-standing strategy of charging a flat fee of 99 cents per song download in favour of a three-tier structure with songs priced at 69 cents, 99 cents and $1.29 to appeal to different market segments.[15]

Some companies prefer to extend their product lines rather than reduce the price of existing brands in the face of price competition. They launch cut-price 'fighter brands' to compete with the low-price rivals. This has the advantage of maintaining the image and profit margins of existing brands. For example, Tesco launched the 'Discount brands at Tesco' range to counter a loss of market share to hard discounters like Aldi and Lidl.[16] Included in the range were staple food items like pasta, bread and tea bags. By producing a range of brands at different price points, companies can cover the varying price sensitivities of customers and encourage them to trade up to the more expensive, higher-margin brands.

Competitive marketing strategy

The pricing of products should also be set within the context of the firm's competitive strategy. Four strategic objectives are relevant to pricing: build, hold, harvest and reposition.

Build objective

For price-sensitive markets, a build objective for a product implies a price lower than that of the competition. If the competition raises their prices we would be slow to match them. For price-insensitive markets, the best pricing strategy becomes less clear-cut. Price in these circumstances will be dependent on the overall positioning strategy thought appropriate for the product.

Hold objective

Where the strategic objective is to hold sales and/or market share, the appropriate pricing strategy is to maintain or match the price relative to the competition. This has implications for price changes: if the competition reduces prices then our prices would match this price fall.

Harvest objective

A harvest objective implies the maintenance or raising of profit margins, even though sales and/or market share are falling. The implication for pricing strategy would be to set premium prices. For products that are being harvested, there would be much greater reluctance to match price cuts than for products that were being built or held. On the other hand, price increases would swiftly be matched.

Reposition objective

Changing market circumstances and product fortunes may necessitate the repositioning of an existing product. This may involve a price change, the direction and magnitude of which will be dependent on the new positioning strategy for the product.

The above examples show how developing clear strategic objectives helps the setting of price and clarifies the appropriate reaction to competitive price changes. Price setting, then, is much more sophisticated than simply asking 'How much can I get for this product?' The process starts by asking more fundamental questions like 'How is this product going to be positioned in the marketplace?' and 'What is the appropriate strategic objective for this product?' Answering these questions is an essential aspect of effective price management.

Channel management strategy

When products are sold through intermediaries such as distributors or retailers, the list price to the customer must reflect the margins required by them. Some products, such as cars, carry margins of typically less than 10 per cent, therefore car dealers must rely on sales of spare parts and future servicing of new cars to generate returns. Other products, such as jewellery, may carry a margin of several hundred per cent. When Müller yoghurt was first launched in the UK, a major factor in gaining distribution in a mature market was the fact that its high price allowed attractive profit margins for the supermarket chains. Conversely, the implementation of a penetration pricing strategy may be hampered if distributors refuse to stock a product because the profit per unit is less than that available on competitive products.

The implication is that pricing strategy is dependent on understanding not only the ultimate customer but also the needs of distributors and retailers who form the link between them and the manufacturer. If their needs cannot be accommodated, product launch may not be viable or a different distribution system (such as direct selling) might be required.

International marketing strategy

The firm's international marketing strategy will also have a significant impact on its pricing decisions. The first challenge that managers have to deal with is that of **price escalation**. This means that a number of factors can combine to put pressure on the firm to increase the prices it charges in other countries. These include the additional costs of shipping and transporting costs to a foreign market, margins paid to local distributors, customs duties or tariffs that may be charged on imported products, differing rates of sales taxes and changes to the price that may be driven by exchange rates and differing inflation rates. All of these factors combine to mean that the price charged in a foreign market is often very different to that charged on the home market. Sometimes it is higher, but it can also be lower if circumstances dictate that low prices are necessary to gain sales, as would be the case in countries where levels of disposable income are low. In such instances it is important for firms to guard against **parallel importing** – this is when products destined for an international market are re-imported back into the home market and sold through unauthorized channels at levels lower than the company wishes to charge. For example, the online music company CD Wow was fined £41 million when it was charged with selling cut-price CDs in the UK that it had imported from Hong Kong. But trading of products across borders within the European Union is legal, so companies like Chemilines have been able to build a successful business importing pharmaceuticals from EU accession states for sale in the UK, where prices can be up to 30 per cent higher.[17]

While most firms seek to standardize as many elements of the marketing mix as possible when operating internationally, pricing is one of the most difficult to standardize for the reasons outlined above. Sometimes the price differences are driven by cost variations, but sometimes they are also due to the absence of competi-

tors or different customer value can lead to accusations of ripping that international prices are much through, for example, the introdu price differences across markets ha more controversial (see Ethical Deb:

Ethical Debate 8.1 What is a fair price?

Price is one of the most hotly debated aspects of marketing. News reports regularly present stories of price variations for products across Europe, leading to claims that some consumers are being unfairly ripped off by companies charging inflated prices. For example, one study found that consumers in Ireland pay €10.99 for four Gillette Mach-3 blades compared with just €6.84 in London, that they pay €9.39 for a packet of Pampers newborn nappies compared with only €4.79 in the Netherlands, and that they pay higher prices for several other well-known brands.[18] These variations are difficult to justify, given the nature of modern consumer markets. Global pharmaceutical companies have been accused of overcharging for critical medicines, particularly in the world's poorer countries where diseases like HIV and AIDS are rampant. Telecommunications companies charge significant premiums for calls made or texts sent while roaming in other countries. And international travellers have complained for years about being ripped off by taxi companies, car hire firms, hotels and other service outlets when they visit new countries.

There are several ways in which organizations can exploit consumers by overcharging for goods and services. One of the most common is price fixing, which is illegal and banned throughout Europe. Rather than compete on price, companies collude with each other to ensure that everyone charges the same or similar prices. For example, 14 retailers in Germany, including leading chains like Metro, Edeka and Rewe, were investigated in 2010 on suspicion of working with manufacturers of products like confectionary, pet food and coffee to fix minimum price levels. It is the job of regulatory authorities like the Competition Authority of Ireland and the Office of Fair Trading (OFT) in the UK to identify and investigate possible price collusion. For example, in 2008, the OFT investigated possible collusion between British supermarkets and their suppliers. The 'big four' supermarkets – Tesco, Asda, Sainsbury's and Morrisons – along with suppliers like Britvic, Coca-Cola, Mars, Nestlé, Procter & Gamble, Reckitt Benckiser and Unilever, were asked to hand over documents. Price fixing is most likely to be found in industries where brand differentiation is difficult, such as oil, paper, glass and chemicals.

Equally controversial is the practice of deceptive pricing – in other words, where prices are not the same as they may first appear. Low-cost airlines have been significant users of deceptive pricing. For example, quoted fares may be as low as 99 cents but when all additional items, such as taxes, baggage charges, fuel surcharges, seat charges and credit card charges, are added in, fares may end up being well in excess of €70. These companies are also users of opt-outs. That is, unless consumers specifically opt out of additional items like travel insurance they will be charged for these as well. Furthermore, many of the headline low-fares offers are very limited in their availability, often restricted to just a few seats. EU regulators have targeted the industry to clean up its act on pricing. Airlines must now give a clear indication of the total price and extra charges have to be indicated at the start rather than the end of the booking.

All this means that consumers need to be very careful when judging the price of a good or service. Ultimately this debate rests on the issue of price and value. Consumers can vote with their feet. If they feel that a price is excessive, in most cases they can switch to substitute products or to other vendors. Consumers need to inform themselves and companies need to take great care in setting price levels. As this chapter shows, pricing must be an integral part of a company's marketing strategy.

Reflection: Consider the points made above and discuss the contention that firms will always charge as much as they possibly can unless forced to do otherwise.

Initiating price changes

	Increases	**Cuts**
Circumstances	Value greater than price Rising costs Excess demand Harvest objective	Value less than price Excess supply Build objective Price war unlikely Pre-empt competitive entry
Tactics	Price jump Staged price increases Escalator clauses Price unbundling Lower discounts	Price fall Staged price reductions Fighter brands Price bundling Higher discounts
Estimating competitor reaction	Strategic objectives Self-interest Competitive situation Past experience	

Managing price changes

So far, our discussion has concentrated on those factors that affect pricing strategy but, in a highly competitive world, managers need to know when and how to raise or lower prices, and whether or not to react to competitors' price moves. First, we will discuss initiating price changes before analysing how to react to competitors' price changes.

Three key issues associated with initiating price changes are: the circumstances that may lead a company to raise or lower prices, the tactics that can be used, and estimating competitor reaction. Table 8.2 illustrates the major points relevant to each of these considerations.

Circumstances

Marketing research (for example, trade-off analysis or experimentation) which reveals that customers place a higher value on the product than is reflected in its price could mean that a price increase is justified. Rising costs, and hence reduced profit margins, may also stimulate price rises. Another factor that leads to price increases is excess demand. This regularly happens, for example, in the residential property market where the demand for houses can often grow at a faster pace than houses can be built by construction companies, resulting in house price inflation. A company that cannot supply the demand created by its customers may choose to raise prices in an effort to balance demand and supply. This can be an attractive option as profit margins are automatically widened. The final circumstance when companies may decide to raise prices is when embarking on a harvest objective. Prices are raised to increase margins even though sales may fall.

In the same way, price cuts may be provoked by the discovery that a price is high compared to the value that customers place on a product, by falling costs and by excess supply leading to excess capacity. A further circumstance that may lead to price falls is the adoption of a build objective. When customers are thought to be price sensitive, price cutting may be used to build sales and market share, though doing so involves the risk of provoking a price war.

Tactics

There are many ways in which price increases and cuts may be implemented. The most direct is the 'price jump', or fall, which increases or decreases the price by the full amount in one go. A price jump avoids prolonging the pain of a price increase over a long period, but may raise the visibility of the price increase to customers. This happened in India, where Hindustan Lever, the local subsidiary of Unilever, used its market power to raise the prices of its key brands at a time when raw materials were getting cheaper. As a result, operating margins grew from 13 per cent in 1999 to 21 per cent in 2003. Subsequently, though, sales fell sharply due to competition from P&G and Nirma, a local brand, as well as consumer disaffection.[19] Using staged price increases might make the price rise more palatable but may elicit accusations of 'always raising your prices'.

A one-stage price fall can have a high-impact dramatic effect that can be heavily promoted but also has an immediate impact on profit margins. When the demand for hotel beds globally fell after the terrorist attacks on New York in 2001, the industry reacted by slashing hotel rates to try to generate business. One of the effects was that it proved to be difficult to raise rates again when the recovery took place.[20] As a result, the hospitality industry has been less willing to make big rate cuts as a result of the global economic downturn. Staged price reductions have a less dramatic effect but may be used when a price cut is believed to be necessary although the amount needed to stimulate sales is unclear. Small cuts may be initiated as a learning process that proceeds until the desired effect on sales is achieved.

'Escalator clauses' can also be used to raise prices. The contracts for some organizational purchases are drawn up before the product is made. Constructing the product – for example, a new defence system or motorway – may take a number of years. An escalator clause in the contract allows the supplier to stipulate price increases in line with a specified index (for example, increases in industry wage rates or the cost of living).

Another tactic that effectively raises prices is **price unbundling**. Many product offerings actually consist of a set of products for which an overall price is set (for example, computer hardware and software, an airline flight, etc.). Price unbundling allows each element in the offering to be priced separately in such a way that the total price is raised. A variant on this process is charging for services that were previously included in the product's price. For example, manufacturers of mainframe computers have the option of unbundling installation and training services, and charging for them separately, while low-fares airlines charge for baggage, check-in, etc. separately. Alibaba.com, the world's largest online platform for trade between businesses, moved from a uniform membership package to a new structure that involved a basic membership fee and charges for additional services such as factory audits and keyword searching – a move that significantly raised the company's profits.[21]

Yet another approach is to maintain the list price but lower discounts to customers. In periods of heavy demand for new cars, dealers lower the cash discount given to customers, for example. Similarly if demand is slack, customers can be given greater discounts as an incentive to buy. However, there are risks if this strategy is pursued for too long a period of time. For example, owing to poor sales of its car models, GM pursued a four-year price discounting strategy in the US market, with disastrous effects.

One iteration of the scheme, which was known as 'Employee Discounts for Everyone', offered buyers a discount averaging US$400–US$500 off the price of a new car. This took the total in incentives available to the buyer to over US$7000, or over 20 per cent off the suggested retail price of the car.[22] The resulting price war with Ford and Chrysler, who followed with similar schemes, hurt profits. But, more worryingly, the effect of the campaign seemed to be that GM customers simply brought forward purchases that they were going to make anyway to avail themselves of the discounts, and customer attention switched to price rather than the value offered by the product.[23]

Quantity discounts can also be manipulated to raise the transaction price to customers. The percentage discount per quantity can be lowered, or the quantity that qualifies for a particular percentage discount can be raised.

Those companies contemplating a price cut have three choices in addition to a direct price fall.

1 A company defending a premium-priced brand that is under attack from a cut-price competitor may choose to maintain its price while introducing a fighter brand. The established brand keeps its premium-price position while the fighter brand competes with the rival for price-sensitive customers.
2 Where a number of products and services that tend to be bought together are priced separately, price bundling can be used to effectively lower the price. For example, televisions can be offered with 'free three-year repair warranties' or cars offered with 'free service for two years'.
3 Finally, discount terms can be made more attractive by increasing the percentage or lowering the qualifying levels.

Reacting to competitors' price changes

Companies need to analyse their appropriate reactions when their competitors initiate price changes. Three issues are relevant here: when to follow, what to ignore and the tactics to use if the price change is to be followed. Table 8.3 summarizes the main considerations.

When to follow

When competitive price increases are due to general rising cost levels or industry-wide excess demand, they are more likely to be followed. In these circumstances the initial pressure to raise prices is the same on all parties. Following a price rise is also more likely when customers are relatively price insensitive, which means that the follower will not gain much advantage by resisting the price increase. Where brand image is consistent with high prices, a company is more likely to follow a competitor's price rise as to do so would be consistent with the brand's positioning strategy. Finally, a price rise is more likely to be followed when a company is pursuing a harvest or hold objective because, in both cases, the emphasis is more on profit margin than sales/market share gain.

When they are stimulated by general falling costs or excess supply, price cuts are likely to be followed. Falling costs allow all companies to cut prices while maintaining margins, and excess supply means that a company is unlikely to allow a rival to make sales

Table 8.3 Reacting to competitors' price changes

	Increases	**Cuts**
When to follow	Rising costs Excess demand Price-insensitive customers Price rise compatible with brand image Harvest or hold objective	Falling costs Excess supply Price-sensitive customers Price fall compatible with brand image Build or hold objective
When to ignore	Stable or falling costs Excess supply Price-sensitive customers Price rise incompatible with brand image Build objective	Rising costs Excess demand Price-insensitive customers Price fall incompatible with brand image Harvest objective

Tactics
  Quick response
  Slow response
	
	Margin improvement urgent
	Gains to be made by being friend
		
		Offset competitive threat
		High customer loyalty

gains at its expense. Price cuts will also be followed in price-sensitive markets since allowing one company to cut price without retaliation would mean large sales gains for the price cutter. This has happened in the UK toiletries market where Boots has failed to follow Tesco in aggressive price cutting on products like shampoo and skin cream. Boots' profits and share price have been falling while Tesco's continue to grow.[24] The image of the company can also affect reaction to price cuts. Some companies position themselves as low-price manufacturers or retail outlets. In such circumstances they would be less likely to allow a price reduction by a competitor to go unchallenged for to do so would be incompatible with their brand image. Finally, price cuts are likely to be followed when the company has a build or hold strategic objective. In such circumstances an aggressive price move by a competitor would be followed to prevent sales/market share loss. For example, Amazon has dropped the price of its Kindle e-reader from $350 in 2009 to under $150 in 2011 in response to price competition from other e-readers such as Barnes & Noble's Nook (see Exhibit 8.5). In the case of a build objective, the response may be more dramatic, with a price fall exceeding the initial competitive move. For example, Vodafone halved the monthly tariff for wireless datacards from £30 to £15, which put it on a par with 3, the industry leader, in a bid to grow its share of the mobile data services market.

When to ignore

In most cases, the circumstances associated with companies not reacting to a competitive price move are simply the opposite of the above. Price increases are likely to be ignored when costs are stable or falling, which means that there are no cost pressures forcing a

Exhibit 8.5 The Amazon Kindle has pursued a strategy of aggressively reducing its price in response to competition from other e-readers

Introducing the
All-New Kindle Family

kindle
$79

kindle touch
$99

kindle fire
$199

general price rise. In the situation of excess supply, companies may view a price rise as making the initiator less competitive and therefore allow the rise to take place unchallenged, particularly when customers are price sensitive. Companies occupying low-price positions may regard a price rise in response to a price increase from a rival to be incompatible with their brand image. Finally, companies pursuing a build objective may allow a competitor's price rise to go unmatched in order to gain sales and market share.

Price cuts are likely to be ignored in conditions of rising costs, excess demand and when servicing price-insensitive customers. Premium-price positioners may be reluctant to follow competitors' price cuts for to do so would be incompatible with their brand image. For example, some luxury brands, such as Lacoste, have suffered heavily because of pursuing a strategy of discounting when faced with excess capacity while competitors chose not to follow.[25] Finally, price cuts may be resisted by companies using a harvest objective.

Tactics

If a company decides to follow a price change, it can do this quickly or slowly. A quick price reaction is likely when there is an urgent need to improve profit margins. Here, the competitor's price increase will be welcomed as an opportunity to achieve this objective.

In contrast, a slow reaction may be the best approach when a company is pursuing the image of customers' friend. The first company to announce a price increase is often seen as the high-price supplier. Some companies have mastered the art of playing low-cost supplier by never initiating price increases and following competitors' increases slowly.[26] The key to this tactic is timing the response: too quick and customers do not notice; too long and profit is foregone. The optimum period can be found only by experience but, during it, salespeople should be told to stress to customers that the company is doing everything it can to hold prices for as long as possible.

If a firm wishes to ward off a competitive threat, a quick response to a competitor's price fall is called for. In the face of undesirable sales/market share erosion, fast action is needed to nullify potential competitor gains. However, reaction will be slow when a company has a loyal customer base willing to accept higher prices for a period so long as they can rely on price parity over the longer term.

Customer value through pricing

Price leadership has become the central value proposition for firms in a wide variety of industries. For example, as we saw in the Marketing Spotlight at the beginning of the chapter, in grocery retailing, the German hard discounters Aldi and Lidl have led the way, in apparel retailing, for example, chains like Penneys and TK Maxx, in air travel low-fares carriers like easyJet and Ryanair, in personal computers, Dell, and so on. Because these firms aim to continually offer the best prices in the marketplace, the various issues described in this chapter take on particular importance. Offering low prices means that profit margins may be tight unless firms can find ways to drive their cost base down or find additional product/service elements that they can charge handsomely for. The three tools that firms have at their disposal to assist in this

challenge are cost management, **yield management** and **dynamic pricing**.

Cost management

Cost control is critical for firms that attempt to lead on price as their success in controlling costs has a direct impact on profit margins. For example, retailers like Walmart and airlines like Ryanair have a reputation about being fanatical in their search for ways of reducing cost. One of the first costs to be removed by some airlines was the practice of selling seats through travel agents and paying them a margin of up to 10 per cent which was incorporated into the price. Most airline seats are now booked directly by customers online. Services like catering and check-in are outsourced, flights go to small regional airports where landing charges are low and, in extreme instances like Ryanair, flight crews buy their own uniforms and pay for their training, headquarters staff supply their own pens, and even electricity sockets were changed to prevent staff charging their private phones at work.

Yield management

Another tool in the armoury of low price competitors is yield management which is the monitoring of demand or potential demand patterns. It is very popular in services businesses like travel and hotel accommodation. Levels of demand are tracked electronically on a daily basis. Therefore, over the course of a year, this information can be stored and used to set prices for rooms or flights which vary from day to day for the next year. It is also possible to track enquiries and use this information to make decisions regarding potential demand levels.

Dynamic pricing

An interesting aspect of many low-price companies is their level of profitability. For example, despite its reputation for low prices, Ryanair is the most profitable airline in Europe. Aside from their attention to costs, a key reason for their success is their flexible approach to pricing which is known as dynamic pricing. This means that prices are adjusted continually, based on demand and potential demand. Therefore, while prices on some flights may be cheap, on others they may be high if these flights coincide with peak holiday periods or major sporting events. Also, if demand for particular flights were to rise quickly for any reason, prices are quickly adjusted upwards. Through the application of technology and the close monitoring of demand patterns, many 'low-price' operators demonstrate a very flexible approach to price!

Marketing in Action 8.3 TK Maxx: luxury for less

Critical Thinking: Below is a review of the operations of the luxury brands discounter, TK Maxx. Read it and critically evaluate the strengths and weaknesses of its approach.

TK Maxx is a discount chain that specializes in selling branded goods at heavily discounted prices. Its first store was opened in the UK in 1994 and by 2010 the company had grown to operate over 250 stores in the UK, Ireland, Germany and Poland. The company specializes mainly in apparel but also carries household goods, gifts and accessories.

The main customer appeal of TK Maxx is that it promises the customer the prospect of finding a bargain – a traditionally high-priced, branded good that is available at discounts of up to 60 per cent. Marketing for the store portrays it as being akin to a treasure hunt. Up to 50,000 items are carried in a typical outlet, with 10,000 new items arriving each week. New stock is placed in the store each day and quantities tend to be limited. This is designed to ensure that customers visit regularly and they are also encouraged to snap up bargains as they are unlikely to be there should they return.

TK Maxx operates using many of the key aspects of a successful low price operator. It runs a no-frills operation and carries no spare stock in storerooms; everything that is shipped goes immediately onto the shop floor. It buys directly from brand owners and designers and carries both current season and out-of-season stock. In recent years, the company has switched its focus from growth throughout Europe to upgrading and expanding its existing stores in order to try to improve its 'pile 'em high, sell 'em cheap' image. However, remaining ahead of many other discount rivals such as Primark, Matalan and the fighter brands of large chains such as Tesco and Carrefour will remain one of its key challenges.

Based on: Anonymous (2007);[27] Chesters (2011)[28].

Summary

Price is a key aspect of the organization's marketing strategy and is also the core value proposition for some businesses. In this chapter the following key issues were addressed.

1. There are three bases upon which prices are set, namely cost, competition and market value. We noted that all three should be taken into account when setting prices. Costs represent a floor above which prices must be set to build a viable business, while competition and customers will influence the overall height of prices.

2. That the pricing levels set may also be influenced by a number of other marketing strategy variables, namely, positioning strategy, new-product launch strategy, product-line strategy, competitive strategy, channel management strategy and international marketing strategy.

3. That marketers need to make decisions relating to initiating price changes or responding to the price changes made by competitors. Whether prices are rising or falling, various factors need to be taken into account and these are important decisions as they affect the overall profitability of the firm.

4. That there are key issues surrounding the ethics of price setting. Price fixing is illegal, and other unethical practices such as deceptive pricing and product dumping are frequently targeted by regulators. Greater levels of price transparency are assisting consumers to avoid being exploited by unscrupulous companies.

5. Price may be the core value proposition offered by some businesses. In these cases organizations employ a combination of cost management, yield management and dynamic pricing to generate high profitability levels.

Study questions

1. Accountants are always interested in profit margins; sales managers want low prices to help push sales; and marketing managers are interested in high prices to establish premium positions in the marketplace. To what extent do you agree with this statement in relation to the setting of prices?

2. Why is value to the customer a more logical approach to setting prices than cost of production? What role can costs play in the setting of prices?

3. How would you justify the price differences for a cup of coffee that you might encounter if you purchase it in a local coffee shop versus a top-class hotel?

4. Discuss how a company pursuing a build strategy is likely to react to both price rises and price cuts by competitors.

5. Discuss the specific issues that arise when pricing products for international markets.

6. Visit www.vodafone.co.uk, www.o2.co.uk, www.orange.co.uk and www.easymobile.co.uk and compare the prices these companies charge for their products. How difficult is it to make an accurate comparison of the cost of a mobile phone package? Why do you think this is so?

Suggested reading

Anderson, E. and **D. Simester** (2003) Mind Your Pricing Cues, *Harvard Business Review*, **81** (9), 96–103.

Baker, W., M. Marn and **C. Zawada** (2010) Do You Have a Long-Term Pricing Strategy? *McKinsey Quarterly*, October, 1–7.

Bertini, M. and **L. Wathieu** (2010) How to Stop Customers from Fixating on Price, *Harvard Business Review*, **88** (5), 84–91.

Davis, G. and **E. Brito** (2004) Price and Quality Competition between Brands and Own Brands: A Value Systems Perspective, *European Journal of Marketing*, **38** (1/2), 30–56.

Mohammed, R. (2005) *The Art of Pricing: How to Find the Hidden Profits to Grow Your Business*, London: Crown Business.

Sahay, A. (2007) How Dynamic Pricing Leads To Higher Profits, *Sloan Management Review*, **48** (4), 53–60.

References

1. **Baker, R.** (2011) Discounters Enjoy Record Market Share, *MarketingWeek.co.uk*, 27 April; **Scally, D.** (2008) The Art of Simplicity, *Innovation*, September, 24–5; **Wood, Z.** (2010) Aldi Founder Theo Albrecht Dies, *Guardian.co.uk*, 28 July.

2. **Lester, T.** (2002) How to Ensure that the Price is Exactly Right, *Financial Times*, 30 January, 15.

3. **Shapiro, B.P.** and **B.B. Jackson** (1978) Industrial Pricing to Meet Customer Needs, *Harvard Business Review*, November-December, 119–27.

4. **English, A.** (2004) Renault to Sell £3200 Car in Romania, *Telegraph.co.uk*, 3 June.

5. **Mackintosh, J.** (2005) Renault's Surprise Romanian Success, *Financial Times*, 29 September, 30.

6. **London, S.** (2003) The Real Value in Setting the Right Price, *Financial Times*, 11 September, 15.

7. **Kucher, E.** and **H. Simon** (1987) Durchbruch bei der Preisentscheidung: Conjoint-Measurement, eine neue Technik zur Gewinnoptimierung, *Harvard Manager*, **3**, 36–60.

8. **Lester, T.** (2002) How to Ensure that the Price is Exactly Right, *Financial Times*, 30 January, 15.

9. **Forbis, J.L.** and **N.T. Mehta** (1979) Economic Value to the Customer, *McKinsey Staff Paper*, Chicago: McKinsey and Co., February, 1–10.

10. **Simon, H.** (1992) Pricing Opportunities – and How to Exploit Them, *Sloan Management Review*, Winter, 55–65.

11. **Cane, A.** (2003) TiVo, Barely Used . . . , *Financial Times*, Creative Business, 25 February, 12.

12. **Anonymous** (2011) Blazing Platforms, *The Economist*, 12 February, 63–4.

13. **Sanchanta, M.** (2007) A Price Cut Too Late for PlayStation 3, *Financial Times*, 6 December, 25.

14. **Stern, S.** (2008) Keep the Focus on Value or You Will Pay the Price, *Financial Times*, 27 May, 12.

15. **Pope, C.** (2009) Has Music Had its Day? *Irish Times*, 27 April, 15.

16. **Rigby, E.** (2008) Tesco Targets Aldi and Lidl with Discount Brand Range, *Financial Times*, 17 September, 22.

17. **Jack, A.** (2005) Drugs Groups Seek Cure for Irritation of Parallel Trading, *Financial Times*, 10 August, 18.

18. **Cullen, P.** (2007) Cheated at the Checkout, *Irish Times*, Weekend Review, 28 July, 1.

19. **Anonymous** (2004) Slow Moving: Can Unilever's Indian Arm Recover From Some Self-Inflicted Wounds? *The Economist*, 6 November, 67–8.

20. **Blitz, R.** (2008) Hotels Keep Door Shut to Big Rate Cuts, *Financial Times*, 27 November, 28.

21. **Hille, K.** (2010) Alibaba Marketing Push Brings Results, *Financial Times*, 11 August, 18.

22. **Simon, B.** (2005) GM's Price Cuts Drive Record Sales, *Financial Times*, 5 July, 28.

23. **Simon, B.** (2005) Detroit Giants Count Cost of Four-year Price War, *Financial Times*, 19 March, 29.

24. **Buckley, C.** (2005) Boots Bears Brunt of Slump, *Sunday Business Post*, Money & Markets, 3 April, 2.

25. **Dowdy, C.** (2003) Wealth, Taste and Cachet at Bargain Prices, *Financial Times*, 9 October, 17.

26. **Ross, E.B.** (1984) Making Money with Proactive Pricing, *Harvard Business Review*, November–December, 145–55.

27. **Anonymous** (2007) Lax Maxx, *Economist.com*, 30 March.

28. **Chesters, L.** (2011) TK Maxx Back with Haymarket Deal after Picadilly Rejection, *Independent.com*, 6 March.

Aran Candy's mission statement:

To produce and market the best gourmet jelly beans in the world, at affordable prices, with a reliable & efficient service, and long term customer care.

Aran Candy specializes in the manufacture and worldwide distribution of high-quality gourmet jelly beans, with 97 per cent of production exported to over 50 markets. The company produces beans under 'The Jelly Bean Factory®' brand at its state-of-the-art plant in Blanchardstown, Dublin, for supply to Europe, the Middle East, the Far East, Australia, New Zealand and Canada. The company has sales offices in Britain and Bahrain and its product is available in over 35,000 stores in the UK alone, including Tesco, Debenhams, and ASDA.[1]

Introduction

In early January 2009, Peter Cullen ('The Old Bean') and his son Richard Cullen ('The Young Bean'), Joint Managing Directors of Aran Candy, sat in the board room of their company reviewing the agenda for the first meeting of the New Year. The key item, given the severe weakness of sterling relative to the euro, was a review of strategic pricing options for their confectionery products in the UK market, one of

their largest export markets. Sterling had weakened by almost 30 per cent vis-à-vis the euro over the previous 12 months, effectively forcing an equivalent cost increase on Aran Candy. The year 2008 had begun with an exchange rate of €1 = GBP£0.74130, by the year end it stood at €1 = GBP£0.95250 (see Figure C8.1). Peter and Richard both knew that even with the right product, promoted correctly and distributed through appropriate channels, the effort was doomed to failure if the product was incorrectly priced. Both were aware that continued action by the Bank of England to depreciate sterling had the potential to inflict grave damage on their export business. A strategic response to the lost price competitiveness in the UK market was urgently needed. Today's meeting they hoped would provide a clear vision of the strategic responses available to them from which one or more could be prioritized.

Background and history

Aran Candy was founded by Peter and Richard Cullen in the late 1990s. Peter had significant prior experience of the confectionery industry. In 1973 he accepted the position of marketing manager and minority 10 per cent stakeholder of Shannon Confectionery, a company in which he was later appointed Managing Director. On leaving the firm in 1985,

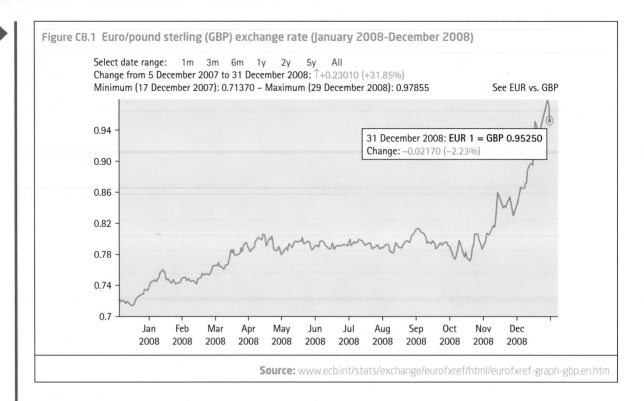

Figure C8.1 Euro/pound sterling (GBP) exchange rate (January 2008–December 2008)

Select date range: 1m 3m 6m 1y 2y 5y All
Change from 5 December 2007 to 31 December 2008: ↑+0.23010 (+31.85%)
Minimum (17 December 2007): 0.71370 – Maximum (29 December 2008): 0.97855

See EUR vs. GBP

31 December 2008: EUR 1 = GBP 0.95250
Change: −0.02170 (−2.23%)

Source: www.ecb.int/stats/exchange/eurofxref/html/eurofxref-graph-gbp.en.htm

his next career move, in partnership with his brother-in-law, was to acquire Clara Candy, makers of Cleeves Toffees, from the receiver. They soon brought it back to profitability. Despite generating up to 9 per cent net profit in its best years, over-exposure to a weakening UK market in 1994 caused the company to run into cash flow difficulties, and ultimately to losses in 1996. On 23 December 1997, as the plant closed for Christmas, Banque Nationale de Paris sent in the receivers. Cullen, then 52, was the largest creditor and lost IR£350,000 (€444,000) personally. Shortly afterwards, Dunhills Plc, a subsidiary of Haribo, a German confectionery firm, purchased the building and machinery of Clara Candy, and took on most of its 105 former employees.[2]

In 1998, Aran Candy was established on a shoestring budget and initially was run from a room in the Cullens' home in Killiney, Dublin. Given his experiences with Clara Candy Cullen had vowed never to manufacture again. All production was outsourced to former rivals in Spain, Belgium and the Netherlands, and sold on a commission basis. Cullen Senior recalls, 'We had one computer, a phone and a fax. We kept costs to nil and took out nothing for at least six months.'[3] Circumstances, however, forced an alternative sourcing strategy on them when, in 2004, their main supplier in the Netherlands decided to sell up. A production facility which became available in the north-east of England looked a likely solution; however, before the deal was signed, the owner sold to a rival bid from a property developer. All was not lost. A sell-off of the factory contents left Cullen in possession of the manufacturing

equipment at a knock-down price. Now all that was needed was premises to house the machinery. After some frenetic searching, a suitable unit became available in the IDA Business and Technology Park in Blanchardstown, Dublin. A fitting-out of the premises followed, staff including some ex-Clara and Haribo employees fully trained in production, safety and hygiene standards were recruited and production began in August 2005.[4]

Production and product range

Jelly beans are believed to be a contemporary variant of Turkish Delight, which itself dates to biblical times. Jelly beans were developed in eighteenth-century France and are linked to Easter, with their egg-like shape symbolizing new birth.[5] Aran Candy is dedicated to producing gourmet jelly beans, a variety produced from a recipe containing sugar, glucose syrup, modified food starches, water, citric acid, fumoric acid, glazing agents shellac bees wax and carnaula wax, flavourings, acidity regulator sodium citrate and colours. The finished bean, which is available in 38 flavours, takes two weeks to produce. Aran Candy Gourmet Jelly Beans are softer, smaller and contain fewer calories than other varieties. The company's 50,000 sq ft factory has the capacity to produce about 2,000 tonnes of beans per annum.

By January 2009 production was running at some 10 million jelly beans per day and sold in a variety of pack sizes and formats. Sachets were available in 25 g and 50 g sizes and the standard tube was 125 g. Jars with an after-use had proved popular with customers, and three jar sizes were

Exhibit C8.1 Selection of products from The Jelly Bean Factory

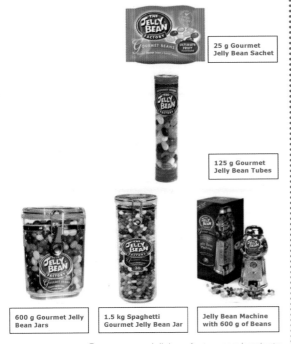

25 g Gourmet Jelly Bean Sachet

125 g Gourmet Jelly Bean Tubes

600 g Gourmet Jelly Bean Jars

1.5 kg Spaghetti Gourmet Jelly Bean Jar

Jelly Bean Machine with 600 g of Beans

Source: www.jellybeanfactory.com/products

Table C8.1 Sugar confectionery company shares 2005–07

% Retail value	2005	2006	2007
Cadbury Trebor Bassett Ltd	24.99	24.85	23.54
Nestlé UK Ltd	11.38	11.12	10.86
Haribo Dunhills (Pontefract) Plc	9.38	10.31	10.41
Masterfoods UK Ltd	6.97	6.52	7.23
Swizzels Matlow Ltd	3.25	3.16	3.35
Ernest Jackson Ltd	3.54	3.38	3.08
Bendicks (Mayfair) Ltd	3.35	3.13	3.00
Chupa Chups UK Ltd	2.54	2.64	2.66
Tesco Plc	2.46	2.44	2.42
Asda Group Ltd	2.13	2.23	2.23
Mr Lucky Bags Ltd	2.08	2.04	1.99
Leaf United Kingdom Ltd	1.60	1.62	1.62

Source: Euromonitor International (2008).

offered in the product range, a 600 g, a 900 g and a 1.5 kg 'spaghetti' jar. In addition, the 600 g jelly bean machine (for which 600 g refill bags were available) had proved popular with customers. All products from The Jelly Bean Factory are GMO, gelatine, gluten and nut free and all are also Halal compliant. (See Exhibit C8.1 for a selection of The Jelly Bean Factory products.)

The UK Sugar Confectionery Market[6]

The UK sugar confectionery market grew by 2 per cent in current value terms in 2008, to £1.6 billion. Cadbury Trebor Bassett Ltd, with 2007 UK sales of £377 million, was the dominant player with a 23.5 per cent share of the market. Nestlé, Haribo and Masterfoods (Mars) were the other main competitors, with 2007 market shares of 10.8 per cent, 10.4 per cent and 7.2 per cent respectively (see Table C8.1).

Unit prices in the sugar confectionery sector rose in 2008, a trend evident across other food stuffs and a response to consistent new product development. A feature of the market during the period was the increasing use of natural ingredients and the move to healthier sugar-free variants. Sugar-free was a rising segment of the sugar confectionery market, growing by 2 per cent in 2008 and by year end comprising 9 per cent of total

value sales. Cadbury Trebor Bassett Ltd had exploited this trend by introducing the Australian Natural Confectionery Company brand of healthier sweets, a product containing no artificial colours or flavours, aimed at parents looking for more permissible treats for their family. They also had introduced a reduced sugar version of their long established. Maynards Wine Gums brand.

Nestlé had announced that they would launch a range of sugar confectionery products containing real fruit juice, with no artificial colourings or flavourings and positioned as a 'better for you' alternative to standard confectionery products. They also launched the Nestlé Go Free promotion, whereby consumers could earn free football, swimming and tennis lessons using vouchers from the packaging of Milkybar, Jelly Tots, Smarties, Fruit Gums or Fruit Pastilles products, taking advantage of the trend towards a healthier and more active lifestyle.

The smoking ban in enclosed public places, introduced across the whole of the UK in 2007, was viewed as having had a positive impact on the sugar confectionery sector, with many adults reverting to consumption of mints and sweets in lieu of cigarettes.

Options

Addressing the meeting Richard Cullen began by outlining a range of strategic pricing options available to counteract the loss of competitiveness due to the adverse movement in exchange rates. What the meeting must now do was consider the pros and cons of each option and judiciously select among them. One option was to withdraw temporarily from the UK market and give priority to exports to relatively strong currency countries. When the sterling exchange rate returned to a more favourable level the UK market could be re-entered. A second option was to trim profit margins and use marginal cost pricing until matters improved. Richard was aware that if sterling valuation continued to be undermined by the Bank of England's quantitative easing process, then this option could prove costly. A third option was to improve productivity and engage in vigorous cost reductions, although Richard was conscious of the challenges of doing this in what was already a lean production facility. Switching sourcing and production overseas to take advantage of more attractive currency exchange rates and factor prices was another option, especially if it was anticipated that sterling would remain weak. Aran Candy could also engage in non-price competition by improving quality and introducing new products. Introducing product with only natural colours and no artificial flavours might not only take advantage of the trend towards natural ingredients but also serve to enhance margins. Another option, relying on the theory of just noticable difference (JND),* would require a reduction in the net weight of product supplied while holding price constant. In line with this strategy Aran Candy might refresh packaging or introduce pack innovations, perhaps a 100 g tube or larger jar sizes. A final option would be to seek a price increase in the UK although Richard was conscious that such a strategy might be resisted by powerful channel partners. Having witnessed the significant adverse effects of the sterling depreciation, Richard knew that Aran Candy jobs depended on making a timely and appropriate strategic response.

* JND refers to the smallest detectable change in a stimulus. In pricing JND refers to the magnitude of a price change before it is noticed by a consumer. In some cases a reduction in product weight may be less noticeable to the consumer than an equivalent increase in price.

References

1. www.aimawards.ie/2009/finalists/finalists.asp?ID=11 (accessed 16 May 2011).
2. **Costello, R.** (2006) How I Made It: Success at Second Bite Tastes Sweet, *Sunday Times*, 4 June, business.timesonline.co.uk/tol/business/article671302.ece?print=yes&randum=12 (accessed 16 May 2011).
3. **Costello, R.** (2006) How I Made It: Success at Second Bite Tastes Sweet, *Sunday Times*, 4 June, business.timesonline.co.uk/tol/business/article671302.ece?print=yes&randum=12 (accessed 16 May 2011).
4. **Daly, G.** (2008) The Jelly Bean Giants, *Sunday Business Post*, 27 April.
5. Adapted from **eHow Careers & Work Editor**, How to Make Jelly Beans, www.ehow.com/how_2084964_make-jelly-beans.html (accessed 16 May 2011).
6. This section relies heavily on data from *Euromonitor International* (2008).

Questions

1. Discuss ways in which changes in the macro-environment has impacted the sugar confectionery market.
2. Discuss the risks faced by an exporting company with a strong domestic currency.
3. List the different pricing strategies Aran Candy may employ in the UK given the severe weakness of sterling relative to the euro.
4. Are there any non-pricing strategies open to Aran Candy to respond to the depreciation in sterling?
5. Which strategy would you recommend for Aran Candy? Justify your choice.

Video See: www.arancandy.com/video.asp for video feature from Ernst & Young Entrepreneur of the Year 2010.

This case was prepared by Dr Michael Gannon, Marketing Group, DCU Business School, Ireland, from various published sources as a basis for class discussion rather than to show effective or ineffective management.

A new Marketing Showcase video featuring an exclusive interview with Diageo's Global Brand Director for Captain Morgan rum is available to lecturers for presentation and discussion in class.

Part 3

Delivering and Managing Customer Value

I was made for the office. To do the serious stuff you have to do, like spreadsheets and timesheets and pie charts. With me, viruses and crashing can be a way of life, but eventually you'll just get used to it. I think computers are meant for work, and fun is just a waste of time. **I'm a PC.**

I was made for the home. To do the fun things you want to do, like photos and movies and music. I run Mac OS X so you don't have to worry about the viruses and spyware that PCs do. And I come with iLife so I can do amazing stuff right out of the box. I think computers should be human and intuitive so, well, that's what I am. **I'm a Mac.**

Chapter 9
Integrated Marketing Communications 1: Mass Communications Techniques

Chapter outline

Integrated marketing communications

Stages in developing an integrated communications campaign

Advertising

Sales promotion

Public relations and publicity

Sponsorship

Other promotional techniques

Learning outcomes

By the end of this chapter you will understand:

1 the concept of integrated marketing communications

2 the key characteristics of the seven major promotional tools

3 how to develop an integrated communications campaign – target audience analysis, objective setting, budgeting, message and media decisions, and campaign evaluation

4 the nature and importance of advertising in the promotional mix

5 the roles of sales promotion, public relations/ publicity and sponsorship in the promotional mix.

Barclaycard

Barclaycard is a global payments company with over 23 million customers across five continents. During its growth, the brand has had some famous advertising campaigns – most notably one that featured the actor and comedian, Rowan Atkinson as a bungling secret agent getting into all sorts of difficulties only to be rescued by his Barclaycard. This campaign firmly established the brand in the public psyche but the momentum was not maintained and both brand equity and business performance declined. By the middle part of the last decade, Barclaycard was further challenged by new market entrants and was suffering a fall in volume transactions while market share had declined from over 30 per cent in 1995 to just 16 per cent by 2007.

In the face of this competition, Barclaycard continued with its favoured approach of using celebrities in its advertising. People like Jennifer Aniston and Jennifer Saunders featured in campaigns which were complemented by price-led messaging that aimed to tackle head-on the challenge posed by new entrants such as Egg and Capital One that sought to attract customers through competitive interest rates. However, this approach did not work and the brand began to be increasingly seen as old-fashioned and out of step with the new generation of credit card holders. Market research indicated that these new customers were young, urban and educated, with an optimistic attitude, active lifestyles and a desire for simple, modern solutions. Barclaycard's promise of being safely able to navigate an uncertain world seemed less relevant.

The brand decided to abandon its celebrity and price-driven approach and create a new positioning around the concept of simple payment. The creative treatment for this proposition was the development of an epic advert featuring a giant waterslide running through a large city that carried a young office worker home to the sound of a classic song. The advertisement was carried on channels and programming suitable to the target market and behind-the-scenes footage of the making of the commercial was carried on YouTube to increase its viral appeal. Further use of social media involved a YouTube do-it-yourself (DIY) competition challenging customers to create and upload their own Barclaycard waterslide. A waterslide iPhone app was also created – a first for the financial services sector. The campaign was also carried in print and on outdoor billboards containing real waterslides and this innovative approach generated a high level of publicity in print and on radio.

The campaign was a huge success. The YouTube video was viewed over 7 million times and the iPhone app downloaded over 12 million times. In post-campaign research, over half of those surveyed could remember seeing the campaign and perceptions of the brand as old-fashioned declined. The popularity of the advert saw it make the Top 10 advertisements of the decade in an ITV viewers' poll and both market share and profitability recovered as a result.[1]

As well as deciding what form of value an organization is proposing to offer its customers, it is also important to make a series of decisions regarding how this value is going to be communicated in the marketplace. As we saw in Chapters 3 and 5 particularly, these are very important decisions owing to the sheer volume of marketing messages that are currently aimed at consumers and the likelihood that many of these messages will not even be attended to, not to mention affect recipients in the ways that might be intended. This makes the study of marketing communications one of the most fascinating aspects of marketing as we seek to answer questions regarding what kinds of messages we should create and how we should communicate them. There are two major classes of tools available to the marketer. Mass communications techniques such as television advertising or sponsorship can be used, and these kinds of techniques will be the focus of this chapter. In addition, many organizations use direct communications techniques such as mobile marketing and social networking, and these direct and online techniques are examined in Chapter 10.

The overall range of techniques available to the marketer is usually known as the 'promotional mix' and comprises seven main elements.

1   *Advertising*: any paid form of non-personal communication of ideas or products in the prime media (television, press, posters, cinema and radio).
2   *Sales promotion*: incentives to consumers or the trade that are designed to stimulate purchase (competitions, special offers).
3   *Publicity*: communications for a product or business by placing information about it in the media without paying for the time or space directly (media interviews, blogs).
4   *Sponsorship*: the association of the company or its products with an individual, event or organization.
5   *Direct marketing*: the distribution of products, information and promotional benefits to target consumers through interactive communication in a way that allows response to be measured.
6   *Digital marketing*: the distribution of products, information and promotional benefits to consumers and businesses through digital technologies. Digital marketing is growing rapidly and is examined in detail in Chapter 10.
7   *Personal selling*: oral communication with prospective purchasers with the intention of making a sale.

In addition to these key promotional tools, the marketer can also use a wide range of other techniques, such as exhibitions, events, product placement in movies, songs or video games and more recent techniques like ambient marketing, guerrilla marketing and buzz marketing. Given the potentially wide menu of communications choices that the organization has, it is important that these decisions are consistent with all other elements of marketing such as branding, pricing and distribution in order to ensure a consistent positioning in the marketplace. If several different communications tools are being used, it is also important that they are consistent with and complement each other. This is what is meant by the concept of integrated marketing communications (IMC).

Integrated marketing communications

Each of the seven major promotional tools has its own strengths and limitations; these are summarized in Table 9.1. Marketers will carefully weigh these factors against promotional objectives to decide the amount of resources they should channel into each tool.

Usually, the following five considerations will have a major impact on the choice of the promotional mix.

1   *Resource availability and the cost of promotional tools*: to conduct a national advertising campaign may require several million euro. If resources are not available, cheaper tools such as direct marketing or publicity may have to be used.
2   *Market size and concentration*: if a market is small and concentrated then personal selling may be feasible, but for mass markets that are geographically dispersed, selling to the ultimate customer would not be cost-effective. In such circumstances advertising or direct marketing may be the correct choice.
3   *Customer information needs*: if a complex technical argument is required, personal selling may be preferred. If all that is required is the appropriate brand image, advertising may be more sensible.
4   *Product characteristics*: industrial goods companies tend to spend more on personal selling than advertising, whereas consumer goods companies tend to do the reverse.
5   *Push versus pull strategies*: a **distribution push** strategy involves an attempt to sell into channel intermediaries (e.g. retailers) and is dependent on personal selling and trade promotions. A **consumer pull** strategy bypasses intermediaries to communicate to consumers directly. The resultant consumer demand persuades intermediaries to stock the product. Advertising and consumer promotions are more likely to be used.

Table 9.1 Key characteristics of seven key promotional mix tools

Advertising
■ Good for awareness building because it can reach a wide audience quickly
■ Repetition means that a brand positioning concept can be effectively communicated; television is particularly strong
■ Can be used to aid the sales effort: legitimize a company and its products
■ Impersonal: lacks flexibility and questions cannot be answered
■ Limited capability to close the sale

Personal selling
■ Interactive: questions can be answered and objections overcome
■ Adaptable: presentations can be changed depending on customer needs
■ Complex arguments can be developed
■ Relationships can be built because of its personal nature
■ Provides the opportunity to close the sale
■ Sales calls are costly

Direct marketing
■ Individual targeting of consumers most likely to respond to an appeal
■ Communication can be personalized
■ Short-term effectiveness can easily be measured
■ A continuous relationship through periodic contact can be built
■ Activities are less visible to competitors
■ Response rates are often low
■ Poorly targeted direct marketing activities cause consumer annoyance

Internet promotion
■ Global reach at relatively low cost
■ Relatively easy to measure effectiveness
■ A dialogue between companies, and their customers and suppliers can be established
■ Catalogues and prices can be changed quickly and cheaply
■ Convenient form of searching for and buying products

Sales promotion
■ Incentives provide a quick boost to sales
■ Effects may be only short term
■ Excessive use of some incentives (e.g. money off) may damage brand image

Publicity
■ Highly credible as message comes from a third party
■ Higher readership than advertisements in trade and technical publications
■ Lose control: a press release may or may not be used and its content distorted

Sponsorship
■ Very useful for brand building and generating publicity
■ Provides an opportunity to entertain business partners
■ Can be used to demonstrate the company's goodwill to its local community or society in general
■ Popular due to the fragmentation of traditional media

As the range of promotional techniques expands, there is an increasing need to co-ordinate the messages and their execution. This problem is often exacerbated by the fact that, for example, advertising is controlled by the advertising department, whereas personal selling strategies are controlled by the sales department, leading to a lack of co-ordination. This has led to the adoption of **integrated marketing communications** by an increasing number of companies. Integrated marketing communications is the system by which companies co-ordinate their marketing communications tools to deliver a clear, consistent, credible and competitive message about the organization and its products. For example, Meteor Ireland's Reindeer campaign for Christmas 2008 was rolled out across television, cinema, outdoor, press, radio, online, social networking, PR, in-store and on-street. A significant proportion of television advertising is currently designed to also have social media applications. The application of this concept of integrated marketing communications can lead to improved consistency and clearer positioning of companies and their brands in the minds of consumers.

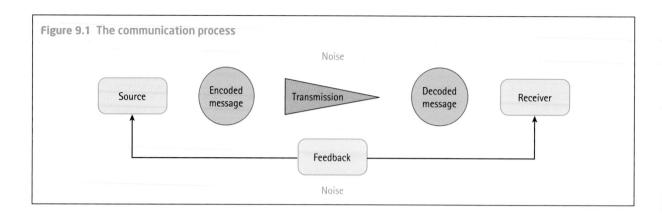

Figure 9.1 The communication process

The traditional model of the communication process is shown in Figure 9.1. The source (or communicator) encodes a message by translating the idea to be communicated into a symbol consisting of words or pictures, such as an advertisement. The message is transmitted through media, such as television or the Internet, which are selected for their ability to reach the desired target audience in the desired way. 'Noise' – distractions and distortions during the communication process – may prevent transmission to some of the target audience. The vast amount of promotional messages a consumer receives daily makes it a challenge for marketers to cut through this noise. When a receiver sees or hears the message it is decoded. This is the process by which the receiver interprets the symbols transmitted by the source. Communicators need to understand their targets before encoding messages so that they are credible, otherwise the response may be disbelief and rejection. In a **personal selling** situation, feedback from buyer to salesperson may be immediate as when objections are raised or a sale is concluded. For other types of promotion, such as advertising and sales promotion, feedback may rely on marketing research to estimate reactions to commercials, and increases in sales due to incentives.

Stages in developing an integrated communications campaign

For many small and medium-sized firms, marketing communications planning involves little more than assessing how much the firm can afford to spend, allocating it across some media and, in due course, looking at whether sales levels have increased or not. It is clear that to avoid wasting valuable organizational resources, marketing communications should be planned and evaluated carefully. The various stages involved in doing this are outlined in Figure 9.2.

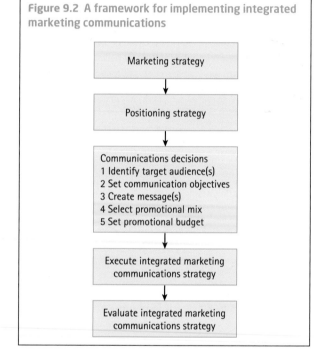

Figure 9.2 A framework for implementing integrated marketing communications

The process begins by looking at the firm's overall marketing strategy, its positioning strategy and its intended **target audience**. What is the firm trying to achieve in the marketplace and what role can marketing communications play? If, for example, the firm is trying to reposition a brand or change consumer attitudes, then advertising is likely to play an important role in this, but it must be integrated with the other marketing mix elements. Objectives need to be set for the IMC campaign and they should be quantifiable. For example, the objective is to increase sales by a given amount or to increase awareness among the youth market by a given percentage. Only after these stages are complete should the company begin thinking about what it is going to say (the message decisions) and where it is going to say it (the media decisions). These are complex decisions, which are discussed in detail in this and the next chapter. A budget for the campaign needs to be agreed, usually at board level in the company. Then after the campaign has been run, it is imperative that it is fully evaluated to assess its effectiveness. We will now examine some of the key mass communications techniques in more detail.

Advertising

Advertising is very big business. In 2011, global advertising expenditure was forecast to reach US$443 billion, with two-thirds of all this expenditure taking place in Europe and North America. There has long been considerable debate about how advertising works. The consensus is that there can be no single all-embracing theory that explains how all advertising works because it has varied tasks. For example, advertising that attempts to make an instant sale by incorporating a return coupon that can be used to order a product is very different from corporate image advertising that is designed to reinforce attitudes. One view of advertising sees it as being powerful enough to encourage consumers to buy by moving them through the stages of awareness, interest, desire and action (known by the acronym AIDA). This is known as the **strong theory of advertising** and it implies that advertising is targeted at a largely passive consumer and is capable of moving them through a series of stages in a fairly linear fashion. An alternative approach – the awareness, trial, reinforcement (ATR) model – sees a key role of advertising as being to defend brands, by reinforcing beliefs so that existing customers may be retained. This is referred to as the **weak theory of advertising**. It implies that most purchase choices are based on habit and that the purpose of advertising is largely defensive. Advertising is likely to have different roles depending on the nature of the product and the degree of involvement of the customer (see Chapter 3).

More recent perspectives from consumer culture theory (see Chapter 3) interpret consumer advertising more in terms of the transfer of meaning. In other words, advertising acts as a source of meanings through which we express ourselves and communicate with others. For example, marketing communications may have social meaning and consumers differentiate themselves from others by consuming particular products (see Exhibit 9.1). Research has found that the brands of clothes worn by people have an impact on cooperation from others, job recommendations and even collecting money when soliciting for a charity.[2] However one chooses to explain it, one should not underestimate the power of advertising. For example, Covergirl's Lashblast mascara advertising campaign featuring Drew Barrymore generated sales that were 70 per cent higher than expected.

Exhibit 9.1 The famous campaign contrasting the PC owner on the left with the Apple Mac owner on the right illustrates the power of marketing communications to transfer meanings

There's more than one choice when it comes to a computer.   Watch Mitchell and Webb as PC and Mac on **apple.com/uk**

Developing advertising strategy

Each of the steps identified in Figure 9.2 is appropriate irrespective of whether the firm is conducting an advertising campaign, a **direct marketing** or **sales promotion** campaign, all that changes is the detail involved. Here we examine some specific advertising issues.

Defining advertising objectives

Although, ultimately, advertising is a means of stimulating sales and increasing profits, a clear understanding of its communication objectives is of more operational value. Advertising can have a number of communications objectives. First, it can be used to *create awareness* of a brand or a solution to a company's problem. Awareness creation is critical when a new product is being launched or when the firm is entering a new market. For example, *The Economist* magazine, which primarily targets wealthy executives, ran a cinema campaign entitled 'The Economist – Let Your Mind Wander' to create awareness among younger readers. Second, advertising can be used to *stimulate trial*, such as car advertising encouraging motorists to take a test drive. Third, and as we saw in Chapter 5, advertising is used to help *position products* in the minds of consumers, such as L'Oréal's repeated use of the slogan 'Because I'm worth it' or Ronseal's 'It does exactly what it says on the tin'. Other objectives of advertising include the *correction of misconceptions* about a product or service, *reminding* customers of sales or special offers, and *providing support* for the company's sales force.

Setting the advertising budget

The amount that is spent on advertising governs the achievement of communication objectives. There are four methods of setting advertising budgets. A simple method is the *percentage of sales* method, whereby the amount allocated to advertising is based on current or expected revenue. However, this method is weak because it encourages a decline in advertising expenditure when sales decline, a move that may encourage a further downward spiral of sales. Furthermore, it ignores market opportunities, which may suggest the need to spend more (not less) on advertising. For example, General Motors cut its advertising expenditure for the first half of 2007 by 27 per cent although sales of its models in the USA had been falling. The company ultimately needed a bail-out from the US government in order to stay in business. Major consumer brands typically spend in the region of 10–15 per cent of sales on marketing.

Alternatively, companies may set their advertising budgets based upon matching competitors' expenditures, or using a similar percentage of sales figure as their major competitor. This is known as the *competitive parity* method. Again this method is weak because it assumes that the competition has arrived at the optimum level of expenditure, and ignores market opportunities and communication objectives. Sometimes firms make a decision on the basis of what they think they can afford (the *affordability* method). While affordability needs to be taken into account when considering any corporate expenditure, its use as the sole criterion for budget setting neglects the communication objectives that are relevant for a company's products, and the market opportunities that may exist, to grow sales and profits.

The most effective method of setting advertising budgets is the *objective and task* method. This has the virtue of being logical since the advertising budget depends upon communication objectives and the costs of the tasks required to achieve them. It forces management to think about objectives, media exposure levels and the resulting costs. In practice, the advertising budgeting decision is a highly political process.[3] Finance may argue for monetary caution, whereas marketing personnel, who view advertising as a method of long-term brand building, are more likely to support higher advertising spend. During times of economic slowdown, advertising budgets are among the first to be cut, although this can be the time when advertising expenditure is most effective. However, research has shown that maintaining or increasing promotional expenditures during a recession can have a positive impact on sales, market share and profitability.[4]

Message decisions

The **advertising message** translates an organization's basic value proposition into an **advertising platform**; that is the words, symbols and illustrations that are attractive and meaningful to the target audience. In the 1980s, IBM realized that many customers bought its computers because of the reassurance they felt when dealing with a well-known supplier. The company used this knowledge to develop an advertising campaign based on the advertising platform of reassurance/low risk. This platform was translated into the advertising message 'No one ever got fired for buying IBM'. As we shall see below, the choice of media available to the advertiser is vast, therefore one of the challenges of message formulation is to keep the message succinct and adaptable across various media. For example, a recent campaign for eBay just focused on the word 'It'. Imagery of the word 'It' appeared on posters, print and television, and migrated online as a viral campaign. The 'It' was finally revealed as part of eBay's slogan, 'Whatever it is, you can get it on eBay'.[5]

Most of those who look at a press advertisement read the headline but not the body copy. Because of this, some advertisers suggest that the company or brand name should appear in the headline otherwise the reader may not know the source of the advertisement. For example, the headlines 'Good food costs less at Sainsbury's' and 'United Colors of Benetton' score highly because in one phrase or sentence they link a customer benefit or attribute with the name of the company. Even if no more copy is read, the advertiser has got one message across by means of a strong headline (see Exhibit 9.2).

Messages broadcast via television also need to be built on a strong advertising platform (see Marketing in Action 9.1). Because television commercials are usually of a duration of 30 seconds or less, most communicate only one major selling appeal which is the single most motivating and differentiating thing that can be said about the brand. A variety of creative treatments can be used, from *lifestyle*, to *humour*, to *shock* advertising.

Exhibit 9.2 **This advertisement for Asics running shoes is a classic example of a strong print ad with powerful visual and a simple headline**

anima sana in corpore sano

running cleanses the mind and body

ASICS.
sound mind, sound body

Cosmetics brands like Estée Lauder have traditionally favoured the lifestyle approach (showing the brand as being part of an attractive lifestyle) to advertising though many have now moved to using top models and celebrities in their advertising (*testimonials*). *Sexual imagery* remains a popular attention-getting tactic in advertising, though recent research casts doubt on its effectiveness.[6] *Comparative advertising* is another popular approach frequently used by companies like low-cost airlines, supermarkets and banks to demonstrate relative price advantages. It can be a risky approach as it often leads to legal battles over claims made, such as the legal action between Asda and Tesco over the former's claim that it was 'officially' the lowest price supermarket.[7]

Volkswagen's 'The Force' campaign uses humour as an effective creative treatment.
www.mcgraw-hill.co.uk/textbooks/fahy

Television advertising is often used to build a brand personality. The brand personality is the message the advertisement seeks to convey. Lannon suggests that people use brand personalities in different ways,[8] such as acting as a form of self-expression, reassurance, a communicator of the brand's function and an indicator of trustworthiness. The value of the brand personality to consumers will differ by product category and this will depend on the purpose served by the brand imagery. In 'self-expressive' product categories, such as perfumes, cigarettes, alcoholic drinks and clothing, brands act as 'badges' for making public an aspect of personality ('I choose this brand [e.g. Tommy Hilfiger] to say this about myself').

Television advertising has long been the staple method of promoting consumer brands, although it now faces many challenges. Technologies like digital recorders enable viewers to avoid watching the commercial breaks and the multiplicity of channels available means that it is harder for advertisers to reach large audiences. The growing trend towards multi-tasking may well mean that consumers are also online at the same time as they are watching television further reducing attention. Advertisers have responded to these trends in a number of ways. First there is the creation of live adverts. For example, Honda and Channel 4 combined to produce the first live television advertisement in 2008. A live sky-diving jump was broadcast in which 19 stuntmen spelt out the car maker's brand name in an advert that had the slogan 'Difficult is worth doing'. The pre- and post-publicity surrounding the initiative also benefited Honda. Second, there is the growth of **consumer-generated advertising**, where brands hold competitions inviting consumers to submit adverts or to participate in the creation of adverts (see Marketing in Action 9.1). The risk of adopting this approach is that some user-generated content may be negative but many organizations feel it is worth giving up some control in order to enhance the relationships that consumers have with brands. The clothing brand Diesel's 'Be Stupid' campaign is designed to inspire consumers to upload videos of their own stupidity online (see Exhibit 9.3). Successful user-generated advertising tends to quickly migrate online as part of a **viral campaign**. Finally, some television advertising invites consumers to go to websites to avail of special offers to take account of consumer trends towards multi-tasking.

Media decisions

Because of the proliferation of media now available to an advertiser, such as hundreds of television channels or radio stations, the media selection decision has become a very important one. Choice of media class (for example, television versus press) and media vehicle (e.g. a particular newspaper or magazine) are two key decisions. Both of these will be examined next.

Marketing in Action 9.1 Heineken Italia – are you still with us?

Critical Thinking: Below is a review of a promotional campaign for Heineken beer in Italy. Critically evaluate using the model of the main stages involved in running a promotional campaign (Figure 9.2) as a guide.

Heineken is one of the strongest beer brands in Italy but was suffering a decline in sales volume due to the recession caused by the global financial crisis of 2008 which resulted in fewer Italians dining out and going for drinks with friends. Although it was tempting to reduce the price or cut back on promotional activity, it decided to continue to aggressively promote the brand with an innovative promotional campaign. The target was older drinkers – those in their late twenties and thirties who were more likely to buy a premium beer – and the objective of the campaign was to build loyalty in this market. The creative approach revolved around the tagline 'are you still with us?' which was designed to touch a nerve with this group that were beginning to leave their fun-filled days behind as they grappled with the responsibilities of maturity.

This message was executed in a number of key and relatively low-cost ways. First, with the use of 200 female accomplices, Heineken gave a group of men a key test of their priorities – miss a Champions League game between AC Milan and Real Madrid to attend a classical music concert with their girlfriends. Fifteen minutes into the concert, the following sentence was beamed on a big screen behind the musicians – 'How could you ever have thought of missing the match? Are you still with us?' The concert gave way to a live telecast of the game. A similar cinema practical joke involved the invitation by direct mail of Heineken drinkers and their girlfriends to the opening of a new romantic film 'Lady Violet's Diary'. Within minutes the movie is interrupted with the 'Are you still with us?' message and movie goers get to watch an action movie with free Heineken. The accompanying 2009 television campaign involved executions that created a sense of betrayal of the beer moment where the culprit was the guy who now had a girlfriend!

The campaign was a huge success. The fake concert was broadcast live on Sky Sports and watched by 1.5 million viewers and over 8 million viewers on news channels the following day. The campaign had a significant effect on brand perceptions with increases in the proportion of consumers reporting that it 'is a brand worth paying for' and 'for drinking with friends' compared with rival brands. Significant improvements were also seen in brand preference and sales value as a result of the campaign.

Based on: Emap Limited (2011).[9]

Table 9.2 lists the major media class and vehicle options (the media mix). The media planner faces the choice of using television, press, cinema, outdoor, radio, the Internet and so on, or a combination of media classes. Creative factors have a major bearing on the choice of media class. For example, if the *objective* is to position the brand as having a high-status, aspirational personality, television or product placement would be better than outdoor advertising. However, if the communication objective is to remind the target audience of a brand's existence, an outdoor or an ambient campaign may suffice.

Each medium possesses its own set of creative qualities and limitations. Television can be used to demonstrate the product in action, or to use colour and sound to build an atmosphere around the product, thus enhancing its image. Although television was traditionally one of the most powerful advertising mediums, concerns about fragmentation of the television audience have led many leading advertisers to move away from it. Furthermore, recent research has again questioned whether viewers actually watch advertisements when they are on, finding that consumers may spend as little as 23 per cent of the time the advertisements are on watching them, with the remainder spent talking, reading, surfing between channels or doing tasks such as cleaning, ironing or office work.[10] Unilever has responded by reducing the amount of advertising it places on television, switching instead to outdoor and Internet advertising. Despite these developments, television is still the largest advertising medium (see Figure 9.3) and some research shows it plays a significant role in brand building.[11]

Exhibit 9.3 The Diesel clothing 'Be Stupid' campaign generated a significant amount of buzz due to its clever graphics and strong headlines

Table 9.2 Media choices

Media class	Media vehicle
Television	Channel 4 News; Eurosport
Radio	Classic FM; Radio Luxembourg
Newspapers	The European; The Guardian
Magazines – Consumer	Hello; Glamour
– Business	Marketing Week; Construction News
Outdoor	Billboards; bus shelters; London Underground
Internet	Google Adwords; YouTube videos
Cinema	Particular movies
Exhibitions	Motor Show; Ideal Home
Product Placement	TV programmes, songs, video games
Ambient	Street pavements; buildings

Figure 9.3 Advertising expenditure by media – Western Europe, 2011

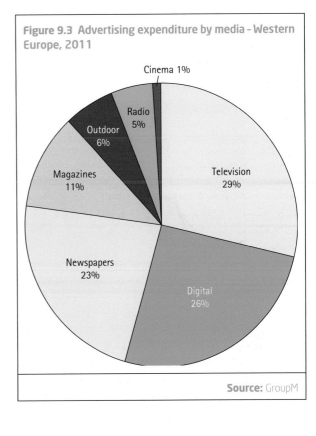

Source: GroupM

Press advertising is useful for providing factual information and offers an opportunity for consumers to re-examine the advertisement at a later stage. Advertisers are increasingly using colour print ads to ensure that their brands stand out. Leaders in this field include the likes of Orange and easyJet, as well as retail chains like Marks & Spencer. Colour advertising in newspapers has risen by 53 per cent as against an 8 per cent growth in mono advertising.[12] Magazines can be used to target particular markets and one growing sector is customer magazines, whereby leading brands such as BMW and Mercedes produce colour magazines of pictures and editorial about their products. Posters are a very good support medium, as their message has to be short and succinct because consumers such as motorists will normally only have time to glance at the content (see Exhibit 9.4). Lavazza, the Italian coffee brand, is an extensive user of poster sites in airports and metropolitan areas where its glamorous, fashion magazine-style adverts are used to build awareness and image of the brand. Outdoor advertising continues to be favoured as the growth of cities, metros and long commuting times make the medium appealing, though it is increasingly subject to regulation. Radio is limited to the use of sound and is therefore more likely to be useful in communicating factual information rather than building image, while cinema benefits from colour, movement and sound, as well as the presence of a captive audience. Cinema is a particularly good medium for brands trying to reach young audiences as is Internet advertising.

A number of other factors also affect the **media class decision**. An important consideration is the size of the *advertising budget*. Some media are naturally more expensive than others. For example, €500,000 may be sufficient for a national poster campaign but woefully inadequate for television. The relative cost per opportunity to see (OTS) is also relevant. The target audience may be reached much more cheaply using one medium rather than another. However, the calculation of OTS differs according to media class, making comparisons difficult. For example, in the UK, an OTS for the press is defined as 'read or looked at any issue of the publication for at least two minutes', whereas for posters it is 'traffic past site'. A further consideration is *competitive activity*. A company may decide to compete in the same medium as a competitor or seek to dominate an alternative medium. For example, if a major competitor is using television, a firm may choose posters, where it could dominate, thus achieving a greater impact. Finally, for many consumer goods producers, the views of the *retail trade* (for example, supermarket buyers) may influence

Exhibit 9.4 This outdoor advert for 3M's Post-it notes shows the visual power of outdoor advertising and its ability to tap into topical issues such as Britain's royal wedding in 2011

the choice of media class. Advertising expenditure is often used by salespeople to convince the retail trade to increase the shelf space allocated to existing brands, and to stock new brands. For example, if it is known that supermarkets favour television advertising in a certain product market, the selling impact on the trade of €3 million spent on television may be viewed as greater than the equivalent spend of 50:50 between television and the press.

The choice of a particular newspaper, magazine, television spot, poster site, etc., is called the **media vehicle decision**. Although creative considerations still play a part, cost per thousand calculations is the dominant influence. This requires readership and viewership figures. In the UK, readership figures are produced by the National Readership Survey, based on 36,000 interviews per year. Television viewership is measured by the Broadcasters' Audience Research Board (BARB), which produces weekly reports based on a panel of 5,100 households equipped with metered television sets (people meters). Traffic past poster sites is measured by Outdoor Site Classification and Audience Research (OSCAR), which classifies 130,000 sites according to visibility, competition (one or more posters per site), angle of vision, height above ground, illumination and weekly traffic past site. Cinema audiences are monitored by Cinema and Video Industry Audience Research (CAVIAR) and radio audiences are measured by Radio Joint Audience Research (RAJAR). Adwords are sold in online auctions where the price of the word is determined by its popularity.

Media buying is a specialist area and a great deal of money can be saved on rate card prices by powerful media buyers. Media buying is generally done by specialist media-buying agencies who may be owned by a full-service advertising agency or part of a communications group. Specialist media-buying agencies have significant buying power as well as established relationships with media vehicles.

Executing the campaign

When an advertisement has been produced and the media selected, it is sent to the chosen media vehicle for publication or transmission. A key organizational issue is to ensure that the right advertisements reach the right media at the right time. Each media vehicle has its own deadlines after which publication or transmission may not be possible.

Evaluating advertising effectiveness

Measurement can take place before, during and after campaign execution. *Pre-testing* takes place before the

campaign is run and is part of the creative process. In television advertising, rough advertisements are created and tested with target consumers. This is usually done with a focus group, which is shown perhaps three alternative commercials and the group members are asked to discuss their likes, dislikes and understanding of each one. The results provide important input from the target consumers themselves rather than relying solely on **advertising agency** views. Such research is not without its critics, however. They suggest that the impact of a commercial that is repeated many times cannot be captured in a two-hour group discussion. They point to the highly successful Heineken campaign – 'Refreshes the parts other beers cannot reach' – which was rejected by target consumers in the pre-test.[13] Despite this kind of criticism, advertising research is a booming business because of the uncertainty surrounding the effectiveness of new advertising campaigns.

Post-testing can be used to assess a campaign's effectiveness once it has run. Sometimes formal post-testing is ignored through laziness, fear or lack of funds. However, checking how well an advertising campaign has performed can provide the information necessary to plan future campaigns. The top three measures used in post-test television advertising research are image/attitude change, actual sales and usage, although other financial measures such as cash flow, shareholder value and return on investment are increasingly being used. Image/attitude change is believed to be a sensitive measure, which is a good predictor of behavioural change. Those favouring the actual sales measure argue that, despite difficulties in establishing cause and effect, sales change is the ultimate objective of advertising and therefore the only meaningful measure (see Exhibit 9.5). Testing recall of advertisements is also popular. Despite the evidence suggesting that recall may not be a valid measure of advertising effectiveness, those favouring recall believe that because the advertising is seen and remembered, it is effective.

Organizing for campaign development

There are four options open to an advertiser when organizing for campaign development. First, small companies may develop the advertising in *co-operation with people from the media*. For example, advertising copy may be written by someone from the company, but the artwork and final layout of the advertisement may be done by the newspaper or magazine. Second, the advertising function may be conducted *in-house* by creating an advertising department staffed with copy-writers, media buyers and production personnel. This form of organization locates total control of the advertising function within the company, but since media buying

Exhibit 9.5 The Virgin Atlantic 'Still Red Hot' campaign in 2009 was estimated to have driven 20 per cent of overall revenue during the campaign

Go to the website to watch the Virgin Atlantic 'Still Red Hot' Campaign.
www.mcgraw-hill.co.uk/textbooks/fahy

is on behalf of only one company, buying power is low. Cost-conscious companies such as Ryanair do most of their advertising work in-house. Third, because of the specialist skills that are required for developing an advertising campaign, many advertisers opt to work with an *advertising agency*. Larger agencies offer a full service, comprising creative work, media planning and buying, planning and strategy development, market research and production. Because agencies work for many clients, they have a wide range of experience and can provide an objective outsider's view of what is required and how problems can be solved. Four large global conglomerates – Omnicom, WPP Group, Interpublic and Publicis – dominate the industry. These corporations have grown in response to major multinational companies like Samsung and Nestlé, who want their global advertising handled by one firm.[14] A fourth alternative is to use in-house staff (or their full-service agency) for some advertising functions, but to use *specialist agencies* for others. The attraction of the specialist stems in part from the large volume of business that each controls. This means that they have enormous buying power when negotiating media prices, for example. Alternatively, an advertiser could employ the services

of a 'creative hot-shop' to supplement its own or its full service agency's skills.

The traditional system of agency payment was by commission from the media owners. Under the commission system, media owners traditionally offered a 15 per cent discount on the rate card (list) price to agencies. For example, a €1 million television advertising campaign would result in a charge to the agency of €1 million minus 15 per cent (€850,000). The agency invoiced the client at the full rate-card price (€1 million). The agency commission therefore totalled €150,000.

Large advertisers have the power to demand some of this 15 per cent in the form of a rebate. For example, companies like Unilever and P&G have reduced the amount of commission they allow their agencies. Given that P&G spent an estimated US$8.7 billion in 2009 it could probably demand very low commission levels, but these companies chose not to exercise all of their muscle as low commission rates ultimately may lead to poor-quality advertising. The second method of paying agencies is by fee. For smaller clients, commission alone may not be sufficient to cover agency costs. Also, some larger clients are advocating fees rather than commission, on the basis that this removes a possible source of agency bias towards media that pay commission rather than a medium like direct mail or online for which no commission is payable.

Payment by results is the third method of remuneration. This involves measuring the effectiveness of the advertising campaign using marketing research, and basing payment on how well communication objectives have been met. For example, payment might be based on how awareness levels have increased, brand image improved or intentions-to-buy have risen.

Another area where payment by results has been used is media buying. For example, if the normal cost per thousand to reach men in the age range 30–40 is €4.50, and the agency achieves a 10 per cent saving, this might be split 8 per cent to the client and 2 per cent to the agency.[15] Procter & Gamble uses the payment-by-results method to pay its advertising agencies, which include Saatchi & Saatchi, Leo Burnett, Grey and D'Arcy Masius Benton & Bowles. Remuneration is tied to global brand sales, so aligning their income more closely with the success (or otherwise) of their advertising.[16]

Ethical Debate 9.1   Informing or misleading?

Advertising is everywhere; it is the means by which organizations communicate with potential customers. But many opponents argue that advertising is at best wasteful and at worst downright misleading, offensive and dangerous. On the other hand, advocates argue that, in modern societies, consumers are savvy enough to be able to assess advertising for what it is.

Misleading advertising can take the form of exaggerated claims and concealed facts. For example, Coca-Cola ran into trouble with the Australian Competition and Consumer Commission for running a 'Myth-busting' campaign about Coca-Cola that used the words 'Myth – Makes you fat. Myth – Rots your teeth. Myth – Packed with caffeine'. The commission forced the soft drinks maker to publish corrective advertisements in seven national and state newspapers charging that its claims were misleading. Similarly, broadband operators have been criticized for advertising promised download speeds that, in reality, were not delivered.

Advertising can also deceive by omitting important facts from its message. Such concealed facts may give a misleading impression to the audience. The advertising of food products like breakfast cereals is particularly susceptible to misleading advertising, such as omitting details of sugar and salt levels, or making bogus scientific claims of health benefits. Some companies, like Kellogg's, use celebrity presenters of science programmes (e.g. Philippa Forrester, presenter of *Tomorrow's World*) to endorse their products, which can give the impression that claims are scientifically grounded. Many industrialized countries have their own codes of practice that protect the consumer from deceptive advertising. For example, in the UK the Advertising Standards Authority (ASA) administers the British Code of Advertising Practice, which insists that advertising should be 'legal, decent, honest and truthful'. Shock advertising, such as that pursued in the past by companies like Paddy Power, Benetton and FCUK, is often the subject of many complaints to the ASA.

Critics argue that advertising images have a profound effect on society. They claim that advertising promotes materialism and takes advantage of human frailties. Advertising is accused of stressing the importance of material possessions, such as the ownership of a car or the latest in consumer electronics. Critics argue that this promotes the wrong values in society. A related criticism is that advertising takes advantage of human frailties such as the need to belong or the desire for status. For example, a UK government White Paper has proposed a ban on junk food advertising at certain times, in the same way as cigarette and alcohol advertising is restricted.

Advertising has always been controversial and it looks as though it will continue to be so for some time to come.

Reflection: Think about your views on advertising. Do you consider it to be mainly informative and entertaining or mainly annoying and misleading?

Sales promotion

As we have already seen, sales promotions are incentives to consumers or the trade that are designed to stimulate purchase. Examples include money off and free gifts (consumer promotions), and discounts and sales-force competitions (trade promotions). A vast amount of money is spent on sales promotion and many companies engage in joint promotions. Some of the key reasons for the popularity of sales promotion include the following.

- *Increased impulse purchasing*: the rise in impulse purchasing favours promotions that take place at the point of purchase.
- *The rising cost of advertising and advertising clutter*: these factors erode advertising's cost-effectiveness.
- *Shortening time horizons*: the attraction of the fast sales boost of a sales promotion is raised by greater rivalry and shortening product life cycles.
- *Competitor activities*: in some markets, sales promotions are used so often that all competitors are forced to follow suit.
- *Measurability*: measuring the sales impact of sales promotions is easier than for advertising since its effect is more direct and, usually, short term.

If sales require a 'short, sharp shock', sales promotion is often used to achieve this. In this sense it may be regarded as a short-term tactical device. The long-term sales effect of the promotion could be positive, neutral or negative. If the promotion has attracted new buyers who find that they like the brand, repeat purchases from them may give rise to a positive long-term effect.[17] Alternatively, if the promotion (e.g. money off) has devalued the brand in the eyes of consumers, the effect may be negative.[18] Where the promotion has caused consumers to buy the brand only because of its incentive value with no effect on underlying preferences, the long-term effect may be neutral.[19] An international study of leading grocery brands has shown that the most likely long-term effect of a price promotion for an existing brand is neutral. Such promotions tend to attract existing buyers of the brand during the promotional period rather than new buyers.[20]

Sales promotion strategy

As with advertising, a systematic approach should be taken to the management of sales promotions involving the specification of objectives for the promotion, decisions on which techniques are most suitable and an evaluation of the effectiveness of the promotion.

Sales promotions can have a number of objectives. The most usual goal is to *boost sales* over the short term. Short-term sales increases may be required for a number of reasons, including the need to reduce inventories or meet budgets prior to the end of the financial year, moving stocks of an old model prior to a replacement, or to increase stock-holding by consumers and distributors in advance of the launch of a competitor's product. A highly successful method of sales promotion involves *encouraging trial*. Home sampling and home couponing are particularly effective methods of inducing trial. Certain promotions, by their nature, *encourage repeat purchasing* of a brand over a period of time. Any promotion that requires the collection of packet tops or labels (e.g. free mail-ins and promotions such as bingo games) attempts to increase the frequency of repeat purchasing during the promotional period. Some promotions are designed to encourage customers to *purchase larger pack sizes*. Finally, trade promotions are usually designed to *gain distribution and shelf space*. Discounts, free gifts and joint promotions are methods used to encourage distributors to stock brands.

Selecting the type of sales promotion to use

There is a very wide variety of promotional techniques that a marketer can consider using (see Figure 9.4). Major consumer sales promotion types are money off, bonus packs, premiums, free samples, coupons, prize promotions and loyalty cards. A sizeable proportion of sales promotions are directed at the trade, including price discounts, free goods, competitions and allowances.

Consumer promotion techniques

Money-off promotions provide direct value to the customer and therefore an unambiguous incentive to purchase. They have a proven track record of stimulating short-term sales increases. However, price reductions can easily be matched by competitors and if used frequently can devalue brand image. **Bonus packs** give added value by giving consumers extra quantity at no additional cost and are often used in the drinks, confectionery and detergent markets. The promotion might be along the lines of 'Buy 10 and get 2 extra free'. Because the price is not lowered, this form of promotion runs less risk of devaluing the brand image. When two or more items are banded together the promotion is called a multi-buy. These are frequently used to protect market share by encouraging consumers to stock up on a particular brand when two or more items of the same brand are banded together, such as a shampoo and conditioner. Multi-buys can also generate

Figure 9.4 Consumer and trade promotions

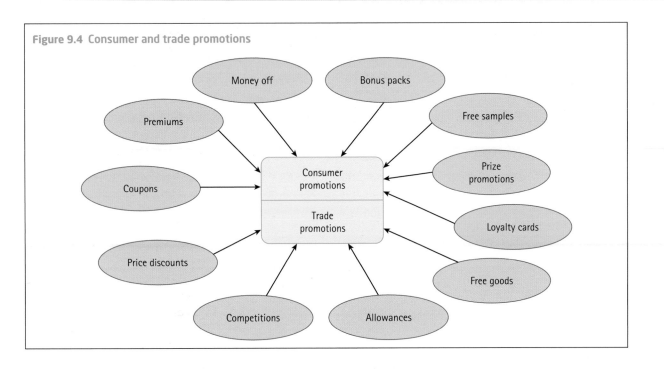

range trial when, for example, a jar of coffee is banded with samples of other coffee varieties such as lattes and mochas. **Premiums** are any merchandise offered free or at low cost as an incentive to purchase a brand; they can come in three forms: free in-pack or on-pack gifts, free in-the-mail offers and self-liquidating offers, where consumers are asked to pay a sum of money to cover the costs of the merchandise (see Exhibit 9.6). The main role of premiums is in encouraging bulk purchasing and maintaining share. Breakfast cereal manufacturers have been extensive users of in-pack and self-liquidating premiums. For example, Kellogg's 'Big Breakfast' promotion for its mini portion packs and cereal bars includes gifts, a scratchcard competition, trade incentives and extensive point-of-purchase support.

Free samples of a brand may be delivered to the home or given out in a store and are used to encourage trial. For new brands or brand extensions this is an effective, if sometimes expensive, way of generating trial. Coupons can be delivered to the home, appear in magazines or newspapers, or appear on packs, and are used to encourage trial or repeat purchase. Increasingly online coupons are being used (see Social Media Marketing 9.1). They are a popular form of sales promotion, although they are usually less effective in raising initial sales than money-off promotions because there is no immediate saving and the appeal is almost exclusively to existing consumers.[21] There are three main types of prize promotion: competitions, draws and games. These are often used to attract attention or stimulate interest in a brand. Competitions require

Exhibit 9.6 Free in-pack gifts have been used by many magazine publishers in a bid to counter declining sales

participants to exercise a certain degree of skill and judgement and entry is usually dependent on purchase at least. For example, in an attempt to revitalize its ailing PG Tips tea brand, Unilever put 'mind game'

Social Media Marketing 9.1 Groupon

Critical Thinking: Below is a review of the business model pioneered by the online coupons company, Groupon. Read it and critically evaluate the role of social media in its business model.

As many sales promotions are all about seeking and finding good deals, it is perhaps inevitable that technology and social media would become popular means through which they are created and delivered. One of the leading organizations in the world in this space is Groupon, a rapidly growing global firm that was founded in the US in 2008.

As the name implies, Groupon 'translates' as group coupon. The way it works is as follows. An affiliate company such as a restaurant works with Groupon and offers a lunch that normally costs €12 for €6 on a given day. Groupon will then contact its registered members in that particular city to inform them of the deal and if enough customers sign up to avail of it, then the deal becomes available. If not, or if the deal is not availed of within a given time, then the offer lapses. This approach has several advantages. If customers want to avail themselves of a deal, they are incentivized to tell their friends about it, in order to ensure that the deal becomes 'live'. Social media like Twitter and Facebook are the ideal vehicles to make this happen quickly. The short lifespan of deals encourages consumers to opt in to receiving regular emails from Groupon. The vendor offering the deal can be confident of a high level of demand and may expect those using it to spend their savings on other goods and services on offer. It may also be important to place a cap on the offer to avoid a situation where demand exceeds supply. The revenue generated from any of the deals on offer is split 50:50 between Groupon and the vendor.

The company has grown extremely rapidly. By the end of 2010, it had over 51 million registered users in 565 cities worldwide generating revenues of US\$760 million and employing over 4,000 people. It sends out over 70 million deal-of-the-day emails to subscribers. Although a privately held company, it was reputed to be profitable within its first year (something unusual for online businesses) and received an offer of US\$6 billion from Google in 2010 which was turned down. This may turn out to not be the best decision it has made as several other major players like Amazon and Facebook have entered this space as have countless smaller operators. An interesting future lies ahead.

Based on: Anonymous (2011);[22] Shayon, (2011);[23] Steiner (2010)[24].

puzzles on the backs of packs and directed entrants to a PG Tips website for solutions. Draws make no demand on skill and judgement, the result simply depends on chance.

Finally, as we saw in Chapters 4 and 7, loyalty cards are a popular promotional tool for service businesses. Points are gained every time money is spent at an outlet, which can be used against purchases at the store in future. The intention is to attract customers back to the store but, as we shall see in the next chapter, loyalty cards are an excellent source of customer information, which can be used in direct marketing campaigns. Loyalty cards are very popular in the UK, with over 90 per cent of people holding at least one card and 78 per cent having two or more. Card schemes can be specific to one company such as the Tesco Clubcard, or a joint venture between several companies such as the Nectar card, which involves companies like Hertz, Sainsbury's, BP, Expedia and Ford, and boasts over 11 million customers. Similarly, online retailers use schemes like MyPoints, which reward shoppers for reading emails, visiting sites, completing surveys and making purchases.

Despite their popularity, loyalty schemes have attracted their critics. Such schemes may simply raise the cost of doing business and, if competitors respond with me-too offerings, the final outcome may be no more than a minor tactical advantage.[25] Shell, for example, reportedly spent £20 million on hardware and software alone to launch its Smart Card, which allows drivers to collect points when purchasing petrol.[26] A second criticism is that the proliferation of loyalty schemes is teaching consumers promiscuity. Evidence from a MORI poll found that 25 per cent of loyalty card holders are ready to switch to a rival scheme if it has better benefits.[27] Far from seeing a loyalty scheme as a reason to stay with a retailer, consumers may be using such schemes as criteria for switching. As we saw in Chapter 7, effective loyalty card schemes are those that are an integral part of an overall relationship marketing strategy.

Trade promotion techniques

The trade may be offered (or may demand) discounts in return for purchase, which may be part of a joint promotion whereby the retailer agrees to devote extra shelf space, buy larger quantities, engage in a joint competition and/or allow in-store demonstrations. An alternative to a price discount is to offer more merchandise at the same price (free goods); for example, the 'baker's dozen' technique involves offering 13 items (or cases) for the price of 12. Manufacturers may use competitions, such as providing prizes for a distributor's sales force, in return for achieving sales targets for their products. Finally, a manufacturer may offer an allowance (a sum of money) in return for retailers providing promotional facilities in store (display allowance). For example, allowances would be needed to persuade a supermarket to display cards on its shelves indicating that a brand was being sold at a special low price.

The pharmaceutical industry is one of the biggest users of trade promotion. For example, in 2004, pharmaceutical companies in the USA spent US$14.7 billion on marketing to healthcare professionals as against US$3.6 billion on direct-to-consumer advertising activities. Trade promotions involve gifts, samples and industry-sponsored training courses. It is a highly competitive business with roughly 102,000 pharmaceutical 'detailers' or salespeople all trying to meet with the top prescribers among America's 870,000 physicians.[28]

The final stage in a sales promotion campaign involves testing the promotion. As with advertising, both pre-testing and post-testing approaches are available. The major pre-testing techniques include **group discussions** (testing ideas on groups of potential targets), **hall tests** (bringing a sample of customers to a room where alternative promotions are tested) and **experimentation** (where, for example, two groups of stores are selected and alternative promotions run in each). After the sales promotion has been implemented the effects must be monitored carefully. Care should be taken to check sales both during and after the promotion so that post-promotional sales dips can be taken into account (a lagged effect). In certain situations a sales fall can precede a promotion (a lead effect). If consumers believe a promotion to be imminent they may hold back purchases until it takes place. Alternatively,

if a retail sales promotion of consumer durables (e.g. gas fires, refrigerators, televisions) is accompanied by higher commission rates for salespeople, they may delay sales until the promotional period.[29] If a lead effect is possible, sales prior to the promotion should also be monitored.

Public relations and publicity

All organizations have a variety of stakeholders (such as employees, shareholders, the local community, the media, government and pressure groups) whose needs they must take into account (see Figure 9.5). **Public relations** is concerned with all of these groups, and public relations activities include **publicity**, corporate advertising, seminars, publications, lobbying and charitable donations. PR can accomplish many objectives:[30] it can foster prestige and reputation, which can help companies to sell products, attract and keep good employees, and promote favourable community and government relations; it can promote products by creating the desire to buy a product through unobtrusive material that people read or see in the press, or on radio and television; awareness and interest in products and companies can be generated; it can be used to deal with issues or opportunities, or to overcome misconceptions about a company that may have been generated by bad publicity; and it can have a key role to play in fostering goodwill among customers, employees, suppliers,

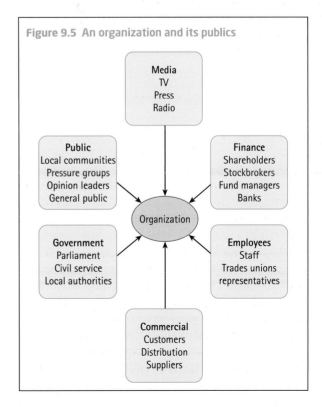

Figure 9.5 An organization and its publics

distributors and the government. For example, Belfast Zoo in Northern Ireland used a rare Barbary lion, Lily, as the centrepiece of their publicity campaign to increase visitor numbers to the zoo. Barbary lions are extinct in the wild and when Lily was rejected by her mother at birth, the cub was hand-reared at the home of the zoo keeper. Belfast Zoo set up an email account for Lily to which children could send messages and press releases and visuals tracked the cub's growth. The campaign caught the public imagination, generating £1.4 million in press coverage and raising visitor levels by almost one third (see Exhibit 9.7)

Three major reasons for the growth in public relations are a recognition by marketing teams of the power and value of public relations, increased advertising costs leading to an exploration of more cost-effective communication routes, and improved understanding of the role of public relations. The dramatic growth of social media has further revolutionized the public relations business (see Marketing in Action 9.2).

Exhibit 9.7 Lily, a rare Barbary lion, became the centrepiece of a public relations campaign by Belfast Zoo

Publicity is a major element of public relations. It is defined as the communication of information about a product or organization by the placing of news about it in the media without paying for the time or space

Marketing in Action 9.2 AEG-Electrolux: the world is noisy enough

Critical Thinking: Below is a review of a publicity campaign run by AEG-Electrolux. Read it and critically assess whether publicity was a more effective way of promoting its Silent Laundry range than advertising, for example.

The ubiquitous presence of noise is a key characteristic of modern urban living and research on domestic appliance customers has shown that they are sensitive to the noise levels of products like washing machines and dryers. In response, AEG-Electrolux, the Swedish white goods firm, introduced its Silent Laundry range that operates almost in silence. In order to communicate this benefit, the company sought not to talk about the brand directly but rather to stimulate a conversation about the issue of noise pollution and to show that the Silent Laundry range offers consumers one option for making their lives quieter.

To execute this message, the company selected locations in key European cities such as Madrid, Brussels and London and by linking poster sites in these cities to decibel meters was able to display on billboards the real-time noise levels in these locations. The data was streamed to five different language sites (such as noiseawareness.co.uk) creating

an awareness of noise pollution and how it varies over days and weeks. The innovative nature of the posters and a well-orchestrated publicity and blog seeding strategy meant that the noise issue became a topic of conversation in the media and among consumers. The PR activity particularly focused on the lead up to and on Noise Awareness Day (15 April 2008) which was a European-wide initiative. Consumers in the key locations also engaged in interesting ways with the decibel meters and authorities in Milan asked for the meter to be turned off each night after midnight after the clientele of a local bar/restaurant began attempts to create the highest readings on the poster after leaving the establishment.

The award-winning campaign generated a significant increase in brand preference for AEG-Electrolux, significant awareness of the issue of noise and an estimated €70 million PR value.

Based on: Burrows (2011);[31] Warc (2008)[32].

directly. The three key tasks of a publicity department are responding to requests for information from the media, supplying the media with information on important events in the organization and stimulating the media to carry the information and viewpoint of the organization.[33] Information dissemination may be through news releases, news conferences, interviews, feature articles, photo-calls and public speaking (at conferences and seminars, for example). No matter which of these means is used to carry the information, publicity has three important characteristics.

1 *The message has high credibility*: the message has greater credibility than advertising because it appears to the reader to have been written independently (by a media person) rather than by an advertiser. Because of this enhanced credibility it can be argued that it is more persuasive than a similar message used in an advertisement.

2 *No direct media costs*: since space or time in the media does not have to be bought there is no direct media cost. However, this is not to say that it is cost free. Someone has to write the news release, take part in the interview or organize the news conference. This may be organized internally by a press officer or publicity department, or externally by a public relations agency.

3 *No control over publication*: unlike advertising, there is no guarantee that the news item will be published. This decision is taken out of the control of the organization and into the hands of an editor. A key factor in this decision is whether the item is judged to be newsworthy. Newsworthy items include where a company does something first, such as a new product or research breakthrough, new employees or company expansions, sponsorships, etc. A list of potentially newsworthy topics is provided in Table 9.3. Equally there is no guarantee that the content of the news release will be published in the way that the news supplier had intended or that the publicity will occur when the company wants it to.

Sponsorship

Sponsorship has been defined by Sleight as:[34]

> a business relationship between a provider of funds, resources or services and an individual, event or organization which offers in return some rights and association that may be used for commercial advantage.

Potential sponsors have a wide range of entities and activities from which to choose, including sports, arts,

Table 9.3 Potentially newsworthy topics

Being or doing something first	
Marketing issues	**Financial issues**
New products	Financial statements
Research breakthroughs: future new products	Acquisitions
Large orders/contracts	Sales/profit achievements
Sponsorships	
Price changes	**Personal issues**
Service changes	Training awards
New logos	Winners of company contests
Export success	Promotions/new appointments
	Success stories
	Visits by famous people
Production issues	Reports of interviews
Productivity achievements	
Employment changes	**General issues**
Capital investments	Conferences/seminars/exhibitions
	Anniversaries of significant events

community activities, teams, tournaments, individual personalities or events, competitions, fairs and shows. Sports sponsorship is by far the most popular sponsorship medium as it offers high visibility through extensive television coverage, the ability to attract a broad cross-section of the community and to service specific niches, and the capacity to break down cultural barriers (see Exhibit 9.8). For example, the Olympics, the biggest

Exhibit 9.8 Specsavers has cleverly sponsored referees and has also been quick to build advertising around major sporting controversies

global sporting event, attracted over US$1.4 billion in sponsorship for the 2004 Athens Games, which represented one-third of the revenue generated by the Olympic Games. Such is the scramble for sponsorship opportunities that even a soccer team's pre-season tour can be sponsored; this was the case with a tour of China by Spanish club Real Madrid, which was sponsored by local cigarette company Hong Ta Shan.

Sponsorship can be very expensive. For example, being one of only six worldwide partners for the 2010 soccer World Cup in South Africa was estimated to cost US$125 million. Therefore organizations need to have a carefully thought-out and well-planned sponsorship strategy. The five principal objectives of sponsorship are to gain publicity, create entertainment opportunities, foster favourable brand and company associations, improve community relations, and create promotional opportunities.

Gaining publicity

Sponsorship provides ample opportunity to create publicity in the news media. Worldwide events such as major golf, football and tennis tournaments supply the platform for global media coverage. Such **event sponsorship** can provide exposure to millions of people. For example, DHL, the German-owned package delivery company, signed a deal to sponsor major league baseball in the USA. This was part of a strategy by DHL to raise its awareness level in the US market where it has a small share and which is also home to its two major global rivals, UPS and FedEx.[35] The publicity opportunities of sponsorship can provide major awareness shifts. For example, Canon's sponsorship of football in the UK raised awareness of the brand name from 40 per cent to 85 per cent among males. Similarly Texaco's prompted recall improved from 18 per cent to 60 per cent because of its motor racing sponsorship.[36]

Creating entertainment opportunities

A major objective of much sponsorship is to create entertainment opportunities for customers and the trade. Sponsorship of music, the arts and sports events can be particularly effective. For example, Barclays Capital sponsored a fashion show at London's Natural History Museum for 450 of its clients that were attending a global borrowers and investors forum. Often, key personalities are invited to join the sponsor's guests to add further attractiveness to the event. Similarly, sponsors of the Global Challenge yacht race, such as Norwich Union, BP and BT, used the event to entertain their best clients on board sponsored boats in desirable locations like Boston and Cape Town.[37]

Fostering favourable brand and company associations

A third objective of sponsorship is to create favourable associations for the brand and company. For example, sponsorship of athletics by SmithKline Beecham for its Lucozade Sport brand reinforces its market position and its energy associations. Both the sponsor and the sponsored activity become involved in a relationship with a transfer of values from activity to sponsor. The audience, finding the sponsor's name, logo and other symbols threaded through the event, learns to associate sponsor and activity with one another. For example, the German lifestyle clothing company Puma has entered a boat (shaped like a shoe) in the prestigious Volvo Ocean race. Footage showing the dangers and thrills faced by yachtsmen and women reflect well on the Puma brand but come at a high price as the cost of participation can reach $30 million.[38]

Improving community relations

Sponsorship of schools – for example, by providing low-cost personal computers as Tesco has done – and supporting community programmes can foster a socially responsible, caring reputation for a company. Many multinational companies get involved in community initiatives in local markets. For example, Nortel Networks, the Canadian telecommunications company, has had a very successful association with the Galway Arts Festival, one of the leading festivals in the Republic of Ireland. Similarly, UBS has sponsorships with the Tate art gallery, the London Symphony Orchestra and some inner-city schools like the Bridge Academy in London.

Creating promotional opportunities

Sponsorship events provide an ideal opportunity to promote company brands. Sweatshirts, bags, pens, and so on, carrying the company logo and name of the event can be sold to a captive audience. One of the attractions of O2's sponsorship of the former Millennium Dome (now known as the O2) was to showcase the latest in mobile phone technology and WiFi services as part of improving the overall visitor experience at the Dome.[39] For example, O2 customers can avoid having to get a paper ticket and instead receive a barcode on their phones that allows them access to an event. By doing so, O2 is hoping to both win new customers and persuade existing customers to buy new services. Similarly, Orange UK provided Glastonbury festival-goers with a 'Text Me Home' tent finder facility as well as a wind-powered mobile phone charger that could be attached to tents overnight.[40]

New developments in sponsorship

Sponsorship has experienced major growth in the past 20 years. Some of the factors driving the rise in sponsorship expenditure include the escalating costs of media advertising, restrictive government policies on tobacco and alcohol advertising, the fragmentation of traditional mass media, the proven record of sponsorship and greater media coverage of sponsored events.[41] Accompanying the growth of event sponsorship has been the phenomenon of **ambush marketing**. Originally, the term referred to the activities of companies that tried to associate themselves with an event without paying any fee to the event owner. Nike has been a particularly successful ambush marketer at various Olympic Games and indeed emerged as the name Asian viewers most closely associated with the Athens Games even though it was not one of the event's official sponsors.[42] The activity is legal as long as no attempt is made to use an event symbol, logo or mascot. For example, Pepsi ran an advertising campaign in 2010 featuring some of the world's most famous soccer players such as Lionel Messi playing local boys on the Serengeti plains. This was a challenge for Coca-Cola, one of the South African World Cup's major sponsors. Regulations are catching up with the ambush marketers, such as provisions in the London Olympics Bill that outlaw the words 'gold', 'summer' and '2012' in advertisements by non-sponsors of the 2012 Olympics.

The selection of an event or individual to sponsor requires that consideration is given to a number of key questions. These include the firm's communication objectives, its target market, the promotional opportunities presented, the costs involved and the risks associated with the sponsorship. The latter point is examined in Marketing in Action 9.3. As with all communications initiatives, the sponsorship should be carefully evaluated against the initial objectives to assess whether it was successful or not. For example, Budweiser beer sales in the UK were up by 18.6 per cent in the second quarter of 2010 compared with the same period in 2009 due largely to its sponsorship of the World Cup in South Africa. Its 'man-of-the-match' vote following each of the 64 games generated 1.5 million fan votes and 2.7 million fans participated in the Budweiser 'paint your face' promotion on Facebook.[43] Similarly, BT estimated that media coverage of its sponsorship of the Global Challenge yacht race covered costs by a multiple of three and the official website attracted more than 30 million hits per race. However, recent research has shown that only 35 per cent of respondents 'always or nearly always' measure their sponsorship and event marketing returns.[44]

Marketing in Action 9.3 The perils of sponsorship

Critical Thinking: Below is a review of some examples of where sponsorships have resulted in negative publicity for the companies involved. Read it and critically evaluate the pros and cons of sponsorship.

Sponsorship is a powerful promotional tool but one that is also not without its risks. This is particularly true when the sponsorship is linked to a celebrity or sports star. One of the most celebrated examples in recent years is that of Kate Moss, one of Britain's top fashion models. She had successful endorsement arrangements with a variety of leading clothing and cosmetics brands but attracted huge negative publicity when video images emerged of her appearing to snort cocaine. She was quickly dropped by a number of brands including H&M, Chanel and Burberry, who feared that their images might be tarnished by association with her. Ironically, before her cocaine scandal, she was earning a reputed £4.5 million per year. But since the scandal, she has been signing a whole new set of endorsement contracts, ranging from one with Nikon cameras worth £1.5 million, to another with Calvin Klein worth £500,000, to others including Bulgari, Longchamp and Virgin Mobile. Overall, her earnings in 2006 were reputed to have soared to £11 million, suggesting that the controversy had done no damage to her brand reputation.

To avoid the risks attached to sponsoring individuals, many organizations choose instead to develop associations with teams or events. However, this can prove to be just as problematic, as demonstrated by the negative publicity generated by the Tour de

France in recent years. The Tour de France is one of the world's most difficult and most famous professional cycling races, and an iconic sports event in its host country. But for some time now the event has been dogged by allegations of drug taking by cyclists and even orchestrated blood doping by whole teams. Each of the major teams in the event has a commercial sponsor. For example, Deutsche Telecom's sponsorship of Team Telekom and later Team T-mobile in the event sparked a cycling craze in Germany after Jan Ullrich, the team leader, rode to victory in 1997. But the relationship turned sour after former cyclists and team doctors confessed to using performance-enhancing drugs when Ullrich failed a drugs test in 2006.

Even sponsoring a television programme has its risks. One of the most successful television shows in recent years has been Channel 4's reality show,

Big Brother. But it became mired in a racist controversy in 2007 during arguments between Shilpa Shetty, an Indian actress, and some of the other contestants, particularly Jade Goody. The media regulator Ofcom received a record 33,000 emails and telephone calls in protest over the alleged racist treatment of Shetty. The programme's sponsor, Carphone Warehouse, suspended its sponsorship of the show, which was worth £3 million, despite market research showing that most people did not blame the sponsor for the controversy. The irony for Carphone Warehouse is that controversies like this significantly increase the viewership of such programmes, although it was unwilling to risk damage to its brand.

Based on: Anonymous (2007);[45] Grande (2007);[46] Vernon (2006)[47].

Other promotional techniques

Because of the fragmentation of traditional audiences such as press and television, a variety of other promotional techniques are becoming more commonplace. Four popular mass communications tools are exhibitions, product placement as well as ambient advertising and guerrilla marketing, which are examined below.

Exhibitions

Exhibitions are unique in that, of all the promotional tools available, they are the only one that brings buyers, sellers and competitors together in a commercial setting. In Europe, the Cologne trade exhibitions bring together 28,000 exhibitors from 100 countries with 1.8 million buyers from 150 countries.[48] Exhibitions are a particularly important part of the industrial promotional mix and can be a key source of information on buyers' needs and preferences.

Exhibitions are growing in their number and variety. Aside from the major industry exhibitions such as motor shows and property shows, more specialized lifestyle exhibitions are emerging in niche markets. For example, the Cosmo show, featuring cosmetics and targeting young women, attracts over 55,000 visitors. The 1999 event was the launch pad for Olay Colour (formerly Oil of Ulay) to reveal its new identity and for the launch of Cussons' new moisturizer, Aqua Source.

Exhibitions can have a variety of objectives, including identifying prospects and determining their needs,

building relationships, providing product demonstrations, making sales, gathering competitive intelligence and fostering the image of the company. They require careful planning and management to ensure that they run smoothly. And a post-show evaluation needs to take place to determine its effectiveness. Fortunately, there are a variety of variables that can easily be quantified, which can be used to measure success. These include number of visitors to the stand, number of leads generated, number of orders received and their value, and so on. Following up the trade show through contact with prospects and customers is also important.

Product placement

Product placement is the deliberate placing of products and/or their logos in movies, television, songs and video games, usually in return for money. While it has been big business in some countries, like the USA, for some time, restrictions preventing product placement have only recently been relaxed in Europe. For example, Steven Spielberg's sci-fi film *Minority Report* featured more than 15 major brands, including Gap, Nokia, Pepsi, Guinness, Lexus and Amex, with their logos appearing on video billboards throughout the film. These product placements earned Dreamworks and 20th Century Fox US$25 million, which went some way towards reducing the US$102 million production costs of the film.[49] Similarly, when the hip-hop artist Busta Rhymes had a smash hit with 'Pass the Courvoisier', US sales of the cognac rose by 14 per cent in volume and 11 per cent in value. Allied Domecq, the brand's owner, claims it did not pay for the plug, but McDonald's is more upfront, offering hip-hop artists US$5 each time they mention Big Mac in a song.[50] The value of product placement deals in the USA grew from $174 million in 1974 and was estimated to be worth $7.6 billion in 2009.[51]

Product placement has grown significantly in recent years for the following reasons: media fragmentation means it is increasingly hard to reach mass markets; the brand can benefit from the positive associations it gains from being in a film or television show; many consumers do not realize that the brand has been product-placed; repetition of the movie or television show means that the brand is seen again and again; careful choice of movie or television show means that certain segments can be targeted; and promotional and merchandising opportunities can be generated on the show's website. For example, the clothes and accessories worn by actresses in popular television shows like *Sex and the City* and *Desperate Housewives* have been in great demand from viewers and some have quickly sold out. Show producers are increasingly looking at the merchandising opportunities that their shows can present. Technological developments in the online gaming sector allow for different products to be placed in games at different times of the day or in different geographic locations, expanding the marketing possibilities available to companies. Product placement is significantly more restricted in Europe than it is in the USA, though the Audiovisual Media Services Directive adopted by the EU in 2007 permits greater levels of placement on EU television programmes but not news, current affairs, sport or children's programming.

While product placement is becoming very popular, it is important to remember that there are risks involved. If the movie or television show fails to take off it can tarnish the image of the brand and reduce its potential exposure. Audiences can become annoyed by blatant product placement, damaging the image, and brand owners may not have complete control over how their brand is portrayed. Also the popularity of product placement is fast giving rise to claims that it constitutes deceptive advertising. Lobby groups in the USA claim that one of the difficulties with product placement is that it can't be controlled by the consumer in the way the traditional advertising breaks can through zapping, and want it restricted.

Product placement is subject to the same kinds of analysis as all the other promotional techniques described in this chapter. For example, in the James Bond movie *Die Another Day*, the Ford Motor Company had three of its car brands 'starring' in the film: an Aston Martin Vanquish, a Thunderbird and a Jaguar XKR. Movie-goers were interviewed both before and after seeing the film to see if their opinions of the brands had changed. In addition, the product placement was part of an integrated campaign including public relations and advertising, which ensured that even people who had not seen the film were aware of Ford's association with it. During the film's peak viewing periods in the USA and UK, Ford's research found that the number of times its name appeared in the media increased by 34 per cent and that Ford corporate messages appeared in 29 per cent of the Bond-related coverage.[52]

Ambient advertising and guerrilla marketing

Two increasingly popular mass communications techniques are **ambient advertising** and **guerrilla marketing**. Ambient advertising generally refers to advertising carried on outdoor media that does not fall into the established outdoor categories such as billboards and bus signs. Therefore advertising that appears on shopping bags, on petrol pump nozzles, on balloons or on banners towed by airplanes, on street pavements, on overhead lockers on an aircraft and so on are classed as ambient. Ambient media is only limited by advertiser imagination.

Closely related to ambient advertising is guerrilla marketing. In essence, the latter is the delivery of advertising messages through unexpected means and in ways that almost 'ambush' the consumer to gain attention. One of the most effective guerrilla marketing campaigns was that used by Carlsberg in the UK which also employed its well-known positioning slogan 'Carlsberg don't do . . . but if they did it would probably be the best . . . in the world'. The company dropped £50,000 worth of £5 and £10 notes all over London on which were stickers containing the slogan – 'Carlsberg don't do litter but if they did, it would probably be the best litter in the world'. For a small advertising investment, the brand received enormous publicity.

Ambient and guerrilla tactics tend to be used by advertisers with limited budgets or to complement a bigger budget campaign. The main strength of these techniques lies in their ability to capture audience attention though they also come in for criticism in that they add to the proliferation of advertising messages in society.

Summary

This chapter has provided an overview of the promotional mix and examined some important mass communications techniques. The following key issues were addressed.

1. The promotional mix is broad, comprising seven elements, namely, advertising, sales promotion, publicity, sponsorship, direct marketing, digital marketing and personal selling. Decisions regarding which combination to use will be driven by the nature of the product, resource availability, the nature of the market and the kind of strategies being pursued by the company.

2. Because of the breadth of promotional techniques available, it is necessary to adopt an integrated approach to marketing communications. This means that companies carefully blend the promotional mix elements to deliver a clear, consistent, credible and competitive message in the marketplace.

3. It is important to take a systematic approach to communications planning. The various steps involved include consideration of the company's marketing and positioning strategy, identifying the target audience, setting communications objectives, creating the message, selecting the promotional mix, setting the promotional budget, executing the strategy and evaluating the strategy.

4. Advertising is a highly visible component of marketing, but it is only one element of the promotional mix. Advertising strategy involves an analysis of the target audience, setting objectives, budgeting decisions, message and media decisions, and evaluating advertising effectiveness. Significant ethical issues surround the use of advertising, which is also undergoing many changes due to developments in technology.

5. Sales promotions are a powerful technique for giving a short-term boost to sales or for encouraging trial. Some of the most popular consumer promotion techniques include premiums, coupons, loyalty cards and money-offs, while discounts and allowances are popular trade promotion techniques.

6. Publicity plays a very important role in the promotional mix. It is the mechanism through which organizations communicate with their various publics. It has more credibility than advertising and incurs no direct media costs, but firms cannot control the content or timing of publication.

7. Sponsorship is a popular form of promotion. The most common types of sponsorship include sports, the arts, community activities and celebrities. Its principal objectives are to generate publicity for the sponsor, create entertainment opportunities and foster favourable brand and company associations.

8. Other important mass communications techniques include exhibitions, product placement, ambient marketing and guerrilla marketing, all of which play different roles in the promotional mix.

Study questions

1. What is meant by integrated marketing communications? Explain the advantages of taking an integrated approach to marketing communications.
2. Select three recent advertising campaigns with which you are familiar. Discuss the target audience, objectives and message executions adopted in each case.
3. It is frequently argued that much promotional expenditure is wasteful. Discuss the ways in which the effectiveness of the various promotional techniques described in this chapter can be measured.
4. Discuss the role of sponsorship in the promotional mix.
5. There is no such thing as bad publicity. Discuss.
6. Discuss the reasons why ambient and guerrilla marketing have become such popular promotional techniques for some product categories. What are the ethical issues surrounding the growth of these mass communications techniques?
7. Visit www.youtube.com. Examine some adverts for a brand or organization of your choice. Discuss the message that the adverts are attempting to convey, as well as the creative treatment used.

Suggested reading

Cornwell, B. (2008) State of the Art and Science in Sponsorship-Linked Marketing, *Journal of Advertising*, **37** (3), 41–55.

Hackley, C. (2010) *Advertising and Promotion: An Integrated Marketing Communications Approach*, London: Sage.

Kitchen, P., I. Kim and **D. Schultz** (2008) Integrated Marketing Communications: Practice Leads Theory, *Journal of Advertising Research* **48** (4), 531–46.

Kohli, C., L. Leuthesser and **R. Suri** (2007) Get Slogan? Guidelines for Creating Effective Slogans, *Business Horizons*, **50** (5), 415–22.

Nunes, P.F. and **J. Merrihue** (2007) The Continuing Power of Mass Advertising, *Sloan Management Review*, **48** (2), 63–9.

Raghubir, P., J. Inman and **H. Grande** (2004) The Three Faces of Consumer Promotions, *California Management Review*, **46** (4), 23–43.

Robinson, D. (2006) Public Relations comes of Age, *Business Horizons*, **49** (3), 247–56.

Tellis, G. and **K. Tellis** (2009) Research on Advertising in a Recession: A Critical Review and Synthesis, *Journal of Advertising Research*, **39** (3), 304–27

References

1. **Turner, C.** (2006) Barclaycard Appoints Communications Chief, *MarketingWeek.co.uk*, 19 January; **Vita, N.** and **H. Probert** (2010) Barclaycard – Sliding our Way into a Greater Share of the Future, *Warc.com*.
2. **Anonymous** (2011), I've Got You Labelled, *The Economist*, 2 April, 74.
3. **Piercy, N.** (1987) The Marketing Budgeting Process: Marketing Management Implications, *Journal of Marketing*, **51** (4), 45–59.
4. **Tellis, G.** and **K. Tellis** (2009) Research on Advertising in a Recession: A Critical Review and Synthesis, *Journal of Advertising Research*, **39** (3), 304–27.
5. **Silverman, G.** (2006) Is 'it' the Future of Advertising? *Financial Times*, 24 January, 11.
6. **Anonymous** (2004) Sex Doesn't Sell, *The Economist*, 30 October, 46–7.
7. **Rigby, E.** (2005) Tesco's Victory over Asda Advert Ends Year-Long Row, *Financial Times*, 18 August, 5.
8. **Lannon, J.** (1991) Developing Brand Strategies across Borders, *Marketing and Research Today*, August, 160–7.
9. **Emap Limited** (2011) Heineken Italia: Are You Still With Us? *Warc.com*.
10. **Ritson, M.** (2003) It's the Ad Break . . . and the Viewers are Talking, Reading and Snogging, *Financial Times Creative Business*, 4 February, 8–9; **Silverman, G.** (2005) Advertisers are Starting to Find Television a Turn-off, *Financial Times*, 26 July, 20.
11. **Terazono, E.** (2005) TV Fights for its 30 Seconds of Fame, *Financial Times*, 20 September, 13.
12. **Grimshaw, C.** (2003) Standing Out in the Crowd, *Financial Times*, Creative Business, 6 May, 7.
13. **Bell, E.** (1992) Lies, Damned Lies and Research, *Observer*, 28 June, 46.
14. **Anonymous** (2005) Consumer Republic, *The Economist*, 19 March, 63, 66.
15. **Smith, P.R.** (1993) *Marketing Communications: An Integrated Approach*, London: Kogan Page, 116.
16. See **Tomkins, R.** (1999) Getting a Bigger Bang for the Advertising Buck, *Financial Times*, 24 September, 17; and **Waters, R.** (1999) P&G Ties Advertising Agency Fees to Sales, *Marketing Week*, 16 September, 1.
17. **Rothschild, M.L.** and **W.C. Gaidis** (1981) Behavioural Learning Theory: Its Relevance to Marketing and Promotions, *Journal of Marketing*, **45** (Spring), 70–8.
18. **Tuck, R.T.J.** and **W.G.B. Harvey** (1972) Do Promotions Undermine the Brand? *Admap*, January, 30–3.
19. **Brown, R.G.** (1974) Sales Response to Promotions and Advertising, *Journal of Advertising Research*, **14** (4), 33–9.
20. **Ehrenberg, A.S.C., K. Hammond** and **G.J. Goodhardt** (1994) The After-effects of Price-related Consumer Promotions, *Journal of Advertising Research*, **34** (4), 1–10.
21. **Davidson, J.H.** (1998) *Offensive Marketing*, Harmondsworth: Penguin, 249–71.
22. **Anonymous** (2011) Groupon Anxiety, *Economist.com*, 17 March.
23. **Shayon, S.** (2011) Groupon Regroups on Mobile, Agency, IPO Strategy, *Brandchannel.com*, 21 March.
24. **Steiner, C.** (2010) Meet the Fastest Growing Company Ever, *Forbes.com*, 30 August.
25. **Dowling, G.R.** and **M. Uncles** (1997) Do Loyalty Programs Really Work? *Sloan Management Review*, **38** (4), 71–82.
26. **Burnside, A.** (1995) A Never Ending Search for the New, *Marketing*, 25 May, 31–5.
27. **Murphy, C.** (1999) Addressing the Data Issue, *Marketing*, 28 January, 31.
28. **Anonymous** (2005) An Overdose of Bad News, *The Economist*, 19 March, 69–71.
29. **Doyle, P.** and **J. Saunders** (1985) The Lead Effect of Marketing Decisions, *Journal of Marketing Research*, **22** (1), 54–65.
30. **Lesly, P.** (1991) *The Handbook of Public Relations and Communications*, Maidenhead: McGraw-Hill, 13–19.
31. **Burrows, D.** (2011) Why Blogs and Tweets Give PR Machine Bite, *MarketingWeek.co.uk*, 24 March.
32. **Warc** (2008) AEG-Electrolux Silent Laundry Campaign: The World is Noisy Enough, *Warc.com*.
33. **Lesly, P.** (1991) *The Handbook of Public Relations and Communications*, Maidenhead: McGraw-Hill, 13–19.
34. **Sleight, S.** (1989) *Sponsorship: What it is and How to Use it*, Maidenhead, McGraw-Hill, 4.
35. **Ward, A.** (2005) DHL Goes For Home Run in Rival's Back Yard, *Financial Times*, 6 April, 31.

36. **Mintel** (1991) *Sponsorship: Special Report*, London: Mintel International Group.

37. **Friedman, V.** (2003) Banks Step on to the Catwalk, *Financial Times*, 3 July, 12.

38. **Mallet, V.** (2008) Retail Brands See Oceans of Opportunity at the Helm, *Financial Times*, 19 December, 12.

39. **Carter, M.** (2007) Sponsorship Branding Takes on New Name, *Financial Times*, 13 March, 12.

40. **O'Daly, K.** (2008) Main Event, *Marketing Age*, November/December, 46–9.

41. **Miles, L.** (1995) Sporting Chancers, *Marketing Director International*, **6** (2), 50–2.

42. **Bowman, J.** (2004) Swoosh Rules Over Official Olympic Brands, *Media Asia*, 10 September, 22.

43. **Farrell, G.** (2010) Sponsors Score with World Cup as Football Promotions Lift Sales, *Financial Times*, 16 August, 15.

44. **Meenaghan, T.** (2011) Mind the Gap in Sponsorship Measurement, *Admap*, February (available online).

45. **Anonymous** (2007) The Cartel of Silence, *The Economist*, 9 June, 71.

46. **Grande, C.** (2007) Big Brother Sponsor Injects New Reality, *Financial Times*, 19 January, 3.

47. **Vernon, P.** (2006) The Fall and Rise of Kate Moss, *Guardian.co.uk*, 14 May.

48. **O'Hara, B., F. Palumbo** and **P. Herbig** (1993) Industrial Trade Shows Abroad, *Industrial Marketing Management*, **22**, 233–7.

49. **Anonymous** (2002) The Top Ten Product Placements in Features, *Campaign*, 17 December, 36.

50. **Tomkins, R.** (2003) The Hidden Message: Life's a Pitch, and Then You Die, *Financial Times*, 24 October, 14; **Armstrong, S.** (2005) How to Put Some Bling into Your Brand, *Irish Times*, *Weekend*, 30 July, 7.

51. **Silverman, G.** (2005) After the Break: The 'Wild West' Quest to Bring the Consumers to the Advertising, *Financial Times*, 18 May, 17.

52. **Dowdy, C.** (2003) Thunderbirds Are Go, *Financial Times*, Creative Business, 24 June, 10.

Company background

Bavaria NV is an independent Dutch brewery which operates in 120 countries worldwide. It was founded by Laurentius Moorees in 1719 but in the mid-nineteenth century Jan Swinkels took over ownership of the brewery and expanded its production and distribution. The Swinkels family are still owners of Bavaria NV which is the largest family-owned brewery in the Netherlands. In addition to its own brewery in Lieshout, the company has a number of subsidiaries, including:

- the Dutch Trappist brewery De Koningshoeven, which produces the beer La Trappe
- Bavaria Horeca, which supplies catering organizations with Bavaria products and services
- Bavaria Events, responsible for supporting events sponsored by Bavaria NV, including Bavaria City Racing, Extrema Outdoor Best, Solar Roermond and Huntenpop.

During 2007, Peter Swinkels retired as chairman of Bavaria NV and handed over his responsibilities to Jan-Renier Swinkels. Peter Swinkels had been with Bavaria since 1972, and acted as Chairman for over a decade. The hereditary management of Bavaria NV continues with six members of the family, five of whom are seventh-generation Swinkels. Sarah Swainson, Bavaria's UK marketing manager, says: 'Bavaria is a brewer steeped in tradition and heritage and has a great reputation for producing top quality beers with a true and

distinctive taste . . . Jan-Renier will follow on from Peter to grow Bavaria's presence in the international beer market and continue to brew Bavaria in the true and unique Swinkels' style.' Bavaria NV produces several different beers in the Dutch and international markets, using the Bavaria label and also produces private label beers. A non-alcoholic beer, Bavaria 0.0 per cent, and Bavaria 0.0 per cent white beer are also produced. In 2007, the company launched a beer, under the name Swinckels' Volmaakt in the Netherlands, an unpasteurized beer that is only available through selected channels. The company owns two malting plants, thus the whole brewing process is conducted in-house. In October 2009, Bavaria NV changed its corporate identity and rolled it out to all its operating countries. A new logo was developed: a compass with the 'S' of Swinkels as the south point. The new house style involved labels which prominently feature the colour blue.

Strategic direction

The business philosophy of Bavaria NV is to consistently maintain the high quality of its beers. This is done by controlling its brewing process in-house, owning natural mineral water sources and two malting plants in the Netherlands. On top of its quality focus, the company also places an emphasis on thematic marketing campaigns, such as its active promotional efforts during the World Cup 2010. Going forward, the dual focus of distinct marketing activities and quality are poised to allow Bavaria NV to stay competitive in the Netherlands beer sector.

▶ # Competitive positioning

Bavaria NV focuses on beer products in the Netherlands and offers a variety of products, including dark beer, domestic standard lager and non-alcoholic beer (see Tables C9.1, C9.2, C9.3).

Bavaria NV uses high-profile marketing campaigns, particularly through sponsorship, to differentiate the company from other beer manufacturers. Some of its key promotions include the following.

Table C9.1 Bavaria NV: competitive position 2010

Product type	% Total volume share	Rank
Beer	8.7	4
Dark beer	1.6	6
Ale	2.1	5
Lager	8.7	4
Domestic standard lager	15.3	2
Non-alcoholic beer	51.3	1

Source: Euromonitor International estimates, 2011.

Red Bull Air Race and Bavaria

Red Bull Air Race and Bavaria entered into a two-year partnership in 2008. Bavaria became the worldwide official beer supplier for the Red Bull Air Races. In total, nine cities around the world will be treated to this spectacular air race. 'The Red Bull Air Race in Rotterdam was the start of a great partnership,' says Bernd Loidl, CEO of Red Bull. Peter Swinkels, member of the board of Bavaria, said: 'We are very proud to strengthen our partnership with a long-term contract for the Red Bull Air Races. The professionalism and the international nature of Red Bull is a perfect fit with Bavaria and the top-class events that we organize.' Bavaria and Red Bull have already worked together in the world of Formula 1, at the Bavaria City Racing Moscow. The Red Bull team was represented by racing driver Mikhail Aleshin during the race through the streets of Moscow city centre.

Television advertising

The UK advertising campaign for the brand centred around the theme of 'real men' – those with a passion for life and extreme sports. The cinematic television trails show men demonstrating their strength and perseverance as they battle

Table C9.2 Company shares of beer by national brand owner 2006-10

% total volume	2006	2007	2008	2009	2010
Heineken NV	43.1	42.5	41.2	39.9	39.1
Grolsch, Koninklijke NV	17.6	18.4	18.0	17.2	16.5
Interbrew Nederland NV	13.0	13.3	13.3	14.1	13.6
Bavaria NV	8.5	8.6	8.5	8.8	8.7
Royal Ahold NV	1.9	1.9	1.9	2.1	2.2
Palm BV	1.9	1.9	1.9	2.0	2.0
Aldi Nederland BV	1.2	1.3	1.4	1.5	1.8
Other Private Label	1.3	1.3	1.3	1.3	1.3
Warsteiner Brauerei Haus Cramer GmbH & Co KG	1.3	1.3	1.3	1.2	1.1
Brasseries Kronenbourg SA	0.6	0.6	0.6	0.7	0.7
Dortmunder Actie Brauerei AG	0.5	0.5	0.5	0.5	0.5
Gulpener Bierbrouwerij BV	0.5	0.5	0.5	0.5	0.5
Leeuw (De) Onafhankelijk-Brouwerij	0.5	0.5	0.5	0.5	0.5
Modelo SA de CV, Grupo	0.5	0.6	0.6	0.5	0.5
Carlsberg Importers NV SA	0.5	0.5	0.5	0.5	0.4
De Leckere BV	0.2	0.2	0.2	0.3	0.3
Alfa Brouwerij BV	0.2	0.2	0.2	0.3	0.3
Super de Boer NV	0.1	0.1	0.1	0.2	0.2
Others	6.7	5.8	7.5	7.9	9.8
Total	100.0	100.0	100.0	100.0	100.0

Source: Euromonitor International from official statistics, trade associations, trade press, company research, store checks, trade interviews and trade sources.

▶

Table C9.3 Company shares of beer by global brand owner 2006-10

% total volume	2006	2007	2008	2009	2010
Heineken NV	43.1	42.5	41.2	39.9	39.1
SABMiller Plc	–	–	18.0	17.2	16.5
Anheuser-Busch InBev NV	–	–	13.3	14.2	13.6
Bavaria NV	8.5	8.6	8.5	8.8	8.7
Palm NV, Brouwerij	1.9	1.9	1.9	2.0	2.0
Carlsberg A/S	0.5	0.5	1.1	1.1	1.1
Warsteiner Brauerei Haus Cramer GmbH & Co KG	1.3	1.3	1.3	1.2	1.1
Oetker-Gruppe	0.5	0.5	0.5	0.5	0.5
Gulpener Bierbrouwerij BV	0.5	0.5	0.5	0.5	0.5
Leeuw (De) Onafhankelijk-Brouwerij	0.5	0.5	0.5	0.5	0.5
Modelo SA de CV, Grupo	0.5	0.6	0.6	0.5	0.5
De Leckere BV	0.2	0.2	0.2	0.3	0.3
Alfa Brouwerij BV	0.2	0.2	0.2	0.3	0.3
Grolsch, Koninklijke NV	17.6	18.4	–	–	–
InBev NV SA	13.0	13.3	–	–	–
Scottish & Newcastle Plc	0.6	0.6	–	–	–
Interbrew NV SA	–	–	–	–	–
Private Label	4.5	4.7	4.7	5.2	5.5
Others	6.7	5.8	7.4	7.9	9.8
Total	100.0	100.0	100.0	100.0	100.0

Source: Euromonitor International from official statistics, trade associations, trade press, company research, store checks, trade interviews and trade sources.

it out to reach a glass of Bavaria beer. The research, fronted by England rugby back row, Nick Easter, revealed that real men spend less than half an hour getting ready in the mornings; work in 'blue collar' trades such as construction or farming; and like football and rugby. Office, 'white collar' jobs were deemed the most unmanly professions. 'This campaign forms part of the larger marketing programme and set out to discover the attributes of real men today,' said Bavaria spokesperson, Sarah Swainson. 'Our research showed that while "metrosexuals" are losing popularity among both men and women, the real man is making a comeback. This theme will also appear in future marketing initiatives as we continue to invest in the Bavaria brand, spreading the word that Bavaria Premium is an imported, great tasting beer, brewed using top-quality malt, the finest hops and the purest of mineral water. A brew for all real men to enjoy.'

Ambush marketing

The increasing cost of hosting major international events, particularly in the sporting arena, has encouraged organizing committees to seek assistance from the corporate sector through the provision of a range of financial or material sponsorship opportunities. In order to avoid dilution of the benefits of the sponsorship through the involvement of direct competitors, category exclusivity is common at major events, for example, just one alcoholic drinks company. However, this creates a dilemma for competitors who wish to use the event for marketing purposes. One solution would be to sponsor a lower category and secure rights of association in that manner. Alternatively, a company could develop a marketing campaign that associates it with the event without making any payment. These approaches can deflect attention away from the main or primary sponsor and have the potential to confuse the public. This represents a growing trend called "ambush marketing" (sometimes termed parasitic or guerrilla marketing).

Ambush strategies

There are numerous examples of ambush marketing, commonly in the sporting context, and often involving global companies. Several examples follow.

■ When American Express (Amex) discontinued its sponsorship of the Olympic Games, Visa took over the category. Amex used former Olympic athletes in its advertising to which Visa responded by publicizing the

▶ fact that Amex was not an official sponsor. This drew a retort from Amex to the effect that it was not necessary to have a Visa to attend the Olympics.

- Billboards showing the Nike name and 'swoosh' brand identifier were erected on a specially constructed building close to the Olympic Park in Atlanta. Reebok was the official sport goods category sponsor.

- The US men's basketball team, known as the 'dream team', was sponsored by Federal Express and the association heavily publicized, although UPS was the Olympic sponsor in the overnight mail category.

- Olympic sprinter, Linford Christie wore contact lenses during interviews with his sponsor Puma's logo. The company was not a sponsor.

- Fuller's Beer placed advertisements during the Six Nations Rugby competition which stated 'Support English Rugby' and showed a picture of rugby posts. As no fee had been paid, the Rugby Football Union argued that this was ambush marketing and complained to the Advertising Standards Authority.

FIFA World Cup 2010 – Budweiser and Bavaria NV

Association Football (Soccer) is the most popular sport in the world and its flagship competition is held every four years. The 2010 event, held in South Africa, attracted a cumulative global audience estimated at 26 billion, spread across 200 countries. Brewer Anheuser-Busch was a major sponsor through its Budweiser brand. At a game between Holland and Denmark, a group of 36 young women entered the Soccer City Stadium in Nasrec, the Soweto area of Johannesburg, wearing the traditional red and white colours of the Danish team. As the game progressed they removed their outer clothing to reveal orange mini dresses, the colour associated with Holland. This episode drew the attention of spectators, coaches and players and represented a media opportunity for television and print journalists, who lost no time in publishing their material worldwide.

The women were ejected from the venue and arrested by the police. A spokesman said the women had been charged under the Merchandise Marks Act and under two sections of the Special Measures Act. The majority of the women were released relatively quickly, although two women, alleged to be the organizers, were detained for a longer period. A FIFA representative suggested that a Dutch beer company, Bavaria, had paid to fly the women to the event and that they were part of an ambush marketing stunt. It was stressed that wearing branded clothing that was from a rival to a sponsor was acceptable, providing it was not part of an orchestrated campaign. The event drew worldwide attention, with the Dutch Foreign Minister stating that 'It is outrageous that the two women have a jail term hanging over their heads. If South Africa or FIFA wants to take a company to task for an illegal marketing action they should start judicial proceeding against the company.' The women were eventually released without charge following an out-of-court settlement between the companies.

Bavaria were in fact on FIFA's watch list as four years earlier they had pulled off a similar stunt. Up to 1,000 fans had to watch Holland's game against Ivory Coast in under-pants because they were wearing orange Bavaria-branded lederhosen (a form of short trousers). They were allowed entry, providing the offending articles were removed.

A spokesman for the Bavaria beer company denied that the women had any links to their campaign, suggesting that the dresses, in the national colours of the Dutch team, were attractive, and that the women should be allowed to wear what they liked. The dresses contained no overt branding, other than a very small 'Bavaria' label. However, prior to the competition, the firm made sure they were instantly recognizable in the Netherlands by arranging to have the dress modelled by top-ranking Dutch model, Sylvie van der Vaart, the wife of Tottenham Hotspur footballer, Rafael van der Vaart. The mini-dresses were produced by the brewery as part of a gift pack, with Bavaria branding, and an estimated 200,000 were sold in the lead-up to the World Cup.

It was estimated that the value of the free media coverage of the stunt would have run into several hundred thousand euros. The Bavaria website traffic increased significantly after the World Cup ambush. According to the Internet analysis company Experian, Bavaria's site in the UK (that previously enjoyed little traffic, if any) rose overnight to the fifth most visited beer site in the country. The majority of traffic was redirected from Wikipedia and Google as the story broke around the world. Bavaria's UK marketing manager Sean Durkan said: 'Brand awareness has definitely increased. There's a lot more activity on Twitter and social media.'

As the cost of sponsorships increase, it is not surprising that some organizations may seek a low-cost alternative. In turn, rights holders will endeavour to maximize their investment to justify the expenditure. The event organizers will also be alert to the damage that ambush marketing can do, if official sponsors are discouraged and remove their sponsorship investments. Major events now rely heavily on sponsorship revenues, without which, the viability of the event may be brought into question. ▶

▶ | # References

Bavaria Company Website, http://int.bavaria.com/
Euromonitor (2011), Bavaria NV in Alcoholic Drinks (Netherlands)
www.marketingmagazine. co.uk
BBC News
YouTube segments

Questions

1. Evaluate the marketing strategies used by Bavaria NV. What is the role of ambush marketing in the company's integrated marketing plan?

   What are the objectives that Bavaria wants to achieve through the ambush activities?

   Is ambush marketing illegal, immoral or a legitimate commercial practice?

2. Imagine you are a category sponsor at a major event:

   (a) What safeguards would you expect the organising committee to put in place to avoid ambush marketing?

   (b) What would you do to protect your own investment?

This case was produced by Dr Des Thwaites, Leeds University Business School, and Dr Yue Meng, Bournemouth University, from various published sources as a basis for class discussion rather than to show either effective or ineffective management.

Chapter 10

Integrated Marketing Communications 2: Direct Communications Techniques and Digital Marketing

Chapter outline

Database marketing

Customer relationship management

Direct marketing

Digital marketing

Buzz marketing

Personal selling

Sales management

Learning outcomes

By the end of this chapter you will understand:

1 the importance of database management as the foundation for direct marketing activities

2 the reasons for the growth in customer relationship management (CRM)

3 the meaning of direct marketing and how to manage a direct marketing campaign

4 the marketing opportunities presented by the developments in digital technologies

5 the emergence of buzz marketing as a popular and innovative promotional technique

6 the role of personal selling in the promotional mix, and the key issues involved in selling and sales management.

MARKETING SPOTLIGHT

T-Mobile

T-Mobile international is the German-based holding company for Deutsche Telekom's various mobile communications subsidiaries outside Germany. In 2011, the brand was present in 10 European countries including the UK (merged with Orange), Austria, Croatia, Hungary, Poland, the Netherlands, the Czech Republic, Slovakia, Macedonia and Montenegro. In the competitive world of mobile communications, the brand had developed a new positioning in 2009 entitled 'life is for sharing'. This was intended not just to be a slogan but also a brand promise and a philosophy for the company.

The T-Mobile 'Royal Wedding' along with its flash mob campaigns have been huge viral hits.
www.mcgraw-hill.co.uk/textbooks/fahy

The challenge was to find an effective way to implement this new positioning across the brand's many diverse markets. While T-Mobile was the clear market leader in countries like Hungary and Croatia, it was a challenger (number two player) in Austria and then a follower (the number four player) in the UK. One of the attractions of the positioning was that it was felt that it was a proposition that would appeal to different age groups with different buying motives in the brand's diverse markets. The key was to find an effective way to communicate the message. The company chose not to focus on traditional advertising alone which would try to show that life was for sharing but rather to create events that would be so appealing that customers would feel compelled to share them. In this way, it was hoped that the events and the communications around them would epitomize the brand proposition.

Events were promoted using teaser announcements such as something will be happening on a given date at a given location on Facebook pages, SMS messaging and rumours on selected radio stations. The intention was that the associated 'buzz' marketing would generate sufficient interest. The London event turned out to be a massive karaoke party featuring the pop artist Pink as special guest which was attended by 13,500 people. Each of the events was recorded for television, radio and poster advertising as well as for content for the brand's YouTube channel and Facebook pages. Consumers were encouraged to upload their own mobile footage of the events and bloggers encouraged to blog about them.

The success of this innovative approach can be assessed in various ways. YouTube footage of the London event was viewed over 5 million times, a dedicated Singalong Facebook group generated 17,000 members and significant press and television coverage of the event was achieved. But equally varied business objectives in the different markets were also attained. For example, a target increase in music downloads of 50 per cent in Austria was well exceeded while a target of 35,000 new pay-as-you-go customers in the UK was exceeded by 42 per cent. Innovative approaches to the delivery of the brand's proposition have continued since with most notably, its highly successful 'flash mobs' in Liverpool St. railway station and Heathrow airport being extensively shared and viewed online.[1]

For many decades, mass communications techniques were favoured by marketers, and the promotional mix was heavily weighted towards tools like advertising and sales promotion. But in recent times, direct communications techniques have become very popular. There are a number of reasons for this. As we saw in the previous chapter, both the audience and the media have begun to fragment significantly, making it very difficult for companies to reach a mass market through the classic 30-second television advertisement, for example. In its place, the emergence of some new technologically based solutions, such as customer relationship management (CRM) and digital marketing, promise a much more direct and interactive relationship with the customer. Also, one of the perennial challenges for marketers has been to justify promotional budgets, and demonstrate the impact of expenditure on awareness and sales. Direct communication techniques such as direct response advertising allow for the more effective measurement of the impact of marketing investments.

This chapter will examine both direct marketing communications techniques as well as the rapidly changing world of digital marketing. Many direct marketing communications techniques rely on the availability of a database of customers, which is the foundation upon which campaigns can be built. We shall first examine database marketing and its evolution into customer relationship management. We then go on to look at the field of direct marketing itself, which has grown out of the old mail-order business. Then we will examine, in some more detail, digital marketing which has been one of the recurring themes throughout this book. Finally, as one of the core objectives of marketing activity is to facilitate a sale, we examine the key activities of personal selling and sales management.

Database marketing

A marketing database is an 'electronic filing cabinet' containing a list of names, addresses, telephone numbers, and lifestyle and transactional data on customers and potential customers (see Exhibit 10.1). Information such as types of purchase, frequency of purchase, purchase value and responsiveness to promotional offers may be held.

Database marketing is defined as:[2]

an interactive approach to marketing that uses individually addressable marketing media and channels (such as mail, telephone and the sales force) to:

- provide information to a target audience
- stimulate demand, and

Exhibit 10.1 A wide variety of businesses such as apparel retailers, gyms and educational establishments run 'bring a friend' promotions as a way of growing their potential database of customers

- stay close to customers by recording and storing an electronic database of customers, prospects and all communication and transactional data.

Database marketing has some key characteristics. The first of these is that it allows direct communication with customers through a variety of media including **direct mail, telemarketing** and **direct response advertising**. Second, it usually requires the customer to respond in a way that allows the company to take action (such as contact by telephone, sending out literature or arranging sales visits). Third, it must be possible to trace the response back to the original communication. The potential of database marketing is enormous. For example, one supermarket analysed its sales and found that it was making a loss on a certain brand of cheese. Before cutting the line altogether, it correlated information about the people who were buying the product and found that they bought other high-ticket items and spent more on average on luxury goods. The supermarket concluded that it would make sense to continue selling the cheese in order to please these high-value customers.[3]

Computer technology provides the capability of storing and analysing large quantities of data from diverse sources, and presenting information in a convenient, accessible and useful format. The creation of a database relies on the collection of information on customers, which can be sourced from:

- company records
- responses to sales promotions
- warranty and guarantee cards
- offering samples that require the consumer to give name, address, telephone number, etc.; for example, some bands give away music for free in exchange for a valid email address
- enquiries
- exchanging data with other companies
- sales-force records
- application forms (e.g. to join a credit or loyalty scheme)
- complaints
- responses to previous direct marketing activities
- organized events (e.g. wine tastings)
- website registrations.

However a key challenge for companies now is how to handle information overload due to the size and complexity of the data available. Winter Corporation's survey of databases found that over 90 per cent of those that it studied contained over 1 terabyte (1000 gigabytes) of data compared with just 25 per cent in 2001. The large US retailer, Kmart had 12.6 terabytes of data covering stocks, sales, customers and suppliers, but this was not enough to save it from bankruptcy.[4]

Collecting information is easiest for companies that have direct contact with customers, such as those in financial services or retailing. However, even for those where the sales contact is indirect, building a database is often possible. For example, Seagram, the drinks company, built up a European database through telephone and written enquiries from customers, sales promotional returns, tastings in store, visits to company premises, exhibitions and promotions that encouraged consumers to name like-minded friends and colleagues.[5]

Figure 10.1 shows the sort of information that is recorded on a database. Customer and prospect information typically includes names, addresses, telephone numbers, names of key decision-makers within DMUs and general behavioural information. Transactional information refers to past transactions that contacts have had with the company. Transactional data must be sufficiently detailed to allow frequency, recency, amount and category (FRAC) information to be extracted for

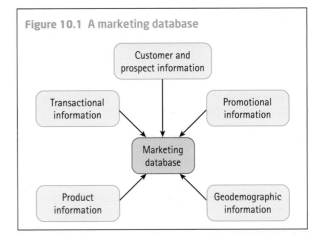

Figure 10.1 A marketing database

each customer. Frequency refers to how often a customer buys. Recency measures when the customer last bought; if customers are waiting longer before they re-buy (i.e. recency is decreasing) the reasons for this (e.g. less attractive offers or service problems) need to be explored. Amount measures how much a customer has bought and is usually recorded in value terms. Finally, category defines the type of product being bought.

Promotional information covers what promotion campaigns have been run, who has responded to them, and what the overall results were in terms of contacts, sales and profits. Product information would include which products have been promoted, who responded, when and from where. Finally, geodemographics includes information about the geographic location of customers and prospects, and the social, lifestyle and business category to which they belong. Cross-tabulating these details with transactional information can reveal the customer profile most likely to buy a particular product. Because of the amount of information held about consumers, data privacy is becoming a major issue, as discussed in Ethical Debate 10.1.

The main applications of database marketing are as follows.

1 *Direct mail*: a database can be used to select customers for mailings.
2 *Telemarketing*: a database can store telephone numbers so that customers and prospects can be contacted.
3 *Distributor management systems*: a database can be the foundation on which information is provided to distributors and their performance monitored.
4 *Loyalty marketing*: loyal customers can be selected from the database for special treatment as a reward for their loyalty (see Chapter 7).
5 *Target marketing*: groups of individuals or businesses can be targeted as a result of analysing the database.

Ethical Debate 10.1 Corporations vs citizens

The advances in data tracking and storage technology mean that the amount of information that corporations and the state hold about us has never been greater. As we increase our usage of technology we leave more and more information trails behind us. Every mobile phone call that we make and the texts and emails that we send are recorded. Some governments are now requiring that operators store all this information for periods of up to three years for security purposes. As we surf the Web, click-stream analysis keeps track of where we go and what we view. Software being pioneered intercepts web page requests to build up a profile of user interests, which can then be used to target advertising. Facebook keeps track of our interests, pictures and conversations. And every time we use a store loyalty card, we enable stores to build up a picture of the kind of customer we are. The key questions that arise are how well do organizations know us, what are they doing with this information and how safe is it.

In answer to the first question, they increasingly know us very well. Database information allows organizations to build up profiles of customers. When organizations share information as, for example, members of the Nectar Card scheme can do, then consumer profiles have the potential to be very accurate because details about grocery shopping (Sainsbury's), online shopping (Amazon.com) and banking (Barclaycard) can all be cross-tabulated and compared. Entry into a loyalty card scheme usually requires the submission of very valuable information like employment status, number of children, number of cars you have, and so on. When all these data are mined, very accurate profiles emerge. The 2008 takeover of DoubleClick by Google also raised significant privacy issues. DoubleClick is one of the biggest users of 'cookies', small digital files that sit on computers and track the websites visited by users. When this information is combined with Google's search records, it can present a very accurate picture of a surfer's interests.

To maximize company profits, this kind of information can be used in different ways. For example, bonus points can be offered to consumers who switch purchases to high-profit items. Second, targeting is improved. For example, Gmail messages are scanned for keywords so if you use the word holiday, you may find that you get advertisements for travel companies. Third, products that offer low margins can be discontinued, which sometimes means that cost-conscious shoppers find their preferred brands are deleted and they may have to shop elsewhere, which is in effect a form of discriminatory pricing. Fourth, price changes can be tested to see how consumers react. For example, the price of a range of products might be increased for a short period and, if consumers do not react adversely, then these higher price levels might remain. Over time, a greater proportion of the store can be dedicated to higher-price items. In intensely competitive markets this is not always possible, but in sectors like grocery retailing the market is becoming dominated by a small number of very large players. Finally, in some industries like insurance, data can be used to identify and weed out high-risk customers.

Once consumer profiles get very accurate, the security of this information is paramount. For example, in the USA, Facebook records and loyalty card data have been presented in legal cases such as divorces to show that one side has the facility to pay more alimony. In 2011, Sony contacted its 70 million Playstation Network users to confirm that hackers had carried out a massive data theft which included names, addresses, dates of birth, passwords, security questions and answers and in some cases credit card details. Security breaches such as this are becoming increasingly common. Facebook too has been criticized for frequently changing its privacy settings or making it complicated to protect one's privacy. For example, the *New York Times* observed that users would need to navigate 50 settings with more than 150 options in order to maintain their privacy on Facebook.[6]

All this adds up to a situation where consumers need to be very aware of what information they give organizations and what permissions they give these organizations with respect to that information. Consumer rights are protected through data protection legislation. Consumers have a right to know what information organizations hold about them and who this information can be passed on to. They also have the right to opt out of marketing databases. But, in an information society, it has effectively become impossible to live a truly private life!

Suggested reading: Turow (2008)[7].

Reflection: Is it reasonable that corporations should be able to build up very accurate profiles of individuals? What are the pros and cons?

Databases can also be used to try to build or strengthen relationships with customers. For example, Highland Distillers switched all of its promotional budget for its Macallan whisky brand from advertising to direct marketing. It built a database of 100,000 of its most frequent drinkers (those who consume at least five bottles a year), mailing them every few months with interesting facts about the brand, whisky memorabilia and offers.[8] It is these kinds of efforts to improve customer relationships that have caused the evolution of database marketing into what is now known as customer relationship management.

Customer relationship management

Customer relationship management (CRM) is a term for the methodologies, technologies and e-commerce capabilities used by firms to manage customer relationships.[9] In particular, CRM software packages aid the interaction between the customer and the company, enabling the company to co-ordinate all of its communications efforts so that the customer is presented with a unified message and image. CRM companies offer a range of information technology-based services, such as call centres, data analysis and website management. The basic principle behind CRM is that company staff have a single-customer point of view for each client. Customers are now using multiple channels more frequently. They may buy one product from a salesperson but another from the company website. Interactions between the customer and the company may take place in a variety of ways – through the sales force, call centres, email, distributors, websites, and so on (see Figure 10.2). For example, Heineken Ireland distributes its products through 8,000 pubs/restaurants and over 1,300 shops and off-licences in Ireland. Presenting a single, up-to-date view on all these customers to all organizational staff, including a field sales force, is what a good CRM system should do.

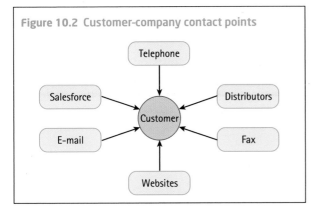

Figure 10.2 Customer-company contact points

Therefore, it is crucial that, no matter how a customer contacts a company, front-line staff have instant access to the same, up-to-date data about the customer, such as his/her details and past purchases. This usually means the consolidation of many databases held by individual departments in a company into one centralized database that can be accessed by all relevant staff. However, CRM is much more than the technology. As we saw in Chapter 7, to be effective, CRM must be integrated into the overall marketing strategy of the company. Staff must be trained on how to use the system, and accurate usage must be continually encouraged and monitored.

The key ways in which CRM systems can be used include the following.

1 *Targeting* customer and prospect groups with clearly defined propositions.
2 *Enquiry management* – this starts as soon as an individual expresses an interest and continues through qualification, lead handling and outcome reporting.
3 *Welcoming* – this covers new customers and those upgrading their relationship; it covers simple 'thank you' messages to sophisticated contact strategies.
4 *Getting to know* – customers need to be persuaded to give information about themselves; this information needs to be stored, updated and used; useful information includes attitude and satisfaction information and relationship 'health checks'.
5 *Customer development* – decisions need to be made regarding which customers to develop through higher levels of relationship management activity, and which to maintain or drop.
6 *Managing problems* – this involves early problem identification, complaint handling and 'root cause' analysis to spot general issues that have the potential to cause problems for many customers.
7 *Win-back* – activities include understanding reasons for loss, deciding which customers to try to win back, and developing win-back programmes that offer customers the chance to come back and a good reason to do so.

To date, CRM initiatives have had a very mixed success rate. Some of the factors that have been associated with success are:[10]

- having a customer orientation and organizing the CRM system around customers
- taking a single view of the customer across departments, and designing an integrated system so that all customer-facing staff can draw information from a common database

- having the ability to manage cultural change issues that arise as a result of system development and implementation
- involving users in the CRM design process
- designing the system in such a way that it can readily be changed to meet future requirements
- having a board-level champion of the CRM project, and commitment within each of the affected departments to the benefits of taking a single view of the customer
- creating 'quick wins' to provide positive feedback on the project programmes.

Direct marketing

Direct marketing is the term that is used to describe the distribution of products, information and promotional benefits to target consumers through interactive communication in a way that allows response to be measured. The origins of direct marketing lie in direct mail and mail-order catalogues and, as a result, direct marketing is sometimes seen as synonymous with 'junk mail'. However, today's direct marketers use a wide range of media, such as telemarketing, direct response advertising and email to interact with people. Also, unlike many other forms of communication, direct marketing usually requires an immediate response, which means that the effectiveness of most direct marketing campaigns can be assessed quantitatively.

A direct marketing campaign is not necessarily a short-term response-driven activity. More and more companies are using direct marketing to develop ongoing relationships with customers (see Marketing in Action 10.1). Some estimates consider that the cost of attracting a new customer is five times that of retaining existing customers. Direct marketing activity can be one tool in the armoury of marketers in their attempt to keep current customers satisfied and spending money. Once a customer has been acquired, there is the opportunity to sell that customer other products marketed by the company. Direct Line, a UK insurance company, became market leader in motor insurance by by-passing the insurance broker to reach the consumer

---

Marketing in Action 10.1 Mothercare: Baby & Me

Critical Thinking: Below is a review of Mothercare's use of database marketing to build a relationship with its customers. Read it and critically evaluate its strengths and weaknesses.

Mothercare is a UK retailer that specializes in products for expectant mothers and for children up to 8 years of age. Its first store was founded in 1961 and it currently operates through retail stores and online in the UK as well as through franchise operations in Europe, the Middle East, Africa and South East Asia. In 2007, the Mothercare group acquired the Early Learning Centre – a company that specializes in games and toys primarily for children up to the age of 6.

For new parents, the most challenging and confusing time can be during the first year of a child's life. Mothercare sought to capitalize on this opportunity by setting up a Baby & Me Club for new mums. Their research had shown that these customers were information hungry – looking for trusted and expert guidance on what to buy for their baby and when. The choice of name was important as it recognized that it was not all just about baby – but mum and dad also. The company set a target of recruiting 200,000 parents-to-be and new parents in its first year. Customers could sign up online or at Mothercare stores and in return they received welcome booklets with advice, information and vouchers to be redeemed against purchases as well as subsequent communications and offers. These were customized to one of five different key life stages within the first year or so of a child's life – all of which bring their own particular challenges and questions.

The club proved to be highly successful, attracting over 360,000 members and generating over £12.5 million in sales. It is also a key element of Mothercare's relationship with its customers at a time when many of its retail stores are struggling with the challenge presented by online retailers such as Amazon and Kiddicare. For example in 2011, Mothercare announced that it was planning to shut one-third of its high street stores to concentrate on out-of-town stores and international markets.

Based on: Direct Marketing Association (2010);[11] Mortimer (2011)[12].

directly through direct-response television advertisements using a freephone number and financial appeals to encourage car drivers to contact them. Once they have sold customers motor insurance, trained telesales people offer substantial discounts on other insurance products including buildings and contents insurance. In this way, Direct Line has built a major business through using a combination of direct marketing methods.

Direct marketing covers a wide array of methods, including:

- direct mail
- telemarketing (both in-bound and out-bound)
- direct response advertising (coupon response or 'phone now')
- catalogue marketing
- digital media (Internet, email, interactive television)
- inserts (leaflets in magazines)
- door-to-door leafleting.

In the UK, the proportion of the promotional budget being devoted to direct marketing has been increasing steadily, with one study finding companies planning to increase their spend on it by over 20 per cent.[13] The potential for growth in the area is reflected by the fact that per capita spend on direct marketing in the UK is US$71 compared with US$152 in the Netherlands and US$428 in the USA.[14] The significant growth in direct marketing activity over the past 20 years has been explained by five factors.

1 The growing *fragmentation of media and markets*. The growth of specialist magazines and television channels means that traditional mass advertising is less effective. Similarly, mass markets are disappearing as more and more companies seek to customize their offerings to target groups (see Chapter 5).

2 *Developments in technology*, such as databases, and software that generates personalized letters, have eased the task for direct marketers. Recent developments like variable data printing (VDP) have enabled different elements within direct mail documents, including text, pricing, offers, images and graphics, to be uniquely personalized.

3 *Increased supply of mailing lists*. List brokers act as an intermediary in the supply of lists from list owners (often either companies that have built lists through transactions with their customers, or organizations that have compiled lists specifically for the purpose of renting them). List brokers thus aid the process of finding a suitable list for targeting purposes.

4 *Sophisticated analytical techniques* such as geodemographic analysis (see Chapter 5) can be used to pinpoint targets for mailing purposes.

5 The *high costs* of other techniques, such as **personal selling**, have led an increasing number of companies to take advantage of direct marketing techniques, such as direct response advertising and telemarketing, to make sales forces more cost-effective.

Direct marketing activity, including direct mail, telemarketing and telephone banking, is regulated by a European Commission Directive that came into force at the end of 1994. Its main provisions are that:

- suppliers cannot insist on prepayments
- customers must be told the identity of the supplier, the price and quality of the product and any transport charges, the payment and delivery methods, and the period over which the solicitation remains valid
- orders must be met within 30 days unless otherwise indicated
- a cooling-off period of 30 days is mandatory and cold calling by telephone, fax or electronic mail is restricted unless the receiver has given prior consent.

Managing a direct marketing campaign

Direct marketing, as with all promotional campaigns, should be fully integrated to provide a coherent marketing strategy. Direct marketers need to understand how the product is being positioned in the marketplace as it is crucial that messages sent out as part of a direct marketing campaign do not conflict with those communicated by other channels such as advertising or the sales force.

The stages involved in conducting a direct mail campaign are similar to those for mass communications techniques described in the previous chapter (see Figure 10.3). The first step is the identification of the target audience, and one of the advantages of direct mail is that audience targeting can be very precise (see Exhibit 10.2). For example, when IBM wanted to grow its data storage solutions business, it knew that it faced a challenge in dealing with chief information officers (CIOs) who saw the company as too big, complex and expensive. But it was able to specifically target its rival HP's customers and focus on return on investment (ROI) – a key metric for these managers. It used direct mail based on a non-corporate character Roi Rapido who disseminated money saving tips and an IBM brochure that was followed up within two days with a telemarketing call.

Figure 10.3 Managing a direct marketing campaign

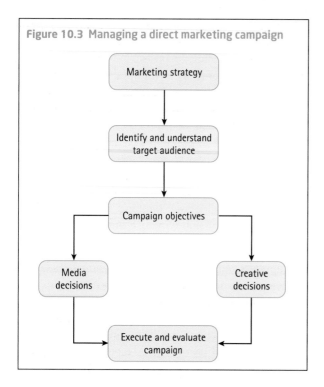

Exhibit 10.2 Boots UK, Christmas 2009 direct marketing campaign (see Chapter 4)

The objectives of direct marketing campaigns can be the same as those of other forms of promotion: to improve sales and profits, to acquire or retain customers or to create awareness. However, one of the benefits of direct marketing is that it usually has clearly defined short-term objectives against which performance can be measured, which makes the evaluation of effectiveness relatively easy. For example, the Spanish car maker Seat, targeted a select list of UK companies in an effort to break into the lucrative fleet car business. A combined direct mail and press campaign generated a 44 per cent increase in new car sales.

The next major decision involves the media to be used for conducting the direct marketing campaign. Each of the major alternatives available to the marketer is discussed below. Once the media have been selected, the creative decisions must be made. The creative brief usually contains details of the communications objectives, the product benefits, the target market analysis, the offer being made, the communication of the message and the action plan (i.e. how the campaign will be run). As direct marketing is more orientated to immediate action than advertising, recipients will need to see a clear benefit before responding.

Finally, the campaign needs to be executed and evaluated. Execution can be in-house or through the use of a specialist agency. As we noted earlier, direct marketing does lend itself to quantitative measurement. Some of the most frequently used measures are response rate (the proportion of contacts responding), total sales, sales rate (percentage of contacts purchasing), enquiry rate, cost per contact or enquiry or sale, and repeat purchase rate.

Direct mail

Material sent through the postal service to the recipient's home or business address, with the purpose of promoting a product and/or maintaining an ongoing relationship, is known as direct mail. For example, Heinz employs direct mail to target its customers and prospects. By creating a database based on responses to promotions, lifestyle questionnaires and rented lists, Heinz built a file of 4.6 million households. Each one receives a quarterly 'At Home' mail pack, which has been further segmented to reflect loyalty and frequency of purchase. Product and nutritional information is combined with coupons to achieve product trial.[15] A major advantage of direct mail is its cost. For example, in business-to-business marketing, it might cost €50 to visit potential customers, €5 to telephone them but less than €1 to send out a mailing.[16]

A key factor in the effectiveness of a direct mail campaign is the quality of the mailing list. For example, in one year in the UK, 100 million items were sent back marked 'return to sender'. So the effectiveness of direct mail relies heavily on the quality of the list being used. Poor lists raise costs and can contribute to the growing negative perception of 'junk mail'. As a result, it is often preferable to rent lists from list houses rather than purchase them.

Direct mail facilitates specific targeting to named individuals. For example, by hiring lists of subscribers to gardening catalogues, a manufacturer of gardening equipment could target a specific group of people who would be more likely to be interested in a promotional offer than the public in general. Personalization is possible and the results directly measurable. Since the objective of direct mail is immediate – usually a sale or an enquiry – success can be measured easily. Some organizations, such as *Reader's Digest*, spend money researching alternative creative approaches before embarking on a large-scale mailing. Factors such as type of promotional offer, headlines, visuals and copy can be varied in a systematic manner and, by using code numbers on reply coupons, response can be tied to the associated creative approach.

Telemarketing

Telemarketing refers to the use of telecommunications in marketing and sales activities. It can be a most cost-efficient, flexible and accountable medium.[17] The telephone permits two-way dialogue that is instantaneous, personal and flexible.

Technological advances have significantly assisted the growth of telemarketing. For example, integrated telephony systems allow for callers to be easily identified. The caller's telephone number is relayed into the computer database and his/her details and account information appear on the screen even before the call is picked up. Technology has also greatly improved the effectiveness and efficiency of outbound telemarketing. For example, predictive dialling enables multiple outbound calls to be made from a call centre. Calls are only delivered to agents when the customer answers, cutting out wasted calls to answering machines, engaged signals, fax machines and unanswered calls. In addition, scripts can be created and stored on the computer so that operators have ready and convenient access to them on-screen.

Telemarketing can be used in a number of roles, and this versatility has also assisted in its growth. It can be used for direct selling when the sales potential of a customer does not justify a face-to-face call or, alternatively, an incoming telephone call may be the means of placing an order in response to a direct mail or television advertising campaign (see Marketing in Action 10.2). Second, it can be used to support the field sales force, for example, in situations where salespeople may find contacting their customers difficult given the nature of their job. Third, telemarketing can be used to generate leads through establishing contact with prospective customers and arranging a sales visit. Finally, an additional role of telemarketing is to maintain and update the firm's marketing database.

Telemarketing has a number of advantages.

1   It has *lower costs* per contact than a face-to-face salesperson visit. But such has been the success of telemarketing that calls to businesses are growing significantly, with many companies moving call centre operations to low-cost countries.
2   It is *less time consuming* than personal visits.
3   The increasing *sophistication of telecommunications technology* has encouraged companies to employ telemarketing techniques. For example, digital networks allow the seamless transfer of calls between organizations.
4   Despite the reduced costs, compared to a personal visit, the telephone retains the advantage of *two-way communication*.

However, telephone selling is often considered intrusive, leading to consumers objecting to receiving unsolicited telephone calls. For example, legislation introduced in the UK in 2004 bans marketing companies from cold calling businesses, with fines of up to £5,000 for violations of the law, although this applies only to call centres located in Britain.

Direct response advertising

Although direct response advertising appears in prime media, such as television, newspapers and magazines, it differs from standard advertising in that it is designed to elicit a direct response such as an order, enquiry or a request for a visit. Often, a freephone telephone number is included in the advertisement or, for the print media, a coupon response mechanism may be used. This combines the ability of broadcast media to reach large sections of the population with direct marketing techniques that allow a swift response on behalf of both prospect and company. For example, direct response advertising is used very regularly by not-for-profit organizations such as the National Society for the Prevention of Cruelty to Children (NSPCC) in order to increase the number of volunteers and donors. Macmillan Cancer Support ran a direct response campaign to drive more callers to avail of its

Marketing in Action 10.2 Expensive phone calls

Critical Thinking: Below are some examples of problems surrounding competitions on popular television shows. Read it and critique the ethical standards of these interactive shows.

In a bid to increase levels of consumer retention, television has become increasingly interactive and is always seeking novel ways of engaging with potential viewers. One of the most popular techniques in recent times is the screening of programmes that invite viewers to enter competitions, or to vote for participants in a competition such as a reality television show. Participating in such competitions or votes usually involves making a phone call. What viewers are often unaware of is how much they are being charged for the call, though regulations increasingly require that this is made clear. What has been much more problematic are instances where consumers pay to enter competitions that they have no chance of winning, as happened with the popular breakfast television show, *GMTV*.

GMTV's phone-in competitions were managed by a telecommunications company, Opera Interactive Technology. However, a *Panorama* investigation discovered that this company frequently chose competition winners before the phone lines were closed and continued to charge callers premium rate prices to enter the competitions. It was estimated that, between 2003 and 2007, 18 million callers had spent £20 million entering competitions that they

had no chance of winning. Ofcom, the television regulator, fined Opera Interactive £250,000 for picking potential winners early. Though *GMTV* argued that it was not aware of the practice, it received a record fine of £2 million for what was described by the regulator as the 'widespread and systematic deception of viewers'. Two *GMTV* executives were forced to resign, it terminated its contract with Opera and offered refunds to disenfranchised entrants.

This is not the first time that television stations have been in trouble over phone-in competitions. For example, the BBC was fined £50,000 for persuading a child to pose as the winner of a *Blue Peter* competition after a technical problem meant that callers could not get through. The company behind the Channel 4, *Richard and Judy* 'You Say, We Pay' competition were fined £150,000 after callers were encouraged to phone in on a premium line after the winners had been chosen. Tens of thousands of text votes for ITV competitions like *Dancing on Ice* and *Gameshow Marathon* were not counted due to technical problems.

Based on: Anonymous (2007);[18] Martin (2007)[19].

financial and emotional support services. It's 'Good Day, Bad Day' campaign significantly increased calls to its helplines (see Exhibit 10.3).

Direct response television has experienced fast growth. It is an industry worth £3 billion globally and comes in many formats, but is not without its controversies, as shown in Marketing in Action 10.2. The most basic is the standard advertisement with telephone number; 60-, 90- or 120-second advertisements are sometimes used to provide the necessary information to persuade viewers to use the freephone number for ordering. Other variants are the 25-minute product demonstration (these are generally referred to as 'infomercials') and live home shopping programmes broadcast by companies such as QVC. Home shopping has a very loyal customer base. For example, Shoppingtelly.com, a website that offers home shoppers news and

information on home shopping products, receives between 20,000 and 35,000 hits per day and some of the leading home shopping presenters, such as Paul Lavers and Julia Roberts, have their own very popular websites.[20] A popular misconception regarding direct response television (DRTV) is that it is suitable only for products such as music compilations and cut-price jewellery. In Europe, a wide range of products, such as leisure and fitness products, motoring and household goods, books and beauty care products, are marketed in this way through pan-European channels such as Eurosport, Super Channel and NBC.

As with many other forms of direct marketing, the effectiveness of campaigns is highly measurable, which is attractive to advertisers, who are also able to avail themselves of the multiplicity of digital channels in order to target adverts more carefully.

Exhibit 10.3 The Macmillan Cancer Support 'Good Day,' campaign encouraged people living with cancer to avail themselves of their support services

Catalogue marketing

The sale of products through catalogues distributed to agents and customers, usually by mail or at stores if the catalogue marketer is a store owner, is known as **catalogue marketing**. This method is popular in Europe with such organizations as Germany's Otto-Versand, the Next Directory in the UK, La Redoute in France and IKEA in Sweden. Many of these companies operate in a number of countries; La Redoute, for instance, has operations in France, Belgium, Norway, Spain and Portugal. Catalogue marketing is popular in some countries where, for example, legislation restricts retail opening hours. A common form of catalogue marketing is mail order, where catalogues are distributed and, traditionally, orders received by mail. Some enterprising companies, notably Next, saw catalogue marketing as an opportunity to reach a new target market: busy, affluent, middle-class people who valued the convenience of choosing products at home.

Used effectively, catalogue marketing to consumers offers a convenient way of selecting products that allows discussion between family members in a relaxed atmosphere away from crowded shops and the high street. Often, credit facilities are available, too. Catalogue marketing was originally popular with consumers living in remote rural locations, obviating the need to travel long distances to town-based shopping centres. For catalogue marketers, the expense of high-street locations is removed and there is an opportunity to display a wider range of products than could feasibly be achieved in a shop. Distribution can be centralized, lowering costs. Nevertheless, catalogues are expensive to produce (hence the need for some retailers to charge for them) and they require regular updating, particularly when selling fashion items. They do not allow goods to be tried (e.g. a vacuum cleaner) or tried on (e.g. clothing) before purchase. Although products can be seen in a catalogue, variations in colour printing can mean that the curtains or suite that are delivered do not have exactly the same colour tones as those appearing on the printed page.

Catalogue marketing is big business. IKEA distributes 46 versions of its catalogue in 36 countries and in 28 languages, accounting for 50 per cent of its total promotional budget. Increasingly, catalogues are being made available online, which reduces the costs of production and distribution, and means that they can easily be updated; 45 per cent of Next Directory's business is now conducted online.

Digital marketing

As we saw in the previous chapter, new developments such as sponsorship and product placement are quickly embraced by the marketing community. Therefore, it is no surprise that the rapid growth of Internet and mobile technologies in society have also generated a great deal of excitement among marketers. At various junctures throughout this book we have examined the impact of these developments on marketing but here we will look at **digital marketing** in some more detail.

The growth of digital technologies over the past 15 years has been remarkable (see Table 10.1). The number of people around the world with some form of access to the Internet is growing rapidly and, in the developed world in particular, consumers have high-speed access through multiple devices. The amount of time being spent 'online' is also growing exponentially. Social networking sites like Facebook and Twitter account for twice as much of the time spent online as any other activity at 22.7 per cent with online gaming accounting for 10.2 per cent.[21] Facebook is a company that was founded in 2004 but it claims over 600 million members making it the fourth largest 'country' in the world. There are 190 million registered Twitter users and between April and July 2010, 15 billion tweets were posted. A 2010 TNS survey found that the most digitally engaged consumers lived in Eygpt, Saudi Arabia and China.[22] The growth in downloadable software applications or 'apps' has also been dramatic. In 2011, Apple's App Store was only three years old but already offered 300,000 apps.[23]

As a result, the types of business and marketing activities taking place through digital media are also developing rapidly. For example, during its early years, organizations tended to use the Internet in a similar manner to which they used other technologies such as television and the press. Company websites were generally like electronic versions of company brochures, describing what the company did and communicating the company's point of view to the marketplace. In addition, communications tended to be mainly one-way, from the company to the customer and were transactional rather than relational in nature. But the rapid growth in the number of websites and the ways in which consumers began to use the web meant that this has changed quickly. Figure 10.4 demonstrates the types of business opportunities that have emerged with the development of digital media.

As we saw in Chapter 3, businesses selling to other businesses (B2B) is a huge part of world commerce and many business-to-business exchanges have migrated to digital media. Corporations and government agencies manage their procurement electronically through vertical and horizontal exchanges such as covisint.com,

Figure 10.4 Digital media business opportunities

	From business	From consumer
To business	B2B covisint.com	C2B Priceline
To consumer	B2C Amazon ITunes Google	C2C eBay Facebook MySpace

Table 10.1 World Internet usage, 2010

World regions	Internet users	Penetration (%)	% growth (2000–10)	% of total users
Africa	110,931,700	10.9	2,357.3	5.6
Asia	825,094,396	21.5	621.8	42.0
Europe	475,069,448	58.4	352.0	24.2
Middle East	63,240,926	29.8	1,825.3	3.2
North America	266,224,500	77.4	146.3	13.5
Latin America/Caribbean	204,689,836	34.5	1,032.8	10.4
Oceania/Australia	21,263,900	61.3	179.0	1.1
World total	1,966,514,816	28.7	444.8	100.0

Source: Internetworldstats.com.

which is a horizontal marketplace for a variety of industries. They also manage their sales to corporate clients through dedicated intranet sites. Business-to-consumer (B2C) activity has also been huge with established retailers such as Tesco setting up home shopping facilities, and a variety of highly successful Internet-based companies, like Amazon, Yahoo! and Google, have emerged to dominate markets. One of the most novel applications of digital media has been the growth of consumer to business (C2B) activity. An example is the facility provided by Priceline.com whereby would-be travellers can bid for airline tickets, hotels and car hire, leaving the sellers to decide whether or not to accept these offers. Finally, digital media has revolutionized how people communicate and connect with each other giving rise to massive growth in consumer-to-consumer (C2C) activity. People trade with each other on eBay and some generate a living through full-time trading. Others make a living playing poker online. The Internet has been a great democratizing tool. Consumers are no longer just the recipients of what businesses have to offer. Innovation is not restricted to the organizations that choose to invest in new product and service development. Anyone with a business idea, a profitable pastime or just something to say now has a forum for doing it.

Digital media have several unique features that have helped to revolutionize marketing communications and these are summarized in Figure 10.5. These unique features make digital media a powerful marketing tool.

1 *Identification*: Digital media users are generally identifiable through processes such as website registrations, social media profiles etc.
2 *Instantaneous*: Through the use of WiFi-enabled devices such as smartphones and tablet PCs, communications are available instantly and content can be updated and changed as necessary.
3 *Interactivity*: We saw in Chapter 9 a linear model of communications where a communicator creates a message and a passive receiver decodes it. In a digital environment, the receiver may be active, participating in everything from one-to-one to many-to-many conversations such as when participating in a discussion on Twitter.
4 *Control*: Linked to interactivity is the notion of control. Digital media places significant control in the hands of the consumer who can decide what information she chooses to receive and has a vehicle for responding to these communications and expressing her opinion.
5 *Co-creation*: Because of its interactive nature, digital marketing content can be co-created through the combined efforts of marketers and consumers. As we saw in Chapter 9, consumer-generated advertising is a rapidly growing sector. Consumers become participants in marketing rather than recipients.

Types of digital marketing

Digital marketing is defined as the achievement of marketing objectives through the use of digital technologies. It can take many forms as shown in Figure 10.6.

Internet marketing

As we have seen throughout this book, marketing on the Internet or online marketing takes many forms. Consumers may respond to online customer satisfaction studies or buy products and services directly from online stores such as Amazon and Hotels.com. The Internet is also a powerful marketing communications tool. The organization's website plays an important role and those of consumer-focused companies try to increase customer engagement through their design, content and regular updates. Online advertising

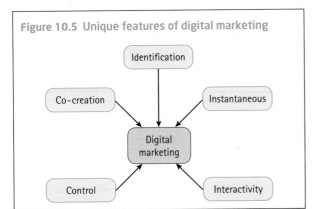

Figure 10.5 Unique features of digital marketing

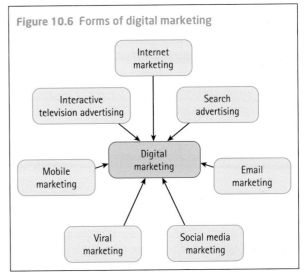

Figure 10.6 Forms of digital marketing

Exhibit 10.4 A highly emotional advertisement for Pantene shampoo made in Thailand became a huge YouTube hit

takes a variety of forms including display advertising (e.g. banner advertisements), rich media adverts (e.g. pop-up advertisements or interstitials – pop-up web pages), email advertising, search advertising (see next section) and online video advertising (e.g. YouTube) (see Exhibit 10.4). It continues to take an ever-growing share of advertising revenue. Internet advertising in the US is worth $23 billion and it comprises over 20 per cent of the advertising market in the UK ahead of outdoor, radio and cinema.[24]

Online advertising has the advantages of being relatively low cost, flexible (it can combine text, audio, video and animation) and it can be targeted at specific groups. Careful targeting of Internet adverts is increasing due to consumer irritation with the intrusiveness of banner advertising and pop-ups. The effectiveness of Internet advertising can be measured through click-through rates (the numbers clicking on a display advert, for example) and conversion rates (the numbers registering on a website, for example). However, click-through rates for banner adverts are now estimated to be as low as 0.002 per cent with the result that innovative new approaches to Internet advertising are being adopted. Simply placing banner adverts on popular websites is being replaced by real-time bidding where advertisement space buyers bid for the 'eyeballs' that are currently online in real time.[25]

Search advertising

The first port of call for most Internet users is the search engine or portal, where leading companies like Google, Yahoo! and Bing help browsers to find the sites that they are looking for. One of the fastest-growing sources of revenue for these companies is word sponsorship. This is the practice whereby the search engine sells key words such as 'holiday' or 'hotel' to the highest-bidding advertiser in an online auction. The buyer then 'owns' the key word, so that when an Internet user searches for that subject, the advertiser's site appears at the top of the list of websites turned up by the search.

'Paid search' advertising commands the biggest share of online advertising spend. Therefore, though web users typically spend only 5 per cent of their time online engaged in search activities, this sector has captured 40 per cent of the advertising revenues. People using search engines are usually looking for something specific and click-through rates are much higher on sponsored searches than on ordinary banner ads. It is also a relatively efficient form of promotion as advertisers pay on the basis of 'price per click'. Every time the user clicks through on a sponsored search link, the advertiser pays a small sum, which can be a few pence, although it can rise depending on the value of the product being sold.

However, it not necessary to buy key words in order to have your site returned in a search. **Search engine optimization (SEO)** is the practice of adjusting the website's structure and content to improve the position with which it turns up in a web search. Generally web users only look at the first page of search results so the position with which a website is returned in a search is very important. The main criteria 'favoured' by search engines are keywords and external links though these are constantly changing with the result that SEO has become big business. The effectiveness of search advertising is measured by click-through rates and revenue/click and it is viewed as being less intrusive than other forms of online advertising such as pop-ups.

Email marketing

Email or electronic mail shares much in common with its paper-based equivalent, direct mail. It is easy to use, costs little to produce and is virtually free to send. However, it also suffers from the same problem – junk mail or spam! Huge volumes of spam clog up email inboxes which has reduced the effectiveness of **email marketing**. It has also given rise to the concept of **permission marketing** which means that consumers opt to receive email communications from organizations. Where email is permission-based and personalized, it is much more likely to be effective. It can be used to communicate information, to build relationships through the content provided in e-zines (electronic magazines) and to generate revenues and referrals. Email communications should include some form of call-to-action (e.g. avail of a limited offer) so that their effectiveness can be measured.

Social media marketing

As we saw above, social media are among the fastest growing components of the Internet comprising social networks (Facebook, LinkedIn), video-sharing websites (YouTube, Vimeo), image-sharing websites (Flickr), blogs and microblogs (Twitter). **Social media marketing** is the use of these social media for communicating with and engaging customers online. Blogs have been popular for many years and remain a favoured way for engaging with stakeholders. Companies like IBM allow employees to blog about their experiences, what they are working on, and it highlights the people behind the products. Facebook is a useful forum to give consumers regular updates about products, with links to videos showing how to solve problems with products and to run competitions. For example, Dell created a social media site IdeaStorm to support their customers and solicit ideas on how the company can do better.

Social media are an increasingly popular vehicle for advertising. For example, advertising on Facebook can be narrowly targeted on criteria like age, gender, marital status, education, location and interests (all criteria that typically form part of an individual's Facebook profile). Advertisers can choose to pay per 1000 impressions or per click through. Similarly, Twitter is developing targeting technology that allows companies to show 'tweets' to users based on the kinds of people and brands that they are following.[26] One of the interesting dimensions of this is that Samsung could show tweets to users that follow Apple, for example. Advertising effectiveness is measured by click-through rates.

Many brands have been quick to adopt social media marketing with mixed results (see Social Media Marketing 10.1). Some key considerations need to be borne in mind when conducting social media marketing campaigns. The first issue is control. Whereas traditional marketing involved the creation and dissemination of marketing messages, social media marketing is co-created. Consumers can and do comment about brands, upload videos and blog and tweet about their experiences (see Exhibit 10.5). Brand managers no longer entirely control what is said about the brand. Secondly, engagement is important. Promotional ideas need to be created on the consumer's terms and need to be engaging in order to ensure consumer participation. For example, Gary Vaynerchuck's video blog, Wine Library TV, has made 1,000 episodes since it started in 2006, has an average of 80,000 viewers per episode and generated sales of US$50 million in 2008. Finally, trust and authenticity are important elements of social media communications in order to ensure consumer participation.

Exhibit 10.5 Dave Carroll's song and YouTube video about United Airlines breaking his guitar has been viewed over 10 million times demonstrating the speed with which negative comment about a company or brand can travel online

Social Media Marketing 10.1 Converting fans to sales!

Critical Thinking: Below is a review of some less than successful social media marketing campaigns. Critique it and consider the essential ingredients of an effective social media campaign.

Social media is truly the new kid on the integrated marketing communications block. Companies around the world are looking at best practice to figure out ways in which they can use popular websites like Facebook, Twitter and YouTube to connect with their customers and increase sales. They are increasingly being told that if they want to remain relevant to new generations of customers, they must engage with them in the media that they are using or else they will be out of touch.

However, many of the early forays of companies and brands into social media have met with decidedly mixed results. Along with the successes that we have highlighted throughout this book, there have been many notable failures too. For example, take the case of Pepsi. In 2010, it decided to shift as much as 50 per cent of its promotional budget into social media. At the heart of this new strategy was the Pepsi Refresh Project where consumers were encouraged to suggest social causes that would 'refresh the world' using social media websites and an iPhone application. Consumers could then vote for their favoured causes and Pepsi would donate millions to them. The consumer response was impressive with over 80 million votes registered, 4 million

'likes' on Facebook and over 60,000 Twitter followers. However, its social media success was accompanied by a fall in sales to its rival Coca-Cola whose Diet Coke brand has replaced Pepsi as the number two best-selling Cola for the first time.

Similarly questionable has been Cadbury's foray into the world of social media with its 'Spots vs Stripes' campaign. Launched in 2010 at a cost of £50 million and as part of its sponsorship of the London Olympics, the campaign had generated just over 200,000 'likes' on Facebook after one year. Just under 4,000 Twitter followers have also signed up. Sustaining interest all the way to the 2012 Games has proven to be difficult. Inevitably, as with all new media, there will be innovative successes as well as some high-profile failures. But social media too, may also have been a victim of its own hype. It would appear that it will become part of, rather than replace, traditional marketing communications, and that its role in an integrated communications mix needs to carefully considered before investments are made.

Based on: Parsons (2011);[27] Ritson (2011a);[28] Ritson (2011b);[29] Taylor, Lewin and Strutton (2011)[30].

Viral marketing

The widespread connectivity among consumers in social networks means that **viral marketing** has grown enormously. Most commonly associated with email and mobile devices, viral marketing is essentially electronic word-of-mouth promotion where jokes are shared among friends, or calls for action such as those in support of the Live8 concerts for poverty relief are publicized. Companies attempt to harness this viral effect by building messages that are suitably engaging and promote an aspect of their company with content that customers want to read and send on. This requires some creativity and a good understanding of the customer base. For example, as part of its 'Campaign for Real Beauty', Dove created a short film entitled

Evolution, which was viewed over 10 million times on YouTube.[31] Viral marketing can be very cheap to produce and highly effective because it is transferred from peer-to-peer and is therefore less likely to be rejected by a recipient than other electronic communications (see Exhibit 10.6).

'Giving something for nothing' is another effective means of increasing the viral effect. Hotmail grew its subscriber base from zero to 18 million in just 12 months by including the message 'Get your FREE email account at www.hotmail.com' at the end of each email. In this way, users of Hotmail became marketers for the company through every email they sent. The same strategy has been employed by Skype, whose software for making free telephone calls over the Internet has been downloaded millions of times since the company was

Exhibit 10.6 The Blendtec 'Will It Blend' series has been a hugely popular viral marketing campaign running since 2006 and has currently generated over 100 million hits on YouTube, Facebook and Twitter pages allow you to suggest items for the next blending challenge

founded in 2003. Companies like 5pm.co.uk send emails promoting specific off-peak restaurant deals, only redeemable through unique links noted on the email, with the intention that these will be passed on to 'new' customers.[32]

Mobile marketing

Mobile marketing refers to the creation and delivery of marketing communications through mobile devices. Early forms of mobile marketing focused on the sending of text messages containing advertising to recipients and this is still very popular. However, the wide variety of visual and Internet-enabled portable devices that are on the market such as smartphones, tablet PCs, e-readers and gaming devices are revolutionizing the mobile marketing business. One of the most rapidly growing forms of mobile marketing is smartphone applications (apps). For example, the deodorant brand Lynx, which is targeted mainly at young males, developed two mobile phone apps designed to help young guys be more successful with girls as part of their 'Get in There' campaign. The apps were downloaded over 350,000 times.

Mobile marketing has several advantages. First, it is very cost effective. The cost per message is between 15p and 25p, compared with 50p to 75p per direct mail shot, including print production and postage. Second, it can be targeted and personalized. For example, operators like Vodafone, Virgin Mobile and Blyk offer free texts and voice calls to customers if they sign up to receive some advertising. In signing up, customers have to fill out questionnaires on their hobbies and interests. Third, it is interactive: the receiver can respond to the

text message, setting up the opportunity for two-way dialogue and relationship development. Fourth, it is a time-flexible medium. Text messages can be sent at any time, giving greater flexibility when trying to reach the recipient. Fifth, it can allow marketers to engage in what is becoming known as **proximity marketing**. Messages can be sent to mobile users at nightclubs, shopping centres, festivals and universities, where recipients can immediately avail themselves of special offers. For example, the US consumer electronics retailer, Best Buy, sends special offers and deals to customer smartphones using a technology that pinpoints when they are entering a Best Buy store. Finally, like other direct marketing techniques, it is immediate and measurable, and can assist in database development.

Interactive television advertising

The growth of digital television has given rise to an increase in **interactive television (iTV) advertising**, whereby viewers are invited to 'press the red button' on their remote control handset to see more information about an advertised product. This form of advertising has a number of advantages. First, its effectiveness is highly measurable – advertisers can track the success of adverts displayed on different channels and at different times of the day. Second, it allows the targeting of niche audiences through specialist digital channels that focus on leisure activities such as sport, music and motoring. Third, it enables the provision of more in-depth information than a single television or press advertisement. Finally, it is convenient, allowing consumers to buy a product without having to use a telephone or computer.

In summary, digital marketing has risen in popularity due to the inherent benefits it offers to customers. The first of these is convenience. Access to a website is available 24 hours a day, seven days a week, and is significantly more convenient than offline distribution channels, which may involve driving, queuing, and so on. Second, the Internet is a global medium. Consumers can get easier access to products/information from different parts of the world than is possible through other channels. Third, it can provide excellent value. Price-comparison technologies allow consumers to search for the cheapest brands and to do immediate, real-time comparisons of the prices being charged by different vendors. Fourth, as the Internet is an information resource, it assists with the buying decision process by enabling consumers to evaluate alternative brands or service providers. Finally and perhaps most interesting of all has been how the Internet has changed so many industries like music, book publishing, travel, and so on. This pattern is likely to continue. Zipcar, an American car-sharing firm, has 400,000 members who choose to rent a car by the hour rather than owning it.[33]

Buzz marketing

The most recent form of direct marketing to emerge is what has become known as **buzz marketing**, which is defined as the passing of information about products and services by verbal or electronic means in an informal, person-to-person manner. For example, in the USA, Nintendo recruited suburban mothers to spread the word among their friends that the Wii was a gaming console that the whole family could enjoy together. Buzz marketing is similar to word-of-mouth marketing, long recognized as one of the most powerful forms of marketing, but it has enjoyed a renaissance due to advances in technology such as email, websites and mobile phones.

The first step in a buzz marketing campaign involves identifying and targeting 'alphas' – that is, the trend-setters that adopt new ideas and technologies early on – and the 'bees', who are the early adopters. Brand awareness then passes from these customers to others, who seek to emulate the trendsetters. In many instances, the alphas are celebrities who either directly or indirectly push certain brands. For example, the Australian footwear and accessories brand UGG became popular in the US and European markets when photographs of actresses like Sienna Miller and Cameron Diaz appeared in the media wearing these products. Celebrities may be paid to endorse products or simply popularize products through their own choices.

Critical to the success of buzz marketing is that every social group, whether it is online or offline, has trendsetters. The record company, Universal, successfully promoted its boy bands Busted and McFly by targeting these trendsetters. It recruited a 'school chairman' who was given the task of spreading the word about a particular band in their school. This involved giving out flyers, putting up posters on school noticeboards and then sending back evidence that this had been done. In return, the 'chairman' – who was typically a 12- to 15-year-old schoolgirl – was rewarded with free merchandise and a chance to meet members of the band.

Developments in technology have allowed the 'buzz' to spread very quickly. As we saw earlier, viral marketing is popular because of the speed with which advertising gets passed on via email. The launch of Apple's iPhone is a classic example of the power of buzz marketing. According to Nielsen's Buzz Metrics, which tracks English-language blogs, the product had more mentions than even the President of the USA around the time of its launch in January 2007, and had an entry on Wikipedia within minutes of it going on show.[34]

Once the target audience has been identified, the next key decisions, like those for all forms of promotion, are the message and the medium. The message may take many forms, such as a funny video clip or email attachment, a blog or story, an event such as a one-off concert, and so on. For example, Diageo launched Smirnoff Raw Tea in the USA with a video clip featuring a spoof hip hop song. The clip, entitled 'Smirnoff Tea Partay', has been one of the most popular on YouTube, with over 3.5 million views. The medium used for carrying the message is frequently online but could also be through offline means such as posters or flyers. But, as with all aspects of buzz marketing, the only limitation is the imagination. For example, many individuals have used parts of their bodies or their private cars to carry commercial messages.

Finally, given its novelty, evaluating the effectiveness of buzz marketing is difficult. Numbers are available regarding how many times a video clip is viewed but marketers will not be able to determine by whom.

Personal selling

The final major element of the promotional mix is personal selling. This involves face-to-face contact with a customer and, unlike advertising, promotion and other forms of non-personal communication, personal selling permits a direct interaction between buyer and seller. This two-way communication means that the seller can identify the specific needs and problems of the buyer and tailor the sales presentation in the light of this knowledge. The particular concerns of the buyer can also be dealt with on a one-to-one basis.

Such flexibility comes at a price, however. The cost of a car, travel expenses and sales office overheads can mean that the total annual bill for a field salesperson is often twice the level of a salary. In industrial marketing, over 70 per cent of the marketing budget is usually spent on the sales force. This is because of the technical nature of the products being sold, and the need to maintain close personal relationships between the selling and buying organizations.

The make-up of the personal selling function is changing, however. Organizations are reducing the size of their sales forces in the face of greater buyer concentration, moves towards centralized buying, and recognition of the high costs of maintaining a field sales team. The concentration of buying power into fewer hands has also fuelled the move towards relationship management, often through key account selling. This involves the use of a small number of dedicated sales teams, which service the accounts of major buyers as opposed to having a large number of salespeople. Instead of sending salespeople out on the road, many companies now collect a large proportion of their sales through direct marketing techniques such as the telephone or the Internet.

The three main types of salespeople are order-takers, order-creators and order-getters. Order-takers respond to already committed customers such as a sales assistant in a convenience store or a delivery salesperson. Order-creators have traditionally been found in industries like healthcare, where the sales task is not to close the sale but to persuade the medical representative to prescribe or specify the seller's products. Order-getters are those in selling jobs where the major objective is to persuade the customer to make a direct purchase. They include consumer salespeople such as those selling double glazing or insurance, through to organizational salespeople, who often work in teams where products may be highly technical and negotiations complex.

Personal selling skills

While the primary responsibility of a salesperson is to increase sales, there are a number of additional enabling activities carried out by many salespeople, including **prospecting**, maintaining customer records, providing service, handling complaints, relationship management and self-management. Prospecting involves searching for and calling on potential customers. Prospects can be identified from several sources including talking to existing customers, and searching trade directories and the business press. Customer record-keeping is an important activity for all repeat-call salespeople because customer information is one of the keys to improving service and generating loyalty. Salespeople should be encouraged and rewarded for sending customer and market information back to head office. Providing service to customers – including, for example, advice on ways of improving productivity and handling customer complaints – can also be a key sales force activity. This is particularly true in cases where the selling situation is not a one-off activity. In general, there has been a rise in the number of salespeople involved in relationship management roles with large organizational customers. Trust is an important part of relationship development and is achieved through a high frequency of contact, ensuring promises are kept, and reacting quickly and effectively to problems (see Marketing in Action 10.3). Finally, given the flexibility of the salesperson's job, many are required to practise

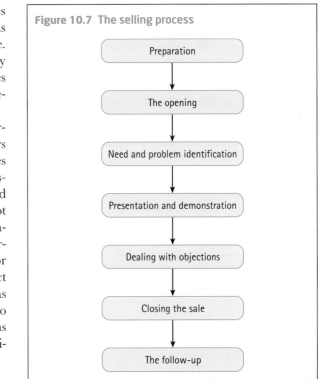

Figure 10.7 The selling process

- Preparation
- The opening
- Need and problem identification
- Presentation and demonstration
- Dealing with objections
- Closing the sale
- The follow-up

self-management, including decisions on call frequencies and journey routing, for example. Many people's perception of a salesperson is of a slick, fast-talking confidence trickster devoted to forcing unwanted products on gullible customers. In reality, success in selling comes from implementing the marketing concept when face to face with customers, not denying it at the very point when the seller and buyer come into contact. The sales interview offers an unparalleled opportunity to identify individual customer needs and match behaviour to the specific customer that is encountered.[35] In order to develop personal selling skills it is useful to distinguish seven phases of the selling process (see Figure 10.7). We will now discuss each of these in turn.

Preparation

The preparation carried out prior to a sales visit can reap dividends by enhancing confidence and performance when the salesperson is face to face with the customer. Some situations cannot be prepared for: the unexpected question or unusual objection, for example. But many customers face similar situations, and certain questions and objections will be raised repeatedly. Preparation can help the salesperson respond to these recurring situations. Salespeople will benefit from gaining knowledge of their own and competitors' products, by understanding buyer behaviour, by having clear sales call objectives and by having planned their sales

Marketing in Action 10.3 Cisco's brave new world

> **Critical Thinking:** Below is a review of some of Cisco's marketing efforts in the Middle East. Read it and critically reflect on the nature of modern personal selling.

Cisco Systems, the networking giant, sees a major part of its future growth coming from massive construction projects in the Middle East. One example is the creation of King Abdullah Economic City (KAEC) in Saudi Arabia. By 2020, the Saudis expect 2 million people to be living in a future metropolis supported by some of the most advanced technology that money can buy. All told, King Abdullah plans to build four brand new cities and upgrade the country's infrastructure at a cost of $6 billion over the coming years.

To tap into this vast potential, Cisco hired a well-connected local person to head the business in the country. He, in turn, hired salespeople and engineers, and got Cisco involved in major government projects. For the KAEC project, senior Cisco executives played host to the King for a demonstration of Cisco technology that allowed a person elsewhere to appear on stage as a holographic image. They realize, though, that Cisco is not just selling technology (a product feature). The real benefit is that it can help countries such as Saudi Arabia modernize their economies and become leaders in the Internet age. The company argues that, by investing in the Internet infrastructure that Cisco sells, these governments can better educate their people, improve healthcare and boost national productivity.

To achieve this, Cisco provides consulting services to help government officials work out how best to use the Internet, and pays for training centres to produce the technicians to implement such plans. Cisco is helping the leaders of countries like Saudi Arabia imagine the future, to bring about 'country transformations' and brainstorm big ideas. One example was the call to Cisco to help with a new broadband network for Sudair city, but a Cisco executive saw the potential of the city as a hub for vast computer data centres, based on its cheap electricity rates. The electricity bill is often the biggest expense in running such centres, which are increasingly important for Internet companies like Google and Amazon. The idea was well received and helped Cisco secure a $280 million contract to create the underlying fibre-optic network for Sudair city.

Based on: Burrows (2008).[36]

presentation. This is because the success of the sales interview is customer-dependent. The aim is to convince the customer; what the salesperson does is simply a means to that end.

The opening

It is important for salespeople to consider how to create a favourable initial impression with customers as this can often affect later perceptions. Good first impressions can be gained by adopting a businesslike approach, being friendly but not overly familiar, being attentive to detail, observing common courtesies like waiting to be asked to sit down and by showing the customer appreciation for having taken the time to see you.

Need and problem identification

Consumers will buy a product because they have a 'problem' that gives rise to a 'need'. Therefore the first task is to identify the needs and problems of each customer. Only by doing this can a salesperson connect with each customer's situation. Effective need and problem identification requires the development of questioning and listening skills. The hallmark of inexperienced salespeople is that they do all the talking; successful salespeople know how to get the *customer* to do most of the talking.

Presentation and demonstration

It is the presentation and demonstration that offers the opportunity for the salesperson to convince customers that they can supply the solution to their problem. It should focus on **customer benefits** rather than **product features**. The salesperson should continue to ask questions during the presentation to ensure that the customer has understood what he or she has said, and to check that what the salesperson has talked about really is of importance to the customer. This can be achieved by asking questions like 'Is that the kind of thing you are looking for?'

Dealing with objections

Salespeople rarely close a sale without first having to overcome customer objections. Although objections can cause problems, they should not be regarded negatively since they highlight issues that are important to the buyer. The secret of dealing with objections is to handle both the substantive and emotional aspects. The substantive part is to do with the objection itself. If the customer objects to the product's price the salesperson needs to use convincing arguments to show that the price is not too high. But it is a fact of human personality that the argument that is supported by the greater weight of evidence does not always win since people resent being proven wrong. Therefore, salespeople need to recognize the emotional aspects of objection handling. Under no circumstances should the buyer be caused to lose face or be antagonized during this process. Two ways of minimizing this risk are to listen to the objection without interruption and to employ the 'agree and counter' technique, where the salesperson agrees with the buyer but then puts forward an alternative point of view.

Closing the sale

The inexperienced salesperson will sometimes imagine that an effective presentation followed by the convincing handling of any objections should guarantee that the buyer will ask for the product without the seller needing to work to close the sale. This does occasionally happen but, more often, it is necessary for the salesperson to take the initiative. This is because many buyers still have doubts in their minds that may cause them to wish to delay the decision to purchase. Closing techniques include simply asking for the order, summarizing the key points and asking for the order, or offering a special deal to close the sale (the concession close).

The follow-up

Once an order has been placed there may be a temptation for the salesperson to move on to other customers, neglecting the follow-up visit. However, this can be a great mistake since most companies rely on repeat business. If problems arise, customers have every right to believe that the salesperson was interested only in the order, and not their complete satisfaction. By checking that there are no problems with delivery, installation, product use and training (where applicable), the follow-up can show that the salesperson really does care about the customer.

Sales management

Because of the unique nature of the selling job, sales management is a challenging activity. For example, many salespeople spend a great deal of their time in the field, separated from their managers, while others may suffer repeated rejections in trying to close sales, causing them to lose confidence. Therefore, the two main aspects of the sales manager's job are designing the sales force and managing the sales force.

Designing the sales force

The critical design decisions are determining sales force size and organizing the sales force. The most practical method for deciding the number of salespeople required is called the 'workload approach'. It is based on the calculation of the total annual calls required per year divided by the average calls per year that can be expected from one salesperson.[37]

There are three alternative approaches to organizing the sales force. A *geographic* structure is where the sales area is broken down into territories based on workload and potential, and a salesperson is assigned to each one to sell all of the product range. This provides a simple, unambiguous definition of each salesperson's sales territory, and the proximity to customers encourages the development of personal relationships. A *product* structure might be effective where a company has a diverse product range selling to different customers (or at least different people within a given organization). A *customer-based* structure is where sales forces are organized on the basis of market segments, account sizes or new versus existing account lines. This structure enables salespeople to acquire in-depth knowledge of particular customer groups.

A growing form of customer-based sales force organization is **key account management**, which reflects the increasing concentration of buying power into fewer but larger customers. These are serviced by a key account sales force comprising senior salespeople who develop close personal relationships with customers, can handle sophisticated sales arguments and are skilled in the art of negotiation. A number of advantages are claimed for a key account structure, including that it enables close working relationships with customers, improved communication and co-ordination, better follow-up on sales and service, more in-depth penetration of the DMU, higher sales and the provision of an opportunity for advancement for career salespeople.

Managing the sales force

The following elements are involved in sales force management: setting specific salesperson objectives; recruitment and selection; training; **sales force motivation** and **compensation**; and **sales force evaluation**. These activities have been shown to improve salesperson performance, indicating the key role that sales managers play as facilitators, helping salespeople to perform better. Sales objectives are usually set in sales terms (sales quotas) but, increasingly, profit targets are being used, reflecting the need to guard against sales being bought cheaply by excessive discounting. The importance of recruiting high calibre salespeople cannot be overestimated. A study of sales force practice asked sales managers the following question: 'If you were to put your most successful salesperson into the territory of one of your average salespeople and made no other changes, what increase in sales would you expect after, say, two years?'[38] The most commonly stated increase was 16–20 per cent, and one-fifth of all sales managers said they would expect an increase of over 30 per cent. Based on extensive research, Mayer and Greenberg reduced the number of qualities believed to be important for effective selling to empathy and ego drive.[39] These are the kinds of qualities that need to be looked for in new salespeople.

It is believed by many sales managers that their salespeople can best train themselves by just doing the job. This approach ignores the benefits of a training programme, which can provide a frame of reference in which learning takes place. Training should include not only product knowledge, but also skills development. Success at selling comes when the skills are performed automatically, without consciously thinking about them, just as a tennis player or footballer succeeds.

A deep understanding of salespeople as individuals, their personalities and value systems, is the basis for effective motivation. Managers can motivate their sales staff by getting to know what each salesperson values and what they are striving for, increasing the responsibility given to salespeople in mundane jobs, providing targets that are attainable and challenging, and recognizing that rewards can be both financial and non-financial (e.g. praise). In terms of financial rewards, sales staff can be paid either a fixed salary, commission only, or on a salary-plus commission basis. Salaries provide security while commissions are an incentive to sell more as they are directly tied to sales levels. Great care must be taken in designing commission and bonus structures. For example, a Chrysler car dealership in the USA found that monthly sales for April were significantly down because salespeople who knew that they would not hit their targets for that month were encouraging customers to delay sales until May in hope of getting the May bonus.[40]

Sales force evaluation gathers the information required to check whether targets are being achieved and provides raw information that will help guide training and motivation. By identifying the strengths and weaknesses of individual salespeople, training can be focused on the areas in need of development, and incentives can be aimed at weak spots such as poor prospecting performance. Often, performance will be measured on the basis of quantitative criteria such as sales revenues, profits generated or number of calls. However, it is also important to use qualitative criteria such as sales skills acquired, customer relationships, product knowledge and self-management.

When you have read this chapter

log on to the Online Learning Centre for *Foundations of Marketing* at
www.mcgraw-hill.co.uk/textbooks/fahy
where you'll find links and extra online study tools for marketing.

Summary

This chapter has provided an overview of direct communications techniques and digital marketing. In particular, the following issues were addressed.

1. The marketing database is the foundation upon which direct marketing campaigns are built. Databases can contain customer and prospect information, transactional information, product information, promotional information and geodemographic information. Technological developments have greatly assisted with database development.

2. Customer relationship management is an outgrowth of database marketing and describes the use of technologies to build and foster relationships with customers. CRM aims to provide an up-to-date single point of view for each customer.

3. Direct marketing is where consumers are precisely targeted through a variety of different techniques including direct mail, telemarketing, mobile marketing, direct response advertising and catalogue marketing. Direct marketing provides many advantages to companies, such as the ability to target customers directly, to run cost-effective campaigns and to allow the effectiveness of campaigns to be easily measurable.

4. Digital marketing continues to grow rapidly. It has five main characteristics, namely, easy identification of targets, interactivity, instantaneous communications, consumer control and co-creation of outputs.

5. There are seven major forms of digital marketing, namely, Internet marketing, search advertising, email marketing, social media marketing, viral marketing, mobile marketing and interactive television advertising.

6. Buzz marketing is an emerging marketing tool that capitalizes on the importance of word-of-mouth promotion. Greater global electronic connectivity has fostered the rise of buzz marketing.

7. Personal selling plays an important role in the promotional mix and salespeople are required to develop a range of selling skills including preparing for the sale, opening the sale, identifying customer needs and problems, presenting and demonstrating, dealing with objections, closing the sale and following up. Sales management involves designing and managing a sales team.

Study questions

1. Discuss the differences between database marketing and customer relationship management.
2. Companies now have a variety of direct marketing media that they can consider when planning a direct marketing campaign. Compare and contrast any two direct marketing media. In your answer, give examples of the kinds of markets in which the media you have chosen might be useful.
3. Discuss the role of social media as marketing tools. How is marketing on social media similar and different from traditional marketing?
4. What is meant by buzz marketing? Discuss the elements of an effective buzz marketing campaign.
5. Salespeople are born, not made. Discuss.
6. Visit www.amazon.com and www.iTunes.com. Review these websites, and compare and contrast the marketing strategies employed by these global Internet leaders.

Suggested reading

Barwise, P. and **S. Meehan** (2010) The One Thing You Must Get Right When Building a Brand, *Harvard Business Review*, **88** (12), 80–4.

Godin, S. (2000) *Unleashing the Ideavirus*, New York: Do You Zoom Inc.

Kaikati, A.M. and **J.G. Kaikati** (2004) Stealth Marketing: How to Reach Customers Surreptitiously, *California Management Review*, **46** (4), 6–23.

Kaplan, A. and **M. Haenlein** (2011) The Early Bird Catches the News: Nine Things You Should Know about Micro-blogging, *Business Horizons*, **54**, 105–13.

Leibowitz, J. (2010) Rediscovering the Art of Selling, *McKinsey Quarterly*, October, 1–3.

Ramaswamy, V. and **F. Gouillart** (2010) Building the Co-creative Enterprise, *Harvard Business Review*, **88** (10), 100–9.

Rigby, D.K. and **D. Ledingham** (2004) CRM Done Right, *Harvard Business Review*, **82** (11), 118–28.

Shankar, V. and **S. Balasubramanian** (2009) Mobile Marketing: A Synthesis and Prognosis, *Journal of Interactive Marketing*, **23** (2), 118–29.

References

1. **Alarcon, C.** (2009) T-Mobile Ads Focus on Value-Added Extras, *MarketingWeek.co.uk*, 4 September; **Emap** (2011) T-Mobile: Singalong, *Warc.com;* **Fernandez, J.** (2010) T-Mobile to Launch User-Generated Music Video Ad, *MarketingWeek.co.uk*, 14 January.

2. **Stone, M., D. Davies** and **A. Bond** (1995) *Direct Hit: Direct Marketing with a Winning Edge*, London: Pitman.

3. **Harvey, F.** (2003) They Know What You Like, *Financial Times*, Creative Business, 6 May, 4.

4. **London, S.** (2004) Choked by a Data Surfeit, *Financial Times*, 29 January, 17.

5. **Nancarrow, C., L.T. Wright** and **J. Page** (1997) Seagram Europe and Africa: The Development of a Consumer Database Marketing Capability, *Proceedings of the Academy of Marketing*, July, Manchester, 1119–30.

6. **Rothery, G.** (2010) About Face, *Marketing Age*, **4** (2), 22–5.

7. **Turow, J.** (2008) *Niche Envy: Marketing Discrimination in the Digital Age*, Boston MA: MIT.

8. **Murphy, C.** (2002) Catching up with its Glitzier Cousin, *Financial Times*, 24 July, 13.

9. **Foss, B.** and **M. Stone** (2001) *Successful Customer Relationship Marketing*, London: Kogan Page.

10. See **Ryals, L., S. Knox** and **S. Maklan** (2002) *Customer Relationship Management: Building the Business Case*, London: FT Prentice-Hall; **H. Wilson, E. Daniel** and **M. McDonald** (2002) Factors for Success in Customer Relationship Management Systems, *Journal of Marketing Management*, **18** (1/2), 193–200.

11. **Direct Marketing Association** (2010) Mothercare UK: Baby & Me Club, *Warc.com*.

12. **Mortimer, R.** (2011) The Best Medicine for a Sick Baby and Child Chain is Retail Therapy, *MarketingWeek.co.uk*, 26 May.

13. **Curtis, J.** (2003) Down, But a Bit Up, *Financial Times*, Creative Business, 15 April, 4–5.

14. **Elgie, D.** (2003) A is for Ad Agency Angst . . . , *Financial Times*, Creative Business, 6 May, 11.

15. **Clegg, A.** (2000) Hit or Miss, *Marketing Week*, 13 January, 45–9.

16. **Benady, D.** (2001) If Undelivered, *Marketing Week*, 20 December, 31–3.

17. **McHatton, N.R.** (1988) *Total Telemarketing*, New York: Wiley, 269.

18. **Anonymous** (2007) GMTV Hit with £2m Phone-in Fine, *bbc.co.uk*, 26 September.

19. **Martin, N.** (2007) Ofcom Fines GMTV £2m in Phone-in Row, *Telegraph.co.uk*, 27 September.

20. **McCann, G.** (2003) Just Like Members of the Family, *Financial Times*, 15 January, 13.

21. **Ostrov, A.** (2010) Social Networking Dominates our Time Spent Online, *Mashable.com*, August 2.

22. **Bradshaw, T.** (2010) Social Networks Dominate Emerging Online Markets, *Financial Times*, 11 October, 24.

23. **Anonymous** (2011) Another Digital Gold Rush, *The Economist*, 14 May, 73–5.

24. **Brennan, A.** (2009) Destination Digital, *Marketing Age*, May-June, 50–4.

25. **Anonymous** (2011) Mad Men are Watching You, *The Economist*, 7 May, 59–60.

26. **Bradshaw, T.** (2010) Twitter Looks to Tweak Service so Advertisers can Target Users, *Financial Times*, 22 September, 24.

27. **Parsons, R.** (2011) Social Media Debate will Continue Until it Enters the DM Fold, *MarketingWeek.co.uk*, 8 August.

28. **Ritson, M.** (2011a) When it Comes to Social Media, Coke Is It, *MarketingWeek.co.uk*, 7 April.

29. **Ritson, M.** (2011b) What if Your Customers are Silent Types? *MarketingWeek.co.uk*, 13 April.

30. **Taylor, D., J. Lewin** and **D. Strutton** (2011) Friends, Fans and Followers. Do Ads Work on Social Networks? *Journal of Advertising Research*, **51** (1), 258–75.

31. **Smith, G.** and **A. O'Dea** (2007) Word of Mouse, *Marketing Age*, Autumn, 20–6.

32. **Anonymous** (2003) EU Rules to Outlaw Spam, *Marketing Business*, May.

33. **Anonymous** (2010) The Business of Sharing, *The Economist*, 16 October, 71.

34. **Grande, C.** (2007) iPhone Presents a Test Case for Media Buyers, *Financial Times*, 30 January, 22.

35. **Weitz, B.A.** (1981) Effectiveness in Sales Interactions: A Contingency Framework, *Journal of Marketing*, 45, 85–103.

36. **Burrows, P.** (2008) Cisco's Brave New World, *Business Week*, 24 November, 57–68.

37. **Talley, W.J.** (1961) How to Design Sales Territories, *Journal of Marketing*, **25** (3), 16–28.

38. **PA Consultants** (1979) *Sales Force Practice Today: A Basis for Improving Performance*, Cookham: Institute of Marketing.

39. **Mayer, M.** and **G. Greenberg** (1964) What Makes a Good Salesman, *Harvard Business Review*, **42** (July/August), 119–25.

40. **Griffith, V.** (2001) Targets that Distort a Company's Aim, *Financial Times*, 21 November, 18.

Case 10 Captain Morgan: the role of social media in building successful brands

Introduction

Previously known as Morgan's Spiced, Captain Morgan Original Spiced Gold is a spirits brand produced by the world's leading premium drinks business Diageo. Diageo is the owner of some of the biggest drinks brands in the world, such as Smirnoff, Johnnie Walker, Guinness, Baileys, J&B, Jose Cuervo, Bushmills, Tanqueray and Captain Morgan. Inspired by the seventeenth-century Welsh buccaneer, Captain Henry Morgan (1635–88) who eventually became Governor of Jamaica, Captain Morgan Spiced Gold was first launched in the US in 1983.[1] The Captain Morgan brand is the third biggest spirit in the US and the fastest growing spirit brand within the top 20 globally.[2]

In 2008, Diageo Ireland announced the relaunch of Morgan's Spiced, under the brand name Captain Morgan Original Spiced Gold, into the Irish market to tie it in line with its brand name and identity in other worldwide markets. Central to its new brand identity is the character Captain Morgan who is used to give the brand a unique identifiable personality. He is promoted as someone with a fun-loving personality, who symbolizes legendary times and fun. Diageo see him as someone who appeals to the target market for the brand – 18- to 24-year-olds. The addition of the Captain Morgan figurehead to the title and the label of the brand is seen to be vitally important in distinguishing the brand in the ever-competitive spirits marketplace.[1]

At the time of its Irish launch, Graham Villiers-Tuthill, Captain Morgan brand manager, emphasized: 'Captain Morgan is an iconic brand which is all about fun and partying. The Captain Morgan character has celebrity status in the US and other markets and we are introducing this rebellious, yet playful personality through our digital and on-trade activity. Captain Morgan will appeal to our consumers not only for being a well-known premium-quality brand, but also as a legendary partner.'[1]

The growth of personal and participation media

When launching Captain Morgan into the Irish market, Diageo were conscious of the fact that the global marketplace was evolving and this affected the way consumers lived and interacted with brands. As the world went online, a whole new media stream opened up to feed a dynamic marketplace. Diageo realized they had to integrate the role of social media into their 360° strategy to build a broader range of engaging activities and two-way dialogue with consumers. In addition, they began to place more emphasis on experiential marketing and social diffusion activities. Diageo wanted to forge ahead of the competition with marketing innovations in viral, digital and experience-based platforms and up-weighted their spend in the digital space.[3]

Diageo wanted to appeal to the target market by involving them in memorable, shared experiences by using social media and online endeavours to promote the Captain Morgan brand in Ireland. Research indicated that their target audience spends significant time online, so creating an Irish

Facebook page was seen as a natural progression for the brand. Facebook was given a specific role within the Captain's communications strategy and the Captain Morgan Ireland Facebook page was established (www.facebook.com/CaptainMorganIreland). The Captain would run the Facebook page and his playful tone would be maintained throughout all communications. A carefully orchestrated online campaign evolved through the 'Dare the Captain', 'The Captain's Cup' and 'The Rose of Tralee' initiatives (outlined later), video and photo collateral and word-of-mouth, driven by social media, all of which have contributed to its success.[4]

The 'Dare the Captain' campaign

The Dare the Captain campaign was launched in Ireland on the 15 October 2009, at a time when the Captain Morgan Ireland fan page had only 1,180 fans. The purpose of the campaign was to drive word-of-mouth and lead to an increase in Irish fan numbers online. The campaign focused on encouraging Irish fans to literally Dare the Captain to do something legendary when he was next in Ireland. The winning dare would be carried out by the Captain, filmed and uploaded on Facebook. The winning darer would win €1,000, with the best two runners-up getting an 8GB new generation iPod Nano.[5]

The competition launched on the Captain Morgan Ireland Facebook page where the Captain appeared in a series of short videos explaining the concept. This activity was complemented by online advertising and by a partnership with Metro AM – Dublin's free distribution and online advertising newspaper. Metro AM has a circulation of 100,000 and represents the perfect media fit for the Captain to reach its target audience in an engaging way. The newspaper content was used to encourage consumers to become a fan and to drive consumers to the new Irish fan page. Captain Morgan posted a reminder clip on Facebook to keep the fans interested and engaged with the idea.[4] This was supported by regular posts and continued interaction with fans as they posted their dare suggestions. Hundreds of dare suggestions were posted and the honour of overall winner went to Carl Malone from Wicklow, who dared the Captain to go to the Wax Museum and scare passers-by! The Captain travelled to Dublin to the Wax Museum and performed the winning dare which was posted on the Captain's Irish Facebook page and went viral on YouTube. The campaign proved very successful for the Captain Morgan brand. Interaction rates increased by 300 per cent during the campaign and the Dare campaign delivered 10,561 fans in two weeks – an excellent result, given little or no heavyweight advertising support. Further evidence of this success comes from the fact that from July to December 2009, Captain Morgan Irish sales increased 102 per cent year on year and the brand grew an entire share point within the total spirits market.[5]

The 'Captain's Cup' campaign

Following on from the success of the Dare the Captain campaign, Diageo were eager to sustain this online and offline interest in the Captain Morgan brand. As a result, another Facebook promotion for the Captain Morgan brand, the 'Captain's Cup' campaign was launched in early 2010. This three-month global initiative was focused on finding four people – an Irish captain and three crew members – to represent Ireland at the Captain's Cup final in South Africa in July 2010. The Irish finalists would join finalists from nine other countries for a fun-filled all expenses paid week with the Captain in South Africa. Competitors wishing to travel to the finals in South Africa first had to complete some fun and quirky challenges online via a competition app on the Captain Morgan Ireland Facebook page to make it to the National Finals. The launch of this campaign and the search for an Irish crew were launched by Diageo via traditional PR, and personalized mail drops were created for the media to generate interest and online coverage.

The competition would see each national team participate in challenges designed to test their team spirit, good humour and adventurous nature, and would reveal the Captain in them.[6] A sold-out National Finals party was held to announce the Irish winning team and this party was exclusively open to Facebook fans only. In total, 448 teams registered for this competition, with 35,000 unique views of the Captain's Cup app and around 1,500 unique Facebook page impressions. There was also good news for the Irish team in South Africa as the Irish team took home the Captain's Cup defeating nine other nations along the way.[5,7]

The 'Rose of Tralee' campaign

In an attempt to connect further with their Irish target market, Diageo wanted to associate the Captain with a uniquely Irish event and the Rose of Tralee International Festival was seen to fit that role. The Rose of Tralee Festival is an annual international competition, which is celebrated among Irish communities all over the world, with the objective of choosing a young woman to be crowned the Rose of Tralee. Each contestant is appointed an escort who accompanies them throughout the festivities. In July 2010, Diageo rallied the Captain's Irish fans to petition to get him made an escort for the Rose of Tralee Festival. Since the Captain is all about the unexpected, it was felt that his appearance at the Rose of Tralee Festival would be a major talking point and would generate media coverage for the Captain and for the brand. A petition was set up for Facebook fans to sign and this was used as a PR hook to campaign the media and the public to get the Captain to Tralee.[5] Following this petition on his Irish Facebook page and negotiations with the festival organizers, the Captain was made an 'honorary escort' at the 2010 Rose of Tralee Festival. His role involved providing mentoring support and relationship counselling to the 32 escorts while also looking after each and every one of the Roses. Captain Morgan was also checking out the festivities in Tralee over the entire weekend. His antics from the week in Tralee were posted diary-style on the Captain's Facebook page and his appearance at the festival generated substantial mainstream media coverage, which proved very positive for the brand. This Rose of Tralee campaign illustrated how a simple Facebook petition could lead to traditional media coverage in the national newspapers.[8]

Conclusion

The year 2010 proved to be very positive for the Captain Morgan brand. Diageo achieved huge exposure for the Captain and the Captain Morgan brand through the use of online and social media campaigns. By the end of 2010, the Captain Morgan Facebook page had 82,000 fans, the highest number of fans per capita of the 23 Captain Morgan markets, including the USA! Building on this success, Diageo is continuing to use the Captain Morgan Ireland Facebook page to further engage with existing fans and to increase their fan base.[5]

The Facebook page is being used to upload videos and photos, to announce weekly competitions, to inform fans of upcoming events and for unprompted fan interaction. For example, the Facebook page is used by the Captain to issue VIP invitations to private bar staff sampling events. These VIP invitations are in great demand as they cannot be bought. All sampling events are also used to recruit additional fans for the page by taking consumers' pictures at the events and uploading them to the Facebook page where consumers can find and tag themselves. This allows the Captain Morgan Ireland content to spread virally throughout Facebook. Photos have proved to be one of the most popular features on the page, with 900-plus daily hits![9] Diageo are also constantly creating new viral video content for their Captain Morgan Ireland Facebook page. As he travels around the world, the Captain creates short films on a flip camera, which are broadcast on the page to create new content and engage specifically with Irish fans (see www.captaintv.ie). The video clips contribute to making the Irish fan page a successful embodiment of the brand and assist in further developing the characteristics of Captain Morgan in the Irish market.[9]

References

1. www.businessleadership.com/marketing/item/ 11577-captain-morgan-lands-in-ire.
2. proof.sltn.co.uk/2011/05/12/captain-aims-to-capture-success/.
3. www.designcognition.com/2010/06/leverging-captain-morgans-brand-packaging-assets-through-new-media/.
4. www.whpr.ie/our_work/digital_marketing_social_media/ captain_morgan_ireland_facebook/.
5. Ogilvy PR Worldwide (2010) Captain Morgan Ireland's First Year on Facebook.
6. www.zimbio.com/Captain+Morgan/articles/txApK7oBkcW/ Captain+Morgan+Needs+YOU
7. www.drinksindustryireland.ie/article.aspx?id=1400
8. www.drinksindustryireland.ie/article.aspx?id=1473
9. WHPR (2010) 'Captain Morgan Ireland Launch on Facebook – Best Use of Online PR', PRII Awards 2010 application.

Questions

1. Evaluate the importance of the Captain Morgan character to the brand's identity. Do you think the character appeals to the 18- to 24-year-old target market? Why?
2. Why do you think Diageo shied away from using 'traditional' advertising media to promote the Captain Morgan brand in the Irish market? Why were online and social media relied upon so heavily?
3. The 'Dare the Captain', 'Captain's Cup' and 'Rose of Tralee' campaigns proved very successful in increasing the brand's online fans. Describe and evaluate the objectives of these social media campaigns.
4. View the Captain Morgan Ireland Facebook page (www.facebook.com/CaptainMorganIreland). Comment on the various initiatives being used on this page to engage with its target market.

This case was written by Marie O' Dwyer, Lecturer in Marketing, Waterford Institute of Technology, Ireland as a basis for class discussion rather than to illustrate either effective or ineffective management. Special thanks to Leighton Wall, Diageo Ireland for his assistance in writing this case.

A new Marketing Showcase video featuring an exclusive interview with Diageo's Global Brand Director for Captain Morgan rum is available for presentation and discussion in class. In the video, Diageo's Global Brand Director talks to Professor John Fahy about how one of the world's largest drinks companies engages with consumers to stay ahead of the competition. Go to **www.mcgraw-hill.co.uk/textbooks/fahy**

Chapter 11
Distribution: Delivering Customer Value

Chapter outline

Types of distribution channel

Channel integration

Retailing

Key retail marketing decisions

Physical distribution

Learning outcomes

By the end of this chapter you will understand:

1 the different types of distribution channel for consumer goods, industrial products and services
2 the three components of channel strategy – channel selection, intensity and integration
3 the five key channel management issues – member selection, motivation, training, evaluation and conflict management
4 the key retailing management decisions
5 the key issues in managing the physical distribution system.

MARKETING SPOTLIGHT

Amazon

Amazon.com was founded in 1995 and with its worldwide presence it has become an Internet phenomenon. The company began life as an online bookstore during the first phase of growth of the Internet. Its distinctive value proposition was relatively simple. Bookstores, even very large ones, were limited by the range of the stock that they could carry and had high fixed costs in buildings, rents, etc., while a virtual bookstore could potentially carry an unlimited supply of books with a much lower cost base. The strength of this proposition became evident when many Internet businesses failed after the dot.com bust of 2000 while Amazon posted its first profit in 2002.

Since then the company's business has expanded enormously and it is now a widely diversified retailer. Music and entertainment products, consumer electronics, toys and games, household items, clothing, sporting goods and even groceries/gourmet foods and cloud computing among many other products and services have become part of the portfolio. A key element of its rapid expansion has been to allow third party partners to sell products and services through the Amazon site. This was a very risky strategy for the company initially as it gave a platform for customers to view the offerings of competitors. However, the company's founder, Jeff Bezos, has consistently argued that Amazon puts its customers first and that the purchase options provided by third-party suppliers improve the customer's experience. By 2004, 26 per cent of Amazon's sales were accounted for by third parties.

High levels of customer service and efficient order fulfilment are critical elements of the Amazon success story. For example, its extensive book collection is available to customers, 24/7, 365 days per year. Improved browsing options, extensive book reviews, 1-click shopping (where customer details are retained) and gift certificates have all been successful customer service initiatives. Given that it is responsible for moving millions of items around the world, it has invested heavily in its supply chain management capabilities. It developed complex algorithms to determine relationships between items that people bought and grouped these items together in warehouses. Increasingly, it sells products that are stored in other people's warehouses, further reducing costs. Amazon is sometimes described as a low-cost operator with a passion for the customer and as a company that is willing to take a small profit on each transaction to build loyalty and trust.

Through offering customers a combination of a very wide selection, shopping convenience, discounted pricing and reliable order fulfilment, Amazon has become a huge global brand. By 2011, the company was valued at US$100 billion generating profits of US$7 billion on revenues of over US$40 billion. Relentless innovation in both products (e.g. its Kindle e-book reader) and services (e.g. the Amazon Prime loyalty programme that offers free shipping of all items within two days for an annual fee) are designed to maintain its lead ahead of both offline and online rivals.[1]

As we have seen throughout the book, several activities need to be conducted in order for organizations to market themselves effectively, including generating customer insights, developing differential products and services, pricing them correctly and communicating with customers. Important decisions also need to be made regarding how products and services are made available to customers. For example, in consumer markets significant shifts in buying habits are taking place such as online purchasing and the increased proportion of expenditure on foods being absorbed by supermarkets. In general, products need to be available in adequate quantities, in convenient locations and at times when customers want to buy them. In this chapter we will examine the functions and types of distribution channel, the key decisions that determine channel strategy, how to manage channels, the nature of retailing and issues relating to the physical flow of goods through distribution channels (physical distribution management).

Producers need to consider the requirements of **channel intermediaries** – those organizations that facilitate the distribution of products to customers – as well as the needs of their ultimate customers. For example, success for Müller yoghurt in the UK was dependent on convincing a powerful retail group (Tesco) to stock the brand. The high margins that the brand supported were a key influence in Tesco's decision. Without retailer support, Müller may have found it uneconomic to supply consumers with its brand. Clearly, establishing a supply chain that is efficient and meets customers' needs is vital to marketing success (see Marketing Spotlight). This supply chain is termed a **channel of distribution**, and is the means by which products are moved from the producer to the ultimate customer. Gaining access to distribution outlets is not necessarily easy. For example, in the consumer food products sector, many brands vie with each other for prime positions on supermarket shelves (see Exhibit 11.1).

An important aspect of marketing strategy is choosing the most effective channel of distribution. The development of supermarkets effectively shortened the distribution channel between producer and consumer by eliminating the wholesaler. Prior to their introduction, the typical distribution channel for products like food, drink, tobacco and toiletries was producer to wholesaler to retailer. The wholesaler would buy in bulk from the producer and sell smaller quantities to the retailer (typically a small grocery shop). By building up buying power, supermarkets could shorten this chain by buying direct from producers. This meant lower costs to the supermarket chain and lower prices to the consumer. The competitive effect of this was to drastically reduce the numbers of small grocers and wholesalers in this

Exhibit 11.1 Eye-level is the best position to have in a shopping aisle and brands will compete aggressively to gain and hold these positions

market. By being more efficient and better at meeting customers' needs, supermarkets had created a competitive advantage for themselves which they have been able to retain for many years.

We will now explore the different types of channel that manufacturers use to supply their products to customers, and the types of function provided by these channel intermediaries.

Types of distribution channel

Whether they be consumer goods, business-to-business goods or services, all products require a channel of distribution. Industrial channels tend to be shorter than consumer channels because of the small number of ultimate customers, the greater geographic concentration of industrial customers and the greater complexity of the products that require close producer/customer liaison. Service channels also tend to be short because of the inseparability of the production and consumption of many services.

Figure 11.1 Distribution channels for consumer goods

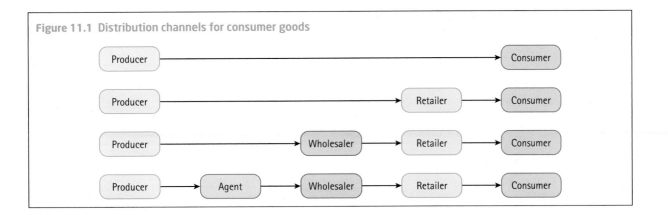

Consumer channels

Figure 11.1 shows four alternative consumer channels. We will now look briefly at each one in turn.

Producer direct to consumer

This option may be attractive to producers because it cuts out distributors' profit margins. Direct selling between producer and consumer has long been a feature of the marketing of many products, ranging from the sale of fruit in local markets to the sale of Avon Cosmetics and Tupperware plastic containers. It is a form of distribution that is starting to grow rapidly again. Concerns over food quality in supermarkets and a growing market for organic foods have seen a rapid rise in farmers' markets in Europe. And of course, in the past 20 years or so, the Internet has been the great new direct distribution medium for products ranging from books and music to DVDs to air travel, and so on. This has had huge implications for traditional retailers like book shops, music shops and travel agents, many of whom have suffered falling sales or have ceased trading.

Producer to retailer to consumer

For a variety of reasons, a producer may choose to distribute products via a retailer to consumers. Retailers provide the basic service of enabling consumers to view a wide assortment of products under one roof, while manufacturers continue to gain economies of scale from the bulk production of a limited number of items. For many people, retailing is the public face of marketing, and large in-city and out-of-town shopping centres have become popular venues for consumers to spend their leisure time. For example, the Mall of the Emirates in Dubai features an indoor ski resort providing a host of winter activities, a Magic Planet family entertainment centre, a shark-filled aquarium and cinemas (see Exhibit 11.2). As we shall see later in the chapter, retailers have become

Exhibit 11.2 Some of the entertainment options available at the Mall of the Emirates in Dubai demonstrate the growing link between shopping and leisure in some parts of the world

increasingly sophisticated in their operations and dominate many distribution channels. For example, supermarket chains exercise considerable power over manufacturers because of their enormous buying capabilities, and have been expanding into other areas of retailing like financial services, music distribution, and so on.

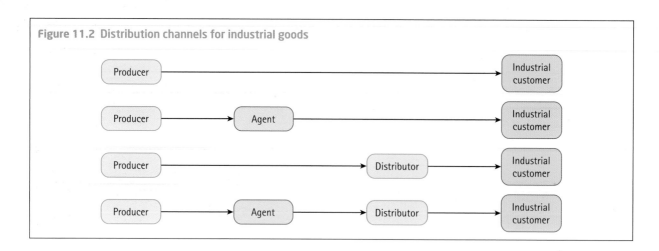

Figure 11.2 Distribution channels for industrial goods

Producer to wholesaler to retailer to consumer

The use of wholesalers makes economic sense for small retailers (e.g. small grocery or furniture shops) with limited order quantities. Wholesalers can buy in bulk from producers, and sell smaller quantities to numerous retailers (this is known as 'breaking bulk'). The danger is that large retailers in the same market have the power to buy directly from producers and thus cut out the wholesaler. In certain cases, the buying power of large retailers has meant that they can sell products to their customers more cheaply than a small retailer can buy from the wholesaler. Longer channels like this tend to occur where retail oligopolies do not dominate the distribution system. In some Asian countries, like Japan, distribution channels can involve up to two and three tiers of wholesalers who supply the myriad small shops and outlets that serve Japanese customers.[2] Many of these wholesalers provide additional services to their customers (the retailers) such as collecting and analysing customer data which can be used to get better deals from producers.[3]

Producer to agent to wholesaler to retailer to consumer

This is a long channel, sometimes used by companies entering foreign markets, who may delegate the task of selling the product to an agent (who does not take title to the goods). The agent contacts local wholesalers (or retailers) and receives a commission on sales. Companies entering new export markets often organize their distribution systems in this way.

Business-to-business channels

Common business-to-business distribution channels are illustrated in Figure 11.2. A maximum of one channel intermediary is used under normal circumstances.

Producer to business customer

Supplying business customers direct is common practice for expensive business-to-business products such as gas turbines, diesel locomotives and aero-engines. There needs to be close liaison between supplier and customer to co-create products and solve technical problems, and the size of the order makes direct selling and distribution economic.

Producer to agent to business customer

Instead of selling to business customers using their own sales force, a business-to-business goods company could employ the services of an agent who may sell a range of goods from several suppliers (on a commission basis). This spreads selling costs and may be attractive to those companies that lack the reserves to set up their own sales operations. The disadvantage is that there is little control over the agent, who is unlikely to devote the same amount of time selling these products as a dedicated sales team.

Producer to distributor to business customer

For less expensive, more frequently bought business-to-business products, distributors are used; these may have both internal and field sales staff.[4] Internal staff deal with customer-generated enquiries and order placing, order follow-up (often using the telephone) and checking inventory levels. Outside sales staff are more proactive; their practical responsibilities are to find new customers, get products specified, distribute catalogues and gather market information. The advantage to customers of using distributors is that they can buy small quantities locally.

Producer to agent to distributor to business customer

Where business customers prefer to call upon distributors, the agent's job will require selling into these intermediaries. The reason why a producer may employ an agent rather than a dedicated sales force is usually cost-based (as previously discussed).

Services channels

Distribution channels for services are usually short, either direct or via an agent (see Figure 11.3). Since stocks are not held, the role of the wholesaler, retailer or industrial distributor does not apply.

Service provider to consumer or business customer

The close personal relationships between service providers and customers often means that service supply is direct (see Exhibit 11.3). Examples include healthcare, office cleaning, accountancy, marketing research and law.

Service provider to agent to consumer or business customer

A channel intermediary for a service company usually takes the form of an agent. Agents are used when the service provider is geographically distant from customers, and where it is not economical for the provider to establish their own local sales team. Examples include insurance, travel, secretarial and theatrical agents.

Channel strategy and management

The design of the distribution channel is an important strategic decision that needs to be integrated with other marketing decisions. For example, products that are being positioned as upmarket, premium items are usu-

Exhibit 11.3 Many consumer service businesses distribute directly to customers. Tony & Guy is one of the best-known hairdressing brands with operations around the world

ally only available in a select number of stores. **Channel strategy** decisions involve the selection of the most effective distribution channel, the most appropriate level of distribution intensity and the degree of channel integration. Once the key channel strategy decisions have been made, effective implementation is required. Channel management decisions involve the selection, motivation, training and evaluation of channel members, and managing conflict between producers and channel members.

Channel selection

Ask yourself why Procter & Gamble sells its brands through supermarkets rather than selling direct. Why does Mitsui sell its locomotives direct to train operating companies rather than use a distributor? The answers are to be found by examining the following factors that influence channel selection. These influences can be grouped under the headings of market, producer, product and competitive factors.

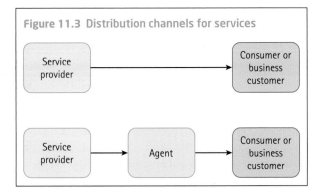

Figure 11.3 Distribution channels for services

Market factors

Buyer behaviour is an important market factor; buyer expectations may dictate that a product be sold in a certain way. Buyers may prefer to buy locally or online. Failure to match these expectations can have catastrophic consequences, as illustrated by the experience of entertainment retailers, who continue to struggle as more and more consumers switch to digital downloading.

The geographical concentration and location of customers also affects channel selection. The more local and clustered the customer base, the more likely it is that direct distribution will be feasible. Direct distribution is also more prevalent when buyers are few in number and buy large quantities such as in many industrial markets. A large number of small customers may mean that using channel intermediaries is the only economical way of reaching them (e.g. department stores). Buyers' needs regarding product information, installation and technical assistance also have to be considered. For example, products that require facilities for local servicing, such as cars, often use intermediaries to carry out the task.

Producer factors

When a producer lacks adequate resources to perform the functions of the channel, this places a constraint on the channel decision. Producers may lack the financial and managerial resources to take on channel operations. Lack of financial resources may mean that a sales force cannot be recruited and sales agents and/or distributors are used instead. Producers may feel that they do not possess the customer-based skills to distribute their products, and prefer to rely on intermediaries instead.

The desired degree of control of channel operations also influences the selection of channel members. The use of independent channel intermediaries reduces producer control. For example, by distributing their products through supermarkets, manufacturers lose total control of the price charged to consumers. Furthermore, there is no guarantee that new products will be stocked. Direct distribution gives producers control over such issues.

Finally, an important decision for producers is whether they want to push their product through the channel or rather market to the end consumer, who then 'pulls' the product through the channel. The former requires investing heavily in trade support to ensure that products are carried and given desired shelf space. The latter means that marketing is targeted at the end user, who through their demand for the product, ensures that it is carried by middlemen. This has raised important ethical issues in the medical profession because of the increased consumer advertising of products by pharmaceutical companies. By building well-known brands like Viagra, Prozac and Vioxx, pharmaceutical companies have been accused of driving consumers to demand products that are not always necessary, in effect pulling them through the channel despite possible objections by medical practitioners. For example, the US drug firms Merck and Schering-Plough have been embroiled in controversy since a study concluded that their joint cholesterol drug, Vytorin, is no more effective than generic versions costing a third of its price. The drug had been aggressively marketed by these two companies.[5]

Product factors

Large and/or complex products are often supplied direct to the customer. The need for close personal contact between producer and customer, and the high prices charged, mean that direct distribution and selling is both necessary and feasible. Perishable products, such as fruit, meat and bread, require relatively short channels to supply the customer with fresh stock. Bulky or difficult to handle products may require direct distribution because distributors may refuse to carry them if storage or display problems arise.[6] A significant proportion of products which can digitized such as books, music, video, software and education are distributed through online channels.

Competitive factors

An innovative approach to distribution may be required if competitors control traditional channels of distribution – for example, through franchise or exclusive dealing arrangements. Two available alternatives are to recruit a sales force to sell direct or to set up a producer-owned distribution network (see the information about administered vertical marketing systems, a topic discussed later in this chapter under the heading 'Conventional marketing channels'). Producers should not accept that the channels of distribution used by competitors are the only ways to reach target customers. Direct marketing provides opportunities to supply products in new ways, as many online companies have shown. For example, traditional channels of distribution for personal computers through high-street retailers were circumvented by direct marketers such as Dell, which used direct-response advertising to reach buyers. The emergence of the more computer-aware and experienced buyer, and the higher reliability of these products as the market reached maturity, meant that a local source of supply (and advice) was less important. However, by pursuing this strategy, Dell was not as effective in reaching corporate customers as some of its major competitors, which continued to use computer resellers. In a break with tradition, Dell announced in 2007 that it was broadening its business model to include computer resellers for the business market as well as Walmart to reach the consumer market in the USA.

The process by which producers or service providers bypass intermediaries and deal directly with final consumers is known as **disintermediation**. In certain sectors and driven largely by online retailing it has been occurring very frequently. For example, travel agents traditionally operated as an intermediary between consumers and airlines and holiday companies charging commissions of up to 10 per cent for their services. Now however, most consumers book their flights and holidays directly online. Bricks and mortar video rental chains like Xtravision and Blockbuster have suffered two waves of disintermediation, first from online video rental firms like Netflix and then from both legal and illegal digital movie websites. Netflix has 15 million subscribers and spends US$600 million per year posting DVDs to customers but wants to reduce this cost by moving them to online video streaming.[7]

Distribution intensity

The choice of distribution intensity is the second channel strategy decision. The three broad options are intensive, selective and exclusive distribution. We will look at each of these now.

Intensive distribution

By using all available outlets, **intensive distribution** aims to provide saturation coverage of the market. With many mass-market products, such as snacks, foods, toiletries, beer and newspapers, sales are a direct function of the number of outlets penetrated (see Exhibit 11.4). This is because consumers have a range of acceptable brands from which they choose and, very often, the decision to purchase is made on impulse. If a brand is not available in an outlet, an alternative is bought. The convenience aspect of purchase is paramount. New outlets may be sought that hitherto had not stocked the products, such as the sale of alcoholic drinks and grocery items at petrol stations.

Selective distribution

Selective distribution also enables market coverage to be achieved. In this case, a producer uses a limited

Exhibit 11.4 Many consumable items like snacks and soft drinks are distributed through vending machines in order that they are available in as many locations as possible

number of outlets in a geographical area to sell its products. The advantages to the producer are: the opportunity to select only the best outlets to focus its efforts on building close working relationships, to train distributor staff on fewer outlets than with intensive distribution, and, if selling and distribution are direct, to reduce costs. Upmarket, aspirational brands like Hugo Boss and Raymond Weil are often sold in carefully selected outlets. Retail outlets and industrial distributors like this arrangement since it reduces competition. Selective distribution is more likely to be used when buyers are willing to shop around when choosing products. This means that it is not necessary for a company to have its products available in all outlets. Products such as audio and video equipment, cameras, clothing and cosmetics may be sold in this way.

Problems can arise when a retailer demands distribution rights but is refused by producers. This happened in the case of Superdrug, a UK discount store chain that requested the right to sell expensive perfume but was denied by manufacturers, which claimed that its stores did not have the right ambience for the sale of luxury products. Superdrug maintained that its application was refused solely because it wanted to sell perfumes for less than their recommended prices. A Monopolies and Mergers Commission investigation supported current practice. European rules allow perfume companies to confine distribution to retailers who measure up in terms of decor and staff training. Manufacturers are not permitted to refuse distribution rights on the grounds that the retailer will sell for less than the list price.[8]

Exclusive distribution

Exclusive distribution is an extreme form of selective distribution in which only one wholesaler, retailer or business-to-business distributor is used in a particular geographic area. Cars are often sold on this basis, with only one dealer operating in each town or city. This reduces a purchaser's power to negotiate prices for the same model between dealers, since to buy in a neighbouring town may be inconvenient when servicing or repairs are required. It also allows very close co-operation between producer and retailer over servicing, pricing and promotion. The right to exclusive distribution may be demanded by distributors as a condition for stocking a manufacturer's product line. Similarly, producers may wish for exclusive dealing where the distributor agrees not to stock competing lines.

Exclusive distribution arrangements can restrict competition in a way that may be detrimental to consumer interests. The European Court of Justice rejected an appeal by Unilever over the issue of exclusive outlets in Germany. By supplying freezer cabinets, Unilever maintained exclusivity by refusing to allow competing ice creams into its cabinets.[9] However, the European Court rejected an appeal by the French Leclerc supermarket group over the issue of the selective distribution system used by Yves Saint Laurent perfumes. The judges found that the use of selective distribution for luxury cosmetic products increased competition and that it was in the consumers' and manufacturer's interests to preserve the image of such luxury products.

Channel integration

Channel integration can range from conventional marketing channels – comprising an independent producer and channel intermediaries – through a franchise operation to channel ownership by a producer. Producers need to consider the strengths and weaknesses of each system when selecting a channel strategy.

Conventional marketing channels

The producer has little or no control over channel intermediaries because of their independence. Arrangements such as exclusive dealing may provide a degree of control, but separation of ownership means that each party will look after its own interests. Conventional marketing channels are characterized by hard bargaining and, occasionally, conflict. For example, a retailer may believe that cutting the price of a brand is necessary to move stock, even though the producer objects because of brand image considerations.

A manufacturer that, through its size and strong brands, dominates a market may exercise considerable power over intermediaries even though they are independent. This power may result in an **administered vertical marketing system** where the manufacturer can command considerable co-operation from wholesalers and retailers. For example, the big Hollywood studios have tried to carefully manage the distribution of movies through a sequence of cinema, video/DVD sale, video/DVD rental to pay-per-view television and finally free television to maximize their returns. While cinema distribution is still somewhat controlled, revenues from DVD rental and pay-per-view television are being significant affected by developments in online distribution as we saw earlier. Pfizer created some controversy when it sought to change its drug distribution arrangements in the UK, which would see all its products distributed through one company, UniChem. Other wholesalers sought to have the action deemed anti-competitive, while retailers were also concerned about the possible emergence of a single, powerful wholesaler.[10]

Retailers, too, can control an administered vertical marketing system. For example, when the retail entrepreneur Philip Green bought the Arcadia group in 2002, he wrote to all suppliers setting out new terms and conditions, imposing a retrospective 1.25 per cent discount and lengthening the number of days taken to pay suppliers from 28 to 30. He then consolidated the number of suppliers completely, delisting some and increasing the work given to others.[11] Many Asian distributors who have profited from the growth of markets like India and China are now acquiring the brands that they previously distributed, such as the sale of the Swiss watch brand Milus to Peace Mark, Asia's biggest watch retailer. As we shall see below, supermarkets have come to dominate food distribution channels and big brands have had to rethink their marketing strategies to cope with these developments as illustrated in Marketing in Action 11.1.

Franchising

A legal contract in which a producer and channel intermediaries agree each member's rights and obligations is called a **franchise**. Usually, the intermediary receives marketing, managerial, technical and financial services in return for a fee. Franchise organizations such as McDonald's, Domino's Pizza, Hertz and the Body Shop combine the strengths of a large sophisticated marketing-orientated organization with the energy and motivation of a locally owned outlet, and hence have been highly successful in building global businesses. Although a franchise operation gives a degree of producer control there are still areas of potential conflict. For example, the producer may be dissatisfied with the standards of service provided by the outlet, or the franchisee may believe that the franchising organization provides inadequate promotional support. Goal

Marketing in Action 11.1 Heinz: reasserting the power of the brand

Critical Thinking: Below is a review of how the Heinz brand has chosen to meet the challenge provided by retailer own-brands. Read it and critically evaluate the pros and cons of the Heinz approach.

The world of marketing has changed dramatically for consumer foods groups like Heinz over the past 30 years. Where once the focus was all about maintaining brand profile and leadership, the challenge is now about finding ways to deal with the enormous power wielded by the big global retailers like Tesco, Carrefour and Walmart. For Heinz, the challenge is particularly acute. Its core products like baked beans, tomato ketchup, frozen foods, soups and pasta meals are the categories in which supermarket own-brands have made the biggest inroads and where significant price competition occurs.

For decades, Heinz has been known for its powerful advertising slogans such as 'Beanz Meanz Heinz' and 'If You've a Family to Feed, Heinz has Everything You Need'. But maintaining this position against a flurry of own-label, lower-price brands aggressively marketed by retailers was going to be difficult. It had several options when thinking about this new challenge. It could engage in price competition (Chapter 8) or it could run sales promotions

to maintain sales during the economic downturn (Chapter 10). It chose instead to build on and re-affirm the emotional connection that it has with its customers.

Its research had demonstrated that though some consumers were deserting the brand, it was often with reluctance. To capitalize on this insight, Heinz developed the slogan 'There are moments when only Heinz will do'. The television campaign showing real-life moments and Heinz's place within them not only appealed to consumers but also created a strong story that the Heinz sales team and wholesale customers could use to ensure effective in-store placement of Heinz products. The combined push and pull strategy was effective in raising brand equity and increasing both sales and market share. Of most satisfaction for Heinz was the fact that its financial gains were at the expense of the own-label brands.

Based on: Howard and Dorsett (2010);[12] Neate (2009)[13].

conflict can also arise. For example, some McDonald's franchisees are displeased with the company's rapid expansion programme, which has meant that new restaurants have opened not far from existing outlets. This has led to complaints about lower profits and falling franchise resale values.[14] A franchise agreement provides a **contractual vertical marketing system** through the formal co-ordination and integration of marketing and distribution activities.

Three economic explanations have been proposed to explain why a producer might choose franchising as a means of distribution.[15] Franchising may be a means of overcoming resource constraints whereby the cost of distribution is shared with the franchisee. It may also be an efficient system for overcoming producer/distributor management problems, because producers may value the notion of the owner-manager who has a vested interest in the success of the business. Finally, franchising may be a way for a producer to access the

local knowledge of the franchisee. Franchising may therefore be attractive when a producer is expanding into new international markets. The biggest franchises operating in Europe are listed in Table 11.1.

Franchising can occur at four levels of the distribution chain.

1 *Manufacturer and retailer*: the car industry is dominated by this arrangement. The manufacturer gains retail outlets for its cars and repair facilities without the capital outlay required with ownership.
2 *Manufacturer and wholesaler*: this is commonly used in the soft drinks industry. Manufacturers such as Schweppes, Coca-Cola and Pepsi grant wholesalers the right to make up and bottle their concentrate in line with their instructions, and to distribute the products within a defined geographic area.
3 *Wholesaler and retailer*: this is not as common as other franchising arrangements, but is found with car

Table 11.1 Europe's top franchises (by unit numbers), 2009

Rank	Franchise	Business	Country of origin
1	7 Eleven	Convenience stores	USA
2	Subway	Food: sandwich bars	USA
3	McDonald's	Restaurants	USA
4	Kumon Institute of Education	Children's education	Japan
5	KFC	Restaurants	USA
6	Europcar	Car rental and leasing	France
7	Pizza Hut	Restaurants	USA
8	Spar	Convenience stores	Netherlands
9	Burger King	Restaurants	USA
10	Jani-King	Commercial hygiene	USA

Source: www.franchiseeurope.com

products and hardware stores. It allows wholesalers to secure distribution of their product to consumers.

4 *Retailer and retailer*: an often used method that frequently has its roots in a successful retailing operation seeking to expand geographically by means of a franchise operation, often with great success. Examples include Subway, Best Western, Pizza Hut and KFC (see Exhibit 11.5).

Channel ownership

Channel ownership brings with it total control over distributor activities. This establishes a **corporate vertical marketing system**. By purchasing retail outlets, producers control their purchasing, production and marketing activities. In particular, control over purchasing means a captive outlet for the manufacturer's pro-

ducts. For example, the purchase of Pizza Hut and KFC by Pepsi has tied these outlets to the company's soft drinks brands.

The benefits of control have to be balanced against the high price of acquisition and the danger that the move into retailing will spread managerial activities too widely. Nevertheless, corporate vertical marketing systems have operated successfully for many years in the oil industry where companies such as Shell, Texaco and Statoil own not only considerable numbers of petrol stations but also the means of production.

Channel management

Channels need to be managed on an ongoing basis once the key channel strategy decisions have been made. This involves the selection, motivation, training and evaluation of channel members, and the resolution of any channel conflict that arises.

Selection

The selection of channel members involves two main activities: first, the identification of potential channel members and, second, development of selection criteria. A variety of potential sources can be used to identify candidates, including trade sources such as trade associations and participation at exhibitions, talking to existing customers and/or to the field sales force, and taking enquiries from interested resellers.[16] Common selection criteria include market, product and customer knowledge, market coverage, quality and size of sales force (if applicable), reputation among customers, financial standing, the

Exhibit 11.5 Planet Beach is a rapidly growing international franchise that combines tanning and day spa services

extent to which competitive and complementary products are carried, managerial competence and hunger for success, and the degree of enthusiasm for handling the producer's lines. In practice, selection may be complex because large, well-established distributors may carry many competing lines and lack enthusiasm for more. Smaller distributors, on the other hand, may be less financially secure and have a smaller sales force, but be more enthusiastic and hungry for success.

Motivation

Once they have been chosen, channel members need to be motivated to agree to act as a distributor, and allocate adequate commitment and resources to the producer's lines. The key to effective motivation is to understand the needs and problems of distributors, since needs and motivators are linked. For example, a distributor who values financial incentives may respond more readily to high commission than one who is more concerned with having an exclusive territory. Possible motivators include financial rewards, territorial exclusivity, providing resource support (e.g. sales training, field sales assistance, provision of marketing research information, advertising and promotion support, financial assistance and management training) and developing strong work relationships (e.g. joint planning, assurance of long-term commitment, appreciation of effort and success, frequent interchange of views and arranging distributor conferences). In short, the management of independent distributors is best conducted in the context of informal partnerships.[17]

Training

Channel members' training requirements obviously depend on their internal competences. Large supermarket chains, for example, may regard an invitation by a manufacturer to provide marketing training as an insult. However, many smaller distributors have been found to be weak on sales management, marketing, financial management, stock control and personnel management, and may welcome producer initiatives on training.[18] From the producer's perspective, training can provide the necessary technical knowledge about a supplier company and its products, and help to build a spirit of partnership and commitment.

Evaluation

Channel member evaluation has an important impact on distributor retention, training and motivation decisions. Evaluation provides the information necessary to decide which channel members to retain and which to drop. Shortfalls in distributor skills and competences may be identified through evaluation, and appropriate training programmes organized by producers. Where a lack of motivation is recognized as a problem, producers can implement plans designed to deal with the root causes of demotivation (e.g. financial incentives and/or fostering a partnership approach to business).[19] It needs to be understood, however, that the scope and frequency of evaluation may be limited where power lies with the channel member. If producers have relatively little power because they are more dependent on channel members for distribution, then in-depth evaluation and remedial action will be restricted. Where manufacturer power is high through having strong brands, and many distributors from which to choose, evaluation may be more frequent and wider in scope. Evaluation criteria include sales volume and value, profitability, level of stocks, quality and position of display, new accounts opened, selling and marketing capabilities, quality of service provided to customers, market information feedback, ability and willingness to keep commitments, attitudes and personal capability.

Managing conflict

Finally, given that producers and channel members are independent, conflict will inevitably occur from time to time (see Marketing in Action 11.2). First, such discord may arise because of differences in goals – for example, an increase in the proportion of profits allocated to retailers means a reduction in the amount going to manufacturers. For instance, when Irish tour operator Budget Travel cut the commissions it paid to travel agents for selling its holidays from 10 to 5 per cent, its subsequent research found that many agents were omitting Budget from the list of choices being presented to customers. Its response was to reach out directly to the end consumer through a €1 million multimedia campaign urging consumers to consider Budget as one of their potential travel choices.[20] However, this campaign was unsuccessful and the firm subsequently ceased trading.

Second, in seeking to expand their businesses many resellers add additional product lines. For example, UK retailer WH Smith originally specialized in books, magazines and newspapers but has grown by adding new product lines such as computer disks, DVDs and software supplies. This can cause resentment among its primary suppliers, who perceive the reseller as devoting too much effort to selling secondary lines. This problem can also work in reverse. Small newsagents in Ireland asked the Competition Authority to review the system

Marketing in Action 11.2 Trouble in the soft drink channel!

> **Critical Thinking:** Below is a review of some changes that are taking place in the distribution channel for soft drinks. Read it and consider the longer-term implications for Coca-Cola, Cola-Cola bottlers and Walmart.

A well-established distribution channel is used to bring popular soft drinks to the marketplace. Leading firms like Coca-Cola and Pepsi Cola manufacture cola concentrate, which is then sold to independent licensed bottling companies, which hold exclusive contracts for particular geographic territories. They in turn manufacture the finished products, which are packaged in bottles and cans, and distributed directly to retail outlets such as shops, supermarkets and vending machines. Over time, bottlers have built up an expertise in serving retailers and many pride themselves on the relationships they have developed with the trade. Some bottlers are extremely large companies and the biggest, Coca-Cola Enterprises, is a publicly quoted company with a market capitalization in excess of US$7 billion.

However, the structure of this supply chain has been threatened by the growth in retailer power and the different systems powerful retailers use to manage supply. For economic reasons, retailers prefer distribution to be managed from large distribution centres rather than having direct delivery to shops by suppliers. Distribution centres are more efficient (see the section on physical distribution later in this chapter) and enable retailers to offer lower prices to consumers. As a result, major global retailers do not need, or favour, the kinds of local supply that Coca-Cola bottlers offer.

Consequently, when Walmart asked that Coca-Cola distribute its Powerade brand to Walmart warehouses rather than to individual stores, bottlers in the USA reacted angrily. Sixty independent bottlers filed a lawsuit against Coca-Cola and Cola-Cola Enterprises, fearing that the move would be the first in a shift away from the direct delivery model and would ultimately threaten their future. Coca-Cola had initially accepted Walmart's proposal as it feared that not doing so would mean that the giant retailer would begin selling an own-label version of the drink. After some disruption to the supply chain, the bottlers settled with Coca-Cola, and agreed to develop and test new distribution and customer service systems.

Based on: Ward (2007)[21]

whereby wholesalers insisted that they carry a full range of magazine titles, with the result that many were left unsold, increasing the costs to the retailer.[22]

Third, in trying to grow their business, producers can use multiple distribution channels, such as selling directly to key accounts or other distributors, which may irritate existing dealers. For example, Alanis Morissette's record company, Maverick Records, created a significant amount of channel conflict in North America when it gave exclusive rights for the sale of her *Jagged Little Pill* album to Starbucks, which was allowed to sell the album for six weeks in its then 4,800 stores before it became available elsewhere. HMV reacted by removing all the artist's music from the shelves of its Canadian stores.[23] For digitized products such as music and software, online distribution is significantly cheaper making it very difficult for physical stores to compete with this channel which is often a source of conflict.

Finally, an obvious source of conflict is when parties in the supply chain do not perform to expectations. For example, DSG International, the owner of the PC World and Currys retail chains, claimed that its poor financial performance in 2007 was partly attributable to a lack of promotional support by Microsoft for its new Vista operating system, which left it with thousands of unsold computers that had to be heavily discounted. This type of conflict is also very common in the telecommunications business where mobile and fixed-line operators buy bundles of time on networks for resale to their customers. Any increase or reduction in these wholesale prices can have a significant impact on their profitability.

There are several ways of managing conflict. Developing a partnership approach calls for frequent interaction between producer and resellers to develop a spirit of mutual understanding and co-operation. First, sales targets can be mutually agreed, and training and promotional support provided. Second, staff may need some training in conflict handling to ensure that situations are handled calmly and that possibilities for win/win outcomes are identified. Third, where the conflict arises from multiple distribution channels, producers can try to partition markets. For example, Hallmark sells its premium greetings cards under its Hallmark brand name to upmarket department stores, and its standard cards under the Ambassador name to discount retailers.[24] Fourth, where poor performance is the problem, the most effective solution is to improve performance so that the source of conflict disappears. Finally, in some cases, the conflict might be eliminated through the purchase of the other party or through coercion, where one party gains compliance through the use of force such as where a large retailer threatens to delist a manufacturer. The merger between Procter & Gamble and Gillette was seen by many as a move to put these two manufacturers on an equal footing with giant retailers like Walmart.

Retailing

Most retailing is conducted in stores such as supermarkets and department stores, but non-store retailing, such as online, mail order and automatic vending, also accounts for a large proportion of sales. Many large retailers exert enormous power in the distribution chain because of the vast quantities of goods they buy from manufacturers (see Ethical Debate 11.1). This power is reflected in their ability to extract 'guarantee of margins' from manufacturers. This is a clause inserted in a contract that ensures a certain profit margin for the retailer, irrespective of the retail price being charged to the customer. One manufacturer is played against another, and own-label brands are used to extract more profit.[25]

Major store and non-store types
Supermarkets

Supermarkets are large self-service stores, which traditionally sell food, drinks and toiletries, but the

Ethical Debate 11.1 Supermarket power

Love them or hate them but you cannot ignore them. Supermarkets are part of the way we live and they have gained enormous power over time. For example, the top four supermarkets in Britain – Tesco, Sainsbury's, Asda and Morrisons – account for over 76 per cent of all grocery purchases. Tesco is the biggest with 658 large supermarkets and over 1,800 convenience stores, and it was able to report pre-tax profits of almost £4 billion in 2011. It takes £1 of every £8 spent by consumers in the UK. In other countries, levels of supermarket concentration are even higher. For example in Australia, the two biggest chains Coles and Woolworths control 70 per cent of the market and 23 cents in every dollar spent by consumers there goes to businesses owned by either of these two companies.

Many critics contend that this level of power is unacceptable. For example, suppliers argue that it puts them in a very difficult position because they are dependent on the supermarkets for their sales. If the supermarket demands lower supply prices, participation in special promotions or is slow to pay, there is usually very little that suppliers can do about it. As a result, many small suppliers cease trading which in turn means that their suppliers also suffer. From society's point of view, this is a worrying development. Branches of large supermarkets may argue that they bring employment to a local community. But over time other local businesses may be unable to compete with these supermarkets and local suppliers may cease trading, resulting in a loss of employment and economic activity in these communities. For example, in the twelve months to June 2005, 2,000 convenience stores closed down in the UK when supermarkets moved in.

Supermarkets also counter that they deliver value to customers by providing a wide range of products at low prices. But again this has led to unsustainable practices such as shipping food products from large scale suppliers in different parts of the world ahead of using local suppliers that leave a smaller carbon footprint. Lobby groups continue to campaign against the growth of supermarkets, and competition authorities around the world regularly conduct investigations of their activities. And in 2011, riots broke out in Bristol, UK, over the opening of a new Tesco store. It would appear that the controversy surrounding supermarkets is likely to run on for some time to come.

Reflection: Consider the arguments for and against supermarkets. Put forward your own point of view.

broadening of their ranges by some supermarket chains means that such items as non-prescription pharmaceuticals, cosmetics and clothing are also being sold. As Tesco seeks further growth beyond groceries, it has moved into a variety of new businesses. For example, Tesco Bank offers savings and insurance products generating sales of £1.1 billion, Tesco Telecoms is a mobile and broadband network with sales of £450 million and Tesco Direct which is an Internet, phone and catalogue business generates sales of £288 million.[26] The main attractions of supermarkets are their convenient locations, wide product ranges and competitive prices. Supermarket operators are skilled marketers who use a variety of techniques such as psychological research, sensory experiences and loyalty schemes to capture a significant share of the market.

Department stores

Department stores are titled thus because related product lines are sold in separate departments, such as men's and women's clothing, jewellery, cosmetics, toys and home furnishings. In recent years such stores have been under increasing pressure from discount houses, speciality stores and the move to out-of-town shopping. Nevertheless, many continue to perform well in this competitive arena through a strategy of becoming one-stop shops for a variety of leading manufacturer brands, which are allocated significant store space.

Speciality shops

As their name suggests, these outlets specialize in a narrow product line. Many town centres, for example, have shops selling confectionery, cigarettes and newspapers in the same outlet. Many speciality outlets, such as Tie Rack and Sock Shop, sell only one product line. Specialization allows a deep product line to be sold in restricted shop space. Some speciality shops, such as butchers and greengrocers, focus on quality and personal service. Speciality shops can, however, be vulnerable when tastes change or competition increases. For example, speciality sports retailers such as JJB Sports and John David Group have been reporting disappointing results as the blending of sportswear and fashion, driven by cultural icons such as David Beckham, has opened up the market to a host of other retailers such as fashion shops and supermarkets.[27]

Discount houses

Discount houses sell products at low prices by accepting low margins, selling high volumes and bulk buying. For example, 'pound shops' sell a wide range of items such as fashion accessories, toys, stationery and tools for £1, and operate on low margins of 2–3 per cent. Good location and rapid product turnover are the keys to success. Low prices, sometimes promoted as sale prices, are offered throughout the year. Many discounters operate from out-of-town retail ware houses with the capacity to stock a wide range of merchandise.

A growing form of discount retailing is factory outlet stores. These are usually out-of-town shopping locations comprising a wide range of manufacturer-owned retail shops that carry out-of-season stock or unsold products from department stores that are heavily discounted. Some of these outlet malls are repositioning themselves as premium outlets (rather than factory outlets) and feature prestigious brand names such as Versace, Gucci, Dolce & Gabbana, Ralph Lauren, Yves Saint Laurent and so on (see Exhibit 11.6).

Category killers

These retail outlets have a narrow product focus, but an unusually large width and depth to that product range. Category killers emerged in the USA in the early 1980s as a challenge to discount houses. They are distinct from speciality shops in that they are bigger, and carry a wider and deeper range of products within their chosen product category; they are distinct from discount houses in their focus on only one product category. Examples of category killers are Toys 'R' Us (toys), Nevada Bob's Discount Golf Warehouses (golf equipment), Woodies (DIY), Halfords (bicycles and auto accessories) and IKEA (furniture).

Convenience stores

Convenience stores, true to their name, offer customers the convenience of a close location and long opening hours every day of the week. Because they are small they may pay higher prices for their merchandise than supermarkets, and therefore have to charge higher prices to their customers. Some of these stores, such as Spar, join buying groups to gain some purchasing power and lower prices. The main customer need they fulfil is that of top-up buying – for example, when a customer is short of a carton of milk or loaf of bread. Societal changes, such as rising divorce rates, decreasing family sizes, long commuting times and time-poor consumers, have all combined to help revitalize the convenience store sector. Consumers are once again favouring quick, convenient purchases, as offered by convenience stores, over a big weekly shop at a supermarket. Consequently, major retailers like Tesco and Sainsbury's have been aggressively buying into this sector.

Exhibit 11.6 Some of the luxury brand names that may be found at a premium outlet centre

Catalogue stores

This type of retail outlet promotes its products through catalogues, which are either mailed to customers or available in-store or online for customers to view on-site (see Chapter 10). Purchase is in city-centre outlets where customers fill in order forms, pay for the goods and then collect them from a designated place in the store. In the UK, Argos is a successful catalogue retailer selling a wide range of discounted products such as electrical goods, jewellery, gardening tools, furniture, toys, car accessories, sports goods, luggage and cutlery.

Mail order

This non-store form of retailing may also employ catalogues as a promotional vehicle, but the purchase transaction is conducted via the mail (see Chapter 10). Alternatively, outward communication may be by direct mail, television, magazine or newspaper advertising. Increasingly, orders are being placed by telephone or over the Internet, a process that is facilitated by the use of credit cards as a means of payment. Goods are then sent by mail. Otto-Versand, the German mail-order company, owns Grattan, a UK mail-order retailer, and has leading positions in Austria, Belgium, Italy, the Netherlands and Spain. Its French rival, La Redoute, has expanded into Belgium, Italy and Portugal. Mail order offers the prospect of pan-European catalogues, central warehousing and processing of cross-border orders.

Automatic vending

Offering such products as drinks, confectionery, soup and newspapers in convenient locations, 24 hours a day, vending machines are particularly popular in some countries, such as Japan. No sales staff are required, although restocking, servicing and repair costs can be high. Cash dispensers at banks have improved customer service by permitting round-the-clock financial services. However, machine breakdowns and out-of-stock situations can annoy customers.

Online retailing

Online retailing is one of the fastest-growing forms of distribution, and is proving particularly popular for products like electrical goods, groceries, clothing/footwear and music/video. It can take any of three major forms. First, in pure online retailing scenarios, the product is ordered, paid for and received online in a completely electronic transaction. As we saw earlier, any product that can be digitized can be retailed in this way. Second, products can be ordered online and then distributed either through the postal system or through the use of local distribution companies in the case of groceries or wine, for example. Finally, most leading retailers have an online presence. For example, the top retailers that have a significant presence both online and offline include Tesco, Marks & Spencer, Argos, Next, Carrefour and Aldi. These retailers work hard to link both channels. For example, Argos customers can select products from the Argos catalogue, order online and pick them up from a local outlet.

Online retailers possess several advantages which help to explain their rapid rise. First is the issue of location which is a central part of the competitive advantage of many offline retailers who made early investments and captured the best locations. However, in an online environment, location becomes less important. Second is flexibility. Online stores are open 24 hours per day, every day of the year, offering customer convenience. Product range is a significant advantage of online retailers. Physical bookstores, video game shops and so on are limited by the number of titles that they can carry making supply choices very important. Online retailers have relatively unlimited carrying capacity as their products are stored in huge warehouses, with other online affiliates or in digital formats such as e-books with the result that they can potentially offer almost any niche product a consumer may be looking for. Fourth, the cost of doing business is relatively lower for an online retailer. Small players can establish a web presence relatively cheaply while offline retailers have to invest in store locations, shop fittings, sales personnel and so on. Finally, online businesses have access to a global market and one of the key marketing challenges is finding ways of driving customers from all over the world to your webstore.

Key retail marketing decisions

A retail outlet needs to be thought of as a brand involving the same set of decisions we discussed when we looked at branding in Chapter 6. Retailers need to anticipate and adapt to changing environmental circumstances, such as the growing role of information technology and changing customer tastes. However, there are a number of specific issues that relate to retailing, and are worthy of separate discussion.

Retail positioning

Retail positioning – as with all marketing decisions – involves the choice of target market and differential advantage. Targeting allows retailers to tailor their marketing mix (which includes product assortment, service levels, store location, prices and promotion) to the needs of their chosen customer segment (see Marketing in Action 11.3). Differentiation provides a reason to shop

---

Marketing in Action 11.3 Repositioning Sainsbury's

Critical Thinking: Below is a review of how the supermarket chain Sainsbury's altered its competitive positioning. Select three retailers of your choice and evaluate their competitive positioning.

In the highly competitive world of UK supermarket retailing, Sainsbury's has built a position as a well-liked, high-quality, upmarket retailer. However, this positioning represented a challenge for the brand during the extensive price competition between supermarkets that took place during the recession following the 2008 global financial crisis. Relative to its peers, Sainsbury's was perceived to be more expensive and this represented a real threat during a time when consumers had become increasingly price conscious.

The challenge for the brand was to convey its price value while not undermining its reputation for quality. The solution it devised was an innovative one that was captured by the slogan 'Feed your family for a fiver'. Its research had indicated that home cooking would remain popular but that consumers were in a rut and looking for new recipe ideas. It developed a range of 50 family meals from Sainsbury's products that all cost less than £5. It was also important that the meals contained products that were at standard prices rather than on special offer and included both Sainsbury's basics and quality items to convey that price value could be obtained across the store. The campaign was launched in 2008 with an initial competition among store staff to generate recipe ideas. A fully integrated campaign using television which featured the celebrity chef Jamie Oliver, magazine, digital and in-store followed.

The campaign caught the public imagination with Sainsbury's receiving the highest recognition of any television advertising that it had done. Within two years, prompted recognition of its slogan had reached similar levels to its main rival Tesco's 'Every little helps'. Brand perception of Sainsbury's prices also improved and ingredients involved in the recipes saw strong sales increases. The company's effectiveness in managing the delicate balancing act of altering its positioning and subsequent sales improvements saw it win the Retail Industry's 'Supermarket of the Year' in 2009.

Based on: Clews (2009);[28] Parsons (2009);[29] Roach (2010)[30].

at one store rather than another. A useful framework for creating a differential advantage has been proposed by Davies, who suggests that innovation in retailing can come only from novelty in the process offered to the shopper, or from novelty in the product or product assortment offered to the shopper.[31] The catalogue shop Argos in the UK has offered innovation in the process of shopping, whereas Next achieved success through product innovation (stylish clothes at affordable prices). Hard discounters like Aldi and Lidl stock primarily own-label products, which are sold at competitive prices (product innovation). This is the dominant retail form in Germany, where discounters have a 40 per cent market share, and is beginning to grow rapidly in other European countries. Toys 'R' Us is an example of both product and process innovation through providing the widest range of toys at one location (product innovation) and thereby offering convenient, one-stop shopping (process innovation).

Store location

Conventional wisdom has it that the three factors critical to the success of a retailer are location, location and location. Convenience is an important issue for many shoppers, and so store location can have a major bearing on sales performance. Retailers have to decide on regional coverage, the towns and cities to target within regions, and the precise location to select within a given town or city. The choice of town or city will depend on such factors as correspondence with the retailer's chosen target market, the level of disposable income in the catchment area, the availability of suitable sites and the level of competition. The choice of a particular site may depend on the level of existing traffic (pedestrian and/or vehicular) passing the site, parking provision, access to the outlet for delivery vehicles, the presence of competition, planning restrictions and whether there is an opportunity to form new retailing centres with other outlets. For example, Starbucks has sought to locate its coffee shops on the side of the street most favoured by commuters going to work, based on the notion that consumers would not cross a busy street for a coffee. Also, two or more non-competing retailers (e.g. Sainsbury's and Boots) may agree to locate outlets together in an out-of-town centre to generate more pulling power than each could achieve individually. Having made that decision, the partners will look for suitable sites near their chosen town or city.

Product assortment

Retailers have to make a decision on the breadth and depth of their product assortment. A supermarket, for example, may decide to widen its product assortment from food, drink and toiletries to include clothes and toys: this is called 'scrambled merchandising'. For example, currently in the UK, supermarkets sell 24 per cent of all CDs, 8 per cent of books and 40 per cent of all newly released DVDs, which has implications for specialist CD/DVD and book retailers.[32] Scrambled merchandising becomes a basis through which retailers can differentiate themselves. Therefore, we see companies like McDonald's offering DVD rentals, Gap selling CD mixes, Starbucks selling music and Tesco selling Starbucks coffee!

Within each product line, a retailer can choose to stock a deep or shallow product range. Some retailers, like Tie Rack, Sock Shop and Toys 'R' Us, stock one deep product line. Department stores, however, offer a much broader range of products, including toys, cosmetics, jewellery, clothes, electrical goods and household accessories. Some retailers begin with one product line and gradually broaden their product assortment to maximize revenue per customer. For example, petrol stations broadened their product range to include motor accessories and, more recently, confectionery, drinks, flowers and newspapers. Services like hot food and car washes offer much greater profit margins than the sale of petrol. A by-product of this may be to reduce customers' price sensitivity since selection of petrol station may be based on the availability of other products there rather than the fact that it offers the lowest price.

Own-label branding gives rise to another product decision. Major retailers may decide to sell a range of own-label products to complement national brands. Often the purchasing power of these large retail chains means that prices can be lower and yet profit margins higher than for competing national brands. This makes the activity an attractive proposition for many retailers. Supermarkets have moved into this area, as have UK electrical giants such as Dixons, which uses the Chinon brand name for cameras and Saisho for brown goods such as hi-fi and televisions, and Currys, which has adopted the Matsui brand name. In both cases the use of a Japanese-sounding name (even though some of the products were sourced in Europe) was believed to enhance the products' customer appeal.

Price

Price is a key factor in store choice for some market segments. Consequently, some retailers major on price as their differential advantage. This requires vigilant cost control and massive buying power. A recent trend is towards the 'everyday low prices' favoured by retailers, rather than the higher prices supplemented by promotions that are supported by manufacturers. Retailers such as B&Q, the do-it-yourself discounter, maintain that customers prefer predictable low prices rather than occasional money-off deals, three-for-the-price-of-two offers and free gifts. Supermarket chains are also pressurizing suppliers to provide consistently low prices rather than temporary promotions. This action is consistent with the desire to position themselves on a low price platform. For example, in France, Carrefour has introduced a system whereby the bonuses of store managers are linked to whether prices are lower than those of comparable retailers. The importance of price competitiveness is reflected in the alliance of European food retailers called Associated Marketing Services. Retailers such as WM Morrison (UK), Ahold (the Netherlands), ICA (a federation of Swedish food retailers), Migros (Finland), Delhaize Group (Belgium) and others have joined forces to foster co-operation in the areas of purchasing and marketing of brands. Their range of activities includes own branding, joint buying, the development of joint brands and services, and the exchange of information and skills. A key aim is to reduce cost price, since this accounts for 75 per cent of the sales price to customers.[33]

Store atmosphere

Atmosphere is created by a combination of the design, colour and layout of a store. Both exterior and interior design affect atmosphere. External factors include architectural design, signs, window displays and use of colour, which create an identity for a retailer and attract customers. The Body Shop, for example, projects its environmentally caring image through the green exterior of its shops, and through window displays that focus on environmental issues. Interior design also has a major impact on atmosphere. Store lighting, fixtures and fittings, and layout are important considerations. Colour, sound and smell can affect mood. Department stores often place perfume counters near the entrance, supermarkets may use the smell of baking bread to attract customers and upmarket shirt companies like Thomas Pink even pump the smell of freshly laundered linen around their stores. In addition, supermarkets often use music to create a relaxed atmosphere, whereas some boutiques use pop music to draw in their target customers. Multi-sensory marketing describes an approach being adopted by retailers to appeal to as many senses as possible.

As we saw in Chapter 7, the rise of experiential marketing has placed a significant focus on store atmospherics as retailers strive to create a shopping experience for consumers. Shoppers are considered to have three attention zones.[34] The first zone operates at a distance of 30 feet from the shopper, and requires the retailer to use a combination of sound, colour, scent and motion to attract potential buyers. At 10 feet what is important is placement on a shelf and an ability to stand out from competitors, placing a premium on how well manufacturers influence the distribution process. And, at 3 feet, the consumer is already holding a potential choice or reaching out for it, so it is the look and feel of the product or its packaging that is important.

Physical distribution

Earlier in this chapter we examined channel strategy and management decisions, which concern the choice of the correct outlets to provide product availability to customers in a cost-effective manner. Physical distribution decisions focus on the efficient movement of goods from producer to intermediaries and the consumer. Clearly, channel and physical distribution decisions are interrelated, although channel decisions tend to be made earlier. Physical distribution is defined as a set of activities concerned with the physical flows of materials, components and finished goods from producer to channel intermediaries and consumers. It is a business that has become increasingly complex as customers such as Walmart, Tesco and others extend their global reach. This has given rise to mergers between logistics companies such as that involving Exel and Tibbet & Britten, as companies seek to provide integrated solutions for their clients ranging from warehouse management to home delivery.[35]

Distribution aims to provide intermediaries and customers with the right products, in the right quantities, in the right locations, at the right time. Distribution problems caused by, for example, a move to a new warehouse frequently impact on corporate performance. Physical distribution activities have been the subject of managerial attention for some time because of the potential for cost savings and improving customer service levels. Cost savings can be achieved by reducing inventory levels, using cheaper forms of transport and shipping in bulk rather than small quantities. For example, Benetton's blueprint for reviving its fortunes has been predicated on getting clothes from the factory to the shop rail faster to enable it to compete with fast fashion retailers like Zara and H&M.[36] Customer service levels can be improved by fast and reliable delivery, including just-in-time (JIT) delivery, holding high inventory levels so that customers have a wide choice and the chances of stock-outs are reduced, fast order processing, and ensuring that products arrive in the right quantities and quality. Physical distribution management concerns the balance between cost reduction and meeting customer service requirements. Trade-offs are often necessary. For example, low inventory and slow, cheaper transportation methods reduce costs but lower customer service levels and satisfaction.

As well as the trade-offs between physical distribution costs and customer service levels, there is the potential for conflict between elements of the physical distribution system itself. For example, low-cost containers may lower packaging costs but raise the cost of goods damaged in transit. This fact, and the need to co-ordinate order processing, inventory and transportation decisions, means that physical distribution needs to be managed as a system, with a manager overseeing the whole process. It can be a very challenging task, as demonstrated in Marketing in Action 11.4.

The key elements of the physical distribution system are customer service, order processing, inventory control, warehousing, transportation and materials handling.

Customer service

It is essential to set customer service standards. For example, a customer service standard might be that 90 per cent of orders are delivered within 48 hours of receipt and 100 per cent are delivered within 72 hours. Higher customer service standards normally mean higher costs as inventory levels need to be higher. In some cases, customers value consistency in delivery time rather than speed. For example, a customer service standard of guaranteed delivery within five working days may be valued more than 60 per cent within two and 100 per cent within seven days. Customer service standards should be given considerable attention for they may be the different-iating factor between suppliers: they may be used as a key customer choice criterion. Methods of improving customer service standards include improving

---

Marketing in Action 11.4 Lego: consolidating distribution

Critical Thinking: Below is a review of changes that Lego made to its physical distribution system. Read it and critically evaluate the role played by physical distribution in an organization's marketing efforts.

For Lego, the iconic Danish building brick toy company, the early part of this century has been the most turbulent since its foundation in 1932. A variety of rapid changes, including competition from electronic toys and games, changing consumer tastes and the growing power of retailers, threatened the very survival of the firm. It reported the biggest net losses in its history in the years 2003 and 2004.

As well as refocusing its efforts on its core markets, the company also knew that it needed to re-examine its supply chain. The Christmas period was the key buying period for toys and with market tastes and preferences likely to change rapidly, Lego needed a distribution system that was responsive to these changes. The company had two huge production sites in Denmark and Switzerland producing a staggering 20 billion bricks per year. The finished Lego products were stored in a 30,000 m² warehouse in Germany from where they were shipped to one of its distribution centres. It used four distribution centres in Europe, two in France serving primarily the UK and southern European markets, one in Germany for the Central and Eastern European market and one in Denmark for Scandinavia and the Benelux.

Fourteen thousand retail customers received direct deliveries from one of these four distribution centres.

Any efforts to rationalize this complex distribution system needed to recognize that product demand roughly doubled during the period from September to November. A further key challenge was to convince company salespeople that any cuts in the distribution system would not impact on levels of customer service. An analysis of the channel revealed that most customers did not need same-day or next-day delivery. As a result the company decided to consolidate all logistics and distribution operations in a massive single distribution centre of 100,000 m² in the Czech Republic, managed by a third party. The logistics company DHL won the contract. After significant teething problems, the decision delivered important cost savings to Lego. For example, during the period 2005 to 2008, Lego sales grew by 35 per cent but logistics costs actually dropped by 9 per cent. On-time delivery rose to 96 per cent from 62 per cent in 2005, showing that cost reductions could be achieved without impacting on customer service levels.

Based on: Wellian, Cordon and Seifert (2008);[37] Wellian, Cordon and Seifert (2009)[38].

Exhibit 11.7 Companies like DHL provide an important physical distribution function

The DHL 'Speed of Yellow' campaign illustrates the value it creates for its customers.
www.mcgraw-hill.co.uk/textbooks/fahy

product availability, improving order cycle time, raising information levels and improving flexibility. An example of raising information levels is the kind of service now being provided online by courier companies like Federal Express and UPS, which offer their customers a facility whereby they can log on and get immediate updates on delivery status (see Exhibit 11.7). However, in modern global supply chains, the outsourcing of activities means a lack of control, which can impact on customer service. For example, a small disruption in its material supplies from Southeast Asia affected Zara's service levels and sales in 2005.

Order processing

This relates to the question of how orders are handled. Reducing time between a customer placing an order and receiving the goods may be achieved through careful analysis of the components that make up order processing time. A computer link between the salesperson and the order department may be effective. Electronic data interchange can also speed order processing time by checking the customer's credit rating, and whether the goods are in stock, issuing an order to the warehouse, invoicing the customer and updating the inventory records.

Inventory control

Inventory control deals with the question of how much inventory should be held. A balance has to be found between the need to have products in stock to meet customer demand and the costs incurred in holding large inventories. Having in stock every conceivable item a customer might order would normally be prohibitively expensive for companies marketing many items. Decisions also need to be taken about when to order new stocks. These order points are normally before stock levels reach zero because of the lead time between ordering and receiving inventory. The JIT inventory system is designed to reduce lead times so that the order point (the stock level at which re-ordering takes place), and overall inventory levels for production items, are low. The more variable the lead time between ordering and receiving stocks, and the greater the fluctuation in customer demand, the higher the order point. This is because of the uncertainty caused by the variability leading to the need for **safety (buffer) stocks** in case lead times are unpredictably long or customer demand unusually high. How much to order depends on the cost of holding stock and order-processing costs. Orders can be small and frequent, or large and infrequent. Small, frequent orders raise order-processing costs but reduce inventory carrying costs; large, infrequent orders raise inventory costs but lower order-processing expenditure.

Warehousing

This part of the distribution chain involves all the activities required in the storing of goods between the time they are produced and the time they are transported to the customer. These activities include breaking bulk, making up product assortments for delivery to customers, storage and loading. Storage warehouses hold goods for moderate or long time periods, whereas distribution centres operate as central locations for the fast movement of goods. Retailing organizations use regional distribution centres where suppliers deliver products in bulk. These shipments are broken down into loads that are then quickly transported to retail outlets. Distribution centres are usually highly automated, with computer-controlled machinery facilitating the movement of goods. A computer reads orders and controls the fork-lift trucks that gather goods and move them to loading bays. Further technological advances are likely to have a significant impact on warehousing and the movement of goods through the supply chain. Warehousing strategy involves the determination of the location and the number of warehouses or distribution centres to be used. The trend is towards a smaller number of ever larger warehouses. For example, the UK electrical retailer Dixons is aiming to cut its distribution centres from 17 to two. Boots is closing its 17 regional distribution centres in favour of a £70 million automated warehouse in Nottingham. At the extreme, some retailers are seeking single distribution centres for the whole of Europe (see Marketing in Action 11.4), with locations such as Moissy-Cramayel in France measuring the size of 350 football pitches.[39]

Transportation

This refers to the means by which products will be transported; the five major modes are rail, road, air, water and pipeline. Railways are efficient at transporting large, bulky freight on land over long distances and are often used to transport coal, chemicals, oil, aggregates and nuclear flasks. Rail is more environmentally friendly than road, but the major problem with it is lack of flexibility. Motorized transport by road has the advantage of flexibility because of direct access to companies and warehouses. This means that lorries can transport goods from supplier to receiver without unloading en route. However, the growth of road transport in Europe, and particularly the UK, has received considerable criticism because of increased traffic congestion, damage done to roads by heavy juggernauts and the impact on the environment. The key advantages of air freight are its speed and long distance capabilities. Its speed means that it is often used to transport perishable goods and emergency deliveries. Its major disadvantages are high cost, and the need to transport goods by road to and from air terminals. Water transportation is slow but inexpensive. Inland transportation is usually associated with bulky, low-value, non-perishable goods such as coal, ore, grain, steel and petroleum. Ocean-going ships carry a wider range of products. When the cost benefits of international sea transportation outweigh the speed advantage of air freight, water shipments may be chosen. But some industries, such as fashion retailing, have seen production move from low-cost countries like China to Eastern Europe and Turkey because it takes 22 days by water to reach the UK from China compared with five days from Turkey. So, although the cost of production is lower in China, the fast turnaround of fashion items makes sea transportation unappealing. Finally, pipelines are a dependable and low-maintenance form of transportation for liquids and gases such as crude petroleum, water and natural gas.

Materials handling

Materials handling involves the activities related to the movement of products in the producer's plant, warehouses and transportation depots. Modern storage facilities tend to be of just one storey, allowing a high level of automation. In some cases robots are used to conduct materials-handling tasks. Lowering the human element in locating inventory and assembling orders has reduced error and increased the speed of these operations. For example, the pharmaceuticals distributor Cahill May Roberts has replaced a paper-based system with Vocollect voice technology whereby material handlers speak to computers to confirm the products that they have collected rather than making paper records. It distributes in the region of 180,000 product units per day to pharmacies in Ireland and accurate records are critical because of the nature of the products being dealt with.[40] Two key developments in materials handling are unit handling and containerization. Unit handling achieves efficiency by combining multiple packages on pallets that can be moved by fork-lift trucks. Containerization involves the combination of large quantities of goods (e.g. car components) in a single large container. Once sealed, such containers can easily be transferred from one form of transport to another.

When you have read this chapter
log on to the Online Learning Centre for *Foundations of Marketing* at **www.mcgraw-hill.co.uk/textbooks/fahy** where you'll find links and extra online study tools for marketing.

Summary

In this chapter we have examined the key issue of delivering products and services to customers. In particular, the following issues were addressed.

1. There are important differences in the structure of consumer, industrial and service channels. Consumer channels tend to be longer and involve more channel partners, while many industrial and service channels are direct to the customer.

2. Channel strategy involves three key decisions, namely, channel selection, distribution intensity and channel integration. These decisions must be made in line with the firm's overall marketing strategy. For example, positioning decisions may drive the number and type of channel members selected to distribute a product and the extent to which they are controlled.

3. The key channel management issues are the selection and motivation of middlemen, providing them with training, evaluating their performance and resolving any channel conflict issues that may arise. Effective support for channel members is often necessary to achieve marketing objectives.

4. There is a diverse range of retail types, including supermarkets, department stores, speciality shops, discount houses, category killers, convenience stores, catalogue stores, mail order, vending machines and online retailing.

5. The key retail marketing decisions include retail positioning, store location, product assortment, price and store atmosphere. Many retailers are strong brands in their own right and need to be managed as such. Technology has enabled some Internet retailers to achieve major competitive advantages in their markets.

6. Physical distribution concerns decisions relating to customer service, order processing, inventory control, warehousing, transportation and materials handling, which impact on the efficiency and effectiveness of the supply chain. Cost and customer service are two conflicting pressures that impact upon the structure and management of the physical distribution system.

Study questions

1. A tour operator has just established a business in the UK selling short-break package holidays throughout Europe. Advise the founder on her options for distributing the company's products.

2. Evaluate the three distribution intensity options that are available to an organization. In what kinds of circumstances might each be used?

3. Describe situations that can lead to conflict between channel members. What can be done to avoid and resolve conflict?

4. Discuss the impact of the growth of online retailing on other retail formats.

5. Discuss the reasons why more and more distribution channels are being characterized by a small number of large central distribution centres rather than by a large number of relatively small outlets.

6. Visit www.starbucks.com and www.costa.co.uk. Compare and contrast these two coffee chains in terms of the major retail marketing decisions such as retail positioning, product assortment, store location and store atmospherics.

Suggested reading

Anderson, C. (2006) *The Long Tail: The New Economics of Culture and Commerce*, London: Random House Books.

Corstjens, J. and **M. Corstjens** (1995) *Store Wars: The Battle for Mindspace and Shelfspace*, New York: John Wiley & Sons.

Ferdows, K., M.A. Lewis and **J. Machuca** (2004) Rapid-fire Fulfillment, *Harvard Business Review*, **82** (11), 104–11.

Jerath, K. and **J. Zhang** (2010) Store within a Store, *Journal of Marketing Research*, **47** (4), 748–63.

Myers, J.B., A.D. Pickersgill and **E.S. Van Metre** (2004) Steering Customers to the Right Channels, *McKinsey Quarterly*, **4**, 36–48.

References

1. **Green, H.** (2009) Can Amazon's Stock Surge Last? *Businessweek. com*, 19 March; **Khanna, R., S. Chhaochharia** and **C. Chattergee** (2009) Leadership: The Amazon Way, *IBS Research Center*; **Streifeld, D.** (2011) Amazon's Profits Fall, but Beat Expectations as Company Invests, *New York Times*, 26 July.

2. **Fahy, J.** and **F. Taguchi** (1995) Reassessing the Japanese Distribution System, *Sloan Management Review*, Winter.

3. **Anonymous** (2011) The Co-op Strikes Back, *The Economist*, 29 January, 58.

4. **Narus, J.A.** and **J.C. Anderson** (1986) Industrial Distributor Selling: The Roles of Outside and Inside Sales, *Industrial Marketing Management*, **15**, 55–62.

5. **Anonymous** (2008) Shock to the System, *The Economist*, 2 February, 67–8.

6. **Rosenbloom, B.** (1987) *Marketing Channels: A Management View*, Hinsdale, IL: Dryden, 160.

7. **Garrahan, M.** (2010) A Pointer to Profits, *Financial Times*, 25 August, 7.

8. **Laurance, B.** (1993) MMC in Bad Odour Over Superdrug Ruling, *Guardian*, 12 November, 18.

9. **Anonymous** (1993) EC Rejects Unilever Appeal on Cabinets, *Marketing*, 25 February, 6.

10. **Jack, A.** (2007) Wholesalers to Seek Injunction on Pfizer's Drug Distribution Plan, *Financial Times*, 1 March, 4.

11. **Voyle, S.** (2003) Supply Chain Feels Fresh Pressure, *Financial Times*, 28 April, 23.

12. **Howard, L.** and **J. Dorsett** (2010) Heinz – It Has to be Heinz: Maintaining Leadership in Uncertain Times, *Warc.com*.

13. **Neate, R.** (2009) Heinz Sees 21 Percent Jump in Baked Beans Sales as Consumers Get Taste for Comfort Food, *Telegraph. co.uk*.

14. **Helmore, E.** (1997) Restaurant Kings, or just Silly Burgers? *Observer*, 8 June, 5.

15. **Hopkinson, G.C.** and **S. Hogarth Scott** (1999) Franchise Relationship Quality: Microeconomic Explanations, *European Journal of Marketing*, **33** (9/10), 827–43.

16. **Rosenbloom, B.** (1987) *Marketing Channels: A Management View*, Hinsdale, IL: Dryden, 160.

17. **Shipley, D.D., D. Cook** and **E. Barnett** (1989) Recruitment, Motivation, Training and Evaluation of Overseas Distributors, *European Journal of Marketing*, **23** (2), 79–93.

18. See **Shipley, D.D.** and **S. Prinja** (1988) The Services and Supplier Choice Influences of Industrial Distributors, *Service Industries Journal*, **8** (2), 176–87; **Webster, F.E.** (1976) The Role of the Industrial Distributor in Marketing Strategy, *Journal of Marketing*, **40**, 10–16.

19. See **Pegram, R.** (1965) *Selecting and Evaluating Distributors*, New York: National Industrial Conference Board, 109–25; **Shipley, D.D., D. Cook** and **E. Barnett** (1989) Recruitment, Motivation, Training and Evaluation of Overseas Distributors, *European Journal of Marketing*, **23** (2), 79–93.

20. **Coyle, D.** (2004) Budget Travel Accuses Agents of Blacklisting, *Irish Times*, 16 November, 16; **Coyle, D.** (2005) Challenges Circle Overhead for Tour Operator, *Irish Times Business*, 7 January, 22.

21. **Ward, A.** (2007) Coca-Cola's Bottlers Settle Dispute Over Distribution, *Financial Times*, 13 February, 2.

22. **Slattery, L.** (2007) Concern at Merger Plan for Distributor Eason, *Irish Times*, 29 January, 18.

23. **Sexton, P.** (2005) A Music Sales Storm is Brewing in a Coffee Shop, *Financial Times*, 21 June, 14.

24. **Hardy, K.G.** and **A.J. Magrath** (1988) Ten Ways for Manufacturers to Improve Distribution Management, *Business Horizons*, November–December, 68.

25. **Krishnan, T.V.** and **H. Soni** (1997) Guaranteed Profit Margins: A Demonstration of Retailer Power, *International Journal of Research in Marketing*, **14**, 35–56.

26. **Rigby, E.** (2010) Tesco Banks on Next Chapter of Growth, *Financial Times*, 22 September, 21.

27. **Rigby, E.** (2004) Sports Specialists Lose Their Way in Quest to be Followers of Fashion, *Financial Times*, 20 August, 21.

28. **Clews, M.** (2009) Sainsbury's Launches Latest Cookery Class Ad, *MarketingWeek.co.uk*, 22 July.

29. **Parsons, R.** (2009) Sainsbury's Attributes Success to Strong Marketing, *MarketingWeek.co.uk*, 13 May.

30. **Roach, T.** (2010) Sainsbury's Feed Your Family for a Fiver: How a Communications Idea Helped Sainsbury's Through the Recession, *Warc.com*.

31. **Davies, G.** (1992) Innovation in Retailing, *Creativity and Innovation Management*, **1** (4), 230.

32. **Rigby, E.** (2006) Supermarkets Prepare to Beef Up Non-Food Ranges, *Financial Times*, 21 February, 5.

33. **Elg, U.** and **U. Johansson** (1996) Networking When National Boundaries Dissolve: The Swedish Food Sector, *European Journal of Marketing*, **30** (2), 62–74.

34. **Roberts, K.** (2006) *The Lovemarks Effect: Winning in the Consumer Revolution*, New York: Powerhouse Books.

35. **Felsted, A.** and **S. Goff** (2004) Going Global is Crucial to Deliver Goods, *Financial Times*, 17 June, 27.

36. **Anonymous** (2003) Benetton Starts 'Dring' Drive, *Financial Times*, 10 December, 33.

37. **Wellian, E., C. Cordon** and **R. Seifert** (2008) Consolidating Distribution (A), International Institute for Management Development.

38. **Wellian, E., C. Cordon** and **R. Seifert** (2009) Consolidating Distribution (B), International Institute for Management Development.

39. **Pickard, J.** (2005) Growing Trend sees Warehouses Swell, *Financial Times*, 17 August, 25.

40. **Lillington, K.** (2008) Giving Voice to New Technology, *Irish Times Health Supplement*, 29 January, 4.

Beach shorts
7.99

H&M

Introduction

H&M is a Swedish company best known for its fashionable but cheap products which are offered to both male and female customers. The target market for H&M products is mainly the 15–30 age group. It offers a range of menswear, children's wear, footwear, cosmetics, home-ware and accessories. It also retails collections of clothing that are designed by well-known designers such as Roberto Cavalli, Karl Lagerfield and Stella McCartney and collections by world-renowned singers such as Kylie and Madonna.

H&M currently operates three main channels of distribution, namely, H&M physical stores, catalogues and the Internet. It has adopted the 'fast fashion' business strategy where efficient supply chains are used to ensure that lead times are reduced and that the range of products on offer is constantly updated. Fast fashion is very much dependent on consumer demand which in turn is influenced by celebrities, print media such as *Now* and *Grazia* magazines, and the Internet including social media such as Facebook and MySpace. Fast fashion products have a limited life span; therefore, the idea is to draw customers into the store on a regular basis to view and hopefully purchase.

H&M operates in one of the toughest industries where recession has seen the closure of many well-known companies. In 2010 alone, H&M opened 214 stores but closed 25 others. However, the brand value of the company increased by 5 per cent in 2010 and *Interbrand* has ranked H&M number 21 in 2009 and 2010. While the company has been highly successful to date, it is facing a number of issues. Is it possible for H&M to maintain 10–15 per cent growth in retail store openings year on year? Will its current distribution system cope with future stores openings and increased online orders? Can H&M compete successfully against new and established online retail stores?

Background

H&M was founded in 1947 by Erling Presson after a trip to the USA where he became interested in the idea of offering customers fashionable but cheap clothing. He opened his first store in Sweden, and in 1964 he expanded to Norway and three years later opened a third H&M store in Denmark. In 1968, Presson acquired a company called Mauritz Widfross which specialized in hunting equipment and menswear. He sold the hunting equipment side of the business and renamed the company Hennes and Mauritz (H&M) and began specializing in clothing for both men and women. Over the next six decades he expanded the product offerings to menswear, children's wear, footwear, cosmetics, home-ware and accessories.

The first UK store was opened in 1976 and further expansion continued in major European cities over the next

Exhibit C11.1 Key H&M brands

COS (Collection of Style)	Weekday	Cheap Monday	Monki
Launched in 2007. This store targets older customers mainly 30 years upwards; the store is more upscale and higher prices are charged for products. In 2010, 35 new stores were opened. COS currently has stores in the UK, Germany, Netherlands, Belgium, Denmark, France, Spain and Ireland	Weekday offers customers clothing products that are creative but affordable. In 2010, 18 new stores were opened	This spin-off from Weekday began by offering customers fashionable jeans but at a cheap price. The company has since expanded its offerings and targets both male and female customers. In 2010 one new store was opened	The aim of this brand is to allow customers to express their personalities through clothing that is environmentally friendly. There is an emphasis on using the least amount of chemicals during the production process. In 2010, 48 new stores were opened

four decades. In 2000, the first American H&M store was opened in Fifth Avenue in New York and since then the retailer has opened over 280 stores. New markets entered in 2010 included South Korea, Israel and Turkey. As well as owning its own retail stores, H&M also operates franchises in nine countries mainly in the Middle East and in North Africa. In 2007 it launched an independent brand called Collection of Style (COS) and in 2008, H&M acquired 60 per cent interest in FaBric Scandinavien AB in 2008 which owned the brands Monki, Weekday and Cheap Monday. These four stores target different types of customers to those that traditionally purchase products from H&M (see Exhibit C11.1).

In 2009, H&M Home was launched which focused on offering a wide variety of home furnishings and accessories. Although this is seen as a separate brand, H&M Home products are sold side by side with clothing stock in selected H&M stores in Europe. In total, the company has in excess of 2,206 stores in thirty-eight markets with a market value of $53.4 billion (see Figure C11.1). It has adopted a unique growth strategy in that it aims to grow the company year on year by 10–15 per cent. For 2011, it is estimated that between 220 and 230 new stores will be opened. Some of these will be in new markets such as Romania, Croatia, Singapore, Morocco and Jordan. H&M operates a policy where all stores are financed from its own cash reserves.

Supply chain management

Traditionally, the clothing industry had a supply chain that was complex and inflexible. Buyers for retailing companies bought stock twice a year and long lead times were the norm. If customer tastes changed during the season, stock could not be altered. As a result retailers were left with a large volume of unwanted stock that was often sold at discounted prices. The traditional

supply chain associated with clothing retailers did not suit the demands of fast fashion companies like H&M. Its success can be attributed to its ability to have flexibility in its design and production which allows the company to react to the very latest fashion trends and constantly changing demands of its customers. H&M's competitors include New Look, Gap and Mango who also offer updated fashion trends to their customers. However Zara, which is part of the Inditex Group, is its key rival. Zara is also renowned for its fast fashion and it controls manufacturing taking charge of what is being produced and how fast it can be distributed to its stores. Currently, Zara takes only 12 days to get a product from the design to a retail store, which contrasts with 21 days for H&M which does not own its manufacturing companies and purchases clothing from over 800 suppliers worldwide. On average about 30 per cent of its suppliers are based in China.

Since H&M operates in an environment where lead times are often short and fashion trends are volatile, which may lead to unpredictable demand, the ability to manage the supply chain efficiently and effectively is crucial to the success of the business. Lead times can vary from two to three weeks to six months. For example, children's clothing and accessories tend to have longer lead times; however, trends based on celebrities tend to be shorter. In order to meet customer demands, the company believes in using a supply chain that is simple, reliable and transparent. However, supply chains also have to be integrated to ensure that costs can be reduced. Integration can be achieved by having ongoing relationships with partners. Currently, H&M has 22 production offices around the world, based in Europe, Asia, America and Africa. The responsibility of each production office is to ensure that orders are placed with the right suppliers who can guarantee specific lead times. Suppliers are chosen not only for their cost effectiveness, but also criteria such as quality and ability to meet short lead times.

Designers use information and design technology such as CAD to enable them to quickly produce new designs.

Figure C11.1 H&M store profile

Market	Year established	No. of stores 30 Nov 2010	New stores during the year	Closed stores during the year	Sales 2010 including vat (Sek M)	Sales 2009 including VAT (Sek M)
Market overview						
Sales including VAT per country and number of stores, financial year 1 December – 30 November						
Sweden	1947	168	10	3	8,365	7,881
Norway	1964	101	9		5,858	5,598
Denmark	1967	87	12	2	4,358	4,254
UK	1976	192	26	1	8,392	7,564
Switzerland	1978	75	2		6,122	6,042
Germany	1980	377	24	9	30,628	30,069
Netherlands	1989	112	10	1	7,387	7,402
Belgium	1992	64	6	3	3,345	3,502
Austria	1994	66	4	1	5,255	5,503
Luxembourg	1996	10	2	1	406	411
Finland	1997	43	6	1	2,567	2,543
France	1998	151	17	1	9,140	8,455
USA	2000	208	19		8,916	7,487
Spain	2000	122	9	1	6,109	6,285
Poland	2003	76	11		2,668	2,466
Czech Republic	2003	22	3		707	677
Portugal	2003	21	1		937	928
Italy	2003	72	8		4,331	3,616
Canada	2004	55	3		2,713	2,190
Slovenia	2004	11	1		568	615
Ireland	2005	12	1		517	557
Hungary	2005	15	5		387	306
Slovakia	2007	7	3		225	187
Greece	2007	18	3		646	480
China	2007	47	20		2,527	1,614
Japan	2008	10	4		1,794	1,111
Russia	2009	11	6		916	373
South Korea	2010	2	2		255	
Turkey	2010	1	1		28	
Franchise[1]	2006	50	15	1	889[2]	591[2]
Total		2,206	243	25	126,966	118,697

1) United Arab Emirates, Kuwait, Qatar, Saudi Arabia, Egypt, Bahrain, Oman, Lebanon and Israel.
2) Excluding VAT.

H&M's supply chain is very much based on a pull strategy from its customers. Point-of-sale (POS) information is used to enable store managers to make decisions regarding issues such as ordering stock levels and identifying individual trends within each store. H&M, like many of its competitors, has two seasons each year – spring and autumn. However, within each season there are many collections. In order to ensure that stores are stocked, the company has a distribution centre in each country in which it has a store and these distribution centres share information with designers and manufacturers.

Multi-channel marketing

The company uses two other method of distribution besides physical stores to gain access to its customers. In recent years an emphasis has been placed on catalogues and Internet sales. In 1980, H&M acquired Rowells which was responsible for the printing of its catalogues. Each year it launches two catalogues in spring and two more in autumn. Throughout the season, smaller seasonal catalogues are launched to ensure that the customer has access to the most up to date fashion trends. Until 2006, the Nordic regions were the only areas where customers could purchase H&M stock through a catalogue, but since then catalogue shopping has been offered elsewhere.

In 1998, the company began its online sales operation. Again, only customers in the Nordic regions, Germany, Austria and the Netherlands were able to order products online. Since then, its Internet markets have expanded to include the UK. Unlike the 'bricks and mortar' store where space is limited, the online customer has access to a wider variety of stock. In 2011, H&M revamped its website to ensure the customer receives as near a 'bricks and mortar' experience as possible. The website is also used as a way of inspiring potential customers by exposing them to current trends and methods of mixing and matching accessories, footwear and clothing using a 'dressing room' facility.

Social media such as Facebook, Twitter and YouTube have also been used to interact with customers. Currently, H&M has nearly 8 million fans on its Facebook page and attracts between 40,000 and 60,000 new fans weekly. Twitter followers discuss current clothing trends and obtain ideas to create their own personal style using clothing from H&M stores. YouTube is also used by the retailer to upload fashion videos. In 2010 more than 5.5 million viewers logged on to watch H&M's fashion videos. The retailer also uses iPhone and iPad applications (apps) to ensure that its followers are kept up to date when new stock arrives in their nearest store. These apps currently have more than 2.2 million downloads. Key competitors like Zara also have a significant Internet and social media presence. It offers online sales to customers in the following countries: Spain, Portugal, France, Italy, Germany, the UK, Austria, Belgium, Holland, Ireland, Luxemburg, Sweden, Norway, Denmark, Monaco and Switzerland.

The future

What next for H&M? As it continues its quest for world domination two key issues need to be addressed. Firstly, it operates in a very competitive environment where one's ability to meet changing fashion trends and price are key to success. However, it cannot ignore the fact that its major competitor Zara is able to get products to the customer much faster than H&M. In order to remain competitive, H&M may have to acquire manufacturers to reduce the time it takes to get clothing from the design stage to the customer?

Secondly, H&M faces new logistical challenges in the coming years if it decides to expand its online sales to all countries where it currently has physical stores and franchises. It will be one of many online retailers trying to attract customers and will need to consider whether to offer the same lines of stock worldwide or have particular lines that are exclusive to customers living in particular regions of the world. Operating in the fast fashion world, it will have to devise tactics to attract customers to its website on a regular basis.

Questions

1 Identify areas of potential conflict in H&M's current supply chain. How should H&M overcome these?
2 Discuss the advantages and disadvantages of H&M purchasing manufacturing companies in order to enable the company to reduce lead times to the customer.
3 Discuss the advantages and disadvantages for H&M of using a multi-channel distribution system.
4 What tactics should H&M employ to ensure that visitors return to its website on a regular basis?

This case was prepared by Valerie McCarthy, University of Limerick from various published sources as a basis for class discussion rather than to show effective or ineffective management.

H&M have used the music icon Kylie Minogue to help build their brand profile.
www.mcgraw-hill.co.uk/textbooks/fahy

Chapter 12
Marketing Planning and Strategy

Chapter outline

The process of marketing planning

Marketing audit

Marketing objectives

Core strategy

Competitive strategies

Tactical marketing decisions

Organization and implementation

Control

The rewards of marketing planning

Problems in making planning work

Learning outcomes

By the end of this chapter you will understand:

1 the role of marketing planning within businesses
2 the process of marketing planning
3 the rewards and problems associated with marketing planning
4 the roles of industry analysis and internal analysis in planning and strategy
5 the different competitive strategies, and the sources of competitive advantage.

Visa

Visa is a global payments company that connects consumers, businesses, banks and governments in more than 200 countries and territories, enabling them to use digital currency instead of cash and cheques. The now famous brand started life as the BankAmerica credit card in California in the 1950s. However as it expanded globally, the need for a single, universally appealing global name was recognized and in 1976 'Visa' was selected. The brand offers customers the promise of convenience, acceptance, flexibility and security in making payments worldwide. To fulfil this promise, it established a global payments system linking card

holders, merchants and financial institutions. This system is supported by fraud detection and prevention features to enable secure payment transactions as well as innovations designed to measure credit risk and to compensate customers in cases where its operations fail. Called VisaNet, the system is capable of 10,000 transactions per second.

Over the years, the company has continually built and supported its brand and in 2010, Visa was ranked as the number 18 most valuable brand in the world by *Brandz* and the clear leader in payment system brands. Central to its success has been its adoption of strong positioning slogans ranging from 'the way the world pays' in the 1970s to 'more people go with Visa' which underpinned its first global campaign in 2009. These propositions have been supported by high profile advertising and sponsorship. It has been the official credit card of the Summer and Winter Olympic Games since 1986, the FIFA World Cup since 2007 and the NFL in the USA since 2005 which gives it access to high profile events such as the Superbowl. It is an extensive user of television, print and digital media and in 2011, it launched Memory Mapper – a social media application that allows consumers to share their travel experiences using photos, videos and blogs.

Visa has been able to capitalize on the rapidly growing market for electronic payments driven by the rise in global commerce, international travel and online purchasing. It successfully became a publicly quoted company in 2008, just at the time when the global financial community was in crisis following the collapse of the investment banking firm, Lehman Bros. Part of its attraction to investors was that it dominates the global payment systems industry and has a unique revenue model which sees it generating income from both banks for issuing cards and merchants for accepting them. It does not issue credit or debit cards or send out bills – this is done by financial institutions. As electronic transactions increase so do its sales and profits. It has been frequently criticized for raising the barriers to entry to new competitors and for squeezing merchants for higher fees. It is the market leader with an estimated 40 per cent share, followed by Mastercard and American Express with Discover Card a distant fourth. By 2010, it was generating revenues in excess of US$8 billion and its share price had doubled since its launch. However, new technological developments on the horizon such as consumers having the facility to pay for goods using smartphones means that its future success is less certain.[1]

In Chapter 1 we introduced the notion of marketing planning. Then, throughout the book, we have examined the nature of customers and markets, and the environmental context within which organizations operate. We have also examined the variety of decisions that need to be taken by marketers. Given the challenging competitive environment in which firms operate, it is important that these decisions are not taken in an ad hoc way but rather in a systematic and rational manner. The process by which businesses analyse the environment and their capabilities, decide upon courses of marketing action and implement those decisions is called **marketing planning**, and it is this that will be the focus of this chapter. Equally, it is important to remember that there must be a strategic element to marketing plans – that is, they must map out a direction for the company over the medium to long term. In this chapter we will also examine some of the popular frameworks used by companies to help them answer key strategic questions, such as where and how to compete, and how to grow. Answers to these questions will be central aspects of any marketing plan.

Marketing planning forms part of the broader concept known as 'strategic planning'; this involves not only marketing but also the fit between production, finance and personnel strategies, and the environment. The aim of strategic planning is to shape and reshape a company so that its business and products continue to meet corporate objectives (e.g. profit or sales growth). Because marketing management is charged with the responsibility of managing the interface between the company and its environment, it has a key role to play in strategic planning.

A firm may be composed of a number of businesses (often equating to divisions), each of which serves distinct groups of customers and has a distinct set of competitors (see Chapter 6). Each business may be strategically autonomous and thus form a **strategic business unit** (SBU). A major component of a corporate plan will be the allocation of resources to each SBU. Strategic decisions at the corporate level are normally concerned with acquisition, divestment and diversification. Here, too, marketing can play a role through the identification of opportunities and threats in the environment as they relate to current and prospective businesses.

The following essential questions need to be asked when thinking about marketing planning decisions:

- Where are we now?
- Where would we like to be?
- How do we get there?

While these may seem relatively simple questions, they can be difficult to answer in practice. Businesses comprise individuals who may have very different views on the answers to these questions. Furthermore, the outcome of the planning process may have fundamental implications for their jobs. Planning is, therefore, a political activity, and those with a vested interest may view it from a narrow departmental, rather than business-wide, perspective. A key issue in getting planning systems to work is tackling such behavioural problems.[2] However, at this point in the chapter it is important to understand the process of marketing planning.

The process of marketing planning

The process of marketing planning is outlined in Figure 12.1. The process provides a well-defined path from generating a **business mission** to implementing and controlling the resultant plans. It provides a framework that shows how all the key elements of marketing discussed so far relate to each other. In real life, planning is rarely so straightforward and logical. Different people may be involved at various stages of the planning process, and the degrees to which they accept and are influenced by the outcomes of earlier planning stages are variable.

Business mission

Ackoff defined the business mission as:

> a broadly defined, enduring statement of purpose that distinguishes a business from others of its type.[3]

This definition captures two essential ingredients in mission statements: they are enduring and specific to the individual organization.[4] Two fundamental questions that need to be addressed are: 'What business are we in?' and 'What business do we want to be in?' In a global, highly competitive marketplace where industry boundaries are constantly blurring, the answers to these questions may not be as obvious as they might first appear. The answers also define the scope and activities of the company, and will be determined by an assessment of the needs of the market, the competences of the firm and background of the company plus the personalities of its senior management.

Including the market and needs factors ensures that the business definition is market-focused rather than product-based (see Exhibit 12.1). Thus the purpose of a company such as Nokia is not to manufacture telephones but to allow people to communicate with

Figure 12.1 The marketing planning process

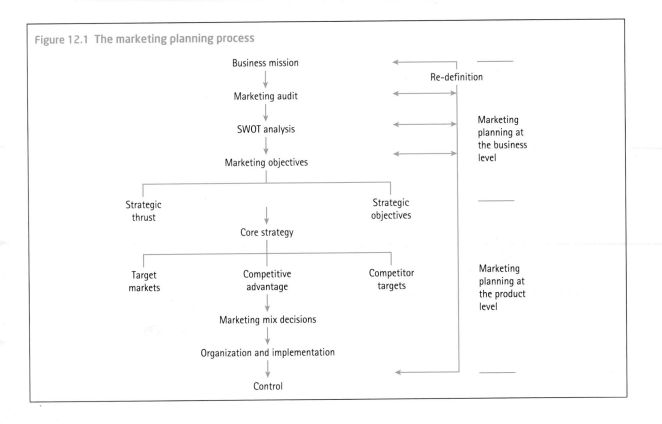

Exhibit 12.1 Vision statements such as these for the consumer products company P&G and the Dutch electronics giant Philips are designed to inspire employees and customers

PHILIPS
sense and simplicity

each other as is exemplified by its slogan 'connecting people'. The reason for ensuring that a business definition is market-focused is that products are transient, but basic needs such as transportation, entertainment and eating are lasting. Thus, Levitt argued that a business should be viewed as a customer-satisfying process not a goods-producing process.[5] By adopting a customer perspective, new opportunities are more likely to be seen.

Management must be wary of a definition that is too wide, although this advice has merit in advocating the avoidance of a narrow business definition. Levitt suggested that railroad companies would have survived had they defined their business as transportation and moved into the airline business. However, this ignores the limits of business competence of the railroads. Did they possess the necessary skills and resources to run an airline? Clearly a key constraint on a business definition can be the competences (both actual and potential) of management, and the resources at their disposal. Conversely, competences can act as the motivator for widening a business mission. Asda (Associated Dairies) redefined its business mission as a producer and distributor of milk to a retailer of fast-moving consumer goods (fmcg) partly on the basis of its distribution skills, which it rightly believed could be extended to products beyond milk.

The background of the company and the personalities of its senior management are the final determinants of the business mission. Businesses that have established themselves in the marketplace over many years and have a clear position in the minds of the customer may ignore opportunities that are at variance with that position. The personalities and beliefs of the people who run businesses also shape the business mission. This last factor emphasizes the judgemental nature of business definition. There is no right or wrong business mission in abstract. The mission should be based on the vision that top management and their subordinates have of the future of the business. This vision is a coherent and powerful statement of what the business should aim to become.[6] The business mission will serve as an overriding influence on the nature of the marketing plan and should also serve to motivate all staff to attain the targets set out in the plan.

Marketing audit

A **marketing audit** is a systematic examination of a firm's marketing environment, objectives, strategies and activities, which aims to identify key strategic issues, problem areas and opportunities. The marketing audit is, therefore, the basis on which a plan of action to improve marketing performance can be built. The marketing audit provides answers to the following questions:

- Where are we now?
- How did we get there?
- Where are we heading?

The answers to these questions depend on an analysis of the internal and external environments of a business. This analysis benefits from a clear mission statement since the latter defines the boundaries of the environmental scan and aids decisions regarding which strategic issues and opportunities are important.

An internal audit concentrates on those areas that are under the control of marketing management, whereas an external audit focuses on those forces over which management has no control. The results of the marketing audit are a key determinant of the future direction of the business and may give rise to a redefined business mission statement. Alongside the marketing audit, a business may conduct audits of other functional areas such as production, finance and personnel. The co-ordination and integration of these audits produces a composite business plan in which marketing issues play a central role since they concern decisions

about which products to manufacture for which markets. These decisions clearly have production, financial and personnel implications, and successful implementation depends on each functional area acting in concert. A checklist of those areas that are likely to be examined in a marketing audit is given in Tables 12.1 and 12.2.

External analysis

External analysis covers the macroenvironment, the market and competition. The macroenvironment consists of broad environmental issues that may impinge on the business. These include the economy, social/cultural issues, technological changes, political/legal factors and ecological concerns (as we saw in Chapter 2).

Market analysis consists of statistical analyses of market size, growth rates and trends, and **customer**

Table 12.1 External marketing audit checklist

Macroenvironment (see Chapter 2)
Economic: inflation, interest rates, unemployment
Social/cultural: age distribution, lifestyle changes, values, attitudes
Technological: new product and process technologies, materials
Political/legal: monopoly control, new laws, regulations
Ecological: conservation, pollution, energy
The market
Market: size, growth rates, trends and developments
Customers: who are they, their choice criteria, how, when, where do they buy, how do they rate us vis-à-vis competition on product, promotion, price, distribution
Market: segmentation: how do customers group, what benefits does each group seek
Distribution: power changes, channel attractiveness, growth potential, physical distribution methods, decision-makers and influencers
Suppliers: who and where they are, their competences and shortcomings, trends affecting them, future outlook
Competition
Who are the major competitors: actual and potential
What are their objectives and strategies
What are their strengths (distinctive competences) and weaknesses (vulnerability analysis)
Market shares and size of competitors
Profitability analysis
Entry barriers

Table 12.2 Internal marketing audit checklist

Operating results (by product, customer, geographic region)
Sales
Market share
Profit margins
Costs
Strategic issues analysis
Marketing objectives
Market segmentation
Competitive advantage
Core competences
Positioning
Portfolio analysis
Marketing operations effectiveness
Product
Price
Promotion
Distribution
Marketing structures
Marketing organization
Marketing training
Intra- and interdepartmental communication
Marketing systems
Marketing information systems
Marketing planning system
Marketing control system

analysis (including who they are, what choice criteria they use, how they rate competitive offerings and market segmentation bases). Next, **distribution analysis** covers significant movements in power bases, channel attractiveness studies, an identification of physical distribution methods, and understanding the role and interests of decision-makers, and influences within distributors.

Competitor analysis examines the nature of actual and potential competitors, and their objectives and strategies. It would also seek to identify their strengths (distinctive competences), weaknesses (vulnerability analysis), market shares and size. For example, firms considering entering the cloud computing business might conduct an analysis of both existing competitors and potential opportunities in this space. Profitability analysis examines **industry** profitability and the comparative performance of competitors. Finally, entry barrier analysis identifies the key financial and non-financial barriers that protect the industry from competitor attack.

A very popular external analysis framework is Porter's 'five forces' model. Porter was interested in why some industries appeared to be inherently more profitable than others, and concluded that industry attractiveness was a function of five forces: the threat of entry of new competitors; the threat of substitutes; the bargaining power of suppliers; the bargaining power of buyers; and the rivalry between existing competitors. Each of these five forces, in turn, comprises a number of elements that combine to determine the strength of each force, as shown in Figure 12.2. So, for example, industries that have high barriers to entry but relatively low levels of buyer/supplier power, low threat of substitutes and relatively benign competition will be more attractive than industries with the opposite set of forces (see Marketing in Action 12.1). For example, high barriers to entry and high levels of competitive rivalry between major players such as Amazon, Sony and Apple may already have made the e-reader business unattractive for some potential entrants. We shall now look briefly at each of the forces in turn, and see how this framework can assist firms in answering the first three key planning questions identified earlier:

- Where are we now?
- How did we get there?
- Where are we heading?

However, since the arrival of the Internet, the industry has been under threat like never before. News (and entertainment) is available online, much of it is free and users can customize the information that they want to receive by selecting particular newsfeeds. As a result, the circulation levels of newspapers have been falling steadily. The affect on advertisers is twofold: falling newspaper sales mean that advertisers reach fewer readers, while online media provide alternative promotional options for advertisers. As a result, in some countries, the industry has been in freefall. For example in the USA, 120 newspapers shut down in 2008 and 16,000 reporters were laid off. Many other titles are losing money and struggling to find models that allow them to disseminate information online and still generate revenues. The industry would appear to be at the most difficult stage yet in its history.

The threat of new entrants

Because new entrants can raise the level of competition in an industry, they have the potential to reduce its

Figure 12.2 The Porter model of competitive industry structure

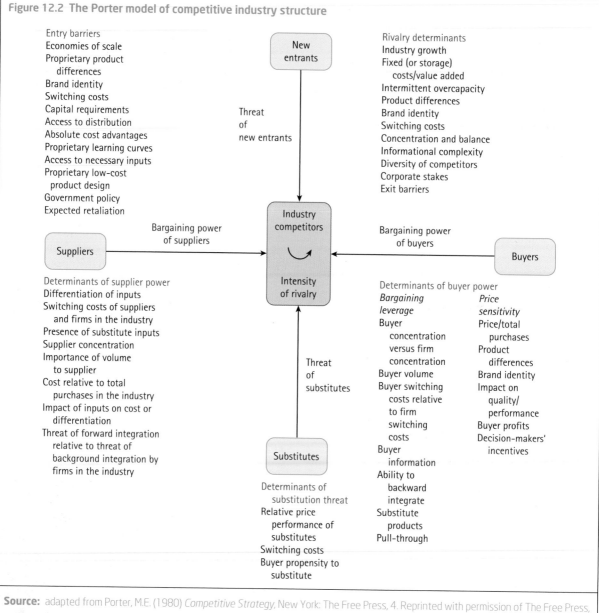

Source: adapted from Porter, M.E. (1980) *Competitive Strategy*, New York: The Free Press, 4. Reprinted with permission of The Free Press, an imprint of Simon & Schuster. Copyright © 1980 by The Free Press

Marketing in Action 12.1 The newspaper industry

Critical Thinking: Below is a review of recent changes in the newspaper industry. Critically evaluate these changes using Porter's Five Forces Model as a guide.

For generations, the newspaper has been one of the key means through which people obtain their news and other information on subjects that interest them. It is an industry that dates back to the sixteenth century when short pamphlets containing news and other information began to be printed and it successfully survived the arrival of new technologies such as radio and television. It is a huge global industry, with the biggest selling daily newspapers to be found in Japan where the *Yomiuri Shimbum* boasts over 10 million readers. The German newspaper *Bild*, is the largest in Europe with a circulation of over 3.5 million.

The production of newspapers is a high-cost activity involving significant investments in labour, printing and distribution. As a result, the industry revenue model involves two components – income from single-copy sales and subscriptions combined with the sale of advertising space. Over time advertising space has become to be the dominant source of income accounting for about 80 per cent of revenue in some markets like the USA since 2000. As a result, the industry tends to be dominated by media giants. For example, Rupert Murdoch's News Corporation owns 175 newspapers around the world while Axel Springer AG owns 150 European newspapers.

However, since the arrival of the Internet, the industry has been under threat like never before. News (and entertainment) is available online, much of it is free and users can customize the information that they want to receive by selecting particular newsfeeds. As a result, the circulation levels of newspapers have been falling steadily. The effect on advertisers is twofold. Falling newspaper sales mean that advertisers reach fewer readers, while online media provide alternative promotional options for advertisers. As a result, in some countries the industry has been in freefall. For example in the US, 120 newspapers shut down in 2008 and 16,000 reporters were laid off. Many other titles are losing money and struggling to find models that allow them to disseminate information online and still generate revenues. The industry would appear to be at the most difficult stage yet in its history.

attractiveness. The threat of new entrants depends on the barriers to entry. High entry barriers exist in some industries (e.g. pharmaceuticals), whereas other industries are much easier to enter (e.g. restaurants).

Key entry barriers include:

- economies of scale
- capital requirements
- switching costs
- access to distribution
- expected retaliation.

The bargaining power of suppliers

The cost of raw materials and components can have a major bearing on a firm's profitability. The higher the bargaining power of suppliers, the higher these costs. The bargaining power of suppliers will be high when:

- there are many buyers and few dominant suppliers
- they offer differentiated, highly valued products (see Exhibit 12.2)
- suppliers threaten to integrate forward into the industry
- buyers do not threaten to integrate backward into supply
- the industry is not a key customer group to the suppliers.

Exhibit 12.2 **Information technology solutions supplier IBM uses advertising like this to demonstrate the value that it provides to buyers**

A firm can reduce the bargaining power of suppliers by seeking new sources of supply, threatening to integrate backward into supply and designing standardized components so that many suppliers are able to produce them.

The bargaining power of buyers

As we saw in Chapter 11, the concentration of European retailing has raised buyers' bargaining power relative to that of manufacturers. The bargaining power of buyers is greater when:

- there are few dominant buyers and many sellers
- products are standardized
- buyers threaten to integrate backward into the industry
- suppliers do not threaten to integrate forward into the buyer's industry
- the industry is not a key supplying group for buyers.

The threat of substitutes

The presence of substitute products can lower industry attractiveness and profitability because they put a constraint on price levels. For example, tea and coffee are fairly close substitutes in most European countries. Raising the price of coffee, therefore, would make tea more attractive. The threat of substitute products depends on:

- buyers' willingness to substitute
- the relative price and performance of substitutes
- the costs of switching to substitutes.

The threat of substitute products can be lowered by building up switching costs, which may be psychological – for example, by creating strong distinctive brand personalities and maintaining a price differential commensurate with perceived customer values.

Industry competitors

The intensity of rivalry between competitors in an industry depends on the following factors.

1   *Structure of competition*: there is more intense rivalry when there are a large number of small competitors or a few equally balanced competitors; there is less rivalry when a clear leader (at least 50 per cent larger than the second) exists with a large cost advantage.
2   *Structure of costs*: high fixed costs encourage price cutting to fill capacity.

3   *Degree of differentiation*: commodity products encourage rivalry, while highly differentiated products that are hard to copy are associated with less intense rivalry.
4   *Switching costs*: when switching costs are high because a product is specialized, the customer has invested a lot of resources in learning how to use a product or has made tailor-made investments that are worthless with other products and suppliers, rivalry is reduced.
5   *Strategic objectives*: when competitors are pursuing build strategies, competition is likely to be more intense than when playing hold or harvest strategies.
6   *Exit barriers*: when barriers to leaving an industry are high due to such factors as lack of opportunities elsewhere, high vertical integration, emotional barriers or the high cost of closing down plant, rivalry will be more intense than when exit barriers are low.

Internal analysis

An internal audit permits the performance and activities of a business to be assessed in the light of environmental developments. Operating results form the basis of assessment through analysis of sales, market share, profit margins and costs. **Strategic issues analysis** examines the suitability of marketing objectives and segmentation bases in the light of changes in the marketplace. Competitive advantages and the core competences on which they are based would be re-assessed and the positioning of products in the market critically reviewed. Finally, product portfolios should be analysed to determine future strategic objectives.

Each aspect of the marketing mix is reviewed in the light of changing customer requirements and competitor activity. The **marketing structures** on which marketing activities are based should be analysed. Marketing structure consists of the marketing organization, training, and the intra-departmental and inter-departmental communication that takes place within an organization. Marketing organization is reviewed to determine fit with strategy and the market, and marketing training requirements are examined. Finally, communications and relationships within the marketing department, and between marketing and other functions (e.g. R&D, engineering, production) need to be appraised.

Marketing systems are audited to check their effectiveness. This covers the marketing information, planning and **control** systems that support marketing activities. Shortfalls in information provision are analysed; the marketing planning system is critically appraised for cost-effectiveness, and the marketing control system is assessed in the light of accuracy, timeliness (whether it provides evaluations when managers require them) and coverage (whether the system evaluates the key variables affecting company performance).

The checklists in Tables 12.1 and 12.2 provide the basis for deciding on the topics to be included in the marketing audit. However, to give the same amount of attention and detailed analysis to every item would cause the audit to grind to a halt under the weight of data and issues. In practice, the judgement of those conducting the audit is critical in deciding the key items to focus upon. Those factors that are considered of crucial importance to the company's performance will merit most attention. One by-product of the marketing audit may be a realization that information about key environmental issues is lacking.

All assumptions should be made explicit as an ongoing part of the marketing audit. For example, key assumptions might be:

- inflation will average 5 per cent during the planning period
- VAT levels will not be changed
- worldwide overcapacity will remain at 150 per cent
- no new entrants into the market will emerge.

The marketing audit should not be a desperate attempt to turn around an ailing business, but an ongoing activity. Some companies conduct an annual audit as part of their annual planning system; others, operating in less turbulent environments, may consider two or three years an adequate period between audits. Some companies may feel that the use of an outside consultant to co-ordinate activities and provide an objective, outside view is beneficial while others may believe that their own managers are best equipped to conduct such analyses. Clearly there is no set formula for deciding when and by whom the audit is conducted. The decision ultimately rests on the preferences and situation facing the management team.

SWOT analysis

A structured approach to evaluating the strategic position of a business by identifying its strengths, weaknesses, opportunities and threats is known as a **SWOT analysis**. It provides a simple method of synthesizing the results of the marketing audit. Internal strengths and weaknesses are summarized as they relate to external opportunities and threats (see Figure 12.3).

For a SWOT analysis to be useful a number of guidelines must be followed. First, not only absolute, but also relative strengths and weakness should be

Figure 12.3 Strengths, weaknesses, opportunities and threats (SWOT) analysis

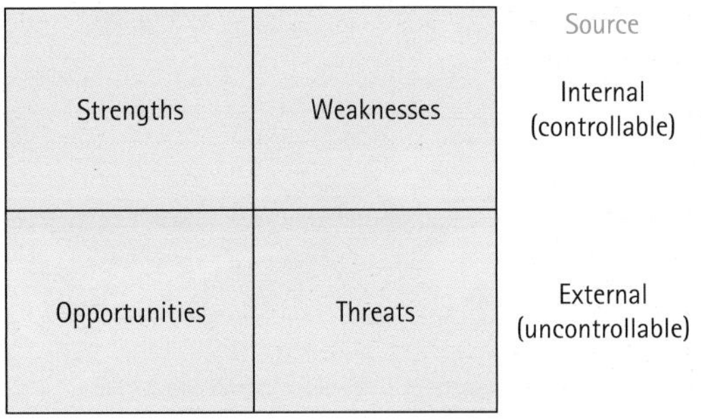

identified. Relative strengths focus on strengths and weaknesses as compared to the competition. Thus, if everyone produces quality products this is not identified as a relative strength. Two lists should be drawn up based on absolute and relative strengths and weaknesses. Strengths that can be exploited can be both absolute and relative, but how they are exploited and the degree to which they can be used depends on whether the competition also possesses them. Relative strengths provide the distinctive competences of a business (see Exhibit 12.3). But strengths need to be looked at objectively as they can sometimes turn into weaknesses. A case in point is Sony, one of whose strengths has been its product innovation capabilities. Such was the success of its products that it seemed to have taken its eye off the market and technological trends. For example, the Walkman has been supplanted by the Apple iPod in the portable audio business and similarly its dominance of cathode ray tube television technology has caused it to miss the trend towards flat-screen televisions.[7]

An absolute weakness that competitors also possess should be identified because it can clearly become a source of relative strength if overcome. If all businesses in an industry are poor at after-sales service, this should be noted as a weakness, as it provides the potential for gaining competitive advantage. Relative weaknesses should also be listed because these may be the sources of competitive disadvantage to which managerial attention should be focused. For example, internal analysis by the DSG group, which owns Dixons, PC World and Currys, found that customer service, the internal layout of stores and product presentation were significant weaknesses.[8]

Second, only those resources or capabilities that would be valued by the customer should be included when evaluating strengths and weaknesses. Thus, strengths such as 'We are an old established firm', 'We are a large supplier' and 'We are technologically advanced' should be questioned for their impact on

Exhibit 12.3 Advertising like this for Tag Heuer watches (with the tagline – The Mikrograph: precise to 1/100th of a second) aims to demonstrate its unique competitive strengths in making precision devices

THE MIKROGRAPH. PRECISE TO 1/100TH OF A SECOND.   **TAG**Heuer   SWISS AVANT-GARDE SINCE 1860

customer satisfaction. It is conceivable that such bland generalizations confer as many weaknesses as strengths.

Third, opportunities and threats should be listed as anticipated events or trends *outside* the business that have implications for performance. They should not be couched in terms of strategies. For example, 'To enter market segment X' is not an opportunity but a strategic objective that may result from a perceived opportunity arising from the emergence of market segment X as attractive because of its growth potential and lack of competition. The ability to spot and exploit an opportunity can lead to success that dramatically exceeds expectations, as demonstrated by the rapid growth of companies like Facebook, Amazon and Google. It also requires the kind of foresight described in Marketing in Action 12.2.

Marketing objectives

The definition of **marketing objectives** may be derived from the results of the marketing audit and the

SWOT analysis. Two types of objective need to be considered: strategic thrust and strategic objectives.

Strategic thrust

Objectives should be set in terms of which products to sell in which markets. This describes the **strategic thrust** of the business. The strategic thrust defines the future direction of the business, and the basic alternatives are summarized in the Ansoff growth matrix, as shown in Figure 12.4. These are:

- existing products in existing markets (market penetration or expansion)
- new products for existing markets (product development)
- existing products in new markets (market development)
- new products for new markets (diversification).

We will now look at each of these in turn.

Marketing in Action 12.2 Live Nation: dominating live entertainment?

> **Critical Thinking:** Below is a review of the rapid rise of Live Nation in the entertainment business. Read it and critically evaluate how it exploited the opportunities created by the changes taking place in the music business. Has its growth strategy been too ambitious?

For some time now, the music industry has been in turmoil. Record sales, which have traditionally been the mainstay of the business, have been falling ever since Napster pioneered the digital downloading of music for free. With a shrinking pie left for recording artists and record labels, the income coming from live performance has become ever more important. From the days when the concert tour was used to promote the album, the industry turned to a situation where the album was used to promote the tour!

Into this growing space have moved organizations like Live Nation, which was founded in 2005 but in a very short space of time has grown to become the largest live entertainment organization in the world. By focusing on the organization and management of concert tours and events, Live Nation placed itself at the heart of where revenue was being generated in the music business – the sales of tickets and associated merchandise at live events. But the company began, and continues, to expand very rapidly. By 2007, it was buying music merchandising companies. It signed thousands of

contracts with artists, including multi-million dollar deals with acts like Madonna, U2, Shakira and Jay-Z. It owns over 150 venues and festival sites around the world and also merged its ticket sales operations with TicketMaster in 2010, making it easily the dominant player in ticket distribution. It is also increasingly offering recording contract services to artists and entertainers and in 2011 agreed a joint venture with Groupon to give discounts on ticket sales.

In a short space of time, Live Nation has gone from being the company that simply managed the concert promotion element of a record label's activities to being at the core of how recording artists now generate their incomes. But the speed of expansion has worried investors. It has suffered several quarterly losses and dramatic drops in its share price, but with an estimated 62 per cent of the live music market, it is likely to be a significant force in the industry for some time to come.

Based on: Carroll (2010);[9] Foley (2008);[10] LaMotta (2008)[11].

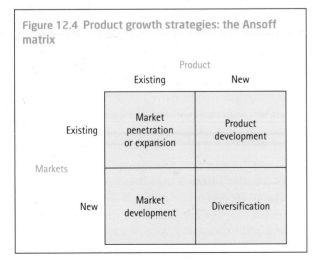

Figure 12.4 Product growth strategies: the Ansoff matrix

1 *Market penetration*: this strategy involves taking the existing product in the existing market and attempting to increase penetration. Existing customers may become more brand loyal (i.e. brand switch less often) and/or new customers in the same market may begin to buy the brand. Other tactics to increase penetration include getting existing customers to use the brand more often (e.g. eat breakfast cereals as daytime snacks) and to use a greater quantity when they use it (e.g. two teaspoons of coffee instead of one). The latter tactic would also have the effect of expanding the market. Market penetration is usually achieved by more effective use of promotion or distribution, or by cutting prices.

Exhibit 12.4 Breakfast cereal manufacturers have moved into the snack food business with products like these

2 *Product development*: this strategy involves increasing sales by improving current products or developing new products for current markets (see Exhibit 12.4). For example, many companies provide additional services to their customers. Faced with pressure on their margins for product sales, drugstores in the USA have started providing walk-in clinics where patients are examined by nurse practitioners who conduct basic procedures such as vaccinations for lower prices than doctors. Global accounting firms like KPMG and Deloitte provide management consulting services to clients.

3 *Market development*: this strategy is used when current products are sold in new markets. This may involve moving into new international markets or moving into new market segments. For example, Nestlé, the world's biggest food group, has been able to grow sales of its brands such as Kit Kat confectionery and Nescafé instant coffee by over 10 per cent in emerging markets such as Africa, Asia and Oceania compared with relatively stagnant sales growth in Western Europe.[12]

4 *Diversification*: this strategy occurs when new products are developed for new markets. This is the most risky strategy but may be necessary when a company's current products and markets offer few prospects of future growth. When there is synergy between the existing and new products this strategy is more likely to work. For example, by developing an online library, Google is aiming to become a content provider rather than just a search engine. It has signed deals with a number of leading libraries around the world, where it will scan thousands of volumes and make them available online.[13]

Strategic objectives

Alongside objectives for product/market direction, **strategic objectives** for each product also need to be agreed. This begins the process of planning at the product level. There are four alternatives:

1 build
2 hold
3 harvest
4 divest.

For new products, the strategic objective will inevitably be to build sales and market share. For existing products the appropriate strategic objective will depend on the particular situation associated with the product. This will be determined in the market audit, SWOT analysis and evaluation of the strategic options outlined earlier. In particular, product portfolio planning tools such as the Boston Consulting Group's growth-share matrix (as outlined in Chapter 6) may be used to aid this analysis.

The important point to remember at this stage is that *building* sales and market share is not the only sensible strategic objective for a product. As we shall see, *holding* sales and market share may make commercial sense under certain conditions; *harvesting*, where sales and market share are allowed to fall but profit margins are maximized, may also be preferable to building; finally, *divestment*, where the product is dropped or sold, can be the logical outcome of the situation analysis.

Together, strategic thrust and strategic objectives define where the business and its products intend to go in the future.

Core strategy

When objectives have been set, a way to achieve them must be decided upon. **Core strategy** focuses on how objectives can be accomplished, and consists of three key elements: target markets, competitor targets and establishing a competitive advantage. We shall now examine each of these elements in turn and discuss the relationship between them.

Target markets

The choice of **target market**(s) is a central plank of core strategy. As we saw in Chapter 5, marketing is not about chasing any customer at any price. A decision has to be made regarding those groups of customers (segments) that are attractive to the business, and that match its supply capabilities. To varying degrees, the choice of target market to serve will be considered during SWOT analysis and the setting of marketing objectives. For example, when considering the strategic thrust of the business, decisions regarding which markets to serve must be made. However, this may be defined in broad terms – for example, 'Enter the alternative healthcare market'. Within that market there will be a number of segments (customer groups) of varying attractiveness and a choice has to be made regarding which segments to serve.

In Chapter 5, we identified a variety of bases for segmenting markets. Information regarding size, growth potential, level of competitor activity, customer requirements and key factors for success is needed to facilitate the assessment of the attractiveness of each segment. This may have been compiled during the marketing audit and should be considered in light of the capabilities of the business to compete effectively in each specific target market. The marketing audit and SWOT analysis will provide the basis for judging the business's capabilities.

The Toyota Yaris 'Treat it with Respect' campaign illustrates its targeting of the economy car segment. **www.mcgraw-hill.co.uk/textbooks/fahy**

Competitor targets

In tandem with decisions regarding markets are judgments about **competitor targets**. These are the organizations against which a company chooses to compete directly, and sometimes the competition is head-on. Weak competitors may be viewed as easy prey and resources channelled to attack them. For example, major airlines are accused from time to time of aggressively targeting the routes used by their smaller competitors, either through heavy promotion or price discounting.

Competitive advantage

The key to superior performance is to gain and hold a competitive advantage. Firms can gain a competitive advantage through differentiation of their product offering, which provides superior customer value, or by managing for lowest delivered cost. Evidence for this proposition was provided by Hall,[14] who examined the competitive strategies pursued by the two leading firms (in terms of return on investment) in eight mature industries characterized by slow growth and intense competition. In each industry, the two leading firms offered either high product differentiation or the lowest delivered cost. In most cases, an industry's return-on-investment leader opted for one of the strategies, while the second-place firm pursued the other.

Competitive strategies

When combined with the competitive scope of activities (broad vs narrow) these two means of competitive advantage result in four generic strategies: differentiation, cost leadership, differentiation focus and cost focus. The differentiation and cost leadership strategies seek competitive advantage in a broad range of market or industry segments, whereas differentiation focus and cost focus strategies are confined to a narrow segment. Seeking one of these positions of advantage is critical to survival. For example, the only players remaining in the fashion business are either megabrands with a billion dollars in sales, such as Gucci, Louis Vuitton, Burberry, Prada and others, or niche brands with sales of between US$1 million and US$100 million, such as Rochas and Balenciaga.

Differentiation

Differentiation strategy involves the choice of one or more choice criteria that are used by many buyers in an industry. A firm then uniquely positions itself to meet these criteria. For example, firms might seek to be better (i.e. have superior quality), be faster (i.e. respond more quickly) or be closer (i.e. build better relationships with customers – see Exhibit 12.5).[15] The aim is to differentiate in a way that leads to a price premium in excess of the cost of differentiating. Differentiation gives customers a reason to prefer one product over another and thus is central to strategic marketing thinking. But it can also be a risky strategy, as demonstrated by the case of Volkswagen. In an effort to develop high-quality cars, it has the highest capital spending of any car manufacturer at 8.2 per cent of sales.[16] This level of investment has not resulted in differentiated brands in the marketplace.

Cost leadership

The cost leadership approach involves the achievement of the lowest cost position in an industry. Many segments in an industry are served and great importance is placed on minimizing costs on all fronts. So long as the price achievable for its products is around the industry

Exhibit 12.5 The online shoe store Zappos has differentiated itself on the basis of its quality of customer service

average, cost leadership should result in superior performance. Thus, cost leaders often market standard products that are believed to be acceptable to customers. Ryanair is a cost leader in aviation and Dell a cost leader in personal computers. They market acceptable products at reasonable prices, which means that their low costs result in above average profits. Toyota is working on a new approach to car design, development and manufacturing in a bid to come up with an ultra-low-cost car. Some cost leaders need to discount prices in order to achieve high sales levels. The aim here is to achieve superior performance by ensuring that the cost advantage over the competition is not offset by the price discount. No-frills supermarket discounters like Costco, KwikSave and Aldi fall into this category.

Differentiation focus

By taking a differentiation focus approach, a firm aims to differentiate within one or a small number of target market segments (see Exhibit 12.6). The special needs of the segment mean that there is an opportunity to differentiate the product offering from competitors who may be targeting a broader group of customers. For example, some small speciality chemical companies thrive on taking orders that are too small or specialized to be of interest to their larger competitors. Similarly, Domino's Pizza has built the world's biggest home-delivery pizza company on the back of a strategy of fast service and consistent quality. The company now delivers a million pizzas a night from 7,300 outlets in 50 countries.[17] Microbreweries have been on the rise around the world to meet niche tastes not catered for by the big brewers. Those firms adopting a differentiation focus must be clear that the needs of their target group

differ from those of the broader market (otherwise there will be no basis for differentiation) and that existing competitors are underperforming.

Cost focus

By adopting a cost focus strategy, a firm seeks a cost advantage with one or a small number of target market segments. By dedicating itself to a segment, the cost focuser can seek economies that may be ignored or missed by broadly targeted competitors. In some instances, competition, by trying to achieve wide market acceptance, may be over-performing (for example, by providing unwanted services) to one segment of customers. By providing a basic product offering, a cost advantage will be gained that may exceed the price discount necessary to sell it. For example, Kiwibank is a low-cost domestic bank that was set up by the New Zealand Government as an alternative to the foreign-owned banks dominating the market. It has proven particularly attractive to low income customers because of its low fee structure.[18]

Choosing a competitive strategy

So it seems that the essence of corporate success is to choose a generic strategy and pursue it enthusiastically. Below-average performance is associated with failure to achieve any of these generic strategies. The result is no competitive advantage: a stuck-in-the-middle position that results in lower performance than that of the cost leaders, differentiators or focusers in any market segment. An example of a company that has struggled to maintain its initial advantage is Starbucks. Throughout its early phase of growth in the 1980s and 1990s, Starbucks had carved out a differentiated position for itself as being more than just a coffee shop chain but rather a 'third place' between home and work, complete with comfortable seating, quality coffee and facilities for downloading music and so on. But as it expanded, it added drive-through facilities, food items and pre-ground coffee which brought it more into competition with low-cost operators such as McDonald's and Dunkin' Donuts. The company's sales and share price dropped dramatically and it brought back its founder, Howard Schultz as chief executive in order to try to recover the ground it had lost by becoming 'stuck in the middle' between low cost and differentiated.

Firms need to understand the generic basis for their success and resist the temptation to blur strategy by making inconsistent moves. For example, a no-frills cost leader or focuser should beware of the pitfalls of moving to a higher cost base (perhaps by adding on expensive services). A focus strategy involves limiting

Exhibit 12.6 Neuroth, the Austrian hearing aid company uses concert tickets in styles from the 1960s and 1970s to remind their clients of how good their hearing once was . . . and could be again through using their products

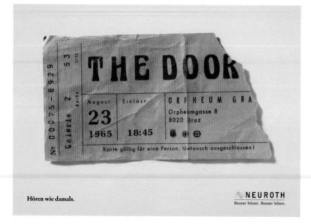

sales volume. Once domination of the target segment has been achieved there may be a temptation to move into other segments in order to achieve growth with the same competitive advantage. This can be a mistake if the new segments do not value the firm's competitive advantage in the same way.

Differentiation and cost leadership strategies are incompatible in most situations: differentiation is achieved through higher costs. However, there are circumstances when both can be achieved simultaneously. For example, a differentiation strategy may lead to market share domination that lowers costs through economies of scale and learning effects; or a highly differentiated firm pioneers a major process innovation that significantly reduces manufacturing costs, leading to a cost leadership position. When differentiation and cost leadership coincide, performance is exceptional since a premium price can be charged for a low-cost product. This is akin to achieving the dual position of high effectiveness and high efficiency discussed in Chapter 1.

Sources of competitive advantage

In order to create a differentiated or lowest cost position, a firm needs to understand the nature and location of the potential sources of competitive advantage. The nature of these sources are the superior skills and resources of a firm. Management benefits by analysing the superior skills and resources that offer, or could contribute to, competitive advantage (i.e. differentiation or lowest cost position). Their identification can be aided by **value chain** analysis (see Figure 12.5). A value chain comprises the discrete activities a firm carries out in order to perform its business.

Exhibit 12.7 Toyota's key resources such as its production expertise, distribution coverage and powerful advertising like this 'lifestyle' campaign have combined to enable it to gain market leadership in the mass car market

Superior skills

These are the distinctive capabilities of key personnel, which set them apart from the personnel of competing firms. The benefit of superior skills is the resulting ability to perform functions more effectively than other firms. For example, superior selling skills may result in closer relationships with customers than competing firms can achieve. Superior quality assurance skills can result in improved and more consistent product quality.

Superior resources

The tangible requirements for advantage that enable a firm to exercise its skills are known as superior resources (see Exhibit 12.7). Superior resources include:

- the number of salespeople in a market
- expenditure on advertising and sales promotion

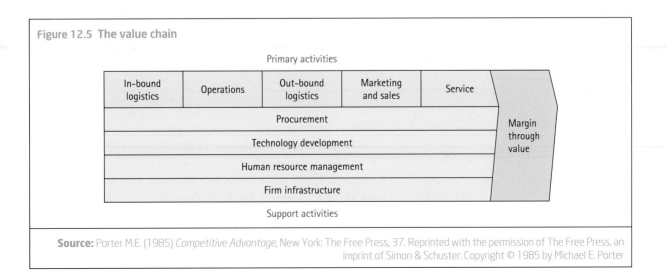

Figure 12.5 The value chain

Primary activities				
In-bound logistics	Operations	Out-bound logistics	Marketing and sales	Service
Procurement				
Technology development				
Human resource management				
Firm infrastructure				

Margin through value

Support activities

Source: Porter M.E. (1985) *Competitive Advantage*, New York: The Free Press, 37. Reprinted with the permission of The Free Press, an imprint of Simon & Schuster. Copyright © 1985 by Michael E. Porter

Marketing in Action 12.3 Uniqlo

Critical Thinking: Below is a review of the growth of Uniqlo into a global clothing brand. Read it and critically evaluate the strengths and weaknesses of its decision to incorporate all elements of the value chain in its business.

Uniqlo is an international clothing brand that is owned by a Japanese company Fast Retailing, and it is Asia's largest clothing retailer. It opened its first store in 1984 selling men's suits but quickly expanded into the sale of casual clothes as well. At this time, the company was simply reselling garments that it bought from other manufacturers but a key turning point for the brand came about when it decided to take on more elements of the value chain and begin manufacturing its own clothes. It actively managed all stages of the creation of new garments from design through to retail. This contrasted with many of its industry peers who outsource different elements of the business. Though Uniqlo manufactures over 80 per cent of its garments in China, these partner companies work closely with Fast Retailing.

In the highly competitive business of clothes marketing, Uniqlo aims to remain distinctive from its competitors by creating basic, functional clothing products at affordable prices. In fact, the Uniqlo brand emerged from a misspelling of its name. It was originally meant to be Uni-clo which stood for Unique Clothing Warehouse but when management saw the mistake, they liked it and the name

has stayed. It uses its capabilities in product procurement and manufacturing to keep its costs low and these savings are passed on to customers in the form of lower prices. Unlike other fast-fashion companies where styles change rapidly and items are disposed quickly, it seeks to create products that are essential to an individual's lifestyle such as fleeces, jackets and polo shirts and its *Heattech* undergarments. A foray into the world of fashion items in 2010 failed badly for the company and it was left holding large quantities of unsold stock.

Since 1991, the company has been busy expanding overseas. As well as its 824 outlets in Japan in 2011, it had over 150 other stores in countries such as the UK, the USA, France, China, Singapore and Russia. Its online sales are also becoming a big part of the business and it is a heavy user of social media in its marketing. By 2011, it had over 600,000 Facebook fans worldwide and in that year, it launched Uniqlooks – a campaign in which members of its community could share images of how they wear the clothes and blog about the brand.

Based on: Corcoran (2011);[19] Fujimura and Ozasa (2011)[20].

- distribution coverage (the number of retailers who stock the product)
- expenditure on R&D
- scale of and type of production facilities
- financial resources
- brand equity
- knowledge.

Value chain

The value chain provides a useful method for locating superior skills and resources. Many firms consist of a set of activities that are conducted to design, manufacture, market, distribute and service its products. The value chain of primarily service businesses may be shorter and involve fewer stages. The value chain

categorizes actions into primary and support activities (see Figure 12.5). This enables the sources of costs and differentiation to be understood and located (see Marketing in Action 12.3).

1 *Primary activities* include in-bound physical distribution (e.g. materials handling, warehousing, inventory control), operations (e.g. manufacturing, packaging), out-bound physical distribution (e.g. delivery, order processing), marketing (e.g. advertising, selling, channel management) and service (e.g. installation, repair, customer training).

2 *Support activities* are found within all of these primary activities and consist of purchased inputs, technology, human resource management and the firm's infrastructure. These are not defined within a given

primary activity because they can be found in all of them. Purchasing can take place within each primary activity, not just in the purchasing department; technology is relevant to all primary activities, as is human resource management; and the firm's infrastructure – which consists of general management, planning, finance, accounting and quality management – supports the entire value chain.

If management examines each value-creating activity, it can pinpoint the skills and resources that may form the basis of low cost or differentiated positions. To the extent that skills and resources exceed or could be developed to exceed the competition, they form the key sources of competitive advantage. Not only should the skills and resources within value-creating activities be examined but the *linkages* between them should also be examined. For example, greater co-ordination between operations and in-bound physical distribution may give rise to reduced costs through lower inventory levels.

Tests of an effective core strategy

The six tests of an effective core strategy are detailed in Figure 12.6. First, the strategy must be based upon a clear definition of target customers and their needs. Second, an understanding of competitors is required so that the core strategy can be based on a competitive advantage. Third, the strategy must incur acceptable risk. Challenging a strong competitor with a weak competitive advantage and a low resource base would not incur acceptable risk. Fourth, the strategy should be resource and managerially supportable. It should match the resource capabilities and managerial com-

petences of the business. Fifth, core strategy should be derived from the product and marketing objectives established as part of the planning process. A strategy (e.g. heavy promotion), which makes commercial logic following a build objective may make no sense when a harvesting objective has been decided. Finally, the strategy should be internally consistent. The elements should blend to form a coherent whole.

Tactical marketing decisions

Decisions regarding each of the elements of the marketing mix make up the next stage of the planning process. These decisions consist of judgements about price levels, the blend of promotional techniques to employ, the distribution channels and service levels to use, and the types of products to manufacture. Where promotional, distribution and product standards surpass those of the competition, a competitive advantage may be gained. Alternatively, a judgement may be made only to match or even undershoot the competition on some elements of the marketing mix. To outgun the competition on everything is not normally feasible. Choices have to be made about how the marketing mix can be manipulated to provide a superior offering to the customer at reasonable cost.

Organization and implementation

It is said that no marketing plan will succeed unless it 'degenerates into work'.[21] Consequently, the business must design an organization that has the capabilities necessary to implement the plan. Indeed, organizational weaknesses discovered as part of the SWOT analysis may restrict the feasible range of strategic options. Reorganization could mean the establishment of a marketing organization or department in the business. A study of manufacturing organizations by Piercy[22] found that 55 per cent did not have a marketing department. In some cases, marketing was carried out by the chief executive, in others the sales department dealt with customers and no need for other marketing inputs was perceived. In other situations, environmental change may cause strategic change, and this may imply reorganization of marketing and sales. The growth of large corporate customers with enormous buying power has resulted in businesses focusing their resources more firmly on meeting their needs (strategy change), which has led in turn to dedicated marketing and sales teams being organized to service these accounts (reorganization).

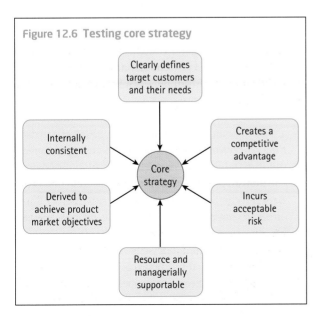

Figure 12.6 Testing core strategy

Control

Control is the final stage in the marketing planning process. The aim of control systems is to evaluate the results of the marketing plan so that corrective action can be taken if performance does not match objectives. Short-term control systems can plot results against objectives on a weekly, monthly, quarterly and/or annual basis. Measures include sales profits, costs and cash flow. Strategic control systems are more long term. Managers need to stand back from week-by-week and month-by-month results to critically reassess whether their plans are in line with their capabilities and the environment.

Where this kind of long-term control perspective is lacking this may result in the pursuit of plans that have lost strategic credibility. New competition, changes in technology and moving customer requirements may have rendered old plans obsolete. This, of course, returns the planning process to the beginning since this kind of fundamental review is conducted in the marketing audit. It is the activity of assessing internal capabilities and external opportunities and threats that results in a SWOT analysis. This outcome may mean a redefinition of the business mission, and, as we have seen, changes in marketing objectives and strategies to realign the business with its environment.

How, though, do the stages in marketing planning we have looked at relate to the fundamental planning questions stated earlier in this chapter? Table 12.3 shows this relationship. The question 'Where are we now?' is answered by the business mission definition, the marketing audit and SWOT analysis. 'Where would we like to be?' is determined by the setting of marketing objectives. 'How do we get there?' refers to core strategy, marketing mix decisions, organization and implementation.

Marketing metrics

A key emerging area of control is that of marketing metrics. The marketing discipline has traditionally been

Table 12.3 Key questions and the process of marketing planning

Key questions	Stages in marketing planning
Where are we now and how did we get there?	Business mission Marketing audit SWOT analysis
Where would we like to be?	Marketing objectives
How do we get there?	Core strategy Marketing mix decisions Organization Implementation

criticized for the quality of its metrics. For example, sales revenues are an important metric but many of the factors influencing sales levels are outside the control of marketers, such as economic conditions or competitor activity. And because marketers have not been good at measuring what they do, they are often poorly represented in corporate boardrooms compared with disciplines such as production and finance. In addition, marketing budgets are often the first to be cut when companies need to make cost savings.

As a result, more attention than ever is being paid to the metrics used to measure marketing activity. A vast array of potential metrics can be identified.[23] In short there are two key elements of marketing measurement, namely, the effectiveness of operational marketing activity and the impact of marketing on the bottom line. Measuring the former is contingent on the type of marketing activity undertaken. For example, distribution activity can be measured by inventory levels, markdowns, facings and out-of-stock levels. But, ultimately, marketing decisions must contribute to increasing profits by increasing sales volumes, increasing prices or reducing unit costs.[24] The most common metrics in use in UK firms are shown in Table 12.4.

The rewards of marketing planning

Various authors[25,26,27] have attributed the following benefits to marketing planning.

1 *Consistency*: the plan provides a focal point for decisions and actions. By reference to a common plan, decisions by the same manager over time, and by different managers, should be more consistent and actions coordinated more effectively.

2 *Encourages the monitoring of change*: the planning process forces managers to step away from day-to-day problems and review the impact of change on the business from a strategic perspective.

3 *Encourages organizational adaptation*: the underlying premise of planning is that the organization should adapt to match its environment. Marketing planning, therefore, promotes the necessity to accept the inevitability of change. This is an important consideration since adaptive capability has been shown to be linked to superior performance.[28]

4 *Stimulates achievement*: the planning process focuses on objectives, strategies and results. It encourages people to ask 'What can we achieve given our capabilities?' As such, it motivates people, who otherwise might be content to accept much lower standards of performance, to set new horizons for objectives.

Table 12.4 The use of marketing metrics in UK firms

Rank	Metric	% using measure	% rating it as important
1	Profit/profitability	92	80
2	Sales, value and/or volume	91	71
3	Gross margin	81	66
4	Awareness	78	28
5	Market share (value/volume)	78	37
6	Number of new products	73	18
7	Relative price	70	36
8	Customer dissatisfaction	69	45
9	Customer satisfaction	68	48
10	Distribution/availability	66	18

Source: Ambler, Kokkinaki and Puntoni (2004)[29]

5 *Resource allocation*: the planning process asks fundamental questions about resource allocation. For example, which products and services should receive high investment (build), which should be maintained (hold), which should have resources withdrawn slowly (harvest), and which should have resources withdrawn immediately (divest).

6 *Competitive advantage*: planning promotes the search for sources of competitive advantage.

However, it should be borne in mind that this logical planning process, sometimes referred to as synoptic, may be at variance with the culture of the business, which may plan effectively using an *incremental* approach.[30] The style of planning must match business culture.[31] Saker and Speed argue that the considerable demands on managers in terms of time and effort implied by the synoptic marketing planning process may mean that alternative planning schemes are more appropriate, particularly for small companies.[32]

An incremental planning approach is more focused on problems, in that the process begins with the realization of a problem (for example, a fall-off in orders) and continues with an attempt to identify a solution. As solutions to problems form, so strategy emerges. However, little attempt is made to integrate consciously the individual decisions that could possibly affect one another. Strategy is viewed as a loosely linked group of decisions that are handled individually. Nevertheless, its effect may be to attune the business to its environment through its problem-solving nature. Its drawback is that the lack of broad situation analysis and strategy option generation renders the incremental approach less comprehensive. For some companies, however, its inherent practicality, rather than its rationality, may support its use.[33]

Problems in making planning work

Research into the marketing planning approaches of commercial firms has discovered that most companies did not practise the kinds of systematic planning procedure described in this chapter and, of those that did, many did not enjoy the rewards described above.[34] However, others have shown that there is a relationship between planning and commercial success (e.g. Armstrong and McDonald).[35,36] The problem is that the 'contextual difficulties' associated with the process of marketing planning are substantial and need to be understood. In as much as forewarned is forearmed, the following paragraphs offer a checklist of potential problems that have to be faced by those charged with making marketing planning work.

Political

Marketing planning is a process of resource allocation. The outcome of the process is an allocation of more funds to some products and departments, and the same or less to others. Since power bases, career opportunities and salaries are often tied to whether an area is fast or slow growing, it is not surprising that managers view planning as a highly political activity. An example is a European bank, whose planning process resulted in the decision to insist that its retail branch managers divert certain types of loan application to the industrial/merchant banking arm of the group where the return was greater. This was required because the plan was designed to optimize the return to the group as a whole. However, the consequence of this was considerable friction between the divisions concerned because the decision lowered the performance of the retail branch.

Opportunity cost

Some busy managers take the view that marketing planning is a time-wasting process that interferes with the need to deal with day-to-day problems. They view the opportunity cost of spending two or three days away at a hotel thrashing out long-term plans as too high. This difficulty may be compounded by the fact that people who are attracted to the hectic pace of managerial life may be the type who prefer to live that way. Hence, they may be ill at ease with the thought of a long period of sedate contemplation.

Reward systems

In business, reward systems are increasingly being geared to the short term. More and more incentives and bonuses are linked not just to annual but to quarterly results. Managers may thus overemphasize short-term issues and underemphasize medium- and long-term concerns if there is a conflict of time. Marketing planning, then, may be viewed as of secondary importance. For example, as it sought to respond to competitive challenges in the personal computer business by emphasizing long-term initiatives that drove sales, Dell Computer Corporation incurred the wrath of institutional investors who wanted to see more emphasis on short-term profits.[37]

Information

A systematic marketing planning system needs informational inputs in order to function effectively. Market share, size and growth rates are basic inputs into the marketing audit, but may be unavailable. More perversely, information may wilfully be withheld by those with vested interests who, recognizing that knowledge is power, distort the true situation to protect their position in the planning process.

Culture

Efforts to establish a systematic marketing planning process may be at odds with the culture of an organization. As we have already seen, businesses may 'plan' by making incremental decisions. Hence, the strategic planning system may challenge the status quo and be seen as a threat. In other cases, the values and beliefs of some managers may be altogether hostile to a planning system.

How to handle marketing planning problems

Various authors[38,39] have proposed the following recommendations for minimizing the impact of these problems.

1 *Senior management support*: top management must be committed to planning and be seen by middle management to give it total support. This should be ongoing support, not a short-term fad.

2 *Match the planning system to the culture of the business*: how the marketing planning process is managed should be consistent with the culture of the organization. For example, in some organizations the top-down/bottom-up balance will move towards top-down; in other less directive cultures the balance will move towards a more bottom-up planning style.

3 *The reward system*: this should reward the achievement of longer-term objectives rather than focus exclusively on short-term results.

4 *Depoliticize outcomes*: less emphasis should be placed on rewarding managers associated with build (growth) strategies. Recognition of the skills involved in defending share and harvesting products should be made. At General Electric managers are classified as growers, caretakers and undertakers, and matched to products that are being built, defended or harvested in recognition of the fact that the skills involved differ according to the strategic objective. No stigma is attached to caretaking or undertaking; each is acknowledged as contributing to the success of the organization.

5 *Clear communication*: plans should be communicated to those charged with implementation.

6 *Training*: marketing personnel should be trained in the necessary marketing knowledge and skills to perform the planning job. Ideally, the management team should attend the same training course so that they each share a common understanding of the concepts and tools involved, and can communicate using the same terminology.

Summary

In this chapter we have examined the important issues of marketing planning and marketing strategy. The following key issues were addressed.

1. The role of marketing planning is to give direction to the organization's marketing effort and to co-ordinate its activities. It helps to answer core questions like, where are we now, where would we like to be and how do we get there.

2. The various stages of the marketing planning process include developing or adjusting the business mission, conducting a marketing audit, conducting a SWOT analysis, setting marketing objectives, deciding the core strategy, making marketing mix decisions, and organizing, implementing and controlling the marketing effort.

3. The marketing audit is divided into an external audit, which examines environmental and competitive conditions, and an internal audit, which reviews marketing decisions and operating results. The information generated by a marketing audit should guide managerial choices regarding future directions for the organization.

4. Marketing objectives need to be decided at two levels, namely, strategic thrusts and strategic objectives. Strategic thrusts deal with the ways in which the organization can grow; there are four core choices, namely market penetration, product development, market development and diversification. Strategic objectives are decided for each product and again there are four choices, namely build, hold, harvest and divest.

5. As well as decisions regarding how to grow, organizations also need to make choices regarding how to compete. Four strategies are available, namely, differentiation, cost leadership, differentiation focus and cost focus. Value chain analysis can assist companies to identify the skills and resources necessary to implement effective competitive strategies.

6. There are a number of rewards to be gained for pursuing careful planning, including consistency, encouraging the monitoring of change, encouraging organizational adaptation, stimulating achievement, resource allocation and competitive advantage.

7. Making planning work is difficult because of office politics, perceived opportunity costs, pressures for short-term results, availability of the necessary information and cultural issues. However, top management leadership, matching planning to organizational culture, reward systems, and communication and training can all help to overcome these problems.

Study questions

1. Discuss some of the difficulties that can be encountered in making marketing planning work in an organization. How can these difficulties be overcome?

2. Discuss the role and limitations of the external analysis phase of marketing planning.

3. Under what circumstances may incremental planning be preferable to synoptic marketing planning, and vice versa?

4. Compare and contrast a cost leadership strategy with a differentiation strategy. Is it possible to pursue both strategies simultaneously?

5. Discuss why it is important for marketers to be able to measure and justify the effectiveness of marketing activities.

6. Visit www.bplans.com, www.knowthis.com/general/marketplan.htm and www.howstuffworks.com/marketing-plan.htm. Review some of the sample marketing plans available on these sites.

Suggested reading

Day, G.S. (1999) *Market Driven Strategy: Processes for Creating Value*, New York: Free Press.

Gulati, R. and **J.B. Oldroyd** (2005) The Quest For Customer Focus, *Harvard Business Review*, **83** (4), 92–102.

Lamberti, L. and **G. Noci** (2010) Marketing Strategy and Marketing Performance Measurement System: Exploring the Relationship, *European Management Journal*, **28**, 139–52.

McDonald, M.H.B. (2008) *Marketing Plans*, 4th edn, Oxford: Heinemann.

Shaw, R. and **D. Merrick** (2005) *Marketing Payback: Is Your Marketing Profitable?* London: Pearson Education.

Sidhu, J. (2003) Mission Statements: Is it Time To Shelve Them? *European Management Journal*, **21** (4), 439–47.

References

1. **Mukerjee, K.** and **K. Chopra** (2009) Visa International: Building a Global Brand, *IBS Research Center*; **Larsen, P.** and **J. Croft** (2006) IPO Plan Reflects Desire to Head Off Critics, *Financial Times*, 12 October, 30; **Steverman, B.** (2008) Visa's IPO Victory, *Businessweek.com*, 20 March.

2. **Piercy, N.** (2002) *Market-led Strategic Change: Transforming the Process of Going to Market*, Oxford: Heinemann.

3. **Ackoff, R.I.** (1987) Mission Statements, *Planning Review*, **15** (4), 30–2.

4. **Hooley, G.J., A.J. Cox** and **A. Adams** (1992) Our Five Year Mission: To Boldly Go Where No Man Has Been Before . . . , *Journal of Marketing Management*, **8** (1), 35–48.

5. **Levitt, T.** (1984) Marketing Myopia, *Harvard Business Review*, **4** (4), 59–80.

6. **Porter, M.E.** (1980) *Competitive Strategy: Techniques for Analyzing Industries and Competitors*, New York: Free Press.

7. **Nakamoto, M.** (2005) Caught in its Own Trap: Sony Battles to Make Headway in a Networked World, *Financial Times*, 27 January, 17.

8. **Rigby, E.** (2008) DSG Contracts with a View to Improved Service, *Financial Times*, 16 May, 17.

9. **Carroll, J.** (2010) Is Live Nation's Day of Reckoning Approaching? *IrishTimes.com*, 23 July.

10. **Foley, S.** (2008) The Rise of the Concert Promoter Live Nation, *Independent.co.uk*, 4 April.

11. **LaMotta, L.** (2008) Live Nation Comes Alive, *Forbes.com*, 29 September.

12. **Simonian, H.** (2010) Emerging Markets Drive Sales for Nestlé, *Financial Times*, 12 August, 20.

13. **Nuttall, C.** (2004) Google Writes its Place in the World's History Books, *Financial Times*, 16 December, 24.

14. **Hall, W.K.** (1980) Survival Strategies in a Hostile Environment, *Harvard Business Review*, **58** (September/October), 75–85.

15. **Day, G.S.** (1999) *Market Driven Strategy: Processes for Creating Value*, New York: Free Press.

16. **Mackintosh, J.** (2004) Volkswagen Misfires: The Carmaker Counts the Cost of its High Spending and its Faltering Search for Luxury, *Financial Times*, 9 March, 19.

17. **Buckley, N.** (2003) Domino's Returns to Fast Food's Fast Lane, *Financial Times*, 26 November, 14.

18. **Fifield, A.** (2003) Kiwibank Can Afford to Hold Critics to Account, *Financial Times*, 24 April, 11.

19. **Corcoran, S.** (2011) Uniquely Made for All, *Marketing Age*, **5** (2), 32–5.

20. **Fujimura, N.** and **S. Ozasa** (2011) Uniqlo: Asia's Top Clothier Goes Back To Basics, *Businessweek.com*, 6 January.

21. **Drucker, P.F.** (1993) *Management Tasks, Responsibilities, Practices*, New York: Harper & Row, 128.

22. **Piercy, N.** (1986) The Role and Function of the Chief Marketing Executive and the Marketing Department, *Journal of Marketing Management*, **1** (3), 265–90.

23. **Farris, P.W., N.T. Bendle, P.E. Pfeifer** and **D.J. Reibstein** (2006) *Marketing Metrics*, Upper Saddle River, NJ: Wharton.

24. **Shaw, R.** and **D. Merrick** (2005) *Marketing Payback: Is Your Marketing Profitable?* London: Pearson Education.

25. **Leppard, J.W.** and **M.H.B. McDonald** (1991) Marketing Planning and Corporate Culture: A Conceptual Framework which Examines Management Attitudes in the Context of Marketing Planning, *Journal of Marketing Management*, **7** (3), 213–36.

26. **Greenley, G.E.** (1986) *The Strategic and Operational Planning of Marketing*, Maidenhead: McGraw-Hill, 185–7.

27. **Terpstra, V.** and **R. Sarathy** (1991) *International Marketing*, Orlando, FL: Dryden, ch. 17.

28. **Oktemgil, M.** and **G. Greenley** (1997) Consequences of High and Low Adaptive Capability in UK Companies, *European Journal of Marketing*, **31** (7), 445–66.

29. **Ambler, T., F. Kokkinaki** and **S. Puntoni** (2004) Assessing Marketing Performance: Reasons for Metrics Selection, *Journal of Marketing Management*, **20**, 475–98.

30. **Raimond, P.** and **C. Eden** (1990) Making Strategy Work, *Long Range Planning*, **23** (5), 97–105.

31. **Driver, J.C.** (1990) Marketing Planning in Style, *Quarterly Review of Marketing*, **15** (4), 16–21.

32. **Saker, J.** and **R. Speed** (1992) Corporate Culture: Is it Really a Barrier to Marketing Planning? *Journal of Marketing Management*, **8** (2), 177–82. For information on marketing and planning in small and medium-sized firms, see **Carson, D.** (1990) Some Exploratory Models for Assessing Small Firms' Marketing Performance: A Qualitative Approach, *European Journal of Marketing*, **24** (11), 8–51; and **Fuller, P.B.** (1994) Assessing Marketing in Small and Medium-sized Enterprises, *European Journal of Marketing*, **28** (12), 34–9.

33. **O'Shaughnessy, J.** (1995) *Competitive Marketing*, Boston, MA: Allen & Unwin.

34. **Greenley, G.** (1987) An Exposition of Empirical Research into Marketing Planning, *Journal of Marketing Management*, **3** (1), 83–102.

35. **Armstrong, J.S.** (1982) The Value of Formal Planning for Strategic Decisions: Review of Empirical Research, *Strategic Management Journal*, **3** (3), 197–213.

36. **McDonald, M.H.B.** (1984) The Theory and Practice of Marketing Planning for Industrial Goods in International Markets, Cranfield Institute of Technology, PhD thesis.

37. **Allison, K.** (2008) Dell's Long View Irks Investors, *Financial Times*, 1 September, 23.

38. **McDonald, M.H.B.** (1984) The Theory and Practice of Marketing Planning for Industrial Goods in International Markets, Cranfield Institute of Technology, PhD thesis.

39. **Abell, D.F.** and **J.S. Hammond** (1979) *Strategic Market Planning*, Englewood Cliffs, NJ: Prentice-Hall.

Case 12 Subway derailed: the case of Germany

Go to the website to see Subway's 'Smokin' BBQ' campaign which reflects the US origins of the franchise.
www.mcgraw-hill.co.uk/textbooks/fahy

The world loves fast food*. And Germany is no exception. Burgers? Pizza? Kebab? Currywurst? There has never been a wider choice of fast food offerings. The average German consumer has developed a healthy (or perhaps unhealthy) appetite for the delights of fast food. According to Datamonitor, the German fast-food market had total revenue of $6 billion in 2009 and is forecast to increase to $7 billion in 2014 (see Table C12.1).

So what is driving fast-food consumption in Europe's largest economy? First, the increase in the number of fast-food outlets means that a quick bite or munch is within easy reach. Second, aggressive pricing strategies have created new snacking occasions. For example, a cheeseburger or a cappuccino at McDonald's costs just €1. Third, consumers are attracted to the convenience of fast food. Hectic lifestyles mean that time has become a scarce commodity. Fast food

* Datamonitor defines the fast-food market as the sale of food and drinks for immediate consumption either on the premises or in designated eating areas shared with other foodservice operators, or for consumption elsewhere.

Table C12.1 German fast-food market value

Year	Dollars (USD) (millions)	Euros (millions)	% growth per annum
2005	5,154.0	3,706.6	-
2006	5,359.1	3,854.0	4.0
2007	5,588.5	4,019.1	4.3
2008	5,782.8	4,158.8	3.5
2009	5,982.1	4,302.1	3.4

Source: Datamonitor

saves all the time and hassle of cooking at home. Next, fast-food outlets have become a social space to spend quality time with family and friends. The Starbucks experience has been extended to other settings such as McCafé where consumers are trading up to enjoy a latte with a muffin or cupcake. Finally, the fast-food industry has responded to consumer health concerns with the introduction of healthier options. For example, a choice of salads and wraps are now available at McDonald's.

Table C12.2 Fast-food key players in Germany

	Turnover in millions of euros			Number of outlets		
	2010	**2009**	**2008**	**2010**	**2009**	**2008**
McDonald's, McCafé	3,017.0	2,909.0	2,835.0	1,386	1,361	1,333
Burger King	750.0	765.5	764.0	707	700	662
Nordsee	286.9	297.5	300.7	344	351	360
Subway	203.0	226.0	205.5	703	798	698

Source: Bundesverband der Systemgastronomie (BdS)

Subway: The Track to Global Success . . .

This would all seem to be good news for the restaurant chain Subway that has been positioned as a healthier fast-food alternative. It is claimed that the sandwich was invented by John Montagu, 4th Earl of Sandwich in 1762. Fast forward more than 300 years. In 1965, Fred DeLuca and Peter Buck opened the first Subway store in the US state of Connecticut and consumers rediscovered a new way to eat sandwiches. The submarine sandwich (known as a Sub) was born. Growth in the USA has reached over 24,200 outlets. The advertising slogan 'Eat Fresh' explains how every sandwich is made to order – right in front of the customer using a variety of baked breads, fillings, toppings and sauces. With all the choices available, there is something for everyone![1]

The Subway Sub may not present a major product innovation breakthrough, but it has become an exponential global market success. Subway opened its first international restaurant in Bahrain in 1984. This was the start of a rapid global expansion plan. The franchise format ensured Subway's expansion, not only quickly, but with limited capital investment required by the franchisee. The yellow and green logo of Subway has since overtaken the golden arches of McDonald's as the world's largest restaurant chain. Subway has currently 34,871 outlets (at the time of writing) in 98 countries including outlets in Afghanistan and Iraq, compared with 32,737 for McDonald's. Subway claims on its website that 'We've become the leading choice for people seeking quick, nutritious meals that the whole family can enjoy'.

Subway Germany: side-tracked?

Subway continues to open new stores across the globe with one exception – Germany. The first Subway restaurant opened in Berlin in 1999 and was able to expand as in other international markets with a franchise model that emphasizes small, low-cost outlets. In 2009, the Subway chain grew to 798 outlets. While Subway was able to capture a growing share of the fast-food dollar in other European markets, German consumers were voting with their feet (or rather their mouths!). According to the Bundesverband der Systemgastronomie (a German industry association), Subway's sales turnover in 2010 was €203 million. This was down almost 11 per cent compared with 2009. Weak sales have hit the bottom line of the franchisee holder. This has forced many outlets to close. 95 Subway outlets closed for business in 2010. The exodus of Subway in Germany has since gained momentum. There are now only 631 restaurants in Germany and Subway is facing competition from many of these former franchise holders who have opened rival chains such as Starsub, Fresh! and Mr Sub. Furthermore, it seems that the banks have also lost confidence in the Subway franchise. In April 2010, it was reported that Deutsche Bank will no longer offer loans to prospective Subway franchise holders.[1]

While McDonald's was able to break the €3 billion revenues barrier in 2010, Subway is fighting to stay afloat at the same time as the German economy is moving ahead strongly. However, the decline of Subway was not unexpected by everyone. In 2007, the President of the Franchisee Association Germany stated that 'A conservative estimate would be that 30 per cent of the Subway franchisees in Germany are just scraping by at the subsistence level'.[2] So why are Germans turning up their noses at Subway?

Subway: can't afford the ticket?

Icon Added Value & Brand Rating reported in a 2007 survey that Subway is perceived as being too expensive by German consumers. This might well be a critical factor as Germans are regarded as being particularly value-conscious consumers. In contrast, McDonald's was rated as delivering excellent quality at a fair price. A Subway 'meal deal' consisting typically of a sandwich, drink and cookie sells for €6.50. This compares with a Big Mac McMenü (Big Mac, fries and drink) of €5.79. Subway has however attempted to boost sales and increase restaurant frequency with the launch of 'sub of the day' ('Sub des Tages'). Customers can enjoy a different sandwich each day for a set price of €2.49. This is supported by a television commercial that shows an athlete throwing a javelin as far as 2.49 metres. (This can be viewed on www.subway-sandwiches.de.) For more information on Subway's competitors in Germany, see Table C12.2.

Crossed rails: culture shock?

German consumers should actually be leading sandwich connoisseurs. Germans eat the most bread in Europe – the average German eating 84.8 kilos of bread each year! However, it may be this passion for bread that is turning the Germans off the Subway sandwich. There are more than 300 different varieties of bread in Germany and it may be that Germans do not wish to compromise on quality and taste. How difficult would it be to sell Californian wine to the French or Australian beer to the Germans? It seemed that too many fillings such as barbecue ribs were too strange and foreign to the German palate. This is in contrast to McDonald's who have adapted to the culinary needs of the German market. For example, more than 1 million sausages, 'Nurnberger' were sold in a three-month promotion in 2010.

Brand image down the tube?

Executives take advantage of having informal meetings in a local Starbucks. Families choose to celebrate children's birthdays in McDonald's. Brands are appealing to the emotions of the fast-food consumer to win over the hearts and minds (and pockets). Is Subway failing to connect emotionally with the fast-food consumer? Subway's brand advertising support has been minimal compared to other fast-food brands. According to Nielsen Media Research, McDonald's Germany spent €172 million in advertising in 2010 in which 65 per cent was spent on television. 'I'm lovin' it' has probably become one of the best known slogans. McDonald's and other fast-food brands have also invested in their restaurant visual design while many Subway outlets still rely on plastic chairs and tables.

Poorly conducted franchise management?

The success or failure of the franchise model is based on a strong working relationship between the franchisee and franchiser. Franchisees at Subway pay a fee of 12.5 per cent of their monthly sales turnover to the franchiser in which 4.5 per cent is put aside for advertising support. The franchisee is able to benefit from Subway's franchise support system that includes training, product development, advertising, purchasing co-operative and field support. However, the Subway franchise model has received widespread criticism.

It is alleged that it has become too easy to become a Subway franchise holder. It has been argued that franchise holders lack the necessary basic management skills and competences to run a successful business. Subway franchisee holders participate in a two-week training course compared to an 18-month training programme at McDonald's. Many Subway franchisee holders have complained that they are not receiving adequate ongoing support from the franchiser. The relationship between franchiser and franchisee is no longer sweet but has turned rather sour.

Competition: a red light for Subway?

McDonald's is undoubtedly the giant of the German fast-food market. However, the fast-food market in Germany remains fairly fragmented and diverse, giving the consumer greater choice. Has Subway underestimated the competitive intensity of the German market? It is estimated that there are between 10,000 and 15,000 independent donar kebab outlets generating an annual turnover of €2.5 billion. Moreover, Subway is not the only restaurant chain to offer so-called 'better-for-you' meals. There are approximately 15,000 bakeries in Germany that can be found on any High Street. For instance, Kamps is Germany's largest single brand bakery chain with 640 retail stores in Germany. These bakeries sell bread rolls (*Brötchen*) that are freshly prepared with conventional fillings such as ham and cheese with a slice of pickle using traditional German bread. Lunchtime queues are not uncommon as consumers seek the convenience of consistent home-style quality closer to their workplace.

Food for thought . . .

Many Subway franchise holders are fighting for survival and are looking towards the franchiser for an action plan to revive their business fortunes. The German market has been traditionally difficult for many foreign retailers. Walmart, Virgin and Gap have all exited from the German market. Will Subway become another casualty or will it be able to prevent itself from sinking into oblivion? The Fourth Earl of Sandwich would certainly prefer the latter; after all, he is bizarrely much less famous for his service to England as First Lord of the Admiralty during the American War of Independence!

References

1. Student & Educator Resource Guide is available at www.subway.com/subwayroot/AboutSubway/StudentGuide.pdf

2. *Probleme bei Subway spitzen sich zu*, www.wiwo.de/unternehmen-maerkte problemebei-subway-spitzen-sich-zu-426518/

3. *Subway Franchisees Unhappy in Germany*, www.businessweek.com/globalbiz/content/mar2007/gb20070319_454968.htm

▶|

Questions

1. Conduct an external analysis of the fast-food market in Germany.
2. Conduct a SWOT analysis of Subway Germany. What are your key findings?
3. What has been Subway Germany's competitive strategy and why has it been ineffective?
4. What specific actions can Subway take to become more competitive in the German market?
5. What future consumer trends should Subway consider in their long-term marketing strategies?

This case was prepared by Glyn Atwal and Douglas Bryson, ESC Rennes School of Business, France, from various published sources as a basis for classroom discussion rather than to show effective or ineffective management.

Glossary

ad hoc research a research project that focuses on a specific problem, collecting data at one point in time with one sample of respondents

administered vertical marketing system a channel situation where a manufacturer that dominates a market through its size and strong brands may exercise considerable power over intermediaries even though they are independent

advertising any paid form of non-personal communication of ideas or products in the prime media (i.e., television, the press, posters, cinema and radio, the Internet and direct marketing)

advertising agency an organization that specializes in providing services such as media selection, creative work, production and campaign planning to clients

advertising message the use of words, symbols and illustrations to communicate to a target audience using prime media

advertising platform the aspect of the seller's product that is most persuasive and relevant to the target consumer

ambient advertising any out-of-home display advertising that does not fall into normal outdoor categories

ambush marketing any activity where a company tries to associate itself or its products with an event without paying any fee to the event owner

attitude the degree to which a customer or prospect likes or dislikes a brand

awareness set the set of brands that the consumer is aware may provide a solution to a problem

beliefs descriptive thoughts that a person holds about something

benefit segmentation the grouping of people based on the different benefits they seek from a product

bonus pack pack giving the customer extra quantity at no additional cost

brainstorming the technique whereby a group of people generate ideas without initial evaluation; only when the list of ideas is complete is each one then evaluated

brand a distinctive product offering created by the use of a name, symbol, design, packaging, or some combination of these, intended to differentiate it from its competitors

brand equity a measure of the strength of the brand in the marketplace

brand extension the use of an established brand name on a new brand within the same broad market

brand stretching the use of an established brand name for brands in unrelated markets

brand values the core values and characteristics of a brand

business analysis a review of the projected sales, costs and profits for a new product to establish whether these factors satisfy company objectives

business mission the organization's purpose, usually setting out its competitive domain, which distinguishes the business from others of its type

buying centre a group that is involved in the buying decision; also known as a decision-making unit (DMU) in industrial buying situations

buzz marketing the passing of information about products or services by verbal or electronic means in an informal person-to-person manner

catalogue marketing the sale of products through catalogues distributed to agents and customers, usually by mail or at stores

causal research the study of cause and effect relationships

cause-related marketing the commercial activity by which businesses and charities or causes form a partnership with each other to market an image, product or service for mutual benefit

chain of marketing productivity the processes through which marketing activities contribute to the performance of the firm

channel integration the way in which the players in the channel are linked

channel intermediaries organizations that facilitate the distribution of products to customers

channel of distribution the means by which products are moved from the producer to the ultimate consumer

channel strategy the selection of the most effective distribution channel, the most appropriate level of distribution intensity and the degree of channel integration

choice criteria the various attributes (and benefits) people use when evaluating products and services

classical conditioning the process of using an established relationship between a stimulus and a response to cause the learning of the same response to a different stimulus

cognitive dissonance post-purchase concerns of a consumer arising from uncertainty as to whether a decision to purchase was the correct one

cognitive learning the learning of knowledge, and development of beliefs and attitudes without direct reinforcement

communications-based co-branding the linking of two or more existing brands from different companies or business units for the purposes of joint communication

competitive bidding drawing up detailed specifications for a product and putting the contract out to tender

competitor analysis an examination of the nature of actual and potential competitors, their objectives and strategies

competitor targets the organizations against which a company chooses to compete directly

concept testing testing new product ideas with potential customers

consumer culture theory (CCT) views consumption less as a rational or conscious activity and more as a sociocultural or experiential activity that is laden with emotion

consumer movement an organized collection of groups and organizations whose objective it is to protect the rights of consumers

consumer panel consumers who provide information on their purchases over time

consumer pull the targeting of consumers with communications (e.g. promotions) designed to create demand that will *pull* the product into the distribution chain

consumer-generated advertising advertising messages created for brands by consumers

continuous research conducting the same research on the same sample repeatedly to monitor the changes that are taking place over time.

contractual vertical marketing system a franchise arrangement (e.g. a franchise) tying producers and resellers together

control the stage in the marketing planning process or cycle when the performance against plan is monitored so that corrective action can be taken, if necessary

core strategy the means of achieving marketing objectives, including target markets, competitor targets and competitive advantage

corporate vertical marketing system a channel situation where an organization gains control of distribution through ownership

culture the traditions, taboos, values and basic attitudes of the whole society in which an individual lives

custom research is research conducted for a single organization to provide specific answers to the questions that it has

customer analysis a survey of who the customers are, what choice criteria they use, how they rate competitive offerings and on what variables they can be segmented

customer benefits those things that a customer values in a product; customer benefits derive from product features (see separate entry)

customer relationship management (CRM) the methodologies, technologies and e-commerce capabilities used by companies to manage customer relationships

customer satisfaction the fulfilment of customers' requirements or needs

customer value perceived benefits minus perceived sacrifice

customer value proposition a clear statement of the differential benefits offered by a product or service

customized marketing a market coverage strategy where a company decides to target individual customers and to develop separate marketing mixes for each

database marketing an interactive approach to marketing, which uses individually addressable marketing media and channels to provide information to a target audience, stimulate demand and stay close to customers

decision-making process the stages that organizations and people pass through when purchasing a physical product or service

depth interviews the interviewing of consumers individually for perhaps one or two hours with the aim of understanding their attitudes, values, behaviour and/or beliefs

descriptive research the systematic examination of a marketing question in order to draw conclusions

differentiated marketing a market coverage strategy where a company decides to target several market segments and to develop separate marketing mixes for each

differentiation strategy the selection of one or more customer choice criteria, and positioning the offering accordingly to achieve superior customer value

diffusion of innovation the process by which new products or services are adopted in the marketplace

digital marketing the achievement of marketing objectives through the use of digital technologies

direct mail material sent through the postal service to the recipient's house or business address, promoting a product and/or maintaining an ongoing relationship

direct marketing (1) acquiring and retaining customers without the use of an intermediary; (2) the distribution of products, information and promotional benefits to target consumers through interactive communication in a way that allows response to be measured

direct response advertising the use of the prime advertising media, such as television, newspapers and magazines, to elicit an order, enquiry or a request for a visit

disintermediation the elimination of marketing channel intermediaries by product or service providers

distribution analysis an examination of movements in power bases, channel attractiveness, physical distribution and distribution behaviour

distribution push the targeting of channel intermediaries with communications (e.g., promotions) to *push* the product into the distribution chain

dynamic pricing the frequent adjustment of prices in response to patterns of demand

economic value to the customer (EVC) the amount a customer would have to pay to make the total life cycle costs of a new and a reference product the same

effectiveness doing the right thing, making the correct strategic choice

efficiency a way of managing business processes to a high standard, usually concerned with cost reduction; also called 'doing things right'

email marketing the achievement of marketing objectives through the use of email communications

environmental scanning the process of monitoring and analysing the marketing environment of a company

ethics the moral principles and values that govern the actions and decisions of an individual or group

ethnographic research an approach to research that emphasizes the observation/interviewing of consumers in their natural setting

event sponsorship sponsorship of a sporting or other event

evoked set the set of brands that the consumer seriously evaluates before making a purchase

exaggerated promises barrier a barrier to the matching of expected and perceived service levels caused by the unwarranted building up of expectations by exaggerated promises

exclusive distribution an extreme form of selective distribution where only one wholesaler, retailer or industrial distributor is used in a geographical area to sell the products of a particular supplier

exhibition an event that brings buyers and sellers together in a commercial setting

experiential marketing the term used to describe marketing activities that involve the creation of experiences for consumers

experimentation the application of stimuli (e.g. two price levels) to different matched groups under controlled conditions for the purpose of measuring their effect on a variable (e.g., sales)

exploratory research the preliminary exploration of a research area prior to the main data collection stage

family brand name a brand name used for all products in a range

focus group a group, normally of six to eight consumers, brought together for a discussion focusing on an aspect of a company's marketing

focused marketing a market coverage strategy where a company decides to target one market segment with a single marketing mix

franchise a legal contract in which a producer and channel intermediaries agree each other's rights and obligations; the intermediary usually receives marketing, managerial, technical and financial services in return for a fee

full cost pricing pricing so as to include all costs, and based on certain sales volume assumptions

geodemographics the process of grouping households into geographic clusters based on such information as type of accommodation, occupation, number and age of children, and ethnic background

global branding adopting a standardized approach to marketing in all the countries that the brand is available

going-rate prices prices at the rate generally applicable in the market, focusing on competitors' offerings rather than on company costs

group discussion a group, usually of six to eight consumers, brought together for a discussion focusing on an aspect of a company's marketing strategy

guerrilla marketing capturing the attention of consumers by the creation of highly unusual and unexpected forms of promotional activity

hall tests bringing a sample of target consumers to a room that has been hired so that alternative marketing ideas (e.g., promotions) can be tested

horizontal electronic marketplaces online procurement sites that cross several industries and are typically used to source low-cost supplies such as MRO items

inadequate delivery barrier a barrier to the matching of expected and perceived service levels caused by the failure of the service provider to select, train and reward staff adequately, resulting in poor or inconsistent delivery of service

inadequate resources barrier a barrier to the matching of expected and perceived service levels caused by the unwillingness of service providers to provide the necessary resources

individual brand name a brand name that does not identify a brand with a particular company

industry a group of companies that market products that are close substitutes for each other

information framing the way in which information is presented to people

information processing the process by which a stimulus is received, interpreted, stored in memory and later retrieved.

information processing approach sees consumption as largely a rational process – the outcome of a consumer recognizing a need and then engaging in a series of activities to attempt to fulfil that need

information search the identification of alternative ways of problem solving

ingredient co-branding the explicit positioning of a supplier's brand as an ingredient of a product

inseparability a characteristic of services, namely, that their production cannot be separated from their consumption

intangibility a characteristic of services, namely, that they cannot be touched, seen, tasted or smelled

integrated marketing communications the concept that companies co-ordinate their marketing communications tools to deliver a clear, consistent, credible and competitive message about the organization and its products

intensive distribution the aim of intensive distribution is to provide saturation coverage of the market

interactive television (iTV) advertising invites viewers to 'press the red button' on the remote control handset to see more information about an advertised product

internal marketing selecting, training and motivating employees to provide customer satisfaction

just-in-time (JIT) the JIT concept aims to minimize stocks by organizing a supply system that provides materials and components as they are required

key account management an approach to selling that focuses resources on major customers and uses a team selling approach

lifestyle the pattern of living as expressed in a person's activities, interests and opinions

lifestyle segmentation the grouping of people according to their pattern of living as expressed in their activities, interests and opinions

lifetime value of a customer recognition by the company of the potential sales, profits and endorsements that come from a repeat customer who stays with the company for several years

macroenvironment a number of broader forces that affect not only the company but the other actors in the environment, e.g. social, political, technological and economic

marginal cost pricing the calculation of only those costs that are likely to rise as output increases

market intelligence the systematic collection and analysis of publicly available information about consumers, competitors and marketplace developments

market segmentation the process of identifying individuals or organizations with similar characteristics that have significant implications for the determination of marketing strategy

market testing the limited launch of a new product to test sales potential

market-driven or outside-in firms seek to anticipate as well as identify consumer needs and build the resource profiles necessary to meet current and anticipated future demand

marketing the delivery of value to customers at a profit

marketing audit a systematic examination of a business's marketing environment, objectives, strategies and activities, with a view to identifying key strategic issues, problem areas and opportunities

marketing concept the achievement of corporate goals through meeting and exceeding customer needs better than the competition

marketing environment the actors and forces that affect a company's capability to operate effectively in providing products and services to its customers

marketing information system a system in which marketing information is formally gathered, stored, analysed and distributed to managers in accordance with their informational needs on a regular, planned basis

marketing mix a framework for the tactical management of the customer relationship, including product, place, price, promotion (the 4Ps); in the case of services, three other elements to be taken into account are process, people and physical evidence

marketing objectives there are two types of marketing objective – strategic thrust, which dictates which products should be sold in which markets, and strategic objectives, which are product-level objectives, such as build, hold, harvest and divest

marketing orientation companies with a marketing orientation focus on customer needs as the primary drivers of organizational performance

marketing planning the process by which businesses analyse the environment and their capabilities, decide upon courses of marketing action and implement those decisions

marketing research is the systematic design, collection, analysis and reporting of data relevant to a specific marketing situation.

marketing structures the marketing frameworks (organization, training and internal communications) on which marketing activities are based

marketing systems sets of connected parts (information, planning and control) that support the marketing function

mass customization the opposite to mass production, which means that all products produced are customized to the predetermined needs of a specific customer

media class decision the choice of prime media (i.e., the press, cinema, television, posters, radio) or some combination of these

media vehicle decision the choice of the particular newspaper, magazine, television spot, poster site, etc.

microenvironment the actors in the firm's immediate environment that affect its capability to operate effectively in its chosen markets – namely, suppliers, distributors, customers and competitors

misconceptions barrier a failure by marketers to understand what customers really value about their service

mobile marketing the creation and delivery of marketing messages through mobile devices

modified re-buy where a regular requirement for the type of product exists and the buying alternatives are known but sufficient (e.g. a delivery problem has occurred) to require some alteration to the normal supply procedure

money-off promotions sales promotions that discount the normal price

neuro-marketing the application of brain research techniques to the study of marketing issues

new task refers to the first-time purchase of a product or input by an organization

operant conditioning the use of rewards to generate reinforcement of response

packaging all the activities involved in designing and producing the kind of container or wrapper for the product

parallel co-branding the joining of two or more independent brands to produce a combined brand

parallel importing when importers buy products from distributors in one country and sell them in another to distributors who are not part of the manufacturer's normal distribution; caused by significant price differences for the same product between different countries

perception the process by which people select, organize and interpret sensory stimulation into a meaningful picture of the world

perishability a characteristic of services, namely that the capacity of a service business, such as a hotel room, cannot be stored – if it is not occupied, there is lost income that cannot be recovered

permission marketing marketers ask permission before sending advertisements or promotional material to potential customers; in this way customers 'opt in' to the promotion rather than having to 'opt out'

personal selling oral communication with prospective purchasers with the intention of making a sale

personality the inner psychological characteristics of individuals that lead to consistent responses to their environment

place the distribution channels to be used, outlet locations, methods of transportation

portfolio planning managing groups of brands and product lines

positioning the choice of target market (*where* the company wishes to compete) and differential advantage (*how* the company wishes to compete)

premiums any merchandise offered free or at low cost as an incentive to purchase

price (1) the amount of money paid for a product; (2) the agreed value placed on the exchange by a buyer and seller

price escalation the additional costs incurred in taking products to an international market, including transportation costs, distribution costs, taxes and tariffs, exchange rates and inflation rates

price unbundling pricing each element in the offering so that the price of the total product package is raised

product a good or service offered or performed by an organization or individual, which is capable of satisfying customer needs

product features the characteristics of a product that may or may not convey a customer benefit

product life cycle a four-stage cycle in the life of a product, illustrated as a curve representing the demand; the four stages being introduction, growth, maturity and decline

product line a group of brands that are closely related in terms of the functions and benefits they provide

product placement the deliberate placing of products and/or their logos in movies and television programmes, usually in return for money

product-based co-branding the linking of two or more existing brands from different companies or business units to form a product in which the brand names are visible to the consumer

production orientation a business approach that is inwardly focused either on costs or on a definition of a company in terms of its production facilities

profile segmentation the grouping of people in terms of profile variables such as age and socio-economic group so that marketers can communicate to them

promotional mix advertising, personal selling, sales promotion, public relations and direct marketing

prospecting searching for and calling upon potential customers

proximity marketing the localized wireless distribution of advertising content associated with a particular place

psychographic segmentation the grouping of people according to their lifestyle and personality characteristics

psychological pricing taking into consideration the psychological impact of the price level that is being set

public relations the management of communications and relationships to establish goodwill and mutual understanding between an organization and its public

publicity the communication of a product or business by placing information about it in the media without paying for time or space directly

qualitative research a semi-structured, in-depth study of small samples in order to gain insights.

quantitative research a structured study of small or large samples using a predetermined list of questions or criteria

reasoning a more complex form of cognitive learning where conclusions are reached by connected thought

reference group a group of people that influences an individual's attitude or behaviour

relationship marketing the process of creating, maintaining and enhancing strong relationships with customers and other stakeholders

repositioning changing the target market or differential advantage, or both

research brief written document stating the client's requirements

research proposal a document defining what the marketing research agency promises to do for its client and how much it will cost

retail audit a type of continuous research tracking the sales of products through retail outlets

retail positioning the choice of target market and differential advantage for a retail outlet

reverse marketing the process whereby the buyer attempts to persuade the supplier to provide exactly what the organization wants

rote learning the learning of two or more concepts without conditioning

safety (buffer) stocks stocks or inventory held to cover against uncertainty about resupply lead times

sales orientation a business approach that focuses on the development of products and services and the aggressive selling of these offerings as the key to its success

sales promotion incentives to customers or the trade that are designed to stimulate purchase

sales-force evaluation the measurement of salesperson performance so that strengths and weaknesses can be identified

sales-force motivation the motivation of salespeople by a process that involves needs, which set encouraging drives in motion to accomplish goals

sampling process a term used in research to denote the selection of a subset of the total population in order to interview them

search engine optimization (SEO) is the practice of adjusting the website's structure and content to improve the position with which it turns up in a web search

secondary research data that has already been collected by another researcher for another purpose

selective attention the process by which people screen out those stimuli that are neither meaningful to them nor consistent with their experiences and beliefs

selective distortion the distortion of information received by people according to their existing beliefs and attitudes

selective distribution the use of a limited number of outlets in a geographical area to sell the products of a particular supplier

selective retention the process by which people retain only a selection of messages in memory

self-concept the beliefs a person holds about his or her own attributes

semiotics the study of the correspondence between signs and symbols and their roles in how we assign meanings

service encounter any interaction between a service provider and a customer

servicescape the environment in which the service is delivered and where the firm and customers interact

shareholder value the returns to a company's shareholders, which grow when the company increases its dividends or its share price rises

social marketing the use of commercial marketing concepts and tools in programmes designed to influence the individual's behaviour to improve their well-being and that of society

social media marketing the use of social media for communicating with and engaging customers online

social responsibility the ethical principle that a person or an organization should be accountable for how its actions might affect the physical environment and the general public

societal marketing concept the idea that a company's marketing decisions should consider consumers' wants, the company's requirements, consumers' long-term interests and society's long-run interests

sponsorship a business relationship between a provider of funds, resources or services and an individual, event or organization that offers in return some rights and association that may be used for commercial advantage

straight re-buy refers to a purchase by an organization from a previously approved supplier of a previously purchased item

strategic business unit a business or company division serving a distinct group of customers and with a distinct set of competitors, usually strategically autonomous

strategic issues analysis an examination of the suitability of marketing objectives and segmentation bases in the light of changes in the marketplace

strategic objectives product-level objectives relating to the decision to build, hold, harvest or divest products

strategic thrust the decision concerning which products to sell in which markets

strong theory of advertising the notion that advertising can change people's attitudes sufficiently to persuade those who have not previously bought a product to buy it; desire and conviction precede purchase

SWOT analysis a structured approach to evaluating the strategic position of a business by identifying its strengths, weaknesses, opportunities and threats

syndicated research research that is collected by firms on a regular basis and then sold to other firms

target audience the group of people at which an advertisement or message is aimed

target market a segment that has been selected as a focus for the company's offering or communications

target marketing selecting a segment as the focus for a company's offering or communications

telemarketing use of telecommunications in marketing and sales activities

test marketing the launch of a new product in one or a few geographic areas chosen to be representative of the intended market

trademark the legal term for a brand name, brand mark or trade character

trade-off analysis a measure of the trade-off customers make between price and other product features, so that their effects on product preference can be established

undifferentiated marketing a market coverage strategy where a company decides to ignore market segment differences and to develop a single marketing mix for the whole market

value chain the set of the firm's activities that are conducted to design, manufacture, market, distribute and service its products

value-based marketing a perspective on marketing that emphasizes how a marketing philosophy and marketing activities contribute to the maximization of shareholder value

variability a characteristic of services, namely that being delivered by people the standard of their performance is open to variation

vertical electronic marketplaces online procurement sites that are dedicated to sourcing supplies for producers in one particular industry

vicarious learning learning from others without direct experience or reward

viral campaigns the creation of entertaining messages designed to be electronically transferred from person to person

viral marketing electronic word of mouth, where promotional messages are spread using electronic means from person to person

weak theory of advertising the notion that advertising can first arouse awareness and interest and encourage some customers to make a trial purchase as well as providing reassurance and reinforcement; desire and conviction do not precede purchase

yield management the monitoring of demand or potential demand patterns with a view to adjusting prices

Author index

Companies and brands index

Note: Page locators in **bold** refer to main entries and those in *italics* refer to illustrations

Subject index